HISTORY OF
THE SECOND WORLD WAR

UNITED KINGDOM CIVIL SERIES

Edited by W. K. HANCOCK

The authors of the Civil Histories have been given free access to official documents. They and the editor are alone responsible for the statements made and the views expressed.

CIVIL INDUSTRY AND TRADE

BY

E. L. HARGREAVES

Fellow of Oriel College, Oxford

AND

M. M. GOWING

B.Sc.(Econ.)

LONDON: 1952

HER MAJESTY'S STATIONERY OFFICE

AND

LONGMANS, GREEN AND CO

First published 1952

Crown Copyright Reserved

HER MAJESTY'S STATIONERY OFFICE

London: York House, Kingsway, W.C.2 & 423 Oxford Street, W.1
Edinburgh: 13a Castle Street   Cardiff: 1 St. Andrews Crescent
Manchester: 39 King Street   Bristol: Tower Lane
Birmingham: 2 Edmund Street   Belfast: 80 Chichester Street

LONGMANS, GREEN AND CO LTD
6 and 7 Clifford Street, London, W.1
also at Melbourne and Cape Town

LONGMANS, GREEN AND CO INC
55 Fifth Avenue, New York, 3

LONGMANS, GREEN AND CO
215 Victoria Street, Toronto, 1

ORIENT LONGMANS, LTD
Bombay, Calcutta, Madras

Price £1 17s. 6d. net

Printed in Great Britain under the authority of H.M. Stationery Office
by Sanders Phillips & Co. Ltd., London, S.W.9

CONTENTS

Page

PREFACE xi

PART I: THE FIRST STEPS IN CONTROL

CHAPTER I: INTRODUCTORY
    i. Pre-War Background 3
    ii. The First Eighteen Months of War . . . 14

CHAPTER II: COMMERCIAL POLICY: IMPORT CONTROL
    i. The Introduction of Control 20
    ii. Import Control in Operation, 1939–40 . . 27
    iii. The Political Problems of Import Control . . 31
    Appendix 1: Import Licensing, 1939–40 and 1940–41 37
    Appendix 2: Note on Import Licensing . . . 38

CHAPTER III: COMMERCIAL POLICY: EXPORTS
    i. Export Problems from the Outbreak of War until
    the Export Drive 39
    ii. The Export Drive 50
    iii. The Changing Emphasis 64
    Appendix 3: Note on Export Licensing . . . 74

CHAPTER IV: PRICE CONTROL: THE FIRST PHASE
    i. Introductory 75
    ii. The Prices of Goods Act, 1939 77
    iii. Retrospect and Prospect 86
    Appendix 4: Some Details of Price Control . . 90

CHAPTER V: RESTRICTIONS ON THE HOME MARKET
    i. The First Experiment 92
    ii. Restrictions Extended 99
    iii. The Implications 110

PART II: THE PERIOD OF FULL CONTROL: FROM SPRING 1941 TO THE END OF THE WAR

CHAPTER VI: INTRODUCTORY   119

CHAPTER VII: EXPORTS: POLICY AFTER LEND-LEASE
    i. Selective Export Policy 137
    ii. The Lend-Lease White Paper 145
    iii. Some White Paper Problems 151

CHAPTER VIII: EXPORTS: PROBLEMS OF ANGLO-AMERICAN CO-OPERATION
    i. White Paper Negotiations Continued . . . 158
    ii. Combined Programming and Planning . . 165

CHAPTER IX: EXPORTS: THE FINAL PHASE
    i. The General Trend 184
    ii. Specific Exports 187
    Appendix 5: Exports of Cotton Piece-goods . . 201

CHAPTER X: CONCENTRATION OF PRODUCTION
    i. The Formulation of Policy 202
    ii. The Procedure 210
    iii. The Achievement 224

CHAPTER XI: THE CONTROL OF FACTORY AND STORAGE PREMISES
    i. The Establishment of the Control . . . 234
    ii. The Control in Action 241

CHAPTER XII: RETAIL TRADE
    i. The Structure of Retail Trade and the Early Effects of War 253
    ii. The Retail Trade Committee 258
    iii. Retail Trade Policy, 1942–45 272
    iv. The Contribution of Retail Trade to the War Effort 279

CHAPTER XIII: THE CONSUMER AND HIS NEEDS
    i. The Needs 282
    ii. 'Tempering the Wind' 292

CHAPTER XIV: CONSUMER RATIONING
   i. What Kind of Scheme? 303
   ii. Clothes Rationing in Operation . . . 314
   iii. Other Distribution Schemes 332
   Appendix 6: Number of coupons needed for the principal articles of adults' and children's clothing at 1st November 1943 . . 339
   Appendix 7: Issue of clothes ration documents by or on behalf of the Board of Trade, 1944–45 . 341

CHAPTER XV: THE TEXTILE INDUSTRIES IN WAR-TIME
   i. The Cotton Industry 343
   ii. The Rayon Industry 372
   iii. The Silk Industry 377
   iv. The Wool Industry 378
   Appendix 8: Cotton Allocations 397
   Appendix 9: Raw Cotton Supplies 398
   Appendix 10: Output of the Wool Textile Industry . 399

CHAPTER XVI: THE CLOTHING AND HOSIERY INDUSTRIES
   i. The Clothing Industry 400
   ii. The Hosiery Industry 414
   Appendix 11: Labour force in the Clothing Industry in Great Britain 421
   Appendix 12: Consumption of Yarn in the Hosiery Industry 422

CHAPTER XVII: CLOTHING POLICY
   i. The General Outline 424
   ii. The Controls in Detail 440
   iii. The Results 470
   Appendix 13: Extracts from BS/BOT 24, the Four-Figure Cotton Cloth Specifications issued by the British Standards Institution, July 1942, under S.R. & O. 1942, No. 1002 . 480
   Appendix 14: Summary of Range of Utility Cloths (excluding wool) 482
   Appendix 15: Cotton Cloth Deliveries, 1944 (by Users) 483

CHAPTER XVIII: CIVILIAN FOOTWEAR
    i. The Control of the Industry 484
    ii. The Shortages 493

CHAPTER XIX: CONTROLS OVER THE MANUFACTURE AND
SUPPLY OF MISCELLANEOUS CONSUMER GOODS
    i. Policy 498
    ii. Examples of Individual Industries . . . 511

CHAPTER XX: CIVILIAN ENGINEERING . . . 540

CHAPTER XXI: PRICE CONTROL: THE EVOLUTION OF
POLICY
    i. The Stabilisation Policy 552
    ii. The Goods and Services (Price Control) Act, 1941 555
    iii. The Formation of Utility Prices . . . 562

CHAPTER XXII: PRICE CONTROL: THE SYSTEM IN
OPERATION, 1942–45
    i. Stabilisation Achieved 570
    ii. Manufacturers' Prices 578
    iii. Distributors' Prices 591
    iv. Control of Service Charges, Hire-Purchase Charges,
       Auctions, Second-hand Prices 607
    v. Review 613
    Appendix 16: Utility Prices 615

CHAPTER XXIII: CONCLUSION . . . . .
    i. Post-War Questions. 618
    ii. Summing-up 625

STATISTICAL APPENDIX 639
INDEX 653

LIST OF TABLES IN THE TEXT

		Page
TABLE 1	Export Credit Department guarantees . . .	59
TABLE 2	Exports of artificial silk, 1938–42	63
TABLE 3	Volume of exports in 1940	65
TABLE 4	Home trade in textiles, 1938–39	94
TABLE 5	Estimates of exportable surpluses and import requirements for cotton piece-goods in 1943 by countries .	178
TABLE 6	United Kingdom exports of agricultural machinery, 1938–46	182
TABLE 7	United Kingdom exports of cotton yarn and cotton piece-goods, 1937–45	192
TABLE 8	United Kingdom exports of woollen and worsted yarns and tissues, 1938–45	194
TABLE 9	United Kingdom exports of artificial silk yarns and tissues, 1938–45	196
TABLE 10	United Kingdom exports of linen and hemp piece-goods and of jute manufactures, 1938–45	197
TABLE 11	United Kingdom pottery exports, 1939–45 . .	200
TABLE 12	Results of concentration of production up to 1st March 1944	225
TABLE 13	Distribution of shops among types of retail organisation	255
TABLE 14	Retail sales of non-food merchandise . . .	263
TABLE 15	Consumers' expenditure at current prices, 1938–45 .	264
TABLE 16	Licences granted under the Location of Retail Businesses Order, 1942–45	278
TABLE 17	Population of various towns as a percentage of the mid-1939 figure	284
TABLE 18	Retail stocks of household goods in Bournemouth and Seaham Harbour	288
TABLE 19	Comparison of wardrobes in terms of coupon values .	330
TABLE 20	Closure of mills in the cotton industry under the concentration of production schemes	364
TABLE 21	Machine capacity and machine activity in running cotton mills, 1940–41	365
TABLE 22	Employment in the cotton industry, 1939–45 . .	368
TABLE 23	Average weekly cotton yarn production . . .	368
TABLE 24	Average weekly production of cotton, rayon and mixture cloths	369
TABLE 25	Employment in the wool industry, 1939–44 . .	395
TABLE 26	Employment in the wool industry, 1944–46 . .	396
TABLE 27	Labour requirements of the civilian clothing industry as at September 1941	403
TABLE 28	Clothing concentration at 30th April 1944 . .	410
TABLE 29	Deliveries of cotton and rayon cloths to the home market for civilian consumption	448

TABLE 30   Proportion of cotton and rayon fabric production represented by utility 448

TABLE 31   Sales of cloth by manufacturers for home trade . . 457

TABLE 32   Percentage of total output of hosiery garments for home civilian use represented by utility 463

TABLE 33   Production of hosiery knitted goods for the civilian market 464

TABLE 34   Supplies of household textiles for the home civilian market 470

TABLE 35   Deliveries of cotton yarn against the Board of Trade allocation 473

TABLE 36   Deliveries to the home market of woven cloth for clothing 474

TABLE 37   Utility furniture production 521

TABLE 38   Index numbers of raw material and rayon yarn prices 570

TABLE 39   Retail margins and expenses 600

STATISTICAL APPENDIX

TABLE I   Numbers employed in certain industries in Great Britain 641

TABLE II   Percentage of total manpower engaged on orders for the Forces and for the home and export markets in June 1944 641

TABLE III   Value and volume of the external trade of the United Kingdom 642

TABLE IV   Retained imports: analysis by classes and selected groups 643

TABLE V   Exports of the produce and manufactures of the United Kingdom: analysis by classes and selected groups 644

TABLE VI   Imports: analysis by source 645

TABLE VII   United Kingdom exports: analysis by destination . 645

TABLE VIII   Woven cloth, household textiles, hosiery and footwear: supplies for home civilian use 646

TABLE IX   Pottery, hollow-ware and brushes: production and supplies for home civilian use 647

TABLE X   Personal expenditure on consumers' goods and services revalued at 1938 prices 648

TABLE XI   Working-class cost-of-living index 648

TABLE XII   Wholesale price index numbers 649

TABLE XIII   Index numbers of wholesale stocks of clothing . . 650

TABLE XIV   Index numbers of stocks of footwear . . . 651

TABLE XV   Index numbers of retail stocks of clothing and footwear 652

PREFACE

THE authors have asked me to write a preface which will explain the general scope of their book and the limits which they have found it necessary to impose upon themselves. They wish me to say, in the first place, that its title is imprecise. But this is my fault; it was the best title I could think of when, many years ago, I was defining the content of a book in this series which would handle salient problems of production and distribution outside the war production zone of the economy. The problems I had in mind were broadly co-terminous with the war-time activities of the Board of Trade. One might describe them as the residuum of a residuum. Up to September 1939 the Board of Trade had been responsible, amidst all their other duties, for planning the war-time management of food and fuel and shipping; but after war broke out they surrendered these responsibilities to new Ministries. The responsibility they retained—for controlling the production and distribution of all consumer goods except foodstuffs and of many consumer services—was still extensive and very intricate.

Within this wide field, the authors have exercised some selection. They have not examined everything the Board of Trade did during the war; their book does not describe the controls over tobacco and matches, laundries and dry-cleaning; nor does it record the activities of those sections of the Board that were concerned with companies, bankruptcy and trading with the enemy. The problems that have been chosen for study are joined to each other within the unity of a larger problem—how to release resources for the war effort and at the same time to ensure to the civilian population an essential minimum of consumption goods, with 'fair shares' for all.

Within this story a place must be found for export policy; early in the war exports were an essential part of the economic effort, because they earned foreign exchange needed to pay for imports; later on, when lend-lease supported the British economy, exports were still essential, though at a lower level, in order to supply the minimum needs of overseas territories of the Commonwealth and of Allied countries. However, as the book proceeds, its emphasis shifts to the measures of internal policy—control over the production and distribution of consumer goods, control of factory and storage space, price control—an immensely intricate system of administrative action whereby the Board of Trade, within their sphere of responsibility, furthered the main objectives of the Government's war-economic policy.

The authors are aware that it is not wholly logical to divorce the history of finished consumer goods from that of the materials and manpower that go to make them, and in some of their chapters (those for example, that deal with textiles and the concentration of industry) they have extended their researches beyond the boundaries of the Board of Trade. However, lines of demarcation must be drawn somewhere, and many of the problems discussed in this book will need to be treated further in other volumes of the series.

The authors are no less aware that the viewpoint of their book is predominantly that of a Government department. They have written the history of the controls, but have not written the histories of the industries which were brought under the controls. In consequence, their book does not contain the answers to some of the most interesting questions: it does not, for example, measure the effect of the controls upon the productivity of industry. To attempt such a task would demand close study of the war-time experience and costs of individual firms.

The disclaimers that have been made fulfil my undertaking to the authors. I feel bound to add that they have performed faithfully the task committed to them. Their book is the first in any language to illuminate an aspect of modern warfare which, though undramatic, is no less significant than military operations or the production of munitions. The labour they have put into the book is immense. In a lecture entitled *The History of Our Times* (Athlone Press 1951) I have remarked that the war-time records of the Board of Trade are contained in twelve million files which occupy sixteen miles of shelf space. The authors have employed a scientific and practical method of drawing from this vast mass of paper, and from the testimony of living people, the material they have needed for solving their historical problems. Their work would have been impossible without the help of Miss V. Acheson in looking after their papers.

Mr. Hargreaves began work in 1942 and covered much ground before the war ended. Then, however, he was recalled to his duties in Oxford and the pace of his research necessarily slackened. At this stage the book might have collapsed altogether had it not been for the loyalty and hard work of Miss M. Gollancz, who assisted Mr. Hargreaves from 1943 to 1947. In 1944 Miss Lucy Brown pioneered the research on retail trade and some other aspects of war-time policy. In more recent years Mrs. Ogilvy-Webb wrote a study of textiles and clothing policy; Chapters XV to XVII are a shorter version of this. Even so, there remained to be done so much research, thinking and writing that Mr. Hargreaves, with his heavy commitments at Oxford, would have been unable to complete the book had he not found a colleague. That it can now be published is due to the remarkable work that Mrs. Gowing has done during the past two years.

March 1951.   W. K. HANCOCK.

PART I

The First Steps in Control

CHAPTER I

INTRODUCTORY

(i)

Pre-war Background

B Y the end of the Second World War civil industry and trade in the United Kingdom were very tightly controlled. Some of the controls were direct—they had been imposed upon prices, imports, exports and upon the manufacture, supply and distribution of consumer goods. Other controls were indirect—manpower had been withdrawn from civilian industries, raw materials had been restricted or even denied and factory premises had been requisitioned. All these controls had originated in a desire to devote as much of the nation's economic power as possible to direct war purposes and, until American aid was assured, to the export trade. Gradually, however, as the war lengthened and dragged on into a third and even a sixth year the controls were designed to serve a new purpose. The complications of pursuing an export drive in war-time had disappeared but other complexities increased. In particular, the dividing line between the war and civilian sectors of the economy had become increasingly blurred. The power of the fighting Services depended not only upon their own efficiency and courage but upon the vast productive effort that supported them. This was the province of the civilians. It was therefore highly important to maintain civilian efficiency and morale at a high pitch—an impossible task unless the Government took care that the minimum essential needs of the civilians were met and that available supplies were fairly distributed. Certain generally accepted social principles added force to this policy: it was, for example, agreed that the costs of war should not fall unduly harshly upon the children.

This close control of civil industry and trade was something almost wholly new. In this sphere the First World War—which had bequeathed so much valuable experience for the control of food or shipping—had left few guides to action. The First World War had, however, provided a foretaste of the problems which the controls over civil industry and trade in the Second World War were designed to solve. Like its successor the earlier war had before long produced a foreign exchange crisis which was primarily a dollar crisis:[1] some of

---

[1] R. H. Brand, *War and National Finance* 1921. Appendix 11 (Memorandum of August 1916). 'The principal danger of the Allies losing the war now lies in a collapse of their external finance, which will cut off some supplies which are absolutely necessary for them.'

the money needed to pay for foreign supplies had been raised by the sale of foreign investments;[1] some of it had been earned by exports, which were in consequence an integral part of the war economy until the United States entered the war in 1917 and granted credits freely to their allies. The intense domestic mobilisation of resources created similar problems in both wars: in 1914–18, as in 1939–45, manpower and raw materials had been withdrawn from civilian industries—this time in order to feed the insatiable army in France with men and munitions and in order to save shipping. The supply of civilian goods fell while incomes were increasing: there was, in fact, inflation.

The problems of the Second World War existed in the First World War; but the controls, as we have said, did not. No direct measures were taken to encourage exports before the United States entered the war in 1917, nor ruthlessly to reduce them once dollar credits were readily available. An export licensing system was administered purely in the interests of the blockade and import licensing operated to save shipping, not foreign exchange. There were no direct controls over finished products to support the controls over manpower and raw materials by ensuring that unessential goods were not manufactured. Nor were there controls to make the process of contraction in civilian industry an orderly one. A strong anti-inflation policy was never developed in the First World War; it is not surprising, therefore, that so little was done towards controlling prices of consumer goods,[2] controlling their distribution or ensuring that the resources remaining in civilian production were concentrated upon making essential goods of reasonable quality.

The little that was done was all done in the last year or so of the war, or even after the war had ended. The only really ambitious scheme was that for 'War-time Boots'. Under it manufacturers were required to produce civilian boots which complied with specifications and prices approved by the Director of Leather. A scheme for standard clothing—hosiery, suits and skirts—and for standard blankets embodied similar principles, but unlike the boots scheme was voluntary: it operated, therefore, only on a very small scale. No general attempt was made to control prices until the war had actually ended and even then the attempt only took the form of an anti-profiteering measure. The Profiteering Act of 1919 gave the Board of Trade power to investigate prices, costs and profits at all stages and to investigate complaints about excessive profits. The Board could either discuss complaints, or, if satisfied that they were just, declare a reasonable price for the article concerned and order the seller to

---

[1] These sales, added to the depreciation of investments in Russia and enemy countries, accounted for a war-time reduction of more than a quarter in Britain's foreign investments. cf. Royal Institute of International Affairs. *The Problem of International Investment*, 1937.

[2] i.e. other than food.

refund the excess paid to the buyer. In 1920 the Act was amended to permit voluntary schemes for limiting profits. Manufacturers and traders could submit such schemes to the Board of Trade: if a scheme were approved, the profits obtained under it were considered reasonable for the purposes of the Profiteering Act. The Board of Trade might then exempt the producers concerned from an investigation into prices, costs and profits.

These beginnings in the control of civil industry and trade were humble and late. Two years after the war ended the cry for decontrol and the post-war slump swept them away. Less than twenty years later problems similar in shape but far greater in size confronted the nation.

Before coming to the experience of the Second World War it will be as well to note the most important of the changes these twenty years had wrought in the United Kingdom's industry and trade. For the country that entered battle in 1939 was very different from the country that had emerged from battle in 1918. In retrospect the year 1914 has seemed to mark the end of an economic epoch. The idea of an epoch is misleading if it suggests that history can be divided into separable slabs or if it ignores the underlying continuity; some of the changes in Britain's economy that were most striking after the First World War had been at work long before that war had begun. By the end of the nineteenth century there had been an awareness that the balance of economic power in the world was shifting. In Western Europe (especially Germany) and in Japan industrialisation had been increasing: in the United States the expansion of productive power had been astonishing. In 1901 'American financiers for the first time' had come 'to the aid of European governments'.[1] At home, there were misgivings about Britain's future. Britain was by no means in the first rank in the new industries such as motor cars and machine tools. In some of her staple industries—on which her export trade largely depended—there was evidence of stagnation.[2]

Such changes were already calling for adjustments in Britain's industry and commerce: the First World War made the process infinitely more difficult.[3] Changes that might have been spread over a generation or more were compressed into a few years. The war produced other changes which would not otherwise have occurred and prevented adjustments which would otherwise have been made. Instead of being gradually adapted to meet foreign competition the staple industries were further expanded to meet a demand that was purely temporary. Post-war demands for the products of Britain's staple industries were indeed lower than those of pre-war years. As a

[1] J. H. Clapham, *An Economic History of Modern Britain*, Vol. III, p. 35.
[2] *Ibid.*, p. 69, and G. C. Allen, *British Industries*.
[3] See A. L. Bowley, *Some Economic Consequences of the Great War*.

B

result of the war, economic nationalism flourished, currencies were unstable, some of Britain's customers were impoverished and other customers had established industries to produce the goods—or substitutes for the goods—that they could not get from Britain during the war. Meanwhile the world centre of economic gravity had shifted further westwards. The war had greatly stimulated the productive power of North America; it had raised the United States to be a great creditor nation and had opened up to the United States new export markets. Many other markets hitherto fed by Britain turned to Japan for supplies.

It would be out of place to include in a book about war-time industry and trade an economic history of the inter-war years. It will suffice to mention three of the most important changes that were at work in the United Kingdom's industry and commerce between the two world wars—the change in Britain's foreign trade, the shift in the balance of British industry and the restriction of competition (which includes the growth of control over trade and industry). All three changes, it must be remembered, were closely connected.

Britain's export trade had reached a climax in the years immediately preceding the First World War.[1] In 1913 the favourable balance of payments on current account was about £200 millions—a large sum which constituted Britain's foreign lending. In the nineteen-twenties this balance on current account, this surplus available for investment abroad, declined: in the nineteen-thirties it disappeared and became a negative quantity. The appearance of an adverse balance of payments was a landmark in the history of Britain's economy. This book cannot explore its many complex causes: it will simply note what actually happened. Most of the figures that comprise the balance of payments showed striking changes between the two world wars. To take one item: the excess of visible imports over visible exports which had long existed was far greater than it had been before the First World War. The figures of values of imports and exports which appear in the balance of payments mask further important changes. They do not, for example, show the changing relationship between import and export prices. Between the wars the terms of trade changed in Britain's favour in the sense that she could buy the food and raw materials she needed by giving a smaller amount of manufactured products in exchange. But these low import prices reflected difficulties and depression among primary producers —that is, among Britain's chief overseas customers. They help to explain another fact which the figures of import and export values conceal—the changing volume of imports and exports. The volume of United Kingdom net imports fluctuated in the inter-war years; it

---

[1] See A. E. Kahn, *Great Britain in the World Economy*.

was however generally higher than in 1913. The volume of net exports was consistently lower—very much lower. Even in the boom years of the late 'twenties, exports were only about eighty per cent. of the 1913 figure; in the peak year of the 'thirties they were only sixty-five per cent. The trough between the two peaks was very low indeed—little over fifty per cent. British exports did not only decline absolutely. They also declined relatively to those of other countries. Britain failed to retain her place in international trade.

An excess of imports over exports was, as we have said, an accepted feature of Britain's economy. For it had been paid for by the net income from invisible exports—shipping, insurance and other services, the interest on foreign investments and so forth. In the nineteen-twenties an increase in this net income had compensated in part for the big increase in the excess of imports over exports. In the 'thirties, this net income fell heavily, a fall which largely accounted for the disappearance within a decade of Britain's favourable balance of payments on current account.

Among all these setbacks the one that caused the greatest public alarm was the decline in exports. The alarm was not so much on account of the balance of payments but on account of the plight of Britain's staple industries which had depended so largely on export markets. This brings us to the second great change of the inter-war years—the shift in the balance of industry. With but a few exceptions the whole inter-war history of the staple industries was gloomy. An increase in home demand could not in general compensate for the great fall in exports; the iron and steel industry, which achieved a new peak of production in 1937 in spite of the halving of its export trade after the great depression, is a rare exception. In most industries the loss of export trade brought a decline in output and the need for contraction. The industries were for the most part highly localised. Since a large proportion of the labour employed in them was immobile, and since their capital equipment was highly specific, contraction was difficult and, in the end, painful.

As an example of this process of decline we can take the cotton industry—not only because its difficulties were outstanding but because this book will be closely concerned with war-time developments in the industry. In the years immediately before the First World War exports of cotton manufactures amounted to about three-quarters of the total output of the industry: additional yarn was also sent abroad in the form of lace and hosiery. Cotton exports amounted to about a quarter of the whole British export trade. In the post-war years cotton exports declined progressively and catastrophically; exports of piece-goods which had been 6,913 million linear yards in 1912 were 1,448 million linear yards in 1938. In the early post-war years the decline in exports mainly affected the cheaper lines, but even before the great slump, depression had spread to almost all sections of the industry. In 1912 the average number employed in the industry was 620,000: in 1938 the number was less than 290,000 and there were over 100,000 unemployed.[1] There was in addition in these years much short-time working.

The inter-war history of the staple industries was almost un-relievedly gloomy and unemployment in them was consistently high. The staple industries, however, were becoming continuously less representative of British industrial life and were providing a pro-gressively smaller proportion of industrial employment. In spite of their decline the volume of physical production in British industry and the general productivity of labour rose in the inter-war years. Between 1911 and 1938 output per man-hour is estimated to have risen by about fifty per cent. which more than offset the effects on the national income of heavy unemployment and the reduction in hours of work.[2] In these years newer industries were rapidly expanding. The most important of the newer industries—electricity supply, electrical goods, automobiles and cycles, aircraft, silk and rayon, hosiery, chemicals and scientific instruments—were together respon-sible for about one-fifteenth of the total net output of British industry in 1907 and for one-fifth in 1935.[3] There was in addition a great expansion in the building industry—particularly in the nineteen-thirties—and in the 'service' trades such as distribution, personal and professional services, catering and entertainment. This changing balance of industry—a shift towards the production of luxuries and consumption goods and away from primary necessities and capital goods—was common to all advanced industrial countries. There were, however, several disquieting features in the British experience. In the first place, rapid though the advance of these new industries was in Britain the advance of other countries was still faster. Secondly, the new industries in Britain were not expanding rapidly enough to absorb the labour displaced from the declining industries. Absorption was in any case difficult because the newer industries were not situated to any great extent in the areas where the decaying staple industries were concentrated. Thirdly, the new industries catered primarily for the home market. The export trade developed by some of the manufacturing industries was, it is true, considerable, but it was not commensurate with the growth in importance of the new industries in the nation's industrial output.

The third of the great changes during the inter-war years with

---

[1] These figures relate to spinning, doubling and weaving; they exclude finishing. See *Cotton Working Party Report*, p. 7. Ministry of Labour figures for insured workers.

[2] Supplementary chapters by G. C. Allen to 1949 edition of W. J. Ashley, *The Economic Organisation of England*.

[3] A. E. Kahn, *op. cit.*

which this book is concerned is the decline of competition and the growth of Government intervention in industry and commerce. Even in the heyday of industrial expansion British Governments had not been ruled by a complete theory of *laissez faire*. But the departures from this principle had occurred for the most part in social affairs: there remained a general assumption against Government control of industry and trade and in favour of free competition among industrialists. In the early years of the twentieth century Government interference in industry and trade was slight and in spite of the growth of combinations of one kind and another British industry was still highly competitive—more so than German or American industry. The First World War was a watershed. Mobilisation of the economy necessitated Government intervention on a broad front: this intervention and the conditions of war-time trade encouraged combination among industrialists. For some time it was thought that these developments were a temporary war-time phenomenon. It was believed that a return to the freedom of trade and industry of pre-1914 days was both possible and desirable. The war left some permanent marks of control—some import restrictions and certain agricultural subsidies considered necessary for strategic reasons. The nineteen-twenties saw other isolated examples of Government intervention in industry. The great changes, however, came with the advent of the nineteen-thirties and of the great depression.

The policy of the British Government in the nineteen-thirties was mainly determined by an anxiety to relieve the depression in the staple industries (including agriculture) and to insulate the domestic economy as much as possible against outside forces. The Government's most important interventions were in commercial policy. In 1931 and 1932, the Government imposed a general tariff, enlarged imperial preference and put a complete though unofficial embargo on new foreign capital issues. Later, import licences and quota schemes were employed to help some domestic industries—most notably agriculture. In addition to helping home industries in the home market the Government tried to promote British exports. To this end it negotiated bilateral trade agreements, established a system of insurance for private commercial credits to foreign importers, manipulated tariffs and assisted British industries to conclude private international agreements of one kind and another. Other countries followed similar policies, though there was evidence just before the Second World War of a reaction against all this restrictionism in international trade and of a disposition here and there to reduce trade barriers.

The sharpest break with the past in British economic policy came in the sphere of external trade. Encroachments by the Government into internal economic affairs were less extensive. They were, however, very important. The main intervention of the Government on behalf of industry was financial—the initiation of a cheap money policy. But the Government also took specific action intended to help certain industries. Subsidies were used, sometimes to strengthen some British industries behind their protective tariffs or import quotas, sometimes to increase the competitive strength of British exports. The Government, moreover, took a hand in the efforts to rationalise the depressed staple industries. The aim of rationalisation was to unify the industries and reduce excessive capacity in them by concentrating production on the most efficient plants. Most of the rationalisation schemes that were drawn up in the staple industries were due to official or semi-official encouragement and assistance. In a few cases the Government used compulsory powers. Here again the example of the cotton industry is worth citing. After earlier unsuccessful attempts at cartelisation large-scale amalgamations began in the spinning section of the industry at the end of the nineteen-twenties. They were intended to secure economies of specialisation, standardisation, bulk-buying and bulk-selling. But this was not enough and Government support for further measures was enlisted. In 1936 a levy was imposed by law upon the cotton spinners and the proceeds were used to buy and scrap excess spindles. In 1939 another Act was passed giving the industry new powers to impose levies, reduce surplus capacity and enforce minimum prices.

These incursions of the Government into fields from which it had for long been barred were not as it happened very felicitous. Whatever their aims the officially encouraged and assisted rationalisation schemes did little to promote economic efficiency or restore the staple industries to health. It was left to the Second World War to bring back prosperity to industries such as coal and cotton, agriculture and shipbuilding. The general result of Government interference was to encourage the decline in competition and to speed the movement towards combination, which was already strong in British industry and commerce. Between the wars and particularly in the nineteen-thirties there was a great increase in cartels—both national and international—for carrying out restrictive practices. The concentration of economic power likewise grew. By 1935 there was a considerable number of commodities whose output was concentrated in one or two firms, and there were many trades in which the three largest units accounted for seventy per cent. or more of employment.[1] Certain marketing devices such as branding goods and extensive advertisement also encouraged the decline of competition.

These, then, were some of the salient developments of industry and trade in the inter-war years. Our survey, though very summary,

---

[1] H. Leak and A. Maizels, 'The Structure of British Industry', *Journal of the Royal Statistical Society*, Parts 1–2, 1945.

has been perhaps sufficient to suggest some preoccupations of the Government in the days of planning for the Second World War.

It is now time to discuss this pre-war planning. The department with which we are primarily concerned is the Board of Trade. Within the Board of Trade there was a good deal of war planning in the nineteen-thirties but most of it was going on in those sections of the Board that were to become new ministries when war actually came —the Food (Defence Plans) Department, the Mercantile Marine Department and the Raw Materials Department.[1] For the wide variety of subjects which were to remain within the province of the Board of Trade throughout the war there had been very little pre-war planning. Before September 1939 preparations were made only for import control and export control. These preparations were in response to three clearly foreseen needs in the forthcoming war. Import control would be necessary to help husband foreign exchange: it was not considered in relation to the need to save shipping space since no shipping shortage was expected. Export control would be necessary in order to conserve scarce materials and products needed for war production and in order to support the economic blockade.

The detailed preparations for these controls can best be considered in the chapters dealing with their early history. Here in this chapter we shall touch upon those preparations that were not made. First, there is export promotion. Since a shortage of foreign exchange was one of the fundamental assumptions about the war economy it is surprising how little thought was given before the war to the wartime problems of the export trade. The only evidence of study of the problem is a memorandum by the Department of Overseas Trade written just before the outbreak of war—in August 1939. This set forth the aims of export trade in time of war—first, the earning of foreign exchange; secondly, the retention of goodwill in overseas markets; thirdly, the use of opportunities provided by the elimination of enemy countries; fourthly, the maintenance of employment in non-war industries. The memorandum also envisaged difficulties in the export trade once war had broken out and suggested various forms of Government assistance—for example, export credits, export subsidies, the use of exchange control, Government marketing of exports and Government purchase of goods for resale in overseas markets. It was with the short-term difficulties that the department was chiefly troubled. The memorandum did however recognise that before long the situation might become one of 'famished' markets; the problem would then be to secure for exporters enough labour and raw materials.

---

[1] The Mines Department remained within the Board of Trade until it was transformed into the Ministry of Fuel and Power in 1942, but it may for our present purpose be considered as an autonomous department.

Perhaps the years of depression and the unhappy history of the export trade after 1918 had dulled the forward-looking habit of mind within the Board. Certainly the Government showed few signs of being aware just how important exports would be should war come. Nor did it relate the need to export with the problems of a war economy. 'The maintenance of employment in non-war industries' could not for long be an important aim of policy in a country aiming at victory. And what of the war industries themselves? The six most valuable groups of exports in 1937 had been cotton yarns and manufactures, machinery, iron and steel, vehicles, woollen and worsted yarns and manufactures, and chemicals.[1] Four of these were, under any definition, war industries, where exports would compete immediately with war production. The fighting Services would also make heavy demands on the two remaining groups, the cotton and woollen textile industries. What then was to be the precedence between exports and munitions production? How was export promotion to be reconciled with export control? What assurance was there that the demands of the export trade for scarce raw materials and scarce skilled labour would be met? What could be done to ensure that the home market did not absorb supplies of scarce raw materials or finished goods which would be needed for the export trade? As it was, in pre-war estimates of raw material requirements, export needs were lumped with home civilian industry under the heading 'civil requirements'. There would indeed have been little point in trying to construct quantitative estimates for the war-time export trade—the uncertainties were too great. It was an awareness of the general problem that was needed and of that awareness there was hardly any sign.

It seems that there was equally little pre-war consideration of the domestic economic problems which were to be the chief preoccupation of the Board of Trade during the war. As far back as 1929 the Committee of Imperial Defence's Sub-Committee on Manpower had expounded the causes and general remedies for war-time inflation. Their report had firmly stated: 'the increase of prices in time of war originates in the increased demand on manpower and the consequent increase in the money circulating as wages and in the increased demand for commodities coupled with the diminishing supply'. The report had advocated drastic taxation, a borrowing policy as uninflationary as possible, control of profits, control of wages and— these were the most important points for the Board of Trade—control of prices, control of imports and rationing of consumable goods. Plans were made, as we saw, for controlling imports. But plans for controlling prices or for consumer rationing were confined to the

---

[1] Respectively £69 millions, £50 millions, £48 millions, £40 millions, £36 millions, £25 millions.

department of the Board of Trade concerned with war-time food policy. Up to the outbreak of war no proposals had been made for controlling the prices of all those non-food consumer goods which formed an important part of the standard of living; nor had there been any discussion about the possibility of rationing such a fundamental necessity as clothing. The Board of Trade's role in a general anti-inflation policy remained unrehearsed in spite of the warning of 1929. Of the Board of Trade's important function in restricting civilian industry in the interests of war production there was no hint or warning. Indeed, Government interference in civilian industry and trade on any appreciable scale was never envisaged.

If the Government had tried to formulate any plans for such interference it would have come up against the major difficulty that was to confront it when the war had started and controls had to be imposed—that is, the lack of sufficient and up-to-date statistical information. The statistics for manufacturing industry were the least inadequate. Ministry of Labour figures for insured workers were of some assistance. There was also the Census of Production. The last pre-war Census was taken in 1935 and in 1937 there were similar inquiries under the Import Duties Act covering a number of trades. But these figures for production had their shortcomings. They did not, for example, include firms employing ten persons or less although in many industries satisfying civilian needs the output of the small firms was substantial. Another shortcoming of the Census was the paucity of information about materials used. And of course by 1939 the 1935 Census was four years old; the results of the 1937 inquiry were available only for the textile industries and the iron and steel trades. Moreover, the officials in the Statistics Department of the Board of Trade were precluded by law from revealing to their colleagues concerned with production policy particulars about any individual firm.

Even more marked were the deficiencies in the statistics about the distributive trades. Before the war there had been some concern about the increase in the number of insured workers in these trades. Ministry of Labour returns, it was pointed out, showed that the distributive trades employed more workers than coal-mining and building together.[1] Britain, some said, was 'overshopped' and some licensing of retail traders ought to be imposed.[2] The statistical foundation for any conclusions about the distributive trades was, however, very shaky. Sample surveys of distribution existed but no census of distribution as a whole; even the estimates of the number of shops varied between the wide limits of half a million and one million. The only regular figures for trade were the Bank of England figures

---

[1] P. Ford, *Economic Journal*, September 1935.

[2] *Ibid.* for a contrary view.

showing percentage changes in retail stocks and sales. These were based on returns about the trade of 'a number of department stores, concerns operating multiple retail shops, independent retailers and a representative section of the retail co-operative societies'. The Bank of England also collaborated with the Wholesale Textile Association in publishing index numbers of trading in textiles.[1] For the finance of distribution there was almost no information at all. Nor was there any detailed knowledge of the way in which consumers in general spent their incomes on non-food commodities, although the Ministry of Labour had conducted an inquiry into working-class expenditures. Some economists had attempted to estimate the distribution of consumers' expenditure between certain categories,[2] but the categories were much too broad to serve as a basis for Government planning.

When the war broke out, then, the Board of Trade, or that part which was to remain the Board of Trade, was limited both in knowledge and preparations.

(ii)

The First Eighteen Months of War

Successive chapters of this part will discuss at length the policies formulated and administered by the Board of Trade in the months between the outbreak of war and the spring of 1941—import and export control, export promotion, price control and restrictions on the home market. But before plunging in among these details it will be as well to recall briefly the general background of the Board of Trade's activities. Export control was designed to aid the economic blockade and conserve scarce commodities. The other controls over civil industry and trade in the first eighteen months of war were imposed as part of the attempts to solve three fundamental problems of the war economy. First, the deficit in the balance of payments was very serious. Secondly, prices were rising; if unrestrained the rise might lead to inflation. Thirdly, resources had to be diverted as speedily as possible from civilian to war production. Clearly these problems were interconnected at several points. The chief cause of inflation and of rising prices in war-time was the diversion of resources away from civilian consumption. And exports would compete with war production as well as with the home market. Nevertheless for our purposes it is sufficient to see how each of the three problems

---

[1] The figures distinguished between home and export sales.
[2] e.g. A. E. Feavearyear, *Economic Journal* 1932 and 1934. Harrison and Mitchell, *The Home Market* 1937, 1939.

presented itself to the Government in the first eighteen months of the war. The eighteen months period falls itself into two divisions with the fall of France as a dividing line.

Foreign exchange difficulties had been foreseen well before the war, but the Government had not realised just how great they would be. In the nineteen-thirties, as we saw, Britain had an adverse balance of payments on current account. But she was still a great creditor nation. Moreover, pre-war discussions ensured that the sterling area would be continued in war-time. This meant that the countries within the sterling area would send supplies to Britain without demanding immediate payment. Exports from the United Kingdom to these countries would pay for some supplies and British capital assets might be sold to pay for others but any balance due from Britain would become a loan to her—in the form of mounting sterling balances in London. When war came some other countries not in the sterling area made payment agreements with the United Kingdom which similarly relieved Britain's anxiety about finding foreign exchange immediately for the overseas supplies she needed. The foreign exchange problem was to find sufficient 'hard' currencies, to find in particular sufficient United States dollars. It was here that the difficulties proved far greater than the Government had expected. The United States Neutrality Act, it is true, had given clear notice that belligerents must pay for any supplies from the United States with dollars and carry them in their own ships. But the Government hoped it would be able to confine dollar purchases within narrow limits. After all, until the Neutrality Act was modified in November 1939 no belligerent could buy arms in the United States. And no one could have foreseen that the war would be as widespread as it finally became. Britain would, it was assumed, still be able to shop in many overseas countries: it was believed furthermore that she would have plenty of ships to carry supplies, however long the haul.

In the early months of the war alarm about the balance of payments—both the United Kingdom's and that of the whole sterling area—grew. Britain could not keep her dollar purchases within narrow confines. She needed goods from America badly—goods that other countries could not supply and goods that could not be procured from distant parts of the world for lack of ships. Dollars, the British and French Governments agreed, would have to be spent on developing American munitions production so that later much-needed aeroplanes and weapons would be forthcoming. By February 1940 a great gap yawned between the two sides of the balance of payments. Estimates, as authoritative as were possible, suggested that the United Kingdom's adverse balance in the first year of war and the sterling area's adverse balance would be about the same—about £400 millions. It was only reasonable to believe that the gap would be far wider in subsequent years. On such calculations the British war effort appeared hopeless—as indeed it would have been had not the United States later on changed their opinion about granting financial aid. Nevertheless, the Government was bound to do anything it could to narrow the gap—anything to earn foreign exchange or economise in its use. This policy had several ingredients. Some of the most important of them, such as exchange control and the sale of foreign investments, are outside the scope of this book. Two ingredients—control of imports and the promotion of exports—will be considered in the following chapters.

The balance of payments was perhaps the chief preoccupation of the Board of Trade in the months between the outbreak of war and the fall of France. Next in importance came price control. Here again the Board of Trade's activities must be seen as part of a much larger picture. The Board were responsible only for the prices of non-food consumer goods. Food prices were a matter for the Ministry of Food and the prices of raw materials and of some intermediate products such as cotton yarn and cloth came within the orbit of the Ministry of Supply. Moreover, price control could never be considered alone. It made sense only if it was related to other parts of economic policy —to taxation, saving, wages policy, rationing, and control of production. Later in the war the Board of Trade's price-control measures were introduced and administered as part of a coherent policy for the restraint of inflation. But in the early months of the war the Board of Trade's effort at price control—the Prices of Goods Act—had a much more limited purpose.

Very soon after the outbreak of war there was a general rise in prices. There were a number of causes for this rise—the depreciation of sterling, increased prices in the countries where imports came from, increased freight rates, war insurance and so forth. In addition, demand for such goods as sandbags, black-out material and torches rose suddenly and prices of them followed. Most of these price increases were of a once and for all type. But they caused the Government a good deal of concern on two counts. First, it seemed necessary to allay public complaints about high prices and profiteering. Secondly, there was the fear that these early price increases might be the beginning of a wages-prices spiral and a general inflation. It was the fear of inflation that dominated discussions about prices and price control for food and raw materials. The main purpose of the Prices of Goods Act, however, was simply to restrain profiteering: its weaknesses were such that it could not be expected to have any real effect on the cost of living. In the spring of 1940 it seemed that more serious price-control measures might be forthcoming from the Board of Trade. The War Cabinet agreed in principle in March 1940 that a scheme for standard clothing and footwear should be prepared and that it should come into operation in the following autumn. But as will be seen later the proposal lapsed.

We have so far considered the balance of payments and the rise in prices. The third problem of the war economy which closely concerned the Board of Trade was the diversion of resources from civilian to war production. As it happened very little action by the Board of Trade was called for in the months before the fall of France. At the beginning of the war there was a wide margin of unused resources in the economy: unemployment figures did not drop below one million until April 1940. Until this margin was absorbed there was little pressure to divert resources from civilian to war production. There were indeed certain special shortages—of particular raw materials and particular types of skilled labour—but general measures of restriction on civilian industry were not the best way to deal with them. From the administrative point of view it was just as well that wholesale measures of restriction were not needed at the beginning of the war. As we have already seen, the lack of adequate and reliable statistical information about civilian industries and about distribution was a serious handicap which was only gradually remedied with the piecemeal application of controls. Moreover, many of the industries for which the Board of Trade were responsible contained an enormous number of small firms. The administrative machinery that existed at the beginning of the war would have been quite unable to cope with many industries at once. As it turned out control over civilian industry was introduced gradually. The first instalment came in order to foster not direct war production but the needs of the export trade. The pull of the home market on textiles was proving too strong —too strong to be checked by raw material control alone. At the same time the Board of Trade were beginning to appreciate the need to conserve stocks of textiles. In April 1940 the first Limitation of Supplies Order was imposed restricting supplies to retailers of cotton, rayon and linen goods.

Before the fall of France the Board of Trade had moved very cautiously in imposing controls over civilian industry and commerce. But in the summer of 1940 Britain was in a mood for throwing caution to the winds. The Board of Trade, like other Government departments, were ready for much more drastic action. In one direction their tasks were lightened. For the new War Cabinet had realised that the balance of payments problem was incapable of solution— and the war incapable of being won—unless the United States gave financial help. Britain must still earn such foreign exchange as she could with her exports, but it was clear that exports must come a good second to war production. The emphasis increasingly shifted away from exports for the sake of earning foreign exchange and towards exports that were necessary to maintain the life of Allies and the overseas Empire. As for import control—the other activity of the Board of Trade concerned with the balance of payments—the fall of France brought a new stimulus to administrative vigour. The shortage of shipping no less than the shortage of foreign exchange made it imperative to exclude all goods that were not necessary for the economic life of the country.

From the summer of 1940 onwards the necessity grew for firm action in the domestic economy. War production was expanding much more rapidly and the unused resources were being absorbed. Raw material licensing on its own was proving inadequate as a control over civilian industry. The Board of Trade therefore felt it necessary to impose increasingly wide and severe restrictions on civilian consumption—restrictions that would free labour, materials and factory space for war production. More goods were brought within the Limitation of Supplies Orders, quotas were reduced and machinery licensing was introduced. For a month or two there were fears that the restrictions were too drastic—that they were freeing resources, especially labour, faster than war production could absorb them. But by the beginning of 1941 the munitions factories were becoming hungry for labour, and the Board of Trade's activities were encouraged. By then too it was clear that the restrictions already imposed would breed further ones. Limitation of supplies was the first step on the production side towards concentration of production and direct control of manufacture and supply, and on the consumption side to clothes rationing and special arrangements for distribution.

As war production grew and civilian production shrank inflation became a very real problem. Supplies for the home market diminished as wages rose. The Government was now resolved to do all it could to restrain inflation. The policy that had begun with food subsidies early in 1940 culminated in March 1941 in the Chancellor of the Exchequer's announcement of the stabilisation policy. Hitherto, the cost of living had been kept in check largely through the control of food prices. Now it became imperative to take firm control of the prices of other consumer goods that entered into the cost of living. The need was most urgent in the case of clothing: clothing was heavily weighted in the cost of living index and clothing prices had been soaring.

This book on civil industry and trade has been divided into two parts, with the spring of 1941 as the boundary between them. One reason why this date has been chosen as a dividing line is that it marked the passing of the Lend-Lease Act. For when this Act was passed export problems entered a new phase. On the domestic front the most important of the Board of Trade's war-time policies were still to be announced and put into force. But the period between the summer of 1940 and the spring of 1941 was one of great advance.

The Board of Trade had developed what had been so singularly lacking in pre-war preparations and in the first nine months of war—a forward-looking mind. They appreciated their war-time problems and were ready for action.

CHAPTER II

COMMERCIAL POLICY:
IMPORT CONTROL

(i)

The Introduction of Control

WE have now introduced generally the problems of civil industry and trade in the first eighteen months of war. Before plunging among the details of commercial policy in this period it will be as well to sharpen perspective by defining more clearly the different phases of British overseas trade over the whole war period. There were three phases. The first is covered by the present study. It is the period up to the inauguration of lend-lease when policy was dominated by anxiety over the balance of payments. The export drive received a marked setback after the fall of France but it was nevertheless still in force. The second phase, from the introduction of lend-lease to the end of 1941, was a period of adjustment. Anxieties about foreign exchange had been immensely relieved but some currency-earning exports were still necessary. In order to use to the best possible effect such resources as could still be devoted to exports, planning and direction of trade were required. Towards the end of 1941, however, exports had to be still more severely curtailed in order to meet American objections to the use of lend-lease materials and scarce materials in exports. In the third phase of commercial policy—that is, after 1941—export manufacture and export connections were unhesitatingly sacrificed to the needs of an all-out war effort. The direction of such trade as remained was changed and much of its pattern was closely planned. Only as the war drew to its close was attention increasingly devoted to plans for resuming freedom to export and for raising export trade from the very low level to which it had sunk by 1943.

In the first, the 'balance of payments', phase[1] of commercial policy import control played an important part. In 1938, alarmed by the prospective adverse balance of payments of the United Kingdom in war-time and in particular by the prospective shortage of hard currencies, the Treasury and the Board of Trade agreed upon the

---

[1] The main features of the balance of payments problems are set out in *British War Economy*, by W. K. Hancock and M. M. Gowing, H.M.S.O., 1949.

need for a war-time import control and the form it should take. At this stage no one seemed to expect a shipping shortage in war-time. It is no exaggeration to say that the sole aim of import control was to be the saving of foreign currencies.[1] Here, import control was to bear a heavy responsibility. For the plans for exchange control were loose. Until the end of 1938, the Treasury had been averse to all schemes for such a control. Their objections were overcome but the scheme that emerged was a partial one. It was intended to control movements of capital[2] and not exchange requirements for normal trading purposes. These requirements were to be curbed in two ways. Some goods were to be subject to import licensing and some foods and raw materials were to come under State monopoly purchase. Exchange was to be automatically allowed for commodities covered by neither of these controls.

Import control was at the outset to cover only a small proportion of the import trade of the United Kingdom. Of a total trade of £920 millions in 1938 the first control Order of September 1939 was later estimated by the Board of Trade to have affected only some £80 millions of imports. By far the greater proportion of imports, it was thought, would be purchased on public account and under monopoly conditions by the Ministry of Supply and the Ministry of Food, though it was possible that these departments would need the help of the import licensing machinery to regulate and enforce their buying programmes.

These assumptions were soon to prove wrong. Admittedly it was intended that import restrictions should be extended as and when experience was gained in administering the control. It would have been dangerous, as the study of export control will show, to overload the machine at the outset. But there was equally no ground for supposing that in the early phases of the war the purchasing arrangements of the Ministry of Supply and the Ministry of Food would have been so fully built up as to be able to deal effectively with the whole range of food[3] and raw material imports. In fact these arrangements tended to be developed from the centre outwards—from the essential and critical items to the relatively inessential and unimportant—with the result that groups of miscellaneous commodities which the country could do without were for a time imported without restriction.

The first instalment of import restrictions was to apply almost entirely to consumer goods. These goods were in three categories—

---

[1] In the saving of foreign currencies is included the economy of avoiding the higher prices which would have resulted from competitive purchases in a free market.

[2] Even here the scheme had gaps. See *British War Economy, op. cit.*, Chapter IV, section (ii).

[3] Some foodstuffs were subject at the outset to import control, but the trade was only estimated at £14 millions and there was a big group of foods subject to control neither by the Ministry of Food nor by the Import Licensing Department of the Board of Trade.

C

luxuries, goods of which large stocks were held in the country, and goods the needs for which could be met wholly or mainly by home production. At first machinery was not to be included in the restrictions. The administration of the licensing of imports under these restrictions was to be in the hands of a newly created division within the Board of Trade, assisted and advised by an interdepartmental committee.[1] Thus the control would rest with a department staffed by civil servants. Some use might, it was thought, be made of trade associations, but there were doubts as to how far these associations could be relied upon to administer such restrictions impartially and efficiently.[2] Where absolute prohibition of import was not imposed the method which would probably be adopted would be to give importers quotas based upon their past trade. At the same time effective liaison was planned between the Import Licensing Department of the Board of Trade on the one hand, and, on the other, the Bank of England (on currency matters), the Ministry of Economic Warfare and the Ministry of Shipping.

The chief troubles to which import control was likely to give rise appeared to be political. How could the restrictions be administered in such a way that they did not cut across the terms of existing trade treaties and agreements, the most-favoured nation clause for example? Few of these treaties made any provision for the imposition of trade restrictions in a national emergency, though the Anglo-American Trade Agreement did allow for prohibitions or restrictions imposed in the event of hostilities.[3] Yet the need to save hard currencies, which was the very basis of the restrictions, could not be satisfied without some pretty drastic discrimination. Nothing apparently could be done about this; the countries affected must be left to register their protests and complaints, and the only reply could be that the controls had been forced upon Britain by the circumstances of the war. So far as the Empire was concerned imports would be admitted freely from the sterling area and the only problem would be Canada. France, too, was a special problem; the restrictions on trade in luxuries would have hit her hard, and, on the proposal of the Foreign Office, it was agreed not to impose cuts of more than two-thirds on former trade with her.

Nevertheless there was perhaps at the time inadequate appreciation of the ill-feeling which would be created abroad by the restrictions of import control. The war-time necessities which lay behind this control were frequently overlooked abroad. In America,

---

[1] There had been some import licensing, it may be noted, in pre-war days, of arms, plumage and dyestuffs, and, in connection with agricultural policy, of beef, lamb, bacon, pork, potatoes and fish.

[2] In the event, as will be seen later, much use was to be made of the services of certain trade associations.

[3] United Kingdom-United States Trade Agreement, 1938, Article 16(g) (Cmd. 5882).

for example, the fact that manufacturers of aircraft and munitions would benefit from British purchases was not allowed to offset the disadvantages incurred by exporters of apples or tobacco. The actual import regulations were often enough to create annoyance. Thus the Swiss in particular were to be much irritated by the absence of any saving clause for goods imported under existing contracts.[1] In all these matters the political consideration—the need to avoid the creation of ill-will in the countries concerned—was predominant.

It was obvious that import control was going to be a delicate matter. Nevertheless the necessary control Order was ready at the outbreak of war. Import control was introduced under the authority of the Import, Export and Customs Powers (Defence) Act, 1939, and the first Order of 3rd September 1939, prohibiting importation without a licence from the Board of Trade, covered textiles, apparel, glassware, pottery, cars, some non-essential foodstuffs and a miscellaneous group of manufactured articles.[2] It was estimated that this would represent trade amounting in 1937 to some £90 millions, and it was intended to reduce the foreign exchange required for this trade to between £6 millions and £7 millions. This would clearly mean a pretty heavy reduction on some of the items; textiles, for example, it was proposed to cut from £18 millions to under £2 millions; imports of women's footwear amounting to about £1 million would be eliminated.[3]

The commodities thus subject to import control were predominantly consumer goods and were in the main either luxuries or goods such as textiles, apparel and footwear for which home production could provide substitutes. The desirability of restricting imports of producer goods, such as machinery, was much more doubtful. When the licensing of imports of all kinds of machinery was in fact imposed at the end of October 1939,[4] it was regarded as an experimental measure to be relaxed possibly if it was shown to be having adverse effects upon British industry. To deal with the licensing problems which would arise a machinery import licensing section was set up; staff with the special technical knowledge required were drawn from the Patent Office. This knowledge was

---

[1] There was, at the beginning of the war, a complete prohibition on the imports of watches and watch movements. Eventually, to meet the Swiss complaint, it was agreed that a fixed sum should be assigned to cover the pre-war orders and this would be allocated by the Swiss Government among traders affected.

[2] S.R. & O. 1939, No. 1054. In addition to the items mentioned, the Order controlled, for example, the import of furniture, clocks and watches, leather goods, office machinery, books, jewellery, toys, vacuum cleaners.

[3] Other drastic cuts would be jewellery from £1,200,000 to £61,000 (Empire £38,000, France £23,000) and toys from £1,800,000 to £10,000 (Empire £7,000, France £3,000).

[4] S.R. & O. 1939, No. 1497.

clearly necessary, since, while the importation of parts could be licensed on a quota basis, applications for the importation of complete machines had to be judged on the merits of the individual case. It might be possible, for example, to secure secondhand machinery in Britain and to recondition it, thus avoiding the need for the import of new machinery. The main problem, of course, was to find out whether home production could meet the applicant's requirements, and close touch was accordingly maintained with the trade associations. A British maker might be fully occupied with Government orders, or on the other hand he might be producing on too small a scale to be able to compete effectively with the foreign product. Finally, as machinery takes time to produce it was necessary to warn importers to make certain of licences before putting in orders.

The main lines of policy to be followed in controlling imports have already been mentioned.[1] Imports of manufactured goods for civilian purposes from hard-currency and dollar sources were as far as possible to be eliminated. On the other hand open general licences would be fairly freely issued for importation from countries within the Empire, though care would have to be taken in drawing up lists of commodities for which such open general licences would be issued to avoid any undue demand for Canadian dollars. As for categories of goods, importation from foreign countries of luxuries and goods substitutable by home production should be cut out. France, however, would be given preferential treatment over other foreign countries, and the maximum percentage reduction—for the luxuries and substitutable commodities—applied to French imports would be $66\frac{2}{3}$ per cent. There were, however, at the outset no open general licences for French commodities, a matter which was to be the source of some indignation and protest across the Channel.

This policy was administered by the application to established importers of quotas of values or quantities based on past trade.[2] Rigid though this arrangement would be under normal circumstances, in war-time it was probably the only practicable way of sharing a reduced volume of trade. Nevertheless, while few imports from foreign countries other than France were completely prohibited,[3] the sources of supply were sometimes so much reduced, either by war or by the licensing policy adopted, that it was difficult to maintain the principle of an equitable sharing among importers of

---

[1] The imports now referred to are those controlled by the first Order of September 1939.

[2] i.e. on trade during the year ending 31st August 1939. No allowance was made for trade with enemy countries.

[3] e.g. pottery, cars, jewellery, vacuum cleaners, toys, luxury foodstuffs. The ban imposed at the beginning of the war on clocks and watches and on glassware was subsequently lifted.

such trade as was left.[1] In some cases a telescoping of the importing organisation occurred, in others the problem was met by the creation of importers' pools. The importer who secured a licence was not charged a fee, though there had been discussion before the war about the possibility of making charges for both export and import licences. It could, of course, be urged that the charging of a fee would be a very reasonable way of skimming off the extra profits that the importer would be making, but there appeared to be several administrative difficulties in introducing charges. Uniform fees would operate unfairly, while *ad valorem* charges, which in any case would be difficult to assess, would not differ greatly from import duties.

There had been doubts, as has been seen, about the use which could be made of trade associations in handling the detailed problems of import licensing. If, for example, the associations were not all-inclusive could they always be relied upon to see that trade was shared equitably between members and non-members? In fact when the import control system came into operation a fair amount of use was made of them. They possessed the technical knowledge without which the licensing of non-standardised commodities could not be effectively administered. Thus the London Chamber of Commerce advised on the importation of domestic glassware, of essential oils, and, through its horological section, of clocks and watches. Other important associations whose services were employed were the Publishers' Association, particularly in connection with the import of books from the United States, and the Wool Textile Delegation. To deal with the problems arising out of the import of torch batteries a Torch Battery Imports Advisory Committee, consisting of battery manufacturers as well as importers, was set up in June 1940; it gave advice on the administration of the newly instituted import control and drew up a list of approved importers.[2] The use of the advice of trade associations in connection with the import of machinery has already been noted. Further use of trade advice and assistance might have proved of dubious advantage, although it would have eased the burden in the first few months of war on an overworked department and might have deflected some of the protests about bureaucratic interference with trade.

During the first few months of war there was a steady addition of commodities to the import list. Mostly, however, these were commodities coming within the purview of the Ministry of Supply controls —flax, paper materials and paper, timber, iron and steel, aluminium

---

[1] For example, trade with France was at first confined to those who had previously imported goods from France, but, since textiles and apparel could be imported from no other foreign country, it was thought necessary to allow other importers some share in the trade in these commodities.

[2] See p. 84. It may also be noted that the administration of the import and export control of postage stamps was entrusted to the British Philatelic Association.

—and the aim of the Orders was often stated to be not so much the restriction of imports as to facilitate the operations of the raw material control. Some miscellaneous foodstuffs were also added to the list at the request of the Ministry of Food.[1]

It was not long before the Treasury saw that, whatever their original intentions, import control would have to be supported by exchange control—for a few special cases at least. Thus the Treasury decided in September 1939 that no dollars should be spent on the purchase of American tobacco, apart from what was required to cover existing contracts. This decision had to be taken because of the trade's practice of buying at auctions well in advance of the actual time of importation. Since, however, arrangements were being made to import small quantities of oriental tobacco this decision was bound to lead to friction with the United States and to give rise to American protests.[2] The United Kingdom tobacco companies were also perturbed by this decision, since it meant in the first place that they would not be allowed dollars to purchase the remainder of the 1939 crop. Their proposals for payment in blocked sterling failed, however, to obtain the approval of the British Treasury. Nor were they happy about the prospect of having to blend Virginian and oriental tobaccos. Moreover, as loopholes had been found in the exchange control it was decided at the end of 1939 to put tobacco under import control.[3] Since tobacco was now freely licensed for import from Empire sources, while American leaf continued to be excluded, this meant further trouble with the United States.

The problem of payment for American films met with an easier solution. A decision was soon reached that import control was not the right way of tackling the matter, since it would not affect the transfer of royalty earnings to the United States by American renter companies in this country. With the help of the American Ambassador the President of the Board of Trade managed in November 1939 to negotiate an agreement with seven American companies which amounted to blocking the transfer of fifty per cent. of their pre-war average remittances for the year 1st November 1939 to 31st October 1940, a sum of approximately $17\frac{1}{2}$ million dollars. Disposal of their remaining revenue was to be supervised by a control organisation representing the companies and the Board of Trade, and what they earned in foreign exchange through overseas distribution of their pictures was to be at their disposal. The companies for their part agreed to export freely to the United Kingdom and not to create an artificial shortage of films.

---

[1] Apples and pears in November (S.R. & O. 1939, No. 1619); bacon, ham and lard in January 1940 (S.R. & O. 1940, No. 35); eggs in November (S.R. & O. 1939, No. 1680).

[2] See p. 32.

[3] S.R. & O. 1939, No. 1874.

(ii)

Import Control in Operation, 1939–40

The significance of import control as an instrument for strengthening the foreign exchange position of the United Kingdom was clearly recognised from the beginning of the war. It was pointed out that whereas Germany had a double control—an exchange control and an import control—in this country there was in effect only one control.[1] An import licence constituted a valid claim to foreign exchange.

Nevertheless it had to be admitted at the end of 1939 that the reduction in imports and the saving in foreign exchange were less than had been hoped. It was true that Ministry of Food and Ministry of Supply purchasing arrangements covered more than two-thirds of imports measured in pre-war values—£630 millions out of £920 millions. Of the remaining imports films and tobacco were subject to special arrangements while import control had been extended to some £120 millions of civilian goods outside the field of State purchase. But there still remained £120 millions of imports not subject to any form of control, including over £50 millions of miscellaneous foods.

There were various partial explanations of the failure to tighten up import restrictions. It had been found necessary, for example, to license additional quantities of certain items—car parts, watches and alarm clocks. Then there had been an agreement with France introducing open general licences for certain French commodities.[2] Furthermore it had been felt from the beginning of the war that as little as possible should be done to interfere with valuable re-export trades. For this reason the imports of undressed furs amounting to £11·5 millions in 1938 had been left untouched.[3] Licences were given for the import of goods held in bond for re-export and for goods on which there would be a drawback of duty on re-export. In December 1939 a stock replacement scheme was introduced, whereby firms exporting from stock might apply for licences to replace the goods so exported.[4]

Yet it was fairly clear that there were far too many loopholes in the arrangements and that control needed to be extended. The gaps

---

[1] Apart from special cases, such as the refusal of dollars for tobacco purchases.

[2] See pp. 34-35.

[3] The open general licence to import undressed furs was revoked in July 1940. A scheme was then introduced, which for a time worked through the Fur Export Group, aiming at obtaining the maximum proceeds in hard currency from the re-export of furs.

[4] To meet Swiss objections it was also arranged that tissues exported for embroidery might be re-imported into this country.

in the Ministry of Supply and Ministry of Food arrangements were particularly unsatisfactory. There were still important raw materials —cotton for example—which, though the subject of a Control, could be imported without licence.[1] There were a number of miscellaneous foodstuffs which the Ministry of Food did not control because they were not essential, and which were not subject to import restriction. The consignment trade in fruit and vegetables, in which the overseas exporter took the initiative in sending the commodities to this country, was an outstanding source of trouble.

Four weighty arguments for extending import control were heard. First, the country ought not to go short of munitions in order to import unessentials; secondly, central control was desirable on exchange and shipping grounds: thirdly, shippers who secured shipping space for unessential imports would tend to raise freight charges, and, fourthly, it would be better if the profits on imports which these shippers made went to the Minister of Food who might use them to subsidise essential foodstuffs.

The case for extending import control to a whole range of food-stuffs, which had been imported in 1938 to a value of about £300 millions, was overwhelming. In March 1940, therefore, an Order was made bringing under such control all foodstuffs and feeding-stuffs for animals, the only exceptions being fish and wines and spirits.[2] For some of these commodities open general licences were issued, either for all countries, for France, or for the Empire. This arrangement not only tidied up the whole problem of control of food imports, but also put an end to the piecemeal addition of foods to the control list which had been a continuous source of friction.

Meanwhile there had been an extension of the scope of import control to include a further group of miscellaneous manufactures and consumer goods—linen and hemp piece goods, certain kinds of hardware, cameras, photographic films and plates and wireless apparatus.[3] With all these extensions of control it was estimated at the beginning of April 1940 that very little of the import trade of the United Kingdom would remain outside the scope of import licensing and Government purchase.

In the spring of 1940 the attitude towards import restriction under-went rapid change. Even the currency problem had altered to some extent: there was a danger in the increase of purchases from the Empire sterling area, since it could not be assumed that Empire countries would necessarily continue indefinitely to invest their sur-plus in sterling balances and sterling securities. More important than

---

[1] On the other hand, by the end of 1939 probably between eighty and ninety per cent. of raw material imports were covered by State purchase.

[2] S.R. & O. 1940, No. 405. Administration of the control lay with the Ministry of Food.

[3] S.R. & O. 1940, No. 343.

this was the emergence of shipping as a shortage with which the import licensing authorities must reckon.[1] For shipping purposes a more realistic import programme had been formulated. Under this programme only 1·15 million tons were allocated to miscellaneous imports,[2] which covered not only civilian consumer goods but things required by the Ministry of Supply such as machine tools and jute sacks. Too much should not be made of this programme. It was only a paper programme, and, moreover, its statistical foundations were slender: the Board of Trade possessed information about the value, but very little about the tonnage, of these miscellaneous imports. Yet the programme encouraged a noticeable change in policy with regard to import restrictions.[3] Lastly, import policy had to conform with home trade policy. Limitations on the supply of textiles and, later, of miscellaneous consumer goods were being introduced in the home market and it was obviously necessary to reduce proportionately imports from overseas sources of supply on which hitherto there had been no restriction.

It was clear now that import control was being so widely extended that it would be administratively a great deal simpler to place a general control on all imports rather than to go on in piecemeal fashion bringing fresh imports under licensing. The latter, the piecemeal procedure, was plainly unsatisfactory because of difficulties of interpretation and definition, which frequently enabled oddments which could well be dispensed with to escape from control. A general control on all imports was accordingly imposed in June 1940.[4]

Hitherto policy had been, it was stated, to license imports of manufactured goods freely from the sterling part of the Empire and from France and French possessions, but, in general, to refuse licences to import goods from other countries unless they were required for re-export or for use in the export trade. The fall of France meant that, to intensify import restrictions, freedom to import from Empire countries would have to be curtailed.[5] Further scope for tightening restrictions lay in the fact that there still remained a number of commodities that could be imported without licence from any source. These were, however, predominantly commodities for which responsibility lay with the Ministry of Supply—raw materials and chemicals. In November the open general licence for wool

---

[1] Even in May 1940 it was stated that the Import Licensing Department had received no definite instructions to take shipping considerations into account.

[2] This figure was later reduced to one million tons.

[3] The introduction of import control for cotton in May 1940 (S.R. & O. 1940, No. 805) was partly a response to the shipping shortage.

[4] S.R. & O. 1940, No. 873.

[5] Open licences were still issued, however, for the import from French Equatorial Africa, French Cameroons and French possessions in India and the Pacific of commodities which could still be freely imported from the Empire.

and hemp was withdrawn, and in February 1941 the similar licence to import certain chemicals liable to key industry duty was revoked.

Eventually also, in December 1940, import restriction was imposed on wines and spirits which it had, curiously enough, been possible hitherto to import freely without licence. The arguments in favour of their free importation had been mainly political and linked with considerations of economic warfare, though it had also been stated that they took up little shipping space. In the summer of 1940 it was agreed that the open general licence for wines and spirits should be continued, though they should receive no shipping priority. However, the Ministry of Shipping protested against these arrangements which seemed likely to permit a considerably larger import tonnage of these commodities than had been provided for in the Ministry of Food's import programme,[1] and the open general licence was accordingly revoked at the end of the year. Imports were, it was agreed, to be limited to 100 per cent. of pre-war, no shipping priority was to be accorded and the Ministry of Food was to advise on licensing.

There were one or two minor ways in which import restrictions were tightened up from June 1940 onwards. In the first place the concessions made for importation undertaken with a view directly or indirectly to re-export were curtailed. In July 1940 it was stated that in future licences would not in general be granted for the importation of foreign goods for re-export to countries within the sterling area of the Empire if the goods were of a kind which would not be licensed for importation for home consumption: nor, where such goods were exported from stock to countries in the sterling area, would licences be automatically granted for imports for stock replacement. A stricter policy was also adopted with regard to the licensing of imports of raw material for incorporation in exports to be sent to the sterling area. These changes of policy were inspired by the desire to avoid further losses of hard currency, but they came up against a deeper problem. Empire countries had not introduced restrictions on the scale on which they had been imposed in the United Kingdom, and until they did so there would continue to be a danger of drain on the central reserves. Import restrictions were tightened, secondly, by directing that goods returned after exportation from the United Kingdom became subject to licence on re-importation. The aim here clearly was to check evasion of restrictions on the home market. Firms had been found trying to evade the Limitation of Supplies Orders by sending goods to Eire and then re-importing them through Northern Ireland.[2] Thirdly, two restrictions

---

[1] 64,000 tons.

[2] This also raised the question of the desirability of maintaining open general licences for goods imported from Eire. Eventually, as the Eire Export Control was found to be working unsatisfactorily open general licences for the import of textiles and apparel from Eire were withdrawn.

imposed in the summer of 1941 may be mentioned; private gift parcels sent to this country were limited to a weight of 5 lb.,[1] and goods shipped to the United Kingdom in transit or for transhipment became subject to import licensing.

(iii)

The Political Problems of Import Control

It had been recognised that import control was bound to raise political difficulties with countries with which the United Kingdom had trade treaties or trade agreements. These problems proved to be quite as awkward as had been expected. Moreover, there were un-. expected protests from France who as Britain's main ally wished for preferential treatment. Most troublesome of all, however, were the objections of the United States.

THE UNITED STATES OF AMERICA

Many foreign countries were adversely affected by the almost complete prohibition on certain imports into the United Kingdom. This was particularly true of the United States, a country with which, quite apart from the pre-war trade agreement, Britain must at almost all costs remain friendly.

The problem could be stated in very simple terms. Prospective purchases of war requirements in the United States, coupled with limited hard-currency resources, inevitably meant that the level of normal peace-time purchases of such things as tobacco and foodstuffs could not be maintained. Yet it was far from easy to persuade the United States—especially the representatives in Congress of districts harshly affected by the restrictions—to understand this problem.

Difficulties arose at the very beginning of the war. In a memorandum to the War Cabinet of September 1939 the President of the Board of Trade, referring to the grave weakness of the country's gold and dollar position and to the need to curtail unnecessary imports, proposed (i) to stop purchases of leaf tobacco from America, (ii) to restrict purchases of apples, pears and canned fruits from the United States and Canada to the level of minimum requirements, and (iii) to reduce, by bargaining with the American film interests, the amount of royalty earnings which they might transfer into dollars.

---

[1] The Post Office's limit on parcels was 22 lb.

The arrangements about tobacco and films have already been described. In November 1939 import licensing was introduced for pears and apples.[1] The Chancellor of the Exchequer, in warning the American Ambassador at the end of October of this move, estimated that the United Kingdom's adverse balance with the United States would amount to £100 millions in the first year of war, and pointed out to him that at a time when dollars had to be refused to the fighting Services the purchase of non-essentials in America would be indefensible. He added, however, that Britain had no intention of using these reductions, forced upon her by the war, to alter permanently the channels of trade, and she intended as soon as possible to revert to her normal peace-time commercial policy as laid down in the Trade Agreement.

Further restrictions were inevitable and were soon to be introduced. Tobacco was placed under import control on 1st January 1940 and was followed by bacon, ham and lard and dried fruits.[2] In February 1940 licensing was extended to frozen and canned meat, and in March to tinned and bottled fruits.[3]

All these measures naturally caused great irritation to the American Secretary of State, Mr. Cordell Hull, the chief exponent of a liberal trade policy, and inconvenience to the Administration who in these matters, at any rate, were anxious to retain the support of the senators and representatives of the Southern states. They were also likely to damage the British cause in the United States, particularly among those who were most ill-disposed to the Axis. Taken by themselves, indeed, they might not have produced any really serious effects, but in conjunction with the proposed British purchases of Balkan tobacco[4] they led to a marked deterioration in Anglo-American relations. There was talk of a denunciation of the Trade Agreement of 1938, and at the end of December 1939 an official protest was made by the United States representative in London, in which the British purchases of oriental tobacco, at a time when American tobacco was excluded from the United Kingdom, were declared to be a violation of the Agreement. So also, it was stated, would be a compulsory mixing of American and oriental tobacco which had been mooted.

---

[1] S.R. & O. 1939, No. 1619. In 1937 imports from the United States of tobacco amounted to £14 millions, of apples to £1·1 million, of pears to £0·6 million, of canned fruits to £3·1 millions, a total of £19 millions out of total imports from the United States of £114 millions.

[2] S.R. & O. 1939, No. 1874: 1940, Nos. 35 and 97.

[3] S.R. & O. 1940, Nos. 193 and 355.

[4] The amounts involved were £870,000 per annum of Turkish tobacco, by way of interest on a twenty-year loan to Turkey, and £500,000 per annum of Greek tobacco. The United States tobacco problem had been solved by the purchase of the remaining portion of the 1939 crop, about two-thirds, by the United States Commodity Credit Corporation.

It was doubtful whether any case could be made out to meet this protest, and, in fact, no reply was ever sent. In London there were conflicting currents of opinion. Some even suggested that the British measures would force the Americans, through the protests of their agricultural interests, to abandon their 'cash and carry' legislation. The Treasury were all for discrimination, as too was the Ministry of Economic Warfare.[1] It was left to the Board of Trade, fearful for the fate of the Trade Agreement, to suggest that if necessary Britain ought to be prepared to buy the oriental tobacco and then burn it; and to resist as far as possible the proposed compulsory blending of the different tobaccos. Meanwhile the tobacco situation was fairly easy—there were two years' stocks in the United Kingdom;[2] and the British companies were thinking up schemes for acquiring the American tobacco without any current expenditure of dollars.

During the early months of 1940 the American Government continued to press for a change of import policy. American opinion, it was urged, would improve if only the British Government would agree to buy certain minimum quantities of American agricultural products. In London, however, it was felt that shortage of hard currency precluded any arrangement of this kind. All that could be done was to point to the increasing expenditure on armaments in the United States, which should indirectly benefit American agriculture, and to assure the Americans, as the Prime Minister did in a speech at the end of January 1940, that Britain intended after the war to return to liberal principles of international trade.

For the time being an increasingly restrictionist policy had to be followed. Not only was cotton brought under import control in May 1940[3] (with an open general licence for imports from the Empire, France, French possessions and Egypt), but later in the year it was agreed that in order to save dollars purchases of cotton from the United States for the second year of war must be drastically reduced. Moreover, in November 1940, the Treasury rejected a request that dollars should be made available to take up options on the United States Commodity Credit Corporation's purchases of the 1939 crop of tobacco, though it was decided that Greek and Turkish tobacco should be bought.[4] Action was, however, suspended for the while, and the whole question was disposed of by two events of the spring of 1941—the passing of the Lend-Lease Bill by Congress and the overrunning of Greece by the Germans.

---

[1] The purchases of oriental tobacco were dictated solely by political or economic warfare considerations.

[2] A stock equal to one year's supplies was, however, considered to be an essential minimum.

[3] S.R. & O. 1940, No. 805.

[4] In August 1940 there had been further purchases of Greek tobacco for political reasons.

FRANCE

As has been seen, provision was made from the very beginning of the war for according to imports from France more favourable treatment than that given to imports from other foreign countries. But the French Government was not satisfied with this arrangement and soon began pressing for a reduction in British import restrictions on French goods. In default of any immediate concessions it retorted in November 1939 by refusing licences for the import of commodities from Britain into France.

The situation was complicated by the fact that the French themselves had already had before the war a system of import quotas which covered the greater part of British trade with them. To return to the *status quo*, therefore, would not mean anything like parity of treatment for imports. However, concessions were immediately made on certain French luxury goods,[1] and from the beginning of 1940 larger quotas were to be given for some imports from France. There followed the Reynaud-Simon financial understanding of December 1939 in which the two countries agreed not to impose restrictions on their mutual trade for the purpose of protecting home industry or for exchange reasons.[2] Doubts were felt about the wisdom of making further concessions. In the first place there was no economic justification for importing French luxuries in time of war, and, secondly, further moves in this direction would give rise to protests from neutrals. Nor had Britain any intention of permanently diverting trade to France. Furthermore, out of a pre-war (1938) trade of £23½ millions more than half the imports were either free or freely licensed. The French had agreed to make concessions in their treatment of imports from the United Kingdom, but it was felt in London that the whole administration of their quota arrangements was unsatisfactory.[3]

Nevertheless the political arguments for meeting the French point of view were weighty, and in February 1940 further steps were taken towards freeing the trade between the two countries. On 16th February an agreement, unpublished in order to avoid arousing the protests of neutrals, was signed. The British representatives agreed to admit a wide range of imports from France without restriction, and for most other commodities to license imports at the rate of 100 per cent. of trade in the base period, 1st September 1938–31st August 1939. Only linen manufactures were prohibited, and this was because

---

[1] An open general licence was issued allowing the free importation from France, Algeria or Tunis of dates, turkeys, crystallised fruit, mimosa.

[2] The wording of the agreement was not clear; did it refer to all restrictions or only to new restrictions?

[3] The French also proposed the setting up of an Anglo-French trade committee, on the lines of the permanent executive committees already created, to facilitate collaboration between the United Kingdom and French trade departments and to arrange for co-operation in export trade. This was not viewed sympathetically by the Board of Trade.

the shortage of flax had meant that no fresh production could be undertaken in Britain for the home market. The French for their part agreed to return to the pre-war position, and if the United Kingdom goods had then been subject to quota to grant quotas in most cases up to at least 100 per cent., on a quantity basis, of the share of the United Kingdom in the total quota, or up to 100 per cent. of actual imports in 1938. Cars, bicycles and linen goods were to be restricted to fifty per cent. of pre-war amounts. The British and the French also undertook to secure for each other liberal treatment in their respective Empires and associated territories, though the United Kingdom representatives had to point out that the Dominions were autonomous in fiscal and tariff policy. The whole agreement was qualified by the understanding that the imposition of restrictions on the home market would justify corresponding restrictions on their trade with one another.[1] This was important for at this time the British Government was contemplating limitations on supplies of cotton, rayon and linen textiles to the domestic consumer.

When the main outlines of this agreement came to be known, some neutral countries, Belgium and the United States for example, were somewhat perturbed. Nevertheless, the French remained far from satisfied. They were not content with the British undertaking to license freely and wished to see the range of open general licences extended. At the end of March 1940 the President of the Board of Trade visited Paris and agreed to make further concessions to the French point of view. Additional commodities, in particular certain fruits and vegetables, were granted an open general licence, and this freedom to import which now covered a long list of goods was to include not only France, Algeria and Tunis but all the French overseas possessions. Supplementary quotas were also to be given for the importation from France of women's and girls' clothing, and for leather gloves.[2] The President further agreed to consider the possibility of importing certain kinds of machinery in which French exporters to this country were interested.

The French authorities conceded supplementary quotas for some commodities imported from the United Kingdom—leather, heavy lorries, jute tissues, photographic paper and films, certain classes of textile machinery. From the British standpoint, however, there remained two thoroughly unsatisfactory features about the whole position. First the French had abandoned the pre-war arrangement whereby the United Kingdom share of their total quota had been administered by British trade associations. Secondly, what had been

---

[1] It was agreed, however, that special concessions should be made in cases where a substantial proportion of imports of the sort of commodities, of which supplies were to be restricted in the home market, had come in the past from what were now enemy countries.

[2] These supplementary quotas represented a portion of the trade formerly done with enemy or enemy-occupied territories.

achieved by these Anglo-French negotiations had been in effect a reversion to the pre-war position. This meant in general an admission of French goods to the British market without quantitative restrictions, whereas on the French side it involved a return to pre-war quotas. Such control as still remained on imports from France into this country was to be used not for restrictive purposes but to secure the effective operation of the controls exercised by the Ministry of Food. There was thus a fundamental lack of balance in the agreements. Nor was it desirable that, merely for political reasons, the United Kingdom should have to agree in war-time to import without restriction the luxuries in which the French trade largely consisted. A solution of the problem would have required, however, a joint planning of the use of the economic resources of the two countries which was quite impracticable at this stage of the war. The sudden and overwhelming catastrophe of the summer of 1940 makes it idle to speculate whether it could have been achieved later.

In the short run, at any rate, there can be no doubt that, if France had remained a belligerent, imports from her would have been subject to a comprehensive measure of restriction, as indeed the agreements permitted. Limitations which were soon to be intensified were being imposed on the supply of commodities in the home market. Moreover, the Ministry of Food was tightening up its controls over imported foodstuffs. In June the French authorities were warned that these measures, together with the diversion of shipping that was now necessary, would mean an alteration in British policy towards imports from France. Had France gone on fighting some of the import relaxations might have had to be maintained, but in general it is clear that concessions to political sentiment would have had to be abandoned in face of the new realities of the war in the west.

APPENDIX I

Import Licensing, 1939–40 and 1940–41

1. YEAR ENDING 31st AUGUST 1940

Commodity	Licences issued	Licences used	Open General Licences
	£ million	£ million	£ million
1. Controlled by Import Licensing Department (other than machinery)	39·908	19·071	28·025
2. Controlled by Ministry of Food and Ministry of Supply controls	104·174	53·291	162·516[1]
3. Silver bullion or coin	1·527	1·177	0·006[2]
4. Machinery	21·775[3]	12·757	12·718[4]
TOTALS	167·384	86·296	203·265

[1] Excluding machine tools.
[2] On Government account.
[3] Of this, £15,081 for machinery from the United States.
[4] Machine tools.

2. YEAR ENDING 31st AUGUST 1941

Commodity	Licences issued	Licences used	Open General Licences
	£ million	£ million	£ million
1. Controlled by Import Licensing Department (other than machinery)	28·939	14·133	66·430
2. Controlled by Ministry of Food and Ministry of Supply controls	121·783	68·158	305·760[1]
3. Gold and silver coin and bullion . . .	1·657	0·885	1·609
4. Machinery[2]	19·253[3]	9·744	35·963
TOTALS	171·632	92·920	409·762

[1] Excluding machine tools.
[2] Including machine tools.
[3] Of this £17,208 for machinery from the United States.

APPENDIX 2

Note on Import Licensing

The main types of import licences issued were as follows:

  (i) The individual licence—the most usual form of licence—covering the importation of a specified commodity to a specified value or quantity.

 (ii) Blanket or block licences authorising the importation of a specified commodity up to a stated aggregate quantity or value in any number of consignments during a given period.

(iii) Open licences, issued to a specified importer, permitting the importation of a specified commodity without limit as to quantity. These licences were usually intended to cover (a) gifts from abroad sent to approved organisations, not involving the transfer of foreign currencies, and (b) commodities coming under Ministry of Supply and Ministry of Food controls.

(iv) Open general licences issued to the Customs, authorising the importation of specified commodities from all countries or from certain specified countries without the production of individual licences by the importers concerned.

Licences were normally valid for three months and were not transferable. Applications for licences were required to be made by the actual importer of the goods. Difficulties were experienced in evolving a satisfactory definition of the importer, but he was normally assumed to be the person primarily liable for making payment to the overseas supplier. Statements of past trading were required from applicants for licences, such statements being accompanied by an accountant's certificate as to their accuracy.

The main items exempted from import licensing requirements were: (1) live quadrupeds, (2) goods for Government departments, (3) goods for privileged persons, e.g. High Commissioners, Ambassadors, (4) goods for Crown Agents for the Colonies, (5) personal and household effects, (6) trade samples.

CHAPTER III

COMMERCIAL POLICY: EXPORTS

(i)

Export Problems from the Outbreak of War until the Export Drive

THE growing emphasis that was placed in the first few months of war upon the need to expand exports and the insistence that manufacture for export was as much a war-winning activity as the making of munitions stand in striking contrast to the almost complete absence of any serious study of the problem of export promotion in official circles before the war. As we have seen, it was as late as August 1939 that the Department of Overseas Trade made a preliminary reconnaissance of some of the problems of export trade in war-time. And, when war-time raw material requirements were being estimated, bulk figures for 'civil' requirements usually made no distinction between export and home trade.[1] The assumption about the export trades in these estimates was that their normal pre-war consumption of raw materials could be taken as the standard of their requirements. This held even for an important exporting industry like cotton.

What had been worked out before September 1939 was the outline of a system for *restricting* exports for the dual purpose of conserving essential materials at home and preventing supplies from reaching the enemy. For many years before the outbreak of hostilities there had been discussions between the departments concerned of the problems of a war-time export control, the form which it should take and the instruments by which it should be given effect. It had been settled, for example, that the Board of Trade should be the responsible authority for administering the control,[2] partly to secure the necessary interdepartmental co-ordination, and partly because of their knowledge of trade and industry and their interest in seeing that no unnecessary restrictions were placed on the export trade in time of war. There was, moreover, a licensing section already in existence in

---

[1] In iron and steel and ferro alloys it was not even possible to distinguish Service and civil requirements.

[2] And not, as had been first proposed, a Ministry of Blockade.

the Board which could be expanded and which would be assisted by an interdepartmental committee. The formal structure of control of the 1914–18 war would be reproduced, and distinction would be made between exports and export markets. As regards the latter: some goods would be prohibited for export without licence to all countries, some to all except Empire countries, and some only to European countries (other than France) and to countries on the Mediterranean Sea or Black Sea.[1]

Probably the more troublesome question was that of the goods to which export control should be applied. Should there be a short list of key commodities or a fairly long list comprising raw materials, foodstuffs and semi-manufactures? The Board of Trade favoured a short list; but it was argued that there would be difficulties with neutrals if the export control list did not correspond fairly closely with the contraband list. Ultimately it was decided that the two lists need not, at the outbreak of war, correspond, but that efforts should be made afterwards to bring them into harmony with one another. In general, considerations of supply and of economic warfare predominated, and the first major export control Order of 1st September 1939[2] was fairly comprehensive. The Board of Trade had frequently made clear their objections to this arrangement. They pointed to the danger of hampering the export trade of the country and they were worried about the burden which would be imposed on the export licensing department, for which, it was pointed out, staff could not be trained in advance. Their fears proved later to be fully justified; in the first few months of war the administrative machinery came near to breaking down under the strain which was imposed on it. However, in pre-war discussion and preparation the Board received no support in their advocacy of a short export control list.

There was also the question as to whether any precautionary measures should be taken before the outbreak of war, and, if so, what form these measures should take. Experience derived from the Munich crisis had shown that there was a danger that important raw materials might be shipped to the Continent before war was declared. Some control was probably necessary—the voluntary co-operation of exporters could not be fully relied upon—but here again the Board of Trade argued that the list should be as short as possible. On 24th August 1939, an Order in Council was published prohibiting the export without licence from the Board of Trade of a number of non-ferrous metals, iron and steel scrap, textile materials

---

[1] Letters were used to denote these distinctions—'A' = all countries, 'B' = all except Empire, 'C' = Europe and destinations on the Mediterranean Sea or Black Sea, other than France or French possessions. The 'B' classification was little used; the only important goods to which it applied were rubber (from the beginning of the war) and, later, machine tools.

[2] S.R. & O. 1939, No. 1024.

other than wool, certain oils, petroleum, mica, rubber, toluol and radium compounds.[1]

Statutory powers for the formidable system of export control that was to be brought into operation on the outbreak of war were acquired under the Import, Export and Customs Powers (Defence) Bill which was hurriedly passed through Parliament on 1st September 1939.[2] This was followed by the first important export control Order of the war.

The arrangements that now came into operation followed fairly closely the pattern of the pre-war plans. They differed, however, in one respect, namely in the absence of any fee for the granting of an export licence.[3] Before the war the Board of Trade had proposed that fees should be charged for licences to exporters able to make good profits by selling at high prices in particular markets, the proceeds being used to subsidise the export of goods to less profitable markets. When war came this proposal was dropped, and indeed at the beginning of the war the pressure on the export licensing department was such that it could not have taken on any additional burden of this sort. However, even had this administrative problem not existed, the difficulties involved in working out a levy-subsidy scheme, which would have been both equitable and advantageous, would have been considerable.

The list of commodities which immediately came under export control was, as has been seen, a long one.[4] The Board of Trade's plea that not too much should be attempted at the outset, and that fresh commodities should only be added as experience was gained and as the resources of the export licensing department expanded was ignored. Thus the list embraced not only raw materials and foodstuffs but also a large number of semi-manufactured and fully-manufactured goods—yarns, semi-finished steel, agricultural implements, certain kinds of scientific instruments and electrical goods, several classes of machinery, vehicles and ships. A wide range of drugs and chemicals fell within it. In the sphere of raw materials it included coal,[5] iron ore and scrap, non-ferrous metals, timber, textile materials, hides and skins, paper-making materials and rubber. In food, drink, etc., it covered meat, dairy produce, grain and flour, fresh fruit and vegetables, wines and spirits, tobacco. Other items were dyestuffs and petroleum.

---

[1] S.R. & O. 1939, No. 945. Wool, dairy produce, tea, coffee, cocoa, and certain hides and skins had also been put forward, but were dropped from the list at a late moment.

[2] 2 & 3 Geo 6, ch. 69.

[3] This was provided for in the Act—see Section 2.

[4] The list at first was divided, like the customs, import and export list, into four sections; in and after January 1940 consolidated export control lists were broken up into sixteen groups.

[5] The export licensing of coal was administered by the export branch of the Mines Department.

All this, of course, was too much for a newly created department to tackle in the first few months of war. Much licensing was naturally done on the advice of the Ministry of Food and Ministry of Supply Controls, though these Controls were often slow to give their advice. But they were not the only departments concerned. In dealing with exports to Europe the Ministry of Economic Warfare had to be referred to. In special cases yet other departments might be involved. Consequently there was delay and congestion. Meanwhile something like 18,000 applications a week for licences were being received. Exporters had been free from this sort of restriction in the past and they were now being urged to increase their sales in overseas markets. They were naturally bewildered and irritated. At the beginning of December 1939 the President of the Board of Trade estimated[1] that about thirty per cent. of pre-war exports to non-enemy countries were covered by export licensing and admitted that the machine was overloaded; it would have been better, he said, if they had started more gradually.

Beyond the improvement of administrative techniques there was little that could be done to ease the situation. The Chancellor of the Exchequer, it is true, was in favour of a drastic reduction of the export control list, but the Ministries of Supply and Economic Warfare, so far from agreeing to this, wished to see it extended. The pre-war argument was revived that it was politically undesirable that the export control list should be shorter than the contraband list. All that could be done, therefore, was to give open general licences for one or two commodities[2]—and to lighten the burden of licensing by transferring some goods from the 'A' category (prohibited to all destinations) to the 'B' or 'C' categories.[3] And it was agreed that most goods could be exported to Eire without restriction. But the fact remained that a comprehensive system of control had been imposed on the export trade of the United Kingdom, and that the invidious task of restriction had been entrusted to the one Government department which had been regarded as concerned with the welfare and promotion of that trade.

Moreover, the effective operation of a scheme of export control raised all sorts of difficulties to which there were no counterparts in, for example, the administration of the import licensing system. Thus the need to take into account considerations of economic warfare made it even less practicable than it was for those in charge of import control to make use of the services of trade associations.[4]

---

[1] H. of C. Deb., Vol. 355, Col. 894.

[2] e.g. cinematograph films (subject to compliance with censorship regulations); S.R. & O. 1939, No. 1053.

[3] Thus machine tools were put in the 'B' instead of the 'A' category. (S.R. & O. 1939, No. 1239.)

[4] For the same reason the scope for bulk licences was much more restricted.

Similarly the global import quotas or rations which were fixed for countries contiguous to Germany raised awkward problems in dealing with United Kingdom exporters. (Most of these problems, of course, disappeared when the Germans overran a large part of Europe.) There were also the difficulties of co-ordination and adjustment with a number of departments with conflicting points of view. It was of no use, for example, for a manufacturer to obtain an export licence and then to find that a Ministry of Supply Control would not give him the necessary raw material;[1] or for the manufacturer who had been allocated raw material to discover that for economic warfare reasons he would not be granted an export licence. Then, again, a contractor for a big plant who was exporting it in sections might find suddenly that some of the parts not yet despatched had been placed under export restriction.[2] One of the ways of dealing with the link between the export licensing department and the raw material Control was to enlist the help of trade advisers who were familiar with the supply position. There were trade advisers, for example, for wool and jute, and at first for cotton. Following the establishment of the Cotton Board in 1940 the administration of export control of cotton textiles was entrusted to its export licensing department.[3]

While the problems of export control were being solved, there grew a preoccupation with export promotion. Soon after the outbreak of war ministers were made fully aware of the country's foreign exchange difficulties and of the need to stimulate exports. The Chancellor of the Exchequer in a memorandum to the War Cabinet of September 1939 recommended the greatest possible encouragement to the export trade. Lord Stamp's committee which advised ministers on economic affairs[4] applied itself continuously to a study of export problems and of the ways in which exports could be expanded. It was at first largely concerned with the obstacles in the path of the exporter, not only the export licensing system, but such things as censorship and Customs regulations, and, above all, the unco-operative or even actually hostile attitude of many of the raw material Controllers. Many of the Controllers, it was said, were refusing to allow raw materials to be used for anything but Service requirements; others would only give raw materials to a manufacturer who could show that he had an order for goods from abroad. The result was a stream of complaints and protests that United

---

[1] There might, of course, be more than one Control involved.

[2] This problem was dealt with by giving 'contract licences' for the whole plant when the scheme had been approved by the production department concerned.

[3] The actual licences were still issued by the Export Licensing Department of the Board of Trade, which consulted the Ministry of Economic Warfare where necessary.

[4] See *British War Economy, op. cit.*, p. 47.

Kingdom exporters were unwilling to quote fixed prices or firm delivery dates. The competitive advantage of the depreciation of the pound against the hard currencies by approximately one-seventh of its pre-war value was being lost. It was arranged therefore that the Minister of Supply should impress on the Controllers the importance that the Government attached to the maintenance and extension of the export trade, and should see how far it was possible to release raw materials for manufacture for export by the employment of substitutes in home and Service uses. On 17th October a memorandum was sent to the Federation of British Industries, the Association of British Chambers of Commerce and the National Union of Manufacturers stating that for export requirements supplies of most raw materials should be fully adequate.

Lord Stamp's committee also went on to consider the part to be played by exports in the economic strategy of the war. Given the existence of idle resources in the export trades, exports were the cheapest and most effective means of satisfying the war requirements of the country—that is, through import from abroad rather than by the diversion of home resources to war production. Later, as the tempo of industrial mobilisation quickened, the exporting industries would tend to lose some of their resources and this would present new and serious problems. The industries affected would be the metal, tool, engineering and vehicle industries which had been responsible for something like a third of total exports in 1937. This pointed yet more strongly to the necessity for expansion of exports by other industries in order to bridge the alarming gap in the balance of payments.[1] Lord Stamp was thus led to emphasise the need for new exports and new exporters. There were a number of manufacturers who sold only in the home market, and the organisation would have to be created which would enable them to sell overseas.

At the same time the Stamp Committee was careful to draw a distinction between different types of exports; they asserted that the encouragement of exports in general was a 'chaotic notion'. There were four considerations to be taken into account in estimating the worth of any particular £1,000 of exports: (i) the margin of export receipts over the import payments involved, (ii) political relations with the importing countries, (iii) the *kind* of exchange, hard or soft, which the exports would yield or which their essential imports would use up, (iv) shipping risks, inwards and outwards, and the 'unseen costs of convoy protection'. Special emphasis was laid on the

---

[1] In January 1940 Lord Stamp estimated that the net adverse balance of payments in the first year of war might reach £400 millions and thought that it would not be safe to draw on reserves of gold and foreign currencies to meet this, to an extent of more than £150 millions a year.

currency factor. Thus on the basis of 1937 values it was reckoned that an additional £100 of exports of cotton piece-goods cost £15 in hard currencies and yielded only £12 in these currencies; whereas an additional £100 of exports of woollen and worsted goods brought in £31 in hard currencies against a cost in them of only £2.

A ministerial sub-committee, which had been set up to look into the matter, and which reported in December 1939, did little to advance the study of export policy. It pointed out that fairly good reasons of one sort or another could be given for most exports, if one took account of the different points of view represented by the Treasury, the Foreign Office, the Board of Trade and the Ministry of Economic Warfare. There were probably few exports which were either particularly desirable or definitely undesirable. But the report made no suggestions as to how exports could be increased.

And, in fact, while much thought was devoted to the problem there was little in the way of action. The Board of Trade set up a new department of Industrial Supplies to deal with priority questions and the provision of raw materials for 'civil' requirements —exports and the home trade. They also initiated discussions with a number of trade associations, asking them about their export plans and export problems and about their raw material requirements. But there were obvious difficulties about any attempt to formulate precise estimates.

The evidence available at the end of 1939 seemed to point to supplies of raw materials as the critical factor for many exporting industries, and proposals for the encouragement of exports included suggestions for special allocations of raw materials or for allocations of raw materials at preferential prices. At the beginning of November 1939, the Wool Control actually introduced a scheme under which a wool ration was fixed for home civilian and export requirements but which gave priority to the export trade, since the Control agreed to replace in full the wool used in exports of woollen and worsted piece-goods and hosiery. However, the pressure of home demand was such that this inducement proved inadequate; reports showed that valuable orders in connection with the seasonal trade to Canada, the United States and South America were being lost. The Wool Control accordingly announced in January 1940 that it would increase the preference by replacing rations used in the export trade at the rate of 125 lb. for each 100 lb. exported for the remainder of the current rationing period.[1] At the same time there was a reduction, as compared with 1938, in the amount of wool made available for the home civilian trade. The scheme was further altered in May 1940 to meet the complaints of those who had not hitherto been engaged in export business, and firms were told that they could take

---

[1] This was subsequently extended to the end of May 1940.

export orders with the assurance that raw material would be available, provided that the rations for which they asked were within their plant capacity after deducting Government orders.

The other great textile industry, cotton, had made little progress in developing plans for the promotion of exports, and, indeed, the pull of the home market seemed to be a powerful factor militating here against the expansion of overseas trade. Before the war, it is true, it had been thought that cotton, in contrast to wool, would not be largely occupied with Government orders and that its main war-time effort would lie in the export field. But discussions had not got much further than the suggestion that the Cotton Industry Board, to be set up under the Cotton Industry Reorganisation Act of 1939, would be the instrument of control with its export trade development committee acting in an advisory capacity: there were few practical suggestions beyond the possibility of an export levy, and of discriminating prices and subsidies to encourage exports to certain markets. With the outbreak of war the operation of the Cotton Industry Reorganisation Act was suspended[1] and a war-time advisory body called the Cotton Board was set up on 18th September 1939 jointly by the President of the Board of Trade and the Minister of Supply. This Board proceeded to set up four committees to deal with raw cotton supplies, production and Government orders, export trade and supplies other than raw cotton.

Some more vigorous and positive policy was soon seen to be required. In the first place there was, as has been mentioned, the growing pressure of the home market. Government orders, too, were loading certain sections of the industry more heavily than had been anticipated; this was true of the spinning of coarser counts, for example. But the most unsatisfactory feature of the position was the status of the Cotton Board. It possessed no more than advisory functions, whereas it wanted something like the functions of a raw material Control and, in particular, powers to take measures to promote export trade. Cotton textile exports might not be very good from the currency standpoint, but they had high conversion value, i.e. a high ratio of value of finished product to imported raw material. The Board accordingly sought four main powers: (i) to lay down fixed prices, not simply maximum prices; (ii) to allocate raw materials; (iii) to call for information about productive capacity, output, stocks, etc.; (iv) to impose a levy on the use of the raw material, the proceeds to be employed for research and promotion of the export trade. Exports, it was also suggested, might be stimulated by 'derogations' from the fixed prices, and, possibly, by subsidies.

On 10th November 1939 a Cotton Controller responsible to the Minister of Supply was appointed. But only just over a week earlier

---

[1] 2 & 3 Geo. 6, ch. 116.

the Cotton Board had protested that 'the President of the Board of Trade and the Minister of Supply, having set up a body for the specific purpose of advising them on the problems of the cotton industry, not only reject its advice but are proposing to take action which appears to reflect adversely alike on its competence and impartiality'. The fact of course was that some of the powers which the Cotton Board was asking for were highly controversial. This was particularly true of the price-fixing powers. The pre-war Re-organisation Act had included provisions for price fixing, but it had also included various and elaborate safeguards. Moreover, the Act referred to peace-time conditions of trade: the conditions now were very different, and what was clearly needed was the enactment of maximum prices. The danger of a revival of what the Cotton Board described as 'destructive price-cutting competition' seemed to be purely speculative. Nor was it perhaps altogether desirable that these powers should be vested in a Board composed of persons interested in the industry.

Eventually the President of the Board of Trade, after discussions with ministers concerned, gave his consent to the proposal that yarn prices should be fixed, though he pointed out that it went beyond the measures of war-time control in other industries and that his doubts had only been resolved by the assurance that the development of the export trade needed a basis of fixed prices. In the first instance, however, price fixing would only cover yarns;[1] weavers' and finishers' charges could be left until later.

The proposal for an export levy too was regarded initially with some mistrust. The levy, it was true, was to be devoted primarily to research and market investigation; only if the deductions from fixed prices, the 'derogations', proved inadequate would the levy be employed to subsidise exports. The President of the Board of Trade, however, thought a power to raise a levy of this sort 'very novel and drastic' and one which should be sparingly used. Export subsidies might provoke retaliation or might quite easily be wasted in markets where there was no need for them.

Before the end of 1939 ministers had decided to agree to the levy though not for the purpose of subsidising exports; they had also agreed to fix yarn prices. At the same time something more effective was clearly needed than the purely advisory body which has been referred to in recent paragraphs as the Cotton Board. Legislation was accordingly introduced early in 1940 to provide for the formal establishment of a statutory Cotton Board.[2] This Board was of course far from being a war-time edition of the Cotton Industry Board

---

[1] An Order was made by the Minister of Supply on 3rd January 1940 fixing margins for single yarns.

[2] 3 & 4 Geo. 6, ch. 9.

which was to have been set up under the terms of the pre-war Cotton Act. For one thing, raw material control and price fixing lay with the Cotton Control. For another, there would appear in war-time to be no need for such things as redundancy schemes.[1] Consequently, the war-time arrangements could be much less elaborate. There would be a Board of twelve members, including an independent chairman, two executive members and nine members drawn from the different sections of the industry—spinning, weaving, finishing, merchanting —with operatives as well as employers. In spite of some objections from the cotton industry—the levy was to be on cotton not on rayon —a member from the rayon industry was added. The chairman and the two executive members—one drawn from the producing section of the industry and one from the merchanting section—were full-time paid members.

The functions of the Board were two-fold. First, to perform certain common services for the benefit of the industry, and particularly for the maintenance and extension of the export trade: advertising, research, experiment, investigation and collection of statistical and other information. Secondly, to advise the Government on questions relating to the industry. Finance for the services which the Board was to provide would come from a levy on raw cotton at the rate of 5d. per 100 lb., but there would be no Government contribution. Thus an instrument was created which was not only to play a considerable part in effecting those adjustments within the industry that were necessary to meet war-time requirements but was also to continue into peace its efforts in promoting the general welfare of the cotton industry.

The immediate problem was how to maintain exports in face of the pressure, partly of Government orders, but mainly of the civilian market. The index number of wholesale textile sales for the home market had risen to 160 in September 1939 and 170 in October (1937 = 100). The Cotton Board was accordingly consulted by the President of the Board of Trade about the best method of limiting home supplies, and discussions ensued which led finally to the Board of Trade Order of April 1940, placing restrictions on deliveries to retail shops of cotton, rayon and linen piece-goods and made-up goods. This was thought to be a more workable and enforceable arrangement than a rationing of raw material supplies to spinners. Meanwhile, it was the Cotton Board's view that there should be a system of priorities in the order Service, export, home civilian demand, and that use might be made of priority certificates. On this suggestion a scheme of voluntary 'preference directions' was introduced in February

---

[1] The nearest war-time equivalent would perhaps be the concentration schemes of 1941, but these were not yet dreamt of.

1940,[1] whereby a merchant placing an order could apply to the Cotton Controller for a direction instructing the manufacturer to give the order priority over other orders not covered by directions. There were to be two types of preference directions: 'A' for Government and essential home services, 'B' for export orders. Here was the beginning of recognition of the relative importance of export and home trade, though expressed in a system of priorities which proved ultimately inadequate to the burden placed upon it of sorting out the different demands.

The necessity for deciding between the home and the export uses of a raw material was raised in its sharpest form in the case of flax.[2] On the one hand there was the valuable linen export trade from Northern Ireland to hard-currency markets; on the other hand supplies were scarce and would deteriorate seriously in the event of any interference with exports from the Low Countries. Flax was, therefore, one of the first materials to be subjected to a fairly rigid allocation scheme. In November 1939 it was decided that no flax should be allocated to home civilian uses; what was available was to be allotted to the export trade, to the Services and to essential home purposes, e.g. Government requirements for hose-pipes. In February 1940 an allocation of 21,000 tons for the first year of war was made to the Northern Ireland export trade.[3] When Belgium was overrun in May 1940, supplies were to fall heavily and a hard fight was to develop to maintain exports against the competing claims of the Services.

In contrast to the arrangements for the major textile materials, plans were being worked out for the allocation of steel between the various war-time uses. A formal allocation scheme did not, however, appear until April 1940, and even then some time elapsed before it could be said to be running smoothly and effectively. What was perhaps most striking about the early estimates was the large provision made for exports of direct steel, i.e. steel in the form of ingots, blooms, tinplates, tubes, pipes, etc., rather than for steel in more highly manufactured form. At the beginning of the war these exports were put at two million tons and were defended on the ground that an eye must be kept on post-war conditions and that it would be disastrous if present customers were lost. But a provision of this sort could hardly be reconciled with the emphasis that was being placed on the conversion value of exports, on the waste that would be incurred in importing bulky raw material and sending it abroad again with very little added value. In any case it was not long before the need was

---

[1] S.R. & O. 1940, No. 196.

[2] Before the war the Board of Trade's supply organisation had estimated requirements for the first year of war as 92,000 tons, of which 30,000 tons would be for export and 30,000 tons for Service uses.

[3] The heavy trade of Dundee in such things as tarpaulins, which went mainly to Empire and sterling markets, received very much less favourable treatment.

felt for a fairly drastic scaling down of steel requirements all round. Thus by April 1940 there had been a heavy reduction in the estimate of export needs, with the weight attached to 'direct' exports much reduced.

(ii)

The Export Drive

Towards the end of 1939 a demand had grown for Government action to co-ordinate and systematise export policy. It looked as though, without something in the way of an official lead, piecemeal efforts to promote exports would be frittered away or even thwarted through failure to integrate Government plans. There was also need for publicity and for appreciation both by the business community and the public of the place of the export trade in the war effort as a whole.

Lord Stamp and his colleagues had at the beginning of 1940 made a further study of export problems, considering them now from the standpoint of the measures which could actually be taken to increase exports from the United Kingdom. They divided these problems into two groups, those where a buyers' market existed, and those, which were coming to be more and more representative of the current situation, of a sellers' market. In the case of a sellers' market the difficulties centred mainly on supplies of raw materials; there was still a considerable volume of unemployment, and apart from certain shortages of skilled men there could hardly be said to be serious labour obstacles to the expansion of exports. The raw material situation could be dealt with in various ways, through allocations of raw materials for export, through differential home and export prices and through guarantee of future delivery at fixed prices. Special attention should also, it was thought, be devoted to the provision of packing materials[1] and of small quantities of materials which were sometimes indispensable in valuable exports. In a buyers' market the problem was primarily that of the relation of home costs to foreign prices, and the two ways of improving this relation were the application of subsidies and the use of exchange discrimination. General exchange depreciation was ruled out, though it was realised that further rises in home costs might make it inevitable. There were objections alike to subsidies and exchange discrimination, the obvious disadvantage of both being the likelihood that they would provoke counter-measures abroad. With subsidies the difficulties would lie

---

[1] Later it was appreciated that there was a case for discouraging exports of certain commodities, glass for example, which made unduly heavy demands on scarce packing materials such as timber. See p. 71.

in deciding whether the exports were worth while and what level of subsidy was necessary in each particular case. The scope for the use of exchange discrimination was considered to be very limited. The views of Lord Stamp and his colleagues on these matters were shared by ministers. In the prevailing market conditions they saw no reason to reduce the supply price either of exports as a whole or of any particular category of exports.

In February 1940 the Government gave its answer to those who had been asking for the end of uncertainty and for a strong lead in export matters. Business had sought for the appointment of a Minister for Economic Co-ordination with a seat in the War Cabinet. The President of the Board of Trade, however, proposed that an Export Council should be created and that a National Export Drive should be launched. On 1st February 1940 the Prime Minister announced the setting up of the Export Council. 'We do not require,' he said, 'to go and search for export trade to-day. It is the export trade which is on our doorstep, asking for goods with which we have difficulty in supplying them.'

On 13th February the President of the Board of Trade informed the House of Commons[1] of the membership of the Council. With himself as chairman and the Secretary to the Department of Overseas Trade as vice-chairman, it was to include officials from the Treasury, Ministry of Supply and Ministry of Economic Warfare, the Cotton and Wool Controllers, Lord Stamp as adviser on economic co-ordination, and representatives of industry, commerce, finance and labour. Mr. (now Sir) Raymond Streat was appointed secretary of the Council. Four of the business members, Mr. (afterwards Sir) F. D'Arcy Cooper, Sir Clive Baillieu, Lord Hyndley and Sir Cecil Weir, formed a full-time executive committee which was to be primarily concerned with pushing on the formation in the different exporting industries of export groups. Each member dealt with particular groups of industries.

In March 1940 a White Paper was issued on the *Aims and Plan of Work of the Export Council*.[2] This stated, first, that the aim of the Council was the promotion of the greatest volume of export trade which could be achieved in war-time, and that the maintenance of the export trade was so vital a factor in the war effort of the Allied Powers that no measure calculated to contribute to the end in view should be excluded from consideration; secondly, that the strongest preference should be given to measures that involved the least interference with the existing channels of trade or with established practices and principles, and that therefore the first objective should be to overcome administrative obstacles in the way of the export

---

[1] H. of C. Deb., Vol. 356, Col. 1347.

[2] Cmd. 6183. See also *The National Export Drive*.

trade; thirdly, that it was essential under war conditions that exporters should receive direction, guidance and support from the central Government to a degree never contemplated under peace conditions; and lastly, because supplies were limited, if for no other reason, the export trade necessary to win the war could only be achieved by some diversion from the home market.

The instruments of the export drive were to be the export groups which individual industries were now called upon to form. The formation of these groups proceeded apace, and by the beginning of the summer something like 200 were in existence.[1] The newly created statutory Cotton Board functioned as the export group for the cotton industry.

Most export groups were formed on the basis of existing trade associations, but it was clearly laid down that every member of an industry interested in the export trade should have the right to join an export group, whether or no he had previously been a member of a trade association. Nor was the joining of a trade association to be made a condition of joining an export group. There were some cases where the export group appears to have been the first comprehensive and representative organisation which had ever existed in the industry.[2] There was also the problem of merchants who might be exporting goods made by scores of different industries. It would have been an intolerable inconvenience to make them join all the manufacturing export groups with which they were concerned, and therefore, with the help of the Chambers of Commerce in the principal cities, a group of general exporters was formed known as the National General Merchants' Export Group.

It is difficult for many reasons to arrive at any clear view of the success achieved by these groups in securing an expansion of the export trade of the United Kingdom, the object for which they had been promoted. There were too many factors outside their immediate control, such as Government economic policies which they could influence but not radically transform. Most important of all, of course, was the drastic alteration in the character of the war which took place in the summer of 1940. This caused an immediate check in certain industries to export work. But the long-run implications were far more serious. Clearly the immensity of the war effort now required would make it quite impracticable to devote more than a small proportion of the country's resources to export activities.

It is therefore more pertinent to consider what results in general followed from the setting up of the Export Council and the creation of export groups. It would be most misleading to suggest that nothing was achieved in the export field. The major textile industries

---

[1] Ultimately approximately 300 groups and sub-groups were formed.

[2] e.g. pencils, oil-burning devices, steel shutters.

and the leather industry developed export plans through their groups, which will be referred to later. Other industries, such as plastics, had comprehensive schemes for co-operative marketing overseas which never got very far simply because the whole export situation was so radically transformed from the autumn of 1940 onwards. Overseas publicity, propaganda, fashion shows and the like were considered and in some cases carried out, though with doubtful success. War-time difficulties were largely responsible, and there was later the general change of export policy in the latter part of 1940 which has just been mentioned.

To a large extent the groups became instruments for the allocation of raw materials and of packing materials among their members. This was particularly true of steel. But even in these matters, when exports were later reduced, there was a tendency for the responsible side of the work, as opposed to the clerical details, to come more and more into official hands. Probably by the end of the war the majority of the groups were performing few if any active functions. Some had actually ceased to exist, and whatever functions they had had reverted to the trade associations.

In investigating the functions which the groups performed there is a danger of overlooking matters of a much less formal character. There can be little doubt of the important part which the Export Council and the export groups played in war as two-way channels of communication between Government and industry. Through them the Government's attitude on matters of economic policy could be interpreted to industry, and industry's views could be made known more clearly and effectively to Government departments. In war-time when rapid decisions had to be taken affecting whole industries the significance of these contacts could hardly be over-emphasised.

The Export Council appealed in the first instance to 'all industry for all exports'. There was indeed hardly anything in the way of a suggestion of the need for discrimination in the export drive. The currency factor was little emphasised, nor was there consideration of the possibility that even a small gain in hard currency might be out-weighed by extra shipping costs or the loss of alternative imports which the importation of the raw material needed for the exports in question involved. Nor again was it stressed that economic policy required the achievement of maximum value in foreign currencies rather than maximum physical volume of exports. What was clear was that there would have to be some diversion of supplies from the home market, and some inducement to manufacturers to export to relatively unprofitable overseas markets. The export groups in their turn were informed that their members could safely accept all export orders. The diversion of trade from one market to another could be left to Government intervention. It was moreover undesir-

E

able publicly to draw attention to the fact that distinctions were drawn between different destinations for exports. Some emphasis was, however, placed on exports of high 'conversion value', particularly in cases where the raw materials had to be imported. But it is plain that the element of propaganda played a large part in the export drive, and the protest of the Chancellor of the Exchequer that the public was being left to suppose that the Government regarded an export to Australia as equally worth while with an export to the United States passed unheeded.

Within the framework of war-time economic policy there was indeed not a great deal that the Export Council could achieve in the way of general plans for the stimulation of exports. The export groups were encouraged to consider how to deal with export prices, and with propaganda and publicity, and to take steps to meet complaints about delivery dates and the failure to quote firm prices. This refusal to quote firm prices had been much too automatic and it was thought that the problem could be met without undue risk by making appropriate additions to prices. But in matters that involved negotiations with Government departments and raw material Controls difficulties of one sort or another were encountered in attempts to make the business of exporting simpler and more profitable. There was, for example, a good deal of discussion about possibilities of substitution for scarce raw materials. It was also asked whether the Service departments could not modify or alter their specifications in such a way as to release some of these scarce materials for the export trade. But in most cases, as will be seen later, these questions were raised in the face of strong opposition from the departments concerned. Moreover, outside the Board of Trade indifference or even hostility to the needs of the export trades was characteristic of most Government departments. In the summer of 1940 this attitude became more marked; firms were then gaining the impression that if they did not carry out the directions of the Ministry of Labour, the Ministry of Supply and other ordering departments, even at the expense of exports, their labour and plant would be taken away from them. The public's estimates of the worth to the country of the export trade were naturally affected, and it was even thought advisable at this time to send out posters with a message to workers from the Minister of Labour telling them that if they were working for exports they were working for victory.

Some account may now be given of the measures and proposals which were put forward in the first months of the war in the interests of the export trade.

LIMITATION OF SUPPLIES

The main contribution of Government policy towards the export drive, as opposed to their attempt to make manufacturers more export-conscious, was a control over home sales in order to divert supplies into overseas markets. This policy was launched by the Cotton, Rayon and Linen Order of April 1940[1] which limited supplies to retail shops of these textiles and of goods made up from them. The Limitation of Supplies Order of June 1940,[2] restricting sales of a number of consumer goods on the home market, had primarily another purpose—the freeing of resources for war production. But it too may have helped exports by making available for war purposes labour and capacity mainly engaged on home production. Indeed, the main aim of the Board of Trade at this time was to induce the supply departments to take the resources they needed from firms engaged primarily on production for the home market and to leave the exporting firms untouched. The major difficulty, of course, lay in trying to get these departments to make use of small firms rather than the bigger firms, frequently exporters, with whom they had established connections.

The results produced by the imposition of these controls were perhaps not very great. The degree of restriction at the outset was not severe, while, as we shall see,[3] actual supplies to home users were limited to an even smaller extent than that prescribed by the Orders. Nor was the basic principle on which they rested acceptable to all exporting manufacturers. Many manufacturers held that a certain level of home trade was the indispensable condition of any export trade. The motor manufacturers had already made the point earlier in 1940, in asking for a bigger allocation of steel for the home market. They argued, in the first place, that reduction in home output meant higher overhead costs per unit of output, therefore higher prices and lower export sales; and, in the second place, that home output was needed to secure a balance of processes and efficient production. Economists tended to reject the first argument, and in particular its assumption that total output must fall off. Overhead costs, it was pointed out, are fixed in the short run for the firm and should not affect its price and output policy; loss of opportunities for sale at home should induce the search for profitable outlets in overseas markets. However, when the Limitation of Supplies Orders came into operation some of the export groups voiced the same sort of criticism. The gramophone record group, for example, pointed out that their trade was speculative and that restrictions on home sales limited the field over which risks could be spread; there could be no production of records specially for overseas markets, since export sales were based on those records which had proved successful in the

---

[1] S.R. & O. 1940, No. 561. See also Chapter V.

[2] S.R. & O. 1940, No. 874.

[3] See pp. 104–5.

home market. Some other groups said much the same thing, and the pottery manufacturers even succeeded in the autumn of 1940 in getting an increase in the quota for the home market.

TAX RELIEF

One of the earliest proposals considered by the business members of the Export Council was that of granting the exporter some relief from direct taxation.[1] There were, of course, formidable difficulties to which Lord Stamp called attention. Quite apart from the general social and political objections to tax discrimination, there was the major administrative problem of distinguishing between the profits derived from exports and the profits from other sources. Then there was the question of firms which did not themselves export but made parts or components for exporting manufacturers. Lastly, there was the objection that it would be wasteful to give relief on exports generally; what was really required was a subsidy on *additional* exports.

However, in March 1940 Mr. (afterwards Sir) F. D'Arcy Cooper wrote to Lord Stamp proposing that the trader should be given relief from Excess Profits Tax in respect of the increase in his export profit in each of the war years as compared with his export profit in the year or years which he had adopted as his standard for the tax. This was a concrete proposal, but it did little if anything to meet the objections, particularly the administrative ones, which could be raised against a scheme of this kind, and Lord Stamp replied that but for the supreme importance which he attached to exports he would be, on fiscal grounds, opposed to it from the outset. The business members of the Export Council tried to take the matter further, but the proposal was rejected on administrative grounds by the new Chancellor of the Exchequer, Sir Kingsley Wood. By this time Excess Profits Tax had been raised to 100 per cent., and the deterrent effect which this was likely to have on firms which were already earning their standard profits was pointed out. Lord Stamp himself thought that it would have a seriously discouraging effect on the export drive to countries where export risks were high, and suggested that in such cases the State should either give the exporter full cover or make itself responsible for the outcome of the transaction, using the exporter merely as an agent.

EXPORT CREDIT INSURANCE

The outbreak of war had witnessed a modification of the system of export credit insurance which had been built up since 1919 by the Export Credits Guarantee Department.[2] Since 1932 the chief

---

[1] The matter seems first to have been raised by Lord Strabolgi in the House of Lords on 23rd January 1940 when he suggested that there should be some tax exemption for profits made from 'abnormal' exports. (H. of L. Deb., Vol. 115, Col. 404.)

[2] What follows is concerned with short-term commercial credit risks. Consideration of guarantees of foreign government credits (U.S.S.R., 1936, Afghanistan, 1937, Turkey, 1938) and of medium-term facilities is excluded.

element in this system had been a solvency policy known as the comprehensive policy which covered, at a flat rate, the whole of an exporter's shipments during a period of twelve months, and insured him against the risk of insolvency of his overseas customers. The proportion of losses against which the exporter was thus guaranteed was seventy-five per cent., and recoveries were shared in the same proportion, i.e. seventy-five per cent. to the department and twenty-five per cent. to the exporter. Then, with currency difficulties and exchange restrictions, the department had introduced a new scheme in what was known as the 'transfer addendum'.[1] This enabled the holder of a comprehensive policy to take out further insurance against the risk that the overseas buyer, while fully solvent, might be unable to remit sterling when the debt was due. Here again the proportion covered, that is of sums unpaid after normally six months owing to exchange restrictions, was seventy-five per cent. But only three months' shipments were insured, and the premium naturally varied from country to country with the exchange risk. In the few years before the war the department's total business had increased considerably, from £7½ millions in 1933–34 to £50 millions in 1938–39. In 1937 Parliament passed the Export Guarantees Act which authorised the giving of guarantees in future without a time limit and raised the maximum liability which the department might incur at any time from £26 millions to £50 millions.[2]

When Poland was overrun in September 1939 the department was faced with claims from holders of policies with 'transfer addenda' for Germany and Poland, and although war risks were not included it was unhesitatingly agreed that these claims should be met. This was, of course, a significant extension of the cover provided by the export credits insurance scheme, and exporters began taking out comprehensive policies, not for the sake of the solvency guarantee, but simply in order to insure against war risks in Europe. Meanwhile premium rates were maintained at more or less pre-war rates in order to help exports.

The altered character of the war and the inauguration of the export drive led, between April and September 1940, to extension and revision of the export credits scheme. In April 1940 the 'catastrophe risk' was specifically included in the 'transfer addendum', while the cover provided was raised from seventy-five per cent. to ninety per cent.[3] But the invasion of Denmark and Norway had revealed a further need of exporters, the need for cover against the risk of having to resell at a reduced value goods specially made for customers in

---

[1] First instituted with reference to trade with Germany this scheme was in 1935 extended to other countries as well.

[2] This was further increased to £75 millions by the Export Guarantees Act, 1939.

[3] The solvency cover remained at seventy-five per cent.

countries subsequently cut off by German aggression. Accordingly, in June 1940 an entirely new 'pre-shipment policy' was issued, available whether or not an exporter held the comprehensive policy, against the risk of loss through failure to ship goods which had been ordered. Under this policy the exporter was required to insure the whole of his turnover, and received cover of seventy-five per cent. of the balance of loss on all non-shipped contracts in the policy year. Thus an exporter could now cover most risks, outside those within the scope of ordinary and war risks marine insurance, from the time of signing a contract to the time when payment fell due.

The President of the Board of Trade, however, and also the exporters themselves, were continually pressing for an extension of these arrangements. They wanted for example a higher percentage of cover and an all-inclusive scheme. Accordingly two changes were made in September 1940. First a new policy was introduced, known as the 'all-in' war emergency policy. This covered the exporter, as to eighty-five per cent. in the case of the insolvency of the buyer, and as to ninety per cent. in all other cases,[1] against loss due to his being unable to deliver or to the buyer being unable to accept or pay for the goods ordered, except where the loss arose through acts of war in the United Kingdom or through United Kingdom Government regulations restricting the manufacture or export of goods. The new policy thus included and extended[2] the cover provided by the insolvency, transfer and pre-shipment guarantees. At the same time an additional policy was made available to deal with the problem of unforeseen changes in freight charges and war risk insurance rates. Important changes in these charges and rates had occurred in the summer of 1940 and it was quite possible that further changes would take place. This had made exporters reluctant to quote firm c.i.f. prices, while overseas buyers were equally unwilling to incur the risks of an f.o.b. contract. The new policy, known as the 'c.i.f. charges policy', insured the exporter selling on a c.i.f. basis against the possibility of increases in these charges.[3]

Thenceforward there were few alterations in the credit insurance schemes. Probably the major change was in February 1942, when it was agreed to cover the exporter against the risk of cancellation or non-renewal of an export licence or of the introduction of export restrictions in the United Kingdom. Previously policies had expressly excluded any event in the United Kingdom which directly or indirectly prevented or restricted the manufacture or export of the goods.

---

[1] The cover in the existing separate policies could be raised correspondingly, the insolvency cover to eighty-five per cent., and the 'pre-shipment' cover to ninety per cent.

[2] By covering extra freight charges due to frustrated voyages, unforeseen transhipment, etc.

[3] The premium was 1s. in the £ of estimated c.i.f. charges.

In the selective phase of the export drive, that is after the autumn of 1940, export credit insurance played its part through the variations in premiums charged on export business in accordance with a currency grading of the various countries. But the Lend-Lease Act and, later, the entry of America into the war transformed here, as it did elsewhere, the assumptions on which policy had hitherto been based. By the end of 1941 the export drive was clearly over, and, as the following figures show, the scope of export credit insurance was contracting:—

Export Credit Department Guarantees

TABLE I		£ millions	
1938–39	49·9	1942–43	64·1
1939–40	63·2	1943–44	50·2
1940–41	95·4	1944–45	50·5
1941–42	108·1	1945–46	71·8

OVERSEAS TRADE NEGOTIATIONS

In April 1940 the business members of the Export Council suggested that trade missions should be sent to the United States and to South America. Such missions, it was true, would not be concerned with actual sales promotion, but they could prepare the ground for subsequent efforts by the individual export groups.

At the moment, however, it appeared doubtful whether much advantage could be derived from sending a mission to the United States. The depreciation of the sterling exchange and the restrictions on American exports to the United Kingdom had caused much dissatisfaction there, and there was a danger that the presence of a trade mission might lead to an attack upon the 1938 Trade Agreement. It was therefore decided that there should only be a mission to the South American countries. This mission under the leadership of Lord Willingdon and including several prominent industrialists sailed on 25th October 1940.

To a considerable extent the aims of the mission were political rather than economic; it hoped to counteract Axis propaganda, to promote an understanding of British war aims and to justify the blockade. In the economic field there were some awkward problems. There was no simple answer to the question of what was to be done with the surpluses that were accumulating in South America as the result of the cutting of the trade of the countries concerned with large parts of Europe. The United Kingdom could not afford to purchase what it did not really require, and did not wish to buy any of the surpluses merely in order to push up its exports. The most constructive line of approach, it was thought, might be through collaboration with the United States and tackling the matter as a problem of triangular rather than bilateral trade. Under a triangular arrangement the United States might make loans to or purchases from Latin America and the dollars arising could be in part, at any rate, earmarked or left open for trade with the United Kingdom. From the British point of view this would have the immense advantage of securing dollars without having to incur the serious difficulties of penetrating the markets of the United States. But it would do little to help the surplus problem. The additional exports arising from the sort of things which the United Kingdom could easily supply and which the Latin American countries would want—textiles, leather goods, pottery, glassware—would probably only yield £15 millions.

Export promotion itself, apart from the wider considerations of triangular trade, turned out, on closer inspection of the position of many of the Latin American countries, to be of dubious advantage. In the case of the Argentine, Bolivia and Venezuela the current balance of payments would be against the United Kingdom, but for the other countries, taking invisible exports into account, there would be no problem in making purchases from them. It was really a question of seeing that they met their financial obligations to the United Kingdom. So far from an export drive being necessary there was a case for reducing exports to these countries to enforce the payment of their debts and debt services. Indeed, while the mission was still abroad action was taken to limit United Kingdom export trade to certain Latin American countries in accordance with the amount of sterling available to them, and in January 1941 control was placed on all exports to Brazil, Chile, Colombia and Peru.[1]

Although the project of a trade mission to the United States had been rejected there were good grounds for believing that something of a less formal and public nature, a direct approach to the United States Government on trade matters, might yield fruitful results. In the summer of 1940, the United States President and Mr. Morgenthau had given the advice that the Government of the United Kingdom should consider 'forcing out British exports' and had suggested that the two countries should co-operate rather than compete in South American markets. On the British side there was the hope that the United States Government might be prepared to consider some extension of the Trade Agreement of 1938, particularly with regard to cotton and woollen textiles. The textile industries seemed to have a better chance than most others of increasing their sales in America; moreover the reduction of the United States' duties on cotton textiles under the 1938 Agreement had been meagre. Furthermore, when purchase tax was introduced in October 1940, there would be an additional handicap on goods exported from the United Kingdom since *ad valorem* duties would be levied on price inclusive of purchase

---

[1] S.R. & O. 1941, No. 192. There was practically a complete stoppage of exports to Peru and Chile.

tax. Accordingly it was arranged that Mr. (afterwards Sir) F. D'Arcy Cooper should go to the United States in October in order to discuss with the Americans the ways in which the dollar earnings of the United Kingdom could be enlarged. British capacity to maintain and expand exports was to be emphasised, and commercial possibilities were to be explored under two main heads. First, was there any scope for a triangular arrangement involving the United States, the United Kingdom and the Latin American countries, the United States undertaking to purchase the surpluses of the latter and thus providing them with foreign currency which they could use to buy British goods? Secondly, could a supplementary trade agreement be negotiated which, through a reduction of United States duties, particularly on textiles, would give greater opportunities to British goods in American markets? Other points which would have to be taken up would be the purchase tax problem[1] and the question as to whether assistance could be given to British exports, for example by reduced freight charges or rates, without attracting countervailing duties.

The political difficulties lying in the way of the Anglo-American discussions which began in November 1940 were considerable. It soon became clear that nothing in the shape of unilateral American concessions could be looked for; the law required that any reductions in United States duties must be such as would at the same time secure the expansion of foreign markets for the products of the United States, and American public opinion would agree to nothing short of this. The American officials therefore sought in return reductions in the United Kingdom margins of preference on Empire fruits and tobacco.[2] Thus it was plain that the Dominions would have to be brought into the discussions and that there would be complicated triangular negotiations. On the other hand it was equally obvious that concessions on the entry of American goods into the market of the United Kingdom could not be introduced in war-time. The dollar situation simply would not permit it. Any agreement made now to lower duties on American goods was therefore in the nature of a deferred liability, and raised the whole question of Britain's post-war financial and commercial policy. Would it really be practicable after the war to dismantle the structure of import and exchange control? Mr. Cordell Hull, the American Secretary of State, a strong liberal in matters of commercial policy, certainly hoped it would be, and the Prime Minister in a speech in January 1940 had given the

---

[1] A Bill introduced into the United States House of Representatives in January 1941, with the aim of excluding purchase tax from the dutiable value of British goods, failed to secure support. Ultimately, in 1946, a final decision was reached in the United States Courts in favour of the British contention that purchase tax should not be included in dutiable value (the Pitcairn case).

[2] The tobacco preference was 2s. 0½d. per pound; it was reduced by 6d. per pound in 1943 in accordance with the terms of the pre-war trade agreement. (See H. of C. Deb., Vol. 388, Col. 972.)

assurance that after the war the United Kingdom would revert to its former economic policy and would support a system of multilateral trade. But there were others, both inside and outside Government circles, who took a different view and doubted the wisdom of giving any such guarantees to the Americans. The negotiations therefore dragged on until in the end they became caught up in discussions ranging over the whole field of post-war economic and financial relations. Then, consideration of the ways in which Article VII of the Mutual Aid Agreement of 1942 could be implemented took precedence over the relatively minor issues of a supplementary trade agreement.

EXPORT COMPANIES AND EXPORT LEVIES

The textile and leather industries were active in the summer of 1940 in putting forward proposals for the raising of export levies and the promotion of export companies. The export company was either to engage in trading operations or to be a non-trading body using its funds for the collection of statistics, for the promotion of research and investigation, and for trade exhibitions and publicity.

The rayon industry had already had before the war arrangements for supplying specially cheap yarns to meet Japanese competition in the Far East and soon after the inauguration of the export drive pushed ahead with more elaborate schemes for the expansion of exports. A company known as the Central Rayon Office[1] was formed by the Rayon Export Group to promote exports assisted by a levy on the trade. The attempt was to be made to extend the pre-war schemes by widening the range of products covered and by including all rayon producers and a larger number of manufacturers, finishers and distributors. A producers' levy of 3d. a pound on rayon yarn was imposed, which was added to prices, and this was supplemented by a contribution from the producers of 1d. for every pound of rayon yarn sold or used by them. This levy fell on the home consumer, for on all exports there was a rebate of 3d. a pound and in addition there were subsidies to assist exports where they were needed. These subsidies, with few exceptions, were limited to standardised fabrics offering bulk turnover with minimum quantities of not less than 50,000 square yards per order. The levy-cum-subsidy scheme was also linked up with voluntary arrangements for reducing weaving, dyeing and merchanting charges. The scheme appears to have led rather to the replacement of Japanese cheap rayons in the soft currency Dominions than to increased earning of much-needed hard currencies. It was, however, effective to judge by the expansion of

---

[1] This company was registered in December 1940. It was stated that up to the end of June 1941 orders for 28 million square yards had been booked through the Central Rayon Office.

rayon exports in the early war years, as shown in the following table:—

Exports of Artificial Silk Yarns and Tissues

TABLE 2

	1938	*1939*	*1940*	*1941*	*1942*
Artificial silk yarns, *million lb.*	8·0	6·9	15·0	20·2	16·3
Tissues of artificial silk, *million square yards*	31·2	43·5	56·3	69·1	102·7

In cotton textiles there was much the same approach to the export problem. There had indeed been a delay of some months in putting into operation the plan of 'derogations' from fixed yarn prices which had been promised when the need for fixed prices was under discussion. However, after the appointment of Mr. (afterwards Sir) Raymond Streat as chairman of the Cotton Board in June 1940, plans for export promotion were pushed ahead. In the first place the Cotton Controller provided for 'derogations' for export orders from the fixed yarn margins, up to five per cent. off the margins on American yarns, ten per cent. off the margins for Egyptian yarns, and five per cent. off doubling margins.[1] The scheme of the Cotton Board was to associate these yarn price reductions with reductions in the later stages of processing and in selling charges, by the formation of export syndicates made up of spinners, weavers, finishers and merchants. These syndicates would each arrange for the production of a particular type of cloth for sale abroad, and the reductions agreed to by the weavers, finishers and merchants, following on the yarn derogations, would ensure that competitive prices could be quoted. Furthermore, an export company, known as British Overseas Cottons, was to be created, its operations being financed by a statutory levy of 5d. per 100 lb. of raw cotton. The company would not itself engage in manufacture but would arrange for the production of standard cloths to be sold to merchants at prices sufficiently low to secure export business. All this was hardly different from a system of export subsidies, but it could be defended on the grounds that its purpose was to facilitate the most economical production and thus to make possible unusually cheap prices. Moreover, there was to be no open subsidy and there would be discrimination in the application of the scheme; not all exports were to be assisted, but only those which would otherwise be lost.

British Overseas Cottons was set up at the end of July 1940[2] and soon afterwards came the formation of export syndicates. A big order for the production of 22 million square yards of cambric cloth for the Dutch East Indies was put through in this way, and the

---

[1] There might be larger derogations for export syndicates.

[2] See S.R. & O. 1940, No. 1210. In its first year B.O.C. handled orders for 41 million yards of cloths for fifteen markets; the value of these cloths was nearly £900,000 and a little over six per cent. of the total value was required to subsidise their production and sale.

Cotton Board reported that syndicates were being formed for pushing exports to the United States, Canada, India, Burma, Chile, the Argentine, the West Indies and the Straits Settlements. Yet it is doubtful whether the plan had more than a limited application. For one thing care had to be taken to avoid interference with existing trade which needed no subvention; for another, as the Cotton Board pointed out, the syndicate arrangement was only suitable for bulk lines. In the event the experiment had only a few months to run, as the impending cut in cotton supplies necessitated in 1941 a complete revision of export plans.

Other industries interested in the raising of export levies and the formation of export companies were wool and leather. In neither case, however, was the company to be a trading body like British Overseas Cottons. Nor were the proceeds of the levies to be employed in any form of subsidisation of export, but rather for the collection of statistics, for research and for overseas publicity and propaganda. Power was taken, in the case of the woollen industry, to impose a levy of one-tenth of one per cent. *ad valorem* on raw wool,[1] and the National Wool Textile Corporation was set up in December 1940. In 1941 a similar arrangement was made for leather. A levy of one-quarter of one per cent. was imposed on raw skins and hides,[2] and the Leather, Footwear and Allied Industries Corporation was created.

In discussing export companies the activities of the Government-sponsored United Kingdom Commercial Corporation should not be overlooked. This company, set up in April 1940 primarily as an instrument of economic warfare in the Balkans and Turkey, helped exporters by arranging for shipping space and by securing export and raw material licences. It subsequently extended its activities to Spain, Portugal, the Middle East and South America, where it undertook in 1940 the financing of goods sent on consignment. For exporters to Turkey it provided a system of guarantee facilities, under which full cover was given and payment was made four months after receipt of the shipping documents. Insolvency, shipment and transfer risks were covered by this arrangement.

(iii)

The Changing Emphasis

The change in the character of the war from May 1940 onwards was bound to have an important effect not only on the volume but also on the composition of the export trade. In the first place it

---

[1] S.R. & O. 1941, No. 148; the yield of the levy was estimated at £50,000.
[2] S.R. & O. 1940, No. 1986.

meant that exports to many markets in Europe and the Mediterranean area were shut off. Exports of coal to France, for example, ceased. Conversely the elimination of flax supplies from the Low Countries had a serious effect on the prospects of linen exports. But, clearly, the major influence of the new situation was upon the activities of home industries, particularly the heavy industries. In the urgency and stress of current events capacity and labour were diverted to war work without much regard for carefully prepared export plans. Again, it was necessary to give precedence over exports to the building up of stocks of such things as aluminium and copper. Finally, in the last month or two of 1940 exports were hampered by the shortage of shipping. The following table shows the fall in the volume of raw material and manufactured exports.[1]

Volume of Exports. (*1935=100*)

TABLE 3

	1940			
	1st Quarter	*2nd Quarter*	*3rd Quarter*	*4th Quarter*
Raw materials .	67	65	28	20
Manufactures .	91	94	67	46

Inevitably, the extension of the war in the west made changes in the system of export control necessary. A new category of 'all goods' destinations was introduced into the control. Thus, by an Order of 12th April 1940, all goods were prohibited to be exported without licence from the United Kingdom to Denmark, Estonia, Finland, Latvia, Lithuania, Norway and Sweden, or to any port in the U.S.S.R. on the Baltic or Arctic Seas.[2] In June a further group of destinations was put on the 'all goods' list: Bulgaria, Greece, Hungary, Liechtenstein, Rumania, Switzerland, Yugoslavia and Black Sea ports of the U.S.S.R.[3] On the fall of France an 'all goods' export control was also enforced with regard to French territory in Europe, Algeria, Tunisia and the French zone in Morocco.[4] Thus by the summer of 1940 no goods could be exported to any European country, except Portugal, Spain and Turkey, without a licence.

An extension of export control was also required to reinforce the developments in exchange control, since there was ground for supposing that valuables of different kinds were being used as vehicles for the export of capital from the United Kingdom. The aim was to prevent export of capital in the form of valuables, while per-

---

[1] A few groups showed an increase of volume of exports, as compared with the pre-war level: cutlery and hardware, pottery and glass, silk and artificial yarns and manufactures, paper and cardboard.

[2] S.R. & O. 1940, No. 551.

[3] S.R. & O. 1940, No. 959.

[4] S.R. & O. 1940, Nos. 1056, 1196.

mitting legitimate trading transactions—a difficult matter since the trader might fail to bring back the full proceeds of his export sales. Prohibition of the export without licence of diamonds, articles of platinum or gold, watches with cases of precious metal and postage stamps came into force on 1st July 1940,[1] and assistance in administering the control was obtained from such bodies as the export groups, museums and from the British Philatelic Association.[2] Licences could thus be given for approved transactions effected in the ordinary course of business, while private individuals were as a rule not allowed to take out with them or to export the articles covered by the Order. Nor were traders allowed to export the stock-in-trade of their businesses except to Empire countries within the sterling area, and care had to be taken to see that what appeared to be normal business transactions did not conceal a transfer of capital abroad. On the other hand provision was made for enabling foreigners and residents in the Dominions or in the Colonies to take out of the country valuables which constituted their personal effects.[3]

The extension of export control was but one contribution to an atmosphere that was growing increasingly unfavourable to the exporter in the summer of 1940. For resources of all kinds were becoming scarce. There was now little hope of retaining for export, capacity and labour which were required by the Service and supply departments. This was particularly true of the engineering industries, where the skilled labour needed for munitions could only be found by diverting it from export work. Before long the whole labour problem became acute. It was inevitable that labour should be taken away from exports to war work, but the transfer was taking place in a haphazard and unselective way. In August 1940 it was agreed that firms whose export business would be severely affected by the transfer of their workers could appeal to the Board of Trade representative on the area board, with whom the Divisional Controller of the Ministry of Labour would consult before any action was taken; but it is doubtful whether this arrangement had much effect. It was not possible, moreover, to include workers in the export trades as such in the schedule of reserved occupations; the schedule at this time took account only of a man's occupation and not of the work he was actually doing. However, the Department of Overseas Trade did devise with the Ministry of Labour a scheme for the reservation of skilled workers in the pottery trades, the percentage of such workers

---

[1] S.R. & O. 1940, No. 1109.

[2] This Association also helped with the administration of import control; see p. 25. Eighty to ninety per cent. of stamps exported were said to be offered on approval.

[3] An advisory committee, assisted by the staff of the Export Licensing Department, was set up to handle this problem and to grant certificates for the export of valuables in place of export licences.

to be reserved varying with the percentage of the factory's output devoted to export. Firms who benefited from the arrangement were required to maintain this export percentage.

Raw materials for exports were also increasingly hard to come by. Indeed, ministers had specifically directed at the end of June 1940 that steps should be taken as soon as possible to reduce allocations of important raw materials entering into the export trade.

In the case of flax, it was thought at first that the loss of Belgian supplies would mean the cancellation of all existing linen export orders. This was avoided, but through the summer of 1940 the only allocation made for the export trade was of the low-grade material— tow—at the rate of 1,000 tons a month. For a short time exports of linen manufactures to all markets were controlled, and there were protests from the Northern Ireland linen industry which had thirty-seven per cent. of its insured workers unemployed.

Attempts to preserve the important hard-currency trade of the linen industry could only succeed through a vigorous campaign for raw material substitution, tow for line and cotton for flax. This was difficult to achieve and there was much opposition from the Service departments. However, it was agreed that for the last three months of 1940 there should be a monthly allocation to Northern Ireland for export purposes of 800 tons of line flax and 200 tons of tow. This concession was only granted on the understanding that the raw material so released would earn hard currency. A scheme had to be devised therefore to ensure that this happened. Under this scheme, which came into operation at the end of 1940, exporters who wished to obtain flax from the raw material Control had first to obtain from the Northern Ireland Ministry of Commerce a release certificate against replacement of goods shipped to the hard-currency markets the United States, Canada, Cuba, Argentina, South Africa—or against orders in hand for these markets.

Of all the raw materials the one most likely to be affected by the new phase of the war was clearly steel. In April 1940 a formal allocation scheme for steel had been introduced on a departmental basis, and in accordance with this scheme steel was being allocated separately to 'indirect' and 'direct' exports[1] under the symbols B.T.4 and B.T.5. Administration of these allocations was at first in the hands of the Iron and Steel Control, though later the Board of Trade took over responsibility for the allocation for 'indirect' exports. This they did through the various export groups concerned, who in turn were responsible for distribution among their members.

In June 1940, when the whole position was re-examined, there was sharp criticism from the Minister without Portfolio of the amount of

---

[1] See p. 49.

steel going into exports.[1] He said that he saw no justification in the situation which had now arisen for exports of steel on a scale equal to one-tenth of the total national steel-producing capacity; for exports of engineering products which in May amounted to almost half as much as that of deliveries to the Ministry of Supply during the same period; or for exports of motor vehicles, the labour employed on which could have produced instead fifty or sixty heavy tanks.

The President of the Board of Trade defended the export of steel goods, partly on general grounds—the need to earn foreign exchange, to maintain goodwill in overseas markets—and partly with reference to special requirements connected with the war effort, such as the provision of machinery for the oilfields. He also emphasised the steps which could be taken to help munitions production without seriously interfering with export activities. He himself, for example, was introducing a machinery licensing Order for restricting the supply to home users of certain classes of machinery and this would assist in releasing skilled engineering labour.[2] It would also be of advantage if armament firms could be brought to face the problem of dilution of labour rather than be allowed to adopt the easy course of taking skilled workers from export trades. Again, multiple shifts could be introduced and more use could be made of plant capacity not fully employed. If there were to be cuts in exports the whole thing should be arranged in an orderly manner. Exports essential to the war effort should be maintained. The system of tendering for Government orders, far too haphazard in its operation, should be replaced by group arrangements and allocation where possible of orders to firms with few or no export connections.

The real centre of the controversy was round the direct steel exports. Was it really worth while to preserve these exports, often at the cost of importing bulky materials from abroad, in view of their low conversion value? Indirect exports, of machinery and spare parts, for example, were agreed to be worth maintaining. Nearly all such exports were of high value, yielding over £100 per ton of crude steel. Clearly also there was good ground for continuing the export of replacement parts. But though the case for the export of direct steel was far weaker ministers found it impossible to agree on an immediate programme of cuts in allocations for this purpose. Some of the exports in question could be defended without difficulty. Tinned plates and sheets, for example, represented highly lucrative exports, employed specialised plant not readily adaptable to other uses, and

---

[1] Allocations of steel for export were as follows, in tons:—

		B.T.4	B.T.5
1940	2nd quarter	189,700	174,400
	3rd quarter	224,100	140,000
	4th quarter	116,500	140,500

[2] See pp. 103–4.

made possible the importation of canned foods from abroad. For the other exports in this category, however, for which there was probably little justification, it was merely decided that if reductions had to be made they should be imposed in the order of ratio of raw material value to value of finished product. It was recognised that before long the cuts would have to come, and that they were simply being postponed for a few months.

The allocation of steel for use in direct exports in the third quarter of 1940 was actually exceeded. The exports which suffered in the pressure of events of the summer of 1940, when the steel allocation scheme broke down, were not the direct exports but the indirect exports of steel. Widespread use of priority of production directions was largely responsible for this adverse effect, partly through causing the capacity of engineering firms to be more fully occupied with Service orders and partly by delaying deliveries of steel to them. A further difficulty arose from the failure to settle steel allocations well in advance of the period in which delivery was to be made, so that firms could not get their orders on to the books of the steel producers until well on in the delivery period. Thus there was a shortfall in deliveries of steel for use in indirect exports. Exports of cars and machinery were also affected by bottlenecks in the production of alloy steel. Finally, in order to assist the effective operation of the steel scheme, the Board of Trade sacrificed 65,000 tons of their allocation, a contribution which was likely to hit hardly the exporters of indirect steel.

By the end of 1940 a much more restrictive policy had been laid down for exports of direct steel. With the exception of tinplates such exports were only to be permitted if they were essential to the war effort, and even then only if no other sources of supply, including hard-currency sources, were available.[1] Nor was it long before the decision to maintain tinplate exports was reversed. In the summer of 1941 it was agreed that overseas requirements in connection with petrol tins and food canning should be met from the United States. Exports thenceforward fell away, and all that was left was a small export of 'wasters' or 'seconds' to the Dominions.

With the growth of war demands on labour and capacity the position of the indirect steel exports became equally vulnerable. The high conversion value of such exports was irrelevant in the face of the pressure on the resources of the engineering industries. Allocations of steel for indirect exports were cut from 224,100 tons in the third quarter of 1940 to 56,153 tons in the second quarter of 1941. A new

---

[1] In the autumn of 1941 this drastic policy towards direct steel exports had to be modified on account of failure to secure deliveries from the United States, through the increasing load on American capacity, the difficulty in diverting small orders for mixed specifications and the time taken to build up an administrative machine to cope with lend-lease orders.

F

method was required for distributing the very limited amount of steel available. Hitherto bulk allocations had been made to export groups for distribution among their members. Exports of this type were now divided into three categories: (i) consumers' goods, mainly of an unessential nature, (ii) goods of an essential nature exported in numbers of small units, such as tools, (iii) heavy capital goods like machinery. Of the total of indirect steel exports approximately twenty per cent. were in the first category, something over ten per cent. in the second and about seventy per cent. in the third. Exports in the former categories could be cut by percentages corresponding to those of cuts on similar goods in the home market. In the case of the heavy capital goods export could only be allowed if it served a purpose directly or indirectly connected with the war effort. This involved the scrutiny of individual orders, since in no other way could manufacturers be prevented from starting on work of an unessential nature. This scrutiny was in certain cases—textile and hosiery machinery, for example—reinforced by the imposition of export control.[1] Thus, even before American protests about the continuance of United Kingdom steel exports had begun to be heard, in the summer of 1941, the decision had been taken that, with few exceptions, steel should only be made available for incorporation in exports if this would contribute demonstrably towards the prosecution of the war.

The problem of steel was an outstanding example of the difficulties that beset the export trade after the military disasters of 1940. By the autumn of 1940 it was clear that the export drive as a whole had lost much of its original momentum. In some directions, it is true, the business members of the Export Council could still report progress. Satisfactory arrangements had been made, with the help of the export groups, towards the provision of timber for packing. Where consumer goods were concerned the Controllers of the requisite raw materials had usually shown themselves alive to the needs of the export trade. But the manufacture of capital goods for export had undoubtedly suffered, and the breakdown of the steel allocation scheme had disillusioned exporters. Moreover, in the new military urgency champions of export interests often found themselves incurring the reproach of not appreciating, or even of actually thwarting, the efforts needed to meet the requirements of the Services; it was indeed very difficult to claim for exports labour, capacity or materials which were said to be required for direct war purposes.

In September 1940 Lord Stamp and his colleagues reviewed the export position and pointed out that some of the basic assumptions of

---

[1] S.R. & O. 1941, No. 523.

export policy had altered. The earning of foreign exchange was still necessary; indeed the country's foreign exchange reserves were almost exhausted. But it had now become a fundamental working hypothesis that Britain should obtain the necessary financial assistance from the United States when occasion arose. Another aim of export policy, hitherto not much considered, was to satisfy, in part at any rate, the essential needs of countries whose economic welfare was of importance to Britain, not merely countries involved in the common war effort, but also countries from which indispensable supplies were drawn. However, against these export considerations— namely the acquisition of foreign exchange and the satisfaction of overseas needs—there now had to be set the much more rapid rate of absorption of resources into war production and the approaching strain on shipping with its threat of serious raw material shortages. Thus two conclusions emerged. First, export trade had fallen heavily in the war-time scale of values. Secondly, the limited capacity that could still be devoted to export must be used to the best advantage. The original idea, therefore, of an undiscriminating export drive aiming at the maximum aggregate volume of exports would have to give way to a more selective policy.

Such a policy would show itself in discrimination between different markets and different types of exports. The differences in the exchange values of exports to different markets was a familiar one, but it was an over-simplification of the problem to divide markets into those yielding hard and those yielding soft currencies. Thus exports to a soft-currency country in the sterling area might replace imports by that country from the dollar area. Moreover, the lists of hard-currency and soft-currency countries were unstable; only exports to the United States and Canada could be assumed to be always desirable. In any case it might be necessary to export to a soft-currency country in order to avert economic distress there or to maintain British prestige. Nevertheless, with all these qualifications, there must be greater selectivity between markets than had been shown in the past.

There was a similar need for discrimination between different types of commodity. Specially suitable for export, for example, were commodities like coal and china clay, consisting of native materials. In general, the criterion of export worth-whileness must be conversion value, and there was a danger that things like machinery which satisfied this criterion in a high degree, and also were good exports from the standpoints of currency and prestige, might be unduly restricted. Some exports were undesirable—glass, for example, which required a relatively large amount of timber for packing.

These principles were useful, but Lord Stamp and his colleagues found it no easier than before to suggest ways in which the right exports could be promoted to the right markets. Export subsidies were ruled out as they had been in earlier discussions of the export problem. All that could be said was that there appeared to be a *prima facie* case for investigating the possibility of bilateral trade agreements between Britain and the countries in which agricultural surpluses were piling up.

When the question of the application of a test of 'essentiality' to exports was being discussed it became quite clear that it involved the whole economic policy of the countries which imported their requirements from the United Kingdom. In the Colonies the position was relatively simple. They had been asked in the early days of the war to introduce import licensing arrangements, and had imposed controls on imports alike from sterling and non-sterling sources. But the problem of the self-governing Dominions of the sterling area was different. If the United Kingdom were to confine its exports to them to 'essential requirements', the Dominions would as a corollary have to pursue a policy of 'belt-tightening'; they would have to eliminate unessential imports. But it was some time before this happened. It was some time before Australia, for example, went in for a fairly rigorous policy of import control. New Zealand, on the other hand, had had before the war, owing to her financial difficulties, a system of import restrictions which she proceeded to extend. These new restrictions, indeed, seemed sufficiently damaging to United Kingdom long-term trading interests for the Board of Trade to issue in December 1940, for the benefit of exporters, a statement of the United Kingdom position. In this statement, after a reference to the diversion of resources to war purposes and to the need for a more selective policy with regard to exports, the policy that New Zealand was asked to pursue was summarised under four heads. First, she should continue to meet her essential requirements as far as possible from the United Kingdom; secondly, restriction on non-essential imports from the United Kingdom should be accompanied by equivalent economies in New Zealand's consumption; thirdly, undue dislocation should not be caused to United Kingdom industries which depended to an important extent on the New Zealand market; and, lastly, the long-term position of the United Kingdom as a supplier of manufactured goods to New Zealand should be safeguarded.

Inherent in this problem was the question of the attitude which the United Kingdom should adopt towards the establishment of secondary industries in overseas countries, particularly the Dominions and the Colonies which had hitherto been dependent upon imports for their supplies of most classes of manufactured goods. War was naturally likely to stimulate such developments through higher freights, transport and supply difficulties and higher costs in Britain. In pre-war years they had been viewed with misgivings, both in business and in some official circles, on the ground that they would limit the market for United Kingdom exports, though the problem had been recognised as a many-sided one. Lord Stamp and his colleagues took the view that to attempt to discourage colonial industrialisation in the name of the export drive would be mistaken. Exports were a means not an end, and such developments should only be resisted when they would involve the importation of expensive machinery from the United States. Even the long-run argument about the need for preserving traditional markets for United Kingdom goods had to be qualified by consideration of the need to diversify the economic structure of relatively simple agricultural communities. For the moment, however, there was in official circles the fear that war-time difficulties of supply and finance would result in overseas countries, and the Dominions in particular, building up secondary industries. It was not until the middle of the war that the older viewpoint underwent profound modification.

APPENDIX 3
Note on Export Licensing

The main types of export licences issued were as follows:—

(i) *Ordinary Licences*, covering the export to a particular consignee of a specified quantity of a certain description of goods. These licences were normally valid for a period of twelve months from the date of issue. The goods in question, if they were to be exported by ship, had to be pre-entered with the Customs, i.e. the exporter had, prior to shipment, to deliver to the appropriate Customs official a shipping bill containing particulars required about the goods.[1]

(ii) *General Licences*, issued to avoid a number of separate applications, and covering the export over a period of an unspecified quantity of goods by a particular consignor to a particular consignee or destination; normally valid for three months.

(iii) *Bulk Licences*, really ordinary licences but distinguished by the fact that they did not specify a particular consignee; normally valid for three months.

These licences were available for the despatch of goods abroad direct by ship or through the parcel post. In the case of the use of shipping, but not in the use of the parcel post, the goods might be sent in instalments. Licences were not transferable; applications had to be made by consignors of goods and not by persons acting on their behalf.

(iv) *Open General Licences* were issued at the beginning of the war to free goods from export control to particular destinations, or to transfer export control to other departments, e.g. coal to the Mines Department and films to the Censorship. Other items, the export control of which lay with other departments, were dangerous drugs (Home Office) and pigeons (Air Ministry). Exemptions from export control varied naturally during the war, but the following are the main items: (a) goods sent to Northern Ireland and the Isle of Man, (b) sample packets by sample post, (c) newspapers, periodicals, etc., (d) aircraft registered outside the United Kingdom or flying under permit, (e) firearms and ammunition for which a firearms certificate had been issued, (f) goods sent abroad on Government account, (g) *bona fide* personal effects, (h) ships' stores and coastwise cargoes, (j) transit and transhipment goods.

The work of the Export Licensing Department was divided mainly among 'goods' sections, corresponding to the various group headings in the export control list. In some cases, e.g. diamonds and proprietary articles, advisory committees including representatives of Government departments concerned and of the trade were set up to help in the administration of the control. Close contact was maintained with other departments, e.g. Ministries of Supply, Food and Agriculture, Ministry of Economic Warfare, Customs, Ministry of War Transport. A liaison staff from M.E.W. worked in the Export Licensing Department.

---

[1] The concession whereby goods pre-entered with the Customs might be shipped after the expiry of an export licence was withdrawn in June 1942.

CHAPTER IV

PRICE CONTROL: THE FIRST PHASE

(i)

Introductory

THE first home-front problem that the Board of Trade had to deal with after the outbreak of war was that of price control —a subject that was to remain one of the Board's chief pre-occupations during the next few years. The Board were broadly responsible for the prices of all consumer goods other than food and fuel. The most important of these goods was clothing which had a weight of sixteen per cent.[1] in the cost-of-living index. Other goods in the index might not be so important but once the prices of articles in common use began to rise the Board of Trade would be the depart-ment answerable to public protests.

Although it had been foreseen before the war that an inflationary rise of prices would seriously hamper the war effort, little thought had been given to methods of price control. The whole task was much more difficult for the Board of Trade than it was for the contracts branches of the supply departments or for the Ministry of Food. For the contract branches had more control over the firms they dealt with and the Ministry of Food closely controlled, from the beginning of the war, supplies and distribution of the most important foodstuffs. The Board never developed a control on this scale—they never bought and distributed clothing in the way that the Ministry of Food bought butter or bacon. As far as the Board were concerned, therefore, effective price control could only be introduced within a wider framework of saving and taxation arrangements, rationing and standardisation of commodities. The war was well advanced before this framework had been built; the first 'realistic' war budget did not come until April 1941, clothes rationing was not introduced until June 1941, utility clothing not until September 1941, and other standardisation schemes not until 1942 and 1943.

There was another obstacle in the way of the rapid development of price control. Methods of control could not operate reasonably successfully without on the one hand the close co-operation of the business community and on the other adequate arrangements for

---

[1] Using 1st September 1939 as the base.

policing and enforcement. Clearly these requirements could not be met easily or rapidly. Apart from the problem created by the very large numbers of traders involved, Government measures had to be applied and enforced in terms of the pricing and costing arrangements of a trading community whose standards of accounting were in many cases low.

A co-ordinated policy of price control was the more difficult because responsibility was parcelled out among a number of departments. While the prices of consumer goods came within the Board of Trade's sphere of responsibility, the prices of raw materials and of certain intermediate products—for example, cotton yarn and cloth, fell within that of the Ministry of Supply. Wages were a matter for the Ministry of Labour; coal prices for the fairly autonomous Mines Department and then later in the war for the Ministry of Fuel and Power. Then the Treasury, which were concerned with price policy as a whole, imposed taxes; the prices of many commodities were to be affected by the levying of purchase tax. Thus the Board of Trade's price-control measures were to be profoundly affected by the activities of other departments. The prices of the factors of production were of crucial importance to them, the more so since a good many price-fixing arrangements were to establish maximum prices on the basis of percentage additions to cost at the various stages of production and distribution. The prices of essential raw materials were in fact gradually brought under control and, later, they were stabilised. The rise of wage rates, however, though it never got out of hand persisted throughout the war as an underlying threat to the stability of the price structure.

It is clear, therefore, that it would be a mistake to attach undue significance to price control of consumer goods taken alone, that is to say outside the general structure of control of prices and consumption of which it formed part. The Board of Trade's measures needed the firm support of restrictions on rises in the prices of the ultimate factors of production. Moreover, it is a matter of elementary economic knowledge that, without effective restraints on demand through rationing, price control in conditions of general shortage is bound to lead to disequilibrium of supply and demand and hence to dislocation and evasion. The first price control measures of the Board of Trade were to underline this lesson as supplies became increasingly scarce from the autumn of 1940 onwards.

The need for some action by the Board had made itself felt immediately after the outbreak of war. For certain influences, some short-term and some long-term, quickly pushed prices upwards. In the first place, the prices of imports rose. Sterling suffered a fourteen per cent. depreciation against the dollar compared with the average rate for January–August 1939, freight charges rose and war risks insurance had to be paid for. The rise in prices was sometimes considerable; cotton prices for example rose by fifty per cent. or more between August and December 1939. In the second place, the sudden demand at the beginning of the war for such things as sandbags, black-out material and torches caused a temporary upward surge of their prices. Movements of this sort were naturally accompanied by public criticism of profiteering.

In the early phases of the war there was no coherent Government policy to deal with these problems. There seem, however, to have been three different strands of thought running through Government departments. First, there was the need to restrain inflation. It was necessary to check undue rises in the cost of living which might lead to wage increases and thus to a vicious spiral of rising costs and prices. But there was as yet no hint of a stabilisation policy and such checks to inflation as were devised were confined to food prices. Working against the anti-inflation policy was a second strand of thought. There were doubts about the desirability of holding strategic prices down below their equilibrium level, partly because of the effect this would have on demand and supply, partly on account of the burden it would impose on the budget in the way of subsidies. These feelings were reflected in policy towards raw material prices. Maximum prices of certain raw materials over which the Ministry of Supply had assumed control were at first fixed at the level ruling in the market at the beginning of the war. For a wide range of other materials for which strong trade organisations existed, it had been arranged that prices would not be raised without consulting the Ministry. Soon, however, rises in costs made it necessary to review the position. It was then decided that prices must be raised to the level, in most cases, of replacement costs. For more than a year the policy of basing material prices on average cost, or even cost plus profit, ruled. The third strand of thought on price policy in the early months of the war was the need to meet public complaints about high prices and profiteering. It was this need that largely inspired the Board of Trade's own first efforts at price control.

(ii)

The Prices of Goods Act, 1939[1]

At the beginning of the war the Board of Trade had asked for the co-operation of various trade associations in maintaining stability of prices, and the major bodies—the Federation of British Industries,

---

[1] 2 & 3 Geo. 6, ch. 118.

the National Union of Manufacturers and the National Chamber of Trade—had circularised their members emphasising the importance of price stability and the need for seeing that increases of prices were only such as could be justified by higher production costs. Politically, however, it was recognised by the Government that something more would be required to reassure public opinion that traders would not exploit the shortages of particular commodities, such as torches and sandbags, which the outbreak of war had caused. An Act of Parliament must be passed in order to convince the public that the Government was taking the matter seriously.

Political considerations thus played an important part in the decision to introduce some form of price control. The hope that the measure might help to check inflationary tendencies was subsidiary. Indeed the economic effectiveness of such a measure, more particularly of the actual Bill which was introduced, was viewed with a certain amount of scepticism. It was even suggested that it would have been better merely to prohibit the charging of unreasonable prices, the courts being left to decide what was and what was not reasonable. The President of the Board of Trade, himself, in his speech in the House of Commons[1] on the Bill emphasised the dangers of a too rigid scheme of price control.

The essential feature of the main provisions of the Prices of Goods Act may be put quite briefly. It limited the profit earned per unit of a commodity to the amount received at the end of August 1939. In the terms of the Act a basic price was fixed for price-regulated goods, being the price at which, on 21st August 1939, similar goods were being offered for sale. Prices of such goods might not be raised above the basic prices except to the extent of the net increase in costs as a whole, the actual costs which might be taken into account being listed in the first schedule to the Act.   These provisions make it clear that the Act was anti-profiteering rather than anti-inflationary in its main intention.

The administration of the Act was entrusted to a Central Price Regulation Committee and to seventeen Local Price Regulation Committees operating in different parts of the United Kingdom.[2] No provision was made for an inspectorate and the main procedure contemplated by the Act was that complaints would be made to the Local Price Committees about overcharging by manufacturers or traders. However, the Central and Local Price Committees were empowered to initiate enquiries of their own.

The provisions of the Prices of Goods Act were open to various criticisms. Some of these had been voiced in the discussion of the

---

[1] H. of C. Deb., Vol. 352, Cols. 1109–1119.
[2] For a list of members of the Central Committee and a list of the seventeen regions see Appendix 4.

measure by ministers before its introduction but others were only revealed by difficulties in administering the Act. The criticisms could be grouped under four main heads.

First, the administrative arrangements themselves were not altogether satisfactory. The lack of an inspectorate was not remedied until the Board's next major price-control measure—the Goods and Services (Price Control) Act of 1941—was introduced and did undoubtedly diminish the effectiveness with which the Prices of Goods Act could be enforced. Complaints from members of the public related for the most part to the grosser forms of profiteering by small shopkeepers in such things as electric torches; traders themselves were unlikely to complain in view of their unwillingness to incur the hostility of their suppliers. Moreover, many traders were probably unaware, if not of the existence of the Act, at any rate of its provisions.

The part played by the Central Price Committee in making the Act a workable instrument of price control was to be an important one. Its activities, however, raised difficult questions of demarcation of function between itself and the Board of Trade. The Board were responsible for general policy, for the making of Orders under the Act, and for decisions about prosecutions, while the Committee was concerned with administration. But the line between policy and administration is in any event a difficult one to draw, and probably more than usually so in the case of an Act whose provisions are of a novel character. The problem of the relations between the two bodies became more acute with the extension of the sphere of price control and was not dealt with until in 1942 the President of the Board of Trade defined the respective spheres of operation of the Board and the Committee.

The second major criticism of the Act was that the 'basic price' grew to be a more and more unsatisfactory datum of price control with the passage of time. It was often difficult to establish what the basic price of any commodity actually was. More important still was the change in commodities since the basic date. New commodities were introduced on the market, and the make-up and design of commodities which were being sold in August 1939 were altered. The Board of Trade were empowered to fix by Order basic prices, but only for descriptions of goods which had come into existence since 21st August 1939 and it might be impossible to prove that no similar article had existed at or before that date.

The third criticism was that the Act assumed, as far as traders were concerned, that the actual costs of retailing could be apportioned without difficulty between the different commodities that were sold. It is clear, however, that almost all of the costs which relate to the services provided by the retailer are not capable of direct allocation.

Retailers are in fact accustomed to price their goods on the basis of varying 'mark-ups' with the aim of securing a satisfactory net profit on their turnover as a whole. The shopkeeper could not say what part of his gross margin on any particular article constituted selling expenses and what part represented net profit. To meet the difficulty the Retail Distributors' Association worked out an elaborate pricing formula, which assumed, however, for the basic date that the proportion of net profit to gross margin for the business as a whole applied to each particular commodity. The formula can hardly be said to have met the requirements of the Act, but it was approved by the Central Price Regulation Committee, and certainly simplified the administration of price control.

The fourth criticism applied to the actual schedule of costs appended to the Act; indeed power was subsequently taken to amend the schedule. During ministerial discussions it was agreed that traders should be allowed to take into consideration the volume of turnover over which the general expenses of the business were spread, and this item was included in the schedule. This seemed at first a reasonable safeguard for the trader, but before long, with increasing limitation of supplies, it provided justification for steadily rising prices based on an uneconomic organisation of retailing as a whole. The period of time involved was another source of difficulty. Over what period should a trader recover his costs? If he had failed to recover them in one accounting period should he be allowed to recoup himself in the following period? The Act threw no light on these problems. Similarly, there was the question whether the cost of his supplies should be the original or the replacement costs. Although the evidence on this point was not conclusive traders maintained that it was their normal practice to price on the basis of replacement values. This could not be considered unreasonable when it had already been agreed that as a matter of general principle the Ministry of Supply should adopt replacement values rather than pre-war values as the basis of pricing. So far, however, as the Prices of Goods Act was concerned, no ruling was given, though the Parliamentary Secretary to the Board of Trade in the debate on the Bill[1] stated that he regarded the practice of averaging the values of stocks bought at different dates as a reasonable one.[2]

The major provisions of the Act, which have thus far been described, applied to free pricing arrangements, that is to situations in which the trader was at liberty to fix the gross margin on commod-

---

[1] H. of C. Deb., Vol. 352, Cols. 1517–18.

[2] Ministers had been in favour of giving traders the option to price on a replacement basis, but the Central Price Regulation Committee thought that this would accentuate inflationary tendencies.

dities at whatever level he might think fit. These provisions did not contemplate the widespread practice of resale price maintenance which had been the subject of a report by a Committee on Restraint of Trade in 1931. This committee had declared that it was 'quite unable to say that the interests of the public would be better served by an alteration of the law which would prevent the fixing of the prices of branded goods'. Yet such arrangements cut across the major provision of the Prices Act, namely that retail prices should not exceed the level which would cover the individual retailer's costs plus his pre-war net profit per unit of commodity sold.

The Central Price Regulation Committee soon came to the conclusion that it would not be practicable to upset the resale price maintenance system. There were thousands of commodities whose prices were fixed in this way, either by individual manufacturers or by trade associations. On the other hand the Committee felt that mere acceptance of this system, which it admitted was contrary to the Act, would involve discrimination between one class of manufacturer or trader and another. It resorted, therefore, to another set of provisions in the Prices Act which enabled the Board of Trade to specify 'permitted prices' for any description of goods. These permitted prices, it should be noted, were not maximum prices but prices which manufacturer or trader might charge with the assurance that legal proceedings would not be taken against him. The procedure of the Central Committee, in order to secure reasonable conformity with the intention of the Act, was to obtain costings from the manufacturers of these price-maintained commodities and data about wholesalers' and retailers' margins, which were checked by a firm of accountants acting on its behalf. This costing procedure could not, it was true, be applied to retail trade, but estimates were made of changes in retail turnover and retail expense ratios. Imperfect as this may appear from the standpoint of a strict enforcement of the Act, it probably represented the most satisfactory compromise that could have been achieved at the time. Prices of many of the goods in question were reduced, and the chairman of the Central Price Committee estimated in July 1940 that the result of specifying 'permitted prices' had been to reduce the level of the prices of the goods affected by at least two per cent.

Before long the Central Price Committee had developed the practice of approving informally, i.e. without resorting to Statutory Orders, a wide range of prices of branded or proprietary articles, costings having been obtained to check the conformity of these prices with the main principle of the Act. Sample costings were taken to check the price lists of such trade associations as the Stationers' Association, the Proprietary Articles Trade Association, the National Pharmaceutical Union. An important agreement, later embodied in an Order[1] was reached with the Wool Textile Delegation of York-shire, covering spinners and manufacturers, as to the *method* of pricing to be adopted and the profit margins appropriate to different sections of the industry.

It can hardly be doubted that these arrangements did much towards making the Act more workable, and in some cases enabling it to operate where otherwise it would have broken down. The Central Price Committee adopted not only this technique but also other methods which made it possible to apply the Act to the special circumstances of particular firms, and by agreements with such firms to extend the area of its effective operation. The success of the arrangements is shown by the way in which they survived after the main structure of the Act had ceased to serve a useful purpose.

The scope of the Prices of Goods Act was at first fairly narrow. The Board of Trade had in mind that the Act should cover the cheaper articles of common use and should apply to the range of goods which a man with a family earning £500 a year might be expected to buy. It was therefore intended to include within its scope many commodities which did not enter into the Ministry of Labour's cost-of-living index number. The main constituents of this index number were, indeed, the responsibility of departments other than the Board: rent, food and fuel and light together accounted for seventy-nine per cent. of the weight in the index. The index number always had a peculiar importance as it was used as a standard in many wage negotiations. But since the index number was based on maintaining unchanged the 1914 working-class standard of living it was recognised as being an increasingly unreal measure of the cost of living in 1940. The Board of Trade had, therefore, to extend their price control activities more widely.

For the application of the Prices of Goods Act an Order had to be made specifying the goods to which it should apply, that is, declaring what goods should be 'price-regulated'. This Order[2] came into force on 1st January 1940 and covered clothing and boots and shoes for men, women, children and infants; piece-goods; pro-tective clothing; household textiles; domestic ironmongery and turnery; table cutlery; domestic glassware and pottery; and miscel-laneous items—knitting yarn, sandbags, electric torches and their accessories. Furthermore, by this Order price control under the Act was applied to all textile and leather materials in fact used in the manufacture of the price-regulated clothing, piece-goods and household textiles except in so far as such materials were already controlled by Defence Regulations. In view of the main aims of the

---

[1] S.R. & O., 1943, No. 1187.
[2] S.R. & O., 1939, No. 1813.

Act it was thought desirable to exclude from control the more highly priced varieties of the finished consumer goods mentioned above, and for all these goods, except certain piece-goods (Italian cloth, sateen and cotton casement cloth), torches and their accessories and sandbags, price limits were fixed. That is, varieties of the commodities selling on 21st August 1939 above the prices specified in the Order were to be free from control.

After a few months' experience of the working of the Act, it was felt by the price committees that this Order needed to be revised. In the first place, it was suggested that the main list of price-regulated commodities ought to be extended. As things stood there was an inducement for manufacturers and traders to produce and sell the more profitable uncontrolled lines of goods. Moreover the indivisibility of most of the trader's expenses rendered the application of the Act to part of his turnover specially difficult. Secondly, it was argued that price limits should be abolished, partly for the reasons already mentioned, partly in order to provide additional protection for the black-coated worker. Thirdly, the control provided for by the Act over the prices of materials and semi-finished goods was inadequate and ineffective. The restriction of its application to such textile and leather materials as had *in fact* been used in the manufacture of price-regulated goods was unduly hampering on account of the difficulty experienced in identifying these materials.

A new Order of 10th May 1940[1] met these criticisms of the existing scope of price control. It abolished price limits. It extended considerably the list of price-regulated goods including, for example, such items as domestic furniture; wireless sets and gramophones; cycles and perambulators; clocks and watches; drugs, soap, candles, matches and mechanical lighters; stationery; brushes for personal use; hand tools; gramophone records; paraffin and kerosene for domestic use. Finally, it extended control over the earlier stages of manufacture by applying the Act to yarn and thread and fabrics made from yarn and thread; leather and leather substitutes; unvulcanised rubber and rubber substitutes; and materials used in the manufacture of haberdashery and mercery.

In spite of these latter extensions of control it was a fair generalisation of the first year of the war to say that price control was enforced more effectively against the retailer than against the wholesaler or the manufacturer. Moreover, control of the prices of intermediate products—yarn, cloth, leather—was probably hampered by uncertainty about the division of responsibility for the industries concerned between the Ministry of Supply and the Board of Trade. But the activities of the Central Price Committee in this field should

---

[1] S.R. & O. 1940, No. 685.

not be overlooked. The agreement with the Wool Textile Delegation was an important piece of work, and in the summer of 1940 the chairman of the Central Committee was investigating the leather tanners' prices with a view to securing proper observance of the Act.

Just as there was some uncertainty about the division of responsibility for some 'intermediate' products, there was for a time some confusion over responsibility for the prices of foods. Some of the Local Price Committees held in 1940 that the prices of various foodstuffs which the Ministry of Food had not yet brought under control should come within the scope of the Prices of Goods Act. This was never done, but for a time the Local Price Committees were appointed by the Ministry of Food as Local Food Price Investigation Committees to receive and inquire into complaints about the prices of uncontrolled foodstuffs. Soon, however, in April 1941, the Local Food Offices took over this responsibility.

Although the scope for action under the Prices of Goods Act was limited, administration of the Act's provisions did sometimes take the Central Price Regulation Committee further afield. This happened in the case of torch batteries, for example. The great increase which the war brought in the demand for torch batteries had led to price rises and market disturbances. Imports of batteries from abroad rose considerably, home supplies were expanded and speculators broke into the normal channels of distribution. The Central Price Committee soon took up the investigation of battery prices. But it did not stop here. It proposed that a schedule of maximum prices which could not easily be introduced under the Prices of Goods Act should be imposed under Defence Regulation 55. Moreover, it also recommended that imports should be so controlled that they were confined to recognised and responsible traders.

Both these recommendations were followed. Maximum prices for batteries were fixed in November 1940 by Orders under Defence Regulation 55. Maximum price schedules were drawn up distinguishing between the larger and the smaller home manufacturers and between different overseas sources of supply.[1] These domestic maximum prices, it may be said in passing, provided an example of what may be regarded as the perversity of a control based on cost since higher maximum prices were fixed for the more expensive but inferior products of the smaller manufacturers.

The Central Price Committee's recommendation about imports was not followed until June 1940. In that month batteries were brought under import control and a Torch Battery Imports Advisory Committee consisting of representatives of importers and manufacturers was set up to assist in the administration of licensing. This

---

[1] S.R. & O. 1940, Nos. 1971, 1972, 2168.

committee recommended that licences should be restricted to firms or individuals who had been engaged in importing batteries or some similar class of electrical goods before the war and had also imported batteries during the previous season.

Before leaving the description of the Prices of Goods Act, it is necessary to mention one complicated problem of detailed administration—the treatment of purchase tax for price-control purposes. The tax, which was to be levied at a rate of one-third or one-sixth on the wholesale value of certain commodities, was introduced in the Finance (No. 2) Act of 1940. It came into operation on 21st October 1940.

The tax was clearly intended to be passed on to the consumer in the shape of higher prices, and as such was felt by the Central Price Committee to be inflationary and to be inconsistent with the Government's aim, embodied in the Prices of Goods Act, of restricting price rises. Though little attention was paid to this view at the time of the introduction of the tax, the remission of purchase tax on utility goods, which will be mentioned later,[1] was to recognise the validity of the principle which it expressed.

The two main problems in the sphere of price control to which the purchase tax gave rise were, first, whether the retailer could charge a *percentage*, e.g. in the shape of a customary 'mark-up', on the tax itself, and, secondly, whether he could write up the value of stocks on which no tax had been paid.

On the first point, it was clearly stated by the Financial Secretary to the Treasury in July 1940[2] that the charging of a percentage on the tax would be inadmissible, i.e. that retailers might raise the prices of their goods only by the *amount* of the tax that they had paid on them. The Central Price Committee, acting on this principle, and arguing that the tax could not be shown separately, published a table showing the appropriate reductions which would have to be made in retail percentage margins in order to leave the retailer the same net cash profit as before.[3] If, as traders maintained, the effect of the tax would be to reduce the volume of goods sold, adjustments could be made later in order to compensate for any reduction of turnover that might arise. This action on the part of the Central Price Committee met the difficulty at the time, but the feeling was strong that traders should not be allowed to make a profit on the tax and that unless the matter was dealt with in a more radical manner they would be tempted to do so. Later in the war, when the structure of

---

[1] See below, p. 606.

[2] H. of C. Deb., Vol. 363, Cols. 1059–60.

[3] These margins had, however, been rounded so as to give the retailer a slight benefit in order to compensate him for the fact that he would be out of pocket between the time when he paid the tax to the wholesaler and the time when he recovered it from the consumer.

G

price control had been more firmly built, it was provided that the prescribed retail margins should be calculated on an ex-tax, as opposed to a cum-tax, basis.

The problem of stocks was somewhat more difficult. The practice of averaging had been accepted as a reasonable one and in conformity with the provisions of the Act. Traders therefore maintained that they should be allowed to average the prices of taxed and untaxed stocks, since it would be awkward to have similar goods selling at two different prices. It would be better, it was argued, to fix a date when the greater part of the untaxed stocks would have been sold, after which traders could price *all* their goods on a cum-tax basis. (This sort of arrangement was afterwards adopted when purchase tax was removed from certain items.) However, the Central Price Committee declared themselves opposed to the averaging of taxed and untaxed stocks. They had naturally rejected any suggestion that traders should be allowed to write up their pre-tax stocks by the amount of the tax, and they felt that there was a danger that any approval of averaging would lead many retailers to do this. They emphasised their point of view by stating that in the case of branded goods for which 'permitted prices' had been specified there would be two prices, for the pre-tax and the post-tax goods respectively. The sanction for the doctrine of the Central Committee was dubious, and it was proposed that the Prices Act should be amended so as to make this sort of averaging illegal. The Law Officers of the Crown declared, however, that the proposed regulation would be *ultra vires*. It had therefore to be admitted that no means were available for preventing certain stores from pursuing their announced intention of averaging the prices of taxed and untaxed stocks of commodities.

(iii)

Retrospect and Prospect

It is clear that there were a good many gaps and inconsistencies in the structure of price control as it developed in the early stages of the war. Certain raw materials and their prices had been brought under control by the Ministry of Supply and these prices were based on replacement values—a policy that had led to a considerable advance in the prices of some materials. As for finished goods, the Prices of Goods Act was being applied over a widening field. Its basic principle however was a limitation of the net cash profit per unit of commodity to that earned in August 1939, while the administrators of the Act had refused to accept the traders' claim to price on the basis of replacement costs. The Prices of Goods Act applied in the main to

traders but some progress had been made in applying it to manufacturers—particularly in those cases where manufacturers or the
associations to which they belonged asked for approval of the prices
of the branded goods they sold.

In the field of 'intermediate' products there was again some
inconsistency and some division of responsibility. The Central Price
Regulation Committee had reached an agreement with the West
Riding wool industry which represented a form of price control
in that it limited the costs of conversion of raw material into yarn
and cloth. A quite different scheme, however, was established over
cotton textiles. Here there was a statutory control operating through
the Ministry of Supply over spinners' margins. And the margins
were fixed not maximum ones. Indeed the whole aim of control
in this case seems to have been different from that of the Prices
of Goods Act. The cotton industry in its different sections had
suffered from price cutting in the period between the wars, and its
representatives had been more concerned with minimum than with
maximum prices. The war had not changed their attitude to this
problem, and as we have seen,[1] it was argued now that fixed prices
were necessary in order to provide a firm basis on which an organised
scheme of price reductions devised to promote cotton exports could
be built up. The 1939 Cotton Industry Reorganisation Act was much
in mind, but this Act had provided reasonable safeguards in connection with its price-fixing arrangement. It was with misgivings
therefore that the arguments of the industry were accepted. Fixed
margins for single yarns were prescribed as from January 1940
though the scheme of 'price derogations' to help exports did not
come into operation until the summer of 1940. One of the conditions
of accepting this principle of fixed margins was that there should be a
periodic review of spinners' profits. Margins fixed were for American
and Egyptian type yarns, based on full-time cost of production in
efficient mills with an allowance of 5s. 6d. per spindle[2] for interest
and depreciation charges, pre-war replacement values being used
in these calculations. The Order did something to restrain the rise,
due to the war, in the prices of the coarser yarns and in certain cases
actually brought a reduction. However, it affected only spinners, and
weavers' margins were not controlled until the spring of 1942.

Amidst the gaps and inconsistencies of price control in these
months a more hopeful proposal had emerged—only to disappear
again. This was a proposal for standard clothing. The idea was first
mooted by Lord Woolton towards the end of 1939. The theory
underlying his scheme was that the pegging of the prices of standard

---

[1] See pp. 46–7.
[2] This was for carded yarns; the figure for combed yarns was 7s. per spindle.

items of clothing would restrain the rise in the prices of non-standard items. Production of the clothing would be secured through the issue of raw material at the lowest price short of subsidy, under a licence which would follow the material through the various production processes and would require manufacture to specification of pre-scribed quantities of particular articles. Mass production of the goods in question, together with a reduction in the margin of the retailer —for he would be free from advertising charges and assured of a steady demand—would contribute towards a reduction of prices.

The Board of Trade pointed out the administrative difficulties of the scheme, in particular the problem of policing the use of the raw material through the successive stages of manufacture and distribu-tion. They would have preferred that the Government should come in as suppliers of cloth to the making-up trade, the makers-up being required to manufacture clothing to specifications at a fixed charge and to sell to retailers on resale conditions providing for a fixed retail price.

There were other criticisms of Lord Woolton's proposal. It was in any case very doubtful whether the scheme could stand alone without the assistance of some form of rationing to restrain demand and without some general measure of price control. If, on the other hand, there was prejudice against standard boots and clothing, there would be much wasted effort and the plan would do little to check the rise of prices. Moreover, it was not clear that really cheap articles—clothing cheaper for example than that offered by the multiple tailors—could be put on the market without some subsidy on raw material prices.

Nevertheless, the War Cabinet in March 1940 agreed in principle to the proposal and decided that arrangements should be made to bring into operation in October 1940 a scheme for standard clothing and standard boots and shoes. Responsibility for the scheme was to rest with the Ministry of Supply.

This did not, however, dispose of the question. In the summer of 1940 discussions took place between the Ministry of Supply and the Board of Trade. The ministers in charge of these departments doubted whether the scheme was necessary for they were agreed that stocks of cloth were at the time ample, and the President of the Board felt that competition among the multiple tailors and between them and the C.W.S. could be trusted to keep the prices of suits low in relation to that of cloth. If a scheme for standard clothing should become necessary, it did not seem that it would get very far for each minister urged that responsibility for preparing and administering it should rest with the other. Thus the scheme was allowed to drop, and nothing more was heard of this type of proposal until June 1941. Much valuable time was thus lost in dealing with a major problem of civilian consumption and little was done to check the rapid rise of the clothing component in the cost-of-living index.

Nevertheless, the standard clothing proposals were an indication of the shape of things to come. Sooner or later the Prices of Goods Act would have to be replaced. By the autumn of 1940 the shortcomings of this Act were becoming more and more noticeable. With the lapse of time the basic price provisions were increasingly difficult to administer, and the lack of an inspectorate hampered administration. And now the forces that were pressing the price level upwards were becoming stronger. Supplies of goods to the home market were being severely cut before there were any means of ensuring that the reduced supplies were distributed as efficiently and economically as possible. Competition could no longer be relied upon to keep prices down. Indeed, the demands of war suggested rather that surplus traders should be eliminated. In these circumstances the Prices of Goods Act, since it permitted traders in fixing prices to take account of diminished turnover, actually encouraged higher prices.

One lesson was becoming clear: a really effective system of price control could not be achieved without powers to fix maximum prices and maximum margins. Such powers would, however, be useless unless they were accompanied by far-reaching measures for the control of production and supply. For maximum prices could not be properly enforced unless the commodities they applied to could be readily identified. If there were to be a comprehensive system of maximum prices, there must first be a considerable amount of specification. And this would undoubtedly have to be promoted by the Government.

The Board of Trade recognised the need for further advances in price control, but were also fully conscious of the problems that would arise. It would not be sufficient merely to prescribe standards and specifications; arrangements would have to be made to ensure adequate production and supply of the goods in question. Further, rationing of consumers would have to be introduced in order to secure fair shares for all of the specified items. Lastly, the fixing of controlled prices on the basis of minimum cost would require concentration of the capacity available for production and distribution.

Thus the next move in price control implied the making of other moves towards utility and standardised production, towards consumer rationing and towards concentration. It will be recorded that, with one exception, these associated moves were made. The exception lay in the sphere of distribution, to which an orderly scheme of concentration was never applied.

APPENDIX 4

1. Original members of the Central Price Regulation Committee:
   RAYMOND EVERSHED, K.C.: Chairman.

   SIR SYDNEY CHAPMAN, K.C.B.: Permanent Secretary to the Board of Trade, 1920–27, and Chief Economic Adviser to the Government, 1927–32.

   O. H. FROST: Director of Messrs. Robinson & Cleaver Ltd.

   J. HALLSWORTH: Industrial General Secretary, National Union of Distributive and Allied Workers.

   LT.-GEN. SIR G. W. MACDONOGH, G.B.E.: Past President of the F.B.I.

   MRS. M. NEWMAN: Alderman of the L.C.C.

   R. A. PALMER: Secretary of the Co-operative Union.

   E. E. SPICER, F.C.A.: Member of Messrs. Spicer & Pegler.

   W. S. WALTERS: Chairman of the Fore Street Warehouse Company.

2. LOCAL PRICE REGULATION COMMITTEES[1]

Region	Headquarters
Northern	Newcastle-on-Tyne
North-Eastern	Leeds
North Midland	Nottingham
Eastern	Cambridge
London (Metropolitan Police District)	London
South-Eastern	Tunbridge Wells
Southern	Reading
South-Western	Bristol
Midland	Birmingham
North-Western	Manchester
South Wales	Cardiff
North Wales	Rhyl
Southern and South-Eastern Scotland	Edinburgh
South-Western Scotland	Glasgow
Northern Scotland	Inverness
North-Eastern Scotland	Aberdeen
Northern Ireland	Belfast

---

[1] For their constitution and organisation see S.R. & O. 1940, No. 25.

3. *Prosecutions* under the Prices Acts, 1939–43 as amended:

Summary of Prosecutions, 1940–46

Year	Number of prosecutions	Convictions	Dismissals	Dismissals under Probation of Offenders' Act	Not proven
1940	31	23	4	3	1
1941	153	139	5	9	—
1942	448	383	29	31	—
1943	836	741	55	32	8
1944	980	898	46	31	5
1945	1,069	1,005	32	28	4
1946	973	917	28	25	3
TOTAL	4,490	4,106	199	159	21

Total fines imposed amounted to £124,407.
Number of cases in which terms of imprisonment were imposed was 32.

CHAPTER V

RESTRICTIONS ON THE HOME MARKET

(i)

The First Experiment

THERE were, as we have seen, no pre-war discussions in the Board of Trade about the need to curb the demands of the home market, much less about the ways and means of doing so. And indeed in the first months of the war there seemed no pressing need to introduce general, direct restrictions on the manufacture or supply of civilian goods. There was still a good deal of slack in the economy and only when this had been absorbed did it become urgent to divert as many resources as possible from civilian to war purposes.

Even in these early months the war did make some inroads upon civilian supplies. Skilled engineering labour was scarce and it was desirable that as much of it as possible should be employed on war work. There were no direct measures to ensure that the necessary transfers of workers were made nor was the capacity of engineering firms compulsorily requisitioned for munitions work. Nevertheless, most firms gladly took on war contracts and sacrificed home trade to do so. It was not long before the supply of civilian engineering goods of all kinds began to decline. Production of industrial machinery fell and such goods as motor cars, refrigerators and vacuum cleaners were difficult to buy. By June 1940 most sections of the engineering industry had only about fifteen per cent. of their workers employed on home trade.

There were, too, a few raw material restrictions that affected civilian supplies from an early stage of the war. For example, supplies of paper, timber and flax for the home market were heavily reduced from the outset. In general, however, raw material control was rudimentary until after France had fallen. Up till then most materials had been distributed far too freely for civilian purposes however unessential.

So in the first period of the war home trade did not suffer very much from restrictions on materials. Even if these restrictions had been tighter they might not by themselves have been conspicuously effective; indeed there proved to be many ways of circumventing the relatively strict controls already in force for timber. War-time experience was in fact to prove that no single control was effective in regulating at once the quantity of civilian goods produced, the quantity of materials used in them and the amount of labour employed for their manufacture. A complicated interlocking system of controls was necessary and in time this was built up. The Board of Trade's contribution to this system was to be control over the supply and manufacture of a wide range of goods.

It was not long after the outbreak of war that the Board first felt the need to experiment with some such form of control. For they received a call for action from the Treasury concerning cotton. The shortage of foreign exchange, or rather of hard currencies, was proving even worse than the Government had expected. At a meeting of the Exchange Requirements Committee in the middle of December 1939 the Treasury and the Bank of England insisted that imports of cotton from the United States must be restricted effectively and swiftly. Owing partly to increased imports but mainly to increased world prices raw cotton had become by far the most expensive single item of British raw material imports. In November 1938 raw cotton worth £2,255,000 had been imported—twelve per cent. of total raw material imports. In November 1939 raw cotton had shot up to £6,538,000—over twenty-seven per cent. of total raw material imports. Cotton imports were quite out of scale with other more important raw materials and dollars could no longer be provided at this rate.

It was the responsibility of the Exchange Requirements Committee to decide the amount of exchange to be made available for cotton purchases. It was the responsibility of the Ministry of Supply and the Board of Trade to consider the machinery for restricting consumption. The Board of Trade indeed already had reasons of their own for wishing to restrain civilian demands upon the cotton industry. For the export trade in cotton goods was not as flourishing as it should have been. Increased expenditure abroad on raw cotton was not bringing an equivalent compensation in increased sales of cotton exports. Owing partly to Government orders but also, to a larger extent, to pressure of civilian home demand[1] the cotton industry had more work than it could do; as a result there was a marked tendency to give priority to the home trade (for which business was more easily obtained and more profitable) at the expense of the export trade. This tendency was very noticeable in the case of cotton and wool, but it seemed probable that it was operating over the whole textile field. Home sales of textiles, as shown by the index numbers of wholesale

---

[1] A contributory factor to this increased home demand was the immense demand for black-out cloth.

trade, which should have fallen to make way for Government orders, had instead risen steeply.

Home Trade in Textiles

TABLE 4

(1937 = 100)	1938	1939
September . .	126	160
October . .	124	170
November . .	120	137

It was quite clear that this development of the textile home trade must inevitably, unless checked, hamper the export trade. The textile industry was so preoccupied with home trade that exporters were unable to guarantee delivery in foreign markets; orders were being lost daily to foreign competitors. The pressure of home demand must then be relieved.

From December 1939 onwards much thought was devoted to finding a remedy. The difficulties were considerable. There was no previous experience for guidance and officials were very much aware that mistakes once made could not easily be retrieved. In particular, excessive control might in its ultimate results be far worse than no control at all. It was especially important to interfere no further with the export side of industry. Export trade in war-time was already difficult enough and exporters might well find further licensing, checking and counter-checking the last straw. 'However well planned on paper may be a scheme of control,' wrote an official, 'and with whatever zeal and understanding it may be administered, in practice control of any kind adds something, perhaps quite a lot, to the height of trade barriers and may make them insuperable to all but the most robust lines of trade.'

There was another important point to be considered—that of price control. Prices would almost certainly rise at the point in the process of manufacture and distribution where supplies were reduced. If supplies for the home market were cut early in the production process there would probably be a cumulative increase of prices through all the successive stages of handling. The prospect of fixing prices to cover the whole of the cotton industry was truly formidable. The Ministry of Supply had so far fixed prices only for cotton yarn. This presented far fewer difficulties than other sections of the cotton industry; even so the yarn prices order ran to fifty-six complicated schedules.

These then were some of the considerations that had to be borne in mind in deciding upon the methods of restriction. The choice lay between two methods. Either supplies of raw material for the home trade could be cut; this would be the responsibility of the Ministry of Supply. Or control could be imposed over the home demand for finished cotton and other textile goods; this would be the responsibility of the Board of Trade. Through the first month or two of 1940 officials explored the advantages and disadvantages of these two proposals. It soon became clear that the balance of advantage lay with the Board of Trade's proposal for control over home demand.

Control over raw material supplies had, of course, something to be said for it. The Cotton Board proposed a system of licensing raw cotton purchases; this would mean rationing the raw cotton used by spinners to fill home-market orders. The quantity of raw cotton normally used for home-market orders would have to be ascertained, the percentage reduction decided and each spinner allowed to buy the restricted quantity. Raw cotton for export orders would be provided freely on proof of export of cotton goods. This method would indeed provide the most certain and effective method of cutting the consumption of raw cotton. In these days, too—it was early in 1940 and an acute shipping shortage was not expected—there were suggestions that it was only necessary to reduce the consumption of United States cotton. It would perhaps be possible to import more cotton from soft-currency areas; in that case, control of raw material supplies would be an effective method of directing this other (possibly inferior) cotton to the home market. There was another advantage in raw material control: a raw cotton rationing scheme would only have to deal with about 500 cotton spinners all of whom were easily identifiable.

The disadvantages of raw material control, however, outweighed these advantages. In particular it might gravely hamper the export trade. If raw material control were loose materials destined for exports might leak into the home market: if raw material control were tight it would place a heavy burden on exporters. There was already evidence that a scheme for rationing raw wool and providing 'bonuses' for exported woollens was, however good in theory, working badly in practice. For cotton the difficulties would be even worse. Cotton and cotton goods passed through many different hands before being shipped off to an export market; often the producer could not know whether or not his product would ultimately reach an export market. The merchant himself might not know until he had had the goods for some time whether they would be exported or not. Theoretically it would be possible, when it was known that goods were to be exported, to pass the information back along the chain of producers to the Cotton Controller in order that he might adjust the raw cotton supplies given to spinners. But merchants were numbered in their hundreds and orders in their thousands. It would be almost impossible to operate and police such a system for the whole export trade. Exporters would be frustrated by delays and might well wonder whether exports were worth pursuing. The Cotton Control's introduction of a system of preference directions to cover Government contracts and export orders did not greatly reduce these objections. The preference directions scheme was very new and had not yet been tried out even as a means of giving priority to export orders. The directions were issued by the Cotton Controller mainly on the strength of evidence from Chambers of Commerce that orders were for export. The applications for such directions could not in any case be checked in detail and to base upon them not merely an order of priority but the actual restriction of trade and production might well cause the whole system to break down.

There were other difficulties inherent in using raw material restrictions to limit home demand. These restrictions would stimulate higher prices for spinning, weaving and finishing cotton besides higher prices in the distributive stages. Moreover, such a scheme was more likely to reduce stocks than consumption. Spinners' stocks of raw cotton were large and there would be nothing to prevent them from using these stocks to keep their home trade going. Wholesalers' stocks might also be dissipated. Orders for the home trade would still pour in to congest still further the spinners' order books.

Most of these disadvantages of raw material restrictions were absent in the Board of Trade's scheme for controlling supplies of goods to the home market. The proposal was to institute control at the first stage in the distribution process—that is, wholesaling—before the products became dispersed among tens of thousands of retailers. After adding producer-wholesalers to ordinary wholesalers probably between 1,000 and 2,000 firms would be coming under control.[1] These people would have to register and they would be prohibited from selling in the home market more than a prescribed proportion of their sales in the home market for a corresponding pre-war period. Such a scheme was far preferable to raw material restrictions if only because it left the export trade entirely free from restriction or regulations. Indeed there was some hope that limitations on home trade might create a strong incentive to work for the export trade. The Board of Trade's scheme would, in addition, produce fewer difficulties of price control. Any undue increase in prices caused by the scheme would take place between the wholesaler and the customer where it could be most easily found and where the Prices of Goods Act—deficient though this was—operated. Another point in favour of the scheme was that it would encourage an orderly disposal of wholesalers' stocks. Administratively, too, the scheme had advantages. It would be simple to run and would not call for a large new administrative machine. Finally there was much to be said for restricting home consumption by a method that could readily be extended to products other than cotton goods.

By the early spring of 1940, therefore, it was decided that the Board of Trade's scheme was the best method of restricting supplies

---

[1] See p. 110 below for actual numbers registered.

to the home market. Decisions then had to be taken on some important details of the scheme. First, should the Order cover other textiles besides cotton? It was finally agreed that rayon and linen goods should be included in the restrictions. It was necessary to limit the sales of rayon goods in order to prevent a switch of consumption from cotton goods, to ease exports and to safeguard raw materials. As regards linen raw material control was supposed to have eliminated new production for the home market, but restrictions on civilian sales would secure an orderly disposal of stocks.

The second question to be decided was the degree of restriction. The Board of Trade felt that it was sufficient to ensure that civilian trade plus Government orders should not exceed the normal home trade: for this it would be enough to limit home trade, excluding Government orders, to seventy-five per cent. of the previous year's trade. A bigger cut would, of course, save more precious foreign exchange: the Exchange Requirements Committee, indeed, would have preferred a reduction to fifty per cent. of previous trade. There were, however, objections against proceeding too far too quickly. Until exports of textiles increased more severe restrictions on the home market might cause an unwelcome increase in unemployment; in those days the unemployed still numbered more than a million. It was, in addition, important to retain the co-operation which the wholesale traders had promised; a more drastic cut might alienate their support. Finally, bigger restrictions might lead to 'panic among consumers, fomented by retailers'. If that happened the scheme might have to be dropped or 'some very unattractive arrangements for rationing the individual consumer' might have to be considered. Certainly if there was any 'panic' the Prices of Goods Act would be a very inadequate bulwark against price increases. Some of these fears reflect the timidity that was prevalent in so many Government circles during the first nine months. In war-time, for example, the argument that a big contraction in supply was undesirable because it would lead to increases in prices was a bad one; such difficulties should simply challenge officials to produce more effective methods of controlling prices and distribution. All the same the size of the restrictions was not the point that mattered most at this period: the Board of Trade felt the scheme was an experiment and that experience in the first restriction period would show whether bigger cuts could and should be imposed.

The Board of Trade's scheme finally emerged as a statutory Order on 16th April 1940. The Order was made under Defence Regulation 55 and was called the Piece Goods and Made-up Goods (Cotton, Rayon and Linen) Order.[1] The Order was designed to ensure that

---

[1] S.R. & O. 1940, No. 561. See also *Limitation of the Home Trade in Textiles: Explanatory Memoranda*, H.M.S.O., 1940.

between the date of the Order and 30th September 1940 the supplies to retail shops of cotton, rayon and linen piece-goods and goods made up from these piece-goods should not exceed seventy-five per cent.— by quantity—of supplies in the period from 30th April 1939 to 30th September 1939. The restriction applied to cotton, rayon and linen goods taken together; but for linen goods taken by themselves there was an overriding restriction to twenty-five per cent. of the pre-war period: in response to protests from the Northern Ireland industry the percentage for linen was soon raised to fifty.[1] In making arrangements for made-up goods it was obviously necessary to calculate the restrictions separately for each individual class of goods. For it would defeat the purpose of the scheme if traders were free to make current sales of, say, table-cloths on the basis of pre-war trade in, say, handkerchiefs.

The mechanism of the scheme was in its essentials simple. It hinged upon the compulsory registration of all wholesalers. There was no restriction over the supply from manufacturers of controlled goods to these registered wholesalers or to any other manufacturers of piece-goods. The restrictions fell upon the supplies to all other classes of unregistered people. That is, supplies from manufacturers or wholesalers to makers-up of piece-goods were limited, and so were supplies to retailers whether from manufacturers of piece-goods or wholesalers or makers-up. Sales of imported goods, it should be added, were affected equally with sales of home-produced goods. One of the objects of these provisions was to ensure that no restrictions impeded any channel of trade leading to an export market. Since wholesalers and manufacturers of piece-goods received unrestricted supplies they were not hampered in supplying for export. In order that makers-up engaged in the export trade should also be free they were invited to register in the same way as all wholesalers: if they registered they would receive unrestricted supplies.[2] Just as export orders were outside the supply quotas so also were any Government orders. This outline of the mechanism of the scheme would be incomplete without a reference to the methods of policing: registered persons and manufacturers of controlled goods were required to make returns, certified by auditors, of their sales of these goods during the specified pre-war period and the period of control.

The Order was in no way concerned with the orderly distribution of the limited supplies among retailers and consumers. Here the Board of Trade hoped for the co-operation of traders and the public. Traders were asked 'to treat their retail customers equitably and not to allow one to benefit at the expense of others'. Retailers were asked to see that wealthy customers did not obtain an excessive share of the

---

[1] S.R. & O. 1940, No. 856.

[2] They would, of course, then be obliged to restrict their home trade.

restricted goods and it was left to the public themselves to limit their purchases to what they genuinely required.

The new Board of Trade Order immediately affected wholesalers' home trade. But it would be some time before the effects were fully felt in the early stages of processing raw material. In the cotton industry some simultaneous action was necessary in order to reduce the swollen order books of the cotton spinners. Early in April the order books were more manageable because spinners were awaiting the announcement of new yarn prices and were therefore reluctant to accept new business. But the Cotton Control knew that as soon as the new prices came into force the congestion of order books would become worse than ever. In spite of the existence of preference directions for Government and export work there was danger that this congestion would prejudice the export trade. It was therefore decided to prohibit for one month the acceptance by cotton spinners of any fresh orders except Government and export orders—that is, any orders not covered by preference directions. This Order[1] came into force at the same time as the Board of Trade's Limitation of Supplies Order.

These first direct restrictions on supplies to the home market came into force in April 1940. The restrictions were not very severe and they applied only to the textile industries. All public announcements about the scheme had emphasised that its purpose was to increase exports and not to slacken activity in the textile industries. The Board of Trade were not trying to force the pace in transferring labour to the armed forces and the munitions industries; indeed in April 1940 the Board, in conjunction with the Ministry of Labour and the Ministry of Supply, were insisting that the main source of labour for war industry lay in the unemployment registers of the employment exchanges. This source, they thought, was unlikely to dry up for a long time and only when it did should attention be given to the deliberate diversion of labour from civilian industries. Even when such diversion did come it would of course be necessary to prevent interference with exports.

(ii)

Restrictions Extended

In May 1940 the climate of opinion changed no less surely in the Board of Trade than in other Government departments and in the nation. Departments now expected the war effort to develop far more swiftly and far more intensely than they had even dreamed of a bare month ago. There was no doubt now that a long, hard war stretched

---

[1] S.R. & O. 1940, No. 556.

ahead. The need to economise in raw materials for reasons of shipping and foreign exchange had grown. The need to husband stocks that were most probably irreplaceable had also grown. And for the first time the immense demands of the war industries for labour were foreseen—demands that the unemployment registers could not possibly fill, demands that would require a great transfer from civilian industries. The Board of Trade were anxious to do all they could to meet these demands of the war economy. 'We cannot afford to live on the scale upon which we are now living,' wrote one high official. 'We must act more ruthlessly than we were prepared to act some months ago.' But while the Board were ready to speed the diversion of resources from civilian production they were still very much aware of their responsibilities towards the export trade. The question now was less how to promote exports than how to protect them in the face of heavy withdrawals of raw materials and labour from civilian industry. The answer however was the same: there must be further restrictions on the home market.

One proposal for diverting resources from civilian to war purposes had to be dismissed simply because it would not protect the export trade. It was suggested that there should be a planned programme for closing down selected factories; this would overcome the difficulties of matching geographically the labour demands and supplies. If the industries concerned had been highly organised and if they had mainly consisted of large units so that the effects of this or that step could be judged fairly, accurately and quickly the scheme might have been practicable. The industries producing miscellaneous consumer goods were not, unhappily, so simple. To take one example: the making-up section of the clothing industry could be expected to yield large numbers of workers; but in it were about 25,000 separate establishments of which nearly 20,000 employed less than ten people each. Theoretically it would be possible to survey the industry and pick out the establishments that were to close; but the survey would take many months. In practice, the Ministry of Labour and the supply departments were much more likely to make a dead set at the seventy or eighty large units employing 500 or more people each—firms whose industrial efficiency was among the highest and whose export prospects were among the brightest.

The Board of Trade were convinced therefore that the best method of restriction was to limit more severely and more extensively the supplies of consumer goods going to the home market. The problem was to decide on the degree of restriction. Two alternative proposals emerged. The first was very drastic. It suggested that when the first Limitation of Supplies Order came up for renewal in September 1940 the quantity of cotton and rayon goods to be supplied to the home market should be reduced to a third of the pre-war level instead of to the three-quarters at present allowed. In addition sales of silk goods should at once be reduced to twenty-five per cent. of the pre-war level and miscellaneous consumer goods to levels varying between fifty per cent. and twenty-five per cent. of pre-war. Restrictions on this scale would, it was thought, release about 400,000 workers; they would, in addition, release considerable numbers from the distributive trades. So drastic a scheme, however, would have its disadvantages. It would perhaps dislocate home trade too severely and there would be unemployment until displaced workers could be reabsorbed. Moreover, such a severe reduction of output would increase costs of production and so reduce the competitive power of British industry in the export markets.

The alternative proposal sought to minimise these difficulties. It suggested that there should be an immediate reduction in the supplies of miscellaneous consumer goods,[1] but not such a big one—supplies would be cut to two-thirds of the pre-war level instead of to a half or a quarter. This scheme would free many workers quickly. It would also provide a framework within which the industries would be obliged to co-operate in choosing factories which could be closed or diverted to war work and workers who could be transferred to munitions production. After the Board of Trade had discussed with the export groups how to obtain still more labour with the least possible damage to manufacturing efficiency and the export trade it might be possible to arrange for a larger cut in home consumption.

The Board of Trade preferred to follow the second, rather slower procedure, and duly recommended it to ministers. At the Ministerial Economic Policy Committee, however, there were doubts whether the Board of Trade's scheme was the best method of diverting resources to war production. Would it not be much better to transfer factories and workers to war industries by positive methods—by requisitioning factories and by direction of labour—rather than by this negative method of contracting civilian industry? Moreover, at the moment—that is in the summer of 1940—there was no general shortage of workers.[2] It was skilled labour that was so very scarce. And here the miscellaneous consumer goods industries could not give much help. Most of these industries—for example lace, mattresses, pottery, toilet preparations—would only yield semi-skilled workers for training. Since it was very doubtful whether exports in these industries could be increased as much as home sales were reduced there would simply be more unemployment. Finally, could not domestic consumption be equally effectively reduced by financial methods—by stiffer taxation and by appeals to saving?

After discussion, however, ministers were agreed that civilian

---

[1] Silk was to be left for the time being. See p. 106.
[2] See *British War Economy, op. cit.,* Chapter XI.

H

consumption must be cut forthwith and that the Board of Trade's limitation of supplies was the most effective method. There was a growing awareness that an intense mobilisation could be achieved only by many controls each buttressing the others. Raw material control was obviously necessary; but it was not by itself enough. It was difficult to control all materials. In some industries there were large stocks of raw materials and it might therefore be a long time before civilian supplies were reduced. Raw material control did not affect the disposal of stocks of finished goods. Moreover the individual Controls themselves possessed administrative defects; some were loosely administered so that evasion was rife; others were rigid and therefore hampered the export trade. High taxation and savings were, like raw material control, obvious necessities in a war economy. But like raw material control these financial measures on their own were neither rapid enough nor effective enough to restrict civilian consumption.

At the end of May 1940, therefore, ministers accepted the Board of Trade's scheme to limit supplies of consumer goods to two-thirds of the pre-war level.[1] The Order—the Limitation of Supplies (Miscellaneous) Order[2]—came into force early in June. It enforced restriction in seventeen classes of goods ranging from essential household goods such as cutlery, kettles, pots and pans, and pottery to toys and jewellery. The annual retail value of these goods at pre-war prices was estimated to be about £250 millions and the number of wholesalers and manufacturers affected about 20,000.

The Order followed the same principles as the textiles Order of April. For the period 1st June 1940 to 30th November 1940 supplies of each class of goods in the Order were restricted to two-thirds of the level in the same period of 1939. Goods supplied for export, for Government orders or to other registered people were exempt. The Order differed in two ways from the earlier textiles Order.[3] First, the restrictions were by value instead of by quantity. The nature of the goods controlled made this administratively essential. It meant of course that since prices were changing it was difficult to estimate the precise effects of any limitation. But the price-changes were upwards: it was therefore safe to assume that the restrictions were stiffer than a quantitative cut of the same figure. At the prices ruling when the

---

[1] In response to protests from Staffordshire the pottery quota was raised, in the autumn of 1940, to eighty-five per cent.

[2] S.R. & O. 1940, No. 874.

[3] There were also minor differences. For example, small manufacturers and manufacturers working on commission were not required to register; in many instances they were therefore affected by limitation of the supplies of materials they received. Small manufacturers were defined as those whose trade (*a*) in at least one month in the year beginning 1st June 1939 did not exceed £250, or (*b*) in any month after that year did not exceed £167.

Order was introduced it was estimated that the 'value' quota of 66⅔ per cent. was equivalent to a 'quantity' quota of fifty-eight per cent. There was another advantage in restricting by value rather than by quantity. Traders were not encouraged to concentrate their reduced trade on the more expensive articles.

The second difference between the textiles and miscellaneous Orders was more formal than real. Under the miscellaneous Order registration of both manufacturers and wholesalers was compulsory. Under the textiles Order manufacturers had not been compelled to register but in practice most of them had been entered on the register. There had been some doubt whether wholesalers should be registered at all under the miscellaneous Order. Wholesalers played a less important part in these industries than in textiles while their numbers would be truly formidable. However, it seemed so important to prevent the wasteful dispersal of stocks in the home market that wholesalers were registered along with the manufacturers.

The Limitation of Supplies Order of June 1940 was not the only contribution by the Board of Trade to the diversion of resources from civilian to war purposes. For the Board of Trade were concerned as much with capital goods for civilian industry as with consumer goods for the home market. The growth of munitions production in the first nine months of war was due far more to diversion within the engineering industry from civilian and export work to munitions than to the industry's expansion. As we have seen, by June 1940 most sections of the engineering industry had only about fifteen per cent. of their workers engaged in home trade. But in the summer of 1940 it was most important to see that no engineering firms were engaged on work that was not essential to the life of the nation. Every skilled worker released from civilian work was needed immediately and urgently to help produce the aircraft, tanks and guns that Britain so sorely needed. Yet in 1940 there was danger that the pressure of home demand on the engineering industry might increase. With the existing limitations on profits manufacturers would tend wherever possible to put their assets into capital goods; this would be especially true in industries where technical improvement was rapid so that manufacturers possessing newer machines would get ahead of their competitors.

In order to forestall such plans and release as much labour as possible the Board of Trade issued an Order empowering them to license the supply of machinery.[1] There were sixteen classes of machines which manufacturers were forbidden to supply unless the buyer had a licence from the Board of Trade. Government and export

---

[1] Machinery and Plant Order, S.R. & O. 1940, No. 875. The department of the Board of Trade responsible for machinery licensing was also responsible for licensing machinery imports; close co-ordination was therefore achieved.

orders were exempt and so were supplies of parts for repair[1] purposes.
By the end of 1940 the Order was more rigorously applied: in July the
number of classes of controlled machinery rose from sixteen to forty
and then later some of the definitions in the Order were more rigidly
drawn.[2] By then, too, the Order could be more strictly administered.
For in the early period of control a good many licences were issued in
order to enable manufacturers to complete and deliver machines
that were taking up valuable factory space needed for munitions
production. Even so the achievements in the first six months of
control were appreciable. On the assumption that machinery valued
at £1,000 represented on the average five tons of iron or steel and the
work of three men (two of them skilled) for one year, refusals of
licences to the end of 1940 represented about 7,850 tons of iron or
steel and 4,710 man-years.[3] In addition, the mere existence of the
control must have prevented many applications for licences. In order
to make the change-over to munitions works in engineering firms as
smooth as possible firms in difficulties through machinery licensing—
usually the smaller firms—were put into touch with the supply departments.

From the summer of 1940 until March 1941—the point chosen as
the dividing line for this history of civil industry and trade—the
story of restrictions on the home market is one of increasing severity.
When the first Limitation of Supplies Order for miscellaneous consumer goods had been discussed in May 1940 the Board of Trade were
already thinking of increasing the restrictions on textiles that had
been imposed in April. They had decided, however, to wait until the
new restriction period began in September. The limitations on cotton
and rayon imposed in March 1940 had been very moderate. A level
of home supplies equal to seventy-five per cent. of pre-war was in
itself generous. But supplies to the home market were in fact much
larger. For the Board of Trade had come up against the problem of
supplying the needs of 'essential persons'—a generic term that
covered such people as hospitals, the Women's Voluntary Services
and ships' stores. The Board had at first assumed that with a cut as
small as twenty-five per cent. there would not be much need for
licensing supplies to these essential persons outside the quota: essential needs could be met by diverting part of the quota from normal
retail trade outlets. But this diversion was impossible without the co-
operation of manufacturers and traders—co-operation which was
against their own interests. Manufacturers and traders were much
more inclined to exhaust their quotas in satisfying the retail trade,
confident that the Board of Trade would be compelled to license

---

[1] 'Repair purposes' were strictly defined.
[2] S.R. & O. 1940, Nos. 1363, 2179.
[3] Nearly half the refusals (by value) were in bakery and textile machinery.

additional supplies for essential purposes. The Board had not realised that the war had greatly expanded essential requirements and that if they were to be met in full within the quota ordinary civilian consumption had to be cut by a much greater percentage than the figures in the limitation Orders. 'Our difficulty,' an official wrote, 'is that a system of base period restriction cannot usefully be applied where essential requirements have multiplied many times since the outbreak of war. The limitation scheme is necessarily in difficulties when it extends beyond ordinary civilian consumption into war-time activities of this kind.' The Board of Trade had tried to link up licensing of quota-free cotton goods with the Cotton Board's preference direction scheme. But this was not enough. By August 1940, when traders had exhausted their textile quotas, the Board of Trade had no alternative but to issue open general licences for supplying free of quota the textiles needed by hospitals, the Red Cross, the Navy, Army and Air Force Institute, the Y.M.C.A., ships' stores dealers and ships' chandlers. In addition individual licences were issued to particular registered traders to supply in excess of quota. This was done, for example, to prevent hardship where the base period was exceptionally unfavourable, to enable supplies to be delivered for indirect Government requirements and, later, for replacing bombed stocks.

Similar arrangements for quota-free supplies had later to be extended to the miscellaneous consumer goods brought under control.[1] It was evident that all these quota-free supplies had seriously diminished the contribution of the limitation of supplies policy to the release of labour and raw materials for exports or war production. Certainly, in the light of these alleviations, quotas of seventy-five per cent. of pre-war for cotton and rayon were excessively high. On the other hand if the quotas were severely cut the problem of essential supplies would become still more difficult.

In June 1940 the Board of Trade were contemplating a reduction of the cotton quota to twenty-five per cent. of pre-war in the next restriction period. However, as a result of protests from the industry, in which it was strongly argued that without a certain volume of home trade, especially in fashion goods, exports could not flourish, the proposal was modified. The new Woven Textiles Order of September 1940[2] reduced the sales of cotton and linen goods between 1st October 1940 and 31st March 1941 to $37\frac{1}{2}$ per cent. of the trade in the equivalent period of the previous year; the overriding restriction on linen goods was to be twenty-five per cent. of the standard period.[3] The restrictions on rayon were much smaller since war demands on

---

[1] See p. 109.

[2] S.R. & O. 1940, No. 1760.

[3] All the textiles restrictions remained on a quantity basis.

the industry were far smaller than for cotton; rayon sales were limited to $66\frac{2}{3}$ per cent. of the standard period. Interchange of quotas between cotton and rayon was no longer allowed. There were suggestions that the Order should be extended beyond cotton, rayon and linen goods to cover woollen and worsted goods, boots and shoes, and silk goods. In the end, however, it was felt that it would be best to consolidate the cotton, linen and rayon scheme before extending it to wool. And since boots and shoes were counted as definitely essential the Board of Trade thought it would be unwise to restrict supplies unless the Ministry of Supply could organise the production of standard boots and shoes.

Silk goods, too, were at first omitted from the Woven Textiles Order. This proved to be a mistake for silk supplies were rapidly diminishing. In October 1940 the Ministry of Supply decided that no more raw silk should be provided for home civilian uses, and the Board of Trade therefore decided to make a supplementary Woven Textiles Order to control the sales of existing stocks of silk goods. The level of sales was to be twenty-five per cent. of the standard period. Simultaneously the Board of Trade announced that from December 1940 supplies of pure silk stockings to home consumers would be completely prohibited except under licence. The silk stocking industry possessed large stocks of yarn and hosiery and the new measure ensured that the yarn would be diverted to more important uses and the hosiery to export markets.[1] Thus came to the women of Britain the first strong foretaste of austerity.

There was one main difference between the Woven Textiles Order of September 1940 and the earlier textiles Order of the previous April: in the later Order the Board of Trade set out to solve the problem of essential supplies which had become so pressing. Licensing was much too clumsy a method of dealing with these supplies: instead an arrangement was needed that would release essential supplies from restriction and take them out of standard period calculations. The new Order included the normal exemptions from control for Government orders, exports and supplies to other registered persons, and added some new ones. First, any goods covered by the miscellaneous consumer goods Order were withdrawn from the scope of the Woven Textiles Order. Secondly, certain essential goods were freed from restriction—for example, adhesive anti-scatter fabric, black-out material, infants' wear, surgical bandages, boiler suits and so forth.[2] Thirdly, the Order gave a list of 'essential consumers' to whom con-

---

[1] In May 1941 a non-profit-making concern, British Silk Stockings Corporation Ltd., was set up with Government support to help manufacturers and wholesalers to export their stocks.

[2] Certain other classes of essential goods remained under control; if these goods had been produced under preference directions from the Cotton Control, the Board of Trade were prepared to license additional supplies outside the quota.

trolled goods might be supplied freely—for example the police, hospitals, local authorities, Y.M.C.A. and so forth. Fourthly, the Order introduced a new category of 'special producers', that is, unregistered people producing certain kinds of finished goods, to whom controlled goods might be supplied freely.[1] The goods for which provision was thus made included many of the essential goods already mentioned above and in addition articles such as motor cars, batteries, books, fire hose and tyres. Supplies to 'special producers' and supplies to essential consumers in the standard period were to be excluded in calculating the quota.

Two other new provisions in the Woven Textiles Order are worth noting. One was to close a loophole: in future registered manufacturers who used controlled goods for manufacturing uncontrolled goods had to count the supplies of controlled goods as part of their quota. The second concerned the transfer of quotas. The Board of Trade could not have effectively prevented the transfer of quotas even if they had wanted to, for registered traders with exhausted quotas could always invoice through other traders with spare quotas. Similarly one manufacturer could easily have made arrangements to produce goods on behalf of another. But in any case, the Board of Trade favoured such arrangements. Quota transfers helped to switch supplies from evacuation to reception areas. They might also help to promote concentration of production. The Woven Textiles Order of September simply said that such transfers must be notified to the Board of Trade. Subsequently an amending Order provided that the Board's consent must be obtained for quota transfers.[2] For quota transfers with their inevitable commissions threatened to push up prices; if it were made compulsory to obtain the consent of the Board this danger would be lessened.

Once the new Woven Textiles Order was issued the Board of Trade had to consider what to do when the restriction period for miscellaneous goods ended in November. By now the needs of the war economy were clearer than they had been in the summer when the first limitations of supplies came into force. Raw materials, for example, were becoming increasingly scarce. Sources of supply had been cut off and shipping was beginning to be a real anxiety. Stocks had to be carefully husbanded and, if possible, built up in case the losses and delays to Britain's shipping grew worse. Meanwhile war production was rising and demanding an ever-increasing share of the supplies available for current consumption. A few raw materials were already so scarce that home-market supplies had to be completely prohibited. The case of silk has already been mentioned: in October

---

[1] People registered as 'special producers' might not supply controlled goods to other people except under licence.

[2] S.R. & O. 1941, No. 76.

1940 it also became necessary to prohibit, except under licence, the supply of domestic hollow-ware made wholly or partly of aluminium. Controllers of all raw materials were scrutinising applications from the home market with increasing severity. But it was still as essential as ever to buttress raw material control with sales control—not only because of the inefficiencies of raw material control but in order to economise in the use of stocks—'a matter of importance', it was remarked, 'since circumstances may arise in which we may have to live on our stocks'.

In the autumn of 1940 the departments of Government were likewise becoming increasingly aware how immense the manpower demands of the Services and the munitions industries would be. A Man-power Requirements Committee had been established in August 1940 to estimate these demands. It did not report until November and December: when it did it said that the Services and munitions industries would need more than three million more men and women by the autumn and winter of 1941.[1] When the Board of Trade were preparing their new measures of restriction they had no precise labour requirements figures before them, but they were aware of the general tenor of the Man-power Requirements Committee's deliberations—that there would soon be a 'famine of men' and therefore a dearth of women. The Board of Trade felt that their restrictions had up to date made an important if incalculable contribution in manpower and that they would continue to do so. But greater releases from civilian industry than were to be expected from the first limitation Orders would soon be needed.

The Board of Trade, then, were anxious to increase the restrictions on the supply of consumer goods. In November 1940 the President of the Board put before his ministerial colleagues proposals which in fact represented a return to the drastic limitation scheme that had been rejected in June: that is, trade was in general to be limited to one-third of the standard period instead of to two-thirds. The cut was by value after excluding purchase tax; when allowance was made for changes in prices permitted trade would be by volume no more than thirty per cent. of the standard period. Restrictions on this scale would, the Board of Trade estimated, release between 75,000 and 100,000 workers—most of them not until the spring of 1941[2]—in addition to an unknown number of workers from the distributive trades.

These proposals were accepted and the new Miscellaneous (No. 5) Order[3] came into force at the end of November 1940. The Board of

---

[1] See *British War Economy, op. cit.*, Chapter XI, Section (i).

[2] Firms did not reduce staff until the quota was exhausted towards the end of the restriction period.

[3] S.R. & O. 1940, No. 2031.

Trade had aimed at restricting supplies in general to a third of the standard period. But the precise percentage of trade permitted for each class of goods covered by the Order[1] varied. Some goods were more essential than others and were given a higher quota—for example corsets were allowed a quota of fifty per cent. and mattresses one of 66⅔ per cent. Pottery was favourably treated with a quota of fifty per cent. because it did not use scarce raw materials. On the other hand undoubted luxuries such as furs had a quota of only twenty-five per cent. Metal furniture was also restricted to twenty-five per cent. because it was imperative to save as much steel as possible.

The new Order went further in discriminating between essential and unessential goods. Each of the seventeen classes of goods included in the Order covered a heterogeneous collection of articles varying in their importance to civilian life. The new Order attempted to distinguish between them by introducing a factor or multiplier. When the Board of Trade wished to reduce the quota for a particular article below the quota for the class as a whole it applied a multiplier greater than unity. Conversely the multiplier was less than unity if the Board of Trade wished a particular article to have a higher quota. An example will make this clear. Class 7 in the Miscellaneous Order embraced such goods as 'cork carpets, felt-base floor coverings, linoleum, floor-cloth, cellulose plastic flooring, oil baize and other oil-cloth and leather-cloth, carpets, carpeting, floor rugs, floor mats and matting'. The quota for this class was fifty per cent. Carpets, however, had a multiplier of $1\frac{1}{2}$—that is, in calculating trade in the restriction period £1 worth of carpets supplied was to count as £1 10s. 0d. In effect, therefore, the carpet quota was only 33⅓ per cent.

In other ways the new Miscellaneous Order followed the same principles laid down in the early Orders and modified by the Woven Textiles Order of September. The licensing of quota-free supplies had been as troublesome with the miscellaneous consumer goods as with textiles. 'All along the line,' wrote the Board of Trade in 1940, 'traders, straining for a maximum turnover, have concentrated their quotas on the least essential portion of their trade hoping to blackmail the Government into licensing additional supplies for any purpose which might be remotely considered as essential. As a result of this policy the Board have, in the past, been forced to issue licences for goods which should have been supplied out of quota.' Licences had indeed been granted on such a 'very generous scale' that it was doubtful whether wholesalers' turnover had greatly declined. The new Order followed the example of the Woven Textiles Order in dealing with this problem—that is, it embodied the device of quota-free supplies to 'essential consumers'. The new Order also provided for the transfer of quotas as the Woven Textiles Order had done.

---

[1] The same classes of goods were covered by this Order as by the earlier one.

(iii)
The Implications

Before this chapter closes, it will have to discuss the part played by the Board of Trade's restrictions on the home market in mobilising the economy for war. It will also have to see these early restrictions in their relationship to the controls over civilian industry that were developed later in the war. But before passing on to these wider questions it is worth pausing to consider these restrictions from a purely administrative angle. Before the war the Board of Trade had never dreamt that they would be drawn into schemes involving detailed administration of civilian industry. Yet when the time came, when the Board appreciated the nation's shortage of foreign exchange, shipping, raw materials and manpower, they swiftly produced proposals for restricting civilian claims on these scarce resources. Once the schemes were accepted the Board were equally resourceful in administering them.

There was, for example, the big problem of compiling registers first for the Cotton, Rayon and Linen Order and then for the Miscellaneous Order. The Cotton, Rayon and Linen Register, which was published only six weeks after the Order, included 4,931 wholesalers, 1,190 manufacturers and 1,068 makers-up of rationed goods for the export trade. The Home Trade Register for the miscellaneous goods, which was published two months after the Order was far bigger still: it contained 55,000 registrations including 10,000 manufacturers.[1] The Cotton, Rayon and Linen Register was compiled by a staff consisting of only one assistant secretary, four part-time principals, a staff officer, ten clerks and two technical advisers. Once the register was compiled it was taken over by a staff of accountants—a body of men who were to play an invaluable part in all the Board of Trade's later essays in control. The Home Trade Register needed a much larger staff. Within a fortnight, 400 people were recruited to deal with it. Administrative staff of sixty-five—including thirty-two university teachers recruited for the long vacation—had to deal with a correspondence which at its peak amounted to 5,000 letters a day. But registration was completed to time and the staff was reduced to 166.

These civil servants, temporary and permanent, had to acquire a detailed knowledge of trade channels and moreover acquire it swiftly.[2] They had to keep track of various types of export merchants.

---

[1] Wholesalers were usually registrable in more than one class: the total number of *names* on the register was about 20,000.

[2] In the autumn of 1940 the Board of Trade office in London which dealt with this work was bombed. The staff and the records had to be transferred to Bournemouth—without any dislocation of current work.

They had to decide what to do when a registered trader appeared as an agent in a transaction between another registered person and an unregistered person: which of the two registered traders should be responsible for applying the necessary degree of restriction? What should be done with 'mixed businesses' where wholesaling or manufacturing was combined with retailing? The civil servants found answers to such questions and the lawyers embodied the answers in legal orders.[1] The Board of Trade even took it upon themselves to interfere with the principle of the sanctity of contracts: their limitation Orders provided for the cancellation of outstanding contracts for controlled goods.[2]

The Board of Trade also came face to face with unfamiliar problems of enforcement. It was possible to evade the limitation of supplies restrictions by a variety of arrangements for invoicing controlled goods through intermediaries. This practice became dangerous as numbers of doubtful characters, many of them with long criminal records for share pushing and other frauds, grew aware of its possibilities. People who had no right to a quota—some, for example, had done no standard period trade—armed themselves with certificates of dubious accountants and registered under the limitation Orders. They then proceeded to inform manufacturers that they had spare quotas and could dispose of their supplies to retailers. The goods were invoiced through the bogus wholesalers but sent direct to the retailers. By the end of 1940 the Board of Trade's accountants were estimating that goods worth millions of pounds had illegally reached the home market, that bogus quota holders had made many thousands of pounds in commission, and that a regular trade had grown up in introducing buyers and sellers of bogus quotas. Air-raids made matters worse, for they made it easy for the bogus quota holders to plead to investigating officers that their pre-war records had been destroyed. In December 1940 a special investigation section was established in the Board of Trade's Accountants Division. The section encountered many difficulties; 'wanted traders', it was reported, 'went out of business and disappeared over night, while other traders who had apparently been dealing in large quantities of goods proved to be mere "blinds" who had never really existed. Faked auditors' certificates were numerous, and attempts were even made to prevent inquiries by offering bribes to the investigating accountants'. Gradually, however, the perpetrators were tracked down. In addition the Board issued directions under the limitation Orders requiring information which would help their investigations. They also dealt with the problem of so-called 'lost' records. In spite of inadequate penalties in the Courts the Board of Trade's investigators, co-operat-

---

[1] e.g. S.R. & O. 1940, Nos. 1022, 1320.
[2] S.R. & O. 1940, No. 1023.

ing with Customs and Excise, the Inland Revenue and Scotland Yard, succeeded in breaking the 'quota racket' by the summer of 1941.

Air-raids presented the Board of Trade with other problems besides those of lost records. The Board had to persuade traders to redistribute their quota supplies in favour of reception areas and away from evacuation areas. They had to arrange for the needs of the bombed-out—mainly through quota-free supplies to local authorities and the W.V.S.[1] They had to arrange for quota-free supplies to bombed retailers and help make arrangements for the marketing of these replacement goods in other premises. Finally the Board had to stimulate the dispersal of wholesalers' stocks in order to avoid heavy losses through bombing.[2]

In general, then, the Board of Trade came well out of their first war-time administrative tests. The faults that appeared—in particular the over-generous licensing of quota-free supplies—were being remedied by the end of 1940.

The Board of Trade's restriction policy raised other problems besides those of administering and amending the Orders. The policy was, as ministers had pointed out, essentially negative. The positive counterpart of the policy lay in the efforts of other Government departments to mobilise for war purposes the labour, raw materials and factory space freed by limitations on civilian supplies. It soon became clear that close co-ordination between the Board of Trade and these other Government departments was necessary. The limitation of civilian supplies was a broad and to some extent clumsy device for releasing resources. Its intention was to achieve a general 'push' of resources from the civilian sector of the economy in order that the 'pull' of the war sector should encounter less difficulty. It was never claimed that limitation of supplies would free resources of the precise kinds and in the precise places that the production departments wanted. The fear that this policy raised in the Government's mind in 1940 was the fear of rising unemployment. What use was there in freeing resources, especially labour, that would simply lie idle? Rising unemployment would be harmful to public morale. It was clear that whatever the forecasts of manpower demands for 1941 might be, war production in 1940 was not expanding rapidly enough to take up the slack in civilian production. Bottlenecks such as skilled labour had to be widened before war factories clamoured, unsatisfied, for unskilled labour. Demands for unskilled labour did exist but they were unfortunately closely concentrated in certain areas. Demands were heavy in the midlands and the north-west. Until the Ministry of Labour was ready for direction and transfer of labour, releases in

---

[1] S.R. & O. 1941, Nos. 185, 335.
[2] See also *Drapers' Record*, 11th January 1941.

London and the south-east, where there was little munitions work, simply went to swell the unemployed.

The Board of Trade's answers to these contentions were definite. Surely, they said, some unemployment was preferable to the use of valuable foreign exchange and shipping for materials for unessential goods on the home market? In any case, could not concerted industrial planning by Government departments mop up pockets of unemployment?

The Board of Trade made certain specific proposals. First, the Board themselves were to establish a special 'keeping step' section to watch the situation and keep in daily touch with the Ministry of Labour and the Ministry of Supply. This section would also be responsible for obtaining from firms subject to the Limitation of Supplies Orders returns showing the current rate of production, the state of their order-books—showing Government, export and home orders separately—and the number of their employees. Secondly, the supply departments would try to ease unemployment by spreading Government contracts. If this was insufficient or if the industry in question produced goods not wanted by the Government, temporary licensing of additional home trade would be considered. Additional home trade would be permitted only if the Ministry of Supply agreed that raw materials could be spared for it and if the Ministry of Labour was clear that additional unemployment in any particular place was undesirable. Thirdly, the Board of Trade would compile, on the basis of their returns from industry, a list of factories available for requisitioning. Such a policy would, the Board hoped, check the development of too much unemployment and help firms in the export trade; for it would divert Government orders to firms if they needed to run full and away from them if they were overloaded, and it would concentrate unessential production as much as possible in areas where munitions production was small.

The policy was carried out and had a fair amount of success. Keeping step inquiries of civilian industries were from the autumn of 1940 onwards taken every two months. This in itself was a great achievement, for hitherto the only information about industry was that in the 1935 Census of Production and, for a few industries, the 1937 inquiries under the Import Duties Act. As more industries were included in the inquiries and as more firms made returns it became possible for the Board of Trade to form fairly reliable estimates of the value of sales and the volume of employment. The particulars sought in the inquiries were varied as special problems arose; for example on the second review detailed information was required about factory premises. The keeping step—or K.S.—returns were studied by the Board of Trade and the Ministry of Labour who thereupon made recommendations to the Ministry of Supply—in most cases recommendations for the diversion of Government orders to certain firms; in areas of heavy labour demand the recommendation was that Government orders should be reduced. Lists of factories which might be requisitioned were sent to the supply departments and lists of machine-tool capacity to the Controller of Machine Tools; by the end of 1940 500 factories had been recommended for requisitioning. There were objections to this policy from the supply departments which were naturally loth to divert orders from efficient specialist firms they knew to small firms whose efficiency was by no means assured. Nor was it easy for the supply departments and the Treasury to modify tendering arrangements for Government contracts. However, it was found possible to administer the tendering system with sufficient elasticity to take account of the Board of Trade's views. The keeping step procedure was also applied to the licensing of ex-quota supplies for the home market. Here, too, attention was paid to the shortage or abundance of labour in the areas concerned and to the firms' export trade.

By the end of 1940 this interdepartmental co-ordination was beginning to serve a new purpose. As war production gathered momentum it became less important to mop up pockets of unemployment and more important to relieve areas where labour was very scarce by diverting orders away from them. In this new phase the Board of Trade tried hard to encourage the supply departments to use the capacity of small firms.

So far we have considered the developing administration of restrictions on the home market. Where did these early restrictions stand in relation to the control over civilian industry that had been achieved by the end of the war? In the period up to the spring of 1941 the limitation of supplies policy was well suited to the needs of the war economy. It protected the export trade and at a time when war production was not expanding rapidly it stimulated the release of labour and raw materials and factory space as quickly as was necessary. Moreover, labour was released where possible in the areas where it was most needed. The first limitations on the home market could afford to be broad and undiscriminating in their method. Nearly all goods, essential and unessential alike, could suffer some reduction.

By the end of 1940, however, it was clear that the limitation of supplies policy was only a first stage in the control of civilian industry. Problems were crowding in from two sides—from the producer and from the consumer. The problems of the producer were to lead to a policy of concentration of production. Concentration was indeed being discussed from the time when the first Limitation of Supplies Order was issued in June 1940. Two kinds of schemes were mentioned. There were at first suggestions for a geographical concentration of production. The Minister without Portfolio, for example, proposed that civilian production should be concentrated as much as possible round London, south-east and eastern England where there was little demand for munition workers. The practical difficulties of such a policy would, however, have been immense. In fact, therefore, discussion centred round industrial concentration—that is, concentration of a reduced volume of production in certain plants. If manufacturers shared the reduced volume of home trade amongst them there would be short-time working and higher unit costs which would damage the export trade. Until the later months of 1940 this danger to exports troubled the Board of Trade more than waste of manpower and factory space. The Board quite certainly hoped that the limitation policy would prepare the ground for schemes of voluntary concentration put forward by industry itself; the Board were prepared to help by licensing the disposal of stocks and the transfer of quotas. In the autumn of 1940 compulsory concentration was regarded as a policy only to be applied in the last resort. Towards the end of 1940, however, concentration became urgent. The new limitations on the home market were drastic and would undoubtedly lead to short-time working before the end of the quota period. In view of the manpower demands foreseen by the Man-power Requirements Committee short-time working could not possibly be allowed.

Limitation of supplies, then, led on to concentration of production. Limitation of supplies and concentration of production together were inevitably followed by a close control over manufacture and supply of civilian goods. Once supplies to the home market were drastically cut and once spare capacity was eliminated, a finer discrimination was necessary. Unessential goods had to be completely prohibited and the capacity available for civilian purposes used only for essential goods.

As limitations on supplies grew more severe the problems of the consumer as well as those of the producer became prominent. In the first discussions about restrictions on the home market the Board of Trade had mentioned consumer rationing as a most unpleasant possibility that was if possible to be avoided. But by the end of 1940 it was doubtful whether it could be avoided for very much longer. Retail stocks had so far cushioned the impact of restrictions on the civilian; but as these stocks dwindled and supplies to retailers were cut a shortage of clothes and other consumer goods was inevitable.

By the spring of 1941 the Board of Trade had embarked on unmapped paths of control that would lead them far and from which there could be no turning back.

PART II

The Period of Full Control: From Spring 1941 to the End of the War

CHAPTER VI

INTRODUCTORY

IN the early months of the war the Board of Trade had remained a fairly peaceful department. But from the summer of 1940 onwards there was, as in all other spheres of Government, a new sense of urgency. Restrictions were tightened, war production increasingly took precedence over exports and new steps in control were being discussed. The policy of the Board developed from this time onwards in an unbroken, broadening stream. The spring of 1941—the line chosen for dividing this history into two parts—may seem an artificial barrier thrust across this stream. There are, however, good reasons for choosing this date. The course of Board of Trade policy was shaped by outside events and in the spring of 1941 there were three important new influences upon it. First, there was the passage of the Lend-Lease Act in the United States. Secondly, the manpower shortage was at last becoming apparent not only on paper but in the factories. All the time, both before and after the spring of 1941, there was a raw material shortage in the sense that the claims of civilian industry had to be reduced in order to meet the rising demands of the Services or in order to conserve stocks. But even in the worst shipping shortages stocks were always sufficient to keep essential activities going. It was manpower that was to be the dominant shortage of the war. The third new influence of the spring of 1941 was the resolute attempt by the Government to formulate an anti-inflation policy.

The effect of lend-lease on the Board's activities was to be profound. It had become increasingly clear from the summer of 1940 onwards that without aid from America Britain could not get the supplies needed for her survival. The export drive which had been gathering momentum since the early months of 1940 could not hope to touch more than the fringe of the problem of external finance. And in any case it had become apparent that the export drive would inevitably be inconsistent with a swiftly mounting munitions production. Nevertheless, through the autumn and winter of 1940–41 the Board of Trade had still been export-minded. Exports still had a general priority over the needs of the home market. For exports earned foreign currency, and more especially the hard currencies which could be put into the barrel which had to be scraped bare before the British claim to assistance from the United States was firmly established.

But with lend-lease the whole emphasis of export policy was to change—not immediately but before very long. Exports for the sake of earning hard currencies were to dwindle away. Indeed, it became a condition of lend-lease aid that they should dwindle even in some cases where the British felt that they could meet the needs of their pre-war customers without impeding war production. The quantity of exports maintained for the sake of currency was very small indeed. Exports were in future to be mainly restricted to those that were essential for the war—essential because the war effort of the Empire and Allied countries would suffer without them. After the United States entered the war attempts were made to apportion the responsibility for these 'war-essential' exports between the United Kingdom and North America. It was still necessary to maintain some currency exports to neutrals who would not indefinitely supply essential goods against claims in sterling. And in a very few isolated cases a trickle of exports of high-quality goods still continued.

The main repercussions of lend-lease for the Board of Trade were those upon the export trade. But there were also some welcome imports of civilian goods as a result of the Act. Over the field covered by the Board of Trade, lend-lease supplies were not of course anywhere near as important as they were in the case of food. There were no mass imports of clothing or household goods. There were, however, a few consumption goods where Britain depended heavily on the United States. These were, in the main, goods which were normally imported in considerable quantities or goods for which demand in war-time was much higher than in peace-time. In war-time capacity could not be increased to replace imports or to meet the new demand. It was, therefore, a blessing when lend-lease brought supplies of, for example, alarm clocks which were needed for war workers, electric bulbs for the hand torches that were a necessity in the blackout, parts for oil stoves, valves for civilian radio sets and wheels and flints for the cigarette lighters needed to replace the elusive match. Dependence on the United States was far greater in the case of some industrial equipment. Most of this machinery—for example machine tools, pumps, agricultural machinery, food machinery, mining machinery—was primarily the concern of departments such as the Ministry of Supply, Ministry of Agriculture, Ministry of Food or Ministry of Fuel (previously the Mines Department). But there were one or two items in which the Board of Trade were vitally interested —office machinery, industrial sewing machines, maple last blocks for boot and shoe manufacture, a minimum of apparatus and film for cinema studios and parts for servicing a whole range of machinery. The lend-lease supplies of 'Board of Trade' goods did not always continue until the end of the war. Production of cigarette lighters exceeded demand so that imports of flints and wheels could fall off. And the definitions of lend-lease eligibility were narrowed. For example, valves for civilian radio sets were in time excluded because they came under the heading of goods for morale and entertainment purposes; they were struck off the lend-lease list towards the end of 1943. Again industrial sewing machines were excluded when a variety of industrial equipment was struck off.

The assured flow of supplies from the United States which was by far the most important result of lend-lease for the supply departments and the Ministry of Food was, however, of minor importance to the Board of Trade compared with the effects of lend-lease on export policy. It was indeed most fortunate that relaxation of the need to export came when it did. For by the spring of 1941 manpower was becoming generally scarce. Hitherto, the Board of Trade's restrictions on the home market had been regarded with misgivings by other departments and by the Ministry of Labour in particular; it was feared that workers might be released before there was alternative employment for them. For as yet war production was impeded not by a shortage of unskilled labour—except in a very few areas—but by shortages of skilled engineering labour, of certain industrial equipment such as machine tools and of certain raw materials. By the spring of 1941, however, the situation was changing. The worst shortages of skilled labour and machine tools were being overcome and new filling factories to be manned by large numbers of women were opening. The shortage of manpower was to gather momentum throughout 1941 until it became the limiting factor on the total war effort. So from the spring of 1941 the Board of Trade were under constant pressure to release as much labour as possible from civilian industries. Labour supply was to govern the level of civilian output. At the same time, however, there was pressure from other quarters for the maximum economy in other scarce resources—factory space, raw materials and, before long, fuel.

From the spring of 1941, then, the Board were more than ever intent on releasing resources from civilian production. Concentration of production launched in March 1941 was a major effort in this direction. A Control of Factory and Storage Premises was established at the same time to meet in an orderly way the demands for space for war production and for storage. Clothes rationing, though primarily introduced for reasons of equity and 'anti-inflation', was also a contribution to the release of labour and materials; in its absence supplies of civilian clothing could not have been cut so low without popular discontent. The controls over manufacture and supply introduced in 1942 were inspired by the desire to squeeze out such resources as were still used for unessential production.

In stimulating the release of resources the Board of Trade no longer had to worry about the export trade as such. A new cause for concern arose. Before the spring of 1941 there had been very little need to worry about the home market for it had fared pretty well. Production of most civilian goods had not yet fallen drastically and such falls as there were had been cushioned by ample stocks. The production of engineering goods for the home market had certainly fallen a good deal but as most of these were durable the effects did not yet seem very harsh. But once manpower began to leave civilian industries more rapidly—whether through concentration or direction of labour or in response to the attractions of the better-paid munitions work— shortages began to appear. When it was the essential goods that were scarce—cups or pans or perambulators or torch batteries or corsets of reasonable quality—the public became insistent in its demands that something should be done. It was no longer enough for the Board of Trade to pursue the necessary but negative activities of restricting supplies. The Board had to assume the responsibility for ensuring that essential consumer needs were met. And not only essential needs at home. For, although the general export trade was dwindling, Allied and Empire countries had to be provided with necessary imports. These responsibilities for civilians at home and abroad inevitably meant that the Board must interest themselves directly in production.

There were other reasons why the Board became far more closely involved in civilian production than had ever been contemplated. During the winter of 1940–41 there had been much discussion in Government circles about methods of attacking the serious inflationary dangers that were inherent in the increasing diversion of the economy to war purposes. In the spring of 1941 these discussions produced a variety of plans which, when translated into action, formed a resolute anti-inflation policy. The focal point of this policy was the budget of April 1941. This raised taxation to what was considered a 'realistic' level. It also introduced the stabilisation policy: in the hope of preventing wages from rising further the Chancellor of the Exchequer announced his intention of stabilising the cost-of-living figure at about its current range of twenty-five per cent. to thirty per cent. above the level at the outbreak of war. The anti-inflation policy had two main implications for the Board of Trade. First, taxation and voluntary savings between them could not hope in war-time to bring personal incomes down to the level where they would absorb the quantity of goods available for personal consumption without increases in prices. Ideally the excess incomes should have been frozen by rationing. But the idea of general rationing proved to be impracticable; all that could really be done was to prevent excess incomes from spilling over on to supplies of essential goods. For if they did there would be serious shortages in the shops, and public discontent. Rationing must therefore be extended to as many essential goods as possible. For the Board of Trade this meant first and foremost clothes rationing which was introduced on 1st June

1941. The difficulties of extending rationing to cover a wide range of household and personal goods proved insurmountable. The Board did, however, manage to introduce a variety of distribution schemes that directed supplies of scarce goods to those who needed them most.

The primary purpose of rationing was of course to ensure fair distribution. But once rationing and similar schemes were begun, they inevitably led the Board of Trade on to production problems. Whatever theory there might be that no ration was a right, the public came to expect, or rather demand, that rations should be honoured. And where rationing covered a wide variety of articles—as the clothing scheme did—the public expected to get not merely something, but the particular articles they wanted. This meant that the Board of Trade had to assume some responsibility for seeing that the right goods were produced in something like the right quantities.

The second implication for the Board of Trade of the intensified efforts to restrain inflation was the need for stricter price control measures. The Prices of Goods Act, passed in the early days of the war, was largely ineffective. There was in particular concern over the movement of clothing prices. For clothing was the one 'Board of Trade' item that had an important weighting in the cost-of-living index[1] and clothing prices had been rising much more swiftly than subsidised food prices. By May 1941 the clothing index was seventy-five per cent. higher than at the outbreak of war and was still rising. It was clear that if the stabilisation policy were to be effective this rise must be curbed. Clothes rationing would, of course, help by reducing demand. But something more was needed. Even before the Chancellor had announced his stabilisation policy, ministers had already agreed that new price-control legislation must be prepared giving the Board of Trade power to fix maximum prices and margins. These powers, which were conferred by the Goods and Services (Price Control) Act passed at the end of July 1941, made possible a fairly close control of prices. But they were not by themselves enough. For it was impossible to fix maximum prices and margins without a clear specification of the goods concerned. Price control, that is, meant control over production. This soon became apparent in the case of clothing where the new powers were first applied. The Board of Trade concluded that the most satisfactory plan would be to encourage manufacturers to produce particular garments from particular cloths at prices to be clearly specified at each stage of production and distribution. This was to be the 'utility' policy. Before long the same policy or something similar was extended to other civilian goods.

This brief summary may have been sufficient to show the 'outside' influences that shaped Board of Trade policy from the spring of 1941 onwards. They set the general theme of the Board's policy—the

---

[1] Its weight was sixteen per cent. if September 1939 is taken as the base year.

decline in the importance of exports as a whole, the anxiety to go on releasing as many resources as possible for war purposes, and the growing need to protect the minimum needs of consumers at home and in Allied and Empire countries. The working out of this theme into specific controls and measures will be studied in the remaining chapters of this book. We shall see the Board working out their new export policy, concentrating production and controlling factory space, trying to find out what the consumer needed, trying to organise a minimum production of essential goods at reasonable prices and trying to improve distribution.

This second part of the book will find the Board of Trade assuming an unfamiliar role—that of a production department.[1] This role was not easy for the Board and the powers attached to it were not comparable with those of the supply departments. To begin with, the Board did not have cut-and-dried programmes of requirements put before them. They had to estimate for themselves what was needed and how much. These were calculations fraught with all kinds of subtleties and all kinds of unknowns. There were undoubtedly great difficulties in drawing up programmes for the Services, but once this was done schedules of requirements for so many destroyers or aircraft or guns or greatcoats could be assembled. But the Board were dealing with the infinitely variable personal and domestic needs of 40 million people or so. At the time when preparations were being laid for the assault on Europe, the Board had to reckon in addition with the demands of American troops for consumer goods and services. There were also the needs of countries abroad to be considered. Physical needs of civilians varied enormously according to where and how people lived and worked, according to their pre-war history and the stocks of goods they possessed. Moreover, standards of judgement about these needs could vary. There was a lot to be said for maintaining minimum standards of comfort among the civilian population —for providing a quantity of clothing sufficient to keep people not merely covered but reasonably respectable, for providing pottery, kettles and saucepans and a certain amount of furniture for those whose need was greatest. But these were not fixed limits that could not be passed. If the needs of war had demanded it, if Britain had been more closely besieged, the population would no doubt have been ready to make more severe sacrifices. As it was, not only physical needs had to be taken into account. By 1941 it was clear that the war would be long. This meant that it would bring a great deal of tedium and anxiety. It would not always be easy in these circum-

---

[1] On this subject see *Lessons of the British War Economy* (National Institute of Economic and Social Research), the chapter called 'The Work of a Departmental Priority Officer' by Richard Pares. Professor Pares very kindly lent the authors some other unpublished work by him on Board of Trade problems.

stances to keep morale high. So frivolities that might seem easy to dispense with in wartime acquired a surprising importance. Women must have lipstick and powder and there must be supplies of footballs and cricket bats. But where was the line to be drawn between keeping morale high and tolerating waste in wartime? Somehow or other by a process of trial and error the Board had to decide such questions. In these matters the Board were quite largely in the hands of the public itself. If the public temper demanded something strongly enough —which it rarely did unreasonably—the Board had to try to meet the demand.

Then, of course, if the Board took an interest in the production of some particular article they had to have some idea of the quantities that should be produced. But there were so few statistics about demand or about consumption or about stocks that for the most part only guesses were possible. And although in some cases techniques were developed for calculating demand—for example for calculating coupon expenditure—guesses remained the order of the day for most goods. Moreover it was not enough to guess at the 'real' demand. For once there was a slight shortage of some particular article, panic hoarding might begin and once this happened nothing would suffice but to stuff the shops with stocks for all to see.

The Board of Trade's difficulties as a production department were not confined to the calculation of requirements. They were equally great when it came to organising production. Industrial statistics were only less scanty than those for requirements. And above all the Board of Trade bought none of the goods whose production they stimulated. They had not therefore the same powers that the supply departments had over their contractors. The Board, for example, had no progress officers except for utility furniture and, for a very short time, for civilian wireless sets. And if industry's ideas of public demand for any goods differed from those of the Board firms could not be forced to undertake production for which they themselves took all financial risk. The example of utility furniture is again relevant here: firms were very slow to produce to the Board of Trade's specifications, partly because they did not believe the public would want the stuff. This intermediate position of the Board of Trade brought other disadvantages. The Board could not develop the same intimate knowledge about the production process and the capacities of individual firms in, say, the clothing industry that the Ministry of Aircraft Production possessed about aircraft engine firms. For the Board did not have the status of a customer. Nor did the Board's programmes have the status of 'war work', at a time when most inducements to manufacturers and workpeople—patriotism, higher wages, profit margins and labour arrangements—made them prefer such work to production for the civilian market.

These handicaps upon the Board of Trade as a production department should be borne in mind when reading about the Board's detailed activities in the following chapters. Programmes could not be much more than estimates and all kinds of incalculable factors were liable to prove the estimates, whether of requirements or production, to be wrong.

There is another point to be remembered when reading the following chapters: they do not give a great deal of attention to the interdepartmental aspects of the Board's work. They do not, that is, go into details of the Board's negotiations to obtain the necessary raw materials, fuel and labour for civilian industry. These negotiations were, of course, most important but the story of which they are part belongs rather to the histories of raw materials, coal and manpower in this series. Here we must confine ourselves to sketching the position as it affected the Board of Trade.

Since Britain depended heavily on imports, her supply of raw materials in war-time was governed chiefly by her ability to procure her requirements overseas and by shipping. In a few cases supplies could be increased by expanding home production. Supplies from overseas were of course much affected by military events. The defeats in Norway in 1940 had struck a serious blow at supplies of iron ore, timber and paper-making materials. The virtual elimination of Europe and North Africa as a supply source deprived Britain of steel and steel-making materials, phosphates, flax, hemp, pit-props and many other essential commodities. The extension of the war to the Pacific at the end of 1941 had even more serious results. Britain lost within a short time the great bulk of her supplies of rubber, tin, lead, hard hemp and some essential chemicals. Some of these calamities were outweighed by the opening up of United States supplies once the Lend-Lease Act had been passed. Once the United States were rearming their own munitions programme was of course a strong competitor for supplies. Nevertheless steel, cotton, timber, chemicals and paper-making materials came across the Atlantic to Britain in a steady flow. Countries of the Empire, notably Canada, also did all they could to replace the overrun sources of supply.

In some cases—notably rubber and some of the non-ferrous metals —absolute shortages of supply governed the quantities that Britain was able to import. But for most materials even more important than shortages at the source of supply was the shortage of shipping. It was for lack of shipping that the quantity of raw material imports fell from 26 million tons before the war to just over 22 million tons in 1940, to 15 million tons in 1941, and 11½ million tons in 1942; after rising to 12·8 million tons in 1943 they dropped back to 11·8 million tons in 1944. Reductions of imports on this scale did not in the event prove as serious as had been expected. Home production of iron ore and steel was buoyant and the felling of domestic timber rose. And, as it happened, raw material requirements proved to have been over-estimated. Nevertheless it was a great achievement that with such a low level of imports the flow of munitions production was never slowed down by a failure in the supply of raw materials. It would not have been sustained if it had not been possible to run stocks down without encroaching on those necessary to maintain distribution. In the period of the worst shipping shortage—between the end of December 1941 and the end of June 1943—stocks of imported raw materials were reduced by $2\frac{1}{2}$ million tons. Nor could munitions production have been maintained—or rather expanded—if there had not been the greatest economy in the issue of raw materials to civilian industry. Indeed it was partly on account of such economy in the period between the fall of France and Pearl Harbour that stocks had been built up to a level where they could be heavily raided without serious consequences.

From the time of the fall of France onwards therefore there was steady pressure to reduce the quantity of raw materials going to civilian industry. This was one of the reasons beneath the Board of Trade's steady attempts to reduce civilian production to what they considered to be the minimum that was compatible with efficiency and morale. But the Board felt that this minimum level of production, once it had been reached, had a strong claim on supplies of raw materials. Usually this claim was met. The Board received, for example, sufficient steel for what they considered to be essential purposes, allocations of raw materials sufficient for the clothing ration[1] and enough timber to fulfil the utility furniture programme. Where materials were critically scarce—rubber was the outstanding example—very few civilian claims at all were admitted.

The machinery for submitting claims to raw materials varied considerably. The interdepartmental authority that handled claims was the Materials Committee which during the war always had a minister as Chairman. One or two materials—notably steel,[2] timber and cotton yarn—were allocated by the Materials Committee between Government departments. Each department was responsible for the detailed distribution of its allocation. Some other materials —for example wool and paper—were allocated very broadly by the Materials Committee between the various end uses; the raw material Controls were then responsible for administering the allocations. When rubber was very scarce after Pearl Harbour it was allocated in great detail by the Materials Committee for specific articles. Another

---

[1] In the last year of the war the Board's allocations of cotton yarn were not adequate; here, however, the difficulty was spinning labour, not raw cotton. See Chapter XVII, pp. 473–6.

[2] Separate allocations were made for alloy steel, drop forgings and tinplate.

case where departmental allocations were inappropriate was that of non-ferrous metals. Here it was very difficult for Government departments to ascertain requirements—for example, departments requiring paint would have no idea of the lead or cadmium content. The Materials Committee reviewed the supply position from time to time, but the detailed control of consumption was left to the Non-Ferrous Metals Control. Much of the consumption was based on known programmes and, for the rest, the Control made enquiries about essentiality of purpose and the possibility of using substitutes.

These differences in technique meant that for some materials the Board had to estimate their own requirements and administer their own allocation. For others they had to interest themselves in the end-use allocations and collaborate with the raw material Controls.

The shortage of coal, like the shortage of raw materials, was from time to time expected to limit production. But, like the shortage of raw materials, it never did in the end. A small number of firms had to stop production temporarily for lack of coal but the shortage never put a general brake on production. This was in part due to the increase of opencast production and in part to heavy withdrawals from stock. There was, too, a third factor—economies in consumption. Industry, both war and civilian, made an important contribution to these economies.[1] From December 1943 supplies of coal to all industrial consumers were cut by ten per cent. There was much less dislocation than might have been expected owing to greatly improved fuel efficiency and the Ministry of Fuel's careful programming of the requirements of industrial firms.[2]

In the end it was neither fuel nor raw materials that limited civilian industries but manpower. If there had been much more manpower shortages of some raw materials might have prevented a considerable increase in civilian production. But on the whole more manpower in civilian industries would have prevented the worst of the civilian shortages with which the Board of Trade had to wrestle.

Up to the early months of 1941 the only direct control that was pulling labour out of civilian industries was military recruitment, operated in conjunction with the Schedule of Reserved Occupations. For the rest the movement of manpower out of these industries was influenced by the activities of the Board of Trade in restricting the level of civilian production, and by a variety of normal economic inducements such as higher wages in the munitions industries and by some war-time ones such as patriotism. With these methods there had been big falls in the numbers of people employed in the most impor-

---

[1] Consumption of coal by industry fell from 45·7 million tons in 1942 to 43·9 million tons in 1943 and 41·6 million tons in 1944.

[2] See *Coal*, by W. H. B. Court (United Kingdom Civil Histories), H.M.S.O., 1951.

tant civilian industries, besides a transfer within those industries to Government work.[1]

The economic inducements to move out of civilian industries were undoubtedly still at work after 1941. And the Board of Trade continued to squeeze out labour by new controls over production. The concentration policy launched in the spring of 1941 in particular attempted to fix specifically the number of workers to be employed by civilian industries and by individual firms in those industries. But from about the middle of 1941 onwards the movements of manpower were increasingly governed by direct labour controls. At the beginning of 1941 the War Cabinet had agreed to three new measures to help meet the growing manpower shortage. These were not, however, in operation until the spring or summer. First, the Schedule of Reserved Occupations itself was revised in the spring. Men were to be combed out of industry by raising the ages of reservation by stages. For each scheduled occupation there would be two ages of reservation the lower of which was to apply only to those employed in the firms registered as being on 'protected work'. These revisions meant the loss to civilian industries of a good many more men of military age. The only 'Board of Trade' firms to be entered on the register of protected work were those working up to eighty per cent. of their capacity on Government and export orders and nucleus firms in concentrated industries.

The second new measure was the Essential Work Order which was designed to prevent high labour turnover and wastage of workers. In undertakings scheduled under the Order, no employee could leave his work or be dismissed without the permission of a National Service officer. Firms were not scheduled, however, unless the Ministry of Labour was satisfied by their welfare arrangements. In the course of time the firms in some eighteen Board of Trade industries were scheduled under the Order[2] and enjoyed the protection afforded by it.

The third measure to which the War Cabinet gave its approval was the use by the Minister of Labour of his powers of registration and direction to whatever extent was necessary to produce enough people for essential work. Powers of industrial conscription had been given to the Minister by the Emergency Powers Act of May 1940 but they had hitherto scarcely been used. From the spring of 1941 onwards successive age groups of women and men outside military age were required to register. Those who seemed suitable for transfer

---

[1] See Tables I and II in the Statistical Appendix.

[2] i.e. ball clay, bookbinding (library rebinding only), boots and shoes, china clay, wholesale clothing, cotton and rayon weaving, cotton and rayon textile finishing, cotton spinning, glass (excluding flat glass and domestic glassware), hosiery, laundries, matches, needles, hosiery needle and fish-hook manufactures, pencil manufactures, potters' millers, pottery and stoneware, utility furniture manufacture.

to more essential work were then interviewed and where possible persuaded to move.

By the end of 1941 the manpower shortage was looking more serious than ever. It was especially difficult to find sufficient recruits for the Services and for the women's auxiliary forces. The War Cabinet therefore decided upon two further modifications of the manpower controls. First, the Schedule of Reserved Occupations was to be abandoned in favour of individual reservations. Secondly, there was to be compulsory service for women in the women's Services and civil defence.

The tightening of labour controls was itself a response to the growing shortage of manpower. And as this shortage increasingly preoccupied Government departments, so the operation of the controls was the occasion for the departments to take a close interest in the detailed labour affairs of the industries and firms for which they were responsible. The Board of Trade for example had to sponsor deferments of men from military service—a task that was particularly heavy when individual reservation succeeded the Schedule of Reserved Occupations. They also had to give their views on the withdrawal of classes of young women for military service or for industry. And they had to sponsor industries for scheduling under the Essential Work Order.

The need to advise on these matters brought up all kinds of production problems. Was a certain product essential? Was output of that product already too low? Was a certain man essential for the production of a firm making that product? Or could a whole age-group of women be safely withdrawn from a certain industry? These precise and detailed manpower questions were not so difficult to answer. By weighing up the essentiality of a product and the signs of shortage or adequacy of supply it was possible to reach a broad classification of industries into those that could not afford to lose any more labour, those that could release women aged 20–25 without prior substitution but which needed to keep those over 26, and so forth. On these lines a whole series of administrative arrangements for handling withdrawals from civilian industries was agreed with the Ministry of Labour.[1]

What was more difficult for the Board of Trade was the manpower budgeting that developed in the later years of the war into the main instrument for allocating the nation's resources between all the different war purposes—between fighting and fabrication of all kinds. Early attempts to measure total demands for manpower and total supplies had been made in 1940 by the Humbert Wolfe Committee and at the end of 1940 and the beginning of 1941 by Sir William

---

[1] The Manpower History in the Civil Series will deal with the whole question of withdrawals of manpower by the Ministry of Labour.

Beveridge. The first real move towards a manpower budget came, however, in the autumn of 1941. Even this budget had not gone into great detail. It stated the manpower demands of the Services and supply departments without examining them closely. There were misgivings in Whitehall as to whether the large numbers concerned could be found without disrupting the civilian economy. But in general it was assumed that by the use of the Ministry of Labour's controls these numbers could be found without intolerable dislocation. And found they were.

By 1942, however, a new technique of budgeting was needed. The manpower to meet the additional demands now being put forward by the Services and supply departments simply did not exist. The Government had therefore to decide on the maximum supplies of manpower that could be obtained from the 'unoccupied population' and by further transfers from civilian industry and then prune demands until they matched supplies. For the first time the Board of Trade were faced with the problem of deciding the maximum amount of manpower that could safely be given up by the industries for which they were responsible. This global arithmetic was a difficult task for the Board. They found themselves trying to calculate the effects on production for war, civilian needs and export of, first, a fifteen per cent. cut in manpower and, secondly, a twenty-five per cent. cut. It was impossible to give answers that made much pretence at accuracy. For the Board controlled only part of the output of most of the so-called civilian industries—most of them by this time had heavy Service orders of one kind or another. And though the Board had extended both their knowledge of and control over these industries neither could be nearly so complete as that of the supply departments. Moreover it was impossible to calculate the effects of labour withdrawals on productivity. If an industry's labour force was reduced by fifteen per cent. and the workers taken were the younger, more active ones, clearly production would fall by more than fifteen per cent.

Other civilian departments shared the Board's difficulties in varying measure. Decisions in the 1942 manpower budget about the maximum supply of labour to be obtained from civilian industries were, therefore, of a hit-or-miss kind. In round figures it was decided that these industries might suffer a net reduction of half a million workers without major changes of policy towards civilian consumption, exports or Service requirements. Of this number over half were to come from food and non-food distribution. The only other industries in which the Board were directly interested which were scheduled for large contributions were wool, clothing, and paper and printing, which between them were to yield nearly 100,000 workers. The remainder of the half-million total was to be made up from small contributions from other industries and from releases from services such as banking and insurance.

This budget for the eighteen months from mid-1942 to mid-1943 was the last to rely upon a substantial supply of manpower from civilian industries. Indeed with the budget there was one new item, 'other essential industries and services', which received an allocation. This recognised that some essential industries not classified under the heading of munitions had contracted too far. The only industry in this list that directly concerned the Board of Trade was cotton. The list, however, was to grow larger in the 1944 budget.

This 1944 budget was based on the assumption that manpower could not be more fully mobilised than it was. Quite apart from further drains by military recruitment wastage from the industrial population was bound to exceed new intakes. Moreover it was recognised that standards and amenities of the civil population could not be further reduced. All that could be done was to make such changes within the diminishing total of manpower as strategy demanded. This did not mean that the labour forces of all civilian industries were to remain stable. Some were still scheduled to decline —retail trade and clothing were still the important contributors among the Board of Trade industries. But for the first time other industries in which the Board of Trade were closely interested— cotton, other textiles, leather, footwear, paper, printing, furniture and laundries—were given an allocation of manpower.

The appearance of these allocations was a landmark. Hitherto— that is up to the end of 1943—practically all Board of Trade industries had lost labour steadily. Attempts had been made to call a halt, but though withdrawals by the Ministry of Labour might cease the other forces at work in industry—an excess of wastage over new recruitment and a voluntary drift towards more attractive employment—could not be ruled so easily. Even the Essential Work Order, powerful though it seemed, could not prevent a steady drift away from these industries. In calculating how far the Ministry of Labour might go in withdrawing successive age-groups of workers or in agreeing to labour releases under concentration the Board and the Ministry together did not make enough allowance for these forces outside their control. But how could they have done? The number of unknowns was too large, and there was too little information about or detailed control over the activities of individual firms. At a time when the Services and all kinds of war production were clamouring for manpower the Board of Trade and the Ministry of Labour could not be excessively cautious in proposing releases from civilian industries. In some industries—pottery, for example, where the decline of the labour force seemed to have gone too far—civil standards were maintained quite well by reorganising production. And even in those industries where lack of labour was a real handicap—in cotton spinning, for example, or laundries or utility furniture—there was a good deal of inconvenience for administrators and for the general public. But in no case, not even in cotton, was the war effort damaged.

In 1942 and 1943, however, it had become clear that if possible the labour forces of certain civilian industries should be re-expanded. The first efforts were made with cotton spinning, but though prolonged they were almost wholly unsuccessful. At first the Board of Trade had not sought specific allocations in the manpower budget for their undermanned industries: the numbers involved were so small relatively to those bandied about in connection with the programmes of the Services and supply departments that it seemed scarcely worth while. As time went on, however, and as manpower margins grew ever narrower, the importance that the Ministry of Labour attached to budget allocations grew. Without allocations the Board found that they stood little chance of getting adequate priority for the labour needs of their industries. And so for the 1944 manpower budget the Board of Trade set down their labour requirements in detail and secured allocations for the industries which must expand. From that time onwards, as peace drew nearer, the Board's claims grew increasingly stronger.

These allocations while the war was still waging did not end the Board of Trade's manpower problems. The allocations for 1944 were very small—5,000, for example, for cotton, 3,000 for furniture, 1,500 for footwear and 200 for paper. But even so it proved extremely difficult to fulfil them. Just as it had been impossible to keep the decline in the manpower of the civilian industries to fixed limits—to say in effect 'thus far and no farther'—so also it proved most difficult to re-expand these industries to the desired level. These industries unaided as most of them were by wage inducements or by good factory conditions did not respond nearly so swiftly to labour controls and to allocation techniques as did the munition industries. They could not be moulded into the shapes that administrators cast for them.

Allocations of fuel, raw materials and manpower were made separately by different Government departments or committees. The authorities allocating one factor or one commodity often knew little about the activities of the authorities allocating the others. The Ministry of Labour did not, for example, take a close and continuous interest in the distribution of raw material. A special responsibility therefore lay upon each Government department to co-ordinate its own requirements for all the different resources. In the Board of Trade this function fell upon the Industrial Supplies Department; into it were canalised all the claims of the Board's production departments for labour, raw materials and fuel. The department had there-

K

fore to develop an intimate knowledge of the Board of Trade's production and export policy and, indeed, advise on its formulation. These activities of the Industrial Supplies Department cannot be recorded separately since they overlap with the subject matter of other volumes in this series. They should nevertheless be remembered as being a most important part of the background to all the discussions and decisions that are described in the chapters that follow.

A word of explanation about the organisation of the other departments of the Board may be found useful. At the height of the war, the work of the Board—excluding work connected with bankruptcy and companies and with trading with the enemy—was divided among six main divisions. Dealing with all overseas trade affairs there was the Commercial Relations and Treaties Division. Internal affairs were split between four 'industries and manufactures' divisions. I. & M.1 dealt mainly with price control and retail trade questions and also with a few miscellaneous subjects, such as films and dyestuffs; it also covered import licensing work. I. & M.2 dealt with all textile and clothing matters. I. & M.3 covered the work of the accountants, coupon control and enforcement and of the consumers' needs branch. I. & M.4 dealt with the control of the miscellaneous consumer goods industries. The Industrial Supplies Department besides handling all priority questions was responsible for civilian engineering and also for the production of a very few miscellaneous goods such as books. As time went on it also absorbed responsibilities for combined export planning and for relief supplies to countries liberated from the enemy. Outside these main divisions of the Board and linked with the Board at the Assistant Secretary level was the Control of Factory and Storage Premises.

In addition to their headquarters staff the Board possessed a regional organisation. The Factory Control had its own regional controllers and regional staff. The Board also had their own representative on each of the regional boards which existed in the civil defence regions. The work of these representatives was to look after the interests of the firms in whose production the Board were interested and to negotiate where necessary with the regional representatives of other Government departments. In practice most of the work of the Board's regional board representatives consisted of negotiations over labour. The regional boards in war-time were of course chiefly concerned with munitions production and the authority of the Board of Trade's representatives was inevitably smaller than that of the supply departments. Towards the end of the war, however, it was obvious that the responsibilities of the Board of Trade regional organisation would increase. There would be all the many problems of reconverting industry from war to peace purposes, including deconcentration, derequisitioning, the sale of Government factories.

And there was to be the new responsibility of securing a better distribution of industry. In order to deal with these increased burdens the Board's regional organisation was strengthened at the beginning of 1945. In each region the office of regional factory controller was amalgamated with that of regional board representative and the man appointed was called a full Board of Trade Regional Controller.

By the middle of the war the Board of Trade were very different from the department they had been in September 1939. They operated controls far more detailed than any that had ever been contemplated in pre-war days. This inevitably meant a large increase in staff. Nevertheless it is surprising that the increase was not greater. Before the war, after deducting the staff employed in sections that were later transferred to other Government departments, the Board employed just over 2,000 people. At the height of the war this figure had grown to 6,500 or so. Of this number only about $4\frac{1}{2}$ per cent. were classed as administrative staff and another $4\frac{1}{2}$ per cent. as professional, scientific and technical staff. Considering the size of the Board of Trade's parish—consumer rationing and control, industrial policy at home, commercial policy overseas, export and import licensing, price control, factory control, permanent regulation functions such as patents, bankruptcy, companies and weights and measures, and special war-time duties such as war-damage schemes and trading with the enemy—these staff numbers seem small. The Board did of course enlist the help of other Government departments in operating their controls. But this in itself was wise and a contribution to economy in war-time administration upon which the Board could congratulate themselves.

The need to draw increased administrative staff from outside normal civil service sources in itself enriched the experience of the Board. The university teachers who became temporary civil servants were often particularly useful. For other new duties connected with the controls the Board leaned upon the accountancy profession and drew upon such people as retired detective-inspectors. For the knowledge of engineering that was required the Board fortunately could make use of the technical ability already existing in their own Patent Office. Unlike other controlling departments the Board did not make a great deal of direct use of businessmen. Where the Board became intimately connected with production—for example in clothing, furniture, and in the miscellaneous controls such as tobacco and dyestuffs—they found their technical knowledge inadequate and they therefore recruited businessmen as directors of production. Factory Control and the Board's regional offices were also staffed with temporary civil servants, many of whom had business experience. These were, however, exceptions. By far the greater part of the Board's work was administered by civil servants and by temporary civil servants not drawn from industry. Nevertheless it was clear that since the Board had to interfere so directly with industrial affairs they needed business advice. This they obtained through the Industrial and Export Council, which included eminent businessmen. Originally set up to help with exports in 1940, the Council assumed in 1941 the new duty of advising on concentration of industry. This gradually extended to giving advice on industrial matters in general. Individual industries were allocated to particular business members of the Council who performed a most useful service in explaining the views of officials to industry and conversely.

From time to time in the following pages references will be made to various high ministerial committees. Those Board of Trade policies that required ministerial sanction were almost all submitted to the Lord President's Committee—the small senior committee which was charged with looking after, on behalf of the War Cabinet, home affairs and economic policy. Only in a few exceptional cases was it necessary to send questions connected with Board of Trade policy up to the War Cabinet for settlement.

This in itself reflects the essential nature of the Board's war-time task and war-time achievements. There was little that was exciting about the work and except for some of the export negotiations very little 'high-powered' glamour attached to it. It was important in the way that so many humdrum tasks competently and quietly performed are important. So much depended in the war upon public morale and public conviction that civil affairs no less than military affairs were well ordered. It was for the Board of Trade to see that, while the civilian economy contributed all it could to the military sector, the civilian himself was maintained on austere but adequate standards and was protected from the less tolerable injustices of war-time inflation.

CHAPTER VII

EXPORTS: POLICY AFTER LEND-LEASE

(i)

Selective Export Policy

THE passing of the Lend-Lease Act greatly emphasised the changed views about exports which had already made their appearance in the summer of 1940. Nevertheless it was some time before the full implications of the Act were felt in export policy. For the time being stress was still laid both inside and outside Government circles on the need to earn hard currencies.[1] *The Economist* for example was emphasising the importance of exports only two months before the Lend-Lease Act was passed.[2] 'It would be tragic and silly', it said, 'if the necessity to export more and more were to be lost from sight in the flood of imports and special payments problems. . . . It is imperative that all non-essential commodities which have suitable markets abroad for ready payment and which do not use labour or plant indispensable for war output should be made and sold freely. It is so urgent that it should not be bounded by merely economic considerations'.

Even after the introduction of lend-lease previous purchases in America and purchases outside the scope of the Act had still to be met through dollar payments. The President of the Board of Trade stated firmly on 3rd April 1941: 'Our need for dollars. . . . remains very great and anything which adds to our dollar earnings is a contribution of first-rate importance to our cause. That is one reason why His Majesty's Government still regard it as a necessity for this country to maintain and extend its exports to the United States and continue to give every assistance to that trade.'[3]

Later in April the President referred to the selective export policy and enumerated four tests which would be employed in deciding whether exports should be encouraged. They were, first, whether the exports earned or saved exchange needed for the payment of

[1] In the winter of 1940 a system of grading of countries, primarily with reference to the hardness of their currencies, had been worked out by officials of the Treasury and Board of Trade in co-operation with the Bank of England.

[2] *The Economist*, 11th January 1941.

[3] H. of C. Deb., Vol. 370, Col. 1168.

essential imports; secondly, whether in the case of the sterling area or Allied countries they were essential to the importing country; thirdly, whether the value of the exported product was high in relation to that of the imported raw material, and, fourthly, whether the article in question could be manufactured and exported without putting an undue strain on resources needed for other war purposes.

In spite of the continuing need to export it was clear that exports would fall still lower in the war-time scale of values. Was there a danger that through lack of a central policy, through piecemeal cutting here and there as shortages of raw material, capacity or labour developed they would fall to a dangerously low level? There was a gap, it might be argued, between the value of imports into the United Kingdom and the non-export sources out of which these imports might be met—lend-lease aid, realisation of overseas assets, invisible items and loans from abroad, including the accumulation of sterling balances in London. Since reserves of gold and dollars had sunk so low this gap could only be covered by exports. The President of the Board of Trade thought that the question needed study. He suggested that the export drive had been helpful in this matter. It had given overseas countries confidence and had induced them to supply the United Kingdom on credit and to hold sterling. Would they continue to do this? Commercial exports in the third year of war, it seemed, would be running at the level of £200 millions, and no one knew whether this would be an adequate figure. The President suggested, in June 1941, that there should be an investigation of what he termed an 'essential export programme' by officials of the Board of Trade, the Treasury and the economic section of the War Cabinet Office. This would not only deal with the problem of the gap but would also break down the total, by commodities and by countries, into the most economical pattern of distribution.

The task of drawing up such a programme would clearly be a difficult one and probably hardly worth the administrative labour which would be involved. In the first place, there were, in addition to the currency-producing exports, the exports which were essential to the war effort.[1] But here everything was guesswork. There could be no precise estimate of the amount of exports from the United Kingdom necessary to sustain the economies of countries which contributed directly or indirectly to the prosecution of the war. It was also clear that the gap in the balance of payments provided no satisfactory basis on which an essential or minimum export programme could be built up. So far as it was a gold or dollar problem it would be largely solved in a few months by the flow of lend-lease supplies. In any case the idea of a gap was significant in relation not to the

---

[1] There were, included in these exports, those that were necessary for political reasons.

United Kingdom alone but to the sterling area, of which London was the monetary centre. Thus it was influenced by the import and export policies of the Dominions who belonged to the sterling area. Finally, in the framing of estimates, a programme of exports would have to take account of the imported raw materials needed in their manufacture. The only conclusion that could be usefully drawn in a changing situation was that some flow of exports was necessary for goodwill purposes, to maintain confidence in the holders of sterling[1] and to keep open markets that would be needed in the post-war expansion of exports. Estimates were in fact made of the minimum level at which exports should be maintained—they varied between £275 millions and £300 millions—but they were perhaps little more than an academic exercise. Meanwhile American protests about the use of lend-lease materials in exports were being heard, and before long the whole nature of the export problem had altered. Policy had thenceforward largely to be directed to controlling and restricting exports, and traditional markets important from the currency stand-point had to be given up.

Before coming to these changes in policy, we shall look at some examples of the application of the selective export policy in 1941.

COTTON

Textiles represented the chief sphere for the application of this selective export policy. Exports of cotton yarn and piece-goods called for urgent consideration, since it had become necessary to cut drastic-ally imports of raw cotton from the United States during 1941. This was in contrast to wool where imports continued and where there were in any case adequate stocks. The cotton industry and the trade in cotton textiles had rapidly to be adapted to this alteration in their raw material supplies. It was clear that the export trade could no longer continue using the 11,300 tons of cotton a month which it had been taking at the end of 1940.

In February 1941 discussion took place between the Board of Trade and the Cotton Board about the control and direction of exports to which the raw material shortage of the industry now pointed. So far as types of goods were concerned it was agreed that restrictions should fall more heavily on yarns than on piece-goods and should not apply at all to the important trade in thread, which possessed a high conversion value, and which was in many markets practically a United Kingdom monopoly. The criteria for judging the importance of different markets would be (a) their value from the exchange standpoint, (b) the desirability of maintaining their goodwill, (c) the possible political effects of a drastic restriction, (d) the extent to which

---

[1] The Argentine was the outstanding example of a country to which exports needed to be maintained in view of balance of payments difficulties.

supplies from the United Kingdom were essential to the well-being of the country concerned. In applying the first criterion currency gradings worked out between the Board of Trade and the Treasury would be adopted.[1]

The amount of yarn expected to be available currently for exports was 22,800 tons a quarter, a figure which was shortly to prove much in excess of deliveries for overseas trade purposes. On this assumption yarn as such was allocated 2,400 tons which would involve a reduction of fifty-seven per cent. on 1940 exports to accessible markets, piece-goods received an allocation of 14,100 tons with a cut on 1940 exports of forty-two per cent., while thread received 1,560 tons of yarn and no reduction was required on its 1940 level of exports.[2] On the basis of 1940 exports of piece-goods the dollar markets, South Africa, Egypt and Iran suffered no reduction. For 'special political reasons' a fifty per cent. increase was planned for the Dutch East Indies. Exports of piece-goods to the Argentine and Uruguay were cut by twenty-five per cent., but the biggest reductions were in exports to the Empire, Australia and New Zealand receiving 33⅓ per cent. and India only twenty per cent. of 1940 supplies of piece-goods from the United Kingdom. The country distribution of yarn exports was similar; supplies to the dollar markets were maintained but other countries' supplies were cut more drastically. There was, for example, no allocation of yarn for India. These arrangements appeared to contemplate a policy of starvation of cotton textiles for Empire countries, and an undue emphasis, after the introduction of lend-lease, on currency. At the outset of the scheme supplementary allocations were granted, first on currency grounds and later on political grounds, for shipment of textiles out of stocks.

This attitude towards exports was soon destined to change. Even in August 1941 the chairman of the Cotton Board stated that he felt bound to admit that currency was becoming a less important factor in exports than the essentiality of the goods to the importing country. This change of view, and later of policy, resulted largely from the shortage of yarn which in its turn derived from the shortage of labour in the spinning section of the cotton industry. Thus allocations of yarn fell short of requirements and deliveries soon fell short of allocations. In the last quarter of 1941 the allocation of yarn for exports was 20,000 tons and this was reduced in the first quarter of

---

[1] There were five grades, viz.:
   1. Dollar countries, South Africa, Turkey.
   2. Argentina, Egypt, Iran, Portugal, Central America.
   3. Dutch East Indies, Belgian Congo and Free French colonies, India, Burma, Uruguay.
   4. Eire, Australia, New Zealand, British East and West Africa, British West Indies, Palestine, Rhodesia, Sudan (Sterling Empire).
   5. Colombia, Chile, Peru, Brazil; other accessible foreign markets.
[2] The balance of the 22,800 tons was accounted for by made-up goods of various kinds.

1942 to 15,000 tons. Coupled with the shortage of yarn was the problem of the gap in overseas supplies following on the economic warfare with Japan—the freezing of Japanese assets and the development of Japanese counter-measures—which broke out in the summer of 1941. Japan had been an important supplier of cheap textiles and in 1940 Commonwealth countries imported over 800 million square yards[1] of Japanese piece-goods. India alone took 368 million square yards, a figure which was only slightly smaller than India's own exports to all destinations of 390 million square yards. There was thus a clear danger that supplies in Empire countries might be reduced to a dangerously low level.

The scheme for export direction of cotton piece-goods was operated on the basis of returns which manufacturer-exporters and merchant converters made of their exports in 1940 to accessible markets. These exporters then received market allocations representing proportions of their 1940 trade. The merchant converter obtained a buying right to new cotton production for export and a quota for each market with which he was concerned. The London merchant was not given an allocation, but the Lancashire converter was required to see that he got his fair share of cloth. Effective control of these arrangements was provided through the introduction of export licensing of cotton piece-goods in May 1941.[2]

Thus the export scheme started on the assumption that orders of goods for overseas civilian needs would go through the normal commercial channels. Though the volume of trade would be much reduced it was expected that the initiative in export sales and production for export would rest as it had done before the war with the merchant converter. This assumption could not in fact be long maintained, and there were many war-time factors which were combining to destroy it. First and foremost this system did not provide for priorities in any particular market nor guarantees for the fulfilment of the more urgent requirements. Dominion governments soon began, through a system of sponsoring, to single out their more important textile requirements and to seek direct ways of meeting them without regard for the commercial arrangements that happened to be operating before the war. The sponsoring system tended to expand and it was reported in July 1942 that all cotton supplies to Australia, most of the supplies to Canada and to New Zealand and a considerable part of those to South Africa had been put at the disposal of the respective governments who now tended themselves to place or sponsor orders, thus in effect overriding the scheme of market allocations to merchants. Another factor operating

---

[1] Fiscal years ending 31st March 1941 in the cases of India and Burma and 30th June 1941 in the case of Australia.

[2] S.R. & O. 1941, No. 551. Export control over yarns was already in existence.

in the same direction was the tendency experienced everywhere as a result of war-time shortages towards standardisation and towards the restriction of requirements to utility types of goods which could best be produced in long runs beyond the range of the small merchant's allocation. In the next chapter an account will be given of the changes made in the export direction scheme on account of these war-time circumstances.

WOOL

The wool industry enjoyed in 1940–41 a much more favourable supply of raw material than did the cotton industry. Stocks were adequate and while there was export control of products which were the result of the earlier processing stages of the industry—yarn, tops and noils—this was mainly on economic warfare grounds. The material was rationed and there was some direction of exports of the semi-processed products, but there was no difficulty in obtaining supplies of wool for manufacture into piece-goods for export. In 1941 a total of 120,000 tons of raw wool was being allocated by the Control, on the basis roughly of 50,000 to the home civilian trade and 70,000 tons for export purposes.[1]

By the autumn of 1941, however, the position had altered. The Minister of Labour was threatening to withdraw 20,000 workers from the wool industry. And there was a prospect of a cut in the imports of wool in the import programme for 1942. Finally there was evidence of a stocking-up of woollen goods in Eire on a fairly large scale. There was little possibility now of cutting home consumption in the interest of the export trade; supplies to the civilian consumer would be barely adequate to meet the ration. Nevertheless there was as yet no question of imposing on the exports of the wool industry the sort of drastic restriction which had been applied to cotton textiles.

Restriction of exports could not, it seemed, be effectively achieved by raw material control alone. Raw material control by itself could not secure direction of exports to the appropriate markets, nor was it practicable in this way to deal with cloth, exports of which were often made in small pieces. Export licensing for woollen piece-goods must therefore be introduced.

The scheme for the direction of exports of woollen tissues and blankets was therefore very much like that for cotton textiles. Returns were called for from exporters showing their exports of these goods by countries in the year ending 31st October 1941 with a view to the granting of market allocations representing proportions of trade in

---

[1] Divided as follows:

		Tons
	Fabrics	40,000
	Yarns	8,000
	Tops	16,000
	Raw wool	5,000

this period. These allocations were given to exporters whether merchants or manufacturers.

An export control Order covering woollen tissues and blankets came into force at the end of November 1941.[1] Meanwhile, as a provisional measure and until a scheme had been worked out, open general licences were given for exports to the United States, Canada, Argentina, Paraguay, Uruguay, Newfoundland, the Philippine Islands, South Africa, South-West Africa and Southern Rhodesia. With regard to other countries, applications for licences were required. Except in the case of Eire, however, they were granted fairly freely since supplies were not seriously scarce and it was felt to be undesirable to create a mass of frustrated exports by the sudden application of export control to goods which were frequently made specially for particular markets and would not be readily saleable elsewhere. The industry was at this time running at a high level of production for export and a large volume of orders was being carried forward into 1942. To help the Board of Trade in the administration of the scheme an advisory committee of representatives of the trade was set up in Bradford.

The scheme did not come fully into operation until February 1942 when the quota arrangements had been worked out, and the open general licence mentioned above was then revoked. Policy at first was directed towards achieving a fairly drastic cut in exports to Eire, a moderate reduction in trade with Empire countries other than Canada and South Africa, while maintaining in general to other countries the level of exports which had been reached in the standard year, 1st November 1940 to 31st October 1941. Bulk licences were issued to exporters except for destinations in which considerations of economic warfare played a part. Meanwhile it had been arranged that yarns, hitherto requiring licences only for 'C' destinations,[2] should not be exported at all without a licence, the export control arrangements being fitted into a rationing and sponsoring system operated through the Wool Control.

Again, as in the case of cotton textiles, the year 1942 was to mark a big change in the planning of wool exports. Here too the same factors were operative: the diminished importance of currency, reductions in supplies and concentration upon standard or utility types of commodity.

*   *   *

---

[1] S.R. & O. 1941, No. 1820.

[2] See p. 40.

The earning of desirable foreign currencies was, at least during the first half of 1941, the major consideration in the formulation of export plans. The problem of directing exports arose in the first place because material shortages meant a reduction in the level of exports and such exports as still remained had to be directed to achieving what were regarded at the time as the most worthwhile results. The direction of exports of cotton and linen textiles has already been described. When supplies of raw jute fell in 1941 a similar programme was worked out for jute piece-goods which were directed to the hard-currency markets of the United States, Canada and South Africa.

It must, however, be emphasised that this export policy was very much the centre of controversy. Allocations for exports which were merely to yield foreign exchange had to be fought for against the opposition of Service and supply departments. Lend-lease had of course transformed the dollar position and the currencies in question were rather those of countries which were important suppliers of the United Kingdom, and who in default of exports to them would be accumulating large holdings of sterling balances. Argentina, for example, in the middle of 1941 was holding special sterling to the extent of £12 millions, and there were doubts as to whether she would continue to sell canned beef to this country in exchange for sterling which she could not use in the purchase of goods. Brazil too was accumulating sterling and the position in Latin America generally gave some ground for concern. Here, as will be seen later, was a dangerous source of misunderstanding between Great Britain and the United States. Other countries which it was thought at the beginning of 1942 might be unwilling to maintain supplies were Portugal and Spain; the latter had indeed set a limit to her holding of sterling balances.

On the other hand it would have been a profound mistake to leave out of account the criterion of 'essentiality' in export trade which was destined in the remaining war years to play the predominant if not the only role. In the cotton scheme, for example, it was certainly a factor for which allowances had to be made. The drastically reduced allocation of steel for export, whether in processed or manufactured form, was governed now by the criterion of essentiality of purpose.

The more rigid control of exports that was now developing was bound to have important repercussions on the structure of the trading organisation. The general problem, which was to become more acute with further restriction of exports in the later war years, was that a reduced volume of export trade could not provide adequate business for the existing merchanting organisation, and there were no plans for the concentration of this organisation as there were for the concentration of manufacturing industry. However, as will be seen later, it was possible in some cases to arrange for pooling schemes between holders of impractically small allocations. There were other similar problems which may be briefly mentioned. Export rations were usually given to manufacturers rather than to exporters generally, and this might in some cases be to the detriment of the merchant. However, it was difficult to alter schemes which linked export control with raw material control, while at the same time it was probable that manufacturers would in their interest look after the merchants with whom they regularly dealt. Another problem of greater difficulty arose from the fact that in all the schemes[1] export allocations were for particular markets with which trade was still possible or permitted, that is, exporters could not switch from one market to another. Moreover, exporters who had previously dealt with markets which were now closed received no share of the trade in remaining markets. However, it was probably true that most firms specialised in particular markets, and it would, at any rate at this phase of the war, have been a waste of time and effort for them to attempt to develop trade with new customers.

(ii)

The Lend-lease White Paper

After March 1941 it was clear that the part to be played by exports in the economic strategy of the United Kingdom would be very different from what had been expected and intended when the export drive had been launched in the spring of 1940. In some fields, particularly where production for export competed for resources with war production, exports were soon drastically cut. This was true, for example, of steel exports. Thus, to take the case of South America, exports of 'direct' steel were being eliminated, except where they served a vital purpose as did those of the tinplate required to bring back canned meat to Britain. Exports of machinery to the South American countries other than the Argentine were also being ruled out; steel had been refused for two big electrification schemes. There was still a flow of spare parts for the maintenance of British-made machinery, and where orders for machinery made to meet the requirements of South American users were in process of manu-

---

[1] The only apparent exception was that for jute piece-goods mentioned above, in which licences were first given on the basis of previous trade to all open markets; but the arrangement was discontinued because it was found that some of the holders had no connections with the particular hard-currency markets in question.

facture it would obviously have been wasteful not to allow them to be completed.[1] Continued exports of steel in these forms and to these markets could indeed be well justified as could the exports of goods containing steel to the Empire and to Allied countries for purposes which were directly or indirectly connected with the war effort. Other exports that did not make the same demands on resources that could be put to war uses had not been restricted in the same degree. The currency criterion was still being emphasised; this was particularly true in the case of the Argentine which was tending to accumulate sterling as a result of the inadequate level of visible and invisible exports to her from the United Kingdom.

However, not long after the passing of the Lend-Lease Act, from the spring of 1941, a growing volume of criticism began to be voiced in the United States concerning United Kingdom exports and export policy. This criticism developed along two main lines. First, it was alleged that supplies of lend-lease materials which were being made available at the cost of the American taxpayer were being used in the export trade of the United Kingdom, thus enabling the British exporter to compete with American manufacturers in overseas markets. Secondly, the complaint was made that materials whose consumption was being restricted in the United States or which were being made subject there to export restriction or prohibition were being obtained by United Kingdom firms and used by them in the export trade.

The first reaction in the United Kingdom to this criticism was to take the view that the American protests were misconceived and exaggerated. It was felt in the first place that there was a tendency for the Americans to overlook the continued importance of certain currency-yielding exports: lend-lease had not solved the problem of paying for supplies of canned meat from the Argentine. Equally there appeared to London to have been a failure in the United States to appreciate the significance of normal commercial exports in sustaining the economies of countries from which Britain drew necessary supplies. Moreover, there was often quite sound justification for certain kinds of exports which continued to flow in spite of the growing tendency of the industries which had made them to con-

---

[1] Exports of (a) machinery, and (b) iron and steel goods to the Argentine, Brazil and Chile were as follows:

£ '000

	Argentina		Brazil*		Chile*	
	(a)	(b)	(a)	(b)	(a)	(b)
1939	1,321	2,447	729	289	171	146
1940	1,380	1,905	845	238	265	163
1941	1,120	1,964	622	121	177	33

* From 6th March to 29th December 1941 there was an 'all-goods' export control on exports to Brazil and Chile.

centrate upon war production. Machinery, for example, and bulkier goods might be going abroad as a result of orders received in the days of the export drive or at a time when restrictions on manufacture for export had hardly begun to take effect. There was also, clearly, a good case for maintaining supplies of spare parts for British machinery installed abroad. Lastly, even when it had been agreed to divert orders for steel to the United States it had been found in certain cases that the Americans were unable to supply, at any rate within a reasonable time, what was required.

There was one problem which, it was realised, was likely to cause trouble, that of the prices at which materials similar to those received under lend-lease were issued to exporters. The issue prices to users of many raw materials were arrived at by averaging over a period the cost of such materials from a number of sources to the raw material Control concerned, and the resultant average might yield an issue price below the notional United States price at which lend-lease materials were entered. To meet the difficulty by introducing differential export prices or levies on exported goods was not at the time thought to be practicable. The problem would become an even more awkward one if, as part of the general policy of internal price stabilisation, it was decided to hold the issue price of some lend-lease material below the current United States price or below the average of that price and the price of similar materials derived from other sources.

Meanwhile in June and July the volume of protests from America had been increasing. British exports of machinery and steel, it was stated, were continuing to the western hemisphere, particularly South America, and there were the relics of the export drive exhibited in the slogan painted on packing-cases, 'Britain delivers the goods'. The hope that the storm which had blown up across the Atlantic would die down had proved to be mistaken. Negotiations had soon to be set on foot to produce a formula which would be acceptable to the United States Administration and American public opinion. Meanwhile in August 1941 the Export Licensing Department of the Board of Trade was already introducing a control over those exports which might be held to be vulnerable to American criticisms.

In the discussions there was at first some talk of the principle of 'substitution' which had played a part in the 1914–18 war. There might, it was pointed out, be some difficulty in physically segregating lend-lease from other supplies. The assurance, therefore, to be required of the United Kingdom should be that it was using at home for war purposes material at least equal in quantity to that which it was receiving under lend-lease. If it were satisfying that condition, then any surplus supplies, from whatever sources they might be derived, should be available for export or for incorporation in exports.[1] Mr. (afterwards Lord) Keynes thought that the Americans would agree to the principle of substitution when the converse of the principle was put to them. That was to say that if they questioned it the reply should be: 'do you mean then that so long as any steel articles are being imported into the United Kingdom, the United Kingdom shall have no steel exports whatever, however large its own output?' Use was made of the principle in the drafting of the British undertaking of September 1941 concerning lend-lease and scarce materials, but it must not be overlooked that even after the entry of America into the war there were United States officials who maintained a much more restrictive view and who held that the United Kingdom should concentrate its resources on war production to the exclusion of the export trade. Furthermore the question was not simply one of lend-lease materials. There was the problem of the scarce materials on which restrictions were being imposed in the United States and which proved in fact to be the more awkward and troublesome matter to handle.

The issue was now that of the form of undertaking which the Government of the United Kingdom should give in order to allay the misgivings that had arisen in the United States. There might, for example, have been a simple assurance that no lend-lease material would be exported or incorporated in exports. But this sort of thing would have been inadequate and would inevitably have left many problems unresolved. It would probably have the awkward consequence of ruling out most of the cotton exports of the United Kingdom. Instead the Treasury decided to draw up a document of a more detailed and restrictive nature, which under the title 'Correspondence respecting the policy of His Majesty's Government in the United Kingdom in connection with the use of materials received under the Lend-lease Act' was published as a White Paper on 10th September 1941.[2]

Those parts of the White Paper which are relevant to this chapter may be given in full:—

(2) Lend-lease materials sent to this country have not been used for export, and every effort will be made in the future to ensure that they are not used for export, subject to the principle that where complete physical segregation of lend-lease materials is impracticable, domestic consumption of the material in question shall be at least equal to the amounts received under lend-lease.

---

[1] If a = supplies of lend-lease materials, b = supplies of similar materials from other sources, c = use of these materials at home for war purposes, then c = a. Under the principle of substitution, if b = a = c, then a is available for use in exports. *Prima facie*, the application of the principle of substitution would have ruled out United Kingdom exports of cotton goods, but it was agreed with the Americans that these exports should be deemed to have been covered out of imports of cotton from other sources, though these imports were in fact of quite different types.

[2] Cmd. 6311. The White Paper consisted of a memorandum addressed by the Foreign Secretary, Mr. Eden, to the United States Ambassador, Mr. Winant.

(3) His Majesty's Government have not applied, and will not apply, any materials similar to those supplied under lend-lease in such a way as to enable their exporters to enter new markets or to extend their export trade at the expense of United States exporters. Owing to the need to devote all available capacity and manpower to war production, the United Kingdom export trade is restricted to the irreducible minimum necessary to supply or obtain materials essential to the war effort.

(4) For some time past, exports from the United Kingdom have been more and more confined to those essential (i) for the supply of vital requirements of overseas countries, particularly in the sterling Empire; (ii) for the acquisition of foreign exchange, particularly in the western hemisphere. His Majesty's Government have adopted the policy summarised below:

(i) No materials of a type the use of which is being restricted in the United States on the grounds of short supply, and of which we obtain supplies from the United States, either by payment or on lend-lease terms, will be used in exports with the exception of the following special cases:

(*a*) Material which is needed overseas in connection with supplies essential to the war effort for ourselves and our Allies, and which cannot be obtained from the United States.

(*b*) Small quantities of such materials needed as minor though essential components of exports which otherwise are composed of materials not in short supply in the United States.

(*c*) Repair parts for British machinery and plant now in use and machinery and plant needed to complete installations now under construction, so long as they have already been contracted for.

Steps have already been taken to prevent the export (except to Empire and Allied territories) of such goods which do not come within the exceptions referred to in (*a*), (*b*) and (*c*) above.

(ii) Materials similar to those being provided under lend-lease which are not in short supply in the United States will not be used for export in quantities greater than those which we ourselves produce or buy from any source.

The memorandum also referred to the distribution in the United Kingdom of lend-lease goods (paragraphs 5 and 6). The remuneration received for this by distributors, it stated, was controlled, and they would obtain no more than a fair return for their services. Food was a special case, since the proportion of the total United Kingdom food supply coming from the United States was small, and it would be impossible to have a separate system of distribution for lend-lease food. The Ministry of Food had, however, established a close control over distributive margins, and no food obtained on lend-lease terms was being sold or would be sold at uncontrolled prices.

L

It is important to note at the outset that this White Paper represented a unilateral statement of policy by the United Kingdom, not a joint statement or bilateral agreement between the Governments of the United Kingdom and the United States. Clearly, however, in interpreting the terms of the White Paper and in administering a policy based upon them there was need for consultation and co-operation with United States officials, principally those of the Office of Lend-lease Administration (OLLA), since the purpose of the undertaking was to forestall criticism likely to embarrass the American Administration or to endanger lend-lease supplies. But co-operation, though necessary, entailed certain obvious disadvantages. It meant at first, until a machinery of consultation had been created, delays in reaching decisions about exports, which hampered the effective administration of export control, and which soon led officials in London to adopt a commonsense interpretation of certain terms in the White Paper, e.g. as to whether a material was 'obtainable' in the United States, in order to avoid a hold-up of trade. More serious, however, was the fact that from the very beginning OLLA regarded itself as a court which alone could decide whether any particular export from the United Kingdom satisfied the terms of the White Paper. In doing so it tended inevitably to adopt a legalistic attitude which hardly seemed to fit the underlying realities of the economic situation, and which, when it was maintained after Pearl Harbour, appeared inconsistent with the pursuit of a common purpose. Moreover, it was soon found that the Lend-Lease Administration had set up a department for 'policing the observance of the terms of the White Paper'. It was irksome for a country like Britain with her long trading experience to have to submit for the first time, albeit from a friendly nation, to this informal control over her exports. But it must be pointed out on the other side that the attitude of officials in Washington was not governed simply by petty considerations or by the desire to interfere merely for the sake of interference. They were acutely conscious of the possibility of criticism from ill-informed or ill-disposed elements in their own country and of the danger that this might cause to the continued flow of American aid and to the prospects of Anglo-American co-operation. The danger was appreciated by ministers and officials in London as well as in Washington. Steps were taken to emphasise the part played by American economic assistance in British war production, and it was arranged that British papers advertising goods should include notices stating: 'the fact that goods made of raw materials in short supply owing to war conditions are advertised in this paper should not be taken as an indication that they are available for export'.

Although the British economy was turning over more fully and more rapidly to war production, the restrictive aspect of much of the

White Paper came as something of a shock to those who were concerned with the export trade either in a business or in an official
capacity. It portended much more definitely than anything that had
happened before the curtailment in many directions of exports from
the United Kingdom. For officials it meant the setting up of additional
export restrictions, which, particularly in the light of the shortage of
staff, would be difficult and troublesome to administer. Committees
were soon created to deal with the general problems involved, a
system of case law was evolved, and finally a code was built up to
guide the operations of the Export Licensing Department. At the
beginning of 1942 there was no disposition to underestimate the
change that had taken place. 'The situation', the Board of Trade
reported, 'is such that we abandon whole sections of the export trade
with open eyes, and the entry of the United States into the war does
not relieve us of our obligations under the White Paper'.

(iii)

Some White Paper Problems

The White Paper of September 1941 was not put forward as a legal
document; had it originally been regarded as such it would have been
drafted with much greater care. But though intended as a general
statement of principles to be followed in the administration of United
Kingdom export policy it came, as has been seen, to be treated as a
code to be interpreted and applied legalistically to individual
instances. In any event awkward problems of export policy and
control would have arisen, but it can hardly be doubted they were
gravely accentuated by the attitude which was actually adopted
towards the White Paper. The major problems which arose are
discussed below.

(i) First of all, there was the problem of how control should be
exercised to prevent the use in exports of materials which were
vulnerable under the terms of the White Paper. This might be
done either through the appropriate raw material Control or
through the machinery of export licensing. Raw material control
was pretty effective in dealing individually with the heavier
types of goods, such as machinery, but it could not be relied on
to prevent the export in lighter goods of vulnerable materials,
because it was not easy to check the use of materials distributed
through bulk allocations and because manufacturers might
already be in possession of small stocks. This meant the extension
of export licensing control to a long list of commodities, and this

had to be done gradually, partly on account of the difficulties of increasing staff capable of handling the new set of problems and partly because a precise definition of each separate item had to be agreed with the Customs authorities. But the setting up of formal machinery of control was a part, and sometimes only a very small part, of the problem of preventing the use in exports of vulnerable materials. When it was a question of exporting actual material or such things as tools and machinery in which steel was obviously incorporated not much trouble arose. But there were many cases in which identification of a scarce material in a finished article was extremely difficult if not actually impossible. Thus manila fibre was not recognisable in paper and the chemical derivatives of a metal might become quite untraceable. Pharmaceutical preparations presented a peculiarly awkward problem, since medicinal tinctures contained a very high proportion of alcohol, a vulnerable material. To have stopped exports of these things, in an attempt to adhere scrupulously to the terms of the White Paper, would have meant cutting off essential medical supplies from many parts of the world. In the end, as the only practicable way out of the difficulty, it was decided that medical supplies should be regarded as essential to the war effort and should be allowed to be exported. The attempt to solve problems of this sort occasioned friction and delay and took up many hours of administrative labour which could ill be spared. And, in spite of all this effort, American 'policing' of United Kingdom exports persisted, and American complaints, some justified and some unjustified, continued to be voiced.

(ii) The part of the White Paper memorandum that gave rise to the major difficulties of interpretation was paragraph four.[1] It was not so much a question of deciding what were scarce materials; these were simply materials which were subject to United States conservation orders, provided that they were being acquired by the United Kingdom from the United States. There were minor problems, of course; for example it was felt necessary to go beyond the actual terms of the White Paper and add aluminium to the list of materials, even though it was not being obtained as such from the United States, on the ground that it was incorporated in aircraft which were being supplied by America. But the serious problems arose over the exceptions recognised in paragraph four, which permitted the use in export from the United Kingdom of vulnerable materials. These will be discussed below. Meanwhile it must be pointed

---

[1] See p. 149.

out that a very wide range of materials soon came under the ban of this paragraph; most metals, many textile materials such as silk, jute and manila hemp and a great variety of chemicals.

(iii) Exports using vulnerable materials were permitted under section (i) (*a*) of paragraph four if they were essential to the war effort of the United Kingdom and its Allies and could not be obtained from the United States. What was essential was obviously susceptible to differences in interpretation and to disagreement. So far as the British Commonwealth was concerned reasonable guides or pointers were provided by the certificates of essentiality issued by the Dominions and by the import licences issued in the Colonies. Some use had already begun to be made of these certificates in directing exports before the lend-lease problem arose. But there was still room for divergence of view as to what exports were covered by this exception. In addition to Commonwealth countries and to recognised belligerent Allies other countries—Egypt, Iran, Iraq, Portugal and Turkey—came to be regarded as Allies for White Paper purposes. Moreover, it could be claimed that goods required to sustain the civilian economies of overseas countries or to provide inducements to producers in those countries from which the United Kingdom drew needed supplies were essential to the war effort, though it was hard to convince the Americans on the latter point.

It may be noted here that in the latter part of 1942 the whole problem became involved in an ambitious scheme devised by the Office of Lend-lease Administration for ascertaining the requirements of all Allied countries for every kind of civilian commodity. OLLA, of course, had to press its demands on the use of United States resources against the competing claims of other American departments and agencies and to do this effectively seemed to call for full statistical information. It therefore invented a standard form on which Allied countries obtaining United States supplies were to estimate their future requirements in detail, quarter by quarter, giving also particulars about domestic production, stocks in hand and minimum stocks, and imports together with information about end uses and justification of the requirements. This turned out to be far too elaborate a scheme as the information sought was quite beyond the capacity of some countries to supply, at any rate within a reasonable period of time. Moreover, the form was unsuited to some requirements such as those for capital goods. Ultimately it proved not only that the data supplied were inadequate but that it had taken so long to complete the forms that the information available was already out of date.

The question whether supplies of things which were being exported under this provision were obtainable in the United States proved even more troublesome. Were officials in the United Kingdom justified in assuming, as they did, that supplies were unobtainable in the United States if they could not be obtained at a reasonable price and within a reasonable time? The Americans themselves were not prepared to concede this point. Again, should supplies be regarded as obtainable in the United States if they were available there but not in British specifications? These were not matters of petty and insignificant detail. Failure to deal with them in a reasonable and common-sense manner might involve wastes and delays which could ill be afforded in war-time. Nor was the trouble ended when it had been agreed that supplies were obtainable in the United States. There was no assurance that the Americans actually would supply the commodity in question, and thus vitally important requirements might go unsatisfied.

At the end of 1941 Mr. Stettinius the Lend-lease Administrator, agreed that, as an interim measure, essential supplies destined for export from the United Kingdom to Empire and Allied countries in the eastern hemisphere might be presumed to be unobtainable in the United States. However, he expected that within a reasonable time general policies would be agreed and that the United States would be 'consulted as to the nature, destination and purpose of the articles to be exported and as to whether we would prefer to export them direct from this country if we determine they are obtainable here'. He also thought that the whole matter should be treated in terms of programmes, rather than, as it was then, on a case basis, and that United Kingdom export programmes should be drawn up with reference to each scarce material, these programmes being integrated with supplies of such material from America.

(iv) The other clauses of the White Paper dealing with components, repair parts and plant and machinery in process of manufacture may now be considered. The exception in favour of 'small quantities of such materials needed as minor though essential components' was interpreted quite arbitrarily as meaning that the scarce components represented not more than ten per cent. by weight of the finished commodity. This interpretation was challenged by the Americans in the case of chromium, nickel, tungsten and vanadium, and the proportion for these materials had to be reduced to five per cent. Here again, administrators faced awkward problems in trying to ascertain whether in any particular case the proportion of the scarce material was more or less than ten per cent. Repair parts were also troublesome. What was a repair part, as distinct from a spare part?[1] Again, there were the obvious difficulties of deciding whether a repair part was exported for 'British machinery and plant now in use'. A lot of repair parts were sent out to firms which held them in stock. Finally, there was the exception in favour of outstanding contracts. In this case it was decided to interpret the White Paper as justifying the export to any destination of goods which had reached a stage of manufacture at which it would have been impracticable to reclaim the constituent materials and use them for other purposes.[2] Otherwise, as was pointed out, there would have been a shocking waste of labour and materials, quite apart from the congestion of factory space involved.

Thus the full rigour of the White Paper, in its effects upon British exports, was modified to some extent by commonsense interpretation of its provisions. The necessity, for example, of ascertaining in each individual case of scarce supply whether a commodity was obtainable in the United States would have introduced a quite intolerable element of delay and friction in dealing with urgent export problems. The difficulty was met by the decision to treat supplies essential to Empire and Allied countries in the eastern hemisphere as 'uno tainable' and therefore admissible for export from the United Kingdom, a decision which, as has been seen, was in effect ratified by Mr. Stettinius at the end of 1941. To require the British Government to consult the Lend-lease Administration in advance about all the exports it wished to make under paragraph 4 (1) (a) of the White Paper would, Mr. Stettinius recognised, 'greatly interfere with our joint war effort'.[3]

In general, however, it would be true to say that the Lend-lease Administration remained the umpire with whom in the last resort the decision lay as to whether any export from the United Kingdom was covered by the provisions of the White Paper, and without its co-operation a workable system of export control could hardly have been evolved. There was, it must be admitted, a measure of friction and disagreement operating throughout the war, but the situation became easier when machinery had been established for regular meetings between British and American officials in Washington. Furthermore the Office of Lend-lease Administration devised a system of 'waivers' to meet cases where exports of goods from the United Kingdom, though not permissible under the provisions of the White Paper, were in the interests, directly or indirectly, of the

---

[1] Tyres and axles were deemed to be spare parts and not, therefore, eligible for exemption.

[2] The date to be taken in applying this ruling was to be either 10th September 1941 or the date of the relevant export control Order, whichever was the later.

[3] Another example of commonsense interpretation was the licensing for export of goods already made before the White Paper came into operation.

common war effort or without which serious hardship would have been experienced. These waivers were of three types: (i) individual waivers, (ii) blanket waivers for the export of a certain type of goods, e.g. card clothing, (iii) quota waivers, in cases where the United States agreed not to object to the export of a certain commodity up to a fixed limit, e.g. radio valves and tainted nickel scrap.

When, after Pearl Harbour, America became a belligerent ally, official circles in London soon began to take the view that attempts ought to be made to replace the White Paper by some bilateral instrument which would deal with the joint allocation of what were referred to as 'critical' materials. The best approach to the problem, it was thought, would be through the Combined Raw Materials Board which had been set up in Washington in January 1942. This Board would be able to compare global figures of requirements with global figures of supplies of raw materials, would then decide what proportion of the requirements could be met and would proceed to make allocations taking into account existing trade channels, economy in shipping, production capacity and availability of man-power. A major advantage of such an arrangement would be that in place of the allocation of raw materials by the United States to the United Kingdom there would be joint decisions and joint control, though with a pooling of resources there would be some loss of the freedom which the United Kingdom then enjoyed with regard to supplies which it did not obtain from America. Another advantage would be that proper attention would be devoted to the requirements of third countries, since at the time it was thought that there was some danger that the United States might devote such a large proportion of their resources to home production, either for war purposes or for civilian consumption, that the urgent needs of Allied countries might be neglected.

The idea of devising joint export programmes for goods made from critical materials was put forward and received support from the United States. But it was clear that a fairly long period was likely to elapse before any programmes could be worked out and put into operation. Meanwhile, as an immediate fact, the obligations of the Whtie Paper remained. Could anything be done to mitigate its irksome restrictions? The British Ambassador thought that the best way of dealing with the interim period, before there were agreed export programmes, would be to have a simple bilateral declaration, which after referring to the joint statement made by the United States President and the British Prime Minister in the establishment of the Combined Raw Materials Board would affirm the mutual dependence of the two countries and pledge them to devote all supplies of scarce materials to the war effort, permitting only such exports to neutrals as would be jointly found to be desirable.

The American authorities, however, took the view that the provisions of the White Paper were still very much in force and that it would be unwise to make any frontal attack on them. They were prepared to agree that where joint export programmes had actually been arranged they should be regarded as overriding the relevant provisions of the White Paper, but they thought it dangerous to go further than this. 'The continuation of the policy indicated in the White Paper', the Lend-lease Administration stated in April 1942, 'is definitely in the interests of both countries. Its retention will reassure the people of the United States that their contribution through lend-lease is being used to the greatest advantage'.

Thus it seemed that the entry of America into the war had made less difference to export problems than had been expected and that the most that could be achieved would be a more liberal interpretation of the terms of the White Paper. The matter was taken up with Mr. Stettinius when he visited London in July 1942. It was pointed out to him that the United Kingdom would have preferred a simple joint declaration concerning the devotion of resources to the common effort, but had recognised that this was not politically feasible. The hope was expressed that there might be some amendment of the troublesome provision of the White Paper about the use in exports of materials that were scarce in the United States. Ultimately the best arrangement would appear to lie in the formulation of joint export programmes for the supply of goods to the non-Axis world.

The discussion of joint export programmes will be considered in the next chapter, when it will be seen how disappointingly slow and inadequate was the progress made in this direction. The persistent efforts made by the United Kingdom during the years 1942–44 to escape from the restrictions of the White Paper will also be examined. Already, however, it had been made clear that the political situation in the United States taken in conjunction with its economic preponderance would make the way out from self-imposed entanglements a difficult one.

CHAPTER VIII

EXPORTS: PROBLEMS OF ANGLO-AMERICAN CO-OPERATION

(i)

White Paper Negotiations Continued

BY the end of 1942 little if any progress had been made towards a broader treatment of the problems raised by the lend-lease White Paper. In November 1942 Mr. Stettinius, the Lend-lease Administrator, pointed out that his assent, given nearly a year earlier, to the presumption by the British authorities that goods which they judged essential to Empire and Allied countries were unobtainable in the United States represented an interim arrangement and that it had been expected that the United Kingdom would 'within a reasonable time . . . inform us of all classes of exports being made' and that joint consultation and programming would be established. In fact the negotiation of export programmes had been an extremely slow business, partly on account of lack of statistics and shortage of manpower, and, thus, 'as a result, the temporary presumption of unobtainability would seem to be lengthening into a permanent arrangement'. Again, it had been temporarily agreed that the United Kingdom might continue exports of agricultural tools to Latin American countries, though United States manufacturers who were familiar with these requirements had sufficient capacity to meet them in full. Steps should therefore, Mr. Stettinius suggested, immediately be taken to make the White Paper effective, pending the formulation of export programmes, by means of advance consultation and agreement on proposed United Kingdom exports. As a first measure the United Kingdom might submit export statistics for 1942, since information of this sort would obviously be needed if the United States and the United Kingdom were to co-ordinate their export policies so as to meet the minimum requirements of third countries.

It was clear that few concessions were being made to the British point of view and at the beginning of 1943 there was growing irritation and uneasiness in Britain over the failure to achieve more positive results from Anglo-American discussions. The uneasiness was mainly about the long-term future. While the war was at its height it was inevitable that exports should contract severely. There was indeed a strong case for maintaining, if not the White Paper itself, at least some agreed restriction on British exports which would protect the United Kingdom from American criticism.

But the British Government had to think further ahead. And it had to reckon with criticism not only from Americans but from its own exporters, who feared that some American firms were exploiting the situation to drive them out of traditional markets, particularly those in Latin America, and were using the British White Paper obligations as a springboard for a post-war export drive. And, indeed, there seemed to be some justification for these fears when it was found that even where export programmes were submitted the Americans began querying them because they were inconsistent with the provisions of the White Paper. By 1943 it had become evident that these restrictions must be swept away within reasonable time in order to pave the way for that post-war expansion of exports which was a condition of the United Kingdom's economic survival.

There were also some short-period considerations. There was the problem of the sterling holdings of South American countries who might be unwilling to go on accumulating sterling in default of exports of goods to them. Chile was already making difficulties about selling nitrates against sterling. It had also been agreed in London in June 1942 that there should be no further significant reduction of United Kingdom exports to Latin America. Then there was always the danger that some country might go short of needed supplies. The fact that a proposed export from the United Kingdom had been ruled inconsistent with the provisions of the White Paper gave no guarantee that the United States would undertake to supply the requirements.

Nevertheless the American scrutiny of United Kingdom exports continued, the Americans contending that in some cases goods were being exported from the United Kingdom on the ground that they were unobtainable in the United States, though they were for all practical purposes identical with supplies currently received on lend-lease. For this reason there was a long and laborious investigation of cranes, hoists and pumps, large quantities of which had been supplied under lend-lease. The inquiry was not completed, but it did show four things. First, the combined manufacturing capacity of the two countries was quite insufficient to meet all essential needs. Secondly, many of the exports were not part of normal commercial trade; for example there was contractors' plant sent overseas for the making of airfields and subsequently re-imported. Thirdly, many of the exports had been approved by American officers reporting to the Combined Munitions Assignment Board, but not by the Office of Lend-lease Administration. Fourthly, the exports listed in the trade returns included parts which were covered by the exemptions laid down in the White Paper.

Meanwhile, at the beginning of 1943, a crisis had arisen over the question whether the United Kingdom should continue its exports of agricultural hand tools and bicycles. When these commodities were discussed by the Combined Export Markets Committee which had been set up in Washington, the American representatives claimed, partly on White Paper considerations, partly on other grounds such as the waste involved in double shipment of steel, that the United States should take over the whole of overseas markets in both.[1]

In May 1943 the President of the Board of Trade decided to put the whole problem of the combined planning of exports and of lend-lease restrictions before his colleagues. He said that he fully accepted the policy of combined Anglo-American planning to meet the minimum civilian requirements of the non-Axis world, but he pointed out three dangers in the current situation. First, there was the increasing restiveness of British industrialists arising from the feeling that their traditional markets were being handed over to American exporters. Secondly, there was the uncertainty as to whether the Americans really would be able to supply the requirements of the non-Axis world as they became more fully mobilised. Thirdly, there was evidence that the Americans were using the White Paper as an instrument for pressing their point of view in the formulation of joint export programmes. He himself wished to see the supersession of the White Paper as soon as possible and its replacement by a joint declaration on the part of the two Governments pledging them to see that sacrifices made by exporters of either nation in the interests of a better planning of resources would not be taken advantage of by the other after the war. Combined planning had seemed to mean in most cases a transfer of the source of supply to the United States. The principle which it ought to embody should rather be that transfers of production should only be arranged when it was clear that a substantial and speedy gain to the war effort would result by doing so.

The special problem of Latin America was also raised at this time in despatches from the British Ambassador in Washington, who had been disquieted by the evidence which had come to his notice of American attempts to eliminate British commercial interests and influence in this part of the world, and to establish there a 'quasi-exclusive United States predominance'. He thought that the time had come to put the British point of view firmly before the danger of a collision of interests had become really acute. The Foreign Secretary and the President of the Board of Trade supported the Ambassador's views and suggested that 'we must begin to prepare the ground, not in any competitive spirit but because we cannot afford to let the

---

[1] For a fuller discussion of these questions see pp. 170–1.

Latin Americans think we have lost interest in them'. It should be explained to the United States that, while the United Kingdom would allow nothing to interfere with the war effort and would not depart from an agreed war-time division of markets or raise its exports above recent levels, it would show its interests in Latin American markets by increasing its 'factual propaganda and prestige advertising' and by reinforcing its overseas commercial organisation.

Ministers agreed that there was a distinction between the short-term problem and the long-term problem. In the short-term there was little if any possibility of expanding exports; that was precluded by the shortages of materials, labour, capacity and shipping. The only trouble here was the introduction of White Paper considerations into discussions about the combined planning of exports. The long-term problem was much more serious. 'The widespread impression', the President of the Board of Trade said, 'of our dependence on the goodwill of the United States for the maintenance of many of our traditional lines of export tends to undermine confidence abroad in our future capacity as a great exporting nation. Nor, when the time comes, shall we be able to expand our exports without friction, if our stocks of raw material in hand are regarded as being subject to the provisions of the White Paper; we have been given to understand that, even when stocks of material obtained from the United States on lend-lease are exhausted, the Americans are not necessarily prepared to allow us a free hand to export products which contain that material because there may still be stocks of products manufactured from material obtained before lend-lease supplies ceased'. Yet to restore exports in the post-war period was essential if the balance-of-payments problem which would then confront Great Britain was even to approach solution.

These views were put to the Ambassador with instructions to press for the supersession of the White Paper or, at the least, for a mitigation of its rigour. The document no longer harmonised with Anglo-American partnership in a common war effort and had become increasingly a source of irritation and friction. Nor was it altogether reasonable that the United Kingdom should be in the position of being unable to modify or withdraw a statement of policy which it had itself put forward. British interests, it was emphasised, would be best served if the White Paper were replaced by a formal declaration made by both Governments to the effect that exports from either country would be determined by the best use of resources for essential war-time purposes and that sacrifices in world markets made by the exporters of either nation in the interests of a better planning of resources would not be taken advantage of by the other after the war. If the Ambassador found it impossible to make progress along these lines —and it was appreciated how difficult it would be politically for the

United States Government to join in a statement of this sort—then he should try to get the Americans to agree to the withdrawal of paragraph 4 of the White Paper, provided that their consent was made public in a statement by Mr. Cordell Hull which would at the same time express agreement with the two principles mentioned in the proposed bilateral declaration.

The attempt to secure modification or supersession of the White Paper proved, however, fruitless, and the next effort to come to grips with the problem was not made until February 1944 when Sir Samuel Beale, a business member of the Industrial and Export Council, went to Washington at the request of the President of the Board of Trade to conduct negotiations. During the months preceding his visit the situation had changed in various ways. In the first place the position of the United Kingdom had been to some extent strengthened by the fact that since July 1943 it had been made clear that the British had not only been receiving lend-lease supplies from America but had themselves been engaged in reverse or reciprocal aid to the United States. Secondly, the discussions centring round the joint programming of exports had broken down and it had been recognised that the field in which combined planning of civilian production could be applied was limited. Thirdly, there had been a shift of emphasis on the American side from 'scarce' materials to manufactured articles received on lend-lease or identical or 'fully substitutable' with goods so received.

After some weeks of negotiation it seemed that Sir Samuel Beale had succeeded in obtaining American agreement to a statement that would considerably ease the situation. There would be a bilateral declaration under which the two Governments would undertake identical and reciprocal obligations, though, of course, as lend-lease greatly exceeded reciprocal aid these obligations would weigh more heavily on the United Kingdom. The British need to export in order to support the common war effort and to obtain from third countries goods required for the prosecution of the war would be recognised. The United Kingdom would be able to resume exports hitherto disallowed under the provisions of the White Paper by taking materials off lend-lease and paying the Americans for them.[1] Both Governments would pledge themselves, however, not to use any material obtained on lend-lease or reciprocal aid in exports without the consent of the other. Finally, machinery would be set up to secure agreement in advance about exports that would raise supply difficulties.

Nevertheless what appeared to be the hopeful beginning of a resumption by the United Kingdom of her export freedom ended in failure. Further discussion showed that the Americans were proposing

---

[1] It was estimated that the cost of doing this would amount to 70 million dollars a year.

to interpret the draft documents in a manner which was both unexpected and unwelcome. They raised for the first time the question of military supplies received on lend-lease terms and similar to those which might be exported. They proposed that agreement should be secured in advance to any exports which were similar to goods *imported on military programmes* into the United Kingdom or the United States. As there were large United States forces in the United Kingdom and there seemed no likelihood of any United Kingdom forces being stationed in the United States the proposal could hardly be regarded as anything but one-sided. In default of any assurance that, if adopted, it would be administered in a reasonable manner there seemed, in view of past unhappy experience with the White Paper, no point in continuing the discussions and the negotiations broke down.

It was evident, however, that the matter would have to be taken up again and that a renewed attempt would have to be made to reach agreement. The opportunity for a new approach to the problem was provided by the conference between the British Prime Minister and the American President at Quebec in September 1944 when the question of lend-lease·and reciprocal aid in the period between the defeat of Germany and the defeat of Japan was discussed. The defeat of Germany would make possible some redistribution of effort in the two countries, and, subject to the requirements of the Japanese war, would presumably permit some recovery of British export trade.

It was agreed at the Quebec conference that mutual aid should continue after the end of the war in Europe and until the defeat of Japan and that a joint committee should be set up in Washington to determine its scope and scale. At the same time the Prime Minister emphasised that, if the United Kingdom were once more to pay its . way in the world, its export trade, which had shrunk to very small dimensions, must be re-established. Naturally no goods obtained on lend-lease or 'identical' thereto would be exported to other countries, but it was essential that the United States should not attach any conditions to supplies delivered to the United Kingdom on lend-lease terms which would jeopardise the recovery of the latter's overseas trade. Mr. Roosevelt expressed his agreement with this point of view.

The way was now open for fresh negotiations, which were conducted by Lord Keynes and which led to agreement in November 1944. This agreement covered the following points:—

(i) The United Kingdom would no longer import on lend-lease terms most manufactured articles for civilian purposes which were 'identical to or fully substitutable' with those which it was likely to export.

(ii) The United Kingdom would be ready to pay cash for any

other manufactured goods which it was receiving on lend-lease, if it found that it was exporting 'identical or fully substitutable' goods.

(iii) A number of raw materials—metals and chemicals—would not be obtained at all from the United States; or, if they were, cash would be paid for them.

(iv) The remaining raw materials would be regarded as subject to the principle of substitution, i.e. if their use in export exceeded supplies from sources other than lend-lease cash would be paid for the excess.

(v) Both countries agreed to take steps to ensure that their exporters did not obtain a competitive advantage over those of the other as a result of the war situation.

The British authorities hoped that the relaxations provided for in this agreement, which would have re-established freedom to export, would come into effect as from 1st January 1945. The assurance was, of course, given to the Americans that the United Kingdom would devote its resources to the prosecution of the wars against Germany and Japan and that there would be no general reconversion of industry or expansion of exports before VE-day. Nevertheless it was the British view that the White Paper would cease to operate as from 1st January and that its provisions would not be invoked so as to prevent the use for export of odd pockets of capacity which might become available. The Foreign Economic Administration, which had succeeded OLLA as the American custodian of the White Paper, took a different view. It held that the White Paper remained in force until VE-day and that applications should continue till then to be made to it for 'waivers' for exports of goods affected by its terms. It affirmed once more that decisions and recommendations of combined boards and committees did not *per se* constitute waivers of White Paper requirements. It did, however, indicate its readiness to take administrative action which would from 1st January secure to the United Kingdom that measure of export freedom which it would have had if the new arrangements had come into force on that date. Thus, in effect, as from 1st January the United Kingdom regained liberty to use in exports certain materials which it was ceasing to take on lend-lease terms—iron and steel, copper, zinc and nickel. The British Government, for its part, undertook that as from the same date it would transfer supplies from lend-lease to cash if it intended to export goods made from materials 'identical or fully substitutable with' these supplies. In point of fact, therefore, the White Paper, though formally retained for political reasons, did cease from the beginning of 1945 to exert any restrictive influence on British export trade. The outcome of the negotiations was communicated to the House of Commons by the Prime Minister on 30th November 1944.

He claimed that 'it would be possible for exporters, henceforward, to make plans with the assurance that they will be able to give effect to those plans with the least possible time-lag when the defeat of Germany releases manpower, capacity and materials'.[1]

In making the agreement, however, the Americans had reserved the right to examine the programme of lend-lease imports in comparison with United Kingdom exports. This was not done with a view to criticising or 'policing' British exports, but in order to arrange for the removal of items from lend-lease in cases in which it appeared that the United Kingdom was exporting goods which were 'identical or substitutable'. By the time that an American representative had arrived—May 1945—to conduct the inquiry, the field of investigation had considerably narrowed. Civilian supplies had been removed from lend-lease, as had also many military items which were no longer required or were required only for shipment outside the country. There remained only the following items which it seemed probable that the United Kingdom was obtaining on lend-lease terms and also exporting: tyres, agricultural machinery, office machinery, some NAAFI stores, motor vehicles' components and spare parts, medical supplies, quartermasters' stores, signal stores. The investigation was a troublesome one; there was the inherent difficulty of deciding whether an item was 'substitutable' and this necessitated prolonged discussions with technical experts. It was also complicated by the shifting basis on which it was carried out, since lend-lease programmes were under constant review throughout the period. In the end it appeared that the list could be narrowed down to tyres, drugs, intermediates for drugs and certain quartermasters' stores, and that these items would have to be removed from lend-lease programmes. The report of the American representative was not in fact completed until after lend-lease had terminated in August 1945. Much time and labour had been devoted to an investigation which had yielded small and unimportant results. Such results, however, as were obtained showed that any exports that were taking place from the United Kingdom of goods 'identical' with those obtained on lend-lease did not in fact constitute a serious abuse of the agreement.

(ii)

Combined Programming and Planning

Having followed the White Paper negotiations through to the end of the war we must now look back again and trace the development of Anglo-American combined programming and planning.

---

[1] H. of C. Deb., Vol. 406, Cols. 69–74.

M

EXPORT PROGRAMMES

The attempt to integrate the export policies and programmes of the United States and Britain developed from two sources. First, the formulation of joint programmes appeared to offer an opportunity of escape from the restrictions of the lend-lease White Paper. The point that such programmes would override the provisions of the White Paper was definitely made in March 1942 in a memorandum of the British Government to Mr. Harriman, and was accepted by the Office of Lend-lease Administration. Secondly, there was a movement in 1942, with much wider implications, towards a joint planning of resources to meet civilian requirements. At this time there seemed to be a danger that the United States in taking steps to concentrate civilian production would pay insufficient attention to the needs of other countries which they alone could satisfy. The job of concentrating American industry became focused in June 1942 on an End (later Standard) Products Committee, a committee of the War Production Board which was set up to consider the requirements and production of finished goods made by industries which either were to be converted to war production or consumed scarce materials. The business of this committee was to estimate minimum total requirements on these industries whether from the United States or from abroad and then either to leave just sufficient capacity in existence to meet them or to close the industry down after having created a stockpile considered adequate to satisfy requirements until June 1944. There seemed to be a serious possibility that the Americans might overdo this concentration, particularly if they did not receive as full and detailed a picture as possible of the minimum requirements of the non-Axis world. In view of the considerable unused capacity for production latent in the American economy these fears proved before long to be much exaggerated, but in 1942 they played a part in the move towards programming, since the Americans would clearly wish to know what proportion of total requirements could be supplied by the United Kingdom. In a memorandum of December 1942 by the Board of Trade, the position was set out as follows: 'until recently cuts in exports could be made in reasonable hope that overseas markets would be able to secure supplies from the United States or other sources. Now, however, rapid conversion of United States industry to war purposes and the as yet rudimentary development of effective Government control over civil supplies in the United States itself has made this an unsafe assumption. If certain vital civil supplies are to be maintained in the United Kingdom and overseas this can only be done by combined planning with the United States.'

As both sides were agreed that some measure of joint programming of exports was desirable it was not long before machinery was set up in Washington to handle the matter. In June 1942 a Combined Export Markets Committee was created to work out commodity programmes for both materials and finished goods.

The advantages to be derived from a co-ordination of the export policies of the two countries were fairly clear. Simply as a matter of effective organisation something of the sort was necessary in order to prevent duplication of effort in supplying the requirements of third countries. More generally co-ordination in the export field would be an integral part of the economic strategy of the war which was concerned to see the optimum use of the resources—labour, materials, capacity, shipping—of the Allied Nations. Political considerations, the White Paper or the treatment of neutrals would be subsidiary to this main aim.

Programming along these lines would of course have been a joint arrangement covering the exports of the United Kingdom and the United States, and co-ordinating with them, where necessary, the exports of third countries; India, for example, would come into discussions of textile exports. It needs therefore to be emphasised that the 'export programmes' actually submitted by the United Kingdom were usually in quite a different category. A number of them were supplied in order to secure the approval of the Lend-lease Administration to broad arrangements covering a certain class of exports; they gave information in general terms about the available surplus in the United Kingdom for export and about overseas requirements, together with justification in certain cases, for example in the Latin American markets, of the exports of the commodity in question. Statements of this sort submitted for American information or approval were clearly something very different from an integration of the export policies of the two countries. In very few cases were joint export programmes formally agreed between the United Kingdom and the United States. There were various reasons for the failure of this attempt at co-ordination.

In the first place there was the statistical and technical problem of formulating requirements. It was repeatedly urged on British representatives by American officials that plans could only be based on fairly comprehensive and detailed statistical information. It was emphasised that joint programming of exports presupposed estimates of the total import requirements of third countries together with information about local production, where that was important, and about United Kingdom capacity to supply. But a large part of the information was frequently not available, and could only be obtained with a disproportionate expenditure of time and clerical labour. For example, lack of adequate statistical data was found to be the major factor limiting the formation of joint export plans in the sphere of chemicals. These difficulties were not surprising: as we have seen, the Lend-lease Administration had been unable to fulfil its ambitious scheme for presenting a complete picture of the demands of the Allied Nations upon the resources of the United States.

There was also the problem of the definitions used in classifying commodities. Thus for hollow-ware, where an export programme was highly desirable owing to shortage of capacity in the United Kingdom, the chief difficulty had been that 'the United States have been employing definitions which involve a degree of precision which the United Kingdom have been unable to emulate'. Again, in dealing with export programmes for paper it was found that the American classification of papers differed materially from that in use in the United Kingdom.

Secondly, there was a number of commodities for which programmes of any sort were quite clearly unsuitable. There were, on the one hand, goods whose demand and supply conditions precluded arrangements of this kind. Most capital goods fell in this category. Some types were normally made to meet special requirements. Others, for which a production programme could have been drawn up, were subject so far as the requirements of any particular area were concerned to irregular demands which made it necessary to approve individual requirements as they arose. On the other hand there were goods for which there could be no question of anything in the nature of a *joint* programme. These were things for the manufacture of which there was a shortage of production capacity in the United Kingdom, and for which therefore the United States must be regarded as practically the sole source of supply. Here the British interest was limited to averting the danger that essential Empire and Allied requirements would not be met.

This British concern points to the third consideration that militated against the successful outcome of joint discussions with regard to the programming of exports. There was often a mistrust, not perhaps so much of American physical capacity, as of the ability of the United States rapidly to build up an administrative organisation which could, without undue friction and delay, arrange for the supply of the wants of countries with whose economies it was unfamiliar. For example, while there had on general grounds been good reason for transferring the burden of meeting various colonial requirements from the straitened economy of the United Kingdom on to the ample resources of the United States doubts soon began to arise as to whether the Americans could supply the goods in time. There were the difficulties of creating a sufficiently flexible administrative machine and of establishing new trading links, to which was added the American insatiable thirst for statistical data which the Colonies were often unable to supply.

Lastly, there was the unwelcome tendency of the Americans to introduce the White Paper as a factor in discussions about joint export arrangements. This was not perhaps actually inconsistent with the understanding that joint programmes, when agreed, would override the provisions of the White Paper, but it conflicted with the British view of the position. Unfortunately for the British case arguments based on the White Paper were sometimes reinforced by general economic considerations which were difficult to answer. Thus in the case of agricultural hand tools the Americans maintained that the United States should supply the needs of the whole non-Axis world, not only because exports from the United Kingdom were precluded by the terms of the White Paper, but also because of the differences in the labour supply situation in the two countries and because of the waste involved in a double shipment of steel.

The problem of the transference of the source of supply in any given case from the United Kingdom to the United States was not a simple one. In rapidly changing conditions it could not be solved, in terms of economic analysis, by an application of the principle of marginal advantage, even had that principle been familiar to the official representatives of the two countries. In fact there had been a tendency on the British side to look to the United States as a residual supplier of the needs of third countries. This tendency had shown itself before Pearl Harbour and it included traditional British markets. Given the differences in the general supply situation in the two countries this was a very proper application of war-time economic strategy. But the balance of argument shifted when it became a question of transferring aggregate demands from the United Kingdom to the United States as a source of supply. The estimate of the advantage to be obtained was much more difficult and any conclusion must be attended by a considerable margin of error. As a war-time principle the British maintained that such wholesale transferences of markets were only justified if they would yield 'substantial and rapid advantage' to the joint war effort. This was a clear statement of a point of view, but how rapid and how substantial was the advantage to be? Nor could the long-term considerations be wholly left out of account. The war would be ending in two or three years and nothing could then be more certain than that the balance of payments situation would require a massive expansion of British exports. This would be the more difficult to achieve if traditional markets had come to lose faith in British exporting capacity and to look to America as their source of supply.

Some months after the Combined Export Markets Committee had been set up the Board of Trade proposed in March 1943 that consideration of joint export programmes should be focused on thirty-nine types of finished goods composed of scarce materials. Twelve of these had already been under discussion by the Export Markets

Committee in Washington. Care had been taken to rule out commodities which were not suitable for programming on the grounds (*a*) that they were non-essential, (*b*) that they were being considered by the Combined Production and Resources Board,[1] (*c*) that United Kingdom exports of them were negligible, (*d*) that they should be dealt with on an *ad hoc* basis.

In June 1943, however, as a result of the difficulties which had been experienced in securing agreement to joint programmes twenty-three of the items which had been put forward were for the time being withdrawn. By the end of the year it had become fairly clear that the Export Markets Committee could make no further progress. It thenceforward ceased to function, pending the outcome of the discussions that were taking place over the supersession of the White Paper. Even then of the handful of programmes which had been put into operation few had formally been adopted by the Committee.

To illustrate the difficulties in drawing up export programmes, two examples may be cited—bicycles and agricultural hand tools.

In 1942 the British representatives had approached the Americans about a joint export programme for bicycles. They appreciated that White Paper provisions would have to be taken into account and they sought some relief from the burden on the United Kingdom industry, which was mainly turned over to war production.[2] They were, however, surprised to find that the Americans proposed that henceforward the United States should supply the whole of world requirements, military and civil, including those of the United Kingdom itself. In the United States, despite the operation of controls, large stocks had accumulated and the manufacturers were pressing for an extension of their markets. In discussion of this proposal the British representatives pointed to the fact that their bicycle exports were restricted to the minimum requirements of the Empire, excluding Canada, and of Allied territories in the eastern hemisphere, and indicated the immense difficulties which would be involved in such a wholesale transfer of markets; for example American repair parts were not interchangeable with those of British models. The Americans, however, were not prepared to accept the view that they should supply only marginal requirements and, in modifying their proposals, still claimed that they should meet all needs of third countries with the exception of Eire.[3] It was eventually agreed to postpone further consideration of the problem until the White Paper had been revised. Meanwhile it was becoming fairly clear that the Americans would

---

[1] See p. 174.

[2] In 1943 it was estimated that eighty per cent. of the industry's capacity was employed on the production of munitions. The export programme was 95,000 complete machines and 184,000 repair-part equivalents.

[3] At one time the Americans suggested that an appeal should be made to the Combined Production and Resources Board on this matter.

find difficulties in supplying third markets and that it was unlikely that they would press the matter any further.

Matchets, agricultural hand tools in wide use in tropical and sub-tropical areas, were a traditional British export and British manufacturers had been accustomed to producing a variety of types to suit the needs of different territories. In November 1942 as a result of requests put forward by the United States, the United Kingdom submitted to the Combined Export Markets Committee proposals for a joint export programme for matchets, suggesting that the United Kingdom should cover the needs of the eastern hemisphere and of the British and Dutch West Indies, while the Americans should be responsible for meeting the requirements of the rest of the non-Axis world. The American representatives on the Committee, however, rejected the proposals, claiming that the United States had sufficient capacity to meet all requirements. In addition to the restrictions imposed by the White Paper there were, they pointed out, the economies to be gained in shipping and labour, and they were not prepared to take into consideration the British argument that the labour employed in the United Kingdom was highly skilled and that the trade was a specialised one. This case, trivial though the resources involved were,[1] was referred to the Combined Production and Resources Board, which in effect supported the British view by concluding that the amounts of steel and labour concerned were negligible and that the combined war programme would not be affected by any transfer of production from one country to the other. In the Board's view the economy in production and shipping from the proposed transfer would not offset the disturbance of markets.[2]

It is thus not surprising that very few export programmes were finally and formally ratified in Washington. Progress was made in dealing with the following commodities: copper sulphate, cinematograph film, sewing machines, steel pen points, crown corks, electric lamps and lamp-making materials. However, even when export programmes had been worked out they were not necessarily formally adopted by the Combined Export Markets Committee. Such agreement as could be secured usually found expression in some sort of zoning arrangement, under which, broadly, the markets in the western hemisphere were assigned to the United States and those in the eastern hemisphere were allocated to the United Kingdom. In some cases, for example dry batteries and typewriters, proposals for joint export programmes broke down because it was found that United Kingdom exports were negligible.

---

[1] It was estimated that 177 persons were employed in the United Kingdom industry, most of them in the Birmingham area; production for commercial export consumed only 2,000 tons of steel.

[2] The matter was ultimately settled more directly through the appropriate controls in London and Washington.

Apart from the activities of the Combined Export Markets Committee steps were taken towards a co-ordination of British and American export policies in certain parts of the non-Axis world. These arrangements were described as 'area programming' as against 'commodity programming', that is to say they aimed at making provision for the supply of the *total* requirements of particular areas through a division of responsibilities between the United Kingdom and the United States. Perhaps the best example of such an arrangement was to be found in the Middle East Supply Centre, which, starting as a purely British piece of administrative machinery, became in every sense a combined organisation with British and American officials serving side by side in all its divisions. The recommendations of M.E.S.C. became the basis of an agreed programme for the division of responsibility for the supply of the long-term requirements of the Middle East territories. Elsewhere attempts at area programming proved on the whole unsuccessful. It was tried in the French and Belgian African territories where tripartite committees, composed of United Kingdom, United States and local representatives, were set up to prepare schedules of total requirements. Programmes took months to work out and, moreover, it was impossible to draw up in advance comprehensive lists of all requirements. Even then agreement about responsibility for supply was frequently unobtainable, because of the intrusion of White Paper considerations, and where agreement was reached programmes were usually not adhered to, largely because the United States did not possess the administrative machinery which could ensure that they would be carried out. At the beginning of 1944 there was a move on the British side to limit the scope of such area programming in order to pave the way for a relaxation of export controls and for restoration of freedom in overseas trade.[1] It was suggested that items such as machinery should be recognised as not suitable for export programming; similarly there was no justification for elaborating programmes for things that were not essential or not scarce. All that was required in such cases was the fixing of general limits in terms of tonnage and of values, the importing country being left to choose its source of supply. A short list was therefore drawn up of essential commodities in limited supply and by the autumn of 1944 programming was, with American acquiescence, confined to it. This arrangement was followed by some demobilisation of the apparatus of control and finally in 1945 by the substitution of a 'reserved commodity list' for the short list, which virtually brought area programming to an end. The reserved commodity list was a list compiled by the combined boards in Washington of commodities which actually were or were

---

[1] Partly, too, there was a desire to avoid the waste of administrative labour in unnecessary and over-ambitious programming of exports.

likely to be scarce and which would have their sources of supply fixed by decision of the boards. This arrangement was to form the basis of policy for supplying the requirements of liberated areas as well as those of the African Colonies.

On the whole, therefore, the results of area programming afforded another example of the failure of over-ambitious and over-rigid plans for Anglo-American co-ordination in the export field.[1] During the war there was perhaps something to be said for attempts to secure an effective organisation of supplies to meet the needs of countries which were dependent mainly on the United Kingdom and the United States. As the end of the war came in sight it was vital to the United Kingdom that there should be no formal limitations which would curtail its opportunities to recover the sectors of overseas trade which it had deliberately sacrificed for the sake of victory.

COMBINED PLANNING

Alongside attempts to devise joint Anglo-American programmes for exports there developed a movement towards a combined planning of resources for civilian production. This movement may be traced to two sources. First, there were the steps, already mentioned, which the United States were taking towards concentration of industry, in connection with which urgent requests had been made for the presentation to them of estimates of forward demands covering all requirements up to 1944. Thus in informing the Dominions of the setting up of the Commonwealth Supply Council in 1942 the United Kingdom authorities stated: 'there is thus an urgent need for prompt steps to be taken to obtain a complete picture of civil requirements from all sources so as to ensure that in co-ordinating production in the United States of America and the United Kingdom the non-munitions supplies essential to the maintenance of the full war effort of all the United Nations are adequately catered for. Otherwise the process of concentration of industry to meet military needs may through lack of planning be carried to such lengths as to endanger essential civilian needs of importing countries.'

Secondly, there was growing recognition of the importance of the civilian sector of the national economy. The Minister of Production, in a memorandum of July 1942 on the creation within his office of a non-munition supplies section, said: ' "war production" can no longer be distinguished from "civil production". What have hitherto been regarded as civil industries have for the most part been cut so far that further contraction would be likely to have harmful effects on the war effort of the country. These industries therefore require as

---

[1] Joint programming of Icelandic requirements was agreed to in the summer of 1942. The arrangement never worked smoothly and its main consequence was unduly and unnecessarily to limit Britain's export freedom. It was abandoned at the end of 1944.

assured an allocation of raw materials, capacity and labour as do those industries producing military requirements.'

Proposals for the setting up of machinery for the combined planning of non-munitions production appeared in June 1942. The need, it was pointed out, was for an assessment of the civilian requirements of the United Kingdom, the United States and the rest of the non-Axis world, which could be translated into demands on raw material and also on capacity, which was more likely to be the limiting factor. The inquiry would be undertaken in terms of individual commodities, items being accorded priority in order of urgency from the supply point of view. A good deal of work was already being done on the problem, but it was not properly co-ordinated, and there was no central point from which estimates could be made of the level below which manufacturing capacity for civilian requirements in the United States and the United Kingdom should not be allowed to fall. Requirements in this connection should cover total requirements, including those of the United States and the United Kingdom, since in a scheme for the proper allocation of resources there should be investigation and control of civilian wants in the two major exporting nations as well as in those of third countries.

The handling of these matters came in 1942 to be focused primarily on two major organisations which will now be discussed, the Combined Production and Resources Board in Washington and the Commonwealth Supply Council in London.

The Combined Production and Resources Board was set up in June 1942, its function being to 'combine the production programmes of the United States and the United Kingdom[1] into a single integrated programme' and in this connection to take account of the need for maximum use of the productive resources available to the United States, the British Commonwealth of Nations and the United Nations, 'the need to reduce demands on shipping to a minimum, and the essential needs of the civilian population'. Thus at the outset the Board seemed to represent the prevalence of grandiose ideas of international planning, and its creation appeared to suggest that the co-ordination which was being achieved in military and munitions matters was equally applicable to the civilian sphere. In January 1943 it set up a committee, the Non-Military Supplies Committee, which was to concern itself with the major economic problem of reducing civilian production in the three countries to a minimum level.[2] This Committee had three sub-committees dealing with medical supplies, textiles and leather and hides.

The Commonwealth Supply Council was set up in October 1942

---

[1] In November 1942 Canada was added to the Board.

[2] This committee became in effect the operating policy committee of the C.P.R.B., its sub-committees becoming full committees and reporting to the Board direct.

on the suggestion of the Minister of Production in order to provide an instrument for focusing Empire requirements and also for translating them where necessary into demands on the capacity of the United States. The Council included the United Kingdom ministers concerned, the High Commissioners of the Dominions (excluding Canada) and Southern Rhodesia and the representative of India at the War Cabinet.[1] It was to act as a co-ordinating body for the British Commonwealth 'in regard to production and requirements of raw materials and of finished goods, including plant, components and other things necessary for their manufacture, in order that they may be presented to the Minister of Production for integration, as the case may be, with the production and requirements either of the United Kingdom or through the Combined Production and Resources Board of North America'.

It was decided that the Council should conduct its detailed work through sub-committees, and four such committees were appointed to deal with munitions, non-munitions, raw materials and machine tools. Later two further sub-committees were set up, one on railway equipment and one on textiles, which was virtually the non-munitions committee in another form. Two sub-committees were also formed jointly with the London Food Council—a fertiliser sub-committee and a food and farm machinery sub-committee. These sub-committees came more and more to do the real work of the Council, which itself met infrequently.

One of the purposes which it was hoped the Commonwealth Supply Council would achieve would be the affording of an opportunity for consultation to the Dominions. There had, of course, in the past been a good deal of informal discussion with Dominion High Commissioners about export policies and programmes for particular commodities, but the aim would now be to have regular and systematic discussions so that the Dominions would have no justification for feeling that their claims were being treated in an arbitrary or partial manner.

The main object, however, in setting up this new piece of machinery was to co-ordinate the demands of the British Commonwealth upon the economy of the United States. There was always the fear that the Americans would, especially if sufficiently detailed information were not supplied to them,[2] make insufficient provision within the framework of their war-time planning for the requirements of overseas countries. 'The pressure from Washington', the Minister

---

[1] It was expected that the Council would also collect information about the requirements of friendly neutrals in the eastern hemisphere, for example through the machinery of the Middle East Supply Centre.

[2] The attempt of the Lend-lease Administration to assemble a library of requirements for non-munitions goods covering a period of two or three years ahead has already been mentioned.

of Production stated, 'for world-wide programmes of requirements is steadily increasing'. The new procedure would mean the assembling of such programmes in London, estimation of United Kingdom ability to supply, and transmission of programmes and estimates to Washington, where the authority of the combined boards might be exerted to ensure that sufficient American capacity was set aside to meet uncovered requirements.

The setting up of the Commonwealth Supply Council led to some discussion with the Dominion Governments of its functions. The Dominions, who had strong missions in Washington, argued that while London might be the proper place for the discussion of what was mainly British supply policy, Washington was the place where consideration should be given to commodities the bulk of which was drawn from American sources. It was pointed out in reply that the object of the new organisation was the complete co-ordination of Commonwealth programmes which, it was thought, could best be done in London because in the past the United Kingdom had been the chief source of supply for the Commonwealth. It was further suggested that a distinction should be drawn between on the one hand the presentation of lists of requirements as a routine matter and the ordinary placing of orders which could be performed by the Dominion missions in Washington, and on the other hand the operation at a high level of combined planning which was to be confined to 'critical' items.

Eventually it was agreed that parallel to the Non-Munitions Committee there should be set up in Washington a committee representative of the United Kingdom and the Dominion supply missions. This involved a division of functions between London and Washington, mainly in terms of the relative importance of the United Kingdom or United States of America as a source of supply. The parallel committee was known as the Principal Commonwealth Supply Committee.

The mention of 'critical' items indicates the more restricted view that was taken of planning in the later phases of the war. Comprehensive planning of all requirements was seen to be too vast a task, particularly in view of the limited amount of manpower available for the job. In the main, moreover, the Non-Munitions Committee in London became concerned with the problem of supplying the Lend-lease Administration with standardised information about Commonwealth requirements. Even when this problem had been reduced to more manageable dimensions by agreement to concentrate on a small number of commodities,[1] the difficulties that confronted the

---

[1] Apart from raw materials and commodities which were held to be more suitable for the Principal Commonwealth Supply Committee in Washington, there were only eight items which were dealt with.

Committee were pretty considerable. And the Americans were disposed to press for a month-by-month programme of new short lists of selected items, a task which was regarded by the British authorities as quite impracticable. Added to this there was disagreement between departments in London about the scope of combined planning. Thus so far as planning was concerned, the Non-Munitions Committee's activities were really confined to cotton textiles. These are discussed below.

Very little, then, had been accomplished in London in the way of combined planning, and attention needs to be directed across the Atlantic to Washington. It had been agreed on the British side that progress would best be made if discussions about planning were restricted in the first instance to a few groups of commodities for which there were or were likely to be supply difficulties. Accordingly, in November 1942 twelve items were proposed to the Americans as a first list of commodities for combined planning: agricultural machinery, textiles, footwear, electric lamps, mining machinery, electric motors, air and gas compressors, pumps, water tube boilers and boiler-house plant, textile machinery, office machinery including typewriters, electric cables. At the same time it was suggested that if the Americans agreed to the list they should try to arrange that no further cuts in the production of any of these items should take place until the matter had been referred to the Combined Production and Resources Board. Soon two further items were added—medical supplies, for which sub-committees were set up in London and Washington, and internal combustion engines. However, after a preliminary investigation it was agreed to reduce the list, and by April 1943 discussions about combined planning had been restricted to agricultural machinery, textiles and medical supplies.[1]

(a) Textiles

The cotton textile problem was, as we have already seen, a serious one. The elimination of Japanese supplies and the reduced output of the Lancashire cotton industry had produced a situation of scarcity in the eastern hemisphere which had only been relieved by a considerable expansion of Indian exports. Now the Indian contribution was falling off, and it was natural that assistance should be sought from the textile capacity of the United States. The Americans were not normally large exporters but their total output was large as a proportion of world supplies. The real problem was the scarcity of cotton piece-goods, though the investigations which were undertaken nominally covered the whole range of textiles.

In Washington it was agreed that the problem was an urgent one

---

[1] The Medical Supplies Sub-committee of the Combined Producton and Resources Board was the first to be established—in November 1942.

and in February 1943 the Non-Military Supplies Committee of the Combined Production and Resources Board set up a textiles sub-committee to go into it. This sub-committee at once reported that the Combined Production and Resources Board should as a first step recommend the national authorities 'to prevent such withdrawal of labour from the textile industries as would result in a loss of production in the industry as a whole'.

As a preliminary to any further recommendations or policy decisions the main task was to draw up estimates of world demands and supplies. This was a difficult job, because of differences in national techniques and in the definitions adopted for statistical purposes. Four questionnaires were, however, devised covering capacity, production and requirements for cotton and rayon piece goods, woollen and worsted fabrics, knitwear and miscellaneous cotton and rayon items such as thread and cordage.[1] The statistical information, for which the United States, the United Kingdom[2] and Canada made themselves responsible, would not cover the requirements of the whole of the non-Axis world—those for relief, for China and for Russia were to be dealt with separately—and the picture that was finally presented must be regarded as an incomplete one. In fact, even such a limited survey as this was only made of the position in cotton piece-goods; the figures for woollen and worsted fabrics covered only part of the field; while for the other items the data supplied were practically confined to the United Kingdom, the United States and Canada.

The 1943 estimates for cotton piece-goods were as follows:—

TABLE 5   Million linear yards

	Production	Requirements	(+) Exportable surplus	or	(−) Import requirements
United States .	11,248	10,068	+ 1,180		
India . . .	6,400	5,800	+ 600		
United Kingdom .	1,901	1,674	+ 227		
Brazil . .	1,300	1,000	+ 300		
Canada . .	320	601	}		− 2,364*
Others . .	1,371	3,340	+ 115 }		
Total . .	22,540	22,483	+ 2,421		− 2,364

* British Empire 1,247, M.E.S.C. 240, French Africa 283, Argentina 150, Others 444.

On the whole, therefore, there was a balance of demands and supplies, the aggregate surpluses of 2,421 million yards being slightly in excess of the aggregate deficiencies amounting to 2,364 million

---

[1] There was also a fifth questionnaire for the purpose of obtaining general information about controls, rationing, quotas, etc.

[2] The information was to be obtained through the Non-Munitions Committee in London, so far as the British Empire (other than Canada and Newfoundland) was concerned.

yards. But it was quite clearly a precarious balance, as no account had been taken of Chinese, Russian or relief requirements which were bound to be large. Furthermore, with regard to the future, it presumed that there would be no marked change in levels of production and consumption, in particular that military demands would not increase and that civilian consumption would be kept down to minimum standards. Finally, there was the problem of the control and redistribution of supplies. What machinery was available, for example, to secure that the United States surplus went, not to domestic consumers, but to relieve the deficiencies of the eastern hemisphere?

The main recommendation of the Textile Sub-committee was that the major exporting countries—the United States, the United Kingdom, Brazil and India—must accept as a minimum figure an aggregate net export of 2,400 million yards. Even so there would be the problem of the needs of the liberated areas, to meet which production could probably not be increased sufficiently and which would therefore call for cuts not only in military but also in civilian consumption. The interest of the sub-committee lay primarily, as has been seen, in cotton textiles. It stated that the production of woollens and worsteds fell short of requirements but it did not think that the deficit was serious.

This report provided a picture of world demands and supplies of cotton piece-goods and afforded a basis for the co-ordination of export policies. But care must be taken in interpreting the phrase 'combined planning'. The Combined Production and Resources Board could make recommendations to national authorities, but it had not the authority nor did it ever attempt to override their decisions. It provided a forum for discussion about scarce commodities, but its ability to secure that its views about the steps to be taken to deal with scarcities should be translated into action was clearly restricted. In America the allocating authority was the Divisional Requirements Committee of the War Production Board, and there the needs of overseas countries had to compete against the strong claims of the domestic consumer and of the military authorities. In the United Kingdom the allocating authority was the Materials Committee.[1] In the sphere of textiles close co-ordination had been achieved with the Indian Government. And if an example of combined planning were to be sought it would be found rather in the relations of Britain and India than in the relations between Britain and America. Thus it turned out that what was really required, namely a transfer of a large part of the burden of supplying the eastern hemisphere with cotton textiles on to the shoulders of the

---

[1] See p. 127.

Americans, was hard to achieve, partly because of the allocation problem[1] and partly because of the difficulty of making new market connections.

In November 1943 a new textile committee was appointed with extended terms of reference. On it were represented the United States, the United Kingdom and Canada, Canada being included not because she was an exporter but because her industry was linked with that of the United States. In April 1945 an Indian representative was added,[2] and at the same time steps were taken to secure co-ordination with Brazil which had become a major exporter of cotton textiles. By this time the position had still further deteriorated. Production in the United States, United Kingdom and India had fallen while military demands had been increasing. The committee felt itself unable to recommend as high an export allocation for either the United States or the United Kingdom for the second half of 1944 as it had done for the first half, and it admitted that its programme would barely meet the most essential needs of the importing countries. Finally, there was the growing problem of the needs of the liberated areas. What prospect was there of meeting them, when exports for 1945 looked like being ten per cent. short of minimum requirements apart from the needs of these areas? Thus there could be no doubt that there would be a desperate shortage of cotton textiles in 1945–46 and that the machinery of control, allocation and co-ordination between the United Nations would have to be maintained if a complete breakdown were to be avoided.

(b) Agricultural Machinery

In taking up at an early stage the question of the combined planning of agricultural machinery British authorities were probably mainly influenced by the fear which has already been mentioned that the United States might, unless the statistical position was fully explained to them, take unduly drastic measures towards concentration of production. For many items of agricultural machinery the United States and Canada were the main sources of supply and in fact the farm equipment industry was the first major industry included in the War Production Board's programme of concentration. Along with this concern about American production policy there was of course appreciation of the increased requirements which would necessarily follow from plans to stimulate local agricultural production in order to save shipping.

In 1942 the agricultural machinery industry in the United Kingdom was not in a position to make a large contribution to overseas

---

[1] At the end of 1943 the Lend-lease Administration agreed to an allocation of 70 million yards of cotton piece-goods for the British Empire and Middle East territories, and this was implemented by the War Production Board.

[2] After the end of hostilities France was also represented on the committee.

requirements. Its main job was to furnish assistance to the home food production campaign, and these efforts had to be supplemented by considerable imports from America. The Ministry of Agriculture accordingly, in consultation with the Board of Trade and with the representatives of the Agricultural Machinery Export Group, had worked out an export programme for items of which North America was not to any important extent a source of supply, for example animal-drawn as opposed to tractor-drawn implements. For each of these items market quotas were fixed, the programme as a whole representing approximately seventy-five per cent. of production for export in 1941, itself a year of low exports.[1] Apart from spares no other exports outside the programme were to be permitted.

The machinery for combined planning was set up in London and Washington by the end of 1942. In London this machinery took the form of a sub-committee of the London Food Committee and the Non-Munitions Committee of the Commonwealth Supply Council, known as the Food and Farm Machinery Committee. It consisted of representatives of the Dominions (excluding Canada), India, Southern Rhodesia, the Colonies, the Middle East Supply Centre, together with representatives of the United Kingdom departments concerned. In Washington an Agricultural and Food Machinery Committee was set up under the auspices of the Combined Food Board, with which from November 1943 the Combined Production and Resources Board co-operated. Eastern hemisphere requirements were collected and scrutinised in London and information was then co-ordinated with that available in Washington. At the outset the major difficulty probably lay in presenting to the Americans the complete statistical picture which they required, not only about agricultural machinery but also about the cropping programmes in the different countries. This had largely been overcome by 1944 and at the same time the prospects of the supply of agricultural machinery had improved.

Towards the end of the war the question arose as to whether combined planning of agricultural machinery could be limited in its scope. Supplies were becoming easier and from the British point of view there was everything to be said for removing export restrictions on the home industry and for securing on the part of the sterling area an economy in dollars. The Board of Trade pressed strongly for the restriction of planning to those commodities which presented supply or shipping difficulties and, for the rest, for allowing importers free choice in their source of supply. British representatives in Washington, however, thought the proposed change premature and were nervous lest with American restrictions on production the breakdown

---

[1] See Table 6.

of combined planning would mean failure to meet requirements on which essential food supplies depended. After victory over Germany had been won attempts were renewed to escape from the limitation on export freedom which, from the British point of view, combined planning seemed normally to involve. It was pointed out that the United Kingdom would no longer wish nor be able to retain production or export controls over all items of agricultural machinery. This time the effort was successful and on 7th June 1945 the Combined Agricultural and Food Machinery Committee decided that as from 1st July all farm machinery should be removed from the reserved commodity list, thus in effect freeing it from combined planning. The committee itself was finally dissolved at the end of September 1945.

United Kingdom Exports of Agricultural Machinery, 1938-46

TABLE 6   thousand tons

1938	*1939*	*1940*	*1941*	*1942*	*1943*	*1944*	*1945*	*1946*
18·6	13·1	10·9	4·1	3·7	4·6	7·6	24·0	55·2

Thus in a limited sphere the achievements of combined Anglo-American planning can be recognised, provided that the expression is not taken to signify an effective control exercised from Washington over the allocation of resources for civilian supply in the United Kingdom and the United States. What was needed in the first place and what was to some extent realised was joint discussion of problems of scarcity which would result in appreciation of critical points in the civilian economies of the Allied Nations and of the remedial measures that were called for. But of all the combined boards the Combined Production and Resources Board was the weakest and it was less likely than the other boards to be able to make its views effective in the centres of decision in Washington and London.

Towards the end of the war new problems began to appear—the problem of relief and the problem of the emergence of surplus capacity as the tension of war demands slackened. There was some suggestion that the Combined Production and Resources Board should include within its activities the 'planning' of the use to be made of surpluses as they arose. But there were obvious dangers and difficulties in this proposed extension of the Board's field of operations. For the United Kingdom it appeared all too likely that planning, if effective, would mean restriction of economic opportunities, whereas what was really needed was maximum possible freedom to resume normal trading operations. Eventually a compromise was reached. It was agreed that the Board should continue its planning activities in the field of scarcities. But if there was a prospect of the emergence of a general surplus the matter should be dealt with by direct negotiation between the United States and United Kingdom Governments. Thus the Board would only be concerned with surpluses in so far as odd pockets of capacity became free from war demands. Here, moreover, it would provide a forum for the interchange of information and for discussion about adjustment of restrictions in the two economies rather than a focus for planning the use of liberated resources. The problem of scarcities was thus the real problem with which the Board had to deal. Even after it had been dissolved at the end of 1945 the Combined Textile Committee continued to function for another year in order to maintain a joint approach to one of the more acute shortage difficulties which had resulted from the dislocation of economies by the war.

CHAPTER IX

EXPORTS: THE FINAL PHASE

(i)

The General Trend

THE year 1941 had been a transitional period in the war-time history of exports. But from 1942 onwards all the forces that were combining to depress the level of British exports (they were to fall to twenty-nine per cent. of pre-war) and to change their nature and their focus were hard at work. Traditional markets had to be sacrificed to an extent unparalleled even in the inter-war period of world-wide depression and trade restrictions.

By 1942 the full effects of lend-lease were felt. The most important of these was the almost complete abandonment of currency as a criterion for exports and the substitution for it of the test of essentiality. This as we have already seen meant changes both in markets and in goods. Partly because Britain no longer needed to worry about her war-time foreign exchange needs, partly because of the American preponderance in the western hemisphere and partly because of the restrictions of the lend-lease White Paper, the United Kingdom's export trade now concentrated very largely on meeting the essential needs of the Empire and the Allies in the eastern hemisphere. Moreover, world-wide shortages naturally tended to make importing countries demand more standardised and more durable commodities and to eliminate the type of trade that had hitherto gone through normal commercial channels.

From 1942 onwards the British economy could in any case spare few resources for export. The diversion of resources to war production was moving steadily towards the peak it was to attain in 1943. And the choice between the use of resources in exports and their use in production for the home market was no longer the simple one it had been in 1939–41. In the days of the export drive the problem had been to restrain the pull of the home market in order to expand exports. This could easily be done without causing any real hardship to the consumer in the United Kingdom. But from 1942 onwards there was serious danger that the home consumer might lack minimum necessities of clothing or household goods. It was no easy matter to balance these domestic needs against some overseas demand which, if unsatisfied, might result in a lower level of food supplies to

Britain. The general problem received formal recognition in export policy when it was decided that exports to Empire countries of certain consumer goods made of metal—for example bicycles and cutlery—should be restricted in the same degree as the limitations on supplies in the home market.

There were two other influences on British export trade in the later war years that must be mentioned—the war in the Far East and acute shipping problems.

One of the main export problems that arose through the outbreak of war in the Far East was that of the 'frustration' of exports destined for countries in the war zone. Frustrated exports were not a new problem. The same difficulty had arisen early in 1941 when a complete export control over goods intended for export to certain Latin American countries had been imposed.[1] It was always liable to occur when a restriction of exports had to be introduced at short notice. When war with Japan broke out there was also the problem of the goods that had been actually shipped and were on their way and had to be diverted.

The frustration of a mass of exports, though at times inevitable, was clearly inconvenient and wasteful. The goods might have been made for a particular market and be unsaleable elsewhere. If not, then attempts would be made to divert them to other markets, or, in the last resort, to allow them to be disposed of on the home market in spite of quota or other restrictions. To settle the problem of cotton textiles intended for the Dutch East Indies an agreement was reached between the Dutch Government, the Cotton Board and the Board of Trade. The goods were diverted to West Africa, which was short of textiles. At the same time the Dutch Government agreed to share as to fifty per cent. in the losses or profits which might arise as the result of the resale of the goods in other markets.

Shipping problems affected mainly exports to South Africa and the Middle East and were associated with the progress of the campaign in North Africa. An acute shortage of shipping developed which necessitated in July and August 1942 the imposition of an 'all goods' control on exports to South Africa and Southern Rhodesia and the cancellation of outstanding export licences.[2]

Already, in the spring of 1942, goods had been piling up awaiting shipment, and it was clear that the waste of labour and material in making goods for which shipping was not available must be prevented as far as possible. The problem was by no means an easy one. South Africa was an important market and encouragement had been given there to the buying of British goods. At first it seemed that

---

[1] See p. 60.
[2] S.R. & O. 1942, Nos. 1375, 1376.

the most practicable arrangement would be for South Africa to institute import licensing for goods imported from the United Kingdom, though there were doubts whether this could be applied with sufficient speed or be operated with the necessary effectiveness to reduce the problem to manageable dimensions. In fact the South African Government showed itself unwilling, for political and administrative reasons, to impose restrictions and control had, therefore, ultimately to be introduced from the United Kingdom end. In July 1942, however, it looked as though a major crisis was developing which would have severe political and economic repercussions in South Africa. There were apparently only shipping facilities available for 5,000–6,000 tons a month, while essential cargoes with high priorities awaiting shipment amounted to 50,000–60,000 tons.

South Africa had already introduced essentiality certificates for imports and linked with these certificates was a system of priority ratings. These arrangements provided the basis for the administration of export control in the United Kingdom. It was agreed that so far as future exports were concerned export licences should only be granted for goods covered by South African certificates of essentiality with priority ratings 1–5.[1] So far as goods awaiting shipment were concerned the Conference steamship lines had established a register, and it was decided that to obtain a place on this register goods must fall within priority ratings 1–8.[2] Export licences, it was agreed, would be given to cover goods on the register.

For the time, however, the shipping crisis afforded some measure of alleviation of supply problems and was thus not without certain compensating advantages. It enabled cuts to be made in allocations for export to South Africa, particularly of cotton, rayon and woollen textiles. On the other hand there was the familiar problem of frustrated exports, though, again, through the diversion of these exports to other markets, including the home market, there was some easing of difficult supply situations.

Somewhat over a year later, in October 1943, there was some relaxation of the export restrictions which had been imposed, but by this time the supply position at home had become a much more serious factor in limiting exports.

---

[1] These priority ratings included goods needed for war purposes and urgent requirements of the more essential industries. There were sixteen ratings in all.

[2] Priority ratings 6–8 covered mainly the normal requirements of essential industries and the more important consumer goods.

(ii)
Specific Exports

The substitution of the 'essentiality' for the 'currency' criterion in the export field involved a striking reversal of policy towards exports generally and particularly textile exports. The most significant aspect of this change of policy was, perhaps, the sacrifice of markets in the western hemisphere. The demands of war production, coupled with the difficulty of compressing any further the standard of living of the British civilian, would in any case have led to a development of trade along these lines; the White Paper, which was interpreted to preclude non-essential exports made of 'vulnerable' materials, took this development further. Essentiality connoted a change not only in markets but, as we have seen, in the types of goods exported. It was inevitable that the manufacturing and trading communities were asked to make sharp and sudden adaptations and readjustments.

In the following pages about specific exports one point should be remembered. A considerable volume of exports went to meet not normal commercial demands but Allied war requirements.[1] Boots for Russia, for example, would be included in the ordinary export figures. Thus any figures given understate the effects of the war on the normal trade relations of the United Kingdom.

COTTON TEXTILES

The cotton position was dominated through the last years of the war by shortage of yarn supplies which made it increasingly difficult to maintain exports even to countries in which there was a 'famine' in textiles. Moreover, the cotton allocation scheme did not work satisfactorily. It broke down on two occasions at the end of 1941 and in 1943—when, so far as exports were concerned, the machine became clogged with arrears and orders for new production had to be suspended. An official of the Board of Trade wrote in August 1944 about cotton: 'in this country over a long period we have never been granted enough to meet our Imperial and other responsibilities on a minimum scale, and our deliveries on the whole have been bad.'

It has been seen how greatly the problem of supplying overseas countries with their cotton textile requirements had been aggravated by the loss of Japanese supplies. If the United Kingdom could not fill the gap was there any other source which could be looked to for an expansion of exports? The one country which seemed able to help and which was strategically well placed for meeting the needs of the

---

[1] From 1942 onwards munitions were shown separately in the export statistics.

eastern hemisphere was India. It had to be recognised that before the war India had been a net importer of cotton textiles, but since the war she had achieved a notable increase in exports of piece-goods.[1] At the end of 1941 the Government of India indicated its readiness to co-operate with the United Kingdom in working out an export programme for cotton textiles, and stated that it had insti-tuted a control over exports of yarn and piece-goods to all destina-tions. Co-operation, in the sense of co-ordination of United Kingdom and Indian programmes, began in 1942 when India started to operate a scheme of market quotas.[2] The arrangement worked well, and India herself was able to achieve a prodigious expansion of exports of cotton piece-goods which rose from 390·1 million yards in 1940–41 to 771·1 million yards in 1941–42 and to 819·2 million yards in 1942–43.[3] After 1942 India's contribution fell away. She herself was suffering from a shortage of consumer goods and a severe inflation of prices and could ill afford to maintain exports at the high level of 1942, particularly in face of a growing volume of internal criticism. Nevertheless the peak figure which she achieved in the early part of the war is remarkable in view of the fact already mentioned that she had been a net importer in peace-time.

Meanwhile in the United Kingdom the drastic cut in the allocation of yarn for export purposes—from 22,700 tons in the last quarter of 1941 to 13,500 tons in the second quarter of 1942—taken in con-junction with the arrears of deliveries which had developed through the faulty working of the allocation arrangements, had necessitated a major revision of the exports direction scheme. In the first place currency-earning exports were eliminated and market quotas were accordingly revised. Secondly, the framework of the scheme itself underwent reconstruction in order to adapt it to the new situation in which Dominion Governments were 'sponsoring' the requirements of their respective countries and thus tending to by-pass the merchant allocation structure. Thirdly, steps were taken to bring about stan-dardisation of fabrics for export and to integrate exports with the production planning of the Cotton Control.

In March 1942 the Cotton Board and the Board of Trade agreed on new arrangements which would be superimposed on, and would to some degree supersede, the system of market quotas for merchant converters. First, orders sponsored by the Dominions—and these

---

[1] Indian exports of piece-goods were as follows:—

			Million square yards
1938–39	.	.	177·0
1939–40	.	.	221·4
1940–41	.	.	390·1

[2] The Indian scheme was, however, unlike the United Kingdom scheme in that the quotas represented 'ceilings' rather than actual allocations.

[3] Seaborne trade of British India. India also increased her exports to Afghanistan and (by land) to Iran from 14·9 million yards (1938–39) to 37·8 million yards (1941-42).

covered, for example, the whole of the supplies for Canada and Australia—were to be taken out of the system. Secondly, practically the whole of the remainder of the cotton yarn allocation for export was to be distributed among merchants on a market basis, but the merchants would have to confine their shipments to approved lists of essential abrics agreed upon in consultation with the authorities in the importing country. Thirdly, some provision could be made on a very small scale for the normal type of merchant trade, since to limit all exports to the first two categories would accentuate certain existing tendencies to leave the cotton industry unbalanced in the demand for certain counts and products. Thus some production of high-class shirtings and fine counts of yarn might enable the industry to run efficiently and at full capacity, and marginal items of this sort might, if opportunity offered and there was no alternative use for them, be exported through merchants in the normal way. Accordingly merchants dealing in markets for which no regular allocations were being made were given token allocations which might be used to maintain trading connections, provided that they were informed that there was surplus production of these types.

The new arrangements recognised in effect that increasing scarcity had undermined the plan for an equitable sharing of markets among the merchants. The Cotton Board had hoped that the existing merchant channels which had conducted the export trade of the industry for so many years would be maintained, but it had to accept 'the Government's attitude . . . that the maintenance of equity amongst all export merchants interested in a particular market cannot be strictly adhered to at the expense of efficiency in the war effort'. In view of the overriding shortage of supplies the allocation that the small merchant would have received for a particular market on a strictly proportional basis would often have been unworkable, and it was therefore laid down that there should be a minimum qualifying allocation per market of 1,000 square yards.[1] Merchants whose allocations would fall below this qualifying limit were advised by the Cotton Board to transfer the quantity concerned to another market in which they had a greater interest or to amalgamate their allocations with those of other merchants. There was also, of course, the problem of the merchants who had been trading with markets which had been completely surrendered, those for example in Central and South America, and there was some talk of compensation for these people out of a specially created reserve of stocks. On the whole, however, the problem did not appear to be a particularly serious one and the compensation arrangement which had been

---

[1] It is interesting to note that at the end of 1941, out of 1,212 allocation holders, 49 were said to do half the business, and 306 were said to do ninety per cent. of the business.

suggested was not regarded as practicable by the Cotton Board.

Working in the same direction was the tendency towards standardisation of export cloths and also towards the inclusion of manufacture for export within the Cotton Control's scheme of planned production. This was already taking place in 1942, for example, with regard to cotton textiles to be exported to West Africa. In May 1943 the Cotton Board announced that all production for export was to be brought within the scope of the Cotton Control's production planning, and that in future for all markets there would be imposed the restrictions on types, yarns, widths of cloth, etc., which such planning required. At the same time, in order to fit in with planning, a minimum figure of 40,000 linear yards would be fixed for orders in any particular cloth. Here again there was a problem for the holder of a small cloth allocation, similar to that which had arisen over the introduction of minimum market allocations. The solution to the problem was sought in the use of the services of British Overseas Cottons Limited, the company which had been set up in the days of the export drive. British Overseas Cottons in effect pooled the orders which were too small to be fitted into planned production and translated them into bulk orders for standardised fabrics. Thus, for example, suitable cloths were planned for the West African market, and in 1943 it was stated that the West African scheme covered over a quarter of the total yardage and of individual merchant allocations. By the end of 1945 B.O.C. had bought 155 million square yards of various cloths, valued at nearly £5½ millions, from 320 manufacturers and had sold them to 680 merchants. Progress had been made towards the establishment of staple cloths and twenty-three such cloths had been in continuous production for one year, thirteen for two years. Some of the merchants, however, preferred not to make use of the services of B.O.C. and they set up instead a grey cloth pool which performed the similar function of pooling small orders.

A striking example of the change which standardisation and bulking of requirements involved was seen in Australia's policy in 1943 when she introduced clothes rationing, which aimed at abandoning the sponsoring of individual orders and at placing with the Cotton Control a programme or budget stated in terms of a list of essential fabrics subject to price control. A compromise was worked out by which a list of textile specifications was drawn up with agreed margins for merchant converters. The merchant system was retained in the sense that, within the general framework of planned production, the budget of requirements was distributed to the market allocation holders.

Towards the end of the war there was a move to break away from the rigid system of market quotas. It was decided that as from the beginning of 1944, some measure of freedom should be introduced by restricting the market quota arrangements to eighty per cent. of the total yardage of cloth available for export, and allowing the remaining twenty per cent. to constitute a 'free export pool'. This pool would be restricted to ten markets,[1] mostly the more important ones, and would be confined to holders of allocations for these markets, but it was expected that some degree of competition between merchants would be revived. The other restrictions on export, however, remained. It was not, for example, until 1946 that an 'open export scheme' was introduced, whereby a certain proportion of the yardage available for export could be switched from one market to another. The proportion at first was only ten per cent., but in 1947 was increased to cover ninety per cent. of production of piece-goods for export.

For the remainder of the war the overriding factor, as has been seen, was the shortage of yarn supplies. Allocations, which in 1944 were stabilised at a level of just over 17,000 tons of yarn per quarter, fell short of requirements, while deliveries fell short of allocations. Such supplies as were available had to be concentrated mainly on meeting the needs of the Dominions and of dependent territories in Africa. Maintenance of exports to the African territories was specially important as a means of securing from them supplies of foodstuffs and raw materials since the native producer would put forth effort only in return for a supply of consumption goods and not simply for money tokens.

It was natural under the circumstances that the United States should be looked to as a source from which the grave deficiency of cotton textile supplies, particularly in the eastern hemisphere, could be filled. The story of attempts to co-ordinate British and American export policies in meeting the needs of the non-Axis world has already been told. Here it need perhaps only be repeated that difficulties, greater than might have been anticipated, were encountered in substituting supplies from the United States for those from Britain, who had had long experience in catering for the needs of the Empire. The types of goods that America could supply were not always suitable, and there was thus a serious danger that, if Britain did not maintain her level of exports, urgent local requirements would not be met.

Even in the western hemisphere the case of Canada showed that there were needs which the United States, in spite of their proximity, could not adequately meet and to satisfy which exports from Britain were still required. During the war the United States substantially increased their exports of cotton textiles to Canada, but despite this and despite a considerable increase in Canada's domestic produc-

---

[1] South Africa, New Zealand, the Rhodesias, British West Africa, French Equatorial Africa, French Cameroons, Belgian Congo, British East Africa, British West Indies, Madagascar and Reunion (not confined to market allocation holders).

tion of yarn and piece-goods the Canadian Department of Munitions and Supplies asserted that Canada was dependent upon a definite allocation from the United Kingdom in order to meet her essential requirements. Canada had, in contrast to other countries which depended upon quarterly allocations, received at the beginning of 1942 the assurance of an annual supply of 5,000 tons of piece-goods and yarn for war purposes, but by 1943 the deterioration in the United Kingdom supply position made it very doubtful whether allocation at this rate could be maintained. The Canadians fought hard for their requirements. They pointed out that civilian standards had been reduced to a level which represented a minimum standard of living consistent with the maintenance of Canada's war effort and national unity of purpose, and that it was politically important to demonstrate that Canada with her Empire connection was able to maintain a standard of living reasonably comparable to that enjoyed by her American neighbour. Consumer rationing, it was argued, would be politically and psychologically impracticable unless corresponding action was taken in the United States. The Americans were indeed ready to help in meeting Canada's needs, but they could give no assurance of a specific rate of supply over a period in view of their already overloaded programme. Goodwill was not enough in the absence of adequate and functioning machinery for implementing American undertakings. Canada, it was stated, could not surrender her connections with Lancashire until such machinery had been created.

Against this very strong Canadian appeal there had to be set the waste involved in shipping raw material across the Atlantic and then shipping it back again in the form of yarn and cloth. It was therefore decided in London that Canada must look to the United States as her source of supply and it was arranged that, as from the end of 1943, the United States should take over the production of Canadian requirements, apart from certain specialities—mainly highly essential yarns—which the United Kingdom alone could supply. The United States, while recognising that Canada was from the geographical standpoint their responsibility, made it a condition of their undertaking that they should be relieved of an equal quantity of British colonial requirements. Canada, however, still urged that, if the United States failed in their undertaking, she should be allowed to revert to British supplies.

United Kingdom Exports of Cotton Yarn and Cotton Piece-goods,
1937–45

TABLE 7

(i) Yarn—million lb.

1937	1938	1939	1940	1941	1942	1943	1944	1945
159·0	123·0	113·7	66·7	28·9	18·8	19·2	19·6	16·1

(ii) Piece-goods—million square yards

1937	1938	1939	1940	1941	1942	1943	1944	1945
1,921	1,386	1,393	976	783	485	374	434	441

WOOLLEN TEXTILES

It has already been noted that exports of woollen textiles were in a different class from exports of cotton textiles. In the first place woollen textiles were better exports from the currency point of view, their raw material coming mainly from the soft-currency area while their markets were largely in the United States, Canada and the Argentine. Secondly, stocks of wool had been adequate and production for export had been running at a fairly high level in 1941; and, indeed, when an export scheme had been worked out it was introduced gradually in order to avoid a mass of frustrated exports.

From 1942 onwards, however, the situation changed profoundly. Raw material supplies for production for export were drastically cut; in 1942 the allocation was at an annual rate of 35,000 tons, of which 21,000 tons were for fabrics and yarn as against 49,000 tons for fabrics and yarn in 1941. The trade in raw wool to the United States and Canada was practically eliminated. Not only were raw material supplies reduced. There was also a big contraction in the labour force available for working up the raw material into finished products.[1]

In consequence of the change in supplies export policy had to be revised. For a time, that is in 1942, exports were maintained largely out of stocks resulting from the previous high level of production. But when stocks had been run down it looked as though it would be barely possible to meet essential Empire requirements.

Thus in 1943 it was decided to issue no further licences for the export of woollen tissues and blankets to the United States or to Latin American countries, with the exception of certain limited quantities of Harris tweeds made by crofter labour. Yarn exports to these countries were also stopped a month later—as from 1st July 1943.[2] This action naturally aroused protests from the trade, both in Britain and in the United States, but it was felt that the policy laid down must be adhered to in view of the deterioration in supplies coupled with the elimination of the currency factor from export considerations.

Exports of woollen textiles were also affected by factors similar to those which had led to a reorganisation of the cotton export scheme. Importing countries tended to focus their demands on the more essential types of goods, and there was also the problem of adapting or adjusting the merchanting organisation to the bulk orders characteristic of war-time arrangements. Canada, for example, wished to make sure that she would be able to obtain the sorts of cloth she wanted at reasonable prices. To meet her requirements it seemed best to operate a voluntary arrangement under which an approved

---

[1] See Chapter XV, section (ii).

[2] Excluding, of course, yarns for which export licences had already been granted.

list of cloths was drawn up with appropriate maximum prices, exporters being called on to concentrate their activities on cloths included within the list. Canada similarly wished to restrict her imports of yarns to fewer types and to put through bulk orders. Her plans would have cut across the system of allocations to exporters, and it was accordingly arranged to set up a company in Bradford which would operate a pool on behalf of those who held rations for the Canadian market. Bulk orders were thus met out of the pool, while profits were shared in agreed proportions.[1]

Woollen hosiery was also an important currency export, but in April 1942[2] it was placed under export control, in view of the difficulty of maintaining supplies to the home consumer. Apart from a small amount of high-class trade which would be permitted for a few months to the United States, it was decided that licences would only be issued for goods of a type completely unsuitable for home consumption.

United Kingdom Exports of Woollen and Worsted Yarns and Woollen and Worsted Tissues, 1938–45

TABLE 8

(i) Yarn—million lb.

1938	1939	1940	1941	1942	1943	1944	1945
34·7	32·0	17·7	13·2	10·5	9·0	8·7	9·0

(ii) Tissues—million square yards

1938	1939	1940	1941	1942	1943	1944	1945
95·8	98·0	86·2	90·9	77·3	46·1	36·5	43·6

RAYON

There was less formal control over rayon, whether for home use or for export, than over cotton and woollen textiles. Export trade had expanded but it was not subject to any measure of direction and it was not clear that the increased exports were going to the right markets from the point of view of general economic policy. Nor was it perhaps desirable, when shipping difficulties were becoming more acute, that there should be much expansion of exports, since rayon required imported raw materials which made an extravagant use of shipping space.

The export levy scheme of the Central Rayon Office, which aimed at producing standardised fabrics and selling them at competitive prices, has already been mentioned.[3] However, with the cessation of Japanese competition the need for subsidising rayon exports seemed to have disappeared, and it was accordingly agreed between the

---

[1] Twenty-five per cent. of the assumed net profit to the actual exporter, the remaining seventy-five per cent., after deduction of expenses, to be shared among the ration holders.

[2] S.R. & O. 1942, No. 602.

[3] See p. 62. From the setting up of the office in September 1940 to May 1942, export business done amounted to 38 million square yards of C.R.O. cloths with a c.i.f. value of £1·6 million.

Board of Trade and the Central Rayon Office in May 1942 that the subsidy should be withdrawn. On exports to certain markets, for example Australia, New Zealand and Cuba, the subsidy was immediately to be removed; but in the case of markets such as British West Africa, British West Indies and the Belgian Congo it was thought that a sudden withdrawal of subsidies would be harmful to native consumers and it was agreed that in these cases they should be taken off in stages terminating in 1943.

Meanwhile it was necessary to consider the complications introduced by the White Paper of September 1941 on the use of lend-lease and scarce materials in United Kingdom exports. It seemed that the principal raw materials used in the manufacture of one sort of rayon or another—cotton linters and ethyl alcohol for acetate rayon and wood pulp for viscose rayon—either were or were likely to become 'scarce' in the United States. In fact, these complications proved less serious than had been expected. Exports were limited rather by supplies in the United Kingdom, which were governed by the shortage of labour for the production of rayon yarn. In accordance with the requirements of the White Paper it was indeed agreed to eliminate exports of rayon yarn to the United States and the Argentine and of staple fibre to all Latin American markets. But the Americans did not object to small quantities of rayon exports to South American countries other than the Argentine or to exports of staple fibre to Canada. At the same time, of course, there were 'essential' rayon exports to the eastern hemisphere which were covered by the general exemption for such exports accorded by the Lend-lease Administration.

In 1942 the United States authorities asked for the submission of a programme of British exports of rayon goods. Data were supplied and in fact information was exchanged between the two countries during the war about their rayon exports, but it could hardly be said that anything like a joint export programme was formally agreed.

Although controls had hitherto been extremely loose the growing shortage, together with the need to meet possible American criticism of rayon exports, led in 1942 and 1943 to the imposition of export control. Rayon piece-goods came under export licensing in July 1942,[1] and an allocation programme was worked out covering a total of approximately 50 million square yards of pure rayon piece-goods for export. Staple fibre came under export control as from 1st March 1943.[2] This was primarily to restrict the export of long staple rayon, large quantities of which were finding a profitable market in Eire in the form of hand knitting yarns.

The picture of rayon exports thus altered appreciably during the

---

[1] S.R. & O. 1942, No. 1135.
[2] S.R. & O. 1943, No. 217.

last years of the war, though not so much as that of cotton and woollen exports. In 1944 exports,[1] amounting in terms of yarn to rather over 30 million pounds or, approximately, to one-quarter of United Kingdom production, were going to Empire markets, but there was still some currency-earning trade to Latin America. Rayon too had been affected, like the other textiles, by the switch to essential types of goods. There were already the standardised cloths of the Central Rayon Office but these covered a limited field. However, there was no question of doing what had been done in cotton, that is to say arranging that the bulk of exports should go in the form of standardised fabrics. There was in fact nothing corresponding to the rigid controls that had been imposed on the cotton industry, both on its production and on its merchanting sides, which would have made such an arrangement possible. All that could be done, therefore, was to call the attention of the trade to the need for concentrating on the more standard types of cloths suitable to war-time conditions, particularly since failure to do so would probably lead to the imposition of controls in the importing countries.

United Kingdom Exports of Artificial Silk Yarns and Tissues, 1938–45

TABLE 9

Yarns—million lb.

1938	1939	1940	1941	1942	1943	1944	1945
8·0	6·9	15·0	20·2	16·3	13·8	15·6	14·2

Tissues wholly of artificial silk and staple fibre—million square yards

1938	1939	1940	1941	1942	1943	1944	1945
31·2	43·5	56·3	69·1	102·7	68·8	81·6	84·2

OTHER TEXTILES

Owing to acute raw material shortages, the currency-earning trade of other textiles—jute, linen and hemp—was largely eliminated. The difficulties experienced in 1940 in securing an allocation of flax for the important hard-currency export trade in linen of Northern Ireland, in the face of stiff opposition from the Service departments, have already been mentioned.[2] From 1942 to 1944 the allocation ceased; all that was allowed by way of fresh production for export was for the purpose of meeting essential Empire and Allied requirements. Trade of course did not necessarily cease, since it could be carried on out of stocks both of raw materials and finished goods. In 1943 a plea was put forward by the Board of Trade for some revival of former currency exports and an allocation of 1,000 tons of low-grade tow was made for this purpose, which was increased later in the year. Lack of labour and of certain types of capacity in the industry had now, however, become the limiting factors.

---

[1] Rayon yarn included in hosiery is excluded here.
[2] See p. 67.

United Kingdom Exports of Linen and Hemp Piece-goods and of Jute Manufactures, 1938–45

TABLE 10

Linen and Hemp piece-goods—million square yards

1938	1939	1940	1941	1942	1943	1944	1945
51·8	67·4	45·4	27·8	22·6	10·5	6·2	8·8

Jute manufactures—thousand cwt.

1938	1939	1940	1941	1942	1943	1944	1945
1,495	1,247	781	475	260	163	124	207

OTHER EXPORTS

It was inevitable that the United Kingdom's traditional exports under the headings of iron and steel, machinery and vehicles, should decline prodigiously. Exports of iron and steel fell from 1·9 million tons in 1938 to 0·2 million ton in 1944. Machinery exports fell from 459 thousand tons in 1938 to 136 thousand tons in 1943. Private car exports were reduced from 44,000 in 1938 to 23 in 1944. Exports of ships and boats were cut to negligible amounts.

Such iron and steel as continued to be exported went out almost entirely in fully manufactured form, as machinery and consumer goods made of metal. For both machinery and consumer goods the overriding limitations on exports were the shortages of labour and capacity and the restrictions of the White Paper of September 1941. Exports were subject to strict licensing control both over raw material and over actual export. Moreover gross statistics of exports of machinery conceal the fact that what were actually exported were frequently repair parts rather than complete machines, and sometimes second-hand rather than new machinery. Thus before the war, in the field of textile machinery, exports of complete looms represented about half the total of looms and parts; in 1943 exports of complete looms were only two per cent. of the total of this class of export.[1]

The advantages to be derived from exporting second-hand machinery did not always prove to be as great as had perhaps at first been supposed. Thus it had been considered that India's enlarged role as a supplier of cotton textiles might be supported by sending her second-hand textile machinery. There were, however, difficulties about doing this. An undertaking had been given to the cotton industry that machinery put out of action through concentration would not be exported. There was also the danger of arousing Lancashire's fears of subsidised competition from India. But there was on the other hand the problem of the desperate shortage of cotton goods in the eastern hemisphere. In fact there was not much to be said for the plan. Indian mills were often equipped with up-to-date machinery, and the supply of obsolescent machinery in small job lots

---

[1] *Board of Trade Journal*, 28th October 1944, p. 390.

O

naturally was not particularly acceptable to the owners of high-class mills. Moreover, in many cases it would have been impracticable on technical grounds to install the second-hand machinery in India. Thus new machinery had to be sent and in view of the difficulties of supply and of shipping, if for no other reasons, a very tight control had to be exercised to ensure that the equipment exported was such as would give exceptional returns in increasing Indian production, either by balancing existing capacity or by speeding up machinery already installed.[1]

For some of the consumer goods containing metal, cutlery and bicycles for example, export programmes with country quotas were devised. Most of the bicycle industry had been turned over to war production, but by 1942 something less than a quarter of the pre-war labour force was still making bicycles and of total output twenty per cent. was going into export. Almost all the exports were going to meet the minimum requirements of the Empire, excluding Canada, and of Allied countries in the eastern hemisphere. As we have seen, however, even in a case like this the restrictions of the White Paper could prove extremely irksome. The Americans it will be remembered went so far as to suggest that they were capable of dealing with all the requirements of the world market, and suggested that the United Kingdom should confine its production to the needs for bicycles in the home market.

In conclusion some account may be given of two groups of United Kingdom exports which had been traditionally important in earning valuable foreign currencies[2]—pottery and china, and whisky. Apart from their currency-earning advantages these two groups of exports possessed special characteristics which could be regarded as giving them some claim to continuance even in an economy that was increasingly being given over to war production. First, let us take pottery and china. Their manufacture used native as opposed to imported materials. This was important as long as shipping and raw materials were the main consideration. But as labour became chief of all limiting factors and as labour in the potteries was needed for the munition factories in Staffordshire the position altered.

Shortage of home supplies was the main direct reason for the introduction of an export control on domestic pottery in May 1942.[3] A ceiling was put on exports, and manufacturers were restricted at first to eighty per cent. and then sixty per cent. by value of their average quarterly exports in 1941. There was no such thing as a formal scheme for the direction of exports. Exporters were given bulk

---

[1] The same control had to be exercised in meeting Australia's demands for machinery for her small textile industry. Here, too, offers of second-hand machinery met with little response.

[2] The important decline in coal exports is discussed in *Coal* by W. H. B. Court.

[3] S.R. & O. 1942, No. 707.

licences, and were encouraged within their total permitted export quota to maintain supplies to the South American markets and, within limits, to the United States[1] and Canada. At the same time it was decided that, although restrictions on the manufacture for home use and for export of decorated ware were being imposed as from November 1942, decorated china and earthenware might still be exported to the United States, Canada and the Latin American countries. This kept decorators who could not be transferred to other work in useful employment and maintained the tradition and skill of decoration, so that this valuable form of export could be expanded after the war.

The continuation of exports of pottery and china was, however, not merely a currency question. Empire countries depended very largely on the United Kingdom for meeting the essential needs of their civilian populations, particularly as Japanese supplies were no longer available. Manufacturers, however, were under no compulsion to supply these needs, and it was clear that they would have objected to any tighter form of export control, even if this only meant division of exports between markets. Meanwhile, the same sort of thing was taking place that had already been affecting textile exports; Dominion Governments were placing bulk orders for such users as hospitals and railways that were competing with normal civilian trade. In consequence of these developments export policy was revised in November 1943. Dominion Government orders were excluded from the general export quotas and were treated as a priority; the Ministry of Works, which was already placing orders for the New Zealand Government, agreed to place orders for the Governments of the other Dominions. At the same time, to create a pool to meet these Government requirements, export quotas for manufacturers were cut from sixty per cent. to fifty per cent. of their 1941 trade in earthenware.

In 1944 there was some relaxation of the various restrictions which had been imposed during the war, with the aim of preparing for a revival of export trade. By the end of the year the prohibition on the export of decorated ware to countries in the eastern hemisphere had been removed.[2] Export quotas were restored to the level of the previous year. Furthermore, manufacturers who did not hold export licences were allowed to apply for licences up to ten per cent. of their 1944 production in order to help them to get a footing in overseas markets. Export control itself was not, however, finally taken off until June 1945,[3] after which date the Government relied

---

[1] The quantity of pottery exported to the United States had increased from 54,600 cwt. in 1939 to 67,300 cwt. in 1941; in value from £295,700 to £486,000.

[2] This did not mean that decorated ware could, within the quota, be exported freely, since some countries had imposed import restrictions on goods of this sort.

[3] S.R. & O. 1945, No. 576.

upon the voluntary co-operation of manufacturers to secure a balanced distribution of supplies between home civilian, Service and export requirements.

United Kingdom Pottery Exports, 1939-45

TABLE II							Thousand cwt.
	1939	*1940*	*1941*	*1942*	*1943*	*1944*	*1945*
Earthenware—total .	485	572	594	427	326	360	174
„ to Australia . .	72	112	101	91	50	100	46
„ to Canada . .	121	170	183	119	111	101	50
„ to United States .	55	55	67	56	37	38	18
„ to Argentina .	33	47	39	24	37	19	6
China and porcelain (other than electrical ware) .	28	52	50	28	23	24	12

As for whisky, the export problem was that of releases from stock. Whisky production took grain supplies for which there were of course important alternative uses. But whisky takes years to mature and supplies come not out of current production but out of existing stocks. The problem of new production hardly concerns us here, and it may merely be noted that allocations of cereals for distilling were first cut and then eliminated from the autumn of 1942 to the autumn of 1944. Whisky, however, remained an important currency export in war-time; in fact it was the major export from the United Kingdom to the United States. Exports of Scotch and Irish whisky to the United States had increased from 4,784 thousand gallons (value £6,985,127) in 1939 to 6,972 thousand gallons (value £10,470,043) in 1940, so that in the latter year whisky exports represented nearly one-third of total United Kingdom exports to the United States. Moreover, these exports were more than half the total of whisky exports. 1940 was, however, a peak year and from then on exports fell sharply away reaching their lowest figure of 4,435 thousand gallons in 1944, of which the United States took 2,570 thousand gallons. In 1944, however, it was decided to allow the distillers to resume operations on a limited scale, and 10,000 tons of barley were allocated for this purpose.

APPENDIX 5
Exports of Cotton Piece-goods

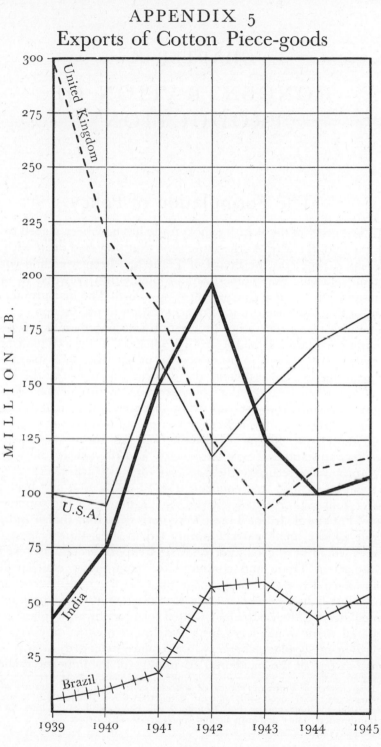

CHAPTER X

CONCENTRATION OF PRODUCTION[1]

(i)

The Formulation of Policy

THE story of the British export trade has now been traced to the end of the war. At the same time that they had dealt with export problems the Board of Trade had been wrestling with a host of industrial and home-front problems that crowded in upon them and it is to these that we must now turn. The first problem in point of time had been that of concentration of production.

The idea of concentrating production into fewer units was not a war-time invention: it had a pre-war ancestry in the rationalisation schemes that had been so prominent in public discussion during the nineteen-thirties. Nevertheless, the descent was not very direct. In purpose and in method the concentration of production of 1941 differed radically from pre-war rationalisation. The primary purpose of concentration was to further the war effort. It was concerned only incidentally with efficiency of production and not at all with long-term reorganisation. It was temporary, and implicit in the scheme was a promise to return to the *status quo* when war was over.

It will be recalled that concentration of production had been discussed from an early stage—from the beginning of the summer of 1940.[2] For the Board of Trade were very conscious that if reduced output for the home market simply led to short-time working resources would be wasted and the cost of exports would rise. At first the Board of Trade had contemplated compulsory concentration as an alternative to limiting the supplies of miscellaneous consumer goods. But it had been necessary to reduce unessential production immediately; if the Board had waited for concentration plans to be prepared there would have been a delay of months or years. The limitation of supplies scheme was therefore extended. It was foreseen that one of the incidental advantages of the limitation scheme

---

[1] This chapter is a general survey of concentration policy. Concentration of the following industries is dealt with in more detail elsewhere: cotton, wool, rayon (all Chapter XV); clothing, hosiery (both Chapter XVI); boots and shoes (Chapter XVIII); furniture, pottery, toilet preparations and sports goods (all Chapter XIX).

[2] See pp. 114–5.

would be the encouragement of schemes to concentrate production. It seemed hopeless to plan a reduction in the number of manufacturers if all of them were pretty well occupied and if each of them hoped that if and when output was reduced it would not be his output. 'To induce such a firm to sign its own death warrant', wrote an official, 'would be a difficult, lengthy and maybe a costly business'. But as supplies were reduced all round manufacturers might be more co-operative. The new limitation scheme should create an atmosphere in which plans for concentrating production could usefully be considered.

In the last few months of 1940 the Board of Trade constantly considered the problems of concentration. The Minister without Portfolio suggested to the President that there should be a geographical concentration of production—that civilian production should be shifted to London, South-East England and other areas where the demands of the munitions industries for labour were low. But attractive though this idea might be in theory, it seemed to the Board quite impracticable. Industrial concentration—the concentration of an industry's output into a few firms—seemed much more promising. The home trade limitation schemes could be used to encourage this kind of rationalisation. They could, by arrangements for the transfer of unexhausted supply quotas, make it easier for a manufacturer to close down his business.

Nevertheless, it was clear that such permissive powers were not enough. A few consumer goods industries were being forced by restrictions—especially raw material restrictions—and by the loss of workers to think of concentrating into their more efficient units and in safer areas. But most industries had no desire to concentrate production. They preferred a share-and-share-alike policy; reduced trade, they thought, should be shared equally among manufacturers in accordance with their previous turnover. If the total home trade were only one-third of the previous trade, all firms should be allowed to work to 33⅓ per cent. of capacity plus export trade and Government orders if any. So the quota concessions were not likely to carry concentration very much further. For the same reason Government exhortations to industry in the autumn of 1940 to prepare concentration schemes met with very little response. The Government got as far as discussing a scheme for one industry—cotton velvet—but the talks were abortive.

By the end of 1940 no formal industrial concentration schemes had been drawn up. The Board of Trade had, however, been following a more promising line of approach—concentration by administrative action. It will be remembered that in the summer of 1940,[1] there were fears in other Government departments that the Board of

_____
[1] See p. 112.

Trade were moving too fast—that the labour released by the limitation of supplies would swell not the munitions industries but the ranks of the unemployed. To dispel these fears the Board had established a keeping step section. Officials of this section and of the Ministry of Labour and Ministry of Supply were to keep constant watch for the development of pockets of unemployment which were to be removed either by using spare capacity for Government contracts or, if necessary, by licensing additional home trade. The chief purpose of these interdepartmental arrangements was to prevent unemployment. But they served other purposes as well. Through this machinery it was possible to divert Government orders to export manufacturers and so assist them to achieve the lower costs of full-time working or, if necessary, Government orders could be withheld where they interfered with export trade. The Board of Trade officials also found it possible to prepare, from their 'keeping step' inquiries, lists of factories engaged on home trade that might be requisitioned for more essential purposes. Meanwhile the Ministry of Labour had a strong interest in turning Government orders away from firms in areas where labour needed to be released for direct munitions work.

This procedure was important in the history of concentration. The careful placing of Government orders helped to prepare the way for the formal concentration schemes that were to follow. Moreover, the information gathered through the 'keeping step' inquiries was an invaluable aid to the administrators concerned with these later concentration schemes.

At the end of 1940 the policy of concentration was invested with a new urgency. The threat of widespread short-time working in the industries producing consumer goods had become much more serious. As we have seen in an earlier chapter the first Limitation of Supplies Orders had not really reduced the volume of home trade very much; but the new orders for textiles and miscellaneous goods that were issued in the last months of 1940 were far more drastic and were bound to affect output. It was now not only a question of keeping export costs down. The time had come when the wasteful use of resources on civilian production could no longer be tolerated. Factory space and manpower, in particular, were by now urgently needed for war purposes.

Factory space was needed both for war production and for storage. Dispersal of war production seemed one answer to bombing attacks and when it began it increased the scramble by Service and supply ministries for space. The most important method of bringing order into the scramble was the establishment of a Control of Factory and Storage Premises.[1] It was also clear, however, that civilian production

---

[1] This will be discussed in the following chapter.

must not be allowed to spread itself thinly over many production units if it could be concentrated into far fewer.

Perhaps the most important of the impulses behind the new drive for concentration of production was the forecast of an acute man-power shortage. Hitherto, the Ministry of Labour had put a restraining hand on the Board of Trade's efforts to contract civilian production. The fear of unemployment died hard. But at the end of 1940 Sir William Beveridge, who had been commissioned to review manpower prospects, made his report.[1] He foresaw that by the autumn of 1941 there would be a 'famine of men' and therefore a great demand for woman-power. This conclusion had important consequences. Chief amongst them was the War Cabinet's approval for new developments in manpower policy—a modification of the Schedule of Reserved Occupations, vigorous use of the powers of registration and direction of labour, and measures to prevent unauthorised movements out of essential jobs.

A lesser but nevertheless important consequence was an approach by the Ministry of Labour to the Board of Trade about labour in civilian production. 'It will be necessary', wrote the Ministry, 'for more extensive measures on the lines of, but not necessarily similar to, the Limitation of Supplies Order—to be applied so as to reduce employment in non-munitions industries and to release labour and factory space. . . . It seems to us that to ensure the maintenance of the labour force required for essential Government and export work and to meet the minimum consumers' requirements in the non-munitions industries, and to secure that this work should be carried on with the greatest possible economy of labour, using women in place of men where practicable, it is essential to introduce measures which would have the following results:—

(1) Concentration of the work which must be carried on in areas where munitions labour demands are least heavy.

(2) That employers and workers are not free to frustrate the intentions of restrictions by organising short time or under-employment.

(3) That the workers should be brought into co-operation so as to provide that the more mobile and adaptable types of labour are released.'

An interdepartmental meeting followed this letter. There it was agreed that concentration should proceed industry by industry. Furthermore it should be determined centrally which firms were to be earmarked as a source of labour for war work and factory space for war production or storage. In choosing the firms particular attention would be paid to the need to reduce non-essential production in those areas where the shortage of labour was likely to be most acute. The Board of Trade and Ministry of Labour agreed to

---

[1] See *British War Economy, op. cit.,* Chapter XI.

make a joint approach to the Ministry of Supply in order that the same principles should be applied to raw material industries.

The next stage was to decide upon the methods of concentration. Clearly the pre-war rationalisation schemes would provide very little guidance. Their conventional method of procedure had been for the industry in question to provide a fund for purchasing redundant businesses for scrapping or cold storage; the fund was fed by a levy on the surviving firms. But several industries had found it difficult or even impossible to agree on such schemes. These pre-war precedents for concentration were 'discouraging enough in their own setting' as one official wrote, and they became quite impossible as precedents in war-time circumstances. Time could not be spared for the months or even years of discussion which might be necessary to obtain agreement within the industries. Moreover, the consumer goods industries which were now concerned were mostly organised on a small scale; discussions with individual firms would be out of the question. Finally, the scale of contraction needed in war-time was far greater than that required in peace. As a first guess it was suggested that four out of every five firms would have to go out of business. It was soon discovered that this was much too high an aim. But undoubtedly many more firms would have to close down than under peace-time redundancy schemes.

For these reasons the Board of Trade felt that it was impossible to adopt the recognised pre-war technique of passing to industrial organisations the responsibility of preparing schemes for concentrating production. The choice before the Board was the same choice they had faced in May 1940 when they decided to frame and apply a limitation of supplies scheme to fifty or sixty industries without consulting a single one of them. Either the Board could play for safety and shelter behind industrial organisations, or they could go ahead and avoid the controversy that any publicity or negotiations with trade associations would necessarily arouse by intensifying administrative action on existing lines.

At first the Board preferred the latter alternative. The domestic pottery industry was put forward as an example of how the policy could be executed. Of 125 firms in this industry, the Board would have liked to see production concentrated on sixty-five to seventy. Of the sixty-five or so firms, forty-five were capable of producing all exports, all Government requirements and some part of the home trade quota; the other twenty to twenty-five firms could produce the balance of the home trade allowed under the quota. The Board were intending to speed rationalisation by recommending the Ministry of Works to concentrate all Government orders on the forty-five 'first-line' firms and by supplying lists of the fifty or so redundant firms to factory requisitioning departments and the Ministry of Labour so that space and labour might be withdrawn. The twenty to twenty-five 'second-line' firms would become redundant as home trade was further contracted.

There was a feeling in the Board of Trade that these methods could be applied to a wide range of civilian industries. If this were done, it seemed quite possible that within a few months the problem of concentrating production would largely have solved itself. Then, no matter whether this did, or did not happen, the Board could complete their control in about six months' time by altering the limitation of supplies scheme and prohibiting supply by manufacturers except under licence.

The proposal for concentration by administrative action instead of by discussions with industry was not, however, adopted. It was important that the Government and industry should co-operate. Ministers and their industrial advisers thought that as a first move it would be too difficult, if only for political reasons, to leave Government departments to select in each industry the firms for survival and elimination. This method of concentration having been rejected, two alternatives remained. An industry might be asked, through its association or representative body, to prepare a scheme to cover all its members. Or individual firms might be encouraged to initiate the desired changes in industrial structure. Right through the discussions on concentration the Board of Trade had been unwilling to contemplate the first alternative. If a trade association was 'making a plan' or 'drawing up a scheme' it was probable that everyone would wait to see what it looked like; weeks, if not months, would then have been lost. In any case some of the consumer-goods industries did not possess representative or comprehensive trade associations. Moreover the production of the firms in each of these consumer goods industries was so diverse that it was impossible to organise concentration centrally. The method of leaving the initiative with individual firms promised to be more speedy and more flexible. It would permit firms to adjust themselves to war conditions and make a rapid return to a peace-time structure. And, not least important, this plan would reconcile 'most completely traditional British economic policy with the requirements of a war-time economy'.

The concentration scheme as it finally emerged was, therefore, based on voluntary arrangements between individual firms. In the ministerial discussions and in the public announcements—in Parliament[1] and in a White Paper[2]—it was emphasised that the new scheme had two purposes. First, it would prevent the wasteful use of resources in civilian industries. In particular it would free labour and factory space for war purposes. There would also be economies in

---

[1] H. of C. Deb., Vol. 369, Cols. 774–776.

[2] *Concentration of Production; Explanatory Memorandum*, Cmd. 6258.

the use of coal, gas and electricity. It was hoped that such economical use of resources would keep costs down and so ease the pressure on prices. Secondly—this was a new point—it would provide a firm basis for post-war reconstruction by leaving an efficient nucleus in full production and by withdrawing the remaining firms into reserve in an orderly fashion; the closed firms would be kept ready to reopen as soon as possible after the war.

The procedure would be as follows. The Board of Trade would inform every industry of the degree of concentration required. They would then expect individual firms to make arrangements with one another that would ensure concentration to this extent. In making these arrangements firms would have to see that production was concentrated, as far as possible, in areas where the demands of munitions industries were least severe. Moreover, the labour released should be adaptable and of a type likely to be readily absorbed in the new employment. The time for the release of labour should, as far as possible, be regulated to the demand. Provided these conditions were fulfilled, any firm that arranged to work full time—whether by taking over and closing down other units or otherwise—could achieve nucleus status. The advantages of nucleus status seemed considerable. The Board of Trade would 'as far as possible' prevent the factories of nucleus firms from being requisitioned and safeguard their raw materials supplies. Government orders would also be given to these firms. Even more important were the labour advantages. The Ministry of Labour would safeguard the labour requirements of these firms 'in appropriate cases upon the recommendation of the Board of Trade'. And nucleus firms would be included in the list of protected establishments. This list had been introduced when the Schedule of Reserved Occupations was revised early in 1941. Firms on the list were entitled to a specially early age of reservation for most of their workers in reserved occupations. In addition, the fact that a firm was on this list would be taken into consideration when applications for deferment were dealt with. One of the chief inducements to concentration disappeared when, at the end of 1941, the Schedule of Reserved Occupations and the list of protected establishments were abolished in favour of individual deferment.

There was then the question of compensation to be considered. One of the attractions of the Board's original idea for concentration by administrative action had been that no problem of compensation would arise. The difficulties of closed firms would be no different from the difficulties of firms which had lost business through the operation of the Limitation of Supplies Orders and the raw material controls. But once formal concentration schemes were encouraged the Government would have to give some lead on compensation. When the President of the Board of Trade put his concentration proposals before his ministerial colleagues, he suggested that closed firms should be eligible for payment under the Compensation Defence Acts if they wished to be requisitioned even though the Board of Trade, as the requisitioning department, might have no immediate use for the premises. This proposal was, however, severely criticised by the Chancellor of the Exchequer who questioned the desirability and legality of creating a title to compensation under the Defence Act. In the following discussions it was therefore agreed that the Government should not pay direct compensation; instead each industry should be invited to formulate its own arrangements for the financial relief of closed firms. The explanatory White Paper made clear this obligation of nucleus firms to compensate closed firms. Similarly, all concentration arrangements had to provide for the plant of the closed firms to be kept intact unless the premises were requisitioned.

The Government could not, however, keep clear of all the financial implications of concentration schemes. It had, in particular, to pronounce on some of the difficult taxation problems that arose. Following discussions between the Board of Trade and the Treasury, a clause dealing with these problems was inserted in the 1941 Finance Bill.[1] This clause meant that, for the purpose of computing income tax and excess profits tax, changes in business activity due to concentration schemes were disregarded. The business of firms closed under these schemes would not be considered 'discontinued' and nucleus firms would not be treated as if they were setting up a new business. Any sum[2] payable as a result of an approved concentration arrangement to a closed concern by a nucleus firm would be allowed as a deduction in computing the nucleus firm's profit and as a trading receipt in computing the closed firm's profits. If in exceptional circumstances an industry set up a central compensation fund fed by levies the amounts paid in by nucleus firms were to be allowed as deductions in computing tax liability[3] and amounts drawn out by closed firms were to be treated as trading receipts.

There was also the problem of wear-and-tear allowances for the machinery and plant of closed firms. Under ordinary income tax law machinery and plant not in actual use for production could not qualify for the normal wear-and-tear allowance; this meant the forfeiture of an appreciable deduction in tax payments. This was clearly a deterrent to concentration and the Chancellor of the Exchequer therefore agreed to ease the burden of closed firms. The Finance Act of 1941 included a provision enabling these firms to claim wear-and-tear allowances just as if they were still producing units.

---

[1] Finance Act 1941, 4 and 5, Geo. 6, ch. 30, Sect. 18.

[2] Except a sum of a capital nature or a sum payable under deduction of tax.

[3] Provided no residue was left in the fund.

(ii)

The Procedure

The concentration scheme was announced at the beginning of March 1941. Which industries were to be covered by it? The Board of Trade were anxious to cover all those industries working substantially below capacity. These consisted of two groups—industries covered by the Limitation of Supplies (Miscellaneous) Order and industries subject to raw material control. The latter group of industries—cotton and rayon, woollen and worsted, paper, boots and shoes and silk—had to be handled in collaboration with the Raw Materials Department of the Ministry of Supply. The Board of Trade had to study the industries covered by the Limitation of Supplies (Miscellaneous) Order to see which were suitable for concentration. Concentration was unnecessary in some of these industries because they were already fully occupied. There was no spare capacity in the industries producing such goods as hollow-ware, office furniture, vacuum cleaners, metal furniture; they were very busy with essential civilian needs, exports, and munitions work. There remained a long list of industries covered by the Limitation of Supplies (Miscellaneous) Order which, it seemed, could usefully be concentrated. The list was concerned only with the existence of spare capacity and did not discriminate between essential and unessential industries. Pottery and hosiery mingled there with umbrellas, toilet preparations and toys. There were a few additional industries covered neither by limitation Orders nor raw material controls which seemed as if they too might be promising candidates for concentration—such industries as brushes and brooms, hats, paints and varnishes and perambulators; on further investigation, however, most of these industries seemed for various reasons unsuitable, at least for the moment. There were other industries with surplus capacity that were likewise considered unsuitable for concentration at this stage. Some, such as printing, were too dependent on local demand. Others, such as clothing and woodworking, were for the most part composed of a vast number of tiny firms; to apply concentration to them at this stage seemed to present too formidable an administrative problem.[1]

Concentration of production was publicly announced early in March 1941. By the end of that month the Board of Trade had approached more than twenty industries and had urged the firms in them to produce concentration arrangements. The first step was a

---

[1] Clothing was, however, tackled in 1942. See Chapter XVI, section (i). Woodworking was also reconsidered at the end of 1941; concentration was attempted, but was unsuccessful, for the larger firms were heavily engaged on Government contracts.

meeting at the Board of Trade with each industry—with manufacturers, officials of trade groups and representatives of workers. The Board of Trade had already decided against the formulation of a concentration plan by a whole industry, and they early established the principle that no trade association as such was to become the only channel of approach to Government officials. Nevertheless the trade associations could be, and often were, most useful in explaining the concentration proposals to their members and in providing a clearing-house for members who needed help in establishing contact with others for the purpose of making industrial arrangements.

The approach to industries and the subsequent discussions were made easier by a development in the Board of Trade's own machinery that has already been mentioned.[1] The Export Council—a body formed to help with the export drive of 1940—was enlarged into the Industrial and Export Council by the recruitment of further eminent businessmen. These men helped to supplement the Board of Trade's knowledge of specific industries. A special concentration committee of the Council was set up under the chairmanship of the President of the Board of Trade to consider both general and particular problems raised by concentration, and a small sub-committee advised on the financial and taxation complexities. The business members gave freely of their time and work. A number of industries was assigned to each of them. After the initial meeting at the Board of Trade the business member would then visit the main centres of production for his industries and help to explain concentration policy to the industries and the views of those industries to the Industrial and Export Council.

The Government had decided that, as far as possible, concentration should be carried out by voluntary arrangements. There were from the start exceptions to this principle; the most notable of these was cotton.[2] Moreover, within a few months it became evident that, although the voluntary principle was surprisingly successful in most cases, it was inadequate for some industries and some firms, so that the Board of Trade were themselves obliged to choose nucleus and closing firms. Before considering the progress of concentration, however, it is desirable to describe the general concentration procedure.

At the initial meetings with industries the Board of Trade had to explain the degree of concentration required; they had to define, that is to say, the condition of 'running full'. There was no common basis for these calculations in all industries. In practice, however, the formula in many of the limitation of supplies industries was the same. A firm was to calculate

(1) the value of its total production during the best month of some fairly prosperous period—sometimes June to November 1939,

---

[1] See p. 136.
[2] Cotton concentration was a special case and is described in Chapter XV, section (i).

sometimes the first quota period under the Limitation of Supplies Order;

(2) its current monthly production.

If production under (1) was, say, £6,000 and production under (2) £4,000, then the firm would have to take over from another firm production of at least £2,000 in order to achieve a condition of 'running full'.

In some large industries more complicated formulæ were required. The boot and shoe industry, for example, could not be dealt with by simple calculations of the value of production. Boots and shoes had not been included in the Limitation of Supplies Orders. Indeed the first direct restriction on the industry was introduced only a few weeks before the announcement of concentration policy: not until the middle of February 1941 did a scheme for rationing upper leather on the basis of past acquisitions and past usage begin to operate.

But this measure did not give the Board of Trade much guidance in deciding upon the rate of concentration for the industry. In fixing this rate the Board of Trade—and the Raw Materials Department which was also associated in this concentration scheme—could not avoid the responsibility for suggesting how many pairs of shoes of different kinds should be produced. It was obviously possible to reduce, quite substantially, the supplies of men's and women's shoes and the supplies of slippers without causing serious hardship. But supplies of boys' and girls' shoes should, it was thought, be maintained. The Board and the Raw Materials Department therefore calculated how many pairs of men's, women's, boys', girls' and infants' shoes and how many pairs of fabric shoes and slippers could be produced for the civilian population from the supplies of raw materials. It was agreed that these various categories should be reduced by the following percentages of home civilian output in 1940:

Men's	18 per cent.
Women's	23 per cent.
Boys' and youths'	No change
Girls' and maids'	No change
Infants'	12 per cent.
Fabric boots and shoes	40 per cent.
Slippers and house shoes	30 per cent.

Concentration groups in the boot and shoe industry had to retain sufficient capacity to produce these quantities of boots and shoes for civilian consumption and, in addition, facilities for Government contracts and for exports. Nucleus factories would be required to work to full capacity—that is at a rate of production equal to the highest monthly rate in 1940, suitably adjusted to a forty-eight hour week.

Decisions about the degree of concentration required involved decisions about production policy in the hosiery industry as well as in the boot and shoe industry. The hosiery industry produces a wide range of goods varying in essentiality—from underwear, socks and children's wear to silk stockings and exotic jumpers; the only common factor between them is the use of the looped stitch.

Some firms manufacture only one or two of these products, others manufacture many of them. Very few firms, however, produce the whole range of articles. Hitherto, the Board of Trade had not been directly concerned with production in the hosiery industry. The Limitation of Supplies Order had been undiscriminating and had simply cut sales of hosiery to shops by a flat rate of fifty per cent. Manufacturers had been free to choose which of their products they would cut—vests, cardigans, scarves or socks. Now that concentration had brought the Board of Trade face to face with the pattern of production in the industry discrimination could no longer be avoided. If productive capacity were to be reduced it must be reduced in the different sections of the industry according to some scale of essentiality. This argument was reinforced from another quarter. Clothes rationing was soon to be introduced and people would then concentrate their purchases far more upon essential clothing. Infants and children would still grow out of their clothes and demands for these would be inelastic compared with parents' demands for scarves and fancy socks. The Board of Trade had, therefore, to assess the probable civilian needs at the reduced level of business and then add to these the requirements of the Services. The Board were then able to hazard a guess at the percentage reductions in production capacity that were necessary in each section of the industry. Altogether there were eleven sections of the industry and each was judged on its merits. The redundancy in the more important sections was fixed as follows:—

Underwear	30 per cent.
Infants' underwear	20 per cent.
Outerwear and fancy hosiery . . .	60 per cent.
Infants' outerwear	20 per cent.
Fashioned hose[1]	30 per cent.
Seamless hose	30 per cent.
Half hose	33 per cent.
Children's half hose	20 per cent.
Other knitwear	75 per cent.

On this basis each firm had to calculate the redundancy in the value of its production. The base period for this calculation was the six months ending 30th November 1940. Redundancy was worked

---

[1] A further redundancy cut was later applied to this section of the trade.

P

out from turnover figures in this period; Government work was included in these figures but exports were excluded. The total redundancy figure for the concentration group—the nucleus and absorbed firms—was then expressed as a percentage of the total gross turnover of the firms in the base period. This percentage gave the redundancy cut to be applied to the group's machines and workers.[1] The Board of Trade insisted that concentration should be at least 100 per cent. The nucleus firms, that is, had to absorb sufficient production after the redundancy cuts had been applied to enable them to work at not less than their capacity in the base period. In addition, the Board of Trade usually required an assurance that the nucleus firms would be working a full forty-eight hour week.

Concentration had at first been intended simply as a means of rationalising production into fewer units. The Board of Trade had not contemplated using concentration as a means of enforcing contraction of production. But it was clear to the officers dealing with concentration schemes that the two processes of rationalisation and contraction could not be separated. For at the time when concentration was introduced the industrial scene was very fluid; the supply of some raw materials was growing increasingly precarious, and great new Government factories were coming into operation. The examples of hosiery and boots and shoes have already demonstrated how concentration confronted the Board of Trade with much wider problems of production policy; the Board had had to decide how far each section of the industry should be contracted.

In other industries, too, concentration and contraction went side by side. In the carpet industry concentration discussions proceeded at first on the assumption that production would continue at about the current level. But within a month or so jute supplies rapidly deteriorated. The combined carpet and rug industry which had used 30,000 tons of jute a year before the war was now told that it would receive only 3,000–4,000 tons for all its trade including exports. This industry had therefore to be drastically contracted at the same time that it was concentrated.

The same thing happened in the pottery industry though for different reasons. When concentration policy was announced in March 1941 the potteries had already lost nearly twenty per cent. of their labour. But the demands for munitions labour in North Staffordshire were still rising and the Ministry of Labour was obliged to ask for a still greater contribution from the potteries. The Board of Trade and the Ministry of Labour therefore agreed to combine concen-

---

[1] Suppose three firms, one nucleus and two absorbed, had a total gross turnover (including exports) in the base period of £104,000 and that after applying the appropriate redundancy rates the three firms had a combined redundancy of £26,000, then twenty-five per cent. of the group's machines and workers would be redundant.

tration with the release of thirty per cent. of the pottery industry's current labour force. At first the Board stipulated that they would only approve concentration schemes that enabled the nucleus pottery firms to work at full capacity after the new withdrawals of labour. Concentration on this scale would have severely reduced the number of pottery firms and the proposal was strongly resisted by the Pottery Federation. This resistance was based in part upon the importance of continuing export trade. Two thirds of pottery output was exported and it seemed desirable to maintain many export patterns which had a goodwill overseas rather than concentrate upon a few of them. For this reason the Board of Trade agreed at length that nucleus firms need only run to seventy-five per cent. of their capacity.

It is clear that decisions about the rate of concentration for an industry were often difficult and that they confronted the Board of Trade with much wider questions of production policy. Once the decisions were made, the initiative lay with the industries concerned. Individual firms were expected to seek out their own concentration partners. Some large firms with several factories could of course concentrate within their own organisation, closing some of their factories and transferring the production to others. Most firms, however, had to combine with one another. Since one of the main objects of the whole concentration policy was to release labour in the areas where it was most needed, firms had to consult the local officers of the Ministry of Labour before they decided amongst themselves which factories should be the nuclei and which should be closed.

In order to make it easier to comprehend at a glance the labour position in various parts of the country, the Ministry of Labour listed all its local office areas[1] as 'green', 'amber' or 'red' (in imitation of the traffic-light colour system) according to the balance of labour demands and supplies in them. 'Green' areas were those in which there was labour that could be transferred to war production elsewhere. 'Amber' areas had neither considerable deficiencies nor surpluses of labour. In 'red' areas there were urgent unsatisfied labour demands. There were too 'scarlet' areas where potential demands were so great that every effort had to be made to avoid placing additional capacity there.

When a group of firms that intended to concentrate together had decided which firms should be nuclei and which should be absorbed, the chief remaining problem was to prepare a satisfactory compensation scheme. For very good reasons the Government had refused to entangle itself in any responsibility for compensating closed firms. It had limited its commitments to measures for easing taxation burdens which might have discouraged concentration. The White Paper on

---

[1] The lists were not published.

concentration announced firmly that nucleus firms must make their own financial arrangements to compensate firms whose works were closed down. There was only one proviso: the arrangement must ensure that the plant of the closed firm be kept intact, unless the premises should be requisitioned.

The compensation arrangements made by firms varied widely. The arrangements between nucleus and closed firms were, it seems, of the following different types:—

1. Production was concentrated within the organisation of a nucleus manufacturer and the arrangements did not affect any other manufacturer.

2. Concentration involved the complete absorption of the 'closed firm' including the acquisition of goodwill and other assets.

3. Concentration did not affect independent manufacturing and trading. The 'closed firm' rented part of the factory space (and in some cases the machinery also) of the nucleus firm; in these cases arrangements about labour costs and certain overhead expenses were necessary.

4. Production was carried out solely by the nucleus firm; the closed firm ceased to trade and the nucleus firm sold (*a*) in its own name and (*b*) in the name of the closed firm for the account of the closed firm. The nucleus firm handed over to the closed firm a share of profits.

5. Production under concentration was carried out solely by the nucleus firm although the closed firm might be operating other factories or might have concentrated other production with other manufacturers. The closed firm in these cases carried on some selling activities. Various arrangements were made about materials and about distribution. The nucleus firm might produce goods for the closed firm only from materials belonging to the closed firm, or from these materials and from its own materials, or the nucleus firm might buy the materials from the closed firm and sell the finished goods to the closed firm. As for distribution the nucleus firm might deliver the goods direct to the customers of the closed firm, invoicing through the closed firm. Or it might deliver the goods to the warehouse of the closed firm which maintained its own selling organisation.

6. The nucleus firm partly manufactured the goods and invoiced the partly finished goods to the closed firm which made its own arrangements for finishing.

7. The closed firm partly manufactured the goods and the nucleus firm completed the manufacture.

8. Something in the nature of a partnership existed between the nucleus and the closed firms. Materials were owned in common and there were usually arrangements for sharing profits.

In a few important industries instead of individual arrangements between nucleus and closed firms there were industry-wide financial schemes. The basis of all these schemes was a levy on nucleus firms to provide a central fund out of which sums could be paid to closed firms to cover the expenses of care and maintenance.

When a group of firms had gone through all the involved discussions necessary for formulating a concentration scheme, the scheme itself had to be submitted to the Board of Trade for approval. At first firms simply gave an outline of their proposals to the Board of Trade. This gave the Board an opportunity to say whether the degree of concentration was sufficient or whether perhaps the production of an extra firm would have to be absorbed by the nucleus before a scheme was acceptable. The Board could also at this stage consult all the other interested ministries to make sure that they were satisfied with the schemes. The Ministry of Labour and the Factory Control within the Board of Trade had an obvious interest. The Ministry of Labour wanted to see how much labour was being released and where. Factory Control would look at the space to be released. If the prospective nucleus factory was modern while the space to be released was decrepit and of little use for storage or production, Factory Control might ask for space in the nucleus factory or even for a switch that would make the decrepit factory nucleus and the modern unit the absorbed firm. The supply departments also had an interest in concentration proposals. They did not wish to see the closure of factories on whose production they set great store. For some industries that held big orders for the fighting Services—hosiery, for example—the supply departments supplied lists of first-line and second-line firms. First-line firms were those regarded as essential and the Board had to see that they were not closed down under concentration. Other firms had to be encouraged to transfer production to them so that they could qualify for nucleus status. Second-line firms were not essential but were regarded as useful; the Board had to see that too many of these firms did not go out of operation.

If a concentration proposal seemed to satisfy all these conditions forms were sent out to the firms concerned for the formal submission of the scheme. The forms showed the material facts about each firm—the value of its production, the type of goods produced, the number and type of its machines and particulars of its labour force together with figures for the division of its production between Government orders, exports and the home civilian market. If the forms submitted confirmed that a scheme was acceptable to the Board of Trade and other ministries, a nucleus certificate, lasting three months in the first instance, was issued to the nucleus firm.

The Board of Trade had hoped that concentration by voluntary methods would proceed fast and that there would be no need to resort to nomination of nucleus and closing firms. This hope was disappointed. A month after the publication of the concentration White Paper only about thirty firms had submitted concentration arrangements based on the closing down of production units and twelve of these proposals came from firms in one industry—the hosiery industry. Over two hundred applications had however been received by the Board of Trade from manufacturers whose establishments were running full and who therefore considered that they could qualify for nucleus status without making arrangements to produce on behalf of another firm. A week or two later applications from 'running full' firms were still flowing in but very few arrangements involving closure had yet been submitted. At the beginning of May the industries controlled by the Limitation of Supplies (Miscellaneous) Order were only slightly touched by concentration; the firms that had submitted promising concentration schemes accounted for only one-sixth of the total numbers employed in these industries.

This reluctance had many causes. In some industries firms were unwilling to throw themselves and their trade secrets into the arms of their competitors. No matter how reassuring the Board of Trade were and no matter how strongly they affirmed that concentration would not encourage monopoly, firms feared that they would be absorbed and that they would not regain their identity after the war. Even when industries fully supported the principle of concentration it needed goodwill and patience to overcome compensation difficulties. When industries felt lukewarm about the whole scheme these difficulties could appear insurmountable; firms might be unwilling either to close or to assume the obligations of nucleus status.

Sometimes the structure or distribution of an industry obstructed the progress of concentration. In some industries, for example paper, separate firms made important and necessary specialities which could not be made by other firms. In some of the consumer goods industries there was a multiplicity of small firms who could, in theory, make concentration arrangements but who rarely wished to do so. Other industries consisted of a small number of firms widely scattered over the country. There were, for example, only fourteen linoleum firms situated in such diverse places as Staines, Lancaster, Wigan and Kirkcaldy. If production were to be transferred skilled workers would also have to be transferred; this would be most difficult. An example of geographical difficulties enhanced by bombing is provided by the light leather goods industry. The industry was centred in Walsall, Birmingham and London. Since Walsall and Birmingham were munitions areas the Ministry of Labour would not allow concentration into either town. But although labour was—at that time —much more plentiful in London the premises of most of the leather goods firms there had recently been destroyed in air raids. It was therefore difficult to find factories in 'easy' labour areas with sufficient surplus capacity to carry out production transferred from Walsall and Birmingham.

There was another reason why concentration applications came in slowly. From the autumn of 1940 the Board of Trade had energetically persuaded the supply departments to divert suitable Government contracts to firms whose output was declining as a result of the Limitation of Supplies (Miscellaneous) Orders. Nor had the firms themselves been idle; they had gone out to seek contracts and sub-contracts. This policy of taking Government work to civilian firms with spare capacity had proved more successful than the Government realised or than the statistics[1] revealed. When concentration was being considered it became apparent that such industries as photo-graphic goods, toys, plastic fancy goods, fountain pens, real jewellery, sports goods, musical instruments, were already largely engaged on Government work of one kind or another. Even such a seemingly 'civilian' industry as lace was mainly engaged on Government orders —in this case, sandfly netting. There was, therefore, very little surplus capacity in these industries.

So it became apparent quite soon that for one reason or another concentration would not yield such great results as were once expected. But even by these more sober standards the results achieved in the first two months or so of concentration were much too small. It seemed that concentration would drag on throughout the summer without any appreciable progress unless the Government took action. The Government had from the outset realised that such action might be necessary. The President of the Board of Trade had announced in the House of Commons[2] that though firms were asked to make their own concentration arrangements,[3] the ultimate respon-sibility for seeing that the necessary degree of concentration was achieved rested with the Government; in the last resort it would be the task of the Government to impose the reorganisation necessary to meet war demands.

At the end of April 1941, therefore, the Board of Trade decided to force the pace by fixing closing dates for the submission of voluntary concentration arrangements. To avoid congestion in the adminis-trative machine these closing dates were staggered; according to the published time-table schemes for nearly all the consumer goods industries should have been submitted by the end of May. The Board of Trade, in announcing these closing dates, made clear their policy towards small firms. The Board did not wish to exclude small firms from the benefits claimed for concentration and they therefore

[1] The K.S. inquiries. See p. 113.
[2] H. of C. Deb., Vol. 369, Col. 776.
[3] The cotton industry was, from the outset, an exception. See Chapter XV, section (i).

emphasised that voluntary arrangements between small firms would be very welcome. It would not, however, be possible to impose concentration on a multitude of small firms; those firms that did not make arrangements of their own would be left to fend for themselves.[1]

When the closing dates for voluntary concentration had passed the Board of Trade did not automatically apply concentration schemes of their own to the larger recalcitrant firms. The progress of concentration was reviewed. It was clear that in some industries voluntary concentration had been successful. In hosiery, for example, voluntary schemes covered about three-quarters of the production of the industry. Small firms and firms which because of special production or location were unsuitable for concentration accounted for another ten per cent. of output. There was no reason why the remaining fifteen to twenty per cent. of production should not be concentrated. The Board of Trade therefore proceeded to nominate nucleus and non-nucleus firms. Nomination was applied to several other industries where further concentration seemed possible and desirable—for example to pottery, boots and shoes, toilet preparations, linoleum and bedding. In some industries, however, it seemed that further releases of labour and factory space would be too small to make nomination worth while.

Nomination was commonly called compulsory concentration. But it must be remembered that there was no specific legislation to apply concentration policy. The policy was essentially one of inducements and sanctions administered through existing controls over labour and raw materials and factory space. For cotton there was a legal sanction; the licences of non-nucleus firms to consume yarn or raw cotton were withdrawn. These firms, therefore, were unquestionably closed down. In other industries subject to a strong central control nomination was effective. But in industries where firms had not found the inducements to concentration sufficiently strong the sanctions were correspondingly weak. Sometimes nominated nucleus firms were unenthusiastic about the advantages attached to their status and were not therefore very concerned to ensure that the supposedly closed firms attached to them did in fact close. And it was often easy for these closed firms to remain open. If their factory premises were requisitioned that was the end of it. But if the premises were not needed for some reason or other the firms could usually struggle on with non-directable labour and with raw materials taken from stock or acquired through the many loopholes in control. A good many firms that were officially closed continued their operations until they came under the closer scrutiny and control imposed when the Board of Trade introduced direct controls over the manufacture and supply of consumer goods.

---

[1] *Board of Trade Journal.* 8th May 1941.

By the end of 1941 there seemed to be little further scope for voluntary or 'compulsory' concentration in the industries covered by the Limitation of Supplies Orders. Concentration activity in the Board of Trade was well past its peak. It was not, however, completely finished. In 1942, for example, the contracts for sandfly netting that had prevented concentration in the lace industry tailed off, leaving surplus capacity to be concentrated. And as part of the growth of control over clothing production, the clothing industry[1] was concentrated in 1942. There was also still some work to be done on the raw material industries.[2] In the autumn of 1941 the Minister of Labour had complained of the slow progress and meagre results of concentration in the wool industry and had asked that the policy should be applied to other industries such as tinplate. In the end the wool industry, like other raw material industries such as paper, was not effectively concentrated in the full sense of the word. Nor were the attempts to arrange schemes for various sections of the iron and steel industry—tinplate, sheets, tube and iron castings—very successful. The jute industry on the other hand, which was asked to concentrate at the end of 1941 in order to release storage space, produced a workable scheme. Unfortunately the scheme had no sooner been prepared than jute imports fell owing to the war in the Far East and reconcentration was necessary. This reduction in jute supplies meant in turn that the nucleus certificates issued to carpet firms and firms making floor coverings had to be withdrawn.

Towards the end of 1942 concentration made a reappearance in ministerial discussions. By this time it was recognised that, provided the shipping crisis was overcome, manpower would be the limiting factor in the British war effort; the current manpower demands of the Services and the supply departments could not possibly be met. War programmes had, therefore, to be reduced. But at the same time it was more important than ever to withdraw any surplus labour from civilian industries. The Ministry of Labour and the Ministry of Production both urged further concentration as a means of drawing off this surplus.

It was not only the general labour scarcity that was causing concern. There were some particular areas where production congestion had become intolerable. Throughout 1942 the Ministry of Production had been trying to ensure that no further work was placed in such areas. The same Ministry in conjunction with the Ministry of Labour had also been urging that, wherever possible, munitions and civilian production should be transferred away from these areas to places where labour was more plentiful. They looked for the co-opera-

---

[1] See Chapter XVI, section (i).

[2] In the food industries, concentration had hardly begun. See R. J. Hammond, *Food*, Vol. I (United Kingdom Civil Histories) (H.M.S.O., 1951), Chapter XXV.

tion of the Board of Trade. For this reason, too, concentration policy came once more to the fore.

In order to release more labour in the areas of acute scarcity the Board of Trade planned to reconcentrate some second priority industries. The industries chosen were light industries which would be easy to move and which were known to have considerable capacity in easy labour areas—leather goods, toilet preparations, sports goods, umbrellas and fountain pens. In these industries nucleus firms in red and scarlet labour areas were told that their nucleus certificates would not be renewed unless the firms moved to approved areas. Further inducements were offered: the Board of Trade had lately introduced firmer controls over the production of consumer goods[1] which made it possible to offer a higher production quota to firms who agreed to move.

Encouraged by some success in reconcentrating these light industries which had already been dealt with once in 1941, the Board of Trade proceeded to deal with other industries which had for various reasons been untouched so far by concentration policy. The first experiment was with the hat industry. This industry was due to contract much further and the Board felt that this contraction should be the opportunity for clearing the industry out of such areas as Luton and the Denton-Stockport-Manchester region where labour was extremely scarce. Firms with branches both in these areas and other places would be required to close the Luton branches; firms established entirely in these regions would be advised to make arrangements with other firms in easier areas. This experiment proved an unhappy one. A storm of local protests at the threats to transfer these industries to other areas broke around the Board of Trade's head. After a week or two the head bowed and the scheme was abandoned.

The hat troubles came in December 1942. They brought to a head a difference of opinion between the Board of Trade on the one hand and the Ministry of Labour and the Ministry of Production on the other about future action—a difference that was carried to the Lord President's Committee. The President of the Board of Trade pointed out that hitherto his department had not pressed small firms to come into concentration schemes since the economies of labour and factory space to be obtained from them would not be worth the administrative trouble and friction involved. In the Board of Trade's view concentration as an instrument for obtaining releases of labour had nearly run its course. Now, however, he was being urged to concentrate for the first time industries that had a very high proportion of unorganised small firms.

---

[1] See Chapter XIX.

There was another point: hitherto, provided the supply of raw materials was adequate, the Board had not compulsorily shut down firms that would not make voluntary arrangements for closing and transferring their production. The Board had simply refused protection to these firms' labour and premises. The President wished to continue this policy. He could not, he said, make himself responsible for throwing people out of work, with the risk that the Ministry of Labour could not find other employment. He was prepared however to do all he could to release labour in difficult areas by refusing licences for manufacturing unessential goods there. Licences would have to be issued to enable those for whom other work could not be found to continue their old trade; the licensing should be undertaken by the local staffs of the Ministry of Labour. As for the production of essential civilian goods in difficult labour areas, the President would urge nucleus firms in concentrated industries to reduce production in the difficult areas and build it up in the easy ones. He would be willing, not to close these firms, but to withdraw their nucleus certificates. Where this was not appropriate there remained the remedy of physically transferring the firms to other regions. But this was a very difficult remedy and should only be used as a last resort when the balance of advantage in favour of a move was very great. When firms were transferred the President asked that the Ministry of Labour and the Ministry of Production should come out openly and share the public responsibility for this unpleasant task.

Some of these propositions of the President's were unacceptable to his colleagues. The Ministry of Labour swiftly brought objections to the main points. The Minister insisted that concentration could be applied to further industries and that small firms should be brought within the scheme. Most of all the Minister objected to the President's proposal that non-nucleus firms should not be closed down. He pointed out that firms remaining in existence, even non-nucleus firms, attracted to themselves labour and contracts, thus establishing claims to keep labour and premises which could not be rejected without strong protests. Moreover if the President's proposals were agreed firms would be closed not according to an individual plan but according to considerations of hardship unrelated to production or the interests of the industry as a whole.

When this disagreement came before the Lord President's Committee the three ministers concerned were asked to meet and sort out their differences. By February 1943 agreement had been reached. Any further civilian industries coming up for examination were to be carefully considered to see whether they could be concentrated, but it was realised that this would be much more difficult than in the case of the industries already dealt with. Where concentration was found to be practicable nucleus firms would in general be nominated.

Where concentration was not practicable arrangements were to be made for the withdrawal of labour on an orderly plan. The proposal of the President of the Board of Trade to allow the production of unessential goods in difficult labour areas only under licence was also welcomed.

Broadly, these decisions were a victory for the Board of Trade's view. The victory was not in itself significant. For, as the Board of Trade had realised, the day of concentration was over. It was no longer very relevant to the problems of economic mobilisation; there was, indeed, very little concentration activity in the Board of Trade during 1943 and 1944. Nevertheless, the ministerial discussions at the end of 1942 and the beginning of 1943 do reveal a confusion of thought about the methods and purpose of concentration which is important in assessing the whole policy. It is to this assessment of policy and its achievements that we must now turn.

(iii)

The Achievement

As a starting point for assessing concentration policy we can take Table 12 which gives the last figures compiled by the Board of Trade to show the releases of labour and factory space laid down in the concentration schemes of various industries.

At first sight the results seem impressive—over 70 million square feet of factory space and over a quarter of a million workers released. But the table should be used with great caution. The figures for releases of space and labour are themselves misleading. When firms submitted concentration schemes they agreed to release a certain number of workers and a certain amount of space from the date when they submitted the scheme. When a nucleus certificate was granted the number of workers and the amount of space to be released were entered in the Board of Trade's 'progress' records as if they were actual figures. But planned releases did not necessarily mean releases achieved. Quite apart from possible errors in the firms' calculations the Ministry of Labour might not wish to take advantage of the proposed release of workers or they might not find anyone who was suitable for munitions work. The factory space released might also be unsuitable or unwanted.

The table of concentration results only covers the 'main' industries. For the purpose of assessing concentration results the table is in one sense too wide and in another sense too narrow. It is too wide because it includes industries which were never really concentrated on the approved lines of the concentration White Paper. It might be

Results of Concentration of Production up to 1st March 1944[1]

TABLE 12

Industry	Number of certificates issued	Number of establishments closed[2]	Gross factory space sq. ft. released[3] '000s	Net labour released[3] '000s
Bedding	69	65	387	0·8
Boots and shoes . .	408	276	3,797	15·0
Carpets	14	57	3,500	10·0
Cardboard boxes . .	91	116	2,035	1·6
Clothing	756	328	2,918	45·0
Conduit tubes . .	5	9	26	0·1
Corsets	39	25	287	1·0
Cotton (all sections) . .	1,533	684	26,000	117·0
Cutlery (including razor blades)	96	85	195	0·7
Furniture	172	—	1,000	8·1
Gas tubes	1	8	—	0·5
Gloves	147	55	195	1·8
Hat hoods . . .	21	27	635	1·9
Hosiery (including warp knitting and dyers and finishers)	415	603	6,129	33·8
Iron foundries . . .	32	30	—	0·4
Jute	58	15	1,761	1·7
Lace	45	88	1,242	2·0
Leather goods . . .	98	180	736	3·7
Linoleum	7	6	980	0·6
Narrow fabrics . . .	147	83	792	6·6
Paint and varnish . .	164	—	200	—
Pottery	85	105	2,418	9·8
Rayon	7	—	1,000	3·5
Silk	56	30	540	1·5
Steel sheets . . .	23	9	600	1·7
Tiles (glazed) . . .	8	11	542	2·0
Toilet preparations . .	37	77	867	1·3
Woodworking . . .	552	68	620	0·4
Wood (all sections) . .	967	234	10,000	12·0
Other industries . .	474	347	1,272	3·9
TOTAL . .	6,527	3,621	70,674	288·4

argued that this in itself is a tribute to the flexibility of administrators in accepting schemes which were not orthodox. But this claim cannot be upheld if the schemes produced results which it was the primary aim of concentration to avoid—that is, spread-over systems and part-time working with no closure of redundant factories. It is therefore fair to say that furniture production was not concentrated—it is clear from the table that no establishments were closed down.[4] The same is true of rayon and paint. Similarly the schemes in the two

---

[1] This table was circulated by the Board of Trade with this heading. It should more accurately have been called 'Progress Report on Concentration Schemes Accepted to 1st March 1944'.

[2] This heading should more accurately have been 'to be closed'.

[3] This heading should more accurately have been 'to be released'.

[4] Some other establishments had been requisitioned before concentration began. See pp. 511–22 for the history of furniture production.

most important sections of the lace industry—lace furnishings and leavers lace—were in no way concentration. The lace furnishings section formed a company, British Lace Furnishings Limited, which received all allocations of raw material and which was responsible for handling all production and sales and all Government contracts. Some machines and some establishments were closed in this process but there were no nucleus firms working full and no closed firms in the technical sense. Basically, the system was one of 'spread-over'.

There is another way in which Table 12 overstates the releases through concentration. The sanctions to ensure that 'closed' firms did in fact close were often weak. Firms could struggle on with raw materials obtained through loopholes in the controls and with non-directable labour. The Minister of Labour in the ministerial discussions on extensions of concentration at the end of 1942 clearly thought that firms closed by concentration schemes were physically shut down. But in some industries, for example cutlery, the 'closed' firms went on working quite happily. This could not be prevented until the Board of Trade introduced their strict controls over the manufacture and supply of consumer goods.[1]

The table of concentration results given on p. 225 is too narrow in that it only sets out to cover 'main industries'. In considering the time and effort spent on concentration and the results achieved it would be only fair to include all the industries covered by concentration or attempts at concentration. Concentration was attempted but formally abandoned in four industries—bicycles, domestic electrical appliances, jewellery and paper. When it was found that industries were unsuitable for concentration they were usually dropped quite quickly. There were, however, exceptions: through pressure from the Ministry of Labour and Ministry of Supply concentration of the iron-foundry and paint industries (both of which are included in Table 12) was pursued long after it was clear that nothing would come of it. We must also remember the additional minor industries which, according to the Board of Trade, were concentrated. These were as follows: braces, fellmongering, football bladders, fountain pens, blown glass, gum, latex, lead sheet and pipe, musical instruments, pencils, photographic goods, pianos, printing ink, rubber footwear, spirit varnish, sports goods, toys and umbrellas. In some of these industries, as in the main ones, concentration had only a paper existence. In all of them together the number of workers 'released'—even in the expansive sense of this word as used in the Board of Trade progress reports—did not exceed a thousand.

It is clear that the Board of Trade's figures give no real guide to the degree of success achieved by concentration. We must therefore

---

[1] Concentration by nomination did not help this difficulty. See p. 220.

discuss the results in more general terms by recalling the twin chief aims of concentration policy[1]—the release of resources for the war effort and the preservation of nuclei for post-war expansion. Let us first take the release of resources and examine the resources separately. First: factory space. The Factory Control considered concentration to be a most useful method of releasing space; it undoubtedly saved the Control a good deal of time and effort in seeking out space to requisition for storage or for war production. But although concentration was immensely useful to the Control it was not essential. Space would have been requisitioned in any case, as indeed it was from many non-concentrated industries. The absence of concentration would simply have meant different methods of interdepartmental procedure. As in the 'keeping step' days of the autumn of 1940 the Board of Trade—and now the Raw Materials Department as well—would have had to recommend which firms should be requisitioned and which should be left alone.[2]

Secondly, how did concentration affect labour releases? The close examination of this question belongs to the history of manpower; only a brief discussion is possible here. Reliable figures of the amount of labour released through concentration considered as a separate policy do not exist. Nor could they. For as the officials who administered it well understood concentration was not an isolated process. It was in essence a scheme for the rationalisation[3] of production. But as we saw earlier it became inevitably and inextricably intertwined with production policy and with contraction of production. The number of workers employed on carpet production and linoleum production, for example, fell chiefly because supplies of jute were dwindling. Pottery production was concentrated not at the industry's current level of output but at a lower level which would free large numbers of workers for munitions production. These contractions would have come even if there had been no concentration.

The labour economies secured through rationalisation alone must have been limited. Short-time working which seemed to be prevalent in some industries before concentration was of course eliminated. But, as events proved, the passage of time would have performed this function: by the end of 1941 the wastage of labour from many civilian industries was proving uncomfortably heavy. In addition to wiping out short-time working concentration was expected to produce

---

[1] For the subsidiary aim of restraining price increases see p. 208. Concentration was never intended to be a method of increasing the efficiency of civilian industry. It is not possible to calculate whether or not the policy had any indirect results on efficiency and productivity.

[2] See pp. 113, 114.

[3] The word rationalisation is used rather loosely here in the sense of concentrating production into fewer units. Rationalisation in economic language is frequently associated with the ideas of efficiency and long-term reorganisation. Concentration was, as we have emphasised, not concerned with these ideas.

economies in the use of key men, maintenance men and managerial and office staff. There must certainly have been some saving in this field. And in some industries, where efficiency depended on the careful organisation of workers into teams, concentration probably helped to restore a balance that had been upset by rationing of raw material or redundancy cuts. However, it is doubtful how big these economies were. For it was a condition of concentration that the plant of closed firms should be kept in working order and this meant that men had to look after the idle machines. Moreover, under several of the most popular concentration arrangements, closed firms were responsible for all their own office and selling work. Indeed in these cases the two aims of concentration policy became difficult to reconcile; the survival of the closed firm's identity was more important than the release of labour for the war effort.

Apart from any claims about the amount of labour released by concentration it was often emphasised that the scheme made orderly those releases that did occur. These claims may have been over-stated. One of the chief attractions of the 'orderliness' of concentration to the Ministry of Labour was the prospect of closing firms in difficult labour areas and encouraging firms in easy areas to be nuclei. But the possibilities of this geographical concentration of production were limited. In April 1941 the Board of Trade analysed the distribution of the main consumer goods industries to be concentrated between 'red', 'amber' and 'green' labour areas and the London area. The analysis showed that at the end of 1940 eighty-five per cent. of the employees in these industries were to be found in 'red' areas and another thirteen per cent. in London.[1] It is therefore clear that the scope for concentrating production in firms in green areas was very limited.

The word 'orderly' as applied to concentration was not only used in a geographical sense. It was also used to imply that the Ministry of Labour could ensure the release of workers of the right kind and at the right time. But this was an empty hope unless the Ministry of Labour could control the movements of workers. From this point of view the timing of concentration was unfortunate. For in the spring of 1941 labour controls were still in their youth. It was possible to keep track of the men of military age. But registration and direction of women and of men over military age were only beginning. As far as women were concerned the whole process of registration, interview and transfer was cautious and therefore slow until the autumn of 1941. The controls over women were not completed until the Control of Engagement Order in February 1942 required all

---

[1] In the spring of 1941 it was still undesirable to shift production to London because of bombing. Later London became one of the most difficult of all labour areas. Other green areas developed into red ones.

employers to engage women aged from eighteen to forty through the employment exchanges. In the summer months of 1941, when the Board of Trade's concentration activities were at their height, there was no guarantee that the labour released passed through the Ministry of Labour's hands for placing. Indeed, of the labour estimated to have been released by concentrating industries between March and August 1941, well over half did not go through the Ministry of Labour's placing machinery.

This was not only due to the looseness of labour controls. Even if the controls had been in full trim the Ministry of Labour might well have found the yield from concentration disappointing. For many of the concentrated industries turned out to be employers on a surprisingly large scale of labour that even by the stern standards of 1943 and 1944 was non-directable—married women with small children, and elderly men. This was indeed partly because the younger and more mobile workers had often left the industry in anticipation of concentration—usually in order to go to war work. It could also be argued that since the Ministry of Labour was reluctant to take steps which might lead to the closing of firms unless this were part of a concentration scheme, concentration was a way of forcing the less easily placed people on to the labour market. But there was of course no guarantee that these people moved to more essential work. Even if they did not there was often an indirect gain in that they took the place of others who were subject to control and were called up. On the other hand many of them left industry, at any rate for the time, rather than move to strange employments further from their home.

In the timing of labour releases, also, concentration did not prove as orderly a process as the Ministry of Labour had expected. When mobile workers were released by concentration schemes, the timing did not very much matter as there were always vacancies for munitions workers somewhere. But if the timing of concentration schemes was not careful the release of immobile labour might not fit in with the demands of local munitions work. Unfortunately variations in the supply of raw materials, or the Factory Control's need for space, or the reactions of individual firms often made it difficult to time labour releases correctly.

Concentration was expected to release other resources besides labour and factory space for the war effort—for example gas, electricity and coal. Even closed firms usually had to use some light and heat in order to keep their machinery in good working order. But as long as 'closed' firms really did close there must undoubtedly have been appreciable economies in the use of fuel and power for civilian production. As coal became increasingly scarce this was a most useful contribution to the war effort. Where the concentrated industry was highly localised in a district where coal supplies were specially difficult these economies were very important in helping the smooth progress of other forms of war production. Cotton concentration undoubtedly helped munitions production in Lancashire in this way.

The release of resources for the war effort was one of the chief aims of concentration policy. Subsidiary to this aim was the expectation that concentration would bring substantial economies in production which would help to keep industrial costs down. It is impossible to say how far this hope was fulfilled. It would be vain to seek for economies achieved through the concentration of production upon the most efficient firms. For the choice of nucleus firms was governed not by efficiency but by the demands of war: it was often necessary to close down the large, modern firms. It was indeed possible that concentration might adversely affect the efficiency of an industry. Nevertheless, it is safe to assume that the nucleus firms themselves produced goods more economically when they were working at full capacity after concentration than when they were working short time. The employment of labour on short time obviously inflated costs; even in the absence of concentration, however, surplus labour would probably have drifted away. The other economies to be achieved by full-time working would vary a great deal from industry to industry according to the burden of overhead costs, the complexity of machinery and so forth. But economies there must certainly have been.

The second main aim of concentration policy was the preservation of nuclei for post-war expansion in the industries concerned. The fear that many producers would be driven into bankruptcy was constantly in the minds of the Board of Trade officials in the months when concentration policy was being planned. The manufacturers themselves were inclined to rate their possibilities of survival higher than the Board of Trade did. And they were not all impressed by the inducements and sanctions which were the basis of concentration. The inducements were indirect—labour, raw materials and factory space would be protected 'as far as possible'. The only real advantage for a nucleus firm was the promise of inclusion in the list of protected establishments which gave it a lower age of reservation from military service for its workers. This advantage disappeared however when the Schedule of Reserved Occupations was abolished at the end of 1941. Unless this benefit while it lasted was of great importance to the firms concerned they might prefer to gamble on the possibility that Government departments would not take away labour and factory space.

The possibilities of survival among firms without formal concentration schemes were in fact quite high. Most producers of consumer goods showed a surprising ingenuity in adapting their production to warlike purposes. And at the end of the war they proved to be adaptable in reversing the process. If, on the other hand, a firm's premises were requisitioned, the compensation payments would prevent financial ruin; in these cases, too, firms were swift in returning to their peace-time production at the end of the war. Even in industries where the factors of production were highly specific and could not be converted to war purposes, it is doubtful whether Government-sponsored schemes were necessary to survival. It was, for example, very difficult to use lace factories for any war purpose once netting contracts declined, since the machinery was large and heavy and could not be moved. But the industry made its own arrangements for avoiding wholesale bankruptcies. Some concentrated firms in restarting production after the war must have received valuable help from their nucleus partners. But the impetus of inflationary pressure must surely have been a more powerful force in the post-war expansion of industry. It is easy, however, to reach this conclusion in retrospect: officials at the time were looking forward and into a misty future.

Lest our assessment of concentration policy seems discouraging we must mention points that weigh more heavily to its advantage. First it can be said that the scheme provided a useful example of co-operation between Government and industry. 'The Government set out the objectives of policy, laid down the conditions that had to be satisfied and established sanctions; but the firms and industries to which the policy was applied were given the task of working out the arrangements in detail.'[1] More important still: in some important industries—in particular cotton, hosiery, boots and shoes, and pottery —the policy was an undoubted success in releasing resources. Indeed, the table printed on p. 225 shows that a large proportion of the results ascribed to concentration is accounted for by these four industries. It is impossible to measure the precise contribution of concentration in these industries, but the releases of labour and space in them during 1941 helped to fulfil the pressing demands of war industries in such difficult areas as Lancashire, the North Midlands and North Staffordshire. There were various reasons for the success of concentration in these industries. All of them were located in clearly defined areas; firms were not scattered far and wide all over the country. All the industries were, too, highly organised. At first this was not necessarily an advantage for at least one of the trade associations concerned obstructed the progress of concentration. But when the co-operation of all the powerful organisations in these industries had been won—as it was—the task of concentration was thereafter simplified. Moreover, once concentration had got under way in three

---

[1] G. C. Allen's article on 'The Concentration of Production Policy' in *Lessons of the British War Economy*.

of the industries—in cotton, hosiery and boots and shoes—there were means of making the schemes effective. For there was a central control over raw material allocations that was in these cases strong enough to ensure that 'closed' firms really did close. For cotton there was, it will be remembered, a legal sanction.[1] In these four big consumer goods industries concentration was in fact as well as in theory a step towards the close control of production that was to be so important in civilian industries in the later years of the war.

In retrospect it seems a pity that concentration as a policy was not confined to the few industries where conditions favoured it and where the results to be achieved were great. As it is, the chief criticism of concentration must be that it was applied too indiscriminately. The sole criterion used was the existence of surplus capacity in an industry, not its essentiality. Here again the timing of concentration policy was unfortunate. Early in 1941 exports were still a matter of importance to the Board of Trade. The debates that were to bear fruit in the Lend-Lease Act were already being held in the United States but the implications of this policy were not yet clear within the Board of Trade. Hence all industries with an export interest were still of value in the Board's eyes. A year later the logic of the British war economy was visible to all; exports were mainly confined to the essential needs of Allies and the production of unessential goods was to be cut to the bone—it was to be, if possible, eliminated.

The fact was that right to the end the circumstances of war were fluid. Shipping prospects fluctuated and military events sometimes changed the prospects of raw material supplies almost overnight. And as for labour, areas that were 'green' in 1941 might become 'scarlet' by late 1942. For these reasons and for some others—such as deficient knowledge in the Board of Trade about the war contracts held by civilian industry—a good deal of time and effort spent on concentration was wasted. One or two of the industries that had been so carefully concentrated had to be closed down. Others had to be reconcentrated to match changes in labour or raw material supply. Every time this happened concentration arrangements and the detailed financial arrangements had to be re-examined, causing more work for Government officials, for industry, and for the overburdened accountants' profession. Moreover, the criteria that had been used in concentrating an industry were superseded sometimes. In the pottery industry, for example, nucleus firms were chosen largely for their importance in the export trade. Later, when there was an acute shortage of articles such as cups for the home market it was found that some of the most useful firms for this type of produc-

---

[1] See p. 220.

tion had been closed. Concentration was in this sense inflexible for once a firm had been closed it was very difficult indeed to reopen it.[1]

The choice of industries to be concentrated and the absence of discrimination between essential and unessential industries had some unfortunate results. The criterion for protecting a civilian firm's labour, materials and space became not so much the importance of its product as its concentration status. For example, as long as the Schedule of Reserved Occupations was in force the only firms to be entered on the register of protected establishments, which conferred reservation at a specially low age, were firms largely working on Government and export work and nucleus firms in concentrated industries. This penalised firms in some industries such as perambulators and hollow-ware which were unsuitable for concentration but which were nevertheless really essential to civilian morale.

Concentration of restricted output into fewer units was in theory an eminently simple and sensible idea. It is impossible to assess its results accurately but it seems probable that its results were in general smaller than those usually credited to it. Except in the few major industries where the scheme was a success the Board of Trade might have done just as well by extending the 'keeping step' procedure evolved in the autumn of 1940 until such time as they were ready for the strict control over manufacture and supply which was introduced in 1942. But these conclusions spring from the backward gaze of history. Early in 1941 the officials of the Board of Trade were engaged in experiments that were quite new and where there was no previous experience to guide them.

---

[1] This problem of reopening closed firms also arose in the cotton industry. See p. 370.

CHAPTER XI

THE CONTROL OF FACTORY AND STORAGE PREMISES

(i)

The Establishment of the Control

AT the same time that the concentration of production was launched a Control of Factory and Storage Premises was established within the Board of Trade. A history of civil industry and trade is not the most logical place for a study of this Control. This study should really form part of a much larger one —a study of the problem of the war-time location of industry. Location problems, however, must transcend the limits of any single history and touch upon many—upon manpower, war production, works and buildings, transport, fuel and power, food. It was not so much for reasons of logic as for reasons of convenience that the control over factory and storage premises became part of the Board of Trade and thereby part of the history of civil industry.

Before the war there had been very little appreciation of the great demands on factory and storage premises that were bound to arise when the war machine was in top gear. Therefore the need for a strict control over the use of premises was almost completely overlooked; the Ministry of Works' central register[1] was no substitute. Right at the beginning of the war a suggestion for some such control was made by the Ministry of Food but it met with scant enthusiasm from the other interested departments. As it happened, the need for the control did not become pressing until the autumn of 1940. In the early months of the war the demand for premises had not been very great. There were no air raids causing damage or fear of damage. The tempo of war production was slow. Stocks of food, raw materials and munitions held in the United Kingdom were increasing very slowly, if at all. But soon after the fall of France there developed a scramble among Government departments and individual manufacturers for space—space for storage and space for production.

When first the Government became aware of this scramble it

---

[1] See p. 236.

examined separately the two problems of space for production and space for storage. It was only after independent studies of both problems had been made that discussions were fused and that the Government realised the urgent need for a control over all premises whether for production or for storage.

The main reason for the increased demand for factory premises was air attack or the threat of attack. The greatest demands for premises came from the Ministry of Aircraft Production for it was supremely important for the survival of Britain that aircraft production should not be crippled by bombing. The answer of Lord Beaverbrook and his Ministry to bombing was dispersal. Sometimes dispersal meant the removal of a vital production unit from one area to another. Sometimes it meant that a large production unit had to be split up into several smaller units. One unit in Chester, for example, was dispersed to twenty-four places and another in Weybridge to thirty-seven places. The Ministry of Aircraft Production pursued its dispersal policy 'with energy and on a very large scale'. As early as October 1940 364 new premises had been acquired for airframe and engine production alone; in addition instrument production and radio manufacture had been partly dispersed. The other supply departments and the Board of Trade—to whom the responsibility for maintaining the supply of essential 'civilian' goods belonged—were less impressed with the value of dispersal but they could not wholly dispense with it. And all production departments had to help the bombed-out manufacturers under their wing to find alternative premises. The bombing of London greatly increased the number of removals.

The search for factory premises in 'safe' areas was not confined to firms producing munitions and other essential goods. There was little to stop private firms, no matter how inessential the goods they made, from taking over any factories they could find. The only check on their moving into factories which might be used for war production was the possibility that the premises into which they went might be requisitioned. It was, as one official committee concluded, 'not a very effective check'.

The scramble for factory space was largely due to air-raid damage and the fear of damage. Other factors, however, intensified it. By the autumn of 1940 the pace of war production had quickened and the supply departments' demands on industry were expanding. These increased demands inevitably produced demands for more factory space. It was no use relying on the wholesale construction of new factories for by this time the building industry was seriously overloaded and the armed forces were casting envious eyes upon the large numbers of able-bodied men of military age employed in it. Moreover, time was short; space was wanted at once, not several months hence. It was obviously better to get hold of existing factory premises than to build new ones.

There was, however, no orderly method for getting hold of factory premises, whether they were wanted for dispersal, bombed-out firms or expansion. Since before the war the Ministry of Works had held a central register of property; Government departments and local authorities could earmark on this list buildings which they expected to requisition later. The department that earmarked a building had first claim upon it and other departments were obliged to hold back. The owner or occupier of the building, however, knew nothing of the earmarking and could dispose of the building to anyone. Moreover, consultation between requisitioning departments was not as close as it should have been. Instances were reported where Service departments had requisitioned buildings suitable for war production in order to use them for offices or billets. Sometimes factories producing for one ministry had even been requisitioned to house a firm producing for another ministry. Again, a department might earmark a building it did not immediately require, thus blocking—however unwittingly—the urgent needs of other departments. In addition to the central register there existed an index of property. It was not the function of the Ministry of Works to find premises on behalf of other departments. But in the late summer of 1940 it had begun to compile a list of buildings—mainly factory premises—that were unoccupied or offered by the owners. Any department wishing to use the Ministry of Works as an estate agent could consult the list and select premises. The Ministry would then requisition the premises on behalf of the department.[1] Finally, the Area Boards had also compiled lists of buildings to be used as pools for rehousing damaged munitions factories from their own areas. But the pools were not protected against requisitioning nor against the infiltration of inessential firms. Nor could they cope with the heavy evacuation to 'safe' areas.

During November and the early part of December 1940 ministers made various proposals for bringing order into the chaotic search for factory accommodation. There were suggestions, though rather vague ones, for some form of control that would restrict the movement of factories and direct such movements as were necessary to places where the least congestion would arise. In addition ministers urged that the machinery of interdepartmental consultation should be improved.

The proposals and suggestions did not receive unanimous approval. The President of the Board of Trade, in particular, thought them

---

[1] Some departments did their own requisitioning. Before requisitioning took place the Board of Trade were meant to be informed to prevent the occupation of buildings meeting export or essential home needs.

misplaced. He felt that the main need was for a 'stay put' policy. Factory owners should, he thought, be strongly dissuaded from transferring their factories away from bombed areas. For such transfers might well develop into a 'refugee movement of industry as dangerous to the industrial life of the country as was the refugee movement of the civil population in France to their army in the field'. The President felt that it was much more important to stop the movement than, simply, as his colleagues suggested, to control and direct it. The only factories allowed to move should be vital war factories that it was essential to restart or to disperse, and bombed factories which produced for export or essential needs in industries where all available productive capacity was already being used. Alternative premises for such factories must be allocated in the same way that raw materials were allocated.

While these discussions about factory premises were going on other discussions were proceeding about storage space. Conditions in the west coast ports first brought this subject to the fore. Diversion of shipping from the south and east coasts to the western ports had produced chaos there. This chaos was made up from many ingredients but one of the chief of them was lack of storage space. When in October 1940 some officers of the Treasury Investigation Section made a general survey of the port of Liverpool in order to discover redundancies and overlapping among officials there, they found the question of warehousing in the port so urgent that they decided to make a special report on it. It seemed highly inadvisable that imports —the country's vital national reserves—should be held in the vulnerable dock area for a moment longer than was absolutely unavoidable. But, as it was, all kinds of people were demanding additional space in the Liverpool area. The Ministry of Food wished to establish twenty buffer warehouses there, the Ministry of Supply wanted to store a growing volume of raw materials and finished goods, the Service departments needed accommodation for stores, and the Port Emergency Committee needed a reserve of vacant space in the dock area lest there should be a hold-up in clearing goods from the port. One thing was clear: warehousing and storage could not be dealt with effectively as a local problem. The possibilities of alternative accommodation would have to be canvassed much more widely.

When these Liverpool problems came before ministers the Minister without Portfolio hastened to point out that this shortage of warehousing space was part of a wider shortage of buildings of all kinds. The same shortage had arisen in the dispersal of food stocks, the billeting or armed forces and the removal of factories from the danger zones. The special difficulties associated with warehousing could be traced to three causes. First, there was the unusually high level of stocks; stocks of imported foodstuffs for example were a million tons higher in November 1940 than in November 1939. Secondly, warehouse buildings were particularly vulnerable to damage by air attack. Finally, there was the diversion of shipping to the west coast ports. This made it necessary to keep a free margin of warehousing space in these ports.

It seemed that it might be possible to relieve the shortage of warehousing space by various methods. But there was one indispensable requirement. It was essential to devise a co-ordinated scheme under which the storage capacity available inland as well as in the ports should be formed into a pool. Space should be allocated from this pool according to the needs of departments and the amounts and types of accommodation available. The existing arrangements for earmarking and requisitioning storage space were the same inadequate ones that governed factory premises—the Ministry of Works' central register of premises and index of property. Moreover, the number of departments seeking storage space was greater than the number seeking factory premises. And the co-ordination of storage arrangements within the separate departments was often weak. The Ministry of Food was by now working towards a system of complete central control of the storage activities of its individual divisions. But the Ministry of Supply, for example, still left separate raw material Controls to look after their own storage problems with almost no central direction.

In November 1940 the Lord President's Committee appointed an interdepartmental committee whose chief task it was to make recommendations about the central and regional organisation necessary to establish a pool of storage capacity. The committee was also of course to study the present storage position and its recommendations were to take account of the needs of the various regions, the suitability of the accommodation available, the economic use of inland transport and the availability of labour.

This committee reported early in December. It confirmed that there was a general scramble for storage space and that this scramble had caused the wasteful use of space. Goods were stored in premises not well adapted to take them, and other goods which these premises might readily have taken had had to be stored equally inappropriately. The use to which space was put and the department into whose control it passed were often matters of chance or they reflected the ruthlessness which individual storage directors were willing to practise. There was in short no coherent system for establishing priority in the use of storage space.

The proposals made by the committee were in substance accepted by ministers and were the basis of the scheme that was finally sent forward for the War Cabinet's approval. There were certain subsidiary proposals for easing the shortage of space. Manufacturers, traders and consumers, for example, were to be encouraged to hold as large stocks as possible. The importance of easing transport by better location of storage space was also urged. And there were recommendations for making more warehousing labour available. But the chief proposal concerned organisation—the establishment of a control. At this point the two sets of discussions on storage and factory space merged. It was recognised that it was impossible to deal with the two problems separately. A unified control was essential. A Controller-General of Factory and Storage Premises was therefore to be appointed.

Many of the main features of the Control were thought out in advance and included in the plan put forward to the War Cabinet. It was generally felt that the Control must be linked with some executive department of State, preferably a neutral one. At that time the Ministry of Works was not strong enough for the task. For this and other reasons the Board of Trade were chosen as the most suitable home.[1]

One of the first tasks of the Controller-General would be to prepare a comprehensive Register of Factory and Storage Premises. A good deal of information was already available. But a special survey would be necessary in order to collect more detailed information about factory and storage accommodation throughout the country including, for example, capacity, suitability for the various processes of manufacture or types of storage, availability of labour, housing, transport and power and the current use of premises. The survey would be extended to accommodation which could if necessary be adapted for storage or factory purposes.

The Control would be responsible for allocating factory and storage space and an interdepartmental advisory committee would help it to decide broad questions of priority. All Government departments would have to obtain authority from the Control's headquarters or from one of its regional offices[2] before requisitioning any premises for manufacture or storage or before requisitioning for other purposes any premises ordinarily used for the purpose of manufacture or storage. Private firms would be urged at once not to transfer themselves from one part of the country to another, except at the request of a Government department. It was contemplated that later private firms would have to obtain a licence from the Control before acquiring premises for any kind of business, manufacture or storage for which the premises had not previously been used. This allocation process would not, it was thought, cause delay. The Control would be able to save departments needing accommodation a great deal of

---

[1] See pp. 249–50.
[2] It was contemplated from the outset that the Control would have a strong regional organisation.

trouble. And once premises were allocated by the Control the department concerned would be protected against competing claims or displacement by other departments or interests.

The Control would not perform the formal act of requisitioning. The legal and financial processes that followed requisitioning would continue to be carried out by the departments already exercising requisitioning power[1]—departments which had the expert staffs for this complicated business.

This outline plan of the Control was ready by the middle of December 1940. But there was a hitch in putting the plan into practice. At the end of November Lord Beaverbrook, Minister of Aircraft Production, had reminded the War Cabinet of the great work performed by his Ministry in dispersing aircraft factories. He had asked for a ruling that 'any premises anywhere' that were not in actual occupation should be at the disposal of the Ministry of Aircraft Production if removal or dispersal were necessitated by enemy action. The War Cabinet agreed to his proposal provided that, if the Ministry of Aircraft Production wanted premises already earmarked by some other department, that department must be informed and must have the right to ask for the premises back.

This decision reflected the continued need for aircraft at almost any cost. But, as some ministers hastened to point out, the decision would make an orderly scheme for allocating accommodation unworkable from the outset. When a week or two later the proposed plan for the Control of Factory and Storage Premises was put before the War Cabinet the Minister of Aircraft Production said that it was unacceptable. He feared that the scheme would involve reference to a number of authorities and would result in delays which would be fatal to the maintenance of aircraft production. The War Cabinet invited the Lord President and the Minister of Aircraft Production to meet and attempt to agree a scheme suitable for immediate operation. Some six weeks passed, however, before agreement was reached and in the end it came only after the intervention of the Prime Minister. Mr. Churchill ruled that the proposed Control should be established, that extreme priority should be given to meeting the needs of the Ministry of Aircraft Production when any factory had been bombed out of action and that he—the Prime Minister—was to be informed of any case in which there was more than forty-eight hours delay in finding new premises.

At last, in February 1941, the way was clear for setting up the Control. The President of the Board of Trade formally accepted executive responsibility although it was agreed that he should work particularly closely in this matter with the Lord President and that he should be

---

[1] i.e. the Ministry of Works and Buildings on behalf of the civil departments; the Service departments; and in emergencies the Ministry of Aircraft Production.

subject to the direction of the Lord President's Committee, particularly in cases of interdepartmental dispute.

The first Controller-General of Factory and Storage Premises was appointed in March 1941 and by the end of the first week in April the first Factory Controller, Storage Controller and all but two of the Regional Controllers[1] had been appointed. In addition to the executive organisation under the Controller-General a new department, headed by an Assistant Secretary, was established within the Board of Trade. It was to act as a link between the Control and the Board of Trade and to deal with questions of policy.

On 15th May 1941 the Control of Factory and Storage Premises began formal operations.

(ii)

The Control in Action

It had been recognised on all sides that the first requirement for a successful control was proper information about factory and storage premises. A register of premises was essential, and the newly established Control quickly set to work to compile one. Or rather, since the problems of factory premises and storage premises differed, the Control had to compile two registers.

The register of factory premises was the easier task. The Board of Trade, among other departments, had powers under the Defence Regulations to request any person to furnish any specified information needed for the efficient prosecution of the war.[2] The legal authorities interpreted this Regulation as referring only to requests for information directed to specific persons. The Board of Trade could not ask owners or occupiers in general to supply particulars about their premises. Only if the Board could send letters direct to individuals could they ask for information supported by the sanctions of the law.

The first thing to do, therefore, was to find a list of factories. The most comprehensive list available was that used for administering the Factory Acts. It was agreed to restrict the inquiry first to those factories where ten or more workers were employed. Even this was an immense field—there were some 70,000 of these factories on the factory inspectorate's list. The field of inquiry was again narrowed by excluding those factories that were most unlikely to have spare capacity in war-time—for example engineering factories. The requests for information had to be directed primarily to the consumer goods

---

[1] Men with business experience were appointed to all these posts.

[2] The authority making the request was legally the judge of what was necessary.

industries which must needs contract in a war economy. Letters asking for returns about factory accommodation were therefore sent only to some 38,000 manufacturers. The replies came in quickly. They made it clear that the scope of the Factory Control's list must be narrowed still further; some factories had been destroyed by enemy action, others had already been taken over by Government departments and others were for various reasons unsuitable. Nevertheless within a year the register contained 32,000 premises and by the end of the war nearly 34,500.

Occupiers of these premises were asked to supply information about their position under concentration schemes, the number of workers employed, the classes of production undertaken, the proportion for Government use and export and the amount of space used for that production and for the storage of goods. Finally, they were asked to give details about the factory buildings themselves, their construction and equipment, the services available and methods of access. The information asked for was sufficient to show easily whether or not a particular factory building would be suitable for a particular production or storage requirement.

The storage register was much less successful than the factory register. No ready-made list of storage premises existed and a new Defence Regulation was necessary to empower the Board of Trade to acquire the necessary information.[1] The next step was the issue of the Storage (Information) Order 1941.[2] With certain exceptions, explained in the schedule to the Order, all owners of premises in the United Kingdom with a floor area of 3,000 square feet or more which had been used at any time since 1938 wholly or mainly for storage were called upon to supply information to the Control. Vehicles and vessels were outside the scope of the Order. So also were premises belonging to local authorities and those owned by all public utilities, except road and water transport undertakings. The premises of these last named undertakings were also excepted from the Order if they were actually occupied by the undertaking and were used wholly for the storage of articles in transit or articles necessary for the proper maintenance of the undertaking. Other premises excluded from the scope of the Order were those used wholly for cold storage or for bulk storage of liquids or grain, those used in connection with a factory and situated within a mile from it, those connected with a retail business, and agricultural buildings. Garages were also excluded, for the Ministry of War Transport was already preparing a questionnaire to be sent to all occupiers of garages with maintenance and repair facilities and it undertook to supply the Control with information about garages of 3,000 square feet or more that were suitable for storage.

---

[1] S.R. & O. 1941, No. 653. This Regulation was known as Defence Regulation 56AA.
[2] S.R. & O. 1941, No. 670.

In contrast to the factory register the storage register was not very successful. Owners of storage premises often pleaded ignorance of their obligations to register their premises. Others did not see the point of the register. Officers of the Control had, therefore, to spend a good deal of time in searching out possible warehouse accommodation. By the end of 1944 over 5,200 premises totalling 67 million square feet of storage space were included in the register.

At the end of 1942 an attempt was made to extend the register to wholesale and retail premises. A new Storage Facilities (Information) Order[1] of December 1942 called for returns from occupiers of premises with a floor area of 10,000 square feet or more which were being used at the date of the making of the Order for any purpose connected with the wholesale or retail sale of articles of any description other than food or drink. Space used as living accommodation, hotels and restaurants were excluded from the Order. The information asked for included such items as the type of trade (wholesale or retail), the type of business (multiple firm, Co-operative Society or single unit establishment), the principal classes of goods sold, area, the number of persons employed. There is no means of gauging how complete the register was. Certainly returns came in very slowly. By the end of 1944 there were rather over 4,000 premises on the wholesale and retail premises register, representing over 121 million square feet.

The whole problem of wholesale and retail premises had been a very tricky one. As the search for production and storage space had grown increasingly difficult Factory Control[2] had obviously turned its eyes on the possibility of acquiring such premises. But the Ministry of Works had remained responsible for the allocation of space for purposes other than production and storage and a good deal of shop space had been requisitioned, for example, for billeting and offices. Meanwhile, the department of the Board of Trade that was responsible for retail trade had become disturbed at the possibility that unco-ordinated requisitioning of shops for every kind of purpose might reduce the number of shops too far. It had been suggested that Factory Control might take over complete responsibility for the allocation of shop premises. This, however, would have cut right across the Ministry of Works' functions. In the end, therefore, it had been agreed that Factory Control should make its own register of wholesale and retail premises and that there should be efficient machinery for tripartite consultations—between the Board of Trade department dealing with retail trade, Factory Control and the Ministry of Works —before any shop premises were requisitioned or allocated.

The collection of information was indispensable to the work of the Control. How exactly did the Control function? Its authority over the

---

[1] S.R. & O. 1942, No. 2264.

[2] For brevity the Control of Factory and Storage Premises will be called Factory Control.

activities of Government departments was complete from the outset. For the War Cabinet's decision that all requests for production and storage space must go through the Control was binding upon departments. The machinery for allocating space depended basically on close co-operation between the following groups of people: Factory Control headquarters, Factory Control regional officers, the head-quarters and regional officers of Government departments needing production and storage space, the headquarters and regional officers of Government departments responsible for providing 'common services' such as manpower, transport, fuel and power, and billeting accommodation. The using and 'common service' departments appointed liaison officers to act as channels of communication between their headquarters and those of Factory Control. When the Control was first set up a considerable number of interdepartmental disputes had been expected, and the liaison officers were formed into a committee which might resolve them. In practice, however, disputes proved remarkably few and the interdepartmental committee only met three or four times to discuss general matters of policy and administration.

A certain amount of form-filling was inherent in this process of mutual consultation. It was important that applications for space from departments should be properly recorded to show the kind of manufacture or storage proposed, the most suitable area for it, the requirements in terms of floor space, minimum head-room, special structures, fuel and power and labour. It was also important that the Factory Control headquarters should know the precise position in the regions. The regional controllers therefore submitted monthly returns showing the applications and allocations they had dealt with and the demands for space that remained unsatisfied. It was no less important that the regional officers should know what was happening at headquarters. A voluminous series of circulars therefore carried to the regions information and instructions on such points as the type of industry and firm most suitable for requisitioning. But although some formality was essential for the purposes of the Control most of the collaboration between departments and headquarters and regional offices was by means of informal discussions, telephone calls and letters.

At first it had been thought that speedy administration could be achieved if the real work of the Control were increasingly done in the regions. It proved impossible, however, to decentralise as far as was hoped. Other departments were often reluctant to give their regional representatives as much authority as the regional factory controllers possessed. But, quite apart from this, a good deal of central planning and administration was unavoidable. For it was necessary to match broadly demands for, and supplies of, space in the separate regions.

Factory Control headquarters, by keeping fully informed of what was happening in the regions, knew the amount of space and the type of premises available in different areas. Headquarters could therefore distribute demands for space to the most likely regions. And they could decide difficult questions of priority. They could also curb the artificial inflation of demands. Using departments were apt to ask for more space than they needed quicker than they needed it; but, if businesses had to be closed in order to satisfy a department's application, exaggerated requests could not be accepted. The extra authority belonging to headquarters made it easier for them than for the regions to sort out the real need from the expressed request.

The normal Factory Control procedure for receiving and meeting demands for space was on the following lines. When a department sent in the appropriate form asking for factory or storage space the request was considered at Factory Control headquarters and sent by them to a region. Departments were asked to avoid nominating particular regions wherever possible so that they could be directed to regions where their requirements could be most easily met. If a region was nominated and was considered to be particularly unsuitable or unlikely to yield the required space, the Control would discuss with the department concerned and try to get it to go to some other region. At the Control's regional office the records were searched for suitable premises to meet the particular demand. As the information on Factory Control's register inevitably became out of date on such questions as the importance of the current work being done by a particular factory, the regional officers inspected the premises before offering them to a department. If the premises were accepted there might be machinery to be moved out. Factory Control would advise on the amount to be moved and would ensure that sufficient space was left for the proper storage of the machinery. When all these affairs had been settled the regional office of the Control issued to the Government department an 'authorisation to acquire'. The Government department was then free to acquire the premises either by private treaty or by requisition.

Control over the acquisition of space by Government departments was not by itself enough. Private firms could not be left free to take up any premises they found. When the work of Factory Control was being planned the existing Defence Regulations did not give the Board of Trade the power they needed to issue an Order controlling the movement of firms. A new Defence Regulation was therefore necessary. Under this new Regulation[1] a Location of Industry (Restriction) Order[2] was signed in July 1941. Until then Factory Control had to rely on the voluntary co-operation of business concerns; private

---

[1] Defence Regulation 55A, S.R. & O. 1941, No. 653.
[2] S.R. & O. 1941, No. 1100.

R

firms were asked in the national interest to refrain from seeking alternative accommodation outside their own area unless it was required for essential war purposes.[1]

The Location of Industry Order made it necessary to obtain a licence from the Board of Trade before using any premises having a floor area of 3,000 square feet or more for the purpose of carrying on a trade or business which would cause those premises to become a factory or a warehouse. It was also necessary to obtain a licence before changing the use of a factory or a warehouse having a floor area of 3,000 square feet or more. 'Warehouse' meant any premises other than vehicles or vessels used for storing articles of any description. If the Order had been completely rigid there would have been difficulties over urgent temporary requirements for storage space. A general licence was therefore issued authorising the use of premises covered by the Order for storing articles for a period not longer than twenty-eight days.[2] Some thought had also to be given to bombed firms. It was felt that no special consideration could be given to bombed firms that wished to move out of their own areas. But special consideration in issuing licences was to be given to applications for licences from firms whose premises had been made unusable by bombing and who sought alternative premises in their own immediate neighbourhood. There were provisos that the premises must be required for an essential purpose and that production could be carried on without new machinery and fittings and without structural alteration requiring a building licence.

In the autumn of 1942 the Order was tightened up.[3] The 3,000 square feet exemption limit was abolished. Moreover, the first Order had simply controlled the use of factory and storage premises; it had done nothing to prevent a firm from acquiring premises by private treaty or otherwise provided there was no change in their use. The new 1942 Order changed this. Henceforward there could be no transfer of business carried on at factories or warehouses without a licence.[4]

This extension of control raises the whole question of the purpose and scope of the Location of Industry Orders. The original Order had been regarded simply as a method of controlling the movement of industry; licences under the Order had been issued very sparingly. In general a firm only obtained a licence if its application was sponsored by a Government department. This meant that there was not very much difference between an 'authorisation to acquire' issued to a Government department and a licence issued under the Location of

---

[1] H. of C. Deb., Vol. 371, Cols. 341–42.

[2] Provided the Board of Trade were informed of the use within ten days.

[3] S.R. & O. 1942, No. 2072.

[4] In addition, premises used for the storage of motor vehicles, pedal cycles, carrier cycles and tricycles were now covered by the Order.

Industry Order to a firm that had the blessing of a Government department.

By the autumn of 1942, however, officials realised that the Location of Industry Order was more than a 'stay put' order. By then most resources—and manpower especially—were becoming acutely scarce, and it was more important than ever to prevent them from being dissipated in unessential or inefficient production. The distribution of manpower and raw materials was of course pretty strictly controlled. But nearly every individual control had its weaknesses and its loopholes. Only by interlocking a number of separate controls could the mesh be drawn sufficiently tightly. The Location of Industry Order, especially after it had been amended, was obviously an important thread in this network. For it could be used to prevent any new entrants into any industry. It was a valuable support to controls over raw materials and labour and over the manufacture and supply of specific goods. Factory Control, acting on behalf of the Board of Trade, was indeed placed in the invidious position of deciding whether or not to license the carrying on of businesses in premises in which it was not interested. The Control was in fact administering the Order mainly on behalf of other Government departments. There was some difference of opinion within the Board of Trade whether it was morally right for departments to use this particular Order for the purpose of preventing a trader from doing something which he might otherwise have been legally entitled to do.

This difficulty was illustrated by the treatment of infringements of the Order. If a firm occupied premises contrary to the Order the Control could of course prosecute. But in such cases the firm would probably be using labour and premises that were not wanted for the war effort so that the case was poor. If the Control did not prosecute it appeared weak. If no other department was much interested in the case, the Control might legalise the firm's action by issuing a licence. But this course was apt to make the whole licensing system seem foolish. There was indeed no escape for the Control from its dilemma.

We have now considered the processes by which the allocation and acquisition of space were closely controlled. In all this work Factory Control did everything it could to promote a more rational location of industry. As long as departments and private firms had been left to scramble for premises there had been no one to ensure that additional production was not begun in districts that were already overloaded and that suffered from particularly severe shortages of labour, transport, fuel and power or billeting accommodation. The departments concerned might have looked into all these matters. But they were generally in a hurry and in such conditions difficulties were minimised or even overlooked completely. Moreover, departments could not tell what the plans of other departments might be. There might be room in a particular area for one factory and not for two, but two departments might independently plan one factory each. Factory Control therefore took upon itself the responsibility for keeping an up-to-date survey of the conditions of labour, electricity, gas and coal in all the different regions. From this departments could see where extra production loads should be avoided and where they should be encouraged. And Factory Control would allocate premises in the overloaded areas for storage—even though they might be model factory buildings—and premises in the easier areas for production—even though they might be decrepit and dingy. When the Ministry of Production was established in 1942 the responsibility for keeping the survey was transferred to it.

Factory Control's primary function was the orderly allocation of space between departments. Ostensibly this function related only to existing premises. But it is obvious that one of the main purposes of making the best possible use of existing premises was to reduce the demand for new premises. This demand was increasingly difficult to meet. Building materials were scarce and the labour force in the building industry was marked down as one of the few remaining sources of able-bodied men of military age. It was therefore important that the control over the use of existing premises and the control over new buildings should be co-ordinated. And so, in the summer of 1941, ministers approved what was called the 'nil certificate' procedure. This meant that new factories or stores could not be built unless the Controller-General of Factory and Storage Premises had been consulted and had given a certificate that no suitable existing building could be made available. Certain forms of new building were exempted from this arrangement—work costing less than £500, applications to erect canteens or any sort of building ancillary to a factory or store as distinct from production or storage space proper, extensions to existing buildings which the sponsoring department agreed must be erected as part of the parent building and any repairs that clearly did not entail the reconstruction of the whole building. Some of these exemptions left pretty wide loopholes in the 'nil certificate' procedure. Factory Control felt, for example, that 'extensions' frequently turned out to be almost new factories and that in these cases existing alternative premises could quite often have been found. Moreover, there was no satisfactory means of ensuring that new works costing more than £500 but less than £5,000[1] had received 'nil certificates'. From time to time attempts were made to tighten the procedure, but without success.

It will be remembered that, although the Control decided which

---

[1] Lists of new works costing over £5,000 were circulated for comment by Ministry of Works headquarters to the headquarters of other Government departments, including Factory Control.

premises should be requisitioned by the various departments requiring space, it was not intended to do the actual requisitioning. This was left to the Service and supply departments or to the Ministry of Works who acted on behalf of the civilian departments. The Control itself requisitioned premises for only two purposes. First it held an emergency reserve of space. It would have been very difficult to perform the functions of a clearing-house for premises at a time of heavy air raids when urgent demands would flood in. It was therefore decided that Factory Control should acquire up to three million square feet of space to hold as a reserve to be used for rehousing factories after bombing or other urgent requirements.[1] As the war went on, however, and pressure on factory space grew and air raids declined it was impossible to keep much of the three million square feet out of action. Most of it was absorbed for current production or storage.

The second purpose for which the Control itself acquired space was tobacco storage. It was necessary to disperse tobacco stocks (which in the autumn of 1941 included heavy imports under lend-lease) from their normal warehouses in the vulnerable port areas. This was not easy, as the alternative buildings had to satisfy fairly exacting technical and Customs requirements. The Control therefore made itself responsible for finding the right premises and for requisitioning them. Nearly half the total imports of American whole-leaf tobacco into the United Kingdom were handled in these warehouses.

We must now turn from describing Factory Control's functions to assessing its achievement. One thing is certain: it was unfortunate that the orderly allocation of factory and storage space did not begin much earlier in the war. By March 1941 a good deal of damage had been done by the uncontrolled scramble for space. The right premises had not gone to the right people. And it had been no one's job to stop departments from pouring into regions where there was neither sufficient labour, power nor transport to feed the production they were undertaking.

When the Control was at length established its place in the machinery of government was perhaps a little anomalous. The Control was attached to the Board of Trade. But its function—the allocation of space for factory and storage premises—was not strictly akin to the other functions of the Board. The Control's work was in a way more nearly related to that of the Ministry of Works which was responsible for allocating space for other purposes—billets, offices, etc.—which controlled the building industry and building programmes and which knew all about the complicated process of requisitioning. Or one might say that the work of the Control was closely related to that of the Ministry of Production from 1942 onwards. For

---

[1] The Ministry of Aircraft Production also held an independent reserve.

that ministry was responsible for those wider problems of location of industry that had loomed large in Factory Control's work. But although Factory Control, in a logical administrative plan, would not have been assigned to the Board of Trade the arrangement in practice produced some strong advantages. It was not simply that the Board were neutral and were not competitors in the search for space; the same could be said of the Ministry of Works and the Ministry of Production. But the Board themselves by their measures of restriction were responsible for releasing most of the space becoming available for war-time needs. The exchange of information between departments of the Board and the Control was easier and fuller than it would have been between the Control and an outside ministry. Moreover, the Board of Trade had a general responsibility for industry; industrialists could feel that the Board would guard against excessive encroachment upon vital industrial needs. It became apparent to industry that the work of space-taking, though heavy-handed, was conducted with a scrupulous fairness and with an understanding of industrial problems.

The best justification of the location of Factory Control is the Control's achievement. Factory Control had to work within fairly narrow limits—for example it had little power to scrutinise the worthiness of demands for space—but within those limits its work could well be called one of the great administrative successes of the war. Figures are not a very useful guide. But it is worth recording that between 1st May 1941 and 31st December 1944 Factory Control allocated to Government departments well over 62 million square feet of space for production[1] and nearly 158 million square feet for storage.[2] Some idea of the order of magnitude involved can be obtained by comparing these figures with the total floor space of all the royal ordnance factories built between 1936 and 1945—that is 35 million square feet. The regions where the greatest Factory Control allocations were given were the North-Western where a total of 40 million square feet was found in this period, London and the South East with 35 million square feet, and Scotland with 25 million square feet. Altogether about 20,000 separate buildings dotted all over the country were requisitioned on the Factory Control's allocation.

These figures are a tribute to the enthusiasm of the regional officers in seeking out space. They went into every corner of their areas, searching for and finding accommodation. When they had satisfied current needs they collected information and planned ahead to meet future demands. They could feel pretty sure that every four walls with

---

[1] 36 million square feet were allocated by means of authorisations to acquire and 26 million square feet by licences under the Location of Industry Order to firms sponsored by departments.

[2] 143 million square feet were allocated by authorisation to acquire and 15 million square feet by licences.

a roof (and even derelict buildings) that could be partially cleared would sooner or later be called into operation.

The operations in which Factory Control was involved were of course very complicated. It was not simply a case of finding a certain amount of space but the right kind of space. The difficulties were greatest in the case of premises for production. The need was mostly for ground-floor factories and for factories with sufficient head-room. It was unusual to find civilian industry buildings—other than engineering factories—with head-room greater than 15 feet and of sufficient strength to take overhead cranes. Buildings of this kind were found in the tinplate industry, in iron-foundries and in film studios. Film studios indeed were eminently suitable for production because of their large head-room, wide spaces and good heating. Unlike most civilian buildings they could even be used for airframe production. Other problems arose over the removal of existing machinery. Textile weaving machinery could be moved fairly easily to make room for other machines, but spinning machinery was much more difficult and as a rule the Control had to leave it in place. In the potteries kilns and moulds could not be moved without gutting the factory. Boot and shoe machinery, the machinery of the clothing industry and circular-type hosiery machines could all be easily shifted. To move fully-fashioned hosiery machines, on the other hand, would be too difficult; it would be even more difficult to put them back.

So it was not easy to find production space. As one Controller-General put it, the dream of the Factory Control was 'an india-rubber Britain with india-rubber buildings which can be stretched vertically and horizontally and still carry a minimum of 5 cwt. per square foot'. Yet the Factory Control could point to such improbable achievements as torpedo production in a boot and shoe factory, aero engine parts from a hairpin factory and aeroplane frames from a toy factory. Tunnels and caves were even used for the manufacture of aircraft. Such examples could be multiplied a hundred times and each had its own problem of structural alterations, machinery removals, etc.

Storage was only a little less complicated. The main difficulty with improvised storage was to get the stocks out. However, the very large variety of articles to be stored allowed flexibility in selecting the right premises. First-class accommodation was needed for, say, flour and sugar, and slightly less superior accommodation for canned goods. But many raw materials could be stored without damage under the most primitive conditions and even under tarpaulins in the open. In finding more and more storage space Factory Control showed ingenuity and pressed into service anything from factories, halls and houses to barns, piggeries and stables. To take one example: one multi-storey weaving factory became a replica of a Devonport Dockyard naval store. Five floors of heavy machinery were cleared, hundreds of steel racks erected, and in three weeks vital stores were moving in from bombed Devonport. Indeed by the end of the war the Admiralty held only 11 million square feet of permanent depot storage space against more than 22 million square feet of requisitioned space. As time went on drastic space-saving methods had to be used. This meant higher piling and smaller gangways in warehouses. Storage in the open became increasingly important until open storage sites equalled in area the requisitioned covered accommodation.

Flexibility was one of the keynotes of the Control's success in meeting demands for space in the right place and at the right time. It was necessary to bear in mind such points as vulnerability to air attack, transport, labour and the lines of communication of the Service departments. As inflammable goods were removed from danger spots, the space was swiftly reallocated to less dangerous materials. Not only had the right space to be found, it also had to be found quickly. In 1942, for example, the movement of American troops began to cause big new demands for storage. These demands were almost always met promptly. In the Bristol area, for example, buildings that only a few weeks previously had been busy in their civilian trades were, in the autumn of 1942, in full operation as United States Army store depots. Upwards of 15 million square feet of storage accommodation was found for the American Army in Southern Command alone. Government departments each yielded some space to meet this demand and equivalent space had then to be found for them in different parts of the country. The activities of the Control reached a *crescendo* as the preparations for D-Day approached; vast masses of stores had to be housed in readiness for these operations.

In the days before the Ministry of Production was established Factory Control could also claim to have done its best to correct some of the worst mistakes in the general location of industry. The trouble had gone too far to be eradicated. But in areas like the Stroud Valley, where intolerable congestion had arisen, Factory Control did its best to turn production away. At the same time it managed to persuade the departments and firms concerned to go to comparatively uncrowded places such as Dundee, where there were surplus resources to make such complicated products as ballbearings and airscrews.

The work of Factory Control was certainly a success. The essence of it was that the officers concerned should keep close touch with everything that was happening at the demand end and the supply end, and that they should show ingenuity in contrivance and improvisation. Perhaps the best tribute to their success is the fact that immediate and imperative demands for covered accommodation were always met. Moreover, although all departments were clamouring for space, complaints about the deeds of Factory Control were rare and there were no appeals to the Lord President's Committee.

CHAPTER XII

RETAIL TRADE

(i)

The Structure of Retail Trade and the Early Effects of War

CONCENTRATION of production had been the Board of Trade's first attempt to concern themselves directly with the detailed affairs of manufacturing industry. The policy had seemed the logical consequence of the Limitation of Supplies Orders and it was undertaken primarily in order to free resources for the war effort. It was inevitable that the question should arise whether similar measures should not also be applied to retail trade which was affected no less than industry by the limitation of supplies. There were, however, all kinds of difficulties in formulating a retail trade policy which would be both practicable to administer and also adequate to war-time requirements.

One of the chief difficulties was the paucity of statistics. No census had been taken of the retail trade, and estimates, for example, of the total number of shops varied widely.[1] What was required as the basis of policy was a statistical analysis distinguishing the main categories of retail outlets, the different types of commodities sold in shops and, further, dividing each class into size-groups based on the annual value of turnover. Nothing of the sort existed. Nor were the labour figures at all satisfactory. The Ministry of Labour data covered the distributive trades as a whole, and did not distinguish between wholesale and retail trade or between food and non-food shops.[2] The war-time Retail Trade Committee—about which this chapter will have a good deal to say—pointed out that the 1931 Census of Population showed nearly 800,000 persons engaged in the non-food retail trades (other than coal) either as proprietors, as managers or as shop assistants; it suggested that these three categories may have formed about two-thirds of all those engaged in these trades. The total in 1931 would probably have been, therefore, about 1,200,000 and this figure might have increased by 1939 by about ten per cent. The Committee said that 'the aggregate number of all shops in Great Britain before the

---

[1] For pre-war estimates see H. Smith, *Retail Distribution* (2nd Edition), p. 35.

[2] The Ministry of Labour figures (estimated) for June 1939 are as follows: of total manpower 2,887,000 in the distributive trades; of employed persons 2,160,400 (1,309,500 males, 850,900 females) in the distributive trades.

war is believed to have been 750,000 or perhaps more', and thought that probably more than half of these were mainly engaged in selling food and drink.[1] Total 1939 retail sales of articles other than food and drink were put at, approximately, £1,200 millions, of which £465 millions or 38·8 per cent. were attributed to clothing and footwear.[2]

The only light shed on this problem during the war was thrown by an inquiry into the shops selling rationed goods which participated in the coupon banking arrangements. Data published in the *Board of Trade Journal*[3] showed that 86,150 shops in the United Kingdom had, at the middle of 1942, opened coupon banking accounts, of which about 81,000 were primarily engaged in selling rationed clothing and textiles, the remaining 5,000 dealing in clothing only as a side-line. The 81,150 shops probably represented ninety per cent. of the shops wholly or mainly selling rationed goods;[4] there were an unknown number who had not opened coupon banking accounts. The details of these returns may be consulted in the *Board of Trade Journal*, but some general facts about the structure of the retail clothing trades, based on the returns and the results of a sample survey, are worth noting. Most significant, probably, is the difference between the distribution of shops among the different size-groups, based on annual turnover and the distribution of sales between these size-groups. Only nine per cent. of the 86,150 shops were in the highest group with turnover amounting to over £12,000 per annum, while forty-three per cent. were in the middle group with annual turnover between £2,500 and £12,000, and forty-eight per cent. were in the lowest group with turnover below £2,500 per annum. The distribution of sales was totally different. The highest turnover group accounted for about two-thirds of the total sales, the middle group for about one-quarter and the lowest group for less than ten per cent. If the ten per cent. of shops which did not open coupon banking accounts were added to the lowest class where they almost certainly belonged, the differences in the distributions would be even more marked.[5] Important also for policy was the evidence as to the distribution of these shops among the different types of retail organisation. The following table shows numbers and percentages:

---

[1] *Retail Trade Committee, Second Interim Report*, p. 2. (H.M.S.O. 1942).

[2] *Retail Trade Committee, Second Interim Report*, p. 3. The National Income White Paper of 1949 (Cmd. 7649) put 1938 expenditure on clothing and footwear at £446 millions.

[3] *Board of Trade Journal*, 3rd June 1944. The figures given here were not available until the end of 1943—that is, they were not available for the deliberations of the Retail Trade Committee which are discussed below. Moreover, it should be emphasised that the figures represent a rather arbitrary selection of shops; there is no reason to expect these figures to be comparable in any way with those of any post-war census of distribution.

[4] Clothing, footwear, hand knitting yarn and dress materials.

[5] The distribution of shops by size-groups would then be eight per cent., thirty-nine per cent. and fifty-three per cent.

Distribution of Clothing Shops among Types of Retail Organisations

TABLE 13

	No.	*Per cent.*
Multiple shops[1]	8,250	10
Co-operative stores[1] . . .	2,460	3
Independent:		
(a) Wholly or mainly clothing .	70,440	81
(b) Other	5,000	6
Total . .	86,150	100

The multiples and co-operatives fell almost entirely in the two upper turnover groups, and their average turnover in rationed goods was greater than that of the average independent shop.

The statistical problem, the problem of estimating the number of shops, related almost entirely to the independent unit shop. Fairly reliable figures were available concerning the larger types of organisation. For the co-operatives a census of 1937 showed 5,827 shops dealing in non-food goods, of which 2,100 sold drapery and 1,236 footwear; 728 shops were engaged in tailoring and outfitting. The Multiple Shops' Federation put the number of multiple branches dealing in non-food goods at approximately 12,500. The number of department stores was only about 300 on a strict definition, but up to 1,000 if smaller stores were included.[2] But reliable and comprehensive information about the numbers of independent unit shops was completely lacking.

The other difficulties that beset retail trade policy were partly economic, partly political. Predominantly they could be said to turn on the enormous variety in organisation, methods and interests among retail traders. In the first place, there were, as has been mentioned, the different types of retail outlet, with frequently widely different selling methods. Secondly, non-food distribution covered an extraordinarily wide range of goods. There was little in common between the tobacconist, the piano dealer and the branch of a footwear multiple, and the effect of the war and of war-time restrictions upon each of these varied considerably. Again, some retailers were specialists, while others dealt in a variety of goods. Nor must the divergence of interest between employer and employee be overlooked.[3]

Next, the retail trades are noteworthy as providing occupation, not necessarily whole-time, for numbers of people with small capital and probably little specialised knowledge, sometimes only with a view to

---

[1] Multiples were defined as firms with more than five branches; each branch counted as a shop. In the case of the co-operatives the number of shops represented the number of addresses, and the number of separate departments selling clothing and footwear was certainly greater.

[2] *Retail Trade Committee, Second Interim Report,* p. 4.

[3] This will be considered again, when the reports of the Retail Trade Committee are discussed.

securing a supplementary income. From the economic standpoint the ease of entering the trade connoted a high 'mortality' among retailers, as compared with those entering other occupations. The closing of shops was not a war-time phenomenon; even in 1938 over forty per cent. of bankruptcies and receiving orders related to non-food retail trades.[1] Politically, this large body of small traders represented a significant influence which, as was frequently shown during the war, could make itself felt in Parliament.

The difference between the manufacturer and the retailer is another point which needs emphasising. The localisation of the retailer in relation to his customers is of vital importance. Further, his shop is a factor in the preservation of his goodwill to which there is nothing comparable in the mill of the manufacturer. For this reason, if for no other, the argument that the concentration policy for manufacturing industry should also be applied to retailing needed to be viewed with considerable scepticism.

Finally, so far as war-time policy was concerned, there were a number of administrative problems. It was generally recognised that the distributive trades offered a large reservoir of labour which could and should be drawn off into the Forces or into war production. The quality of the labour, it was true, varied considerably, but was there any need to do more than let the Ministry of Labour, subject to the usual safeguards, take away from retail distribution the labour that it required for the war effort? Was it really administratively practicable, given the structure of these trades, to devise an orderly plan for what was sometimes called a 'telescoping' of retail distribution, while preserving a reasonable balance between the different types of retail outlet? The problem, it was agreed, was not that of the retail trades as a whole; the circumstances of the food traders were very different. But did that make the problem much easier? There were some who argued that, if a scheme including measures of compensation were put forward, the food traders who had not suffered under Limitation of Supplies Orders ought to contribute along with the rest.

In the first few months of the war there could hardly be a clear view of the way in which the retailer was likely to be affected. The effect of evacuation would, it was thought, be to transfer trade mainly from shopkeepers in big towns to shopkeepers in country districts. Restriction of supplies, when it came, appeared likely to have more serious consequences, but there had been nothing much in the way of restriction as yet and no plans or proposals were put forward to deal with it. With regard to the retailer's obligations in connection with debts, mortgage payments and rates the Courts (Emergency Powers) Act

---

[1] In 1938 there had been 1,280 bankruptcies in the non-food retail trades; in 1941 there were only 161 bankruptcies. See H. of C. Deb., Vol. 382, Col. 220.

seemed likely to afford him only limited protection if he found himself in difficulties.

The bombing which began in the latter part of 1940 created some new problems,[1] partly through the evacuation which then took place and partly through the destruction of retailers' premises and stocks. Most of these problems are concerned with the distribution of supplies among the civilian population and are dealt with elsewhere in this volume. All that need be said here is that the retailer was enabled to replace his bombed stocks[2] and equipment and that unsuccessful attempts were made to initiate mutual assistance schemes among traders in the blitzed towns. Under these schemes it was proposed that the bombed trader, who might be unable for some time to resume his activities, should hand over his replacement stocks to a retailer who had not suffered damage, profits on the sale of these stocks being shared. In one case, at any rate, the inducement of additional supplies was required to secure agreement to a scheme of this kind, since the bombed retailer usually preferred to keep his stocks against the time when he could set up shop again rather than surrender them to a trade competitor.

Limitation of supplies clearly seemed to raise much more serious problems for the retailing community in general than any destruction of stocks by bombing. The problems would be especially difficult for small traders. (In raids which were usually directed to the centres of towns the larger organisations—the department stores, the multiples and the co-operatives—suffered often more heavily than the unit shops.) With the more drastic restrictions that were imposed in the autumn of 1940 complaints began to be received, from both traders and the public, and these complaints increased in volume in the first half of 1941. The case of the small trader was taken up in Parliament, where he was declared to be 'the backbone of this country'.[3] The small man, it was argued, was particularly affected by the limitation Orders because manufacturers and wholesalers found it easier, and more profitable, to concentrate their quotas on the larger stores and the multiples.[4] The individual retailer himself, of course, had no quota, though there was frequently misunderstanding on this point.

Along with this growing concern for the small trader there was developing a line of thought which pointed towards some scheme of concentration for the retail trades. The *Drapers' Record*, a trade paper, was in March 1941 advocating something of this sort. 'Local retailers', it was suggested, should 'mutually arrange for a contraction of their

---

[1] As did also the invasion threat of the summer of 1940.

[2] Licences were given authorising manufacturers and wholesalers to supply bombed retailers with goods in excess of their limitation of supplies quotas.

[3] H. of C. Deb., Vol. 371, Col. 1684.

[4] See *Drapers' Record*, 8th February, 22nd March 1941.

number, those continuing to make an allowance to those who drop out.'[1]

The announcement in March 1941 of concentration proposals for manufacturing industry prompted, as we have seen, the idea that there should be some form of concentration to bring about the orderly contraction of the retail trades. One proposal put before the Board of Trade would have introduced a retailer's quota, based on trade in a standard period, which would have formed the basis of payments and compensation arrangements. The quota would have been a saleable commodity, and could have been surrendered by the withdrawing trader at a fixed price to a central pool, which would resell to traders remaining in business, preference being given to reception areas. Some scheme, it was argued, was necessary because otherwise retailers would hang on, even though they were incurring losses. The evil results of the absence of a scheme would be rises of retailing costs and prices, bankruptcy among traders, and the failure to secure a speedy and effective transfer of labour to war work. The difficulties even of a scheme of this kind, with its provision for a guarantee of re-entry to the withdrawing trader[2], were not perhaps fully appreciated; the divergences of interest among an enormous variety of traders were not adequately recognised. Yet the emergence of proposals of this sort showed that the need for a policy and a plan for the retail trades was being felt.

(ii)

The Retail Trade Committee

Inquiries in the House of Commons in March and April 1941 elicited the fact that the departments concerned had no plan for dealing with the retail trades, but in a short space of time political pressure had produced a change of approach to the subject. It was decided that the matter was urgent, and that a committee should be set up to investigate and report as soon as possible. The appointment of a Retail Trade Committee was announced by the President of the Board of Trade on 13th May 1941.[3]

The terms of reference of this Committee were 'to examine the present problems of the retail trade in goods other than food, having

---

[1] *Drapers' Record*, 8th February 1941. Again on 15th March 1941 this paper said: 'The suggestion is repeated and re-emphasised that steps be taken right now in each district for the war-time "marriage" of shops on terms mutually agreed, as the only way to avoid extermination and widespread insolvency.'

[2] All traders were to be registered and there was to be a ban on new firms which would continue for a defined period after the war.

[3] H. of C. Deb., Vol. 371, Cols. 1068–69.

regard both to the immediate needs of the conduct of the war and to the position after the war', but the President also said that he regarded it as essential that 'any measures which may be taken to deal with these urgent and important problems should secure a fair and equitable balance between the different trading interests concerned both small and large'.[1] The exclusion of the food trades was in deference to the views expressed by the Ministry of Food and the principal trade organisations. A much more serious matter was the vagueness of the Committee's terms of reference.[2] Thus the trade members of the Committee tended to take the view that the Committee's concern was with the fate of the retail trader, the individual shopkeeper, and that such matters as the release of labour from the distributive trades were for the Ministry of Labour to deal with. The broad economic problem of securing the maximum release of labour for the war effort while maintaining efficient distributive services got pushed into the background. The Committee's approach to its problems was thus distorted in such a way as seriously to diminish the value of its reports and recommendations. The President's statement also had a restrictive influence on the Committee; it could not recommend anything that would upset the balance of interests in the retail trades.

Another difficulty lay in the composition of the Committee. Probably it would have been best to have had a small committee consisting of three or four independent and expert members who would have taken evidence from traders and trade organisations. Politically, however, it would have been difficult to avoid what was actually done, namely the setting up of a larger committee including direct representation of the different elements in the retail trades. Twelve members were appointed, of whom three were of independent standing, three were representatives of labour, and six were trade members. These latter included members of the Multiple Shops' Federation, the Retail Distributors' Association, the Co-operative Union, the Drapers' Chamber of Trade, the National Chamber of Trade and the Scottish Chamber of Trade. The diverse interests and attitudes of this unwieldy body were soon to show themselves. The chairman of the Committee was Mr. Craig Henderson, K.C., M.P.

The Committee proceeded to issue a questionnaire to the retail trade associations, partly with a view to obtaining information about the size and strength of each association, and partly to ascertain their views about the desirability or otherwise of concentration in the retail trades. On this latter subject they aroused a good deal of opposition. There was hostility to the idea of a compensation arrangement, while

---

[1] *Ibid.*

[2] See also *The Economist*, 4th July 1942. The terms of reference had been left deliberately vague.

those who spoke for the small trader seemed to think it the function of the Committee to help him to keep going rather than to devise plans for the closing down of shops.

The Committee therefore turned to discuss the less controversial proposal for a measure of control over the opening of new shops. Here they found widespread support from the trade associations. They themselves were generally agreed that something of the sort was desirable, though one member who thought control unnecessary was prepared to suggest that the question of the opening of new shops was a racket worked up by the shopkeepers in the reception areas who disliked the idea of competition. However, it was agreed that if this restriction were imposed it should be continued after the war so long as supplies were limited and prices controlled. Furthermore, it was agreed to recommend that the licensing authorities which would have to be set up under this arrangement should be the Local Price Committees with the addition of a trade representative from the non-food trades and a representative of one of the two trade unions concerned.[1]

The Committee presented its first interim report on 13th October 1941. It argued that the opening of new shops in war-time involved a diversion of labour, goods and transport, which could only be justified if it could be shown 'that the number of retail outlets is insufficient to provide for the essential needs of the population'. Furthermore, a multiplication of outlets might 'seriously disturb the relation between sales and selling costs and tend to make a rise in prices inevitable or, by the incursion of newcomers, to force existing traders out of business'. It therefore recommended:

(1) Except under licence no person should be permitted to establish a retail business in premises not hitherto used for the category of trade which it was proposed to set up.[2]

(2) There should be no restriction on the sale of existing businesses. Persons taking over existing businesses should not be required to take out licences unless they proposed to deal in new categories of goods.

(3) Traders who had lost their premises through bombing should be entitled as of right to a licence, provided that they applied for it within thirty days, that they intended to carry on the same category of trade as before, and that they re-established themselves within a mile of their former premises.[3]

(4) Licences should also be required for the sale of goods of a character materially different from those formerly sold at given prem-

---

[1] Alternatively, the Committee recommended that the authorities should be specially constituted local tribunals consisting of four members appointed by the Board of Trade—two independents, one trade member and one representative of the unions.

[2] Retail trade was taken to include hairdressers' shops and sales by auction of non-food goods. Premises should be understood to include stalls, booths and domestic premises.

[3] These conditions were to be waived in the case of emergency shops let out to traders by the local authority.

ises. A schedule was attached to the report listing the broad categories of goods which would be covered by this recommendation.

(5) The licensing authorities should be the Local Price Committees with the additions already mentioned.

The main principle of this report—the restriction on the opening of
new shops—was readily accepted. There might be some doubt about
the subsidiary recommendation of the Committee that shopkeepers
should not be permitted to extend their activities into new categories
of goods without a licence. Could such a restriction be enforced?
Would it help the small shopkeeper? The chain stores, for example,
could compete more effectively by abandoning their price limits than
by extending their range of goods. However, in the framing of the
Location of Retail Businesses Order of 1941,[1] both points were
incorporated.

The effect of this Order was to prohibit without licence as from
1st January 1942 the opening of new retail premises[2] and similarly to
prohibit persons from selling goods or performing certain services
which they had not sold or performed in the basic period, 1st December 1940–23rd October 1941. The Order applied only to the non-
food retail trades, but it included a few services—hairdressing, beauty
treatment and those performed by circulating libraries and auctioneers—as well as goods sold over shop counters. The goods were
listed in forty-eight categories for the enforcement of the transfer
restriction, e.g. a trader could sell tumblers if he had previously only
been selling china, but he required a licence to enable him to switch
from china to jewellery. The licensing authorities were to be the
Local Price Committees without the addition which had been recommended by the Retail Trade Committee of a trade member and a
trade union member. The Local Price Committees were advised to
restrict the granting of licences to two general cases: first, where an
essential consumer need in a particular area could be demonstrated,
and, secondly, to meet the position of traders who had lost the use of
their premises through war damage.

This measure did not dispose of the broader problems that had been
remitted to the Retail Trade Committee. Here the Committee soon
found that it could make little progress without fuller and more
accurate information. A compensation scheme, for example, could
not be worked out without estimates of the proportion of shops which
were likely to close and of the liabilities that would fall upon a
central fund. Accordingly, it set up an investigation sub-committee.[3]

---

[1] S.R. & O. 1941, No. 1784.

[2] No licence was required when a business was sold (or its goodwill acquired) provided
that the person to whom it was sold did not extend his operations into lines of goods
not previously sold at the premises in question.

[3] The members of this sub-committee were Mr. Mathias (chairman), Mrs. Tate, M.P.,
Professor Sargant Florence, Mr. Neal, Mr. Hann.

This sub-committee, which became responsible for the preparation and drafting of the second and third reports of the main committee, proposed to carry out its inquiries under two main headings. In the first place, an investigation was to be made into war-time restrictions affecting retail trade, which would cover not only the limitation of supplies and price control policy, but also the Ministry of Labour's plans for the withdrawal of labour from the distributive trades. Secondly, the sub-committee proposed to make a survey of the situation in retail trade, which would include detailed study of conditions in sample towns and discussions of retailing problems with the trade associations.

The first investigation yielded results forming the basis of the second report of the Retail Trade Committee, which presented a gloomy picture of the prospects facing the retailer. 'Our survey', the Committee said, 'reveals a bleak prospect for shopkeeping in 1942.' Emphasis was laid, in the first place, on the reduction in supplies that was occurring in almost every line of non-food goods, on the measures of commodity standardisation that were being imposed, and on the more rigid control of prices that was being introduced. On labour matters the Committee took an almost equally gloomy view. Working from the occupation tables of the census of 1931 it estimated that, of men engaged in the non-food retail trades sixty-three per cent. came within the scope of the armed forces and National Service Acts, and of women twenty-six per cent. between twenty and twenty-five, and eleven per cent. between twenty-six and thirty were in the field for withdrawal. These classes together represented half of the entire labour force, including the more vigorous and efficient workers in the trades.

There was hardly anything in the report to suggest a lightening of this sombre prospect. Different areas might be differently affected; the trader in Oxford or Rugby would not fare as badly as the trader in Dover or Hull.[1] Again, in the first two years of war the trader might have had some freedom of manœuvre, and had shown some resilience, but when 'the full effects of contraction, previously masked and delayed, begin to operate the retailer's position will rapidly deteriorate'.[2] The department stores, the multiples, the chain stores and the co-operatives might be somewhat better placed; they might be able to effect an internal concentration, either by concentrating within their own site or by closing down a proportion of their branches. But the small independent shopkeeper had not these possibilities. He must face up to three alternatives: '(i) As he not infrequently puts it himself, he can decide to "hang on no matter what happens", or (ii) he can try to arrange a temporary "marriage" with one or more fellow-

---

[1] But the emphasis throughout the report was on contraction, e.g. 'It is . . . evident that the severity of the reduction in evacuation areas far outdistances the reduction in reception areas.' (*Second Interim Report*, p. 21.)

[2] *Second Interim Report*, p. 22.

retailers, or (iii) he can close down either for the war's duration or permanently.'[1]

What was perhaps most noticeable about the report was that it approached the situation with which it had to deal entirely from the retailer's angle.[2] The need for the release of resources, particularly labour, from the retail trades for the war effort was barely recognised, nor was any attempt made to compare the hardships of the retailer with the sufferings which other sections of the community were undergoing or might be expected to undergo. 'The report in a number of places reads as though it were written by shopkeepers for shopkeepers, without regard for the general public', was one of the verdicts on it.

It is, however, more relevant at the moment to consider whether the Committee had in fact presented a reliable picture of the retailer's position and of his problems as they were developing in 1941–42. The first point that emerges in an examination of the report is the error made by the Committee in focusing attention on the *volume* of supplies to the retailer rather than on the *value* of his turnover. It is clear that the profitability of the retailer's business depends on two things—the gross margin which he obtains, as a percentage of money turnover, on the commodities which he sells, and the expenses which he incurs in order to secure that turnover. Given the fact that, with a reduced volume of supplies, prices were rising retail turnover might not fall off and might even increase. The Bank of England's figures of retail trade and turnover,[3] unaccountably ignored by the Retail Trade Committee, give the following picture:

Retail Sales of Non-Food Merchandise

TABLE 14

(1) *Retail Sales* (Non-Food Merchandise) in Great Britain; percentage change as compared with previous year.

year[4]	
1939–40	+1·8
1940–41	+4·2
1941–42	−5·4
1942–43	−0·1
1943–44	−6·0
1944–45	+6·9

(2) Annual Index Numbers of retail sales of non-food merchandise in Great Britain.

1942 = 100

1939	100
1940	105
1941	98
1942	100
1943	93
1944	101

---

[1] *Second Interim Report*, p. 24.

[2] The addendum of the labour members of the Committee will be referred to later.

[3] The only qualification to be made to the Bank's figures was that they were derived almost wholly from the department stores, the multiples and chain stores, and the co-operatives.

[4] Trading year February–January inclusive.

A more detailed picture is provided by the figures from the National Income and Expenditure White Papers, analysing consumers' expenditure at current prices. They are as follows, in £ millions.

Consumers' Expenditure at Current Prices[1]

TABLE 15 £ millions

	1938	1939	1940	1941	1942	1943	1944	1945
1. Durable household goods								
(a) Furniture	152	146	139	128	114	83	68	92
(b) Hardware	82	77	73	69	60	58	59	80
2. Other household goods								
(a) Matches	10	12	12	11	10	10	10	9
(b) Soap	30	30	31	31	28	28	29	29
(c) Other	14	14	16	15	15	14	16	18
3. Clothing								
(a) Footwear	73	78	90	91	97	87	90	91
(b) Men's and boys' wear	127	131	137	116	123	101	125	130
(c) Women's and girls' and infants' wear	246	249	269	245	267	241	279	293
4. Books, etc.								
(a) Books	10	9	8	13	17	20	21	23
(b) Newspapers	36	36	36	37	38	40	43	45
(c) Magazines	18	18	18	18	18	19	21	23
5. Other goods	177	181	187	189	184	190	201	229
Total	975	981	1,016	963	971	891	962	1,062

The general picture presented by these tables is much the same, a rise of turnover up to the end of 1940, followed by a fall, with the lowest point reached in 1943, which was followed by a rise from then onwards. Apart from the year 1943 there was no marked fall in aggregate money turnover; it did not differ appreciably in 1941, 1942 and 1944 from what it had been in 1938. There were, of course, very noticeable differences in the experiences of different trades. There was a big reduction in the expenditure on furniture, for example, though it must be remembered that these tables make no allowance for second-hand goods, expenditure on which increased considerably. On the other side of the picture there was a steady rise in the value of footwear sales and a striking increase in the expenditure on books.

While the Retail Trade Committee erred in failing to distinguish between volume and value of retail turnover, it also neglected to draw the obvious conclusion from the withdrawal of labour from the retail trades, namely that it would enable the shopkeeper to economise in his expenditure on labour. The people who would suffer would be not the traders but the members of the general public who would be standing in queues.

---

[1] These figures include purchase tax, of which the following sums were raised:—

	£ millions		£ millions
1940–41	26·2	1943–44	91·7
1941–42	98·5	1944–45	98·4
1942–43	110·5		

With the drafting of the second report completed the investigation sub-committee of the Retail Trade Committee undertook the remaining part of its inquiry, which was directed towards a study of conditions in the retail trades. On the one hand information was sought from the Multiple Shops' Federation, the Co-operative Congress and the Retail Distributors' Association about reductions which had taken place in floor space (department stores), in numbers of branches (multiples and co-operatives) and in staff.[1] On the other hand, a survey was made of shopping conditions in seven towns—Derby, York, Newport (Monmouthshire), Oxford, Ispwich, Gravesend and Rugby, with aggregate pre-war resident population amounting to just over 600,000.[2] Oxford and Rugby were reception areas, but none of the towns had been blitzed or suffered heavily from evacuation.

The results of these investigations may be briefly summarised. In the country as a whole the department stores had suffered a loss of over twenty per cent. of floor space, mainly through enemy action. The net closing of shops by multiples was fully ten per cent.,[3] that by co-operatives was considerably less. Staff reductions amounted to fifteen per cent. for co-operatives, twenty-two per cent. and twenty-six per cent. for multiples and variety chains, thirty-three per cent. for department stores.[4] The seven towns study completed the picture by providing data about the medium-sized and the small unit shop. In these towns the total reduction of shops between the outbreak of war and March 1942 had been ten per cent. By categories of trade chemists and footwear shops had fared best, while in jewellery and in furniture and furnishings there had been reductions of fourteen per cent. and twenty-one per cent. respectively. However, the large organisations—the department stores, the co-operatives, the multiples and the variety chain stores—and the large unit shops had maintained their numbers.[5] The shops which had suffered reductions in numbers had been the small shops.

A sample survey of shops in Glasgow and Leeds made about this time[6] appeared to reinforce the argument that the small shopkeepers had suffered severely as a result of the war. The conclusions of this survey were that about one-fifth of the shops in Glasgow and Leeds

---

[1] The results of this inquiry were published as an appendix to the third report of the Retail Trade Committee.

[2] The results of this survey were also published in the appendix to the third report.

[3] Complete closing of branches by variety chains represented only four per cent. of 1939 shops.

[4] The comparison in all figures is between 1st September 1939 and March 1942.

[5] The contrast between the experience of the large organisations in these seven towns and their experience in the country as a whole was ascribed by the committee partly to the fact that these towns had not suffered air-raid damage, which elsewhere had been concentrated on main shopping areas.

[6] 'War and the Small Retail Shop'; *Oxford Institute of Statistics Bulletin*, 4th April 1942.

which were open in January 1940 had closed by the end of 1941; that the smaller shops were most affected (in Leeds twenty-five per cent. of small shops had closed, thirteen per cent. of medium-sized and eleven per cent. of large); and that non-food shops were more affected than food shops (twenty-four per cent. against fourteen per cent. closed in Leeds).

All these figures needed care in their interpretation, and it should not have been readily assumed, as the Retail Trade Committee appears to have done, that the closing down of small shops was mainly, if not solely, due to the war-time hardships suffered by the retailer. It was probably true before the war that there were annually a large number of failures among the many small men who with little capital and experience had entered the business of shopkeeping. Moreover, the average earnings of these small traders had been pretty low, and there can be little doubt that the rise in wages in the war must have induced many of them to shut up their shops and seek more remunerative employment in industry. The case which the Retail Trade Committee was trying to make was clearly not proven, and, indeed, in the light of subsequent developments the picture it was painting of the retailer's prospects appears a distorted one.

Already, in the drafting of the second report, the internal strains and stresses within the Committee had begun to make themselves felt. The trade union members of the Committee considered that the report tended to exaggerate the difficulties of the trader's position; it ignored the effects produced by the closing down of shops, the existence of considerable stocks, and the labour economies which had been or would be effected. They believed that the report as it stood would be used by employers as an argument against improvements in wages which, they themselves considered, were badly needed. They produced an amendment along these lines and were only at length persuaded, in deference to the views of the trade members, to withdraw it and to substitute an addendum to the main report. In this addendum they stated it as their view that the current difficulties of the retail trades were 'to some extent due to the absence in the past of any planned economy, which meant that anyone was free to open a shop without regard to the actual requirements and needs of the public'. They then proceeded to give their warning about wages. National Joint Industrial Councils had recently been set up, but they had been hampered by the fact that in the past the economy of the retail trades had been based on low wages. 'Accordingly', ran the addendum, 'nothing in the main report must be read as barring representations by the trade unions concerned for improvement in the present wage scales and working conditions at such times and in such cases as they may think proper'.[1]

---

[1] *Second Interim Report*, p. 29.

Another set of stresses emerged when the drafting committee tried to press on with proposals for some form of concentration scheme for the retail trades. The second report had already pointed in this direction. Temporary war-time 'marriages' of traders were mentioned with approval, though the obstacles to such 'marriages' were recognised. The report also referred to the possibility of a mutual compensation scheme based on a levy on traders remaining in business, though it had to admit that the replies which had been received to this suggestion from the trade organisations had not been encouraging.[1] The Committee now proposed to go more deeply into these questions, and to get the trade organisations to look at them again in the light of a steadily worsening position.

Before examining the Committee's scheme it will be as well, first of all, to look at the awkward problems confronting any plans for concentration and compensation in the retail trades. The major problem, undoubtedly, was to devise a scheme which, while meeting the national requirements for labour and storage space, would preserve essential distribution facilities and could at the same time be reconciled with the conflicting interests of the distributors themselves. For example, the Multiple Shops' Federation claimed that the concentration of the available supplies of goods into the hands of the larger organisations was desirable, because they were more economical of manpower and other resources; they could adjust their labour requirements more accurately to the changing volume of supplies, and they had the advantages of bulk buying. The representatives of the small independent shops contended that they, on the other hand, tended to be run by elderly people who would be of little use in war industries, and that the only storage space of any value was to be found in the large retailing organisations.

The problem of compensation was almost equally formidable. The Government had ruled in September 1940 that there should only be compensation for those suffering from direct war damage.[2] Therefore any compensation for withdrawing traders would have to be met by a levy on those remaining in business. This, in the first place, increased the difficulty of arranging any concentration scheme which would meet with approval from all sections of the retailing community. It also raised the objection that any adequate measure of compensation could not be provided without a raising of retail prices.

Nor were the administrative difficulties of a concentration plan to be underrated. Could any Government department tackle the problem of dealing with thousands of traders about whom so little was known? To handle the question of 'marriages' between retailers

---

[1] *Second Interim Report*, p. 27.
[2] H. of C. Deb., Vol. 365, Cols. 42–3.

would require local knowledge which was not and could not easily be made available in Whitehall. Again, the Committee was reporting in 1942, by which time many traders had gone out of business. To leave them out might appear inequitable, but it would have been administratively quite impracticable to include them within concentration and compensation arrangements.

The fact that, in spite of these difficulties, the Retail Trade Committee put forward in its third report a scheme of concentration is a measure of the gravity with which it viewed the whole position in the retail trades. The principles underlying this scheme were:

(i) Withdrawal from trade should be voluntary. There was no support on the Committee for any measure of compulsory closing of shops. Nor would the small traders have agreed to compulsory closure; they were even disturbed at the idea that they should be encouraged to withdraw from business.

(ii) Continuing traders would be registered and would be liable to a compulsory levy. This should be all-embracing; the possibility of contracting out should be excluded.[1] After some discussion of the basis of a levy, which might be, for example, on profits, wage bills, number of employees, or turnover, it was agreed to recommend a levy on turnover, at the rate of one per cent. on the previous year's turnover.[2] There might of course be difficulties about this—the smaller traders probably did not keep accurate records of turnover and it would be difficult to separate food and non-food turnover. It was proposed that the very small trader should have the option of contracting out of the scheme. This levy should be allowed as a business expense both for taxation and for price-control purposes.

(iii) Compensation should be arranged so as to cover only the withdrawing retailer's contractual obligations. These included rent and rates, and such things as maintenance and fire-watching costs, insurance and payments under the War Damage Act. Compensation should be assessed, like the levy, on turnover; the rate recommended was five per cent. of annual turnover, to be paid annually for the duration of the scheme.[3]

The main liability to be accounted for was rent, and the major problem was the assessment of the amount of this liability. Compensation at the rate of five per cent. of turnover seemed adequate for most traders and more than adequate for some. However, for retailers with highly rented premises in central areas this would be insufficient,

---

[1] Except for the very small trader—see below.

[2] This was recommended for the beginning of the scheme; the levy could be adjusted from time to time to meet changes in the total of turnover represented by withdrawing traders.

[3] If the obligation to pay rent came to an end, however, the compensation should automatically cease.

and to meet their case an extension of the facilities of the Liabilities (War-Time) Adjustment Act 1941 was recommended.[1]

In its report the Committee proposed that as an alternative to the scheme of compensation just described, termed 'standard benefit', there should be provision for 'special benefit' available to those without contractual obligations or with only very short-term contractual obligations. This special benefit would be calculated at the same rate as standard benefit, would be allowable for a fixed term of six months, but, as a maximum, should only apply to the first £5,000 of turnover. The trader could either take this benefit out in cash or leave it invested in the compensation fund at an agreed rate of interest. This was intended to operate as a special inducement to speedy withdrawal from business.[2]

(iv) The withdrawing trader should be afforded prior rights of re-entry after the war. Withdrawal would include the closing of a unit shop, of a branch of a multiple store, or a floor of a department store, or 'marriage' of two traders. Although it was difficult to make the scheme retrospective, the Committee thought that the possibility of allowing similar rights of re-entry to those who had, before the introduction of the scheme, ceased trading as a result of the war should be considered.

The general principles of this concentration scheme were discussed in February and March 1942 with representatives of a number of the trade associations concerned—forty-seven in all—and of the two trade unions. Of these associations only one, the Drapers' Chamber of Trade, appears to have given unqualified support to the scheme. This body, as has already been noted, had even before the appointment of the Retail Trade Committee been advocating some form of concentration among traders. The investigation sub-committee of the main committee also made a short provincial tour, in which it studied local retailing problems at first hand, conferring with local Chambers of Trade at Ipswich, York, Plymouth and Edinburgh.

Put in its simplest terms the main reason why most classes of traders were opposed to these proposals was that they felt that they could do better by carrying on independently rather than by entering into arrangements for a levy and compensation for withdrawing traders. Turnover in many cases had risen rather than fallen, and it was felt that the Committee had over-emphasised the bleakness of the pros-

---

[1] This Act provided that a person might apply to the Court for an adjustment of his affairs if (a) he were unable to pay his accrued debts, or would be unable after payment of his accrued debts to meet future liabilities in respect of obligations already incurred, or (b) he were in such a position that if he were required to pay his accrued debts or to meet, as they fell due, his future liabilities he would have no reasonable prospect of preserving or recovering his business or would otherwise lose his means of livelihood (Sec. 3, Sub-sec. 1).

[2] It was recommended that, to qualify for special benefit, withdrawal should take place within six months of the scheme's inception.

pect facing retailers. Some dealers in goods, supplies of which had been restricted, for example motor-cycles and radios, thought that extra servicing and repair work would compensate for the decrease in the volume of new goods for sale.

Objections to particular points in the scheme were, first, that it excluded the food traders, an artificial and inequitable arrangement; secondly, that the benefit of the compensation would simply go into the pockets of landlords and mortgagees; and thirdly, that the levy on turnover was fixed at too high a rate. Cutting across these objections were the clashes of conflicting interest between different sections of the retailing community. The small trader, represented by the National Chamber of Trade, thought that the scheme favoured the large organisations and feared that it might have the result of driving him permanently out of business. His fears were indeed somewhat justified by the attitude of those large organisations who held that a really effective scheme, operated in the national interest, ought to aim at the concentration of retailing in efficient large-scale units. The Co-operative Congress maintained throughout an uncompromising hostility to the proposals. The co-operatives preferred to carry their own burdens, arranging, if necessary, an internal concentration scheme, rather than come into a general plan.[1] They were the only body to suggest that the levy on turnover would be passed on to the consumer in the shape of higher prices. The National Union of Shop Assistants, alone of all the bodies interviewed, favoured a compulsory concentration which would place available supplies in the hands of the larger shops, which were not only more economical and efficient but could guarantee good conditions of employment. These criticisms all represented first reactions to the Committee's proposals. When the Committee's third report was published in June 1942, the hostility of the various sections of the retail trades was more widespread and violent.

Of equal significance with the hostile reception of the report by the trading community was the change of attitude towards the whole problem which had taken place in the Board of Trade. So far as the traders' claim to special consideration was concerned, the official view now rather was that their difficulties had been exaggerated, and that, in general, the small retailer was but one example of a very large class of people who had been adversely affected by war conditions. The closing down of small shops was not perhaps so very surprising; it was the sort of thing which had been taking place through the pre-war years. Nor was there much fear that the closing of shops would endanger that minimum of retailing facilities which even in war it was essential to provide.

---

[1] *Vide* the minority report to the third report of the Retail Trade Committee signed by the Co-operative representative on the committee.

Economically, the arguments in favour of concentration were not very strong; they were a good deal weaker than the arguments which could be advanced on behalf of the concentration of manufacturing industry. The amount of shop space outside the larger stores suitable for requisitioning for storage or office purposes was not large. Much of the labour in the smaller shops was personally attached to the business to a far greater extent than in industry and was in consequence much less mobile. The labour released from these shops by a voluntary concentration scheme would consist largely of elderly and immobile workers.[1] Thus a closing of the larger shops and branches of the large retailing organisations would really do much more towards yielding useful resources for the war effort than the withdrawal of the small shopkeeper which was being advocated.

Politically the scheme bristled with difficulties. The conflict of interest between traders dealing in different lines of goods, between the large and the small shops, between these again and the multiples and co-operatives, in conjunction with the lukewarm, if not hostile, attitude of labour in the retail trades would have been enough to throw doubt upon the desirability of going ahead with the plan.

The details of the scheme, if put into operation, would have presented awkward problems. The exclusion of the food trades was unsatisfactory, but, quite apart from trade views, the Ministry of Food would not have agreed to their inclusion; it was opposed to the bringing even of sweet shops within the scope of the compulsory levy, although it did not object to their being given the option of joining the scheme.[2] Again, there would have been difficulties in collecting the levy on turnover, particularly from the smaller shops which did not keep accurate records. The Inland Revenue stated that they could not use their machinery for collecting the levy and that they could not, without special legislation, disclose the records in their possession even to another department. The proposal, moreover, of the Retail Trade Committee that the levy should be allowed as a business expense for taxation and price-control purposes cut right across official policy towards price-fixing under concentration schemes; the Board of Trade and the Central Price Committee had taken the line that concentration levies should come out of the profits of nucleus firms and should not be treated as costs. Finally, there was the whole question as to whether the scheme would work. Would the compensation be sufficient to induce a large number of traders to withdraw from business rather than hang on hoping for the best?

---

[1] The Minister of Labour had no doubt that he would get much more of the sort of labour he wanted by withdrawing workers by age groups than through the scheme propounded by the Retail Trade Committee.

[2] The Retail Trade Committee in its third report proposed that sweet shops should be included in the plan, on the ground of the close association of the sugar confectionery business with the newspaper and tobacco trades (*Third Report*, p. 22).

Meanwhile divergences of points of view had made themselves felt on the Committee itself. The representative of the co-operatives stated that he was unable to accept the conclusions of the report and submitted a minority report, which repeated the views of the co-operative movement. The labour representatives did not like the report, but they signed it as they could think of no satisfactory alternative to the main scheme. They insisted, however, on the inclusion of an addendum which again stressed the need for a planned economy and a limitation on the number of retail outlets. The representatives of the small trader were far from satisfied. They thought the concentration scheme played into the hands of the large organisations; there was all the difference in the world between a multiple closing one of its branches and the small man shutting up his shop, his sole source of livelihood. They would have liked to see the scheme made retrospective, more even distribution of supplies and some control over the expansion of multiple businesses. One of them submitted an addendum emphasising the position of the small shop as a 'valuable element and indispensable unit in the economic and social life of the country'.[1]

In October 1942 the President of the Board of Trade made it plain that he was not prepared to accept the main proposals of the Retail Trade Committee. At the same time he put forward the outlines of a policy which would be adopted to meet retail trade problems. Thereupon three members of the Retail Trade Committee, who had been engaged in the investigations and in the drafting of the Committee's report, resigned in protest.[2] On 2nd November 1942 the Committee itself was disbanded.

(iii)

Retail Trade Policy, 1942–45

With the collapse of the scheme put forward by the Retail Trade Committee the course of policy was altered. A policy was inaugurated which rejected the ideas of concentration and withdrawal of traders from business and attempted instead to redress the balance between different trading interests by deliberate discrimination in favour of the small man. This policy, adopted by the President of the Board of Trade and approved by ministers, was to be effected in three ways: first, by withdrawing labour chiefly from the larger shops; secondly, by meeting the needs for office and storage space by requisitioning part or the whole of larger shops; and, thirdly, by the introduction of arrangements to secure for small retailers a fair share of the

---

[1] *Third Report*, p. 30.

[2] Mrs. Tate, M.P., Professor Sargant Florence, Mr. A. H. Mathias.

limited supplies.[1] The only feature of the third report of the Retail Trade Committee which the President proposed to retain was the provision for controlled post-war re-entry, by which the interests of withdrawing traders would be to some degree safeguarded. The lines of the new policy were clearly indicated in the President's statement in the House of Commons on 13th October 1942. 'There is a real danger', he said, 'that a large number of the smaller shops may be squeezed out of business. For many reasons this is undesirable. I have therefore come to the conclusion that some positive action is needed to assure to the small retailer his fair share of available supplies.'[2]

This policy conflicted openly with the view that an effective compensation and concentration scheme was needed both to meet the needs of the war effort and also to avoid the collapse of the small trader. The fair shares scheme, it was argued, was a delusion because the supplies would not be available on a scale adequate to keep all the small shopkeepers in business. It was, *The Economist* said, 'a cat and mouse policy, and the problem of what to do with the small retailer when he is finally squeezed out for lack of business remains entirely unsolved'.[3]

The case for spreading the limited supplies of goods rather than concentrating them in fewer shops was put on four grounds—the dependence of rural areas on small shops, the importance of dispersing stocks to reduce the risks of air-raid damage, the need for shops near people's homes, and the need to requisition office and storage space from the larger shops. Given these assumptions, however, the question still remained as to what evidence existed for unevenness in the distribution of supplies.

The smaller shopkeepers had for some time been complaining that they had not been getting their fair share of current supplies. They maintained that manufacturers and wholesalers found it more economical and simpler to dispose of their limited quotas to the multiples and chain stores. After rationing had been introduced some retailers said that they had a coupon surplus for which they could get no supplies. More information was needed and it was decided to appoint a special investigator to look into the problem.

The commodities selected for investigation were clothing, pottery and hollow-ware. The wholesalers, for their part, tended to deny, and on the whole the evidence seemed to support their case, that they had discriminated against the small trader. They put the blame to some extent on the manufacturers. But the problem was due, in many

---

[1] A plan for a 'retail trades war-time investment fund', in which withdrawing traders would invest the proceeds derived from the realisation of their stocks, was deferred for further consideration.

[2] H. of C. Deb., Vol. 383, Cols. 1478–79.

[3] *The Economist*, 19th December 1942.

cases, to the very low level to which supplies had been reduced. The simple fact was that there was not enough of some things to go round, fully-fashioned stockings or flannel trousers for example. It would have been futile and wasteful to attempt to arrange that each shop-keeper should receive a share of the commodities that were very scarce indeed.

Although this investigation hardly supported the complaints of the small shopkeeper, it was decided that there was sufficient ground for action. Two possible courses seemed to be open. The first was the formation of retailers' buying pools under which retailers would pool their purchases and distribute them locally among themselves. This proposal was dropped because it met with little approval either from wholesalers or retailers. The scheme came up against the individ-ualism of the retailer and his unwillingness to give his competitors information about his suppliers and his business methods. It would, however, have helped to save labour and transport, both valuable war-time resources.

The other possible course of action was carried out under the name of the 'Fair Shares' or 'Minimum Parcels' schemes. These schemes were applied to pottery, clothing and hollow-ware and provided that small retailers of these commodities might claim from their suppliers a percentage of their purchases in a standard year. These percentages would be fixed with reference to the relation of current supplies to supplies in the standard year and would vary from area to area to take account of war-time movements of population. The schemes were to be voluntary to meet the objections of the wholesalers who had protested against the extra amount of work involved. The details were to be arranged by three committees consisting of manufacturers, wholesalers and retailers.

These committees reported in December 1942, and the schemes came into operation as from the beginning of January 1943. The details of the schemes may be seen in the following table:

Membership of the scheme		*Standard year*
Retailers with a turnover of less than:		
Clothing	£5,000 per annum	1939
Pottery	£3,000 per annum	1st December 1940–30th November 1941
Hollow-ware	£2,500 per annum	1st June 1939–31st May 1940

The clothing scheme covered all clothing except footwear, and in-cluded other drapers' goods, such as household drapery and haber-dashery. The hollow-ware scheme covered domestic cooking utensils and buckets and dustbins, but excluded general hardware. The per-centages of standard period purchases varied between the schemes and between different areas.[1]

---

[1] Thus in the clothing scheme traders in evacuation areas on the Kent coast were assigned a percentage of 50, while those in reception areas in the West of England were given a percentage of 100 of standard period purchases.

The schemes met with a good deal of criticism. They naturally had no support from the large traders. But in any case the benefit of these arrangements to the small trader was doubtful. They would not satisfy his requirements for particular brands or varieties of commodities in keen demand; the larger shop would still be able to improve its position relatively because it could offer a better selection. However, no difficulty was experienced in putting the fair shares schemes into operation, and this in spite of, or perhaps partly on account of, their voluntary character and the absence of any legislative sanctions. There is possibly some further indication here that the extent of the maldistribution of supplies had been exaggerated.[1]

The chief fear of the small trader had been that he would be permanently squeezed out of business. What security had he that if he withdrew from trade he would be able to reopen his shop after the war? To meet this difficulty it was announced that a register of withdrawing traders would be set up. The register was formally opened in January 1943. It was confined to traders in the non-food trades dealing in the goods and services covered by the Location of Retail Businesses Order. Only shopkeepers would be eligible for registration; stall-holders, credit traders and people trading from private houses would be excluded from the scheme. Furthermore, to qualify for registration, a trader must have closed his shop after 1st September 1939 and must have been in business for a minimum period of twelve months' continuous trading before closing. A trader who had sold his business as a going concern was not eligible for entry in the register, but would be included in a supplementary list.

Application for registration was of course voluntary, and it was important that every effort should be made to secure publicity for the scheme. Extensive arrangements were made to advertise it, but by June 1945 only 17,427 names were recorded as being on the register. As there was no evidence as to the number of traders who had withdrawn from business, it is impossible to say whether the size of the register should be explained as a result of widespread ignorance of the scheme or as an indication that there was no real need for it, and that traders were faring better than had been anticipated. Of 11,490 registrations recorded by March 1944, 2,663 were branches of multiples, 173 were branches of co-operatives, and 8,654 were shops of all other types, figures which hardly supported the thesis that the unit shop was suffering much more heavily than the large organisation.

The plan for a register of withdrawing traders was naturally closely linked with the control imposed by the Location of Retail Businesses

---

[1] The only change that need be recorded was the modification of the clothing scheme to meet the needs of ex-Servicemen who had been granted licences to set up shop again. They were given a uniform percentage of 100 of standard period purchases, and assisted to find new suppliers if they had lost touch with their old suppliers.

Order, since the purpose of the register was to secure for the traders who made use of it prior rights of re-entry after the war. With the discharge from the Forces of increasing numbers of disabled ex-Servicemen there was a danger of a conflict between the political necessity of doing something for these men and the need to guarantee the rights of those whose names were entered on the register. Disabled ex-Servicemen formerly retail traders had been automatically granted licences to return to their old businesses, but up till the end of 1943 no decision had been taken about men discharged from the Forces who wished to enter retail trade for the first time. On 14th December 1943 a statement was made about post-war licensing policy.[1] Licensing both of food and non-food shops would continue after the war, but would not be made a permanent arrangement. Licensing of non-food shops in the transition period would be operated so as to facilitate the return of persons on the register. This meant that they would automatically be granted licences to return to their former businesses, or, if their old premises were bombed or let to other tenants, to premises in the same neighbourhood. No special facilities would be given to traders on the register who wished to set up in a different line of business.

The introduction of the Location of Retail Businesses Order at the end of 1941 has already been described. It was inevitable that, in the course of the war, there should be some change in the purposes for which this control was used. It had emerged in the first place from the deliberations of the Retail Trade Committee and was to some degree associated with the Committee's later proposals for concentration of retail distribution. No one, it was recommended, who had ceased trading should be allowed to resume business without a licence. Later, after the disbanding of the Committee, the idea of preserving a balance between different sections of the retail trades may have been reflected in the administration of the Order. Finally, the Order was instrumental in arrangements for securing controlled entry and re-entry into retailing towards the end of the war.

There were bound to be difficulties of administration, interpretation and enforcement in a control of this sort. A few of these may be mentioned here. It was clearly not easy to define or to enforce the provisions restricting existing traders from extending the range of goods which they were selling. An amending Order,[2] which prohibited a trader from selling without licence a category of goods unless he had previously been selling a 'substantial proportion' of goods in that category, proved inadequate to deal with traders who, for example, because they had previously been selling boracic acid as a

---

[1] For discussion about post-war policy with regard to the Location of Retail Businesses Order see below, pp. 278–9.

[2] S.R. & O. 1941, No. 1933.

side-line, considered themselves entitled to launch out into the whole range of 'drugs, medicines, medical and surgical appliances'. It was impossible to define what constituted a 'substantial proportion' of a category of goods. Difficulties also arose over the acquisition of goodwill. It had been provided that a trader taking over a shop who had legally acquired the goodwill from the former occupant should not require a licence.[1] Then it was found that the purpose of the Order was being circumvented by traders who went round the country buying up fictitious goodwill at nominal prices. Accordingly, a consolidating Order of August 1942[2] attached the right to trade in a certain category of goods not only to certain premises but also to the trader who had done business in those premises in the standard period. Finally, there was a group of administrative problems arising out of the fact that the Order covered not only the ordinary retail shop, but market stalls, booths, sales from private houses, mail orders, etc. The turnover of the market trader was proportionately not large, but he was often engaged in black market activities and he was peculiarly difficult to control.

The principles on which licensing was administered naturally underwent some modification. The fundamental principle was set forth under the title of the consumer needs test. The goods or services which an applicant for a licence proposed to put on the market must be shown to be 'reasonably required to provide for the essential needs of the public in the area concerned',[3] and the onus lay on the applicant to prove that this was the case. Some help in the matter could be given by publicity, for example in the local press, but to a large extent local licensing committees relied, in coming to a decision, on advice received from the Board of Trade's area distribution officers.[4]

The exceptions to this principle may be summarised under four heads:

(i) Traders whose premises had been bombed or requisitioned were to be given licences to set up in new premises.[5]

(ii) Favourable treatment was to be given to traders who wished to move to other premises, provided that they stayed within the same shopping area and that there was no change in the size or character of the business.

(iii) There was no wish to make the new provision about goodwill in the consolidating Order of 1942 bear harshly on a trader who

---

[1] This was to give effect to the recommendation of the Retail Trade Committee that nothing should be done to restrict the sale of existing businesses.

[2] S.R. & O. 1942, No. 1619. This Order was not made retrospective; see S.R. & O. 1942, No. 1828.

[3] Notes for guidance of local licensing committees.

[4] For a description of the functions of these officers see pp. 294–6.

[5] Provided they satisfied certain conditions with regard to, e.g. proximity of new premises to the old and time limit for making applications.

wished to dispose of his business. Local committees were therefore recommended to grant licences without reference to the consumer needs test where they were satisfied that there had been a genuine transfer of goodwill.

(iv) In the latter part of the war growing attention had to be paid to the problem of men discharged from the Forces who wished to enter or to re-enter retail trade. The case with regard to ex-Servicemen whose names were on the register of withdrawn traders was clear; they were automatically to be given licences to reopen their former businesses. Nor was there any difficulty, on the other hand, in deciding that an ex-Serviceman not formerly a retailer, who had not suffered disablement, should receive no preferential treatment but should be required to satisfy the strict consumer needs test. The disabled ex-Servicemen fell into two categories. Those who had previously been engaged in retailing were to be granted licences to open shops in any area, in any line of business, provided that the grant of a licence to operate in an area other than that in which they used to trade would not prejudice the interests of retailers on the register. Disabled ex-Servicemen who had not formerly been retailers were to be treated in the same way, except that the licensing committees were to consider, with the advice of the Ministry of Labour, whether in each case retailing afforded good prospects for the applicant.[1]

The following table analyses the figures of licences granted for the period 1st January 1942–30th September 1945[2]:—

Licences Granted under the Location of Retail Businesses Order
TABLE 16

(i) Licences granted for the opening of new businesses (non-food trades) . . .   17,849 { 327 multiples / 94 co-operatives / 17,428 other traders

(ii) Licences granted for the acquisition of goodwill of existing businesses (non-food trades) . . . . . .   17,146 { 370 multiples / 338 co-operatives / 16,438 other traders

Total .   34,995

In the last six months of 1945 15,989 licences were granted for England, 1,808 for Scotland and 776 for Wales; of these 6,993 were in respect of the acquisition of goodwill and 1,746 were for the transfer of businesses.[3]

The whole question of the future of the Order came under consideration in 1943. Was it desirable that there should be some restriction on the opening of shops in the post-war period, operating

---

[1] These relaxations of the consumer needs test were extended to cover war-disabled civilians.

[2] See H. of C. Deb., Vol. 416, Col. 1321; figures exclude canteens, market stalls, etc.

[3] H. of C. Deb., Vol. 426, Col. 494.

as a permanent measure? Temporarily, of course, the Order would have to continue to allow the resettlement of traders who were on the register. But in the matter of a continuing control over retailing it was not clear where the interests either of the nation as a whole or of the trading community lay.

Already in pre-war days, when there had been much talk of Britain being 'over-shopped', proposals had been put forward for a control by licensing over the retail trades.[1] These proposals reflected not only the interests of existing shopkeepers, but also a feeling on the part of some at any rate of the workers that their conditions could not be improved under the circumstances of unrestricted competition. Now, in 1943, there was a new and additional factor to be considered—the possibility that the post-war period might see a flood of ex-Servicemen pouring into the retail trades. Many traders could remember the misfortunes which had overtaken ex-Servicemen of the First World War who had invested their gratuities in shops.

However, the Location of Retail Businesses Order could hardly be regarded as a suitable instrument for the planning of the retail trades in the post-war world. And, indeed, the great majority of the retail trade organisations, which were consulted on the matter, were opposed to the idea of its being retained as a permanent measure of control. In December 1943 it was stated by the ministers concerned that while licensing would continue after the end of the war it would not be retained permanently. Two years later the President of the Board of Trade announced that the Order would be revoked at the end of 1945 and that the register of withdrawn traders would be closed. Sufficient time had then elapsed since the end of the war to allow ex-traders to resume their former businesses.[2]

(iv)

The Contribution of Retail Trade to the War Effort

As we have seen, schemes and policies for retail trade came and went. The whole subject had bristled with difficulties. Some had been caused by inadequate knowledge and others had been political; together they had pushed to the foreground of retail trade policy the problem of the retail trader himself—his chances of survival and the

---

[1] See H. Smith, *Retail Distribution*, 2nd Edition, pp. 184 *et seq.*

[2] Special steps were, however, to be taken during the first three months of 1946 to assist the priority classes—ex-traders and war-disabled persons—through the granting of building licences and coupon floats. H. of C. Deb., Vol. 417, Cols. 896–97.

balance between different kinds of trading interests. The two other problems involved—services to the consumer and the release of resources for the war effort had tended to disappear into the background.

The abandonment of all schemes for concentrating retail trade meant that manpower and space were withdrawn piecemeal as they were wanted. It was clear that shopping in war-time had to continue. But it was more important to maintain a reasonable number of shops selling food—and a reasonable number of people serving in them— than the numbers of shops and people selling other consumer goods. Everyone had to buy food and buy it frequently; other goods were bought at much more irregular intervals.

The labour engaged in selling food therefore had more protection than that engaged in selling other goods. Right up to the end of the war the Board of Trade and the Ministry of Labour felt confident that the non-food retail trades still provided a reservoir of labour that could be diverted to more useful purposes. Withdrawal of labour from retail distribution seemed to them far preferable to the withdrawal of labour from manufacturing industry.

Even in the early months of the war non-food retail trade received no protection for its male labour of military age. The trade was not included in the Schedule of Reserved Occupations and those engaged in it could be called up freely, subject only to the hardship arrangements whereby applications for deferment could be made by owners of one-man businesses or by employees appealing in the interests of their employers.

When the drive to recruit women for war service began in earnest in 1941, the retail trades lost more of their young labour. Women in the 20–25 age-groups could be withdrawn wholesale. There were, however, arrangements to defer key workers in the 26–30 age-groups. An employer could apply for the deferment of a woman in these groups if the shop concerned would suffer serious dislocation by her withdrawal and if no reasonably satisfactory substitute was available. It was necessary to take account of the general value and experience of the woman in her particular job and also 'the character of the business in relation to the maintenance of reasonable shopping facilities'. The machinery for administering and advising on these arrangements consisted of a central panel and local committees, all composed of representatives of employers and employees in the trades.

In time these arrangements had to be changed. The Ministry of Labour was not satisfied with them and felt that more women would have to be taken away from the shops. Meanwhile the Board of Trade from 1942 onwards took a more active interest in the release of labour from retail trade. They were concerned now to protect the small trader and to see that labour was withdrawn mainly from the larger retailing organisations. They were also feeling that they must make sure that a minimum of retail shops was maintained. For a time the Board were not prepared to take the responsibility of advising which particular shops were essential and which were not. In 1942–43 however there was a scheme under which the retail trades were divided into two lists, the more essential and the less essential. In the first list women could be withdrawn up to the age of thirty-five, in the second list up to the age of forty-five. At the same time the definition of key or pivotal workers was tightened and the maximum period of deferment was limited to six months. In 1943 it was necessary to withdraw even more women. The Ministry of Labour proposed either that all shops should be closed part-time, thus releasing women for part-time work or that all women up to the age of forty-five should be called up; pivotal workers would be deferred.[1] The second alternative was preferred and was put into operation.

These arrangements were much less generous than in the food trades where the age of reservation was twenty-seven for women and where there was no withdrawal without prior substitution. But they were no doubt adequate. The hardship and deferment plans served their purpose. And as its directable labour was withdrawn, retail trade drew upon a large reserve of juvenile, part-time and elderly workers. In a few areas where there had been heavy bombing or where large numbers of munition workers were housed there may have been real hardship through lack of shops and labour to serve in them. But in general the consumer suffered no more than a reasonable amount of discomfort from queueing in non-food shops.

The release of space was a less pressing problem than the release of labour. For the small and medium-sized shopkeepers about whom there was such political controversy had little to offer that was of much use for storage or office purposes. The obvious course was to take the space required from the larger shops and the larger organisations and this fitted in with the post-1942 retail policy of the Board of Trade. In December 1942 a register was opened of wholesale and retail premises with an area of 10,000 square feet or over.[2] Nearly 4,200 premises were registered with 121 million square feet of floor space.[3]

After all the tumult of retail trade policy the reduction of the trade was operated through these humble administrative means.

---

[1] A new category of 'super-pivotal' workers was invented at this time; these were women who had acquired special knowledge of a particular type of essential work, e.g. buying or accounting, or who were responsible for the training or supervision of young and inexperienced workers.

[2] S.R. & O. 1942, No. 2264. See also p. 243.

[3] Over a quarter of this was in London.

CHAPTER XIII

THE CONSUMER AND HIS NEEDS

(i)

The Needs

WAR-TIME retail trade policy was inspired in part by a concern for the needs of the consumer—that is, of the ordinary buying public. But shopping facilities were by no means the greatest of the consumer's problems. More important was what he or she could find in the shops. During the first months of the war the home consumer still fared very well. It was not until the summer of 1940 that the Board of Trade needed to show much interest in him. By then, however, the first Miscellaneous Limitation of Supplies Order had been issued. As one official put it the Board had done 'a rash thing'; their action in cutting the supplies of almost all everyday goods except food had 'verged on irresponsibility'—or would have done but for the cushion of stocks in the shops and in people's 'bottom drawers'. Their necessarily crude and unscientific methods, inevitable though they had been in the new mood of exuberant haste, would in time undoubtedly produce all kinds of consumption problems. To understand these problems consumer inquiries would be necessary.

In June 1940, therefore, a first inquiry was made[1] to see whether and where the shoe was unduly pinching the consumer. The answer was that, apart from a shortage of kitchen utensils in some places, the consumer had very few complaints so far. He—or she—had not yet felt the effect of restrictions in supply whether they were caused by the Board of Trade's Orders or by shortages of materials. The stocks held by manufacturers, wholesalers and retailers were in general higher than they had been a year previously. Indeed the recommendations of this June inquiry were all concerned with intensifying the restrictions. The first inquiry was a very rough and ready affair—a 'kind of lucky dip' as its author remarked. But there was a lot to be said for refining the methods and conducting a continuous investigation into the impact of restrictions on consumers and traders. This would check the results of Board of Trade policy and furnish material for future decisions. For, as the first inquiry pointed out, the state of trade opinion and public opinion, the amplitude of stocks, the availability of raw materials, the effects of Orders and the

---

[1] It was made by a specially recruited expert, Mr. (now Sir) Francis Meynell, who later became Adviser on Consumer Needs to the Board.

incidence of consumer demand were all in constant motion. The Board needed 'a moving picture of equally moving events'.

It was not until the autumn of 1940, however, that events began to move swiftly enough to cause the Board of Trade renewed anxiety about consumer problems. Supplies of labour and raw materials were becoming scarcer and the Board were as anxious as anyone to transfer resources from civilian production to the war effort. They were therefore preparing much more drastic Limitation of Supplies Orders both for textiles and for miscellaneous consumer goods. Once these restrictions had become really severe two kinds of consumer problems were bound to arise. In the first place, as we have already seen, the Limitation of Supplies Orders were clumsy in that their restrictions did not distinguish sufficiently between essential and unessential articles. The Board gradually recognised that it was as important to maintain a minimum supply of essential goods as to free resources by ruthlessly cutting supplies of unessential goods. This policy was to bear fruit in the control of manufacture and supply Orders for clothing and other consumer goods. But first it was necessary to identify those articles that even in the midst of war proved to be indispensable to a civilised community. The Board could do this only by keeping in constant touch with the consumer.

The second consumer problem that arose as restrictions on supply were pulled more tightly was the problem of distribution. Part of the answer to this problem was rationing, which will be discussed separately. But rationing did not begin until June 1941 and then only covered clothing. Meanwhile, under the limitation Orders, manufacturers or wholesalers were confined to their quotas of trade but they could distribute the quotas as they wished. There was no reason why the goods should necessarily find their way to the places or to the consumers whose need was greatest.

Before plunging into details about the various administrative devices by which the Board of Trade tried to help the consumer it is necessary to survey the problems of the consumer—the pattern of war-time consumer needs—in more concrete terms.

First, let us take this problem of distribution. What changes in the pattern of demand had war brought? One most obvious change was brought by the air raids. Towns that had been bombed needed exceptionally high quantities of consumer goods to replace those destroyed in private homes or in shops. In addition the war brought an unprecedented movement of population about the country. From the outbreak of war to the end of 1945 there occurred in England and Wales some 34,750,000 changes of address in a civilian popula-tion of about 38 millions.[1] In the year 1940 there were nearly 7¾

---

[1] See R. M. Titmuss, *Problems of Social Policy* (United Kingdom Civil Histories) (H.M.S.O., 1950), p. 413.

million changes of address and in the year 1941 over 6¾ millions. These figures of course overstate the more lasting shifts of population between different towns and districts. For a good deal of the movement was to and fro; people did not necessarily stay put in new places. Nevertheless the population of many places did expand or contract by pretty large percentages. Sometimes the expansion or contraction lasted for most of the war; sometimes it lasted only for much shorter periods. The following table shows the changes in the civilian resident population of certain towns and districts.

Population as a Percentage of the Mid-1939 Figure:

TABLE 17

	Dec. 1940	Aug. 1941	Dec. 1942	June 1943	Dec. 1944	Sept. 1945
London Region	71	71	76	76	73	81
Inner N.E. zone of London	50	46	53	53	51	59
Alsager (Cheshire)	106	108	157	156	167	157
Stone (Staffordshire)	111	115	135	135	133	125
Southend-on-Sea	42	48	56	58	70	84
Clacton	32	35	43	44	94	95
Birmingham	93	88	91	92	95	96
Malvern	124	122	125	125	124	119
Keswick	149	143	126	123	107	100
Liverpool	91	78	82	80	82	83
Hoylake	111	125	116	113	107	105
Lyme Regis	125	119	103	100	112	106
Southampton	86	65	67	67	74	81
Lynton (Devon)	179	168	130	131	128	113
Amersham	149	140	122	119	122	114
Stroud	124	124	118	116	117	112

The decreases in population were largely due to evacuation of one kind and another. As air attack declined or as the coastal areas became safer the populations in evacuation areas gradually grew once more, though not to their pre-war size. The increases of population, on the other hand, had various causes. In some places such as Keswick, Lynton and Amersham the influxes of population were mainly due to evacuation, whether official or unofficial. Here, too, as air attack diminished the population returned to something nearer —though not necessarily very close—to its original normal size. In other places, such as Alsager, Stone and Stroud, the increased population consisted of workers in new or expanded munitions works; often of course the workers brought their families with them. It would be possible to pick out other town such as Harrogate, Colwyn Bay and some of the North Lancashire coastal towns which became the war-time home of large branches of Government departments.

Problems of distribution did not arise simply through changes in population numbers. The newcomers to a town might present a

pattern of demand quite different from that of 'the natives'. Towns
that received evacuees found their child or adolescent population
greatly increased. In theory the clothing of the children might be
expected to come mainly from parents in evacuation areas but in
practice a good deal of the demand had to be met locally.[1] When a
reception area received a secondary or public school *en bloc* the
increased demand might be particularly difficult to meet because it
was concentrated on either boys' or girls' clothing. Again the
difference in urban and rural habits of life was reflected in the
different shopping demands of the evacuees and the inhabitants of
the reception areas. For example, a shopkeeper in Aylesbury said
that the local townsfolk had never used wellington boots but that
London evacuees wanted them badly when they arrived in the
country. Moreover evacuees from, say, a poor part of London might
arrive in a fairly prosperous county town and demand cheaper goods
than the local shops were used to supplying. On the other hand
some remote and poor areas of Scotland received influxes of the
wealthier, unofficial evacuees. The problems of towns where war
production greatly expanded differed in detail though not in kind
from the problem of these reception areas. Such towns experienced
unaccustomed or greatly increased demands for such items as
industrial clothing.

So far we have been talking only of changes in the resident civilian
population. But these people were not the sum total of the shopping
population. In particular, the armed forces, who were of course
unevenly distributed about the countryside, also went buying in
civilian shops. In theory the soldiers, sailors and airmen should have
been able to meet most of their needs in their own N.A.A.F.I.
canteens. But N.A.A.F.I. did not always seem to be popular with the
troops except as a food and drink canteen. There were therefore frequent reports that members of the Forces were buying up civilian
supplies of such things as razor blades. Moreover before clothes
rationing was introduced there was evidence that some soldiers dis-
carded the underwear supplied to them by the War Office and
bought in the shops the kind they were accustomed to. Sometimes,
too, Service messes (run on a voluntary basis) turned to local retailers
for crockery and linen which was not issued to them officially.
A phenomenon often remarked but rarely explained was that every
time—and how often!—a Service unit moved it needed to renew its
domestic equipment.

Indeed the general problem of local bulk buying whether by the
Services, works canteens or local institutions was a difficult one. At
first under the Limitation of Supplies Orders such bodies as Government departments, local authorities and institutions had been able to

---

[1] See R. M. Titmuss, *Problems of Social Policy*, for evacuation problems generally.

buy from registered manufacturers and wholesalers outside quota. But local interests had demanded a procedure for purchase from retailers who could in theory subsequently get quota-free replacements. As the 'limoso'[1] arrangements were superseded by other controls over manufacture the procedure for replacement—if any—became much more uncertain. Consequently, 'the littlest little man' —as one official called the consumer—sometimes found himself losing in the competition for supplies.

Some towns had influxes of shoppers peculiar to themselves. There were, for example, the problems of the west coast ports. From the autumn of 1940 most of the merchant shipping coming to Britain had to discharge at ports in the west instead of at those in the south and east. In a town like Greenock the buying population was greatly swollen by the floating population of seamen. Another kind of problem arose in Fleetwood, a fishing port. Here Icelandic trawlers came in considerable numbers and the fishermen, short of consumer goods at home and earning high war-time wages, bought lavishly in the local shops.

The distribution problems caused by changes in the population were further complicated by changes in shopping habits. Before the war inhabitants of small market towns and villages frequently went for their heavier shopping—clothing and domestic equipment—to the nearest large town. These excursions were usually social as well as utilitarian in purpose and they were generally made by bus. But in war-time people were often too busy to shop so far afield. And shopping expeditions were no longer pleasurable in themselves. War-time transport services were a strong deterrent to unnecessary travel: bus queues were long and cheap railway tickets were withdrawn. Moreover, the variety and quantity of goods for sale in the larger towns declined and shopkeepers tended to reserve scarce goods for known and regular customers to the disadvantage of the rural visitor. So it happened that Dingwall shopped less in Inverness, Petersfield less in Portsmouth and Kenilworth less in Birmingham, Coventry and Leamington. Such changes meant of course an additional strain on supplies and shopping facilities in the smaller towns.

There was another major cause of changes in the pattern of war-time demand for consumer goods. The war had brought to the country as a whole full employment and—in spite of the Government's strenuous efforts to curb inflation—higher spendable incomes. Demand for consumer goods was buoyant in all the areas where high wages were being earned in munition industries. But the change in demand was most noticeable in those areas that had suffered most from pre-war economic depression. For example, agriculture and fishing were no longer depressed and the districts and towns depen-

---

[1] The popular abbreviation for 'Limitation of Supplies Orders'.

dent on these industries reflected their new prosperity. Even more radical was the change in the condition of the pre-war 'special areas' such as South Wales, Northumberland, Durham and Cumberland. In these districts pre-war unemployment had been tragically high and coal-mining, where wages were particularly low, still absorbed a high proportion of those who were employed. The working-class houses in these areas had no stocks of clothing nor of household goods to cushion the impact of war-time scarcity. And the goods that had been bought were of the cheapest qualities and wore out quickly. During the war unemployment vanished even in these areas and wages were high. Sometimes there seemed to be ingrained habits in the families with bad employment history that did not lead them to make great efforts to improve their pitifully low standards in domestic possessions. More often, however, there was anxiety to improve these standards at the first opportunity. Reports flowed into the Board of Trade of these changes. For example, instead of the cheap clothing sold before the war in these areas, better quality garments were now demanded. And families that had been unable to afford anything more than cotton blankets for their beds—if those —were now asking for woollen blankets.

Enough has been written to show that in war-time the distribution of consumer goods needed to be particularly flexible. But as it happened distribution became more rigid. Manufacturers and wholesalers, anxious to distribute their reduced supplies equitably, usually allocated them according to the percentages bought in some pre-war base period. It seems that the initiative of individual shop-keepers still reaped rewards. A 'go-getting' technique by retailers prepared to spend a good deal of time in searching out supplies paid dividends. And more than one well-stocked shopkeeper was heard to say, 'I look after the traveller and he looks after me'. On the other hand some retailers complained that they did not receive their fair quota of supplies, and shopkeepers in remote country districts said that wholesalers' travellers had stopped calling. An evacuated town like Southend could complain that it was forgotten as firms thought it was dead and travellers were impeded by the police. Moreover, the concentration of production produced distribution problems, for a nucleus firm might refuse to supply the customers of a concentrated partner. There was another difficulty; in times of shortage goods tended to go straight from the manufacturer to the large retailers in the large centres of population. The result of this was that whole-salers as a class were sometimes starved and so in turn were the rural areas and small shops.

On the whole, however, manufacturers and wholesalers seem to have dealt fairly with their customers according to their lights. But it was obviously anomalous that goods should be distributed not

according to war-time need but according to the pre-war prosperity
and population of different areas or to the accidental over or under
ordering by shopkeepers in an arbitrarily chosen base period. As far
as clothing was concerned rationing did of course help to distribute
supplies more fairly. But in spite of the Board of Trade's efforts to
see that the different articles of clothing were produced in the quantities needed some items always remained scarce in relation to
demand. Distribution problems therefore persisted even for clothing:
for household equipment they were always present. Some towns—
and not usually those where need was greatest—were far better
stocked than others.

In the early summer of 1943, for example, the Board of Trade
compared the position of Bournemouth—formerly a popular seaside
resort—and Seaham Harbour—a coastal mining town in Durham.
The current population in Bournemouth and its contiguous satellite
towns (which had their own independent shopping centres) was
121,500; the current population of Seaham, whose nearest large
town was seven miles away, was about 23,500. In Seaham Board of
Trade representatives counted stock in all the retail outlets—eight
drapers and ten hollow-ware dealers. In Bournemouth they visited
only four drapers and five hollow-ware dealers, all situated in one of
the main shopping streets. They found the following stocks:—

*Retail Stocks of Household Goods in Bournemouth and Seaham
Harbour*

TABLE 18

	Blankets		Sheets	Pillow-cases	Mat-tresses	Towels	Tea towels
	Wool	Cotton					
Bournemouth . . . (four outlets only)	946	465	414	5,448	76	3,988	6,900
Seaham . . . (all outlets)	1	0	0	28	3	64	606

	Kettles	Sauce-pans	Frying-pans	Buckets	Wash-bowls
Bournemouth . . . (five outlets only)	431	77	14	388	62
Seaham . . . (all outlets)	0	27	3	6	4

This example compares two towns of different size and very
different pre-war history. The results are striking: plentiful stocks of
everything in Bournemouth but only one blanket, no sheets and no
kettles in Seaham. Disparity in distribution is striking even if towns
of equal shopping population and roughly equal pre-war prosperity
are compared. For example, over three months in 1943 Ashbourne

(shopping population 15,940) received deliveries of 63 woollen blankets, and Newton Abbot (15,730) received 338, Truro (21,000) had 799 saucepans delivered and Ludlow (21,520) had 204. Stowmarket (9,000) received 1,505 kettles and Richmond, in Yorkshire, (9,000) only 284.

Such cases could be multiplied. In some towns this disparity of supplies caused really serious hardship. Let us look briefly for example at one of the towns that caused the Board of Trade most concern—Whitehaven. This coastal town in Cumberland had suffered severely in the pre-war depression and therefore its base period supplies were low. In war-time, however, the town flourished and several important industrial plants employing skilled labour were established in the surrounding countryside. Very few of the workers who came to man these plants lived in hostels; they were nearly all billeted on existing families or housed in new houses built for the purpose. Travel restrictions prevented the use of Carlisle as a market centre. Thus a heavy burden was thrown on the exiguous local supplies of household goods. It is not surprising therefore that a survey for the Board of Trade of stocks of domestic equipment in Whitehaven homes disclosed a disturbing number with less than 'essential minimum' supplies. That is, twenty per cent. of the houses surveyed had less than two saucepans, nearly twenty per cent. had less than one cup and two plates per person, seven per cent. did not have a kettle and twenty-three per cent. did not have a scrubbing brush.

We must now leave these distribution matters and come to the second bundle of consumer problems: severe restrictions on the supply of consumer goods had only been in force a short while when it became apparent that some were in danger of going too far. In theory it might have been true that even essential goods could be dispensed with in war-time. If men could not buy razor blades they could have grown beards. The genius of improvisation that soldiers displayed in deserts or prison camps might have been invoked to deal with the shortage of pots and pans and crockery in civilian homes. But neither the Government nor the people envisaged this degree of austerity, except perhaps in the event of a German invasion. There was, of course, a good deal of improvisation and austerity among civilians; there was a general campaign of make-do and mend and as we shall see later many of the civilian goods produced were of very economical design. But Britain was after all a civilised community and was fighting a long war whose moments of excitement were divided by long dreary periods of wearying toil. In these conditions it was extremely important to maintain civilian efficiency and morale at a high pitch. People wanted to maintain the decencies of life; unless adequate supplies of essential consumer goods were available much time and energy and temper were wasted in shop-to-shop hunts.

We shall soon turn to describing the administrative measures for identifying the essential goods that were scarce and were badly needed. But first it is worth spending a few paragraphs in discussing the needs themselves. Some needs were obvious. For example, the Board of Trade early accepted the responsibility for ensuring adequate civilian clothing supplies; as we shall see later this came to mean adequate supplies of different garments for all ages and sizes —woollen underwear or boys' turnover socks or girls' liberty bodices or outsize garments. Similarly the need for the common items of general household equipment—saucepans, kettles, frying-pans, cups, saucers, blankets and sheets—was fairly apparent.

But there were many important needs that were not so easy to appreciate. Some were for small articles of common use that could be easily squeezed out of production as factories undertook war contracts—such things as press studs or hair-grips. Into this category too came the equipment necessary for babies and young children. Insufficient production added to increased demand on account of the rising birth-rate were to produce an acute shortage of such items as prams, babies' baths and chambers, teats for feeding-bottles and fire-guards. Again it might seem that the scope for improvisation in some of these articles would be great. But housewives in war-time were heavily burdened. Moreover the qualitative importance of the shortage of children's equipment far outweighed the quantitative aspect. The difference between real shortage and a satisfactory state of affairs might be no more than 100,000 of an article like babies' baths. On the other hand such deficiencies helped to lower those standards of infant hygiene and welfare which in the past had often been all too low. And one of the firm assumptions beneath the nation's food and social policy was that the war should not impair the health of young children.

For other articles the war brought a new or increased demand. Sometimes the increase was unexpected: for example the Services demanded higher standards of shaving than some of their members had been accustomed to in civilian life and this was believed to be a contributory cause of the shortage of razor blades. Again, changes in social habits caused a greatly increased demand for sanitary towels which made it essential to increase production; for a time, too, large quantities were imported from the United States. Other increases in demand such as those for torch batteries and blackout material were more obvious. It was really imperative that these demands should be met. Torch batteries were, of course, needed not only by ordinary civilians but by war workers; for example at Middlesbrough the big steel works was about three miles from the residential district and all the shifts either began or ended during blackout hours. Consumption of torch batteries was therefore exceptionally high and without batteries the workers' attendance at the steel works might suffer.

The war also brought to light many essential needs of particular districts or particular occupations. Before the war the Board of Trade had not been called upon to take much interest in the nation's living and working conditions; they could not, therefore, be expected to foresee the kind of troubles that war-time shortages would bring. They did not know for example how many houses in country districts and in towns lacked bathrooms, water-heating facilities, gas or electricity and adequate and modern lavatories. And it was not therefore until shortages had actually arrived that the Board became aware of the urgency in some districts of providing sufficient galvanised baths, heavy large kettles, oil stoves and wicks, sanitary pails and sanitary pans and chambers. The example of two towns will show how essential these needs were. In Middlesbrough there were 36,000 houses; of these 18,000 had no bathrooms and 28,000 had no indoor sanitation. In Stockton there were 18,000 houses; 10,500 of these had no bathrooms and 12,000 had no indoor sanitation. In country districts the proportionate need was even higher. Or to take another example: in Chester-le-Street, a mining area of Durham, a very few miners lived in council houses but the others had no washing facilities other than water from a community tap serving five or six cottages. Pithead baths existed at only one or two collieries. In such a district a shortage of galvanised baths caused real distress.

Gradually an infinite variety of local needs became apparent. For example many people in towns might be able to dispense with floor coverings. But it was essential to have some matting for the stone floors of Northumberland farms (only matting would do since the floors quickly rotted lino) and matting or heavy lino for the tiled floors in the Kettering-Wellingborough-Corby districts which were tramped by quarrymen's boots.

The variety of working needs was equally bewildering. Civil servants had to become familiar with such problems as the relative advantages and needs for fustian, moleskin, kersey flannel, corduroy, cotton tweed or Derby tweed trousers in different occupations. They had to understand the various needs of the miner—pit socks, pit pants, pit trousers or drawers, sweat cloth, safety boots, boot studs and so forth—and the variations in need according to whether certain pits were wet, dry, hot or cold. Many groups of workers had special needs. To take only one group, the agricultural workers round Morpeth; these men needed a special variety of 'shepherd boot' of special leather and construction; ordinary boots were of little use as they became soaked immediately on crossing the moors and slipped on the hills. As final examples of working needs that had to be met even in war-time we can mention drinking-flasks, lunch tins, thermos flasks and alarm clocks.

These pages have perhaps been sufficient to show the kind of consumer problems that confronted the Board of Trade in war-time. In the interests of morale and efficiency the Board had to temper the wind to the shorn lamb. As officials hastened to point out the lamb in this context *had* been shorn; indeed he *must* be shorn in war-time. The Board were interested in consumer needs and not in consumer wants although it was not easy to make the distinction and the criteria were often questioned. The Board were interested in identifying these needs and in organising production to meet them and in making distribution less disorderly. We must now turn to see how these functions were performed.

(ii)

'Tempering the Wind'

The Board of Trade's first measures to try to adjust the distribution of consumer goods in accordance with consumer needs came in November 1940. The Board had been perturbed about those distribution problems caused by changes in population that we have already mentioned—that is, about the tendency of wholesalers and manufacturers to distribute their supplies according to pre-war purchases in spite of the fact that the population of some towns had greatly increased or decreased. In discussions with the Board the Wholesale Textile Association pointed out that its members could hardly adjust supplies when they had no information about the shift of the population. The Board therefore set out to supply such information. Up-to-date statistics about alterations in population seemed surprisingly hard to come by. Later the most accurate figures of the buying population of towns were obtained from the number of sugar registrations; but in the meantime the only figures available were rather unsatisfactory ones from the Registrar-General's Department. From these figures a circular was compiled giving lists of towns or areas and the proportions by which supplies to them should be increased or decreased.[1] The first circular was issued to wholesalers at the end of November 1940 and revised versions were published at intervals throughout 1941.

It is doubtful how successful these arrangements were. Even with all possible goodwill on the part of the wholesalers their effect could

---

[1] The Ministry of Home Security would not permit the actual population figures to be circulated.

not have been very great. For few wholesalers had a truly 'national' distribution and those who had were often 'strong' in some areas and 'weak' in others. Those who attempted to adjust their supplies by areas according to the Board's wishes did it mostly by travellers' territories which might or might not fit into the regional groupings listed by the Board. Even where they did awkward questions of equity would arise—it seemed hard to cut one traveller's quota more than another's. And sometimes of course wholesalers were not willing to assume the extra work that these circulars required. It may of course have been true that the Board of Trade received a distorted picture of the situation since they only received complaints. Nevertheless it seems that most districts were expressing complete scepticism about the effects of these circulars.

Later in the spring of 1941 there were proposals for a scheme by which wholesalers would have been forbidden to send more than a certain percentage of their supplies to retailers in London. It was, however, abandoned partly because there was no adequate information about the numbers of wholesalers supplying London and the provinces and partly because it was feared that such a scheme would strengthen the multiple traders' position against that of the small trader.

While attempting to adjust the distribution of supplies to match population the Board had also been faced by the distribution problems caused by the air raids. When the various Limitation of Supplies Orders were issued it was realised that some special provision for heavily bombed areas would be necessary. They would need additional supplies of bedding, clothing and hollow-ware at a time when local supplies and local shops might have been destroyed. Under the various Orders, therefore, general licences were granted to wholesalers and manufacturers to supply controlled goods outside their quotas to bombed retailers. Retailers were allowed replacement not only of the whole value of their stocks but also of equipment owned in the course of business up to the total loss finally agreed for the retailer's war risks insurance claim.[1]

With the heavy raids on provincial towns at the end of 1940 — beginning with the raid on Coventry in November—something more than these general licences became necessary. In these towns the damage to goods and property was so heavy in relation to the total stocks of goods and to traders' premises that it was difficult to meet consumer need both immediately after a raid and later on. Under the new Limitation of Supplies Order of November 1940 essential consumers—a category that included local authorities and the Women's Voluntary Services—might be supplied free of quota with certain goods such as clothing, pottery, cutlery and domestic hollow-

---

[1] Purchase tax was excluded from the value of goods to be replaced.

U

ware. They were able therefore to relieve the essential needs of the bombed-out on the day after a raid. Apart from this provision the Board seem to have depended for the maintenance of supplies to the public on quick marketing by retailers of their replacement stocks. For the Board were reluctant to increase supplies of controlled goods by special licences. It was hoped that retailers who had been so badly damaged that they would not be able to resume trading for some time after a raid would transfer replacement stocks to unbombed traders in the neighbourhood, the unbombed trader handing over a proportion of his profit to the bombed trader as compensation. This type of arrangement was known as a mutual assistance scheme.

These arrangements were tested in the heavy raids on Coventry and Southampton. In both cases the Board were faced with widespread complaints of shortages which were blamed on the limitation Orders. The complaints seemed to the Board to be exaggerated. There were however certain inherent difficulties in the Board's policy. Mutual assistance schemes were unattractive to bombed traders who wished to keep their replacement stocks until they could themselves set up shop again and who were loth to surrender supplies to their principal trade rivals. Additional supplies were needed as an inducement to enter these schemes. Moreover it is clear that these policies safeguarded the position of the retailer rather than that of the consumer. The retailer, provided he could obtain alternative premises, would not suffer serious hardship but the consumer was wholly dependent on the initiative of the local authority in obtaining and distributing supplies or on the willingness of retailers to replace —and sell—their stocks at once. It therefore became clear that some machinery was necessary to direct adequate supplies where they were needed rather than give an automatic right of replacement. It was equally clear that the Board needed some specially trained officials who could assess the needs of individual bombed towns and who could explain the machinery for replacement of stocks and other administrative details in bombed areas.

For this reason, if for no other, it was clear that the Board of Trade needed some form of regional organisation to deal with distribution questions. But there were other reasons: in particular, the Board of Trade needed to keep in touch with the effects of the drastic limitations of supplies introduced in November 1940. The Board needed in short an intelligence service. In February 1941, therefore, four area distribution officers were appointed and in April a further eight. This provided one officer for each civil defence region and the strength was reinforced by further recruitment both from within the Board and from outside during the following two years. At the Board's headquarters a Consumer Needs Branch was established.

One of the most important tasks of the area distribution officers was always post-blitz work. In the early days of their work this involved explaining to traders the mechanism whereby they could exercise their rights to full replacement of bombed stocks, encouraging them after they had been bombed to place their replacement stocks in the market as quickly as possible and authorising the supply of goods ex-quota where it was found to be necessary. The area distribution officers were also responsible for supervising the formation of retailers' mutual assistance arrangements, and for seeing that the shopping premises remaining in the town were adequate. Later, as we shall see, these responsibilities for mitigating the effects of bombing were to become more elaborate.

Apart from these functions the primary duty of the distribution officers was to bring the Board into contact with what was happening in shops in different regions, to provide an answer to the question 'What really happens to the consumer when we (the Board) issue an Order?' and to give the Board the first warnings of supply and distribution problems that might become critical later. Allied to this duty was that of educating traders in the purposes of the Board's necessarily unpopular policies.

This work of liaison between the Board and traders and consumers inevitably became more complicated as the war went on. In the early days of their appointment the distribution officers found that there were general shortages of one or two types of goods—certain classes of clothing such as underwear, corsets and girls' stockings and certain items of hollow-ware goods such as kettles and saucepans. Some areas, too, had their own particular difficulties. But in general the conclusion was that the consumer was 'only just beginning to feel there's a war on'. It should be added that the distribution officers' point of contact with the supply position was the retailer and to some extent the wholesaler—not the consumer. This approach was dictated partly by the limitation of numbers—even when the organisation was at full strength there was only one distribution officer to about a million consumers—and partly by the distribution officers' responsibility for watching the flow of distribution.

In the first few months of their existence the main evidence of the distribution officers' activities was a weekly summary which was circulated to the production departments of the Board. This gave a condensed account of the retailers' and to a less extent the manufacturers' and wholesalers' problems that had been encountered and a 'moving picture' of the main trends and tendencies. The distribution officers reported not only difficulties in respect of shortages, maldistribution, trading-up[1] and so forth but also coupon and quota

---

[1] i.e. the manufacture or sale of more expensive and more profitable goods at the expense of cheaper lines.

problems, the special needs of various occupational groups, transport difficulties and special problems arising from bombing, the transfer of labour and the closing of 'concentrated' suppliers.

New developments in the consumer needs work of the Board of Trade followed swiftly upon the introduction of the Consumer Rationing Order in June 1941. This Order marked the opening of a new era in the Board's policy—an era of much closer control over the production and distribution of consumer goods, in which the Board were responsible for ensuring that the necessary minimum of goods was manufactured and fairly distributed. It was now not enough to keep a general eye open for hardship. For the new, detailed methods of administration the Board needed more precise information about consumer needs. As the Adviser on Consumer Needs wrote, 'If in peace-time no soap-maker would dream of bringing out a new line without interviewing thousands of housewives and hundreds of shopkeepers, asking them for their experiences, their preferences, their habits of use and expenditure, so in war-time it was a million times more necessary that this great super-industry at the Board of Trade—which had no benefit of trading experience, which had to deal with an incredible multiplicity of goods quite apart from clothing, which had a responsibility to the consumer, to the manufacturer, and above all to the needs of the war—should know the effect of what it did, and calculate the effect of what it proposed to do'. The Board now needed to know the answers to questions such as these: what civilian goods were there whose manufacture should be prohibited? What articles in time of war were essential for civilians? What quantity of each article should be produced or should be named as a target in each industry?

New kinds of inquiry were, then, essential. The Board's researches had somehow to be conducted on a scale that would make them capable of statistical analysis. For the distribution officers' early methods of reporting did not give a sufficiently accurate or objective picture of developing shortages. Their method of approach was to discuss the shortages with traders often in response to complaints— a method which tended to exaggerate shortages. It had also to be remembered that once a shortage of a necessity had developed it appeared even greater than it was, not only because people tended to hoard but also because people went from shop to shop asking for the commodity so that individual demands were multiplied. Moreover in their summaries of shortages the officers often grouped together difficult items because they formed a class in the Limitation of Supplies Orders. This made it difficult to obtain a clear picture of shortages of individual items: braces and corsets for example were in the same class in the Order, but it was unlikely that these two items would be equally scarce.

In August 1941, therefore, a new system was introduced. All retailers interviewed by distribution officers were questioned about the stock position of certain individual items selected beforehand by the Board of Trade and known to be scarce. From this was developed a retailers' panel from which the Board obtained monthly figures of the number of retailers without stock of many essential articles.

It was not easy to form this panel. It was difficult to take a representative sample of retailers when, in the absence of a census of distribution, the Board had no knowledge of the total number of retailers in any branch of the trade. The sample in the panel included finally about 1,500–1,600 retailers grouped as 'large', 'medium' or 'small' according to the number of persons employed. The selection of shops within these groups was a random one.[1]

The other main difficulty over the panel lay in obtaining from shorthanded retailers the necessary detailed information about a large variety of goods. To simplify this it was decided first that retailers should only be asked to state if they were entirely out of stock of each article, and secondly that officials of the Board should call regularly on the members of the panel to get the information on the spot.[2]

The value of these figures lay not so much in comparing relative out-of-stock figures for different items as in enabling the Board to watch continuously the trend of shortage for any particular article. The figures gave no impression of the total quantities of supplies since they took no account of the flow of goods through the retailers' hands. The Board felt however that over a period of several months the figures (which were embodied in a monthly report) gave a satisfactory and accurate gauge of the trend of shortage.

As the Board of Trade's methods of controlling manufacture and supply were strengthened and refined it became necessary to extend researches to the consumer level and these researches, too, had to be capable of statistical analysis. The most important of these consumer researches was the consumer panel for clothing which began in August 1941 and lasted for the rest of the war. The panel recorded the numbers of various articles of clothing bought and the prices paid. It was thus the means of establishing both the rate at which the public were spending their coupons and the way—in types of garments—in which they were taking up their ration.[3] This information was indispensable as the basis of the clothing budget and production

---

[1] See *Board of Trade Journal*, 5th May 1945, p. 198.

[2] From May 1943 onwards the work of collecting these figures from the members of the panel was contracted out to a commercial agency, the British Market Research Bureau.

[3] From the outset the material was collected and tabulated by the British Market Research Bureau.

planning,[1] and the information about prices was used by the Board for calculating retailers' turnover in rationed goods.

This panel was the most important of the consumer surveys. But there were others. Special surveys were made for the Board of Trade by the War-time Social Survey or commercial agencies to establish the need for things such as outsize garments, special corsets, pottery, perambulators and other nursery requisites and various kinds of sanitary towels. These surveys were usually helpful but they were not always sufficiently accurate to provide answers with even reasonable certainty. In addition there were regular monthly, and later two-monthly, inquiries into housewives' shopping difficulties, chiefly in the purchase of unrationed goods. The inquiry covered 3,000 consumers chosen at random who were asked which of thirty items (all known by the Board to be rather scarce) they had tried to buy, whether they had been successful and if not how many shops they had visited in the attempt. In addition these people were asked to name other items they had difficulty in buying. This inquiry therefore enabled the Board to discover early the growth of new distribution problems. Moreover the inquiry showed not only where the consumer was unable to buy because goods were unobtainable but also where he or she was unwilling to buy—for example because prices were too high.

Besides watching consumer purchases Consumer Needs Branch—again through outside agencies—surveyed from time to time consumers' stocks of rationed and unrationed goods. The most notable of these were three 'wardrobe checks' in April 1942, December 1942 and April 1944 made on the stocks of clothing held by the members of the Consumer Panel. There was however no regular method of continuously reporting changes in consumers' stocks.

As Consumer Needs Branch developed its technique of measuring consumer and retail shortages statistically and as the routine work of collecting and tabulating information from the various panels was transferred to market research agencies, the work of the area distribution officers changed. Their primary function remained informatory. They still explained and justified the Board's actions to traders and reported the trader's reaction back to the Board—not only his mental reaction but also the line of conduct he seemed likely to follow in the circumstances of a new Order, regulation or licence. And when flaws appeared in the structure of control the distribution officers were first to note and report them. Moreover, the distribution officers still did many special investigations for departments of the Board. For example, in the early months of 1942 before the utility furniture scheme was brought forward, these officers investigated the prices and availability of second-hand furniture. But the time of the distri-

---

[1] See Chapter XVII, section (i).

bution officers was increasingly taken up by executive duties of one kind or another.

The distribution officers, of course, still had their responsibility for helping bombed towns. The original arrangements for replacement of bombed traders' stocks and the authorisation of ex-quota supplies became obsolete as controls over manufacture and supply were substituted for the limitation Orders. For the bombed traders' replacement right could only be honoured because of the existence of wholesalers' and manufacturers' stocks immobilised by the quota system. With the introduction of controls over manufacture these stocks in time disappeared and the traders' replacement rights became illusory. Moreover, as supplies grew scarcer during 1942 and 1943 it was more difficult than ever for towns to recover without help from the Board of Trade; even small-scale bombings threatened to produce supply crises.

To meet these needs a new form of procedure was introduced at the beginning of 1943. Instead of licences designed primarily to safeguard the retailer certificates were issued for emergency supplies to be sent at once to bombed areas on a basis of consumer need. On receiving news of an air raid the distribution officer would visit the bombed town and quickly check stocks of essential goods damaged and destroyed, stocks remaining and the probable size of the demand from homeless people. From these facts he could calculate the quantities of goods required to avoid undue hardship and arrange for them to be sent to unbombed traders. Arrangements for supplying goods against emergency certificates varied from product to product. For clothing and household textiles, for example, emergency stocks were held by selected wholesalers in each civil defence region.[1] For pottery and hollow-ware, on the other hand, the distribution officer sent the emergency certificates to wholesalers who would supply the chosen retailers. The wholesalers passed the certificates back to the manufacturers who supplied these goods over and above the normal allocation. Needless to say, the operation of this scheme depended on the close co-operation of Consumer Needs department with the production departments of the Board.

The distribution officers were also responsible for seeing that shopping facilities in bombed towns were maintained. In 1941, after the heavy raids on provincial cities of the previous winter, arrangements were made for stocks of temporary shops or booths to be stored regionally and let out to traders when the need arose. As it happened the booths were never needed. It was always possible to avoid a crisis in distribution by traders moving into empty shops or sharing premises or by quickly repairing damaged shops.

---

[1] The immediate clothing needs of the bombed-out were met by local authorities and the Women's Voluntary Services.

The other main duties of the distribution officers in the later years of the war concerned retail trade—the officers were asked to advise on the granting of licences under the Location of Retail Businesses Order,[1] the requisitioning of shops, etc., and the distribution of un-rationed goods. As the war progressed, the distribution of certain important goods—clothing, utility furniture, alarm clocks, rubber boots, and so on—was controlled. But there remained three important groups of scarce goods that were essential and the distribution of which could not be easily controlled—first, household textiles, blankets and bedding; secondly, domestic hardware, hollow-ware, brushes, etc.; and, thirdly, pottery.

In their anxiety to be fair to the small trader the Board introduced in January 1943 the Fair Shares Scheme for pottery, hollow-ware and clothing. This, as we have seen,[2] guaranteed each small shopkeeper a percentage (varying according to the needs of the area) of his pre-war supplies. The Board hoped that this scheme would also help to make the distribution of these goods between areas rather more equitable. But the Fair Shares Scheme by itself was not nearly enough. For it was becoming increasingly clear that the distribution of these goods be-tween areas was grossly unequal. Unfortunately the machinery for meeting shortages could not throw light on this question—the re-tailers' panel did not provide material for comparing supplies between different areas nor did it show deliveries over a period. It was thus extremely difficult for the Board to assess complaints of shortage at their true value or compare two complaints from different places with one another.

In an attempt to meet this difficulty Consumer Needs department evolved a laborious method, known as 'town assessments', for meeting particularly bad local shortages. The task of assessment fell on the distribution officers. When a complaint of shortage was received the officer called on every trader in the town dealing in the particular class of goods surveyed and collected figures of his present stocks and his deliveries over the previous three or six months. These assessments began early in 1943 and revealed the striking inequalities in supply that we have already noted.

From the results of a number of these assessments of local scarcities, from other assessments made in towns not suffering hardship and from information held by the Board on current production a standard level of supplies was calculated for pottery and hollow-ware. This represented the level of supplies per thousand of the population which the average town should receive. This standard level provided a yardstick against which future complaints of shortage could be

[1] See p. 277.
[2] See p. 274.

measured and gave a sound basis for refusing assistance to areas whose shortage problems were found to be exaggerated.

In the same way the department calculated a 'critical level' of supplies which represented a severe shortage of the goods in question. Where a town, on assessment, was shown to have fallen to this level or below it the department, in consultation with the production branch of the Board, arranged to increase supplies. This technique was known as 'patching'. A 'patch' was defined as 'a specified quantity of cups, plates, teapots, kettles, saucepans or frying-pans sent to a town in consequence of an established deficit in the supplies available to consumers'. It was arranged by the production branch through the wholesalers or manufacturers who normally supplied retailers in the town. It was designed to make good the deficit in the last two or three months; its sole purpose was to relieve acute need among the towns-folk, the extent of need being determined by shop and consumer sur-veys. The patching system was a voluntary arrangement[1] and was used fairly extensively; it was pretty effective in practice and even more effective politically.

'Patching' was not applied to household textiles and bedding, which grew acutely scarce in the latter part of the war. The only action taken by the Consumer Needs department was when second-hand blankets were released by the Services or the Ministry of Works; these were directed to the areas that needed them most. In 1944 the same classes that were entitled to utility furniture were given a priority claim on available supplies of household textiles. But nothing was done to redistribute supplies between areas.

After the 'patching' system had been in existence for some time Consumer Needs department concluded that in some areas the prob-lem was not one of haphazard distribution but one of chronic under-supply. This applied with particular force to the pre-war special areas whose needs have already been discussed in this chapter. Four out of every five patches had gone to towns in the North, in Wales and in Northern Ireland.

The patching system was not adapted to deal with conditions of chronic shortage. Accordingly, in January 1944, suppliers were ap-proached by the Board and asked to increase permanently their deliveries to regions—largely the pre-war depressed areas—where there was real under-supply. All hollow-ware manufacturers were asked in January 1944 to step up their supplies to wholesalers supply-ing these districts. In the case of Cumberland the request was to treble, in the cases of Northumberland and Durham to double, the

---

[1] Under the Hollow-Ware and Kitchen Hardware Order of July 1942, S.R. & O. 1942, No. 1456, however, registered manufacturers were obliged to 'comply with any directions issued by the Board of Trade regulating the descriptions and quantity of any such hollow-ware which may be supplied by him to an area in the United Kingdom and to registered and unregistered persons respectively'.

supplies they would otherwise have sent. These 'stepping-up' requests were deliberately set high and many were not fulfilled. But the special areas did receive in 1944 something like a seventy per cent. increase in supplies over those received in 1943.

This achievement was satisfactory if not spectacular. And, indeed, this conclusion might well be applied to the work of the Consumer Needs department of the Board considered as a whole. The general scarcity of consumer goods was too great in the later years of the war to make elaborate schemes for redistributing supplies worth while, or to prevent acute shortages of articles that were essential. But the department's rough-and-ready schemes for switching supplies did undoubtedly mitigate some of the worst inequities. And the department's contact with distributors and consumers did undoubtedly provide information about needs and shortages that was invaluable in formulating production policy within the Board. Moreover, the contacts between the department and retailers were most valuable; they contributed to the understanding and acceptance of the Board's various regulations dealing with distribution.

Consumer Needs department became a most useful two-way channel of information between the Board and its distributing and consuming public. The development of production, distribution and consumption statistics made some of the original functions of the department unnecessary. But on all other aspects of distribution policy on which statistics threw no light the distribution officers were the only source from which the Board could draw an objective or dispassionate opinion on a situation. For the most part the Board's policies were naturally and necessarily unpopular with retailer and consumer alike, even when the Board were trying to mitigate the effects of a shortage over which they had no control. Other vehicles of public opinion were not therefore wholly trustworthy as a source of information. The trade press was in general so full of criticism that its strictures were not much help in showing the Board where things were really going wrong. The protests issuing from the post-bag, deputations and M.P.s were apt to arise only when the situation was out of hand. The great value of the distribution officers was that they could be relied upon to sound a warning in good time before a situation was past repair.

CHAPTER XIV

CONSUMER RATIONING[1]

(i)

What Kind of Scheme?

IN pre-war plans no detailed consideration had been given to rationing consumer goods other than food and fuel. In 1929 the Treasury, in their memorandum on the Course of Prices in a Great War, had included 'rationing of consumable goods' among the ingredients of an anti-inflation policy. But a sub-committee of the Committee of Imperial Defence reporting on these matters in 1933 concluded that for goods such as clothing, boots, soap, domestic ironmongery, brushware, pottery and tobacco, rationing might not be necessary and might moreover be impracticable on account of the variation of needs.

In the first year of war rationing of consumer goods had been mentioned once or twice in the Board of Trade, but only as something to be avoided if at all possible. Indeed the institution of such rationing in Germany was regarded as a sign of the enemy's weakness. But in these early weeks rationing was not necessary. Civilian supplies had not yet been seriously reduced and incomes were not rising steeply. The problem of unfair distribution had not therefore become pressing. The figures for wholesale and retail stocks of textiles are sufficient proof of this: in July 1940 wholesalers' stocks were 116 per cent. by volume of the 1937 monthly average, and there was also evidence that retail stocks of most textile goods were higher in July 1940 than they had been a year earlier.[2]

By the autumn of 1940, however, prospects were changing. The feverish activity in war industry of all kinds meant higher incomes in the country. And more severe restrictions on supplies of consumer goods were being planned. Moreover, the announcement of the introduction of purchase tax from the end of October 1940 seems to have inspired a certain amount of anticipatory buying; the retail value of clothing sales for October was sixteen per cent. above that of the previous month. There was, therefore, some anxiety among the public and a feeling that a further disparity between supply and demand

---

[1] See also the article on this subject by W. B. Reddaway in *Lessons of the British War Economy*.

[2] See *Board of Trade Journal*, 5th September 1940: Article on Retail Trade.

would lead to serious shortages of consumer goods and a rise in prices which would put them beyond the reach of poorer people. In November newspapers such as the *Manchester Guardian, The Economist,* and the *Financial News*[1] were urging the need for some kind of rationing scheme to ensure that everyone received a fair share of the necessities of life. About the same time the President of the Board of Trade in a talk with the Federation of British Industries and the Press expressed a hope that with the co-operation of all those concerned in distribution it would be possible to avoid rationing. But if not he would face any difficulties and introduce a scheme.

Officials of the Board were clear that even though rationing was only a possibility careful planning of a scheme should begin without delay. For the Board would get into serious trouble if they attempted any improvised arrangements at short notice. Before the end of November the first proposal for a rationing scheme was being discussed. The Board of Trade had to think out the problem on their own. They could not simply copy the Ministry of Food which relied mainly upon the equitable allocation of foodstuffs to the various wholesalers and retailers and which placed very little emphasis on the disposal of the coupons. For the differences between the supply of food and the supply of other consumer goods were great. The Ministry of Food had physical possession of all those commodities that were rationed at this stage of the war and distribution to wholesalers and retailers was closely supervised by its agents. The Board of Trade, on the other hand, had only a loose control over supply by private wholesalers and manufacturers.

The first rationing proposal in November 1940 suggested that there should be individual rationing for the dozen or so essential goods (out of the 800 goods controlled by the limitation schemes) that were becoming scarce. The following were cited as typical examples: stockings and socks, underwear; kettles and pans; knives, spoons and forks; cups, saucers, plates and dishes. The idea was that coupons would fix the value of the annual purchase in each class. The value would represent working-class expenditure at the £3-a-week income level on the item concerned. Retailers would collect coupons from consumers and would have to surrender these to wholesalers and manufacturers in order to secure further supplies.

In the discussions that followed this proposal certain points were agreed from the outset. For example, everyone thought it would be a serious mistake to require the consumer to register for the supply of these rationed goods at a particular shop. Apart from the nuisance to the consumer, it would be highly undesirable to allow the retailer a monopoly in supplying particular sections of the community. Once

---

[1] *Financial News* of 11th November 1940, *Manchester Guardian* of 16th November 1940, and *The Economist* of 23rd November 1940.

competition between retailers was abolished either an impossible burden would be thrown on the Prices of Goods Act or the Government would have to undertake price-fixing for a range of goods where price-fixing was always difficult and sometimes impossible. Given a system which limited a retailer's turnover not according to his supplies of goods but according to his ability to attract customers, the price difficulties would to some extent be solved. The emphasis would change from shortage of supplies which meant high prices to shortage of demand which must make for lower prices.

Outside this common territory there was wide scope for amendments and alternative suggestions to the original rationing proposal. Some of the economists who were temporary civil servants at the time were especially helpful. One suggested at the outset that the German points system should be used. For as it stood the original scheme did not provide for any freedom of choice as between different rationed articles. Moreover, once the scheme had to be extended to a largish number of articles it would be unwieldy since each article would involve a different type of coupon. Under the points system, on the other hand, coupons would be interchangeable at fixed rates between different articles. Even though the scheme only covered a few articles at the outset it could easily be expanded.

The same economist doubted whether the original proposal to confine the ration to the amount consumed out of a working-class income of £3 a week would be politically feasible. He therefore suggested that the general issue of coupons should be made on an absolutely rock-bottom basis, but that further coupons should be available to anybody who cared to buy them for a very high fee (say the equivalent of a purchase tax of 200 per cent. or so). This would amount to a penal taxation on consumption with an exemption limit so chosen as to enable the essential consumption of the poor to escape all taxation.

These ideas were only amendments to the initial proposal. From another economist in the Board there came suggestions for a different kind of scheme altogether. In the background there would be drastic taxation and a compulsory saving scheme to mop up as much purchasing power as possible. The rationing scheme would then take the shape of a general limitation on the value of goods an individual could buy. This should greatly reduce the chaos which would otherwise prevail in the unrationed field. If only a few individual commodities were rationed, leaving consumers free to buy as much as they could of others, demand would become concentrated on the others, particularly substitutes; more and more of the semi-necessities would then become scarce and have to be rationed. Moreover, rationing could work only if it covered a fairly wide field. For people's need to buy individual items varied enormously particularly if the unit period was as short as a year.

This seemed the fundamental objection to the original rationing proposal. Of the items proposed only stockings and socks and underwear were suitable for rationing by themselves. On each of the other items, the majority of people (including most of the rich) spent almost nothing in most of their lives, though occasionally they spent a lot—for example when setting up house. If the ration were fixed on any level based on an average the result would be absurd: a year's ration would not suffice to buy more than about one unit of the cheapest article included. To take one example: the retail value of the permitted supplies of all kinds of domestic hollow-ware worked out very roughly at 1s. per head per annum. For people setting up house or really needing to replace kettles or pans this would be intolerable. But if the ration were raised to say 5s. per annum or whatever seemed to be a reasonable limit for anybody's purchases there would not be the goods to honour the ration and unessential purchases would not be restricted at all.

The alternative rationing proposal, when it was worked out in more detail, was on the following lines. Everyone, including children, would have a ration of £6 10s. per half-year to spend on all goods other than food and drink, cigarettes and tobacco, coal, gas, electricity, petrol, motor accessories and newspapers. There would, of course, have to be arrangements for authorising certain additional necessary purchases. The existing system of raw material controls and limitation Orders would continue side by side with this rationing in order to secure some control over the types of goods produced and also to reduce the need for very careful enforcement of rationing by retailers. For the idea was that retailers would simply cancel the appropriate value tokens in the ration book. If, however, the retailer could not get supplies he would have little incentive to sell outside the ration.

These then were the ideas that were floating about in the formative discussions about rationing. Gradually opinion crystallised about the form the scheme should take. One guiding principle was that to be workable the scheme must be as simple as possible—simple for the public to understand and simple to administer and enforce. Before long, therefore, it was agreed that the scheme should not attempt to cover more than clothing. Certain other points were also decided quite quickly. For example, the suggestion of extra rations to be bought for a high fee was turned down—not only would it be politically difficult, but it would keep consumption above the essential minimum.

One of the most difficult points to decide was whether the ration should be by value or by quantity. In some ways there was a great deal to be said for a value system. It had the enormous merit of simplicity. It was more equitable and was likely to release more resources for the war. For in fixing a quantity ration a sufficient number of garments would have to be permitted to cover the essential needs of the man or woman buying the cheaper, less durable goods. The person who could afford to buy the more durable ones would get more than his minimum needs. On the other hand, there were dis= advantages in a value ration. It would destroy higher quality trade. It would be difficult to keep in step with changes in prices. And enforcement would be very weak for in the absence of any link between quantities supplied to the retailer and quantities sold by him it would be difficult to detect evasions. Finally, therefore, about the end of January 1941 officials agreed to plan for a quantity ration which would be on the German points system and which would involve the passing back of coupons by retailers in order to obtain further supplies.

The next step was to decide just what should and should not be included in the scheme. Then the size of the ration and the points schedule had to be fixed. As far as scope was concerned the final decision was to cover all cloth made wholly or mainly from any textile (other than jute), wearing apparel including handkerchiefs, footwear and hand knitting wool. A longish list of textile goods was excluded[1] —headgear, fur garments, household textiles, second-hand goods, infants' garments (appropriate to children under four), and miscellaneous textile goods not suitable for clothing—e.g. tracing cloth, surgical belts, black-out cloth, mending wool and ribbons. To meet the needs of industrial workers clogs, boiler-suits and workmen's bib-and-brace overalls were exempted from rationing.

The task of fixing the size of the rations and the pointing was entrusted to the Board's statistical department. It was a difficult calculation, for the available statistics were scanty. For estimating clothing supplies there were only the Census of Production figures for 1935 and 1937, together with some figures collected from wholesalers under the limitation Orders. As for demand, there was nothing to go on beyond some figures of clothing purchases by different samples of people in 1938.

The statisticians approached the problem from the demand side. They did not at first attempt to estimate existing supplies of clothing, and divide them out among the population. They aimed instead at determining the clothing needs of the population in war-time. By using the Census of Production and a good deal of inspired guesswork and common sense they managed to estimate the quantity of different items of clothing consumed in a pre-war year by an average male and an average female. The guesswork and common sense were indis-

---

[1] Some of these were brought within the rationing scheme later in the war, e.g. fur coats, some household textiles, secondhand goods, infants' clothes and some industrial clothes. See Section (ii) of this chapter.

pensable for some of the Census figures were only expressed by value
and sometimes different items of clothing—for example socks and
stockings—were lumped together in one heading. And there were no
figures at all in the Census to suggest how much material was sold
across the counter for making up at home.

With the figures for pre-war consumption before them the statisticians decided what would be a reasonable level of war-time consumption. As a broad guide they thought that at first consumption as
a whole might be reduced to two-thirds of the peace-time level. But
quite clearly it was not possible to assume a reduction of two-thirds
—no more and no less—in the consumption of every single item.
Women could undoubtedly cut down a pre-war consumption of four
dresses a year by more than a third and at a pinch men could do without pyjamas and waistcoats. Items such as shoes and socks, stockings
and shirts, on the other hand, could not be cut so heavily. So again
common sense came to the rescue and a schedule of the average war-
time consumption of each item of men's and women's clothing was
drawn up.

These figures gave the size of the initial ration. Next it was necessary to translate the ration into points. The first points schedule was
in no sense an attempt to price the various items of clothing so that
demand for them was brought into a rough balance with supply. It
aimed instead at matching the points values as nearly as possible with
the yardage of material required to make each garment. This system
was indeed essential if coupons were to be passed back by retailers
and wholesalers in order to obtain further supplies. Otherwise the
people who made up clothing and who had to surrender points for
their cloth supplies would find themselves with intractable surpluses
or deficiencies of coupons.

As a basis for the points calculations a yard of woollen cloth
36 inches or so wide counted as three coupons and a yard of any
other material as two coupons; woollen goods had higher points
values because they are more durable. The points values of different
articles of clothing were then fixed by estimating the amount of
material in an average-sized garment. In a few cases, such as dressing-
gowns and woollen pyjamas, points values and yardages were deliberately not matched. If they had been, the number of points required
would have been very high and retailers' stocks would almost certainly have been immobilised. Production would then have been
discouraged. But it was equally discouraged by giving lower points
values for these goods than the yardage required—manufacturers
could not replace their material. By adopting this course, however,
existing stocks were freed.

The pointing of goods made from woven textiles was fairly straightforward. But the clothes ration was also to cover hosiery—that is to

say, all kinds of knitted garments—and footwear. Yardage could be used as a very rough guide for such things as underwear, but it was no use in deciding the points values of other articles such as socks and stockings and footwear. These values were in the end settled at what seemed a reasonable and sensible level in relation to the woven garments. For example it was recognised that women consumed more stockings than men consumed socks by fixing the former at two points and the latter at three.

Once all the points values had been fixed they could be multiplied against the estimates for war-time consumption to give—with some rounding off and adjustment—the total coupon ration. This worked out in the end at sixty-six coupons for the first rationing year.[1] It was obviously desirable that children's rations should go further than adults'. This was done by lowering the pointing for children's garments, which had already been defined for exemption from purchase tax as those of sizes generally worn by boys and girls under fourteen. This of course accorded perfectly well with the principle of matching yardage and points. Children who needed adult sizes of clothing were to be given extra coupons.

During the remaining years of the war the total number of points was reduced and the pointing for particular items was varied quite a lot up and down. Often these changes were 'price' changes in the sense that they tried to adjust demand for certain items to supply. But the general structure of the points schedule remained firm throughout the war. This in itself is a tribute to the achievement of those who drew the schedule up in so short a time with so little information to guide them.

The ration was not at the outset calculated with any close reference to supply. But when the ration scale had been worked out, a rough cross-check was made to see whether the ration seemed roughly comparable with the scale of the current restrictions on supply. An estimate was made of the average amount of woven cloth,[2] hosiery and boots and shoes available under the current restrictions for each member of the civilian population. These amounts were translated into points and compared with what seemed reasonable male and female clothing budgets on the sixty-six coupon ration. The result of the analysis was to suggest that under the current restrictions supplies would be just about enough for the sort of ration envisaged. If anything the ration seemed likely to be in excess of available supplies; but stocks were still ample enough to make the deficiencies good. No doubt there was a considerable margin of error in the calculation; all the same the two sets of figures fitted together miraculously well.

---

[1] To spread purchases over the year it was agreed that twenty coupons should be invalid until the 1st January 1942 (assuming rationing began on 1st June 1941).

[2] i.e. the amount of woven cloth used for clothing. This meant subtracting from available supplies the cloth used for household and industrial purposes.

W

While the size of the ration was being planned there were a good many other difficulties about the scheme to be solved. There were, for example, various problems about the machinery of control. First, was it necessary to continue the Limitation of Supplies Orders[1] alongside rationing? On the whole it seemed necessary to keep them going for a time, for the Board wanted to be able to control the output of cloth for the home market; although the consumer was to have as much individual choice as possible, the Board also needed to control to some extent the nature of production.[2] Finally, limoso[3] was a certain safeguard against forgery of coupons or any other unforeseen failure of the rationing system that might lead to excess production for the home market. If limoso were abolished, the Board of Trade would be taking a leap in the dark. There was, however, little doubt that quota control should be dropped as soon as possible. Raw material control plus sales control was bad enough, but these two with consumer control on top were not to be tolerated except as an interim measure. Moreover, the additional burden on retailers of finding wholesalers with unexhausted limoso quotas might be considerable. To solve this last difficulty it was proposed to license any person who had exhausted his legal quota to make additional supplies against the surrender of coupons. A close check could be kept on these licensing figures to see whether or not the ration was out-running available supplies.

Another problem that seemed very perplexing for a time was that of the maker-up. It will be remembered that it had been a central point of the accepted ration scheme that the maker-up of garments would receive coupons from the shopkeepers equivalent to the garments sold and would pass them back to the weaver in order to obtain piece-goods to make more garments. But difficulties arose because, no matter how skilfully the statisticians had done their work, the pointing for made-up goods could not be equated exactly with the pointing for constituent piece-goods. It would be quite impossible, for example, to match the multiplicity of sizes and styles of made-up goods with an immensely long list of pointings. Makers-up might, therefore, accumulate large surpluses or deficits of coupons. They might be tempted to sell the surpluses or they might cease to make large sizes. Various suggestions for changing the system for passing back coupons were therefore proposed. Might some organisation be set up to give the maker of large sizes more coupons than he had surrendered and the small-size maker less? Or should makers be registered and the small-size makers be made to disgorge their excess coupons and the

---

[1] The Order limiting the supplies of textiles and most clothing was by now called the Woven Textiles Order. See p. 105.

[2] The control over production permitted by the limitation Order was of course only indirect.

[3] See footnote on p. 286.

large-size makers be given more? Or perhaps makers-up who were registered for purchase tax should not be required to surrender coupons when renewing piece-goods supplies; they would keep books showing sales of garments and the Board would check these records against the coupons the makers-up held. The first two suggestions seemed hopeless. The third seemed more promising until it was realised that the Board of Trade's accountants who were already severely strained would have to look after another 10,000 firms. Since it was most important that the scheme should be as simple as possible it was decided in the end to stick to the original plan. Makers-up were to surrender coupons in order to obtain supplies of piece-goods.[1] And pointings for piece-goods and made-up goods were to match as closely as was possible.

When the scheme was in operation some of the maker-up problems inevitably arose. In particular supplies of large sizes were inadequate. But this difficulty was met on the rationing side by issuing extra coupons to manufacturers in trouble and on the production side by stimulating output.[2]

There were also the manufacturers who used rationed goods in the manufacture of unrationed household articles, such as mattresses, upholstered chairs or bed linen to be considered. How were they to obtain the piece-goods they needed? It was decided that the Board of Trade should issue coupons to them based upon a proportion of the cloth they used in the year ending 31st March 1940. The Board were not prepared to issue coupons for making goods that they considered to be unessential.

In addition to all these problems about the structure of control there were many points to be settled about the mechanics of the rationing scheme. Ration cards, for example, had to be issued to the population. Since secrecy was essential for the success of the scheme it was impossible to arrange to print and distribute proper clothing cards before the scheme was introduced. Luckily, however, there were in the current food ration card twenty-six unused margarine coupons and the Ministry of Food agreed that these should be used as a first instalment of clothing coupons.

When it came to planning the distribution of the clothing books proper the Board of Trade were hampered by their lack of a local organisation. The Board had, therefore, to turn to other departments for help. The Ministry of Food said firmly that its own local offices were overworked and could not do the job. The Post Office was also overworked, but was persuaded to undertake to distribute the main

---

[1] When the coupons, or rather coupon vouchers (see p. 312), reached these suppliers or those who registered under the Woven Textiles Order they had to be passed on to the local Board of Trade accountant's office.

[2] See below, Chapter XVII, p. 465.

clothing books,[1] and also the supplementary cards which were being planned for children needing adults' sizes of garments, and for replacement of lost cards.[2] The Post Office also promised to operate a voucher scheme whereby retailers would bring packets of loose coupons and exchange them for vouchers worth 500 coupons which they could use to send to their suppliers. The Post Office was not expected to count coupons but simply to send the sealed packets to the Board of Trade which would carry out spot checks and then have the coupons pulped. The Ministry of Food did agree in the end to help with some of the 'trimmings' of distribution—it was to issue cards to newborn babies, look after immigrants and emigrants and accept from the Registrar of Births and Deaths the clothing cards of the dead. Coupons for the replacement of wardrobes of the bombed-out and those who suffered theft or fire were to be issued by the Assistance Board and Customs and Excise Department. It was also necessary to decide on methods of checking traders' coupon transactions. Manufacturers of unrationed goods and registered traders were therefore to be required to submit to the Board of Trade accountants returns showing the acquisition and disposal of rationed goods and of all coupons and vouchers. They were also to send all their surplus coupons to the accountants to be destroyed.

So far we have been following through the administrative plans for rationing. But it will be remembered that when the preparation of these plans had begun in November 1940 rationing was still something that was to be avoided if at all possible.[3] By February 1941, however, the President of the Board of Trade was prepared to submit his department's preliminary proposals to the Lord President's Committee. The Committee accepted the proposals in principle but reserved a final decision until the administrative arrangements had been completed. In May the President put the full scheme before the Committee and recommended that it should begin upon 1st June. The Committee in turn recommended to the War Cabinet that the scheme be adopted. At this stage, however, it seemed possible that the scheme might be turned down. There seem to have been fears that the plan would be unnecessary, unpopular and unworkable; the Prime Minister in particular doubted the wisdom of the scheme. Could not sufficient clothing be made available for civilians to avoid rationing?

The arguments of the Board of Trade in reply to these criticisms were powerful. The scheme itself was not intended to restrict the quantity of clothing available for the public—that had already been done. The sole object of the scheme was to provide fair distribution

---

[1] These books were to be issued in exchange for a used 1940–41 food ration card.
[2] The Post Office was not to check these claims but issue them in exchange for forms signed by the appropriate authority.
[3] See p. 304 above.

of available supplies. Without it the first sign of shortage might produce panic buying by the well-to-do. And shortages would not long be delayed. For wholesale and retail stocks had fallen very substantially since the summer of 1940. Retail stocks were about forty per cent. lower and were now, in May 1941, only about two-thirds to three-quarters of their pre-war volume. Wholesale stocks were, by volume, probably under half the peace-time average. If, on the other hand, rationing and shortage alike were to be avoided, at least 200,000 additional tons of cotton and wool a year and at least 350,000 additional workers would have to be provided for civilian clothing. These points were strong enough to win the day and on 27th May—four days before the date planned for beginning the scheme—permission to go ahead was at last given.

The Consumer Rationing Order was signed on 29th May 1941[1]. It will be as well to summarise its main provisions. Rationed goods and the appropriate number of points for each article were defined in a schedule. Traders were forbidden to supply retail customers or any other traders and manufacturers of unrationed goods with any rationed goods except against the surrender of the appropriate number of coupons. Retail customers, except when ordering goods by post, could not offer loose coupons. There were exceptions to the rule that goods could only be supplied against coupons. Rationed goods could be supplied coupon-free under the authority of a licence from the Board of Trade for the execution of contracts of a Government department, for export, to a local authority or to the Women's Voluntary Services for civil defence, and by one trader registered under the Limitation of Supplies Order to another such person.[2] And in order to maintain supplies in the interval between the time the retailer took the first coupons and the time these reached the registered supplier rationed cloth could be supplied to traders without coupons up to 28th June and other rationed goods up to 21st June. But no trader could supply in this way goods worth more than 10,000 coupons and a trader registered under the limitation Orders could not supply more than one-sixth of his current quota for this purpose. Coupons were not transferable except where the Order specifically allowed it, i.e. between traders and for the purchase of uniforms by employers for their employees. Finally there was the usual provision empowering the Board to ask for information and returns.

The President of the Board announced the introduction of rationing to the public in a broadcast at 9 a.m. on Whit Sunday, 1st June. The choice of this date made it possible to advertise the scheme widely

---

[1] S.R. & O. 1941, No. 701.

[2] In the case of rationed goods supplied to the Women's Voluntary Services or local authorities, a statement showing the number and description of the goods and the coupon value had to be certified by the authorities. It was then a 'coupon-equivalent' document.

on the Sunday and Whit Monday (a bank holiday) while the shops were shut. In the meantime 150 envoys had been trained to address meetings of traders throughout the country. In addition a large supply of explanatory leaflets was distributed. The secret had been well kept—there were indeed one or two leakages right at the very end[1] but nothing sufficient to impair the success of the scheme. And the scheme was a success. Although the Board of Trade had been working so much in the dark and had been unable to enlist the advice of any outside bodies the scheme had obviously been soundly planned. It proved workable and flexible and was to last with little major change for nearly eight years.

(ii)

Clothes Rationing in Operation

Although the basis of the rationing scheme stood firm there were of course a good many modifications in scope and methods. And the size of the ration itself inevitably changed. It was not to be expected that the consumption considered appropriate in the spring of 1941 when civilian austerity was in its early stages could be maintained in 1942, 1943 and 1944—the years of severe stringency. Indeed, even in the first year of rationing the basic ration of sixty-six coupons could only be maintained at the expense of a reduction in stocks.[2]

In March 1942, therefore, the President of the Board of Trade submitted proposals to the Lord President's Committee about the size of the 1942–43 ration. The new clothing books had been printed with sixty coupons. Should they be valid for twelve months, for thirteen months (which would be an effective annual ration of fifty-five coupons), for fourteen months (equal to an annual ration of about fifty coupons) or even longer? The President himself recommended a ration of about fifty coupons. Anything much below this level seemed likely to cause real hardship and would produce many individual appeals. On the other hand, stocks were running down and the supplies coming forward were not enough to maintain even a sixty-coupon ration. If the ration were fixed at sixty coupons there would be serious danger that the ration could not be honoured, which would produce all the evils of shortages and queues that rationing was de-

---

[1] The main leakage was the result of advance notice of the scheme which was given highly confidentially on 30th May to a very limited meeting of trade association representatives.

[2] The Board of Trade index figure of wholesalers' stocks of textiles by value was 82 in May 1941 and 91 in May 1942. The index figure of prices of clothing sold by representative department stores rose by about twenty per cent. in this twelve months and a similar price rise would occur at the wholesale stage. The quantity of stocks therefore declined.

signed to prevent. Consumption at the fifty-coupon level, after taking account of the additional supplementary issues that would be necessary, was estimated to involve 50,000 fewer workers in textiles and clothing and 30,000 fewer tons of shipping space than a sixty-coupon ration. Ministers had little hesitation therefore in agreeing that the ration should be fifty coupons or thereabouts.

In the end the 1942–43 clothing coupons had to last fifteen months, thus giving an effective annual rate of forty-eight coupons. What this ration meant to the ordinary consumer who had no supplements is illustrated by the following figures: with a forty-eight-coupon ration a man could buy one pair of socks every four months, one pair of shoes every eight months, one shirt every twenty months, one vest and one pair of pants every two years, one pair of trousers and one jacket every two years, one waistcoat every five years, one pullover every five years, one overcoat every seven years, leaving about three coupons a year over for odd items such as handkerchiefs. From time to time the Board of Trade wondered whether this small ration should not be further reduced. But in the end forty-eight coupons were considered to be the minimum level to which the ration should drop. The task of meeting the ration fell of course upon those who were organising textile and clothing production.[1] They managed to fulfil it until the very end of the war. In 1944 clothing stocks fell dangerously[2]—so much so that the twenty-four coupons which were to last for the latter six months of the 1944–45 rationing year (1st February–1st August 1945) had to last seven months instead. This was equivalent to an annual rate of just over forty-one coupons. Thereafter the ration was for a time reduced to an annual rate of thirty-six coupons.

In addition to planning the size of the ration it was necessary to control the rate of expenditure of coupons. Unless they were spent at a steady flow there might be 'runs' on the shops or deficiencies or surpluses at the wholesale or retail stage. In the 1941–42 rationing year this was prevented by issuing the proper clothing books only when the margarine coupons had been spent and by making twenty of the forty coupons in the clothing book usable only after 1st January 1942. This seems to have been successful although complaints were made by the trade that the rationing year did not coincide with the trading season. This was put right in the 1942–43 year, when it was provided that not more than twenty coupons could be spent before 12th October 1942 and not more than forty before 15th March 1943. Coupon expenditure was similarly evened out in 1943–44. It should be added that coupons, except for 'margarine' coupons, did not have to be spent in the year for which they were issued. There was always a time lag before they were invalidated.

---

[1] See Chapter XVII below.
[2] For an explanation see pp. 472–6.

To compare the size of the ration in different years in terms of coupons is not very useful unless the value of a coupon remained fairly stable. As we have already seen, the main structure of the pointing schedules did remain firm during the life—certainly the war-time life[1]—of the rationing scheme. Certainly the Board of Trade were aware of the need to make as few changes as possible in coupon values. There were, however, bound to be many adjustments in points values and in the exemptions from the rationing Order, particularly in the early days. It was only a month after the introduction of the scheme that a new and much enlarged points schedule was issued. This was the fruit of consultation through a Retailers' Advisory Committee and Trade Suppliers' Committee (representing wholesalers). The new list distinguished individual items of clothing and their points ratings more clearly, altered some of the original values and revised the exemptions. For example, furnishing fabrics which had been rationed by implication under the heading of 'cloth' in the original order were now exempted. Another general adjustment to the points schedule was made after the scheme had been going for six months.

Later changes in points values and exemptions were, however, made largely in an attempt to produce a better balance of supply and demand. For one thing men and women proved very quick to pick up points bargains or to use exempted goods for unaccustomed purposes. Even in the first adjustment to points value made in July 1941 it had been necessary to withdraw the general exemption for second-hand goods and apply it only to such goods sold below a certain value. Before the end of 1941 it was also necessary to ration workers' bib-and-brace overalls which had proved useful for housework or gardening. Similarly coupon-free furnishing fabrics proved a good substitute for rationed dress fabrics so that in June 1942 most of these fabrics had to be rationed. The manufacture of the heavy fabrics that remained unrationed was at the same time forbidden and existing supplies could only go to such purposes as export and Government orders.

Other instances of adjusting supply and demand through the rationing scheme may be mentioned. In October 1942 women's fully-fashioned stockings, whose manufacture required more labour than unfashioned ones, were raised from two to three points; unfashioned stockings remained at two. It was also in October 1942 that towels were for the first time included in the ration. And in August 1943 a serious shortage of leather led to a general up-pointing of footwear.[2] Then, too, towards the end of the war certain unpopular

---

[1] After the war, one important feature of the original scheme disappeared when the pointing of woollen goods was brought down to the same level as that of non-woollens.

[2] This meant that the 'outsize child' system had to be extended to children with large feet.

austerity garments,[1] for example short socks and trousers with no turn-ups, were down-pointed.

Another of the more important changes in pointing was made partly to balance supply and demand and partly for rather different reasons. One very clear result of clothes rationing was the demand for better coupon value. This public demand, arising from an increased capacity to pay higher prices for a greatly restricted number of garments, was powerfully reinforced by the natural tendency of distributors and manufacturers to secure the maximum profit for a reduced turnover. As a result distributors complained about frozen stocks of articles which the public refused to buy and clothiers jibbed at taking up allocations of material for which demand was sluggish. There was therefore on these grounds a case for lowering the coupon value of lower-priced goods. This case was reinforced by another argument. Poor people had been accustomed of necessity to buy 'often and cheap'. And although the proportion of the community who could not afford any but the cheapest goods had diminished in war-time, it was still significant. Rationing hit these people hard, for the goods they bought were perforce poor coupon value. The solution to this problem was fairly simple. As from 1st September 1943 certain low-grade woollen goods were reduced to the non-wool pointing, and another still lower rating was applied to low-grade non-woollen goods.

Perhaps the most noticeable change in the rationing scheme after its introduction was the great extension of 'special schemes' which would meet the needs of those with specially heavy demands for clothing. By the end of the war there were all kinds of provisions for industrial workers, civilian uniform wearers, the Services, stage productions, inmates of institutions, sufferers from certain diseases, diplomats, prisoners, and so forth. The original scheme, however, had only provided for supplementary issues of coupons to children wearing adult sizes of garments.[2]

The arrangements for issuing coupons to children were settled early in the history of rationing. In November 1941, twenty extra coupons were issued for the 1941–42 rationing year to children whose age at the beginning of rationing was 15 years 10 months to 16 years 5 months, and forty coupons to those whose age at the beginning of the scheme was 13 years 8 months to 15 years 10 months. Children whose age at the beginning of rationing was under 13 years 8 months, but who were of more than normal size or weight, were also entitled to forty extra coupons. These arrangements meant that extra coupons had to be issued to more than two million children. 'Outsizes' were

---

[1] See pp. 436–9.

[2] i.e. in addition to the obvious need to replace clothing for the bombed-out, etc. These replacements were based on assumptions by the Board of Trade about the coupon value of a minimum wardrobe.

weighed and measured and their coupons issued at school. Older children still at school also received their extra coupons there. Those engaged in industry received theirs from Post Offices on presenting their unemployment books, and those neither at school nor in industry received theirs from the Post Offices on presenting a form signed by a Justice of the Peace or some such person; in these cases their current food ration books had also to be presented and marked as a check against duplicated issues.

When ministers agreed that the 1942–43 general ration should be reduced they also agreed that children should be compensated by a special allowance. In 1942–43 and subsequent rationing periods each child under eighteen[1] therefore received ten coupons in addition to the adult ration. The extra issues to older children were maintained. Those aged 13 years 5 months to 15 years 10 months and the younger 'outsizes' got twenty coupons on top of the 'flat ten', and those aged 15 years 10 months to 16 years 5 months got ten coupons on top of the ten. The issue of these children's coupons was simplified. The Ministry of Food issued the coupons on production of food ration books. Outsize children still had to be weighed and measured at school, but the Food Offices issued the coupons on production of certificates signed by head teachers.

When rationing was first being planned it had been contemplated that in addition to older and outsize children expectant mothers should receive extra coupons. But when it was decided to make infants' clothes coupon-free, the extra coupons seemed unnecessary. The idea was that the mother should buy ready-made garments or make the baby's clothes out of material bought on her own ration. For when the baby was born the mother should be rich in coupons as the baby would receive a pretty full adult's ration with little to buy out of it. It soon became clear, however, that this scheme did not adequately meet the needs of mothers who either preferred to make their own baby's clothes at home or could not afford to buy ready-made garments and were therefore obliged to use coupons for buying materials. From the beginning of August 1941, therefore, every expectant mother was entitled to fifty extra coupons to be obtained on a doctor's or midwife's certificate from the Public Health Department. At the same time infants' clothes ceased to be coupon-free.

The special schemes that caused the Board of Trade most trouble were those for industrial workers. The original sixty-six coupon ration was liberal for the bulk of the population and adequate for the essential needs of nearly all of it. But a universal enforcement of the strict ration on clerks and blast-furnacemen alike would have made the Board's 'fair shares' propaganda unconvincing. Not only did workers

---

[1] Ages on 1st June of 1942 and subsequent years.

in some occupations require more clothing than other people, but they also needed special types. Many trades had specialised needs of their own which varied from one district to another. Moreover, in some industries certain articles of clothing were compulsory under the Factory Acts in order to protect the health or safety of workers. Naturally enough the Board of Trade knew very little about all these complexities and in the conditions of haste and secrecy under which the rationing scheme was prepared the Board did not explore them. The only concession to the needs of industrial workers in the first rationing Order was the exemption of clogs, bib-and-brace overalls and boiler suits from rationing and the pointing of fustian trousers at five coupons as against a standard rate of eight. There were no concessions for the innumerable other kinds of clothing such as protective boots and there were no provisions for extra coupons for heavy workers.

It soon became clear that these arrangements were wholly inadequate. The concessions were open to abuse by non-industrial workers and they did not meet the industrial workers' needs. From November 1941, therefore, bib-and-brace overalls, boiler-suits and clogs were all put on the ration, but they and all other industrial overalls already rationed were given low points values.[1] The problem of industrial workers was now approached from the point of view of the individuals concerned. To some extent this was done by allowing workers to buy certain special garments coupon-free upon the production of some such authority as a Factory Inspector's certificate. The certificate method also had to be widely used when towels and tea-towels were rationed in the autumn of 1942. Permits to buy towels and tea-towels without coupons had to be issued to a whole range of people—caterers, factories and food-shops, who were under a statutory obligation to provide towels for their workpeople,[2] and individuals such as doctors, dentists and midwives.[3]

In general, however, the needs of industrial workers for extra clothes were met by issuing supplementary coupons. Indeed, very soon after the introduction of rationing, the Trades Union Congress took the stand that if sixty-six coupons represented a fair share of clothing production for the sedentary worker it could not be equally fair to the industrial worker. They had therefore suggested an immediate cut in the basic ration with a corresponding supplement to in-

---

[1] Employers who were legally required to provide overalls for their workers had to collect the appropriate number of coupons from their workers. This was not always easy and the Board had to prosecute some recalcitrants. Employers could obtain coupon loans or floats from the Board with which to buy overalls.

[2] The towel shortage was so bad that the issue of permits could not be extended to some of the users with statutory obligations—public houses, non-food retail shops and chemists.

[3] Towel needs of workers in very dirty occupations were dealt with in the general negotiations for supplementary coupons.

dustrial workers generally. The Board refused this on the grounds
that the ration was calculated as a fair share for the 'average active
man and woman' who represented the bulk of the population. The
Board agreed, however, that there were some types of workers for
whom sixty-six coupons could not possibly be adequate and promised to examine any claims for supplementary coupons which the
T.U.C. put up. There were just two principles. One was that the
expenditure of the number of coupons required for two or three overalls—or any other occupational clothing of about the same value—
should not entitle anyone to a supplement. The second was that no
award of less than ten coupons should be made to any worker since
the administrative problems of assessing awards to within a coupon
or two would be intolerable.

The T.U.C., like the Board of Trade, knew very little about the
practical problems of workers' clothing needs. As one official wrote,
'our awards were therefore fated often to be anomalous and nearly
always erratic'. But the chances of success were bedevilled from the
outset by the first award to the miners. While the T.U.C. were still
collecting claims for industrial awards, the Board had for political
reasons to make a quick decision on the appropriate supplement for
the miners. Pressure from the Mineworkers' Federation and the
Mines Department combined with the Board's ignorance to produce
what was later admitted to be an 'astonishing' award of sixty coupons
to every underground miner. It was also admitted that the results of
this award were unfortunate. The T.U.C., who had been ignored in
the negotiations, acquired a distrust of the Board which took a long
time to eradicate. Every subsequent industrial claim was made in the
knowledge that the miner, by no means the worker most heavy on his
clothes, had got sixty extra coupons.

In trying to sort out the claims from all other industrial workers the
Board consulted factory inspectors, employers and any other source
of expert advice they had time for. But the whole field was so completely new that no one could really do more than prevent the Board
from making very obvious mistakes. The Board believed that only the
solid and resolute—though necessarily unofficial—support of the
T.U.C. in cutting down exaggerated claims prevented the whole
award system from foundering long before the end of the rationing year.

The Board were quick to grasp the lesson of this experience. First
they realised that the cardinal sin in the eyes of the workers was not
harshness but unfairness. Secondly, they realised that they had created
'a system of enormous complexity and fundamental inaccuracy'. As
one official added, 'the more we strove after accuracy, the deeper we
floundered in complexity'. In the second rationing year, therefore,
the Board determined to take a much broader view of the problem
and to try to find some means of devolving the final distribution of

coupons on to men who knew more precisely what workers needed —men on the spot. In addition it was realised that all decisions should be much more carefully explained to industry.

For the second rationing year, with the cut in the basic ration, it was decided that there should be a general occupational supplement of ten coupons to all manual workers.[1] There remained, however, certain heavy workers for whom further supplements would be essential. It was decided that these extra supplements should be given very sparingly; in the end they were confined to workers in nine industries —mining, quarrying, heavy chemicals, iron and steel, non-ferrous metals, carbon, coke and by-products, gas production and shipbuilding. These additional supplements were given in the form of coupon pools to individual factories. The size of a factory's coupon pool was not to exceed five times, or in the case of quarries and ship-yards, four times the number of its manual workers.[2] The coupon pools were then left to be distributed by the works committee to the workers who really needed them.[3] Some extra help was given to miners and heavy chemical workers by making certain of their working garments coupon-free.[4]

The issue of all the industrial coupons in the first rationing year as well as later was accomplished through the help of the Ministry of Labour. The employers of workers eligible for extra coupons—or in the case of coupon pools the works committees—applied and received the coupons through the local employment exchanges.

The new 1942–43 scheme for industrial supplements worked extremely well. It was accepted as fair and its administration was flexible and decentralised. Its cost in coupons was also much less than had been expected. It had been thought that the number of workers eligible for the general occupational supplement, 'the industrial ten', would be rather more than 13·2 millions; it turned out to be about 12·2 millions. The number of workers eligible for the coupon pools —inaccurately dubbed 'the iron ration'—was estimated at two millions in some 12,000 undertakings, and it was thought that the pools would cost about 15 million coupons. In fact, only 7,000 undertakings applied for the 'iron ration' and took only eight million coupons. And works committees seemed to be very scrupulous in sending back unused coupons. Moreover, very few coupons had to be issued to

---

[1] A list of these was agreed without much trouble.

[2] In addition to these arrangements new entrants to certain industries were provided with coupons to enable them to buy clothing.

[3] Sometimes the coupons were divided among all the factory workers instead of according to need. But usually the scheme worked well.

[4] Miners, for example, could get pit pants and one pair of safety boots per annum coupon-free. Unfortunately in the case of safety boots this encouraged new demand for a product the output of which could not be increased. In 1943–44 therefore certificates were issued which gave miners either a pair of coupon-free safety boots or six coupons' worth of other types of men's clothing.

individual undertakings who found the ration inadequate for certain groups of their workers. The gross ration received by some workers fell very sharply as a result of the new arrangements. Miners who received 126 coupons in the first rationing year received 68 in the second, workers in heavy industry had 111 in the first and 61 in the second, workers in light industry were reduced from 81 to 56 coupons. Nevertheless, the new arrangements were generally accepted as fair and did not cause a single strike.[1]

Another example of the kind of problem which the Board had to face after rationing had been launched was that of civilian uniforms. Certain employers were under a legal obligation to provide clothing and many public employees found it necessary to wear uniforms for reasons of health or safety or as a sign of authority. Besides these there were the members of civil defence organisations and of a large number of voluntary organisations all of whom naturally wished to wear uniforms without giving up coupons. Many of the public authorities concerned were, under the rationing Order, able to obtain their supplies coupon-free. And in the early months of rationing the Board of Trade made it possible for a good many voluntary organisations to obtain coupon-free uniforms in the same way as members of the fighting Services[2]—by signing the back of traders' bills or by obtaining chits from superior officers. It soon became obvious that these concessions might seriously weaken the rationing scheme. The dangers were made still clearer in September 1941 when the Minister of Supply proposed to buy uniforms for women employed in filling factories to wear when off duty and to sell the uniforms coupon-free at cost price. This, it was hoped, would make the munitions industries as attractive as the women's auxiliary Services. The President of the Board of Trade voiced a strong opinion that any departure of this kind would open the door to such a flood of parallel claims from other essential workers that it might prove impossible to honour the ration. The proposal was therefore dropped.

At the same time the Board tightened up existing provisions. In October they made public their view that the wearing of uniforms by civilians was to be discouraged. Those who wore such 'voluntary' uniforms would have to surrender the full number of coupons whether they bought them or received an issue. For some duties, however, uniforms were considered necessary, and members of certain organisations[3] were therefore to be allowed to give up a reduced number of

---

[1] The scheme was continued broadly unchanged in subsequent years. Certain additional industries, e.g. brickworks, glass manufacture, wet-battery manufacture, became eligible for the iron ration.

[2] See next page.

[3] Civil Defence Services, Fire Services, Police Force, uniformed staff of Government departments, local authorities, N.A.A.F.I. and such undertakings as transport, gas, water and electricity and such classes of nurses as the Board might specify.

coupons for uniforms with which they were issued. Whole-time members of these organisations had to give up coupons without regard to the quantity of uniform actually issued to them each year but related to the type of garments worn as uniform. The coupons represented not the coupon value of the articles of uniform actually issued but the saving of one year's wear and tear on ordinary clothes as the result of wearing uniform.[1]

These arrangements kept the uniform problem within bounds, but it remained tiresome. In the face of pressure from other Government departments on behalf of special uniform wearers, it was not easy for the Board to insist that uniform wearing should be discouraged and that the uniform coupon concessions could not be extended as an inducement or reward for undertaking a particular job. Moreover, the Board had the tedious job of sending out directions to surrender coupons to uniform wearers who failed to make their annual contribution. Sometimes the directions had to be followed up by visits from enforcement officers or in the last resort by prosecutions. In 1943 the Board did attempt to replace the uniform concession by the simpler system of supplementary coupons and the surrender of the usual number of coupons for all items of uniform. This proposal foundered, however, on opposition from other departments. So the old system continued until the attempt to enforce it was gradually abandoned. The first relaxation was in August 1944 when it was agreed that people who had worn uniforms for two years or more should be excused the surrender of coupons for twelve months.

The Board of Trade were concerned not only with the coupon problems of the civilians, but also with those of the Services. For commissioned officers were expected to provide and maintain a set of uniform appropriate to their duties out of their allowances and pay. And while other ranks received nearly all their personal clothing from the Services they had been used to buying for themselves minor articles such as handkerchiefs and pyjamas. In planning rationing these needs had been overlooked. When the general scheme was announced it was therefore agreed that as an emergency measure officers and cadets of the Services and women's Services should be allowed to obtain supplies of rationed goods simply by signing the back of traders' bills. Other ranks could obtain minor items through a document signed by their commanding officers and stating that the goods in question were essential personal articles of a type not supplied by the Services. These documents became 'coupon equivalents' to traders and offered magnificent opportunities for abuses which increased as

---

[1] In one or two cases, especially where the distinction between 'uniform' and 'occupational clothing' was very blurred (for example the Women's Land Army and Women's Timber Corps), uniforms were still issued to new members without any surrender of coupons.

this scheme was extended to members of Dominion, American and other Allied Services. Negotiations were therefore soon begun to replace the scheme by proper Service clothing coupons. These were issued from 1st March 1942 to men and women officers of the Army and Air Force and to nursing sisters. Each officer received sufficient coupons to cover wear and tear of uniform and undergarments and amenities, and newly commissioned officers received an outfit allowance.[1] Other ranks were not issued with coupons but were still allowed to obtain handkerchiefs coupon-free by chits from their commanding officers;[2] women 'other ranks' received ten coupons a year.

In the beginning Service coupons were valid only for a restricted range of items of outfit and it was strictly forbidden to share them with other members of the family. The Service departments pressed the Board to relax the restrictions so that officers could buy 'leisure' clothing. At the end of 1942, therefore, the Services accepted a reduction of twenty per cent. in the maintenance ration on condition that the Board allowed the use of twenty-one coupons a year for a restricted set of other garments.

The Admiralty had held that it was entirely impracticable to bring the Navy into the rationing scheme owing to the continuous movements in and out of the country and their consent to the issue of Naval Service coupons was not given till early in 1944.[3]

Coupon issues were also necessary for prisoners-of-war. From September 1942 each prisoner's registered next-of-kin was supplied with a book of forty coupons as soon as the Red Cross reported his presence in a camp, followed by an issue of twenty coupons each quarter until release; released prisoners also received a coupon grant.

Before the end of the war plans had also to be made for clothing demobilised men. It was decided to provide each male member of the Services with an issue of clothing coupon-free and free of charge (its wholesale value was about £12) and in addition with ninety clothing coupons.[4] Demobilised women were given coupons and cash instead of the free outfit.

The Merchant Navy provided rationing difficulties of its own. For while merchant seamen served in conditions which were in many respects like those of the Royal Navy, they clung to their civil status. The standard officer's uniform was not compulsory and was not worn

---

[1] e.g. a male Army officer received an outfit allowance of 225 coupons plus a maintenance allowance of eighty-eight per year. An additional allowance was given for tropical kit.

[2] These chits were very easy to forge and in 1945 were replaced by Board of Trade forms.

[3] Certain adjustments were also necessary for naval ratings and W.R.N.S. who received a money allowance for the maintenance of their outfits.

[4] Later a supplementary issue of twenty-six was given to men demobilised after 1st June 1945.

much on deck and very little on shore. Moreover, there was no strongly defined line of demarcation between the Merchant Navy itself and the tangle of miscellaneous occupations connected with the sea. It took a long time[1] to sort out the anomalies of seamen's food ration books and identity cards before the Merchant Navy itself could be sufficiently well identified to be issued with a special clothing book giving a normal annual maintenance allowance of 109 coupons. New entrants to the Service received an initial issue of 150 or 200 coupons with a reduced maintenance allowance of 54 coupons for the first year thereafter. The needs of non-seagoing people on the fringe of the Merchant Navy were met by uniform concessions to Trinity House men and the marine staff of railway companies, the certification of coupon-free oilskins and rubber boots for inshore fishermen and dock workers, and the issue of the industrial ten when practicable.

It is impossible to detail all the arrangements that had to be made to meet the needs of all kinds of special groups of people: the examples that have been given are perhaps sufficient to show the complexity of 'consumer' problems. These problems were not the only ones that had to be sorted out after the rationing scheme was launched. For example various changes had to be made in the mechanism of coupon control. One of the most important of these was the introduction of coupon banking.

Rationing had been in force for only a month when the Board of Trade realised that the actual mechanism of passing back coupons was most unsatisfactory. There had been one simplification in that batches of 500 coupons could be exchanged at Post Offices for vouchers. But even so the drawbacks of the scheme were numerous. In the first place it involved an intolerable amount of counting and re-counting of coupons, vouchers, etc., every time these changed hands. The Board realised that the number of coupons in circulation in the first year of rationing would amount to several thousands of millions. Practically all of them would change hands three times and in many cases there would be no less than seven transfers—from consumer to retailer, retailer to Post Office (coupons), Post Office to retailer (vouchers), retailer to wholesaler, wholesaler to unregistered maker-up, maker-up to cloth supplier, cloth supplier to Board of Trade for cancellation. These transfers would breed all kinds of disputes between traders and between traders and the Board of Trade over shortages revealed by counting. The system also made for weaknesses in security. As soon as coupons or their equivalents came into retailers' hands they became bearer documents which needed continuous control and safeguard at every stage. The Board had no real redress against a registered trader who claimed to have lost coupons

---

[1] Till early in 1943.

X

which he was required to surrender for cancellation. And 'lost' coupons might all too easily find their way back into circulation. Moreover, anyone could obtain a 500-coupon voucher by presenting an envelope suitably certified at the Post Office; if the contents of the envelope were found to be waste paper the 'retailer's' name and address also turned out to be false. In general, any measures to alleviate the difficulties of counting and re-counting coupons looked as if they would weaken the control and measures designed to strengthen control would tend away from simplification and economy.

All these difficulties pointed to one solution and one solution only —a coupon banking system.[1] This would mean that all but the smallest traders in rationed goods would open coupon banking accounts, retailers would bank their coupon takings in the same way as their cash takings, and thereafter all coupon transfers except those in the category of 'petty cash' would be effected by 'a/c payee—not negotiable' coupon cheques. This system would relieve traders of almost all counting of bearer paper except at the consumer-retailer stage, of all inter-trade disputes over the number of coupons and of many security measures. The saving of clerical labour to traders would be immense. The Board of Trade would benefit from an immeasurably strengthened control. Bearer paper would be largely eliminated and in case of need the banks' books would provide a complete duplicate record of all but the smallest coupon transfers. With this strengthened control the possibilities of removing quota control from textiles and relying on coupon control would be strengthened.

As 1941 wore on the Board of Trade found that an increasing number of envelopes exchanged for vouchers at the Post Offices contained forged coupons or torn-up newspaper.[2] The need for a banking scheme was thus increasingly urgent. Delays in getting started had, however, arisen. First there had been long discussions over the agency to be employed. The Board felt sure that the joint stock banks were the most suitable people to operate the scheme, but it was some time before this was finally agreed. Some further time was taken up by deciding how the banks should be paid. It was eventually agreed that the cost of the scheme should fall on the Exchequer and that as the scheme was to be compulsory no attempt should be made to recover money from the traders.

The scheme was launched in June 1942.[3] Coupon banking was compulsory for all transactions involving more than seventy-five

---

[1] Such a system was already in operation in Germany.

[2] In one week in November, as much as four per cent. of the envelopes exchanged in the London area contained 'bad paper'.

[3] S.R. & O. 1942, No. 1120.

coupons apart from the purchase of rationed goods by local authorities and similar bodies. Later it was also made compulsory for traders to pay 'coupon equivalent' documents into their accounts.[1]

Another development in coupon control was the extension of advances or 'floats' of coupons to manufacturers. The general principle of coupon control was that it should be a self-regulating mechanism, the issue of coupons being balanced by a supply of rationed goods. But it had been obvious from the first that the Board of Trade would themselves have to allocate coupons for such purposes as export and the manufacture of unrationed goods from rationed material. As time went on special provision also had to be made for issuing extra coupons to people such as makers of outsize garments, traders who had lost coupon capital by the down-pointing of their stocks and businesses which had been closed down but were restarting (for example, on the return of ex-Servicemen from the Forces).

Another change in the rationing scheme after its inception was in the methods of distributing ration books. In the first year of rationing the Board had overcome the disadvantages of having no local organisation of their own by making use of existing services. The Post Office had distributed the basic rations, and the Food Offices, the Assistance Board, Customs and Excise and the Ministry of Labour had all helped with special distributions. Advice and information had been disseminated through Citizens' Advice Bureaux, the Women's Voluntary Services and Chambers of Commerce. The arrangements for the special distributions were in most cases maintained unchanged. The trouble in the second rationing year was the distribution of the basic books. Owing to increasing staff difficulties the Post Office simply could not manage counter distribution again, and for some time the Ministry of Food was adamant that it could not take on the job. Finally, however, the Ministry of Food relented; from 1942 onwards the basic clothing ration books were issued from Food Offices; from 1943 they were in the same cover as food ration books, but detachable from them, thus halving the Ministry's ration book stock record work.

One consideration that was most important in all discussions about the mechanism of clothes rationing was enforcement. Coupon banking was begun in order to reduce illegal activities. And in negotiating with the Ministry of Food about the distribution of ration books the Board of Trade emphasised strongly the need for safeguarding the books from theft. The fact was that clothes ration books had a black-market value that increased as clothing grew scarcer. A clothing book was much more valuable to an unscrupulous person than a food book. No registration of customers was required for clothing and the coupons were valid for at least a year (against two weeks for food).

---

[1] S.R. & O. 1944, No. 800.

Moreover, the cash profit to be derived from the sale of clothing represented by one ration was considerable. Then, too, there were virtually no unrationed goods and no provision for coupon-free sales comparable to the sale of food in restaurants. The black-market price of the 1941–42 clothes ration book was at one time 2s. 6d., but the price in 1944 was more like £5 a book or 2s. 0d. a coupon. The Board were constantly trying to increase the security of their ration documents. The possibility of forgery of books, if not of other ration documents, was almost eliminated by the introduction of security printing for the second and subsequent years' books. In addition, all clothes ration documents and most coupon-equivalent documents bore serial numbers so that it was possible, with the co-operation of the issuing agents, to identify the rightful holder of any book. The internal checking systems in offices that issued coupons were also improved. And of course efforts were intensified to protect bulk supplies of coupons in issuing offices from theft. To help in all its attempts to beat evasions the Board had to appoint special enforcement officers. The Board's accountants still did the major part of the work of checking traders' accounts and so forth. But the enforcement officers did 'field work'. They worked in teams under the guidance of an ex-police officer investigating specific complaints, making test purchases without coupons or with loose coupons,[1] providing ocular evidence to traders that they were being watched. They also educated traders by supplying information about the various Orders.

In spite of all precautions the possibilities of evading the rationing Orders always remained great. There was always a risk that the coupon-free supplies of rationed goods for export or for special consumers such as local authorities might be diverted to the home market. Then there was the problem of lost ration books. In the first rationing year lost books were replaced without much scrutiny; 800,000 people who were alleged to have lost their books received 27 million coupons. The Board were very worried as to where this course would lead. In the second rationing period, therefore, declarations of loss had to be signed by a J.P. and accompanied by a 1s. 0d. stamp. Moreover, a distinction was made between careless losers and those who suffered loss through no negligence of their own and whose claims could be checked. This latter category included loss by bombing and theft reported to the police. All other persons had to fill in a further form giving full details of their present wardrobes and received only enough coupons to bring them up to the basic standard in each class of clothing. As a result replacement of losses in the second rationing year amounted to only $14\frac{1}{2}$ million coupons issued to some half a million people.

These replacements were very small in relation to total coupon

---

[1] And taking care to avoid charges of Gestapo methods.

issues—less than a half per cent. in 1942–43. The whole question of lost coupons, however, illustrates two fundamental points about the success of the clothes rationing scheme. Well planned and well drafted though the scheme and the Orders were they would have been at least a partial failure if sufficient people had been determined to get round them. It was impossible to close every loophole and check all coupon transactions. As it was, rationing, like other detailed controls, worked for two reasons. One was bluff—that is, giving the public the impression that their activities were being checked more closely than was the case. Second and even more important was the goodwill of the great majority of the public. They were convinced that rationing was fair, that it was a contribution to the war and that it should therefore be made to work.

Having described some of the more important aspects of clothes rationing in operation, we must now sum up its effects.[1] The forty-eight coupon ration provided ordinary adults who received no supplementary coupons with something like half their pre-war consumption in terms of quantity. Children's consumption, on the other hand, probably fell by little compared with before the war. Since demand shifted from cheaper to more expensive articles the purchases of clothing valued at 1938 prices fell less than the quantity bought. Personal expenditure on clothing in the years of rationing was about sixty per cent. of the pre-war level.[2]

Three times during the war—in April 1942, December 1942 and April 1944—the Board of Trade made a check of the coupon value of the wardrobes of the panel of consumers.[3] These checks showed that the tendency to buy better quality goods and the pressure to make goods last longer combined to keep wardrobes from falling very much. Over the two years 1942–44 there was little change in the coupon value of either men's or women's wardrobes averaged over the country as a whole, but there was wide disparity in the experience of different classes of the population. The most well-to-do increased their wardrobes by four per cent. for women and six per cent. for men, while the poorest section experienced falls of seven and eight per cent. respectively. Moreover, in spite of coupon supplements the average industrial worker had in April 1944 a wardrobe smaller than those in receipt of the basic ration only. Men with the basic ration only had a wardrobe worth 251 coupons, but men with the 'industrial ten' and 'iron ration' had only 213 and 200 respectively.

---

[1] The whole question of honouring the ration—planning production and maintaining stocks—is dealt with in Chapter XVII.

[2] This figure covers purchases out of personal income. It therefore includes expenditure by officers—including Allied officers—stationed in this country but excludes clothing issued by the Government to the Services. Owing to the uneven incidence of coupon releases 1943 was a particularly lean period.

[3] See p. 297.

Altogether the evidence is that clothes rationing made a substantial contribution to the war effort by making it possible to reduce civilian production without impairing morale. At the same time although it caused inconvenience it did not cause serious hardship.

Comparison of Wardrobes in Terms of Coupon Values

TABLE 19

(a) Coupon Value of All Wardrobes Checked

	April 1942 (first check)	April 1944 (third check)
Men[1]	225	223
Women[1]	223	219
Youths (14–17)[2]	176	176
Maids (14–17)[2]	185	185
Boys[3]	90	90
Girls[3]	114	118

[1] Weighted by AB Class five per cent., C Class fifteen per cent., D Class sixty-five per cent. and E Class fifteen per cent.

[2] Unweighted averages as no class data are available for the first check in April 1942.

[3] Weighted according to the class distribution obtained in April 1942 since no national estimates are available.

(*b*) *Comparison of Wardrobes in Terms of Coupon Values by Classes*

	AB Class		C Class		D Class		E Class		Weighted total	
	Average coupon value (at 1942 values)	Percentage change April 1944 cf. April 1942	Average coupon value (at 1942 values)	Percentage change April 1944 cf. April 1942	Average coupon value (at 1942 values)	Percentage change April 1944 cf. April 1942	Average coupon value (at 1942 values)	Percentage change April 1944 cf. April 1942	Average coupon value (at 1942 values)	Percentage change April 1944 cf. April 1942
Men First check .	318		258		218		194		225	
Third check .	330	+ 4	265	+ 3	215	− 2	180	− 7	223	− 1
Women First check .	303		265		216		184		223	
Third check .	320	+ 6	269	+ 1	211	− 3	170	− 8	219	− 2

It was estimated that

A)
B) } Classes represent well-to-do classes (five per cent. of total population).

C Classes represent middle classes (fifteen per cent. of population).

D Classes represent industrial workers (sixty-five per cent. of population).

E Classes represent poorly paid workers (fifteen per cent. of population).

(iii)

Other Distribution Schemes

As all kinds of household goods became increasingly scarce during the middle years of the war officials and the public were constantly asking whether they could not be rationed. But the objections remained very much the same as they had been when proposals for general consumer rationing had first been formulated.

There were, for example, all kinds of problems of equity. These were particularly intractable in the case of household goods because of the infrequent intervals at which most of these goods were bought, the great importance of a household's initial stocks and the very low level of supplies. There were bound to be a great many special cases and there would also be an awkward problem of equity between large and small households. The difficulties of administration would inevitably be appalling for it would be impossible to deal with the special cases by a bulk issue of a supplement once a year, like the 'industrial ten' for clothes. Discretion would often be needed in applying any general rules and some check would have to be made on applicants' statements. Local offices would be essential. Almost worse than the administration of special issues to private households would be the problem of business and institutional users.

Other difficulties were more familiar—the rationed field would have to be defined, a pointing list would have to be drawn up that would be administratively workable and the machinery of passing back and collecting coupons would have to be established. Then there was the question of 'honouring the coupon' in particular lines. Cups and bed linen were in no sense interchangeable and the public would expect some freedom of choice in using their coupons. Yet it would be very difficult to adjust supply and demand.

Some of these problems could have been solved and the effort of solving them might have been worth while if the size of the proposed ration had been reasonably large. But if the rationed field were to cover bed-linen, bedding, hollow-ware, crockery, glass-ware and table cutlery, the total value of rationed goods in 1943 would be only about £20 millions a year retail after deducting the share of business users. This was only about one-twentieth of the value of goods under the clothes ration which required far less administration than would be needed for household goods, and even less than half the value of the sweets ration. After allowing for the special claims of new households, the value of the general ration might be about 7s. 6d. per head per year. Apart from drinking-vessels and plates there could not even be one per person of all the articles of hollow-ware, bed-linen, crockery and glass-ware put together.

Moreover, the labour force engaged in making all these articles for the home market was probably—in 1943—only about 30,000. Yet the staff needed for administering a rationing scheme would run into thousands. Altogether the effort would simply not be worth while. Provided the Board of Trade enforced price control and secured a reasonably fair geographical distribution, the scramble of housewives for goods would probably produce as good a fit between real needs and actual purchases as any administratively possible 'ration'.

Rationing of household goods was for all these reasons 'out'. Instead a variety of measures were taken to match supplies and demand more closely.[1] To meet the most serious shortages—such as cups and essential kinds of hollow-ware—supplies were increased.[2] And to reduce unessential demands[3] the production of some articles was confined to unattractive types—grey instead of white blankets and plain white crockery (for a time with a high proportion of handleless cups) instead of decorated ware. In addition there developed a number of distribution schemes to direct scarce essential goods to the people who needed them most.[4] Such schemes were necessary even within the fairly self-regulating clothes rationing system. Indeed, the first ones were all for different articles of industrial clothing, where supplies were adequate only for those whose need was undeniable; in some cases they were inadequate even for these people.

The chief examples of such schemes were rubber garments of all kinds. For after Pearl Harbour rubber was acutely scarce and consumption had to be heavily cut. The first directed distribution scheme was worked out for rubber gloves. Sales to people whose needs were not essential were forbidden and buying permits were issued to those qualified to obtain them. Beyond an understanding with the authorities who issued permits (the Ministry of Labour, Ministry of Health, etc.) that only essential needs should be met, no absolute limit was imposed on the number of permits to be issued. Even so, after the introduction of the scheme, demand for gloves contracted by over eighty per cent.

An even more stringent permit system was needed for rubber boots. The number of buying permits had to be carefully regulated to match the very limited supplies. Each of the ministries responsible for a group of essential consumers received, therefore, a predetermined block allocation of serially numbered permits and had to decide for

---

[1] It was not till after the war that sheets were put on the clothing ration.

[2] See Chapter XIX.

[3] In addition to saving labour in some industries such as pottery.

[4] This section does not deal with the geographical distribution of supplies (for this see Chapter XIII), but with distribution to individuals.

itself the degree of necessity that warranted the issue of a permit to a particular individual. Broadly speaking, the issue of boots was confined to those who had to work in deep mud or water or in certain chemicals. In some cases employers were enabled to hold a communal pool of boots for use by workers when engaged in jobs for which boots were indispensable.

In 1942 and 1943 the number of distribution schemes tended to increase rapidly. The permit system was extended to other articles of clothing such as plimsolls, goloshes and rubber aprons. There were schemes for directing windfalls such as surplus Service goods, frustrated exports and goods sold by the Admiralty Marshal. For example reconditioned battledresses were distributed for the benefit of agricultural, timber and chemical workers, and surplus parachutes went to hairdressers to make capes. Towels were directed to colliery canteens for miners without pithead baths. Supplies of imported alarm clocks were reserved for workers who had to rise early. Retailers were asked to keep strainers for invalids and infants. Moreover, the controls over the manufacture and supply of consumer goods that were being developed made it possible for the Board of Trade to stipulate the people to whom supplies of certain goods should go. For example some kinds of sports goods were reserved for the Services, schools and other youth organisations and sports associations. Some musical instruments were reserved for the B.B.C., the Forces, prisoners-of-war and the Salvation Army. Steel trunks were reserved for officers and nurses going abroad. Some types of electrical equipment were reserved for people with doctors' certificates.

Amidst the variety of formal and informal distribution schemes one method—the priority docket—became particularly favoured. The strict buying permit, although a valuable emergency measure, was criticised by retailers as inflexible, for permits were not always presented regularly and stocks were sometimes frozen on retailers' shelves. One alternative method—direct supply to consumers—was used as little as possible because retailers obviously disliked it. The priority docket, on the other hand, did not have these objections. It entitled certain classes of consumers to priority for certain goods. And it encouraged the retailer to grant the priority by giving him a priority right to replacement of supplies sold in this way. On the other hand, existing stocks were not frozen because the retailer could sell to the general public anything surplus to the needs of priority purchasers. The first priority docket scheme was introduced in 1943 for sweat cloth—a form of towelling used by furnacemen. The principle was then extended to such goods as industrial clogs which had become so popular through the Board of Trade's publicity that demand was much higher than supply. Priority dockets were later sometimes used as an intermediate step, as supplies increased, between buying permits and complete freedom of sales; this happened for example in the case of rubber boots.

Perhaps the most important group of buying permit and priority docket schemes was that for the major household goods needed for setting up home—that is for furniture, curtains, linoleum, sheets, blankets and mattresses. The first item to be dealt with was furniture. By 1942 production of furniture was already very low—low enough to cause serious difficulties for people such as newly-married couples and victims of enemy action who really needed reasonably priced furniture. Accordingly in 1942 the utility furniture scheme was begun. Manufacture of furniture except under licence was prohibited. The only manufacturers who received licences were those who undertook to make specified articles of furniture to simple, specified designs. The furniture was strictly price-controlled and was to be sold only against buying permits issued on behalf of the Board of Trade. It is with the methods of distribution that we are now concerned.[1]

Buying permits were issued by the Assistance Board[2]—on behalf of the Board of Trade—to 'certain priority classes'.[3] In the early days of the scheme—that is, at the beginning of 1943—the priority classes were defined as people who proposed to marry and set up house within three weeks or who had married on or after 1st January 1941, people who were setting up house because they had, or were about to have, young children, and people who had lost furniture through enemy action. Very soon the definition was extended to people who had set up house since September 1939 and refugees from abroad who had arrived since the outbreak of war, were married and were likely to set up a permanent house in Britain.

There was no basic ration of furniture to all qualified people. The various articles of furniture were valued in units roughly corresponding to the quantity of material used for them[4]—on the same lines as the 'pointing' for clothes—but the number of units allotted to each applicant depended upon his or her needs and the amount of furniture already owned. The maximum issue to any person was sixty units.

Furniture was produced and distributed under very different conditions from clothing. At the outset of the scheme there were of course no retail stocks of utility furniture; nor was production high enough during the war to build up such stocks. And since furniture was scarcer than clothing the temptation to sell supplies on the black market was correspondingly greater. It was therefore necessary to introduce a more rigid system of control than that of the clothes

---

[1] The utility furniture scheme is discussed in more detail in Chapter XIX.

[2] In May 1945 the issue of permits was transferred from the Assistance Board to a special utility furniture office.

[3] Permits were not necessary for nursery furniture.

[4] For example, a 4-feet wardrobe cost twelve points, a tallboy eight, a sideboard eight, a dining-table six, and an armchair six.

rationing scheme. The retailer had to get the buying permit or right number of units from his customer before he could deliver the furniture in order to be able himself to get delivery from the manufacturer. Moreover, permits were valid only for three months. If any units were unused in that time or if the circumstances of the holder so changed that the information given on his application was no longer relevant —for example an engagement might be broken off—the permits had to be returned to the Assistance Board. There were other provisions in the Order designed to tighten control. In order to prevent retailers from forcing suites of furniture on people who only wanted odd items conditional sales were expressly forbidden. The Board also took power to ask holders of permits what they had done with them.[1]

The distribution of furniture was further complicated by the problem of transport. Furniture is bulky and road and rail transport were heavily strained. It was therefore necessary to introduce a zoning system whereby manufacturers had to limit their supplies to traders in a particular area. In addition each buying permit was marked with an 'area of validity' outside which it could not be spent.

The early history of the utility furniture scheme was not altogether happy. Production was not nearly adequate to meet the permits issued. It was impossible, however, to limit the issue of buying permits; the Assistance Board could not discriminate between *bona fide* applicants from the priority classes. In July 1943, therefore, a six weeks' ban had to be imposed on new applications and when supply was resumed permits had only a maximum value of thirty units— barely enough to furnish one room.[2] By July 1944, however, production was reaching nearly 450,000 units a week. The classes entitled to buy utility furniture were therefore extended to include people who needed extra furniture for growing children.[3] At the same time the permits were valid for six instead of three months and the Assistance Board could renew expired permits. Although production steadily increased—to 1,200,000 units by July 1945—demand also rose through enemy action and through more people setting up house at the end of the war. It was not therefore until February 1946 that the ration was restored to sixty units.[4] Sales of utility furniture were not made free for all until June 1948.

From September 1943 people in the utility furniture classes were also entitled to obtain without coupons enough furnishing fabric to curtain one living-room. It was important to ensure that these curtain permits should enable the retailer to replace his stock, but there was some difficulty because the coupon-pointing of furnishing fabrics

---

[1] Utility Furniture (Supply and Acquisition) Order 1942. S.R. & O. 2580.
[2] Pointings for bed-settees, divans and bed-chairs were, however, reduced. S.R. & O. 1943, No. 1205.
[3] S.R. & O. 1944, No. 836.
[4] S.R. & O. 1946, No. 243.

varied.[1] In the end the buying permits referred not to coupon values but to yardage and it was on this basis that retailers were enabled to replace their stocks. Further difficulties arose in 1944 for manufacture of any kind of curtain material was extremely low and stocks were quickly being used up. Retailers could not always honour the permits, and even if they could they were not always willing to do so. For permits were not coupon-equivalent documents and could not be used for goods other than curtains; retailers therefore preferred to sell to non-priority consumers who offered coupons. The only real solution was increased production and this was authorised from June 1944. In addition the permit for priority classes was replaced by a combined priority docket and coupon-equivalent document. The priority docket was passed back by the retailer to obtain replacement and the coupon-equivalent document with a standard value of thirty coupons could be paid into the retailer's coupon bank and the coupon capital be used for any rationed goods.

From June 1944 priority classes for utility furniture could also obtain priority dockets for linoleum and felt base floor coverings. Previously, from the beginning of 1944, retailers had simply been asked to give priority to holders of utility furniture permits and to restrict each purchaser to 20 square yards. This had, however, been unsatisfactory—retailers had no documents to pass back to manufacturers entitling them to priority of supply, since people had parted with their furniture permits and the unscrupulous could go from shop to shop ordering 20 square yards.

The main need of 'new households' in addition to furniture, floor coverings and curtains was bedding. Production had fallen low and it was very difficult to find any bedding in the shops. From June 1944, therefore, priority dockets were issued for sheets, blankets and mattresses to people in the utility furniture classes who could prove their need to the Assistance Board. The scheme for sheets and mattresses worked well. As regards sheets, the Cotton Board ensured that sufficient production was reserved for priority orders and they operated a clearing-house for these orders since otherwise they would have fallen unequally among holders of reserved production.[2] The wool manufacturers, however, did not organise a reserve pool of stocks, so that difficulties did arise over blankets. To overcome this the responsibility for maintaining a pool of reserved supplies was transferred to wholesalers; an agreed percentage of price-controlled blankets was sent to the pool.

In 1943 the Board of Trade had become rather alarmed at the proliferation of special distribution schemes. All of them made demands on manpower and certifying authorities were becoming restive

---

[1] See above, p. 316.

[2] Only about one sheet in five was sold against priority dockets.

at increased burdens on their depleted staffs. Moreover, the schemes were growing up haphazard without much co-ordination within the Board of Trade. It was clearly desirable that there should be joint consultation as to whether, for example, manpower should be used to direct the distribution of one article rather than another or about the channels to be used and the choice of an issuing authority. This co-ordination was achieved by establishing a Special Distribution Committee under the chairmanship of the Parliamentary Secretary.

Another major administrative problem had arisen over the distribution schemes. Under the Goods and Services (Price Control) Act of 1941 conditional sales or discrimination between customers were illegal unless the condition or discrimination were imposed by law. The only way of overcoming this difficulty was by passing an Act[1] which empowered the Board to issue licences permitting traders to restrict the sale of certain specified goods to particular classes of consumers.

Clothes rationing in particular, but also the distribution schemes and the efforts of the Consumer Needs department of the Board of Trade,[2] did do a great deal to promote as close a fit as was possible in war-time between needs and supplies. For the goods where neither rationing nor distribution schemes were practicable—notably household goods—consumers were left to compete in the shops. But in general the public were convinced that the Board of Trade were doing their best to pursue a policy of 'fair shares' and morale was strengthened accordingly.

Amidst the mass of detail about these policies it is worth remembering two things. First, however simple and streamlined any scheme might originally be—and clothes rationing was eminently so—the complexities of life were such that it could not remain so for long. To close loopholes in control and to meet individual needs outside the average an administrative detail was necessary that is reminiscent of the Elizabethan State. We have seen children being weighed and measured in school and declaring the size of their feet, and we have seen people declaring the amount of furniture they possessed. 'Fair shares' promoted high morale. This made the administrative costs worth while, but they should not for that reason be underestimated.

The second point worth emphasising is that rationing and distribution schemes were only part of a much wider policy. They had an important place in the 'fair shares' policy of war-time, but they would have been of little avail without the battles being fought against inflation on other fronts—food control, price control, and even more important the general financial policy of the Government.

---

[1] The Goods and Services (Regulation of Disposals of Stocks) Act became operative in November 1943.

[2] See above, Chapter XIII.

APPENDIX 6

Number of coupons needed for the principal articles of adults' and children's clothing at 1st November 1943[1]

Group I[2] covers the following types of goods: woollen (i.e. containing more than fifteen per cent. by weight of wool) except certain specified[3] utility cloths, fur (including imitations), leather (including imitations), corduroy (except certain specified[3] utility cloths), velvet, velveteen, and all pile fabrics except towelling.

Group II covers all goods not in Group I or Group III.

Group III covers certain specified[3] utility rayon cloths.

	Man	Woman	Child[4]
Overcoat, raincoat, etc.:			
Mackintosh, raincoat, overcoat, cape (except cycling cape), cloak:			
(a) if unlined, single texture and not Group I . .	9	9	7
(b) if fully lined and Group I or of double texture material not woven in one process of which the outer fabric is Group I	18	18	11
(c) Other than those in (a) and (b)	16	15	10
Jacket, cardigan, waistcoat or pullover:			
Jacket, blouse-type jacket, sleeved waistcoat, blazer, cycling cape, woman's half-length cape, woman's bolero:			
(a) if lined and Group I	13	12	8
(b) if unlined, single texture and not Group I . .	6	6	4
(c) if unlined, blouse-type and knitted . . .	8	8	5
(d) Other than those in (a), (b) or (c) . . .	10	8	6
Sweater, jersey, jumper, pullover, cardigan, bed-jacket, if Group I and weighing at least 10 oz. (7 oz. for children)	8	8	5
Cotton football jersey	4		2
Waistcoat, pullover, jumper, cardigan, bed-jacket, jersey, sweater—other than those described above . . .	5	5	3
Trousers, shorts or skirt:			
Trousers, slacks, over-trousers, breeches, jodhpurs:			
(a) if lined and Group I	11		8
(b) if unlined and not Group I	5	5	4
(c) other than those in (a) and (b)	8	8	6
Shorts:			
(a) if fully lined and Group I	6	6	4
(b) if not fully lined and not Group I	3	3	2
(c) other than those in (a) and (b)	5	5	3
Skirt, divided skirt—of Group I		6	4
Skirt, divided skirt·not Group I		4	3
Kilt	16	14	8
Dress, gown, frock:			
Dress, gown, frock—Group I		11	8
Dress, gown, frock—Group II		7	5
Dress, gown, frock—Group III		5	4

[1] This table does not cover all details of pointings nor does it cover infants' clothing, industrial overalls and footwear, officers' special uniform garments, nurses' special garments. For full list of pointings see S.R. & O. 1943, No. 1100.

[2] For the purposes of the groups see p. 317 above.

[3] i.e. specified in S.R. & O. 1943, No. 1100.

[4] i.e. young children's wear of a size, style, character which is exempt from purchase tax, even if not utility.

	Man	Woman	Child
Shirt, shirt-blouse or shawl:			
(a) Shirt, unlined and not Group I, with sleeves less than elbow length	4		3
(b) Shirt unlined and not Group I, other than in (a)	5	5	4
(c) Shirt, lined and/or Group I	7	7	6
Blouse, shirt-blouse, shawl, plaid—Group I		6	4
Blouse, shirt-blouse, shawl, plaid—Group II		4	3
Blouse, shirt-blouse, shawl, plaid—Group III		3	3
Blousette		2	2
Overall or apron[1]			
Apron	1	1	1
Smock overall—not Group I		4	4
Sleeveless overall with tie fastening and closed back—Group II		4	4
Sleeveless overall with closed back—Group III		3	3
Sleeveless overall with open back—Group III		3	3
Sleeveless overall with open back—Group II		2	2
Overall with sleeves other than smock overall—not Group I	7	7	5
Dressing-gown, house-coat, pyjamas, nightdress, etc.:			
Dressing-gown, house-coat—Group I	8	8	7
Dressing-gown, house-coat—not Group I	7	7	6
Pyjama jacket or trousers—Groups I and II	4	4	3
Pyjama jacket or trousers—Group III		3	2½
Nightdress—Groups I or II		6	5
Nightdress—Group III		4	4
Undergarments, etc.:			
Combinations, petticoat, slip or like garment—Group I	7	6	4
Combinations, petticoat, slip or like garment—Group II	5	4	3
Combinations, petticoat, slip or like garment—Group III		3	2
Suspender belt, brassiere, modesty vest		1	1
Corset	3	3	2
Men's or boys' non-woollen vest with sleeves, non-woollen pants with legs of knee length or more	4		2
Woollen vest without sleeves, woollen pants with legs less than knee length	5	3	2
Woollen vest with sleeves, woollen pants with legs of knee length or more	6	3	2
Knickers or pantees or men's legless trunks—Group II	2	2	2
Vest, knickers, cami-knickers—Group III		2	1
Socks, stockings, collar, tie, handkerchief, etc.:			
Pair of women's or girls' stockings—not woollen and not fully fashioned		1½	1
Pair of women's or girls' stockings—woollen and/or fully fashioned		3	2
Pair of three-quarters hose or woollen socks of more than ankle length or foot length more than 9½ inches	2	2	
Pair of three-quarters hose or socks other than above	1	1	1
Collar, pair of cuffs, man's tie	1	1	1
Small handkerchief (less than 1 sq. ft.)	¼	¼	¼
Large handkerchief not more than 2 feet in length or breadth	½	½	½
Bathing costumes:			
Bathing costume	3	3	2
Bathing trunks	3		1
Footwear, leggings, etc.:			
Pair goloshes, rubber overshoes, rubber bootees, plimsoles, rope-soled shoes, low-heeled slippers, children's sandals, football, hockey, running, boxing, cycling or bowls boots or shoes	5	5	2
Pair of wooden-soled footwear, certain specified[2] utility women's and girls' footwear	7	5	3
Pair of boots, bootees, shoes, high-heeled slippers, men's or women's sandals or footwear not described above	9	7	3

[1] Other than nurses' and industrial garments.

[2] As specified in S.R. & O. 1943, No. 1100.

APPENDIX 7

Issue of clothes ration documents by or on behalf of the Board of Trade, 1944–45

(*1st August 1944 to 31st August 1945*)

NOTE: Complete figures for the issues of various kinds of coupons do not exist for the years before 1944. The year 1944–45 includes, of course, a few months of peace. Nevertheless the figures are a guide to the order of magnitude of the coupon issues for various purposes.

A. *Issues of clothing ration documents to consumers*

	Coupon value	Coupon value
1. Coupon value of basic ration clothing books to civilians less coupons withdrawn from recruits to H.M. Forces, the dead, etc.		2,059,980,918
2. Coupon value of supplements issued to civilians		483,151,305
(i) Industrial awards including issues for awards under the 'Industrial Ten' and 'Iron Ration' schemes, expenditure of coupons on civilian uniform concession, provision of towels, etc.	180,561,838	
(ii) Supplementary issues to children	81,207,413	
(iii) Supplementary issues to expectant mothers	58,111,175	
(iv) Issues to people who lost clothing through war damage, accidents or theft (including issues of certain material certificates to priority classes)	95,534,600	
(v) Issues to people demobilised from Forces	34,913,035	
(vi) Expenditure of coupons by organisations (e.g. W.V.S., Red Cross, N.A.A.F.I.)	21,258,827	
(vii) Other supplements (e.g. emigrants, people with special needs, entertainment purposes, sports clubs, Foreign Office requirements, etc.)	11,564,417	
3. Coupon value of ration documents issued to H.M. Forces (including Merchant Navy) less coupons withdrawn from people leaving Services		109,106,596
4. Coupon value of clothing ration documents issued in replacement of those lost		21,024,085
		2,673,262,904

B. *Issues of clothing ration documents to traders*

	Coupon value	Coupon value
1. Coupons issued to traders for various purposes		199,903,986
For acquisition of rationed goods by manufacturers of unrationed goods	22,974,829	
For acquisition of rationed goods for export	118,817,902	
For replacement of coupons for rationed goods supplied to Government departments	28,496,955	
For replacement of lost ration documents and rationed goods	13,686,385	
For other purposes, e.g. coupon deficiencies and making up, provision of additional coupon capital, rationed goods for industrial purposes, etc.	16,927,915	
2. Percentage allowance on coupons deposited in coupon bank accounts[1]		59,351,879
		259,255,865

[1] The allowance from June 1942 to May 1946 was two per cent.

Y

C. *Issue of coupon equivalent documents*

Coupon value

Coupon value of coupon equivalent documents issued by local authorities and other bodies licensed by Board of Trade (estimated)[1]   58,823,886

TOTAL ISSUES OF CLOTHING RATION DOCUMENTS TO CONSUMERS AND TRADERS   2,991,342,655

D. *Losses of clothing ration documents*
Losses of clothing coupons by Board of Trade agents, deficiencies on agents' accounts and losses by banks . .   7,630,142

---

[1] These authorities were not required to submit statements of coupon expenditure to the Board. This figure was reached by a test check of documents deposited in coupon bank accounts.

CHAPTER XV

THE TEXTILE INDUSTRIES IN WAR-TIME

Textiles loomed large in war-time export policy and on the home front the provision of adequate supplies of civilian clothing at reasonable prices was the most important single task of the Board of Trade. We shall therefore examine at some length the war-time history of the industries concerned and the methods of controlling them. This chapter will deal with the individual textile industries (cotton, silk, rayon and wool), Chapter XVI with the hosiery and clothing industries and Chapter XVII with general policy and production planning.[1]

(i)

The Cotton Industry[2]

ITS STRUCTURE AND CONTROL

Until 1938 cotton had been Britain's largest manufacturing and export industry. Between 1924 and 1938, however, it had greatly declined. Yarn production had fallen by one-third, cloth production had been halved and exports of piece-goods had fallen by two-thirds. There had been half a million employees at work in 1924 but by 1938 there were only 300,000[3] and about another 100,000 insured cotton workers were unemployed. Among those in work there were wage reductions and short-time working. Even though capacity had been reduced by about thirty-five per cent., only sixty-five per cent. or so of the machinery installed was running. Fierce price-cutting had left little margin to cover even running costs still less to modernise machinery or improve working conditions. Labour relations were embittered and exceptionally strong sectionalisation in the industry had helped to delay solution of the main problems. When the Second World War broke out the cotton industry, as summed up by an official of the war-time Cotton Control, was 'unbalanced, unstable, unprofitable and unattractive to labour'.

---

[1] Chapter XVII will cover utility cloth as well as utility clothing.

[2] This study has been greatly assisted by the considerable body of information supplied by the Cotton Control.

[3] These figures relate to spinning, doubling and weaving only.

Before we turn to see how an industry with this background adjusted itself to war-time conditions, it may be useful to describe briefly its structure. The main processes are *spinning* raw cotton, waste or other fibres into yarn, *doubling*, which is twisting together two or more strands of yarn into a single thread,[1] *weaving* yarn into cloth and *finishing* the yarn or cloth by bleaching, dyeing, printing, etc. Each of these four main sections is almost a separate industry, with one firm usually concentrating on one process. All the cotton does not go through all the processes. And the processes themselves may vary considerably according to the types of goods produced.[2]

The separation of function is reflected in local specialisation. The industry itself is highly concentrated in Lancashire and the adjoining areas. Within this district, Oldham and Rochdale are, for example, the chief spinning centres for coarse counts[3] and Bolton for fine counts. Or, again, Blackburn and Burnley weave plain cloths and Preston weaves 'fancies'. The finishing works, on the other hand, are widely scattered and often in remote valleys where there is an ample water supply.

Distribution in the cotton industry is usually separate from production. Manufacturers mainly work to the orders of 'merchant converters' who order the cloth, buy it at the grey or loom-state stage, have it finished on commission and market it at home or abroad. There are many converters—in 1946 there were 1,750—but a small proportion of them handles a large part of the business; over ninety per cent. of the trade, whether home or export, is done by about 500 firms.

Before the war the cotton industry had not been highly organised on an industry-wide scale. There had been a Joint Committee of Cotton Trade Organisations which had helped to prepare the Cotton Industry (Reorganisation) Act of 1939. This Act, which was to establish a central Cotton Industry Board, did not, however, reach the Statute Book until a month before the outbreak of war and the main principles were never put into operation.[4] But the war itself produced two central bodies concerned with cotton—the Cotton Board and the Cotton Control.

We have already seen[5] that a Cotton Board drawn from the various sections of the industry including the workers was set up soon after the war began and that at first it was purely advisory and had no funds of its own nor proper organisation. These shortcomings were increasingly noticeable and in March 1940, it will be remembered,

---

1 For statistical purposes doubling is often treated as part of the spinning section.
2 See e.g. the description in the *Cotton Working Party Report*, p. 36.
3 Counts refer to the thickness of the yarn.
4 Cotton Industry (Reorganisation) (Postponement) Act, 2 & 3 Geo. 6, ch. 11.
5 See pp. 46–48.

the Cotton Board was reconstituted. It was still a representative body, but it now had an independent, salaried chairman and powers to raise funds by a levy on all raw cotton purchased by spinners.[1] The new Board was to advise the Government on any questions concerning the industry that might be referred to it and to encourage the export trade. When the export drive petered out the functions of the Cotton Board changed. For example, it administered the financial arrangements of all the cotton concentration schemes and handled the concentration of the finishing sections. Moreover, it gradually undertook a good deal of administrative work on behalf of the Board of Trade, especially in connection with export control and utility clothing. Towards the end of the war the Cotton Board took a great interest in post-war problems of all kinds. Its success in persuading the various sections of the industry to collaborate and in negotiating between the Government and the industry was sufficiently great for its own post-war future to be assured.

The Cotton Control was established in November 1939 by the Ministry of Supply on the same lines as the other raw material Controls.[2] Its tasks were the control of prices, and the administration and control of the industry; as war-time problems multiplied so also did the Control's functions. Its general responsibility for raw material supplies, production, prices and statistics developed into concern with allocation schemes, preference directions, labour affairs, yarn and cloth planning. In theory the Ministry of Supply controlled cotton up to the finished cloth stage. In practice, however, the Control only concerned itself with production up to the grey cloth stage—that is, with the spinning, doubling and weaving industries; the affairs of the finishing industry were for the most part delegated to the Cotton Board.

In connection with the export drive a third organisation was established in the cotton industry—British Overseas Cottons Ltd. This company, it will be recalled,[3] had been established in July 1940 in order to encourage exports by forming a link between producers and merchants for bulk production of finished cloth on special terms. This it was hoped would make it possible to attack new export markets. The company performed its task by bulking orders from merchants and thus giving long runs to producers and by negotiating 'derogations'[4] from controlled prices where necessary. It was at first covered against losses by a levy on raw cotton sales; this levy ceased, however, in August 1942,[5] for funds had accumulated after the collapse of the

---

[1] Cotton Industry Act, 3 & 4 Geo. 6, ch. 9.
[2] i.e. the Control was financed by the Ministry of Supply and the staff were therefore employed by the Government.
[3] See p. 63.
[4] *Ibid.*
[5] S.R. & O. 1942, No. 1597.

export drive. After the export drive the company's functions inevitably became less important. Nevertheless, as we have seen,[1] it continued to act as a useful clearing-house for small holders of export allocations and the advantages of the system were sufficiently strong for the grey cloth merchants to emulate it by organising a similar pool for themselves. Towards the end of the war British Overseas Cottons helped the Government in another way, by disposing of surplus textiles abroad. The organisation as a whole was clearly considered useful, for the Cotton Board's Post-War Committee recommended that something similar to it should be set up after the war.

This brief description of the central organisation in the cotton industry has been carried through to the end of the war. We must now turn back to see the impact of war on the cotton industry. In the autumn of 1939 the industry found itself working with full order books for the first time for years. Home trade was unrestricted, exports were being encouraged and on top of these Service contracts poured in for a host of war stores—from Service clothing to tyre fabrics, webbing, tarpaulins and medical gauze. There was indeed 'business for every spindle that could run'.[2] From the outset there were warnings of problems ahead. There was already some difficulty over raw material. Heavy orders for coarse yarns for war purposes were increasing the demand for American cotton at a time when shortages of hard currency made this particularly undesirable. Attempts had therefore to be made to relax specifications so that Indian and Egyptian cotton could be used more extensively.[3] There was also difficulty over labour. Men and women left the industry for the Forces and munitions industries so that despite unemployment in certain towns a shortage of the right labour at the right points limited output almost from the first. For this reason, only ninety per cent. of the spindles in place could, in fact, run. A still larger percentage of looms was idle.

For the first four or five months of war the demands of the Services, exports and the home market were left to compete with one another. Any efforts to influence production were spasmodic and unrelated to any general plan.[4] Soon, however, as order books became over-

---

[1] See p. 190.

[2] See the article by Sir Ralph Lacey (the war-time Deputy Cotton Controller), 'Cotton's War Effort', *Manchester School of Economic and Social Studies*, Vol. XV, No. 1, January 1947. This is a published version of a lecture by Sir Ralph Lacey to the Manchester Statistical Society in November 1946.

[3] This was not only to save hard currency but to make use of the capacity adapted for these yarns.

[4] Sir Ralph Lacey in 'Cotton's War Effort' gives several examples. For instance, one morning the Cotton Control got an urgent telephone request for an astonishing quantity of inch-wide tape for defeating the magnetic mine. A week-end of telephoning revealed that nothing could be done in time if the tape was to be woven. Bulk deliveries were begun within a week by cutting up wide cloth on a machine designed for cutting paper strips.

crowded, yarn prices began to rise and closer control was clearly necessary. In February 1940 the Cotton Control introduced a system of preference directions[1] to give Government and export orders priority over civilian requirements. Firms were still free to accept what contracts they liked, but the Minister of Supply now had power to direct any firm to give preference to a particular contract, even if this meant setting aside non-preference work.[2] Preference A was for direct Government orders and essential home services[3] and preference B was for export orders identified by chambers of commerce or by trade associations. The normal home civilian market had no priority.

This system was rather hit or miss, but it did do something to direct production away from less essential needs. After a year or so, however, it threatened to break down because the number of preference orders became too great to be manageable. It became almost impossible to get a new contract accepted unless a preference direction followed. The home market was hard hit; by the spring of 1941 this priority system, combined with the Limitation of Supplies Orders, was causing shortages of clothing which were reflected in rising prices.[4] The real blow to the preference direction system was, however, the concentration of the cotton industry. By that time about eighty-five per cent. of total output was covered by these directions and, as concentration was to reduce output by about a third, only preference A contracts would have much hope of fulfilment. Some other system had to be devised to give a share of the inadequate total to other demands besides those of the Services.

In the spring of 1941 the Materials Committee began to allocate raw cotton between Government departments. But this was not very satisfactory and in August 1941 an allocation of cotton yarn began, coupled with an approved order system—twin controls that lasted until the end of the war. The allocations were made at quarterly intervals by the Materials Committee on the basis of the expected output of the industry. Allocations were made by the Materials Committee to various Government departments, to industrial groups,[5]

---

[1] S.R. & O. 1940, No. 196.

[2] Preference directions were issued at the request of the firm. They were supposed to give protection to firms against claims for breach of contract where non-preference contracts were set aside. The point was never tested in the courts.

[3] A heading that included such miscellaneous items as burnishing mops, cleaning cloths, shrouds, sewing thread, typewriter ribbons, tracing cloth, hydraulic packings, filter cloths, industrial gloves, tarpaulins, officers' clothing, anti-scatter net and insulating material.

[4] See p. 313.

[5] Industrial groups included most of those industries which consumed cotton goods on a substantial scale, e.g. cordage and tyres, insulated cables, boots and shoes, surgical dressings, wool, jute, plastics, hosiery, etc. Their requirements were sponsored by a Government department, often the relevant raw material Control, or sometimes by a recognised trade association.

essential home services,[1] civilian home trade and exports. Allocation holders were free to place or authorise orders within their allocations and firms were free to accept any authorised ('approved') orders. Deliveries of yarn were licensed only against approved orders.[2] At each stage of a contract or sub-contract the buyer made a return to the Cotton Control signed by the seller and the yarn licence was issued only if the returns were in order.

This system had its disadvantages. First, it was cumbrous. The returns at each stage meant that serious delays occurred between the approval of the original contract and the final licensing of the yarn. Moreover, since each approved order was licensed right through individually, some licences were ridiculously small—sometimes for as little as $\frac{1}{2}$ lb. of yarn. The second and more serious disadvantage was that the only common measure for calculating allocations was by weight of single yarn. The main war-time increase in demand was, however, for coarse counts of cotton, especially for heavy canvases. Therefore, although the aggregate allocations roughly balanced output, allocation holders were trying to acquire coarse counts in excess of production, while some producers of fine counts had difficulty in getting enough approved orders to absorb all their output. There were other similar difficulties and the Cotton Control could do little about them because it did not yet fully control production; it did not know where or what orders were placed. The difficulties were the more pronounced because production was continually, though slightly, falling. The ability of firms to vary their production declined with their rate of activity and the ability of consumers to vary their demands declined as allocations became increasingly inadequate.[3] The only solution was central planning of the yarn and cloth production. And this indeed became one of the main functions of the Cotton Control after mid-1942.

Production planning will be discussed in detail in Chapter XVII. It is, however, worth summarising in advance the working of the control system as a whole. When the Materials Committee met to allocate cotton for any quarter, it had before it statements of requirements and expected output and comparisons of current allocations and deliveries.[4] In practice, since production was always disappointing, allocations for each quarter consistently exceeded output. Each allocation from the Materials Committee entitled the department

---

[1] See the note on the previous page. This allocation, perhaps five per cent. of the total, was administered by the Cotton Control.

[2] S.R. & O. 1941, No. 1174.

[3] See Sir Ralph Lacey, 'Cotton's War Effort', *op. cit.*

[4] Each department or purpose that had an allocation had a symbol, e.g. M.S. for Ministry of Supply or E.H.S. for Essential Home Services. Records were kept of yarn licensed and of deliveries made against these symbols. The difficulty over the shortage of heavy canvases was eventually solved by having a separate allocation for them.

—or other authority—to buying rights in the quarter concerned up to the amount of the agreed allocation. It also carried with it forward buying rights to enable departments and the industry to make long-term plans. The forward buying rights were normally eighty per cent. of the allocation for delivery in the subsequent quarter and about sixty per cent. for delivery in later periods.[1] In practice, however, departments did not use all their buying rights at once but preferred to keep something in hand for emergencies; the load on the industry's order book did not therefore reach the maximum that was theoretically possible under the allocation system.

Once planned production was in operation, each department or authority,[2] as soon as it knew its allocation and therefore its buying rights, placed a programme of its cloth requirements before the Cotton Control. The Control in turn translated these general cloth requirements into specific demands on the industry for yarns, raw cotton, etc. Since output always fell below the level of allocation the Cotton Control had to ensure that the shortfall was spread fairly between departments. The sanction behind the Control's activities was a strong one: spinners could not deliver yarn—or, in the case of a firm that both spun and wove, use yarn—without a licence.

The procedure for direct Government orders was as follows. A contracting department's quarterly cloth programme might have to be modified by the Cotton Control to take account of technical difficulties in the industry. But once the programme was settled, the Cloth Planning Department of the Cotton Control arranged for its production with suitable weavers who nominated the yarn suppliers they preferred. These nominations and yarn details then went to the Yarn Planning Department of the Control who finally selected the spinner, licensed the delivery of the yarn and informed the weaver and the department concerned. The department then placed its contract with the weaver. The Control always exerted its influence towards the longest possible runs and repeat orders were placed with firms wherever possible before the old contracts ran out. The Control did not deal with orders of less than 2,000 lbs. of yarn. Small orders were delivered from stock and the supplier obtained from the Cotton Control a form promising replacement. These forms were transferable and could be accumulated until they added up to more than 2,000 lbs. of yarn; the Control could then be asked to plan an equivalent weight of cloth. As for finishing the cloth, departments arranged this themselves or through merchant converters.

Sometimes Government departments bought made-up cotton

---

[1] After a time departmental needs became so well known that there was not likely to be a change of more than twenty per cent. in any allocation between one period and the next.

[2] This procedure applied to nearly all allocation holders. There were, however, one or two exceptions. For example, the wool industry took its cotton in the form of yarn.

articles or were responsible for an allocation even though they did not buy on their own account. For example, the Ministry of Food was very interested in the supply of flour bags to millers even though it did not buy them. In these cases the department issued an authority to the firm concerned to acquire cotton and sent a copy to the Cotton Control, who invited the firm to nominate its preferred suppliers. Matters then proceeded as for direct Government orders. Much the same system worked for the allocations to industrial groups. Each group came under the authority of a Government department or trade association which was responsible for approving firms' buying programmes and forwarding them to the Cotton Control. The cotton allocation for essential home services, on the other hand, was administered by the Control itself. As the range of items was so wide, treatment varied. In some cases the Control, in consultation with the firms, succeeded in confining the demands to a limited range of standard cloths. For the most part, however, demands were too small and scattered and firms applied for the approval of individual orders.

The home civilian allocation—which after 1942 consisted mainly of utility cloths—was of course administered by the Board of Trade and will be dealt with in detail later on.[1] For the most part the production was planned by the Cloth Planning Department of the Cotton Control on behalf of the Board of Trade in much the same way as direct Government orders. But the Cotton Board Utility Cloth Office arranged the allocation of grey, unfinished cloth to merchant converters and its subsequent sale to garment makers or wholesalers. The Cotton Board told the converters which weavers would be making the cloth and the Control gave the weavers the corresponding information. The converters and weavers then linked up.

The Board of Trade were also responsible for the export allocation of cotton, though this again was administered for them—this time by the Cotton Board. We have already seen[2] that within the main allocation there was a system of allocation both for markets and for individual exporters. The Cotton Board obtained a return from each exporter of his shipments of cotton goods using 1940 as the basic year. Every quarter each individual exporter received his allotted yardage market by market and then arranged his own source of supply. The Cotton Board was responsible for seeing that the exporter did not exceed his allocation and for getting the necessary spinning and weaving licences from the Cotton Control. The Board of Trade export licensing system ensured that the authorised yardage for each market was not exceeded. During the last two years of the war, it will be remembered,[3] a small part of the export allocation was set aside for

---

[1] See Chapter XVII for a discussion of cotton utility schemes.
[2] See Chapter VII, pp. 139–42 and Chapter IX, pp. 187–92.
[3] See p. 191.

'free exports'. Manufacturers could make tentative arrangements with exporters and apply to the Cotton Control for yarn licences. The Control only authorised sufficient total production to absorb the 'free export' allocation and the allocations to particular markets.

It was not usually possible to programme export demands a long time ahead.[1] In order to secure the economies of long runs, however, export orders were (with a few exceptions) not planned for lengths less than 40,000 yards. The many individual allocation holders who held smaller allocations than this were able to use the services of British Overseas Cottons Ltd. which offered a wide range of standard cloths. Or they could use the merchants' grey cloth pool. Sometimes, of course, the Cotton Control was obliged to restrict export requirements for certain particularly difficult counts of yarn or widths or construction of cloth.

The main history of the cotton allocations was one of a struggle between a whole variety of essential needs—from the Services, from industry, from civilians and from overseas—for their share in the constantly declining output of the industry. The total amount that was allocated fell from 104,000 tons in the last quarter of 1941 to 78,000 tons in the second quarter of 1945.[2] These allocations, moreover, were higher than actual output. In the remaining sections of this chapter we shall be studying the reasons for this decline in output. Early in 1941 it had been feared that a shortage of raw material would limit cotton output. But as the table in Appendix 9[3] shows, this did not happen. Imports of raw cotton were exceptionally low in 1941. Thereafter they were far more than the cotton industry could consume and stocks of raw cotton rose steadily. The fall in the cotton industry output was wholly due to a shortage of labour. This shortage was heavily accentuated, even if it was not actually caused, by the concentration of the industry.

CONCENTRATION

The concentration of industry policy has already been generally discussed. Here we shall look more closely at concentration of the cotton industry, partly because it was one of the largest and most thorough schemes and partly because it affected the industry so profoundly.

Until the beginning of 1941 the cotton industry had no problem of surplus capacity. By then, however, it seemed that the shipping shortage would reduce cotton imports to a level barely sufficient to

---

[1] Sometimes governments abroad could programme demands, e.g. Dominion direct government purchases and Australian civil demands. In these cases the export programmes were planned on the same lines as home civilian production.

[2] See Appendix 8 at the end of this chapter.

[3] At the end of this chapter.

meet seventy per cent. of the industry's requirements. And indeed in 1941 cotton imports were to be only 364,000 tons compared with 633,000 tons in 1940. The shortage was aggravated by the loss of 33,000 tons of raw cotton in the bombing of warehouses in Manchester and Liverpool; at one point during 1941 stocks were to fall to 105,000 tons, which was much lower than at any other time during the war. Early in 1941, therefore, it was clear that cotton consumption must be reduced immediately.

The question was how to deal with surplus capacity. The White Paper on concentration had not yet been published and it was necessary to decide whether the reduced production should be concentrated in two-thirds of the mills running at maximum capacity or whether all mills should continue to run at a reduced rate of activity. In the 1914–18 war, when shortage of raw cotton created surplus capacity, the industry had chosen the latter alternative; a rota system of working had been introduced whereby operatives were obliged to take regular periods of enforced holidays with pay.[1] This system had worked when no alternative employment was available for cotton workers, but it was obviously unsuitable in 1941 when munitions factories in north-west England badly needed workers and the armed forces were clamouring for men and women. Nevertheless, the industry favoured some such plan. The chairman of the Cotton Board suggested that the cut to be made in production in 1941 could be achieved by giving all firms a basic ration of raw material equivalent to twenty-five per cent. of their full capacity and firms with a high proportion of essential work up to sixty per cent. of their full capacity. As it would not be worth while for firms with a twenty-five per cent. ration to carry on, their ration could be bought up by other firms and they would close down with some compensation.

The Board of Trade did not feel that this piecemeal reduction of capacity would release enough labour or factory space at the right time or in the right places. To them the arguments in favour of concentration as opposed to the spread-over system were overwhelming from the outset. This view was not, perhaps, made sufficiently clear to the industry, which believed until the concentration White Paper was actually published that they had a choice between concentration and a spread-over system. Although the industry would still have preferred a spread-over system they were very willing to co-operate once the decision to concentrate had actually been announced. They felt, however, that a central authority would have to nominate the firms to run or close if concentration were to proceed fast and far enough.

---

[1] Paid for by a levy on employers, especially in the Egyptian section, because only American type cotton was scarce. See H. D. Henderson, *The Cotton Control Board* (Oxford University Press, 1922).

For it was clear that there would be a good many complications in concentrating the cotton industry. First, the demands for labour in the cotton areas were particularly heavy; the Ministry of Labour estimated in April 1941 that the war factories in this district would need 126,000 workers in the next few months and that at least half would have to come from cotton. In order to provide this number for munitions and to allow for the inevitable loss of some workers to other occupations the Control estimated that at least 100,000 workers would have to be displaced.[1] Secondly, it was feared that shortage of raw materials might be so serious that half the industry's plant would have to close. Thirdly, over sixty per cent. of the industry's output was for Government and other essential orders calling for rigid specifications or standards of performance. This limited the possibility of transfer, the more so since there was so much local specialisation in the industry. It would thus be very difficult for one firm to find other 'matching' firms and it was unlikely that the number of matching firms would be sufficient to release the required number of workers or achieve the required degree of concentration.

In view of these difficulties the Government agreed with the industry that the cotton industry could not for the most part be governed by the White Paper principle of voluntary arrangements between firms; a central authority would have to select firms to close or run. The Board of Trade[2] were to decide the degree of concentration necessary in each main section and after a brief initial period to permit voluntary arrangements the Cotton Control was to nominate firms to close and run.

The most urgent task was to concentrate the spinning section of the industry, for on 1st March 1941 the issue of raw cotton by the Cotton Control to spinners was substantially cut.[3] There was little time for consultation with the trade on the choice of mills to run or close. Decisions were therefore taken by regular and frequent meetings in the region between the Cotton Control and the Ministry of Labour. These decisions were difficult. It was necessary to take into account 'the areas in which labour was required for other war purposes, the extent to which mills were already engaged on essential work or were set out for such work as was likely to be required, their flexibility in dealing with different types of raw cotton, the amount of transport necessary to keep them running and the proximity of other mills which could absorb or supply experienced labour'.[4] Where possible the Control chose as nuclei firms that used mostly ring spindles which

---

[1] See Table on p. 368 for the number actually lost by the cotton industry—130,000 between the end of 1940 and the end of 1942.

[2] The Ministry of Supply, of which the Cotton Control was a part, insisted that the Board of Trade should take responsibility for the Cotton Control's concentration activities.

[3] For example, licences to consume cotton were refused to about sixty spinning firms.

[4] Lacey, *op. cit.*, p. 33.

were worked by women rather than mule spindles which were worked by men.[1] Where other things were equal, the firms chosen as nuclei were those with the largest number of preference directions. Voluntary arrangements between firms were not entirely excluded, and at least 19 mills were closed in this way. The Cotton Control could ensure that closed mills really did close by withdrawing firms' licences to consume cotton and cotton waste.

Concentration of spinning went forward swiftly. Out of a total of about 520 cotton-spinning mills,[2] over 200 were closed between March and December 1941; between March and July mills had been closing at an average rate of approximately ten a week. The closed mills had a capacity of over 14 million m.e. spindles or thirty-eight per cent. of the total spindle capacity of the industry.[3] As had been intended, some spinning areas suffered more than others. For example, in Chorley and Preston, which were near the big new Lancashire filling factories, over sixty per cent. of the m.e. spindles ceased to work.[4]

By October 1941 yarn output had been reduced to about sixty per cent. of its preconcentration figure and between December 1940 and December 1941 the cotton-spinning industry had lost nearly 18,000 men and 30,000 women.[5] Even before the end of 1941 there were fears that the industry had been over-concentrated. In December the President of the Board of Trade admitted to his colleagues that concentration had probably been carried too far, especially in the spinning section, and that the remaining capacity appeared to be inadequate to meet requirements.[6] The Cotton Control had estimated that supplies of cotton would be sufficient for not more than 22 million spindles,[7] but by the end of 1941 there were only 20·5 million spindles in the running mills. And by then the raw material shortage—which had been the most urgent reason for quick and drastic concentration—had eased. During 1942 raw cotton imports were 162,000 tons higher than in 1941. Now, however, the industry could not absorb these quantities. The labour force of the industry

---

[1] Ring spinning is a continuous process and mule spinning an intermittent process, so that a ring spindle produces more yarn in a day than a mule spindle on the same counts. For the purpose of measuring spinning capacity one ring spindle is treated as equal to one and a half mule spindles, i.e. mule equivalent spindles.

[2] Other figures give 450 for the total number of mills. It depends what is counted as a separate mill. Where two or more mills were on one site the Board of Trade usually counted them as one if there was only one power house.

[3] Forty-four per cent. of the total number of mule spindles in the industry were in closed mills and twenty-seven per cent. of the ring spindles.

[4] For district figures see Lacey, *op. cit.*, Table 8.

[5] It is impossible, of course, to link figures of labour lost directly with concentration. See p. 227.

[6] It is arguable, however, that what went wrong was not the amount of concentration but the labour supply of the nucleus mills. See pp. 364–7.

[7] Actual spindles not mule equivalent.

declined steadily and even the nucleus spinning mills were never fully manned; as early as August 1941 these mills were running at only seventy-eight per cent. of capacity. For this reason yarn production remained below demand for the rest of the war.

Concentration of the waste spinning section was accomplished fairly easily. Waste cotton is a by-product obtained mainly, though not entirely, in the course of raw cotton spinning and it is spun by specialised mills. In the spring of 1941 the reduction in the supply of raw cotton and the increased demand for waste for use in explosives made it clear that waste spinning capacity would have to be concentrated. The concentration was carried out very largely by voluntary arrangements. Over 40 out of 125 mills were closed; the closed mills held about a quarter of the section's total spindleage. During 1942 consumption of cotton waste by the industry was about forty per cent. less than it had been just before concentration. By the end of 1941 the labour employed was only about sixty-four per cent. of the figure at the end of 1940.[1]

Concentration of the doubling section of the cotton industry also proceeded smoothly. Redundancy had not been heavy in this section before the war and during the war the ratio of doubled yarn to single yarn had to be increased owing to heavy military demands for coarse yarns for canvases, tyres, webbing, etc. The section was indeed hard pressed to meet these demands, for even before concentration it had lost a good deal of labour. Only a relatively small proportion of the doubling spindleage had, therefore, to be closed down. It was thought that at least seventy per cent. of productive capacity should be allowed to run. The section possessed a wide variety of processes and machinery and to some extent this complicated concentration. On the other hand, however, the machinery of many mills could be adjusted to twist a heavier or lighter thread. Moreover, most doubling spindles were owned by combines or multi-unit firms so that a large proportion of the industry was concentrated by voluntary arrangement. Finally, though the main centre of doubling is in Lancashire, there are substantial numbers of mills in other places such as Yorkshire and Nottinghamshire where the labour shortage was less acute.

By the beginning of 1942 just over 80 out of a total of nearly 270 mills had been closed; these closed mills had about twenty per cent. of the total spindleage of this section of the industry. Labour losses were not very heavy; at the end of 1941 the labour force was only about twelve per cent. less than it had been at the end of 1940.[2] In order to ensure that closed mills did close, the Cotton Control had

---

[1] Cotton waste consumption before concentration—4,100 tons a month.
Cotton waste consumption in 1942—2,424 tons a month.
For labour figures see Table 22 on p. 368.
See Lacey, *op. cit.*, Table 9, for analysis of concentration by districts.

[2] For labour figures, see Table 22 on p. 368.

to introduce licensing for doubling spindles.[1] Licences were only given to nucleus firms and to firms which performed doubling as an ancillary operation to such things as rope or lace manufacture.

Concentration of the weaving section was a much bigger task than concentration of doubling. In May 1941 the Cotton Controller had said that the quantity of yarn likely to be available for weaving would not keep running more than half of the 480,000[2] looms in the cotton- and rayon-weaving industry. Heavy concentration of capacity in the weaving section was therefore necessary and labour displacement was likely to be serious. The progress of concentration in the weaving section could not, however, be so rapid as in the spinning section owing to the wide range of cloth produced, the many types and widths of looms and the large number and small size of the weaving units.[3] A further difficulty was presented by the number of very small firms renting only 'room and power' in a shed shared by several other firms. On the other hand, the labour problem was rather easier than in the spinning section because the weaving industry was less highly localised. In some weaving areas outside Lancashire—for example, in south Scotland—labour was relatively plentiful.

At first there was some doubt about the best method of concentrating the weaving industry. The Cotton Control, the Cotton Board and the consultative committee of the industry favoured compulsory concentration. This would mean that loom licensing would have to be introduced so that firms could be compulsorily closed by withdrawing their licences to weave. The Board of Trade, however, generally preferred voluntary concentration schemes. They felt that the strong reasons for compulsory concentration of cotton spinning did not apply to weaving; indeed, weaving was so varied in form and design that discrimination between firms would be largely a matter of personal opinion. To the Cotton Controller this multiplicity of types of cloth and machinery seemed a major obstacle in the way of voluntary schemes.

In the end weaving firms were given an opportunity between March and May 1941 for suggesting voluntary schemes. Many firms responded and with the help of the Cotton Control in the negotiations over one-third of the firms in the industry were covered in this way. But at the end of May 1941 the status of over 230,000 looms —most of them in Lancashire—was still undecided. It seemed clear that without compulsion concentration would not be completed and

---

[1] S.R. & O. 1942, No. 127.

[2] Even in the early war months not more than about 360,000 looms ran. The section would not expect to work at 100 per cent. nominal capacity because different looms are needed to make different types of cloth and some are bound to stand idle.

[3] In 1940 over forty per cent. of weaving firms owned fewer than 200 looms each and only five per cent. owned more than 1,000. The average number of workers employed per firm was under 200. (*Cotton Working Party Report*, pp. 41 and 49.)

the large numbers of workers needed for munition factories in the weaving districts would not be found. Loom licensing therefore began in June 1941[1] and the Cotton Control decided which looms should run and which should close. Under the concentration arrangements for weaving very few firms went out of business altogether —only 70 out of a total of 900. Firms might have their own mills closed and looms stopped but they had licences to run looms in someone else's mills. In general, the units which only rented 'room and power' in sheds shared with other firms[2] were not granted nucleus status unless the rest of the shed was also made nucleus. Even in these cases they were only granted nucleus status for specialised types of cloth.

Concentration of the weaving section was finally completed by October 1942. Four hundred sheds with 166,000 looms were completely closed and a further 70,000 looms in running mills were unlicensed. The labour force of the weaving industry fell by about 58,000 between the end of 1940 and the middle of 1942.

One of the most complicated problems to be settled in concentrating the cotton industry was compensation. The White Paper on concentration had emphasised the individual responsibility of nucleus firms for compensating closed firms. The Board of Trade had been reluctant to encourage industry-wide compensation schemes; these would mean compulsory levies and someone would have to decide the rate of the levy and the firms which were to contribute. It was soon clear, however, that the cotton industry must be an exception to the Board of Trade's rule. Since the Cotton Control had to close down some spinning firms immediately without giving them time to make private financial arrangements, an industry-wide or rather section-wide compensation scheme would have to be set up.

At first there was a suggestion that the necessary funds should be raised through a levy on the price of raw cotton. This scheme was, however, unacceptable. For as all raw cotton was owned by the Ministry of Supply, any assistance given out of a fund created by an addition to the price of raw cotton would be from a public fund. This was ruled out by a Government decision that closed firms should not receive compensation from any Government fund.[3] The only means of raising money for a compensation fund was therefore by a levy on the nucleus mills calculated on the number of machines installed.

One principle of the compensation schemes was that all closed plant and machinery should be maintained in a condition to start

---

[1] S.R. & O. 1941, No. 843.

[2] Before concentration there were sixty-one such sheds, i.e. about 4·3 per cent. of the total number of weaving units. They contained 69,000 looms. (*Cotton Working Party Report*, p. 41.)

[3] See Chapter X.

z

again after the war. The one exception to this rule—the weaving industry—will be discussed a little later. The general anxiety to maintain plant and machinery may seem surprising in an industry like cotton where pre-war redundancy had been so great. Would not the best interests of the industry have been served if the less efficient mills had not been allowed to reopen? Such a use of the concentration scheme was, however, ruled out by the Government's pledge in the White Paper on concentration that closed firms would receive every assistance to reopen. Moreover, a reserve of plant had to be kept ready in case of air-raid damage to running mills. In any case the criteria for closing mills in war-time were not the same as those for the permanent elimination of redundant capacity. The balance of demand was different in peace and war. And in war-time some of the most efficient firms had to be closed since they were in areas where the demand for munitions labour was heaviest; on the other hand, it was desirable that units in remote areas where there were reserves of immobile labour should continue to run even if they were not very efficient.

Central compensation, or care and maintenance, funds were set up for eight sections of the cotton industry[1] and were administered by the Cotton Board. All these funds had a similar basis. A theoretical figure was built up for the cost of maintaining a typical closed mill[2] and closed firms received payments on this scale. These payments were made from a central fund in each section which was fed by subscriptions from nucleus firms. These subscriptions were calculated either on the units of machinery or on turnover and were fixed by the Cotton Board at a level sufficient to meet the agreed monthly payments to closed firms. Contributions from nucleus firms began when the section's fund was set up, but payments to closed firms began only from the date of closure. The total amount received and distributed by the Cotton Board exceeded £16 millions. In some cases closed firms were able to build up, from the payments they received, funds to help them with the expenses of reopening after the war.

It is worth examining in some detail the working of one of these care and maintenance schemes; since the spinning scheme was the largest, we shall use it as our example. The Cotton Board had to

---

[1] Spinning, waste spinning, doubling, weaving, yarn processing, piece dyeing, finishing-and-raising and piece bleaching (not calico printing).

[2] This figure was arrived at by estimating, for example, the cost of maintenance of plant; remuneration for a manager and secretary and other staff, auditors, office and engine-room staff, warehousemen, watchmen, overlookers, firewatchers; payments for coal, water, gas, electricity, telephone, oil, grease, etc., and water rights; fire insurance, ground rent, health and unemployment insurance and workmen's compensation of remaining staff; commodities war-risk insurance on stocks, Schedule A tax and local rates; repairs and maintenance on buildings. But the items varied considerably with the type of mill, etc. The theoretical figure was not intended to cover interest on capital or capital commitments under Part 2 of the War Damage Act nor payments to directors, stockholders or debenture-holders.

work out the details of the scheme very quickly before firms were closed. It had no previous experience to guide it in making preliminary estimates of the right figure for the rate of levy and the rate of compensation. The difficulty was to find a proper balance between them so that neither closed nor running firms should suffer severe financial loss nor running firms seek an undue rise in prices. Fortunately contributions and payments were on a monthly basis and could be changed at short notice if necessary.

Compensation was based on the cost of maintaining a mill of 100,000 mule equivalent spindles which was estimated at £7,000 per annum—a figure that was accepted by the industry's consultative committee on concentration subject to revision after an experimental period of a year. The basis for payments into, and withdrawals from, the fund was spindleage. Payments to closed firms worked out at 1·4d. per month per mule equivalent spindle and contributions from nucleus mills were whatever was required to produce this rate at any one time. The contributions from nucleus mills were calculated by the total number of spindles installed whether actually running or not. They were changed fairly frequently but were in the neighbourhood of 1d. per month per spindle. Nucleus firms might not ask for an increase in yarn prices on account of their subscriptions.

At the end of a year's experimental working the spinners' care and maintenance scheme was revised in certain ways. The maintenance rate for a mill of 100,000 m.e. spindles was raised from £7,000 to £7,500 per annum. Since maintenance had proved proportionately heavier for small factories, a sliding scale in reverse proportion to the number of machinery units installed was introduced to give increases ranging from ten per cent. to twenty-five per cent. in the normal rates of payment for all mills with fewer than 60,000 spindles. Under the revised scheme closed firms were allowed to keep for their own use any sums they could save out of the fund. They could also keep any income they received from the requisitioning or sub-letting of their factory space without any abatement of their receipts from the fund.

One question of principle arose when the spinners' scheme was revised. The cotton industry had been the first to be concentrated and the Board of Trade had insisted that compensation payments should provide only for care and maintenance; compensation for loss of profits was to be excluded. Other industries, however, obtained concessions and the cotton spinners shared them when their scheme was revised. It was agreed that closed firms should share in the profits of nucleus firms in order to cover other expenses such as depreciation of plant and buildings. Expenditure on maintaining the closed firms would be wasted if they were unable to begin again after the war because they had used up their working capital upon necessary payments not covered by the care and maintenance allowance. The

Board of Trade agreed that £10,000 would be a reasonable figure for a unit of 100,000 m.e. spindles allowing £7,500 for maintenance and the rest for a reasonable share of profits. This, together with the other revisions, made the rate of compensation to closed mills 2d. per spindle per month and the rate of contribution from nucleus mills 1·2d. per spindle per month.

The care and maintenance schemes in other sections of the cotton industry were similar to that in spinning. An important variation in the weaving section must, however, be mentioned. In general, as we have seen, closed firms were obliged to maintain their equipment in a condition to begin work again. In the weaving industry, however, some closed looms were scrapped. The initiative came from the Factory Control who badly needed space occupied by idle looms in the weaving mills. The Control made a special arrangement by which weaving firms whose space was taken over were offered a sum of £2 per loom in addition to scrap value and also a commuted payment of ten months' care and maintenance; the Cotton Board had first to agree that the looms were suitable for scrapping. The scheme seemed in the interests of the care and maintenance fund which was relieved of the obligation to maintain old machinery, in the interests of the industry which could get rid of redundant looms and in the interests of the nation which needed scrap metal as well as factory space. The scheme was therefore extended to any firms which wished to scrap their looms, even if their premises were not requisitioned. A limit of 50,000 was set to the total number of looms to be scrapped. In fact, however, probably not more than 4,000 were destroyed.

The rate of care and maintenance payments made to closed firms in the cotton industry was on average probably about right. Some firms found it adequate. Some did not. Some closed mills paid small dividends during the war, some claimed that even when an element of compensation for profits was introduced the amount they received only just covered their outgoings. Some built up a certain amount of reserve against the expenses of reopening after the war. On the whole, indeed, most closed firms did not suffer great financial loss. What they did lose was the opportunity the nucleus mills had of making increased profits during the war, their goodwill and more particularly the opportunity for installing such amenities as canteens. The owners of the closed mills had to suffer 'the hardship of seeing their competitors coining money, improving their mills and strengthening their position for the post-war period'. For most nucleus mills showed greatly increased profits during the war. With a few exceptions, their contributions to the care and maintenance funds though substantial were no more than they could afford.

We have not yet discussed the concentration scheme of the finishing section. This section of the cotton industry is really a separate industry and its concentration differed from that of other sections. The whole process was handled by the Cotton Board instead of the Cotton Control and the care and maintenance schemes were from the outset an integral part of the concentration arrangements.

Finishers were given six weeks—until 10th June 1941—in which to prepare voluntary concentration schemes. The Board of Trade decided the degree of concentration needed in each of the five subsections of the industry—piece bleaching, calico printing, cloth dyeing, finishing-and-raising and yarn processing—and the industry was then asked to prepare schemes in consultation with the Cotton Board. Very few firms, however, came forward with voluntary schemes. The Cotton Board felt that progress might be quicker if care and maintenance schemes could be approved in advance. The Board of Trade did not object and each section therefore drew up proposals for such schemes. Many acceptable private arrangements were made and the Cotton Board nominated other firms to run or close in order to bring capacity down to the required level.

The concentration arrangements varied between each section of the industry. Calico printing, for example, had suffered from particularly heavy redundancy before the war and, as Service contracts made few demands on the printing section, it was necessary to concentrate printing to fifty per cent. of its capacity.[1] Since printers specialised in different types of work, it was agreed that a closing firm should be allowed to divide its work among several nucleus firms according to the specialities of each. The printers drew up an agreement about concentration covering all kinds of points such as post-war plans, prices and also, of course, compensation. The combination which covered about half the industry—the Calico Printers' Association—joined in the agreement with the rest of the industry. Under the industry's compensation scheme, which was not administered by the Cotton Board, closed firms were to receive a share of the nucleus firms' takings calculated afresh each year, based on their proportion of the total turnover in sterling of all members during a standard period. There was thus an element of profit-sharing in this scheme from the outset. This departure from principle was justified on the ground that printers' factories had never run to full capacity; if they did so owing to concentration the economies would be so great that the nucleus firms would be placed in an unusually favourable position compared with the closed firms. By the time concentration was completed there were twenty-one nucleus establishments and thirty closed ones.

In the bleaching section of the finishing industry about thirty-five per cent. of the normal capacity was closed down. The section was

---

[1] In all the finishing sections capacity was usually measured by the annual value of work of which the firm's plant was capable.

dominated by a combine which possessed thirty-four branches as against the ten independent firms. Of these combine branches nine were closed, and five which mainly bleached yarn were dealt with under the concentration of yarn processing. Four of the independent firms were closed. There was no care and maintenance scheme for the whole section, but the Cotton Board operated a care and maintenance scheme based on turnover for the independent firms. Running firms made payments into a pool to provide care and maintenance for closed firms and also allowed closed firms a discount on work done on their behalf.

The dyeing section presented some of the most difficult concentration problems in the finishing industry. Its boundaries were not clearly marked—some firms dyed not only cotton and rayon but also wool and silk—and many firms were independently minded and stood aside from the trade association and trade arrangements. Moreover, the Service departments made heavy demands on certain types of processing; to make up for almost full running in the sections working for the Services other sections had to be heavily contracted. At first the Board of Trade wanted to reduce total capacity by forty per cent. For technical reasons, however, the Cotton Board wished to keep a high proportion of certain machines. The cut in capacity was therefor reduced to twenty-five per cent. At first the proposals for compensation were hindered by the industry's desire to tie the arrangements to a scheme for statutory price control, which the trade association had advocated before the war. The Board of Trade, however, would not contemplate statutory minimum prices and compensation proposals eventually followed the usual lines. Nucleus firms paid into a fund a percentage of their 1940 turnover[1]—the initial contribution was one per cent. Closed firms might receive payment at the initial yearly rate of seven per cent. of their 1940 turnover. These sums were later adjusted as necessary. Altogether seventy-eight dyeing establishments were granted nucleus status and forty-four were closed.

In the yarn processing section (which bleached, dyed, mercerised and sized cotton yarns) voluntary concentration was very difficult to arrange. The larger units of the section including the big combine of the industry were only engaged in yarn processing. The other units,

---

[1] 1940 turnover meant, in the case of a firm whose sole business was that of dyeing and/or finishing on commission, the total charges made and invoiced to customers for such dyeing and/or finishing, including ancillary processes, after making percentage additions to or deductions from the basic prices, but before deducting cash discount. Charges for work given out, trade discounts, special discounts and rebates; charges for boxes, cases, packings or wrappings included in the invoice were to be deducted in arriving at the turnover figure. Firms which combined piece dyeing and finishing with other production or merchanting were required when calculating their turnover to adjust their charges as if the work had been done on commission and deduct from total sales the original cost of cloth plus merchanting profit. If a firm's accounting period ended at a date between 30th September 1940 and 31st March 1941, that firm might submit for the 1940 turnover a turnover for the twelve months ending at a date between these two dates.

however, were part of firms that did spinning or weaving—sometimes both—as well as yarn processing. Many of these vertically organised firms were mainly interested in branded goods and specialised products in which design played a large part. For this reason, established trade connections and goodwill were particularly important and voluntary arrangements correspondingly difficult. Before concentration went ahead compensation terms were settled. Running firms paid a levy on their turnover in 1941 and later years—originally the rate was four per cent. of the 1941 figure—and closed firms received care and maintenance payments based on 1940 turnover—this rate was originally fifteen to sixteen per cent. In addition, up to forty per cent. of the capacity of running firms was to carry out work on behalf of the closed firms at ten per cent. discount.

Capacity in the yarn processing section was reduced by a third under concentration. Out of 110 firms 59 became nuclei. In addition nucleus certificates were granted to certain vertical firms for their yarn processing departments on the understanding that they released labour and factory space and that their output did not exceed limits set by the Cotton Board. The general principle that all nucleus firms in concentration schemes must run at full capacity did not apply to the yarn processing scheme. For seven of the largest units were from the beginning specifically permitted to run at sixty per cent. of their capacity. If they had been closed the industry would have been crippled and if they had run at full capacity all the small units would have had to close. The mills could, it seemed, run economically at this level and still release useful labour and factory space; since they were in particularly difficult labour areas it would probably have been impossible in any case to man them fully. This rather unusual spread-over system was therefore adopted.

The finishing-and-raising section was not concentrated until all the other sections of the finishing industry had been dealt with. Very few firms made voluntary arrangements and the Cotton Board nominated twenty firms to run and twenty to close. The finishing and raising sections of eleven vertically organised firms were granted nucleus status on condition that they participated in the care and maintenance scheme and reached a satisfactory agreement with the Cotton Board about the volume of their production. Altogether capacity was reduced by forty per cent. The compensation scheme was almost identical with that of the dyeing section and the rate of levy and of payments to closed firms was initially the same.

Broadly speaking, concentration in the finishing trades was completed by September 1942. Out of 413 firms 169 were closed and 244 were granted nucleus status. The numbers employed fell from 54,000 in December 1940 to 35,000 in December 1942.[1]

---

[1] See Table 22 on p. 368.

It is now time to appraise the results of concentration in the cotton industry as a whole. Its aim was to produce an orderly reduction of capacity with the minimum disturbance to war production and the maximum economy of labour, materials and space. Was this achieved?

Altogether about one-third of the cotton industry's mills were closed down.

Cotton Mills Closed by Concentration

TABLE 20

	Total	Closed by concentration
Spinning . .	520	200
Waste spinning .	125	40
Doubling . .	267	83
Weaving . .	1,400[1]	400
Finishing . .	413	169

It will be remembered that the original reason for concentrating the cotton industry to this extent had been the shortage of raw cotton. By the autumn of 1941, however, it seemed that raw cotton supplies would be more plentiful than had been expected; the shipping shortage had eased and the passing of the Lend-Lease Act was an assurance that cotton imports from America would not be restricted for lack of dollars. Concentration had, however, proceeded in order to release factory space and labour. The labour releases we shall deal with shortly. As far as factory space was concerned, cotton concentration certainly helped the war effort. It is impossible to obtain accurate figures of the amount of factory space made available for war purposes,[2] but the best guesses put the figure between 20 and 30 million square feet. It is doubtful whether much of this space would have been forthcoming if all mills had remained at work; it would have been much more difficult to requisition half of two running mills than to requisition one stopped mill.

Concentration had other undeniable advantages. The reduction in the number of mills at work must have produced savings in coal, gas, electricity and transport.[3] These were important since all these resources were particularly scarce in Lancashire. Concentration must also have kept the overheads and costs of cotton mills lower than they would otherwise have been. There were other incidental benefits. Later on planned production of cotton was made easier by the consolidation of the industry and the incidental collection of statistics brought about by concentration. And of course if surplus mills had

---

[1] It is difficult to distinguish in weaving between the technical units (the weaving sheds) and the financial units (the firms). The figure given here refers to the sheds but it does not completely cover the whole weaving section. This explains the discrepancy between the figure here and the figure for the number of weaving firms on pp. 356 and 357.

[2] The records of the Control of Factory and Storage Premises were kept by regions and not by industries.

[3] Unfortunately there are no figures to show the savings produced by concentration.

been forced out of business without compensation schemes individual hardship would have been much greater.

All these items may be put to the credit of concentration. But we must also remember that after concentration the output of the cotton industry was never again sufficient to meet what were considered to be the essential needs of war—Service, industrial, civilian and export needs. The war was of course never in danger of being lost through lack of cotton goods, but vexatious shortages of these goods caused overburdened administrators much trouble and anxiety. In part this was due to increases in demand which could not be foreseen at the time when concentration began. Russia's entry into the war caused an increase in demand. Then when Japan entered the war Lancashire had to make good the loss of Japanese goods in Africa and Asia. At the same time tropical warfare brought increased demands for cotton. Even apart from these increased demands, however, there would have been a shortage of cotton. The production of cotton yarn fell well below the level aimed at in the plans for concentrating spinning.

The root of the problem was labour. There was never enough labour in the nucleus mills to keep them running at full capacity. Indeed one critic could assert 'that the final production position reached after one of the worst upheavals in the industry's history was the spread-over system which was in the first place recommended by the trade's leaders but rejected by the Government'.[1] It was true that before concentration rather less than eighty per cent. of the industry's plant was running and that after concentration only about eighty per cent. of the licensed plant in running mills was working.

Machine Capacity and Machine Activity in Running Mills, 1940–41

TABLE 21

	Cotton and staple fibre spinning M.E. spindles (millions)		Waste spinning spindles (millions)		Doubling spindles (millions)		Weaving looms (thousands)	
	Installed in running mills	Running	Installed in running mills	Running	Installed in running mills	Running	Installed in running mills	Running
1940	39·00	28·95*	0·96	0·76†	3·75	3·00†	500	372†
1941	24·34	19·49	0·58	0·54	3·05	2·49	343	293

* Fourth quarter.　　　　　　† Estimated.

Without concentration, of course, the spread-over would have been thinner. But it is impossible to say how much thinner. For it is arguable that concentration itself was mainly responsible for the

---

[1] *The Economist*—Commercial history and review of 1941.

excessive loss of labour from the cotton industry; in this sense it is possible to speak of the industry as being over concentrated.

Concentration drove workers from the cotton industry in two ways. First, it encouraged—as indeed it was meant to encourage—cotton workers to go into munitions work. North-west England had been growing into a big munitions centre and from the early months of the war there had been a drift from the cotton mills, with their relatively unattractive pay and working conditions, into the radar, aircraft and shell-filling factories. When talk about concentration began, the drift became an avalanche. Cotton workers anticipated Government action and found their own alternative employment. Without the cotton workers war factories in the north-west could not have been manned. Nevertheless the numbers that left the cotton industry were much greater than the Government had bargained for.

Secondly, concentration drove some cotton workers away from employment altogether. The industry had always employed a large proportion of women, including many married women. Those with children under 14 were not subject to Ministry of Labour direction and there is some evidence that a good many of them left industry altogether when their mills were closed rather than move to more distant work. One small, interesting proof may be cited—the 'penny membership' of the trade unions. Trade union members who retire from the cotton industry can retain certain financial benefits on the payment of one penny a week. In the Oldham Card Room Union —which has one-third of the total card-room membership in Lancashire—this penny membership increased by 2,000 between March and October 1941. The penny membership of other unions organising women showed similar increases. The experience of the Cotton Control when deconcentration began also showed that there were many women who had stayed at home during the war but were ready to go back to their 'own' mills when these reopened. It is probable that other married women from the cotton mills did not stay at home but went into occupations, such as retail trade, that were considerably less important than cotton. For this reason the war effort might have been better served if fewer cotton mills had been closed. More use could then have been made of immobile labour. Production would of course have been uneconomical in the sense that it would have been spread even more thinly than it was. But as it turned out this was not necessarily the most important criterion. If it had produced more cotton the spread-over might have been worth while.

One thing is quite certain: wherever the labour from the cotton industry went—into munitions or back home—the results for the cotton industry were very serious. Between December 1940 and December 1941, when concentration mainly took place, the cotton industry lost 112,000 people or nearly thirty per cent. of its workers.

The spinning section lost nearly 50,000 or something approaching forty per cent. of its labour force. In later years of the war these figures were to be reduced even lower as wastage from the industry exceeded new intakes. It had proved impossible for the Government to concentrate the cotton industry to a predetermined level. The Government might say 'thus far', but the shrinkage in fact went a good deal further. Concentration so accelerated the movement from the industry that it could not easily be stopped.

In the end, then, an appraisal of concentration in the cotton industry must depend on the balancing of intangible items. On the one side are the contribution to the munition industries, the release of factory space, and the economy in fuel and power and overheads. On the other side are the waste of labour through women going back to their homes or to less essential occupations, the anxieties of trying to share out the inadequate war-time cotton output between many urgent claims—anxieties which were after all no different in kind from the anxieties of allocating the munitions made by the war factories in the north-west—and the excessive shrinkage of the cotton industry. Who is to say which side weighs the more heavily?

MANPOWER

The surplus labour that was available to the cotton industry had drifted away in the early months of the war. After concentration the drift, as we have seen, became an avalanche. Thereafter the manpower story is one of unavailing struggle to maintain the slowly declining labour force. These manpower movements are clear from Table 22. Between December 1939 and December 1944 150,000 workers left the cotton industry and as this figure takes no account of the 50,000 unemployed in September 1939 the total loss to the cotton industry was 200,000 or nearly half the pre-war labour force.

The loss of labour to the Services and to war factories inevitably meant that the average age of the insured labour force steadily increased. In 1939 nearly a quarter of the industry's women workers were under twenty-one. By 1945 only a fifth were under twenty-one and nearly a third were over forty. As for men, nearly half of them in 1939 were between twenty and forty years old. By 1945 over half the men were over forty and less than a quarter were between twenty and forty. This contributed to the war-time fall in the productivity of the cotton industry's labour force. The high proportion of women—many of them married—in the industry[1] made it particularly difficult to enforce longer hours and overtime.

---

[1] In 1937, 238,000 of the 432,600 workers in cotton spinning and weaving (insured in the industry, including unemployed) were women between 18 and 59. Of these 124,000 were married or widowed, i.e. out of every 100 workers, roughly fifty-six were women, thirty of them married. In 1943 138,000 of the 223,800 insured workers were women; of these 71,000 were married or widowed, i.e. out of every 100 workers, sixty-two were women, thirty-three of whom were married. Ministry of Labour figures.

Employment in the Cotton Industry (in thousands)[1]

(*Operatives at work*)

TABLE 22

		Dec. 1939	Dec. 1940	Dec. 1941	Dec. 1942	Dec. 1943	Dec. 1944	Dec. 1945
Cotton and staple fibre spinning	Males	47·8	46·0*	28·2	27·3	25·3	24·9	29·3
	Females	80·9	79·0*	49·2	51·0	46·6	45·7	55·1
	Total	128·7	125·0	77·4	78·3	71·9	70·6	84·4
Waste spinning	Males	4·6	4·5*	2·9	2·9	2·8	2·7	3·0
	Females	2·8	2·8*	1·9	1·8	1·8	1·8	1·9
	Total	7·4	7·3	4·8	4·7	4·6	4·5	4·9
Doubling	Males	9·5	9·0*	6·1	5·8	5·4	5·2	5·3
	Females	22·2	22·0*	21·1	19·8	20·0	20·2	19·6
	Total	31·7	31·0	27·2	25·6	25·4	25·4	24·9
Total yarn production (spinning, waste, spinning, doubling)	Males	61·9	59·5*	37·2	36·0	33·5	32·8	37·6
	Females	105·9	103·8*	72·1	72·6	68·4	67·7	76·6
	Total	167·8	163·3	109·3	108·6	101·9	100·5	114·2
Cotton and rayon weaving	Males	57·1	55·0*	33·2	30·8	28·5	30·6	31·7
	Females	107·3	105·0*	75·0	72·8	65·4	76·1	76·1
	Total	164·4	160·0	108·2	103·6	93·9	106·7	107·8
Cotton and rayon finishing	Males	39·4	39·0*	34·0*	23·0*	23·0*	21·2	23·9
	Females	15·5	15·0*	14·0	12·0*	10·0	8·8	9·8
	Total	54·9	54·0*	48·0*	35·0*	33·0*	30·0	33·7
GRAND TOTAL (all sections)	Males	158·4	153·5	104·4	89·8	85·0	84·6	93·2
	Females	228·7	223·8	161·1	157·4	143·8	152·6	162·5
	Total	387·1	377·3	265·5	247·2	228·8	237·2	255·7

* Estimated.   *Source:* Cotton Control

The decline in the labour force and in its productivity was reflected in falling cotton production. The most severe labour shortage in the cotton industry throughout the war was in the spinning section and particularly in the card rooms. Inadequate output in other sections of the industry was masked to some extent by the yarn shortage.

Average weekly cotton yarn production

TABLE 23   million lbs.

	1939	1940	1941	1942[2]	1943	1944	1945
Average for year	21	22·9	15·8	14·76	14·11	13·39	12·01

[1] Owing to differences in the definition of the cotton industry, the figures of the Cotton Control do not agree with those of the Ministry of Labour. Trends are, however, the same.

[2] The figures from 1942 onwards include spun rayon and mixture yarns.

Average weekly production of cotton, rayon and mixture cloths

TABLE 24						million yards
	1940 (from August to the end of the year)	*1941*	*1942*	*1943*	*1944*	*1945*
Average for year	67·1	47·2	39·5	39·2	37·3	35·6

As production fell and cotton became seriously scarce ideas about the status of the cotton industry in the various scales of priority were altered. During the early part of the war the gloomy pre-war history of the cotton industry had been prominent in officials' minds. Munitions production had been developed in north-west England partly because of its relative safety but also because of the surplus skilled labour available there. This surplus was indeed soon sucked into war production, but it was some time before a new and startling fact sank in: the cotton industry no longer had a reservoir of labour on which to draw. As cotton output became inadequate for essential needs it was clear that cotton could no longer be regarded as primarily a civilian industry. It was in every sense vital to the war effort.

Concentration in the cotton industry had not yet been completed when it was recognised that the industry's labour force must be protected. The first task was to prevent wastage. Later, attempts were made to recruit more labour and to increase the output of the existing labour force.

To prevent wastage the Essential Work Order was applied to the industry. The Cotton Control asked for it to be applied early in the concentration process, but the spinning and doubling sections of the industry were not scheduled under the Order until October 1941, the weaving section until January 1942, and the finishing section until May 1943. Where the industry received advance notice of the Government's intention to apply the Essential Work Order the drift from the mills was for a time positively accelerated. But once the Order was in force it may well have acted as a brake on further movements from the industry. The manpower figures make it clear, however, that the Order was not enough to prevent the industry's labour force from falling.

Scheduling under the Essential Work Order was intended to stop the drift into other industrial occupations. Meanwhile the Cotton Control was urging that the loss of cotton workers to the Services should also be stopped. Since men were mainly supervisors or mechanics, the call up of a man might seriously damage a mill's output. It was not until 1944, however, that the Ministry of Labour felt able to apply this protection to male cotton workers.

At the beginning of 1942, however, the cotton industry had been granted a form of protection that ranked high in manpower circles. The spinning, doubling and weaving sections had been placed on the list of vital war industries. This meant that women employed in the industry were exempt from being called up and could not be transferred to other work; moreover, men and women registered under the Registration for Employment Orders could be directed into the industry if they were suitable. Probably this move had some good psychological effects and did something to reduce wastage. But its main results were disappointing; by May 1942 output had declined again.

The Ministry of Labour and the Cotton Control now decided to take positive steps to increase the labour force. It was agreed that about 3,000 key workers, mostly men, should be released from the Royal Ordnance factories and other war factories in Lancashire in order to return to the cotton industry. Other cotton workers were to be released from non-essential industries. Another step was to reopen a few of the mills closed under concentration in areas where there were pockets of immobile labour.

A minor move was to begin spare-time shifts wherever possible. A few spinning mills which were very short of card-room workers started evening shifts; former card-room workers who could not work during the day were employed between 5.30 p.m. and 9.30 p.m. for five days a week. Although the number of these evening shift workers was small—probably not more than 400 at any one time—they had more than a proportionate effect on production because they filled vacancies in certain crucial processes and enabled the firms to employ their day-time labour to better advantage.

All these attempts to increase the cotton industry's labour force met with some small success. In December 1942 there were 1,000 more workers in the spinning section and another 1,000 more in weaving than there had been in May. But wastage was still so high that efforts to recruit more workers had to be intensified if the labour force was not to drop again. In early 1943 therefore further measures were agreed. The Cotton Board established a Recruiting and Training Department to encourage the recruitment of juveniles.[1] Ex-cotton workers who became available were to be returned to the industry and all ex-cotton workers employed in closed mills on maintenance work were to be directed back to production work. In September 1943 a special registration was carried out of all women aged eighteen to fifty-five who had had at least six months' experience as cotton workers since 1935. It was hoped to direct a large proportion of the 95,000 women who registered back to work in the cotton mills even if they were working in munitions. The results, however, were very meagre. About seventy per cent. of the women were either

---

[1] After the first year of the Department's life 716 juveniles entered the industry in the first quarter of 1944 compared with 245 in the first quarter of 1943 (*The Economist*, 13th August 1944).

married women with young children or were medically unfit to return to the industry. Of the rest, only about one in ten could be
persuaded or directed back to cotton.

In 1943 the supply departments also agreed to help the cotton industry by releasing workers under a quota system. The Ministry of
Supply would release 350 a month from munitions factories working
for them, the Ministry of Aircraft Production 50 and the Admiralty
50. These quotas proved difficult to apply partly because of the
effect on urgent munitions work, but even more so because many
workers, even when released by the supply departments, could not be
directed to the cotton mills.

In all the attempts to get labour back to the cotton industry the
lesson was the same. The cotton industry was by now unpopular and
when it competed with munitions work it could not attract additional
labour. Despite all the efforts of the Ministry of Labour the industry's
labour force continued to fall and only increased very slowly when
munitions work in Lancashire declined.

Side by side with the effort to get more labour into the cotton mills
there had been attempts to increase the output of the labour already
there. In 1942 the cotton industry was asked to work longer hours,
train substitutes, improve amenities, etc. Overtime was introduced in
the spinning sections in 1942, 1943 and 1944; during the summer
months hours were extended from forty-eight to fifty-two a week. The
results were small. In each of the three years weekly production increased by 6 per cent. when overtime began compared with an
increase of $8\frac{1}{3}$ per cent. in working hours. The weekly gain then
declined until just before overtime stopped, when it was hardly
noticeable. When overtime ceased production fell by 6 per cent. and
then gradually recovered. On balance there was a small net gain in
production per operative per annum, but probably more important
than this increase were the consequent earlier deliveries of yarn. Overtime was not generally worked in the other sections of the cotton
industry.

The Cotton Control took the lead in encouraging firms to improve
amenities and welfare facilities. It helped them to find billets, open
day nurseries and arrange transport for workers. Mills undertook
many schemes designed to improve or install air conditioning and
dust-extraction plant, canteens, lavatories, first-aid rooms, etc.

No dramatic attempt was however made during the war to increase
productivity in the cotton industry. The whole subject was brought
to the fore in the summer of 1944 by the publication of the Platt
Report.[1] When in combined discussions between London and
Washington it seemed that joint cotton textile supplies would be too

---

[1] *Report of the Cotton Textile Mission to the United States of America, March–April 1944.*
(H.M.S.O. 1944.)

low for Allied needs, it was suggested that a small mission led by the Cotton Controller should go to the United States to investigate cotton production methods there; productivity of the British industry might be increased by adopting some of these methods. The Controller, Sir Frank Platt, therefore led a mission of seven cotton experts to the United States. Their report on American and British production methods drew some startling conclusions. They concluded that in normal conditions British production per man per hour was less than in America by eighteen to forty-nine per cent. in spinning and by fifty-six to sixty-seven per cent. in weaving. It followed that for a given output a much greater labour force was required in British mills.

It would be out of place to analyse here in any detail the conclusions of the Platt Report. The central argument was that American production methods were highly mechanical and were geared to economise labour. British methods, on the other hand, were geared to prodigality of labour and economy in machinery. At a time when the days of a cheap and plentiful supply of labour seemed to be over for Lancashire these conclusions and arguments about their validity were most important. But they were important rather for the days of reconstruction. However much anxiety the labour shortage in the cotton industry was causing it was clearly impossible to re-equip the industry with high-speed automatic machinery and modernise or rebuild the mills in war-time. The big debate was left for the future and Government officials meanwhile had to struggle with humdrum and piecemeal, and usually unsuccessful, efforts to stop the cotton industry's labour force from falling.

(ii)

The Rayon Industry

ITS STRUCTURE AND CONTROL

Rayon production is a chemical rather than a textile process, but its history follows logically after cotton because most rayon was spun or woven on cotton machinery and because rayon yarns and cloths were largely controlled by the Cotton Control and Cotton Board. Rayon is also used in the silk, linen and woollen industries, but in smaller quantities. It is produced in two forms—*rayon staple* consisting of short lengths of fibre which have to be spun into a yarn, and *continuous filament* which is already yarn but needs further processing, such as throwing (doubling and twisting) or winding before it can be woven or knitted. This preparation of the filament is usually carried out by the rayon producers so that it is ready for immediate insertion in the loom. Continuous filament was before the war the more im-

portant of the two fibres; in 1939 120 million lbs. of continuous filament were produced and 60 million lbs. of rayon staple. There are two
main types of rayon produced in the United Kingdom—viscose
(which represented before the war eighty-five per cent. of production)
and acetate. Rayon was an expanding industry before the war; in the
ten years up to 1939 production increased from 56 million lbs. to
180 million lbs. Production of rayon in the United Kingdom is in the
hands of only ten firms, two of which produce a major proportion of
the entire output.

During the war rayon output fell. Rayon staple production, which
is economical in the use of labour because it needs no winding or
throwing, maintained its 1939 level until 1942 when it fell to a steady
annual rate of 50 million lbs. Continuous filament production had
fallen from its pre-war level of 120 million lbs. to 70 million lbs. by
1943. Rayon supplies were however relatively plentiful in the early
war years and no direct control was imposed on the industry until
the introduction of clothes rationing made it necessary. Service
requirements for ordinary rayon (as against rayon strong yarn, which
will be discussed below) were small; as late as 1942 it was estimated that
the home and export markets took ninety per cent. of rayon production.

Until the summer of 1941 rayon supplies were restricted at only
two points. From April 1940 onwards the supply of rayon cloth to the
home market was restricted with the other textiles under the Limitation of Supplies Orders.[1] In addition the rayon producers exercised a
voluntary control over the supply of rayon yarn by fixing allocations
for the home and export trades and also for each rayon-consuming
industry. This was not very satisfactory for the Board of Trade who
had no precise information about the size of these allocations or the
consumption of rayon by the weaving, hosiery or other industries. In
June 1941, for instance, the Board of Trade said the producers' allocations for export appeared to be considerably higher than for a
corresponding period in 1940,[2] while home trade was only getting
about two-thirds of the limitation of supplies quota; 'it is not by any
means certain', thought the Board, 'that the ratio so decided on is in
the best national interest'. Moreover, as there was no control over the
use of rayon there was no assurance that rayon output, which was
now declining, would go to meet essential needs. As soon as the
Board of Trade became responsible for honouring the issue of clothes
coupons they felt they must be able to guarantee a supply of rayon
for the home market and therefore to restrict the uses to which rayon
was put. The utility scheme, together with planned production in the
cotton industry, made closer planning of rayon yarn and cloth
production inevitable.

---

[1] See Chapter V.
[2] See p. 63 for the expansion of rayon exports.

2A

The first problem—the allocation of rayon in accordance with Government policy—was simplified by the small number of producers in the industry. The Board of Trade, together with the Ministry of Supply,[1] agreed to supervise an unofficial control run by the producers rather than impose an official one. The producers agreed under a voluntary arrangement to deliver supplies in accordance with allocations approved by the two departments. For this purpose they set up at their own expense in November 1941 a Rayon Allocation Office in Manchester which controlled the uses to which rayon could be put by a system of approved orders as in the case of the cotton industry. The work of the Rayon Allocation Office will be discussed in detail in Chapter XVII. Briefly, the Board of Trade, in consultation with the producers, agreed the level of output for each four-monthly period, taking into account the estimated coupon requirements, Service needs and export demands for rayon and the level of production of the previous period. Regular figures of current production and estimates of future production were supplied to the Board by the producers. The total estimated output of rayon was then allocated through the Rayon Allocation Office to the various consumers—the export trade,[2] the cotton- or wool-weaving industries, the hosiery, lace and narrow fabrics industries, etc.

The bulk of continuous filament rayon was supplied to cotton weavers and the bulk of rayon staple fibre was spun and woven by cotton firms. Smaller quantities were, however, spun or woven on silk or woollen machinery. This rayon was controlled through the Silk and Rayon Controller and the Wool Controller respectively. Allocations of rayon, to be used for approved purposes only, were made to firms which had used rayon in the standard period. The only exception was long staple yarn (rayon spun from staple more than 3 inches in length) which was controlled when spun on silk- or cotton-spinning machinery, but was not controlled until almost the end of the war when spun on woollen or linen machinery. The Wool Control allocated it to the spinners but maintained that the total quantity involved was so small that it was not worth while setting up complicated administrative machinery to restrict the use of the spun yarn to essential purposes. This small loophole in control led to a disproportionate number of complaints throughout 1943 and 1944. Weavers in Lancashire and in Northern Ireland could get long staple yarn from the Yorkshire spinners while the Lancashire spinners had their production of rayon yarn completely controlled. The Board of Trade also complained that sheets made with the long staple yarn were

---

[1] The Ministry of Supply was interested in rayon, partly because of the rayon strong yarn programme and partly because the Cotton and Silk Controls were its responsibility.

[2] Exports were fixed at their 1941 level, but no export licensing system was introduced at first.

selling at too high a price—nine guineas a pair. On 1st March 1945, owing to the shortage of wool-spinning capacity, the Wool Controller prohibited the spinning of any non-wool yarn on wool machinery except under licence. This did not diminish the quantity of long staple yarn being spun nor restrict its price,[1] but it did restrict its use to purposes which the Control could approve. One of the results of this 'free' long staple yarn combined with the shortage of flax was that Northern Ireland became a pioneer in the development of long staple rayon cloth, not as a substitute for wool, but as a textile in its own right.[2]

Rayon waste was controlled from November 1942 onwards in order to make sure that it was used for essential purposes. Spinners and weavers had to sell it to one of three selected waste merchants who had to make monthly returns to the Cotton Control and to sell all spinnable waste back to the cotton industry at a fixed price. There were similar arrangements with the Silk and Wool Controls.

Perhaps the most important rayon programme outside the province of the Rayon Allocation Office during the war was that for rayon strong yarn. This yarn is of very high tensile strength and is produced by a relatively easy adaptation of ordinary rayon machinery. Its chief use was for heavy-duty tyres. After the loss of Malaya, when economy in crude rubber became urgent, rayon strong yarn tyre fabric was technically approved for the heavy military and aircraft tyre programmes because it stands up to the higher temperatures generated by synthetic rubber tyres better than cotton casings. Other uses for rayon strong yarn were for a fine, very strong yarn for supply-dropping parachutes[3] and as a silk substitute for insulating delicate wires in radio, signalling and other electrical apparatus. Some rayon yarn was also needed for essential home needs such as surgical sutures, oiled rayon instead of oiled silk, and rayon grit gauge for the abrasives industry and for conveyor belting in mines and quarries. A small quantity of rayon strong yarn was allocated for export under Board of Trade direction as to quantity and destination.

Production of rayon strong yarn did not get well under way until the end of 1942. Output rose from 710,000 lbs. in 1941 to 4 million lbs. in 1943 and to nearly 10 million lbs. in 1944. From 1942 this programme competed, especially for labour, with the ordinary rayon production for civilian uses; inevitably civilian consumption bore the

---

[1] It was costing 4s. to 5s. a pound to spin in Yorkshire. It could have been spun for 2s. 9d. a pound in Northern Ireland, but the Board of Trade would not agree to any reduction in the flax-spinning programme.

[2] See the article by H. E. Wadsworth, 'The Utility Cloth and Clothing Scheme', *Review of Economic Studies*, Vol. XVI (2), No. 40.

[3] Nylon was the only approved silk substitute for man-carrying parachutes. Nylon was an entirely new material to United Kingdom industry; production rose in the war from nothing to one million lbs. a year, none of it for civilian consumption.

brunt of any general short-fall in production. The rayon strong yarn programme as a whole was the direct responsibility of the Raw Materials Department of the Ministry of Supply, not the Board of Trade. No direct control was imposed, but early in 1943 the Ministry of Supply made an agreement with the half-dozen or so firms producing rayon strong yarn whereby they made returns of stocks and output to the Silk and Rayon Controller who issued licences to acquire rayon strong yarn to all users. This arrangement continued until July 1945 when the allocation of rayon strong yarn became a function of the Rayon Allocation Office.

LABOUR

The rayon industry was never concentrated in the accepted sense of the word. For any normal scheme applied to the rayon industry would have forced production entirely into the hands of the two main producers; the combined output of all the small firms would have been insufficient to meet essential demands. Moreover, rayon plants would have deteriorated very severely by acid corrosion if left idle for any prolonged period. Instead of concentration, therefore, there was a spread-over system. One small rayon firm was closed down, but for the rest each producer's output was cut; in one case the cut was as much as forty per cent., but more usually it was about fifteen per cent.

The amount of labour supposed to be released as a result of this agreement was about 3,500. As long as rayon production was thought to be above minimum needs, rayon producers were expected to make further labour releases. Immediately before the outbreak of war 33,000 workers were employed in the production of rayon staple and in the production and processing of rayon yarn. By the end of 1944 the figure (including those working on rayon strong yarn) was 19,500.

By the end of 1943, indeed, there were strong complaints of labour shortage. Rayon producers said they could not meet minimum essential requirements for the civilian programme unless they received help in making up labour wastage. Any labour available was going to the production of rayon strong yarn and the labour force of ordinary production was continuing to fall even though working conditions and wages were reasonably good. Poor quality recruits and the loss of experienced rayon workers were also lessening output despite the long hours worked—fifty-six hours a week on shifts.

Something was done by transferring some production to easier labour areas. But it was also necessary to ask the Ministry of Labour for definite help. By September 1944, after protracted discussions, an 'approved labour force' was fixed for each factory.[1] Any labour over

---

[1] Later some approved labour forces were increased to include rayon strong yarn operatives.

the approved labour force could be withdrawn by the Ministry of Labour; but, if there was no excess, labour could only be withdrawn by prior substitution, except for men of military age.

By April 1945, when munitions cuts were releasing labour, the Board of Trade with the Ministry of Labour agreed to increases in the approved labour forces for the rayon producers varying from ten per cent. in difficult to twenty per cent. in easy labour areas. The purpose of these increases was to build up rayon production to meet a forty-eight coupon ration and to offset the shorter working hours now proposed for the industry. It was hoped to increase production by fifty per cent. Regional or second labour preference was given where necessary to build up the labour force to the expanded approved labour force or even over it in areas where there were few competing demands. In addition, ex-rayon workers released from munitions industries received priority in order of discharge and were sent back into the rayon industry unless they were needed to fill skilled preference vacancies. The expanded approved labour force figure had in fact now become a target—a target which must be hit if rayon were to get its share of the post-war export trade.

During the war rayon and cotton cloth production had been handled by the Board of Trade and the Cotton Control largely as one problem. Utility fabrics in rayon and cotton had, as we shall see, been planned together and substituted for each other when necessary.[1] This had masked to some extent the problems of the rayon industry's relationship with the cotton industry, but during the last two years of the war there were attempts by rayon producers to seek a certain amount of autonomy. This was one of the problems that the textile industries had to face in the immediate post-war years.

(iii)

The Silk Industry

A study of the war-time textile industries is not complete without a reference to silk. This industry is divided into two main sections. The raw silk industry weaves or knits the continuous silk thread which has been reeled on to bobbins from the cocoon and has then been 'thrown' (twisted, etc.) by silk throwsters. The spun silk industry uses 'waste' silk, i.e. the shorter ends from the cocoons which are combed into sliver, spun like other textile fibres and then woven or knitted.

For the first year of the war there was no problem of supply and the civilian and export trades continued on a peace-time basis. Service

---

[1] See Chapter XVII for a discussion of rayon utility.

requirements were relatively small, exports could be justified on currency grounds, and alternative sources of employment were not very readily available for the labour engaged on silk. The only restriction was that imports of raw silk for the civilian and export trades were kept at their pre-war level of 5 million lbs. These favourable circumstances rapidly disappeared. Service requirements expanded, munitions and the Services began to absorb a large part of the industry's labour force, and direct purchases from Japan became increasingly difficult. The Treasury did not consider the foreign currency gained by silk exports sufficient to recompense dollar expenditure on indirect purchase of raw silk through the United States. At the end of 1940 imports were cut by a half. As soon as Japan entered the war all waste silk stocks were immobilised for Service use, the use of raw silk for the export trade was forbidden, and a veto was imposed on the use of raw silk for all but essential civilian purposes.[1] One of the essential purposes for which silk was still permitted was silk bolting cloth (used in flour milling, abrasives and in textile printing trades) which had previously been imported from Switzerland. Its manufacture was now developed satisfactorily in this country for all essential requirements, except for some of the finest sizes. The silk processing industry, in a considerably concentrated form, was chiefly engaged on silk substitutes—mainly nylon and rayon. Consumption of raw silk fell to less than one-tenth of its pre-war level. The Silk and Rayon Control licensed all imports and issued licences to firms to convert silk into yarn and yarn into cloth.

These restrictions continued until 1944 when a technical decision made by the Ministry of Aircraft Production on the superiority of nylon compared to silk for parachutes released a certain amount of labour and capacity from Service needs and enabled the silk export trade to be partially resumed, with an upper limit of 300,000 lbs. annually. This limit was removed in August 1945 when raw and waste silk production was restored to private firms on the understanding that they would export two-thirds of the manufactured raw silk and half of the waste silk.

(iv)
The Wool Industry

ITS STRUCTURE AND CONTROL

The great bulk of the wool manufactured in Britain is processed in the West Riding of Yorkshire, though there are also smaller centres of the industry in Scotland, the West of England, Leicester and

---

[1] The use of silk was not even permitted for medal ribbons or dental floss.

Lancashire.[1] The total 1938 labour force of the industry was about 230,000 (about sixty per cent. of the pre-war cotton labour force).[2] In 1938 nearly 48,000 insured workers were unemployed, but by 1939 this figure had dropped to 14,000. The wool industry, like cotton, is particularly dependent on women workers. The average ratio in the wool industry was before the war 130 women to every 100 men employed compared with a national ratio of 35 : 100.

Raw wool, which can be either merino or crossbred,[3] is received by the woolcomber in the state in which it was packed in the country of origin. Yarn can be manufactured either on the 'woollen principle' or on the 'worsted principle'. These are differentiated partly by the manufacturing processes employed and partly by the raw materials used. In the worsted section of the industry wool and other fibres such as mohair and alpaca go through a series of processes of which the intermediate products are tops and noils. The raw material must be of good even length and is usually merino or fine crossbred wool. After sorting, blending and scouring the wool is carded and then combed to separate the shorter fibres or noils from the long fibres or tops. The noils are disposed of to the woollen trade or the feltmakers while the tops become the raw material for worsted yarn spinning the object of which is to keep the fibres as nearly parallel as possible. The worsted section is organised horizontally in the sense that the manufacture of tops, yarns and cloths is nowadays usually undertaken by separate firms. In the woollen section a wide range of materials, chiefly raw wool but including fibres recovered from rags, is spun into yarn without any intermediate product corresponding to tops. The proportion of crossbred material used is higher than in the worsted section. Although some firms mix in recovered wool (shoddy or mungo) and other materials, other firms use raw wool almost exclusively. In woollen manufacture the fibres are of varying lengths and lie more irregularly than in worsted spinning. The industry is organised vertically in the sense that all the processes are usually undertaken by one firm.

After yarn manufacture the weaving and finishing processes of

---

[1] Before the war ninety-two per cent. of the worsted section and two-thirds of the woollen section were in the West Riding. In towns like Bradford and Huddersfield forty per cent. of the insured population is employed in the wool textile industry.

[2] Ministry of Labour figures for insured workers.

[3] Merino is a fine, long staple, soft-handling wool which is all imported, mainly from Australia but also from South Africa. The modern tendency is to use it increasingly. The proportion of merino tops produced has increased from twenty-seven per cent. in 1924 to fifty per cent. in 1937 and sixty-five per cent. at the end of the war (*Wool Working Party Report*, Table 23). Crossbred is coarser, short-stapled, brighter in appearance and crisp to handle and is imported mainly from New Zealand. The home clip (about ten per cent. of total wool consumption) is also crossbred. There was a shortage of crossbred wool during the war owing to the demand for it for Service contracts, e.g. greatcoatings, etc. See *Wool Working Party Report*, Appendix VIII, for a full description of the various wool processes.

both woollen and worsted materials are similar. Cloth made from worsted yarn is usually hardwearing and of very good quality. It is used extensively for men's suitings, etc. Although cloths made from woollen yarn are in general less expensive than worsted cloths, they are not necessarily inferior. More varied effects in colour and design and finish can be obtained with woollen cloths—for example, in overcoats, women's dresses, tweeds, blankets and billiard cloths.

In the wool industry generally associations of employers are exceptionally strong.[1] In 1919 a Wool Textile Delegation had been formed of representatives from each of the main trade associations.[2] In 1937 the Board of Trade asked the Delegation to prepare a scheme for the control of the wool industry in the event of war. A scheme for a Wool Control was approved in the following year; it was worked out in considerable detail so that the Control could, if necessary, become the sole owner and importer of all raw wool on the day war broke out. The Control was to distribute the wool either in its raw state or in the form of tops and noils. On the production side the Control was to be responsible up to and including the finished cloth stage. Premises for the Control were earmarked, the necessary licences and forms were printed, arrangements were made for setting up advisory committees for each main section of the industry and a list was prepared of wool industrialists who would be capable and willing to staff the senior posts in the Control. Early in 1939 some of these officials-designate were asked to arrange the bulk purchase of the materials and the production of woollen cloth necessary to equip the newly-enrolled 200,000 National Servicemen and 270,000 additional Territorials.

On 4th September 1939 the Wool Control came into being. Like the other raw material Controls, it was part of the newly-established Raw Materials Department of the Ministry of Supply and the Controller was responsible to the Minister. Under the ægis of the Ministry the Control exercised its most important functions—the importation of raw wool and the distribution of wool, tops and noils in the United Kingdom. The Control also had close relations with the departments responsible for clothing and equipping the various Services, for the Control in effect placed all Government contracts.[3] Early in the war, too, the Control began to have close contacts with the Board of Trade about the problems of the export trade. There was also consultation about civilian needs—about the quantity of raw wool that should be provided for the home market. But the Board did not for some time concern themselves closely with other aspects of the problem of

---

[1] *Wool Working Party Report*, p. 119.

[2] Except commission dyers and finishers.

[3] To be precise, the contracts were placed by representatives of the contracting departments stationed in the Control. But these representatives normally did little more than ratify what the Control had done.

clothing the civilian in war-time, such as the production of the right types of cloth at the right prices. From the summer of 1941 onwards, however, this problem came to the fore and as the Board of Trade developed their clothing policy they became dependent upon the Wool Control as well as upon the Cotton Control and the Cotton Board for implementing it.

It is impossible to do justice to the activities of the Wool Control within the narrow limits of this chapter. We are concerned primarily with those aspects of the Control that were important to the Board of Trade. We shall therefore describe very briefly the methods of allocating wool, and the history of the concentration scheme and of labour withdrawals; in Chapter XVII there will be a fuller discussion of utility wool cloth. Thus we can do no more than mention in passing the greatest achievements of the Control—its operations as a merchant and its handling of Government contracts. As we have seen, these activities of the Control had begun before war broke out. They very soon became much more widespread. The Control was responsible for buying raw wool overseas and at home and in the early days of the war the wool clips of Australia and New Zealand were purchased and the home clip requisitioned.[1] The Control was also responsible for arranging imports. As for internal distribution, within three months of the beginning of the war the Control was operating as a top maker[2] and was the sole importer and primary distributor of all wool, tops and noils in the United Kingdom. The Control was the absolute owner of all wool up to the top stage. The Government contracts that the Control handled were very various; they were not only for many different types of clothing—ranging from equipment for arctic conditions to jungle-green equipment for Burma—but also for such things as special fabrics for self-sealing petrol tanks and fabrics which could be substituted for rubber. Some of these fabrics were entirely new to the wool industry; for example, the fabric for petrol tanks was two and a half times the thickness of blanket cloth and the Ministry of Aircraft Production required for it an accuracy within engineering limits.

In general, it can be said that the Wool Control delivered the goods. Service, civilian and overseas demands were in total met and the output of the industry continued to increase until about 1942, despite large-scale labour withdrawals. This was no mean achievement when the complexity of the industry, the diversity of the raw materials, the different and changing demands, and, above all, the sheer volume of work handled by the Control is considered. During the war, for example, the Control purchased $10\frac{1}{2}$ thousand million

---

[1] Arrangements covering the South African clip were made about a year later.

[2] In this context a top maker means a merchant, not a manufacturer. The Wool Control had wool combed on commission, but did not itself own and operate wool-combing plant.

lbs. of raw wool, placed Government contracts for 540 million linear yards of cloth and 76½ million blankets and produced and sold 1,138 million lbs. of tops and noils.[1]

The Control was divided into two sections—a Directorate of Wool Supplies which was responsible for all raw materials and the making of tops and a Directorate of Wool Textile Production which was responsible for the production of all manufactured and semi-manufactured articles. Tops were made on commission for the Control —the rates being settled by the Ministry of Supply costing officers. Top-makers[2] were organised in groups with a parent top-maker responsible to the Control for the whole group's output. Committees staffed by Control officials and the industry examined samples and reduced the great number of peace-time top qualities to a limited number of standardised 'pool' tops which were an adequate variety for war-time production. Tops were sold by the Control direct to the user without the intervention of the merchant (except as the direct agent of the user for purposes of selection, sorting, warehousing, etc.).[3]

We must now consider how wool was allocated, how rations to firms were issued, and how the civilian and export allocations were handled. The Materials Committee did not introduce for wool a system of detailed departmental allocations with 'symbols' as in the case of cotton; for there was never a serious gap between total output and minimum demands. Total supplies of raw wool were plentiful throughout the war, though difficulties were caused by shortages of crossbred wool; the demand for this type of wool rose in the war as it was used for heavy garments such as Service overcoats. And until the end of the war the wool industry did not suffer from a general labour shortage; only in worsted spinning did labour shortage cause serious trouble. The wool programme was discussed from time to time by the Materials Committee and the stock position and import programme were broadly related to the demands for Service contracts, export requirements and (after the first year) the home civil programme. Usually the gap between demands and production was met by reducing stocks; but sometimes additional shipping was allocated or the demands were scaled down.

The Materials Committee's allocations were only a rough guide to make sure that demands were not outrunning supplies. The discussions in the Committee no doubt deterred departments from entering into too fierce competition with each other; but the determining fac-

---

[1] As an official of the Wool Control wrote: 'The magnitude of the administrative task will be appreciated when it is realised that the mass of wool recorded consisted of some thousands of different types, each lot of which required consideration before processing with consequent detailed recording at each stage until finally sold by the Control.'

See Appendix 10 for figures of the war-time activities of the wool industry.

[2] Similar arrangements were made for other sorters and commission combers.

[3] The wool merchants remained out of business until the end of March 1945.

tors in meeting demands for wool were the programmes discussed by departments individually with the Wool Control and the amount of wool and other raw materials released to the industry each period by the Wool Control through a Joint Rationing Committee.[1] The Control was perfectly prepared to take full responsibility for meeting demands once it had agreed them.

So far as direct Government orders (which included A.R.P. and the fire services as well as the armed forces) were concerned, an allocation of wool was made in full by the Control to a firm which had been given a contract. In order to distribute contracts as widely[2] as possible the Control was advised by trade committees on the capacity available in each main section of the industry. The Control also co-operated with the buying officers of the various Government departments to break down the somewhat rigid specifications insisted on originally. Later on the Control succeeded in obtaining a good deal of discretion in the actual choice of mixtures suitable for a particular use. Many firms without previous experience in this class of work—Service cloths are in most cases heavier and coarser than average wool cloths and use a higher proportion of crossbred wool—were assisted to adapt their machinery and methods. The Control progressed the contracts and was responsible for keeping delivery dates. Branches of the Ministry of Supply Contracts Department and of the Ministry of Supply Costing Section were set up within the Control to facilitate the placing of the formal contracts. In this way the Wool Control was able to plan production and balance the use of raw materials on a long-term basis. Despite difficulties such as labour losses the supply of Service cloth was maintained throughout the war without resort to compulsory powers.

The Wool Control delegated its responsibility for other production to the Joint Rationing Committee which thus became responsible for all production in the wool industry except Government contracts and top-making, although the Wool Control staff did the detailed administrative work. The Joint Rationing Committee consisted of two representatives appointed by each local rationing committee together with three representatives of the trade unions. The members of the local rationing committees were nominated by the appropriate employers' organisations in each section of the industry (e.g. spinning) or each geographical area (e.g. the West of England). The committees were trade bodies with no legal authority; they depended therefore on the co-operation of the industry.

---

[1] See also Chapter XVII, pp. 451-9.

[2] For technical reasons it was inefficient to concentrate Government orders on some firms and leave others to supply civilian and export needs. As Government cloths are heavier than average, a spinning firm, for example, engaged on Service contracts would find itself short of enough preparatory machinery to keep all its spindles running. The Control's aim was therefore to use as many firms as possible.

The Joint Rationing Committee distributed wool and other subsidiary textile raw materials[1] for all home and export requirements to the sectional and area rationing committees in accordance with the pre-war consumption of the respective sections and districts. The local committees then made allocations to each individual firm. The total volume of materials to be available in each four-monthly period was decided by the Controller himself—in consultation with the Wool Advisory Council[2]—in the light of the stock position, expected imports, the probable demands for Government contracts, etc. The ration for each individual firm was then worked out. Machinery employed on Government contracts was excluded from the calculations. Machinery engaged on export work was then provided with rations according to the quantities that had been made available to the Rationing Committee. Machinery producing for the home market was the residuary legatee, receiving such percentage dividend of pre-war consumption as could be provided out of the material available.[3]

This rationing system was essentially a 'fair shares' scheme whose general object was to make sure that no firm suffered more than another. Although the firms with modern and efficient machinery and a high output per unit got more generous rations than the less efficient firms, the chief defect of the scheme was that it kept the least efficient firms in being when it might have been more in the national interest to concentrate rations (and therefore labour) on the firms whose output per machine was highest. The chief merit of the scheme was probably its elasticity, which enabled it without major alterations to cope with the various problems created by changing war-time conditions such as labour withdrawals, the utility programme, the demobilisation clothing programme, etc. The Wool Control did not have to extend its power over firms or alter its original rationing arrangements; throughout the war the industry itself planned its own

---

[1] The materials rationed fell under twelve heads: wool, tops, noils, worsted yarn, woollen yarn, worsted waste, woollen waste, and shoddy. Raw cotton, cotton waste, cotton yarn and rayon yarn were rationed by the Committee within the global allocation given to the wool industry by the Cotton Control.

[2] This consisted of representatives of employers, employees and officials of the Control.

[3] The process of arriving at this 'percentage dividend' was complicated. In the spinning and weaving sections the raw material used in a pre-war year by a particular firm was divided by the number of active machines in use, thus giving a theoretical consumption figure per unit of machinery per year on the type of work the firm was doing before the war. The number of machines required for Government contracts was then excluded, and the number of active and inactive machines was then multiplied by the theoretical consumption figure per unit, and a theoretical consumption figure obtained for all the machines in a firm available for home and export production. The raw material available in a particular period was then related to the total theoretical consumption figure for all the firms in an area or section, and the resulting proportion applied to the theoretical consumption figure of each firm. Thus a ration for each firm was achieved. The rationing system for other sections of the industry was broadly similar, but, for example, in the wool-combing and top-making sections the ration was based on the actual consumption of raw material in a two- or four-year pre-war period and not on a theoretical consumption figure.

production, in accordance with the Control's changing instructions, under the Joint Rationing Committee schemes. To officials in the Board of Trade the position was not altogether satisfactory. For some time, indeed, they could not discover the rate at which rations of wool were actually being distributed to the industry and consequently they found it difficult to be satisfied that the home market was not getting either too large or too small a proportion of the total output. After the introduction of clothes rationing the Board of Trade did manage to obtain fuller information[1], but not as much as they would have liked.

How were the civilian and export allocations made? The first discussions of the Materials Committee (in the early months of the war) about the allocation of wool were concerned with Service and export requirements only; the home market was left to look after itself. Manufacturers were understood to be receiving enough wool to keep between eighty-five and ninety per cent. of their machinery running to cover both home and export requirements. In order to encourage them to concentrate on exports, manufacturers got 100 per cent. raw material replacements for their export orders and the civilian ration therefore had to bear the full brunt of the cuts—at least on paper. In fact the home market proved more attractive to manufacturers and there was some evidence that home trade wholesalers and retailers were building up stocks of wool textiles while Canadian, United States and other buyers were having difficulty in getting their orders accepted. The ration of raw materials for exports was therefore increased by the Control in March 1940 to 125 per cent. of requirements, provided that the extra raw materials were used in the production of additional exports. At the same time the supplies of wool for the home trade issued by the Control were cut to fifty per cent. of pre-war consumption. Thereafter they were progressively cut, until in February 1941 they were only twenty-two per cent. of pre-war consumption. It is doubtful, however, whether the arrangements for policing these civilian and export allocations were effective.

By the middle of 1941 the general picture had changed: certain large Government contracts had been completed; lend-lease had diminished the importance of the export drive; there was a belief that stocks for the home market in the hands of wholesalers and retailers were by now falling rapidly. Civilian supplies were therefore increased again to thirty-five per cent. of pre-war consumption, a rate which represented 50,000 tons (greasy) of raw wool. The Board of Trade were now more anxious to avoid a shortage of civilian cloth rather than a surplus and, as this rate was insufficient to meet the clothing ration that had been introduced in June 1941, the allocation was

[1] See Chapter XVII, pp. 451–9.

raised to 70,000 tons. In February 1942 it was again increased to 80,000 tons in order to cover errors in the original estimates.

The programme for wool utility cloth,[1] when it was introduced in September 1941 was included in the allocation of raw materials for the home market. Firms that wished to make utility cloth applied to the Wool Control, which was responsible for seeing that applications were sufficient to make the Board of Trade's programme effective. There was, however, no planned production of civilian requirements; orders continued to be placed through normal commercial channels.

It must be emphasised again that the figure allocated by the Materials Committee to the home market was in fact a paper allocation used more as a general guide than as a working figure. The actual rate of supply of cloth did not necessarily match it very closely. As we have seen, the Board of Trade could not discover the rate at which rations of wool were actually being distributed by the Control to the wool industry; but they felt sure that the rate for the home civilian market was much higher, at least until 1942, than the Materials Committee allocation.

Further discussion of the home civilian ration[2] will be found in more detail in Chapter XVII; but it should be noted here that the supply problem was eased for the Board of Trade by the fact that the introduction of utility in February 1942 coincided with a considerable reduction in the Service demands for wool cloth.

So far as exports are concerned, we have already seen that before 1941 manufacturers were encouraged to accept export orders by being given 100 per cent. and later 125 per cent. of their raw material needs. In order to obtain more export orders, two organisations were set up in 1940—the Export Group of the National Wool Textile Executive and the National Wool Textile Export Corporation. These two organisations were, broadly speaking, under the same management.[3] The National Wool Textile Export Corporation was financed by a levy of one-tenth of one per cent. on the value of all wool sold by the Wool Control for processing in the United Kingdom,[4] and its function was to promote the sales abroad of the products of the industry. The function of the Export Group was to encourage such exports, the necessary finance being supplied by the Corporation.[5]

When the export drive temporarily ceased and export licensing was

---

[1] See below, Chapter XVII.

[2] And of the wool utility scheme.

[3] So far as can be discovered each section of the wool trade had its own committee of exporting firms known as a sub-group. These sub-groups elected the Export Group of the National Wool Textile Executive. The second organisation, the National Wool Textile Export Corporation, was composed of sixteen members, seven elected by the Export Group, just mentioned, and five by the Wool Textile Delegation. The other members were either co-opted or represented the Scottish manufacturers and hosiery manufacturers.

[4] Report of the National Wool Textile Export Corporation, 1944–45.

[5] *Board of Trade, Working Party Reports: Wool* (H.M.S.O. 1947), p. 93.

introduced in November 1941, the two organisations were of some assistance to the Board of Trade in fixing market allocations and the individual exporters' allocations. The system was, as we have seen,[1] similar to that for cotton. The Board of Trade fixed an allocation for each market and the Wool Control through the Joint Rationing Committee allocated export quotas to individual manufacturers within the totals determined by the Board. In addition, each market's allocation was divided between all the exporters who had previously traded there. The declared purpose of this arrangement was to preserve all possible export channels. The exporter received an allocation which was a percentage of his base period trade (that is trade in the twelve months ending 31st October 1941). He was then issued with export licences up to the total of his allocation. The allocations could not be interchanged, but if a firm's allocation was less than 500 lbs. it could be transferred to an exporter of cut lengths to whom 500 lbs. might represent a worthwhile trade. There were a few exceptions. Export licences were sometimes issued to firms holding stocks, even if they had no market allocation, or to firms exporting to countries like Abyssinia where there had been no base period trade.[2]

This system continued until the end of the war. In the autumn of 1944 the Export Group opened its own office in New York to publicise British wool textiles and to provide for United Kingdom exporters a market research service supplying up-to-date statistics and information. This was in preparation for the post-war export drive.

We have been considering the allocation of wool between different demands—that is, the core of the control system. Before going on to consider the labour problems of the industry it may be worth reflecting for a few moments on the nature of the control over the wool industry and upon some of the differences between it and the control over the cotton industry. Plans for the Wool Control had been approved a long time before the war and therefore when the Control was born on the outbreak of war it was born with all its teeth; in this it differed basically from the Cotton Control whose teeth were cut one at a time over the first two years of war. This early start was in most ways an advantage; in particular, it was an important reason, if not the only one, why the supply of raw material for the wool industry went through fewer vicissitudes than the supply for the cotton industry.

In the latter part of the war there was little difference between the completeness of the authority exercised by the Wool Control and the Cotton Control over raw material supplies. The two Controls differed fundamentally, however, in their methods of controlling the production of cloth. Cotton was allocated by more formal methods and by

---

[1] See pp. 142-3.

[2] Annual report of the National Wool Textile Export Corporation, 1944-45.

much narrower categories than wool. And the Cotton Control from mid-1942 onwards interfered with normal commercial methods on a scale that was far more drastic than anything the Wool Control contemplated. For the Cotton Control by then was planning the production, mill by mill, of all cotton yarn and cloth requirements whether for Government, export or civilian purposes. The Wool Control placed Government contracts with the cloth manufacturers, but it did not plan the production of yarn or cloth for export or civilian purposes. Instead it gave general directives to the industry and relied upon the machinery of the Joint Rationing Committee to implement them.

Thus the methods of the two Controls were very different. Inevitably the Controls' relations with the industries over whom they were in authority also differed. The goodwill of the industries was needed—and was forthcoming—in both cases, but the Wool Control relied more heavily upon it than did the Cotton Control. Voluntary co-operation was indispensable to the Wool Control, which relied upon the normal commercial practices of the industry to fulfil wartime demands; the Cotton Control had largely superseded such practices and relied for its control over production on that legal instrument, the licence. The Wool Control received co-operation in plenty; it was one of the Control's virtues that the industry was so ready to 'play ball'. The Control did of course possess pretty strong sanctions should any firm prove recalcitrant—it owned all raw wool and was responsible for allocating it to each firm; it placed all Government contracts and it allocated all subsidiary raw materials.[1] But the Controller rarely found it necessary to apply these sanctions.

Both the Cotton Control and the Wool Control held their authority from the Minister of Supply. Neither was formally responsible to the President of the Board of Trade though both were very closely concerned in the Board's clothing policy. The Board did not, however, have the same day-to-day relationships with the two Controls; their relations with the Cotton Control were rather more intimate than those with the Wool Control. Information about cotton—about the industry, and about the working of the Control—was exchanged more freely than information about wool. The Board were in an even closer relationship with the Cotton Board.[2] Consequently the Board of Trade ended the war with a much deeper knowledge of the cotton industry than of the wool industry. The Wool Control, on the other hand, was self-sufficient. It was the sole line of communication between the Government and the industry and its members tended to be impatient of interference from Whitehall despite friendly personal rela-

---

[1] For example, rayon and cotton. The Control allocated bichromates from 1940; coal, starch and dextrines from 1941; and sulphur from 1942.

[2] See p. 47.

tions between the officers concerned. The Control felt that the technical problems of the industry were so complex that laymen were ill-advised to meddle with them. The Control would answer specific questions, but it did not like to supply the Board with general information which might be used wrongly by officials who lacked the necessary technical knowledge of the trade. When the Wool Control disagreed with policies suggested by the Board—the close specification of utility cloths, for example, or the control of rayon long staple yarn—it was difficult for the Board to know how weighty the technical objections raised really were.

The reasons for the differences we have found in the approach of the Cotton and Wool Controls to their tasks are various. They lie partly in those questions of personality that are not discussed in this series of histories.[1] They also lie partly in the nature of the industries controlled. For example, the raw material of the two industries is basically different; raw cotton has many varieties but raw wool, being an animal fibre, has far more.[2] The structure and pre-war history of the two industries differed equally greatly. The extreme sectionalisation of the cotton industry stood in contrast to the closely-knit organisation of the wool industry. Moreover, the effects of the pre-war depression had lain more heavily on Lancashire than on Yorkshire. This may account in part for the more legalistic and precise nature of the war-time control over the cotton industry. Then, as we have seen, the war-time fortunes of the industries were also different; until the end of the war raw materials and labour were more plentiful in the wool industry than in the cotton industry. For all these reasons the informal methods of control that were considered sufficient in the wool industry would have been hopelessly inadequate in the cotton industry.

CONCENTRATION

We must now turn back in time to 1941 and the problem of concentration in the wool industry. The White Paper[3] setting out the general principles to be adopted had been published in March; but the Wool Control was not satisfied that wool output could continue to meet demands if concentration was applied too vigorously to the industry. It felt that in view of the great variety of products which was required from the wool industry even in war-time and the differences in the equipment of the machines in the industry,[4] any attempt at mass concentration would inevitably result in serious

---

[1] See the editor's preface to *British War Economy, op. cit.*

[2] See *Wool Working Party Report,* p. 31.

[3] See Chapter X above.

[4] Apart from commission dyeing and finishing plant. The wool dyeing and finishing industries were in fact concentrated in consultation with the appropriate trade associations.

disorganisation of essential output. The Wool Control continued to maintain this view despite pressure from the Board of Trade and the Ministry of Labour.

However, the Wool Textile Delegation undertook to work out a scheme which while maintaining essential production would release storage space and labour 'in similar proportions to those which were being released by other industries'. A Central Concentration Association, in which about ninety-eight per cent. of the industry participated, was set up to administer a voluntary concentration scheme. Under this scheme about 160 firms or factories had been closed by early 1942[1] and about 680 had received nucleus status. It is unfortunately impossible to give any reliable figures for the labour released by the scheme. This figure of closed firms must, however, be qualified by the definition of 'closed' peculiar to the wool industry. The policy was to keep all firms very much alive and a closed firm remained in business and remained entitled to its share of Government contracts and to its rations from the Joint Rationing Committee. The closed firm therefore retained its managerial, warehouse and despatch staff and farmed out its work to one of the nucleus firms who undertook to place at the disposal of the closed firm 'an amount of machinery similar to that which they were operating at the time of vacation' (of their premises). The nucleus firm was also to make a substantial contribution towards any special expenses incurred by the closed firm as a result of concentration. In return the nucleus firm was to receive the productive labour formerly employed by the closed firm as well as its rations and contracts. In many cases the labour did transfer, but—especially where the nucleus mill was many miles away from its partner—a good deal of the labour drifted away, the younger women to go into munitions and the older women to stay at home.

Thus the wool industry did have a formal concentration scheme on a voluntary, not compulsory, basis. Twenty to twenty-five per cent. of its mills closed, that is about fifteen per cent. of the machinery in the worsted spinning and weaving sections and about six per cent. of the woollen plant[2] was laid up and the premises made available to the Factory Control.

Output was thus concentrated under fewer roofs; but the results of the wool concentration scheme were open to two criticisms: first, that the closed mills went on employing many workers and, secondly, that there was too much idle machinery in the nucleus mills. These points were strongly pressed by the Ministry of Labour and also by the Board of Trade. They could also argue, as a subsidiary point, that the

---

[1] Excluding woollen carpet yarn spinners, many of whom closed a little later when the carpet industry was closed down.

[2] It was difficult to move and store plant from woollen and combing mills if it was ever to be of use again.

practice of allocating contracts and rations to both closed and nucleus firms meant that within the same nucleus factory there were many different lines being produced at once without the economies of long runs or mass production methods.

So far as the closed firms were concerned the Wool Control maintained that the labour retained by them to carry on their business —as distinct from their production—was only doing work for which the nucleus firms would otherwise have to take on additional staff and that no more than $2\frac{1}{2}$ per cent. of the labour force was involved.

The Ministry of Labour calculated that about 4,000 workers were thus employed by 'closed firms', apart from administrative staff; it argued that the nucleus firms could have done the work with only a small proportion of this number. A Ministry of Labour survey of the wool industry at the end of 1942 also found that some 'closed' firms had not in fact ceased production. In the Leeds area, for example, about ten per cent. of the 'closed' firms were still in full production and a further ten per cent. still in partial production. In other cases 'closed' firms said they were forced to continue some processes because they found that their nucleus firms were unable to undertake them.

The second line of criticism—namely that nucleus firms had a high proportion of idle machinery—was not denied by the Wool Control, although it gave no figures. The Control maintained that, owing to the very high peace-time variety of products, a certain amount of idle machinery was inevitable and that the real war-time problem in the wool industry was the proper balance between groups of machines. The two narrowest bottlenecks were the milling machine section on the woollen side of the industry (because Service cloths needed four to eight times the amount of milling[1] required by the average civilian cloth) and the drawing machinery section on the worsted spinning side (because Service cloths were more than double normal thickness). All the industry's milling capacity, the Control argued, was worked to its fullest extent with double shifts and overtime wherever possible; since it was not practicable to transfer milling machinery[2] to other mills, a proper balance of machinery and the maximum use of scarce capacity were better obtained by spreading the active machinery over a number of units than by running the same amount of machinery in fewer mills. In the Wool Control's view concentration had gone as far as was useful. To press it further would be to decrease production without any compensating savings in labour. The Control pointed out that one operative could only attend a certain number of machines whether the unit was large or small. The small units were not wasteful of supervising staff because, owing to the labour shortage, managers and foremen were operating

---

[1] Milling or fulling is a shrinking process.
[2] Additional power, drainage, water and steam-piping would have had to be installed.

machines themselves. Moreover, if some mills were closed their labour would not necessarily go into the remaining mills.

The Ministry of Labour and the Board of Trade did not altogether accept these views. The Ministry of Labour found that in some sections of the industry—for example, among the blanket firms—there was so much unused capacity in the nucleus firms that half of them could have closed without disrupting production. There was doubt whether production had been cut to the bone and the Ministry urged that the industry should be drastically reconcentrated in order to release more labour. The blanket firms were reconcentrated, but no further progress was made in the industry as a whole. After 1942 labour withdrawals were made piecemeal from each factory.

Concentration in the wool industry (as in some other civilian industries) proved to be really a modified form of spread-over. In view of the experience of the cotton industry, this does not seem in retrospect so serious a shortcoming as it appeared to Whitehall at the time.

LABOUR

In the early months of the war the wool industry was able to meet its new commitments without difficulty. The industry had a reservoir of unemployed and under-employed labour on which to draw, a reservoir largely composed of married women who were willing to be 'stood off' from time to time to look after their homes for a period.[1]

Up till the autumn of 1941 the wool industry had not lost an excessive amount of labour. Whereas in cotton the labour force had fallen by mid-1941 from about 340,000 pre-war to 276,000, in wool the drop over the same period was only from 208,000 to 195,000.[2] Moreover, a large proportion of these workers was available for civilian work because the numbers engaged on Service contracts fell considerably during the summer of 1941 and the export drive had passed its peak.[3] It was therefore not surprising that wool was classed as one of the civilian industries which could be expected to make a considerable contribution of its labour to the general pool.

Concentration must have released some labour though it is impossible to say how much. Then in October 1941 it was agreed to withdraw 10,000 women of the twenty to twenty-five age group from

---

[1] See p. 379.

[2] These are Ministry of Labour figures and relate to insured workers not registered as unemployed in June each year, i.e. males 14–64, females 14–59, and exclude non-manual workers earning over £420 per annum, but include part-timers. They are therefore not strictly comparable with the figures for cotton on p. 368.

[3] *Operatives employed in the wool industry*

			Government	Export	Home market	Total
						Thousands
1940	December	.	107·0	40·7	64·4	212·1
1941	June	. .	80·2	45·3	69·8	195·3
1941	December	.	66·7	40·2	69·2	176·1

the wool industry. Firms engaged seventy-five per cent. on Government contracts or on utility could appeal to the Wool Control and Ministry of Labour against withdrawals and something could be done to retain key women and to time the releases conveniently; but the industry as a whole had to produce the full 10,000. In practice therefore the cuts were inevitably distributed with little regard either to the type of output or the labour position in a particular firm. In some firms production was embarrassed, while others still held a large pool of labour which allowed them to continue to work short hours. Few firms, it seemed, made an effort to train workers as substitutes. These methods of withdrawal hit the worsted spinning section particularly hard. For here the work was normally performed by young women on low wage rates who were eventually upgraded to worsted weaving. While women in the twenty to twenty-six age group formed only ten per cent. of the women in the wool industry as a whole, in the worsted spinning section they formed forty per cent. It is not surprising therefore that worsted spinning never recovered from this 'comb-out'. By mid-1942, although the output of the woollen spinning and weaving sections was still about 5·5 per cent. in excess of estimated requirements, the output of worsted spinning showed a $17\frac{1}{2}$ per cent. deficit. This had serious effects on the hosiery industry, which was largely dependent on worsted yarn supplies.

The Ministry of Labour had not finished with the wool industry. In the early summer of 1942 there developed a struggle between the Ministry and the Wool Control, which felt that the industry's labour force had now fallen far enough. The Control believed that the wool industry could not release large additional numbers of workers unless Service and civilian demands on the industry were cut. The Minister of Labour, on the other hand, complained of a peacetime attitude to production in the wool industry. He declared that the older women being trained as substitutes were too few, that no overtime was being worked, that there had been little real concentration and that almost no part-time labour had been introduced. There was also disagreement about the precise numbers of workers employed in the industry at the time. Finally, however, it was agreed that between mid-1942 and the end of 1943 the industry's labour force should be reduced to 160,000; that is, according to the figures then available, between 16,000 and 20,000 workers should be released. Any part-timers could be kept in addition to the 160,000. It was hoped that productivity in the industry would be increased by more overtime and by applying the Essential Work Order to prevent unnecessary turnover and absenteeism. None of the reduction was to fall on worsted spinning. With this proviso, the Board of Trade felt that output would be adequate to meet requirements.

Before long it was clear that some of the strongest controversy between the Wool Control and the Ministry of Labour had been un-necessary. For the mid-1942 manpower figures, when they were ready in the autumn of 1942, were to show that the labour force in the wool industry was lower than either the Ministry or the Control had believed; it was in fact already very near the 160,000 level which it was to have reached by the end of 1943. There had, however, been other miscalculations; in particular, the Wool Control had over-estimated production requirements by exaggerating the export pro-gramme. The current rate of export was roughly 40 million lbs. of piece-goods per annum, but it was now discovered that half of this was coming out of stocks; the annual rate of production required for export during 1942 and 1943 was not more than 20 million lbs. The agreed withdrawals of about 16,000 workers from the wool indus-try therefore went ahead. They appeared to cause few difficulties. Indeed, cloth output in January 1943 was higher than in July 1942 despite the loss of thousands of workers.

In the spring of 1943 the question of labour withdrawals was re-opened by cuts in the Services' clothing programme.[1] These cuts were expected to release 3,000 workers in the worsted spinning section and a further 4,000 in the worsted weaving and woollen sections in addi-tion to the 16,000 already to go or gone. The Board of Trade now found themselves in a disagreement with the Ministry of Labour. They were ready to see the 4,000 additional workers released from worsted weaving and woollen production, but they felt strongly that the workers released from Service contracts in the worsted spinning section should be transferred to civilian work there. The Board were most concerned about hosiery supplies which were far below require-ments and which had increasingly been made of rayon and cotton yarn in order to release wool for the Services. The result had been repeated complaints from all quarters—despite a very mild winter—that reasonably warm underclothing was unobtainable. Absenteeism and illness were feared unless supplies of warm underclothes could be increased. The Board wanted to keep the workers released from spin-ning worsted yarn for the Services in order to improve the quality rather than the quantity of hosiery. They were prepared to release other workers by cutting cotton and rayon yarn supplies to the hosiery industry and by releasing some workers from the hosiery industry itself.

In the end it was decided that 1,000 of the 3,000 workers released in worsted spinning by the Service cuts could be kept for civilian worsted yarn. Another 1,000 were to be taken from worsted spinning for cloth-making so that worsted hosiery yarn would in fact only lose 1,000 workers. In spite of fears to the contrary these withdrawals did not prove excessive. Service requirements for worsted yarn were less

[1] See p. 412.

than the Wool Control anticipated and worsted spinning output was higher.[1] Moreover, the prospects of crossbred wool imports from New Zealand improved so that the Board of Trade could be given woollen yarn as a substitute for the expected deficit of worsted yarn.

Altogether then the wool industry lost a great deal of labour during the war—partly by withdrawals and partly by a drift to the more attractive munitions work. The diminishing labour force is shown in the following table:

Employment in the Wool Industry

TABLE 25		Thousands Employed[2]
Mid-1939	.	207·6
Mid-1940	.	222·3
Mid-1941	.	195·3
Mid-1942	.	162·1
Mid-1943	.	143·5
Mid-1944	.	129·1

Source: Ministry of Labour

Thus about 80,000 workers left the wool industry. On top of the decline in the labour force productivity had fallen. The average age of men employees had increased by eleven years during the war and the average age of women workers by four years. There was much absenteeism and reluctance to work overtime. Moreover, there was some evidence that the efficiency of the expanding and progressive firms suffered most; they had attracted the younger workers in peacetime and were therefore the first to lose labour in war-time.

By the end of 1943 there were fears that the fall in the labour force had gone too far in wool as in other civilian industries. Further falls in wool production could not be permitted, especially in view of relief demands and the importance of wool exports after the war. Early in 1944, therefore, it was agreed that workers with one year's previous experience in the spinning and weaving of wool were to be given priority of release when redundancy occurred in a war factory. They were to be returned to the woollen mills unless required to fill particularly urgent war demands. This move had some small effect. Nevertheless it was not enough. The Prime Minister was anxious in the spring of 1945 that, in order to avert a critical shortage of civilian clothing after VE-Day, twenty per cent. of the manpower engaged on military cloth should be diverted to civilian cloth. By July 1945 the Service and supply departments had released the equivalent of 7,000 workers; most of them, however, were from blanket rather than from apparel cloth production.

---

[1] Partly as a result of restricting production of rayon hand-knitting yarn on worsted machinery.

[2] Males under sixty-five and females under sixty, but excluding non-manual workers earning over £420 per annum. Part-time female workers are included, two being counted as one unit.

By the end of the war the labour force of the wool industry was still inadequate to meet the needs of a demobilisation clothing programme, the civilian programme and the export drive. The woollen spinning section had become a bottleneck no less narrow than worsted spinning had been; shortage of labour there prevented full absorption of recruits into the weaving sections. For these reasons the wool industry was given labour preferences in order to help it in building up its labour force. The aim was to recruit 22,000 additional workers before the end of 1945. These hopes were, however, disappointed. There was certainly an upward trend in the labour force, but it was not as big or as swift as had been hoped.

Employment in the Wool Industry

TABLE 26		Thousands
		Employed
Mid-1944	.	129·1
Mid-1945	.	129·8
Mid-1946	.	148·6

We can see that the wool labour force followed a similar but less violent course to that of the cotton labour force, passing from a relatively easy position during the first two years of war through compulsory withdrawals and natural drift to munitions work in the following two years to an increasing struggle to rebuild the labour force during the last two years of the war. The war-time problem was complicated by a lack of reliable information about the size or the use of the labour force which led to interdepartmental arguments and made very difficult the decisions on the steps necessary at any one time. The end of the war found the industry with an inadequate labour force and no certainty that it would be attractive enough to draw the necessary recruits.[1]

---

[1] On this point of 'attraction' see *Wool Working Party Report*, pp. 43–64.

APPENDIX 8
Cotton Allocations

Thousand tons

	1941 IV	1942 I	1942 II	1942 III	1942 IV	1943 I	1943 II	1943 III	1943 IV	1944 I	1944 II	1944 III	1944 IV	1945 I	1945 II	1945 III	1945 IV
Total Government departments	30·7	29·0	29·3	30·5	26·9	26·9	25·7	26·1	24·6	24·5	23·7	23·5	23·2	22·5	23·1*	20·0*	17·4*
Industrial groups	28·7	26·7	25·0	25·4	27·0	26·7	27·0	25·6	26·0	25·1	24·1	24·6	24·0	23·2	20·8	20·9	21·8
Essential home services	10·5	13·0	14·0	10·8	7·0	7·0	6·3	6·0	6·4	5·7	6·3	5·2	5·3	5·3	4·7	5·0	6·0
Civilian home trade	13·8	14·0	14·0	13·0	15·0	15·0	15·8	15·8	15·0	15·0	15·0	14·5	15·1	15·5	15·0	17·0	19·5
Overseas Allied requirements	20·0	15·0	13·5	15·1	16·1	16·7	18·5	18·5	18·0	18·0	19·0	18·0	18·0	18·0	14·1	14·1	18·5
TOTAL	103·7	97·7	95·8	94·8	92·0	92·3	93·3	92·0	90·0	88·3	88·0	85·8	85·6	84·5	77·7	77·0	83·2
Production	92·4	93·3	90·8	87·2	91·4	87·8	85·7	87·1	93·0	88·3	84·8	79·7	80·5	76·4	75·2	69·7	79·1

Source: Cotton Control

* Including military requirements for the Far East.

It must be emphasised that this table does not give an exact division between Service and civilian requirements. For instance, many Government departments' demands were not for Service contracts but for civilian needs, and some industrial groups' requirements were for Service needs as well as for home industry. In the last quarter of 1942, for example, the true Services' requirements totalled 32·3 (thousand tons); civilian and essential home services for home trade totalled 42·7 (thousand tons); exports totalled 17·1 (thousand tons). Other periods would show a similar proportion.

APPENDIX 9

Raw Cotton Supplies[1]

Thousand tons

	Imports	Re-exports	Losses by enemy action or fire — At sea or abroad	Losses by enemy action or fire — In United Kingdom	Consumption	Stocks — At end of period	Stocks — Highest	Stocks — Lowest
1937 . . .	741·1	27·3	—	—	639·0	308·0	—	—
1938 . . .	538·7	20·4	—	—	495·0	311·0	—	—
1939 . . .	571·4	19·1	4·7	33·4	588·0	275·0	—	—
1940 . . .	633·2	5·4	13·6	1·8	620·0	228·0	—	—
1941 . . .	364·1	—	46·6	0·1	430·7	178·7	204·5	105·2
1942 . . .	525·9	—	11·2	1·1	419·2	290·5	346·7	183·4
1943 . . .	440·8	—	5·2	0·7	394·8	348·6	348·6	190·7
1944 . . .	360·3	—	—	—	358·7	349·5	372·1	303·3
1945 . . .	400·0	14·3	—	—	319·7	411·1	411·4	331·3
1946 Jan.–June	190·2	3·8	—	—	175·3	416·2	416·2	399·1

[1]The figures for each year do not balance exactly because of small differences between the time when imports were entered with the Customs and the time when they were marked as added to stock.

APPENDIX 10

Output of the Wool Textile Industry

1. *Wool Consumption*

12 months September to August 1939–40	*Total million pounds clean wool*
Woollen spinning . . .	412·2
Topmaking	367·3
1940–41	
Woollen spinning . .	382·5
Topmaking . .	262·8
1941–42	
Woollen spinning . .	308
Topmaking . . .	236·3
1942–43	
Woollen spinning . .	269·7
Topmaking . . .	189·7
1943–44	
Woollen spinning . .	241·1
Topmaking . . .	158·3
1944–45	
Woollen spinning . .	230·0
Topmaking . . .	153·0

2. *Deliveries of Worsted Yarn (million pounds)*

	Government	Home civil (including Utility)	Export (yarn and fabric)	Hand knitting	Total
1942	79·1	44·3	19·5	9·4	152·3
1943	55·1	50·0	16·8	8·6	130·5
1944	44·3	53·3	17·4	8·0	123·1
1945	42·0	53·5	21·8	9·6	126·9

3. *Deliveries of Woven Wool Fabrics*

(For this purpose the number of yards of fabrics 36 inches wide and below has been halved. A linear yard is approximately 54 inches wide.)

In million linear yards	Government	Home civil (including Utility)	Export	Total
12 months September–August				
1942–43	74·2	131·2	31·0	236·4
1943–44	59·7	118·6	23·4	201·7
1944–45	53·5	111·6	25·9	191·0

Source: Wool Control
See *Board of Trade Journal*, 18th May 1946

CHAPTER XVI

THE CLOTHING AND HOSIERY INDUSTRIES

(i)

The Clothing Industry

THERE are two ways of making clothes. A length of cloth can be cut out and the pieces sewn together; or a length of yarn can be knitted into a garment or into shaped pieces for sewing together. This is the basic difference between the clothing, or making-up industry and the hosiery industry.[1] The clothing industry's raw materials are principally cotton, wool and rayon cloth; the hosiery industry's raw materials are principally cotton, wool and rayon yarn.

The clothing industry has a variety of production methods—the domestic, outworker and factory systems all exist in it. One or more processes are carried out in almost every town in England; main centres do exist, however, such as Leeds for mass-produced outerwear, Manchester for waterproofs and for overalls and infants' wear and London for all types of clothes, but predominantly for women's outerwear fashion goods.[2] The industry employed before the war about 440,000 people[3] who were spread over about 24,500 establishments. If firms employing ten or less workers were omitted, the number of firms would be reduced to about 5,000. Of the firms employing more than ten workers, forty-six per cent. were found during the war

---

[1] Some firms, however, are engaged in both the light clothing and the hosiery trades.

[2] In a census taken by the Board of Trade in June 1942 London employed twenty-seven per cent. of the industry's labour force, the Manchester area twenty-three per cent. and the Leeds area sixteen per cent.

[3] Tailoring, dressmaking and millinery trades only, excluding outworkers. Figures are from the Census of Production 1935. See *Board of Trade, Working Party Reports: Heavy Clothing* (H.M.S.O. 1947), pp. 77, 79.

Accurate statistics of employment are particularly difficult because the definition of 'clothing industry' varies so considerably. For example, the 1935 Census of Production divided the industry into six sections, of which only the first, 'tailoring, dressmaking and millinery', could strictly be classed as clothing (others were boots and shoes, hats, umbrellas, etc.). The Ministry of Labour sometimes divides the industry into six different sections, five of which are shown in Appendix 11 (boots and shoes we have omitted) but Ministry of Labour figures often also omit the dressmaking, millinery and other dress industries, as in the figures given in the *Statistical Digest of the War*. The Board of Trade 1942 survey of the clothing industry divides the industry into ten sections, giving for example proofed garments, infants' wear, industrial overalls, etc., separately (e.g. see *Heavy Clothing Working Party Report*, p. 124).

to be employing less than twenty-six workers and only six per cent. over two hundred. These largest firms, however, employed thirty-eight per cent. of the total number of employees.[1] Trade in the industry was, in peace-time, highly seasonal.

Broadly speaking there are two sections in the clothing industry. The heavy clothing section produces men's suits and coats, women's tailored suits and coats, rainwear, shirts, pyjamas and industrial overalls. The light clothing section produces women's dresses, blouses, underwear, nightwear, domestic overalls, baby clothes and certain types of men's underwear. The heavy clothing section employed nearly half of the insured workers in the clothing trades in 1939. The difference between the two sections is real. Production methods, machinery and materials are completely different and there is little interchange of labour between them. The light section uses thin wool, silk, cotton and rayon materials, usually weighing less than six ounces to the yard, and light flat sewing machines; the processes include a good deal of decorative stitching and the industry is much influenced by fashion changes. The heavy section uses heavier materials and machines and tailoring rather than dressmaking methods. It employs more men than the light industry, especially in the cutting and pressing sections. Its output, being less vulnerable to fashion changes, is more suitable for mass production methods.

The complexities of the clothing industry—in particular the very large number of small firms—had protected it from control during the early part of the war. Its output had not been directly affected by the Limitation of Supplies Orders for the quotas on the supply of piece-goods applied to the registered manufacturers of cloth and the quotas on made-up goods applied to the registered wholesalers of these goods. Between these two points of restriction the clothing industry was free to produce whatever it could. Moreover, when clothes rationing was introduced in June 1941 there had as yet been no attempt to concentrate the clothing industry. The sequence of events in the industry was therefore quite different from that in the other industries concerned with textiles and clothing. In the textile, hosiery and boot and shoe industries limitation of supplies was followed by concentration, and concentration was followed by Government intervention in the control of production, or intervention designed to extract the maximum from an industry already more or less severely

---

[1] Board of Trade war-time census:—

Size of firm	No. of firms as percentage of total	No. of employees as percentage of total
10–25 workers	46	12
26–50 workers	23	13
51–100 workers	17	18
101–200 workers	8	19
Over 200 workers	6	38

contracted. In the clothing industry, on the other hand, the production policy and consumption policy were framed first and the Board of Trade were able to guide the contraction of the industry so as to implement these policies.

The impetus to control the clothing industry came partly from the introduction of clothes rationing and the need to honour the ration and partly from the demands made by the Ministry of Labour on the industry. By the autumn of 1941 employment in the heavy and light clothing sections had fallen substantially, but the making-up trades as a whole still had more than enough labour to handle all the cloth the textile industries could supply. The surplus was not, however, evenly distributed. Government orders for heavy and proofed clothing had kept these sections busy and persuaded labour to remain in the industry, while the light clothing section had lost a large number of women through a voluntary drift into the Services and munitions. The production of children's wear, which was unpopular work mostly located in munitions areas, suffered especially—so much so that by the middle of 1941 there was a serious general shortage of this clothing.

In the summer of 1941 clothing contracts for the Services were reduced by about forty per cent. The Board of Trade therefore seriously contemplated concentration of the industry. The difficulties, however, proved too great for the time being. It was not possible to confine concentration to the firms where redundancy was serious—the firms that had been working on Government contracts; yet firms engaged on export and civilian orders were still pretty fully occupied. There were moreover the complexities of the industry to be reckoned with and these were accentuated by the absence of reliable information about the industry. The Board felt that unless they were to ignore all but the largest firms concentration of the clothing industry would be beyond their administrative capacity.

The Ministry of Labour, however, needed to withdraw labour from the industry. In September 1941, without prior consultation with the Board of Trade, the Ministry of Labour had agreed with the industry that all its women workers between the ages of twenty and twenty-five should be withdrawn. The Board of Trade now had to interest themselves directly in the production affairs of the clothing industry. For these withdrawals, although justified in view of the industry's labour surplus, threatened seriously to disrupt the output of some garments —such as essential working-class clothes and children's wear—that were already scarce. Some firms, for example shirtmakers, who employed large numbers of young workers were likely to lose the lot. The Board had therefore to ask the Ministry of Labour to defer the calling up of women from some firms making those garments that were already scarce. The Ministry of Labour wished to go even further in withdrawing women from the clothing industry in London and here again the Board had to put out a restraining hand.

These growing requests for deferment gave the Ministry of Labour cause to fear that the agreement with the trade was being whittled away. The Board of Trade on the other hand saw that a piecemeal policy of labour deferments in individual firms to meet a temporary shortage of particular clothes must be superseded by a long-term policy which would make sure that there was enough labour in the industry to meet the population's essential clothing needs. The Board therefore worked out in the autumn of 1941 the designation policy. It was decided to nominate or 'designate' firms which were predominantly engaged in Government or essential civilian work and to offer them some form of labour protection.

The Board of Trade and the other interested departments had first to know how many workers would be needed to satisfy essential Service and civilian needs. The Service needs were known and the Ministry of Supply knew how many workers were wanted to meet them. By this time too the utility scheme had begun and the Board were gaining a clearer idea of essential civilian needs. But they did not know how many workers would be required to meet them and they still had very little information about the number of workers in the clothing industry. During September 1941 therefore they took a census of 1,400 clothing manufacturers—that is those firms employing more than fifty workers each, or about seventy-five per cent. of the total labour force. The firms were asked to state not only their labour force and its age distribution but also their production in the previous quarter. This census gave the Board the information they needed in order to advocate the designation policy to the Ministry of Labour.

It was decided that the labour requirements of the whole civilian clothing industry were as follows:—

Labour Requirements of the Clothing Industry
TABLE 27

	Estimated percentage of pre-war capacity now required	Estimated labour now required[1]
Heavy outerwear and proofed garments	38	92,000
Men's shirts and nightwear	67	41,000
Women's light outerwear and underwear	42	18,000
		151,000

With the Ministry of Supply the Board then agreed a list of

[1] This labour estimate proved too low. See p. 412.

designated contractors who were of interest to them both. To be included in this list firms had to employ more than ten workers and had to be engaged up to at least seventy-five per cent.[1] of their capacity on the production of utility clothing and/or Government contracts. They also had to undertake to control their production of specific garments at the Board of Trade's direction. These firms were promised that their premises would not be requisitioned. They were also to receive preferential treatment in the supply of cloth and their labour would only be withdrawn if substitutes were first provided. Owing to shortages of light clothing no women over twenty in this section were to be withdrawn without prior substitution. In the rest of the industry designated firms were to lose the 20–25 age groups, but women over twenty-five were not to be withdrawn without prior substitution. Designation did not prevent a firm from increasing its labour force by taking on juveniles, part-timers or women over registration age. Nor did it affect the freedom of individual workers to leave if they wished. Conversely designation did not guarantee reservation from military service for a firm's employees.

The Ministry of Labour agreed these proposals with one reservation. The Board of Trade and Ministry of Supply had tried to avoid designating firms in areas where labour was particularly scarce. The Ministry of Labour asked however that such firms as were designated in four particularly difficult areas—Leicester, Manchester, Bristol and Nottingham—should have their labour forces reduced by one-sixth. Manchester firms were also to be told that their designated labour forces were to be regarded as a maximum. Early in 1942 it was necessary to reduce the labour protection a little further. The protection of the 20–25 age group in the light clothing section was abolished; designated firms who could show that half or more of their production was of children's clothing were however granted prolonged deferment in order to train and recruit substitutes. Then a little later it was agreed that the labour protection to firms to be designated in particularly bad labour areas—the 'scarlet' areas—should only apply to those workers not required by the Ministry of Labour for transfer to munitions.

Designation went ahead steadily and was complete by the middle of 1942. The final list, excluding Northern Ireland, covered 1,863 factories and protection was given to 216,200 workers.[2] Of these, about 117,000 workers and 1,400 factories were employed on civilian work. About sixty-seven per cent. of the total labour that was protected was employed in tailoring and dressmaking, ten per cent. on

---

[1] The utility margins had been worked out to allow a reasonable profit for a fairly large firm working about eighty per cent. on utility production.

[2] These figures exclude a small number of Ministry of Supply contractors who had special labour agreements with the Ministry of Labour.

proofed clothing, fifteen per cent. on shirts and underwear, and eight per cent. on industrial overalls. Ten per cent. of the total labour employed in designated factories was in firms with 11–49 workers, thirty-five per cent. in firms with 50–199 workers and fifty-five per cent. in firms with over 200 workers. Thus designation maintained the relative importance of the medium-sized firms, but placed a certain emphasis on the larger firms at the expense of the small-to-medium firms.

The designation scheme had begun primarily as a method of protecting labour in a few firms whose output was particularly important to the Board of Trade. But it had developed into something more. By the offer of protection the Board of Trade had received from designated firms undertakings to produce a high proportion of utility goods and to obey the Board's directions. Designation had indeed become one of the chief means of working the utility scheme.[1] For fulfilling this wider purpose, the policy had, however, certain defects.

In the first place, undesignated firms were unreasonably badly treated. Not only were they liable to lose their most efficient labour but by mid-1942 arrangements had been made to route eighty per cent. of utility cloth and seventy per cent. of all cloth to designated firms. Undesignated firms—who were on the whole the smaller firms —might be forced into bankruptcy; this would accord ill with the principles that the White Paper on Concentration had laid down for contracting industries. Firms had been designated arbitrarily by the Board of Trade and the excluded firms had had no redress and no opportunity to amalgamate with other firms. Moreover, the Board of Trade still required a substantial volume of production from the undesignated firms if the ration were to be honoured.

Secondly, it seemed unlikely that the releases of labour and factory space under the designation policy would prove sufficient. The Board of Trade had agreed with the Ministry of Labour and with the supply departments that the total number of workers required in the clothing industries to meet civilian and Service needs[2] would be about 300,000. The labour force of the industry in mid-1942 was, however, 346,000. It seemed unlikely that over 40,000 workers could be withdrawn as long as so many of the directable age groups remained protected within the designated firms. Factory Control likewise pointed out that it had considerable claims on the clothing industry which could not be met if designated firms continued to be protected from requisitioning. For example, in the Leeds area the

---

[1] The rest of the apparatus of control for operating the utility scheme will be discussed in Chapter XVII.

[2] i.e. in designated and undesignated firms and for all types of production including non-utility.

Control required a quarter of the four million square feet occupied by the heavy outerwear industry; yet the individual firms on the Control's list were all designated. The Control believed that the designated firms could be packed into three-quarters of the space they occupied without restricting their output.

For all these reasons the Board began to doubt whether the designation policy was the last word in the control of the clothing industry. Concentration on normal lines would now be a better and fairer method of rationalising the industry. Through designation concentration had become much more feasible than it had been in 1941. The Board now knew much more about the industry, especially about the type and volume of output and the efficiency of the designated firms—firms which represented a potential body of nuclei. The task of dealing with over 25,000 firms which had looked so formidable a year earlier had now become much more manageable. Moreover, the utility programme and therefore the total level of production required from the clothing industry had been finally settled during the summer of 1942. Then, too, another method had been devised for enforcing the utility programme—the method of key certificates for the allocation of cloth;[1] this was expected to be more effective than threats of labour withdrawal or offers of labour protection.

The concentration scheme was therefore launched. At first it was proposed to proceed regionally in each of the main clothing areas—London, Manchester, Glasgow and Leeds. The first experiment was made in Leeds. A census was taken of all the clothing firms in the district, the district was divided into eleven zones and a committee of local manufacturers was formed. The committee, with the Board of Trade's officials, then arranged the concentration. Firms to qualify as nuclei must be 'running full'—that is, employing ninety per cent. of the labour used on the premises on 1st June 1940. No conditions were imposed on the size of nucleus undertakings. Like designated firms nucleus firms had to undertake that not less than seventy-five per cent. by value of their production should be utility, Government contracts or other production approved by the Board of Trade (for example, exports, police uniforms, etc.). As for the release of resources for the war effort, factory premises were more important than labour. The Ministry of Labour had relatively few urgent immediate demands to fill in the Leeds area and the concentration scheme did not therefore provide for specific labour releases. Factory Control, however, made a list of the premises it required and obtained the million square feet of space that it was seeking in the area. The concentration committees had been free either to amalgamate firms under one management or to move them into new

---

[1] See below, p. 445.

premises. In fact there was not very much amalgamation; for the most part two units produced side by side under the same roof.

After the Leeds scheme was complete, the Board of Trade in November 1942 took a census of the rest of the clothing industry. All firms employing more than ten workers at the end of June 1942 had to state the numbers employed in each age group, their floor space, their methods of production, the value of production of each type of clothing and the value of production for Government, export or civilian orders. The results of this census were not available until March 1943; they then provided the necessary statistical basis for concentrating the rest of the clothing industry.

Meanwhile, a new consideration had entered into concentration policy. In the autumn of 1942 the Ministry of Production and the Ministry of Labour had decided that less important industries—including making-up—should be removed from 'scarlet' labour areas and should be built up in the 'green' labour areas.[1] This made it impossible to concentrate the clothing industry regionally. Any scheme would now have to be a national one.

It is doubtful whether the removal of all clothing production from scarlet areas was at all practicable. Two of those areas—Birmingham and Leicester—were main centres of the clothing industries and other scarlet towns such as Crewe, Nantwich and Warrington had important clothing industries. It was unlikely that the green areas—Glasgow, North-East England and the East and West Ends of London—had ample reception capacity and even more unlikely that the different grades and types of production traditionally associated with each area could be matched up.[2] A major upheaval of this kind might well have been disastrous for the clothing ration. Moreover, labour shortages were fluid. Areas that were only red might quickly become scarlet; clothing production could hardly be uprooted every few months to keep pace with changing labour conditions. Nevertheless, in the autumn of 1942 the Board of Trade was ready to try to combine concentration with the restriction of production in scarlet areas. Rather than physically transfer firms from scarlet areas the Board were to try to choose nucleus firms in green areas. These nuclei would be associated with closing firms in scarlet areas.

In the end, however, little concentration was achieved during the winter of 1942–43. A few regional schemes got under way. But there were various obstacles in the way of progress. As we have seen in an earlier chapter, the Board of Trade were becoming reluctant to concentrate industries with large numbers of small firms and they

---

[1] See p. 215 for explanation of these areas.

[2] There were other difficulties—for example, the higher wage rates in London deterred firms from transferring their production there and Government departments from transferring contracts there.

were certainly unwilling to close firms compulsorily. There was nothing to be gained by doing so. Even if all usable labour were withdrawn from clothing, it was clear that a small residue would remain in most firms, and there would also remain a considerable number of firms too small to join in concentration schemes. So long as this labour could not be used elsewhere, these firms were likely to be useful pockets of production. On the other hand, the inducements being offered to nucleus firms did not seem sufficient to attract firms into voluntary schemes. Manufacturers were to be persuaded into the scheme mainly by the promise of supplies of 'steered' cloth, but by the end of 1942 cloth production and deliveries were not yet working out according to the cloth budget. Supplies of non-utility cloth were unexpectedly plentiful and there were even sufficient surpluses of utility cloth to give undesignated firms a fairly adequate supply. Some designated firms complained that they were penalised because they were limited by their key certificates in the total quantity of cloth they could obtain, and could not avail themselves of these surpluses.

The biggest of the obstacles to the progress of concentration was uncertainty about the labour withdrawals to be made. Not until the spring of 1943 was it settled how big the total clothing labour force should be and where the withdrawals were to be made. This uncertainty was largely due to fluctuations in the volume of clothing production required by the Ministry of Supply.[1] For a time it seemed that the clothing industry's labour force was shrinking too fast and that no labour should be withdrawn. By the beginning of 1943, however, it had become clear that withdrawals could continue. It was then necessary to agree on the protection to be given to nucleus firms. It was decided that nucleus certificates should in future state an approved labour force covering both Service and civilian contracts. Within this number withdrawals could only be made if the Ministry of Labour provided substitutes. Conversely, if a firm recruited labour over and above its approved labour force,[2] the Ministry of Labour might withdraw an equivalent number of workers, which it might choose as it wished. In order to encourage firms in scarlet areas to move to green areas, their approved labour force was divided into two parts—the residual labour force (workers whom the Ministry of Labour could not transfer to war work) and an authorised labour force which the firm might engage in a green area.

---

[1] e.g. estimates of the labour force required to carry out Ministry of Supply contracts varied from 90,000 in 1941, up to 149,000 in the summer of 1942, when deliveries were seriously in arrears, down to 80,000 in March 1943 when the temporary crisis had been overcome, and again down to 50,000 by the end of 1943. Concentration could not go ahead while the Ministry of Supply was trying to increase production to meet its requirements.

[2] Juveniles were not counted as part of the approved labour force until they had completed six months' training (later nine months).

The Board of Trade usually issued nucleus certificates to cover the firms' residual labour force if their efficiency was not below normal standards. In addition they were allowed to recruit sufficient juveniles to balance their labour force. Firms in green areas were given an approved labour force of the numbers actually employed plus a recruitment figure for any additional production undertaken on behalf of a firm in a scarlet area. Employment of women in the 1915–23 age groups was to be avoided whenever possible. Thus firms in scarlet areas were not to be compulsorily closed nor compulsorily moved. Instead, the Ministry of Labour was to remove all the labour in these areas which it could use on more important work.

Under this scheme concentration was carried out in two groups of scarlet towns during the spring and summer of 1943—the Greater Birmingham area and a group of towns in the southern counties.[1] In Birmingham itself, for example, out of forty-seven clothing firms employing 2,400 workers, thirty-five were concentrated into fifteen units with a residual labour force of 623; the nucleus firms might recruit such juveniles as they needed to form balanced working units making not more than 700 workers in all. The other firms either remained outside concentration or had their whole production made for them, at cost, in a reception area. The results of this policy in scarlet areas were not, however, so spectacular as had been expected. This was partly due to the changes in the labour demands themselves. In the Birmingham area, for example, the Ministry of Labour had expected to take eighty per cent. of the industry's labour force, but changes in war production requirements modified the unfilled labour demands to such an extent that by August 1943 the outlying towns in the area, such as Stourbridge, Dudley, Bilston and Walsall, were declared to be scarlet areas no longer.[2]

By the autumn of 1943 most of the clothing industry had been concentrated. The only areas where no concentration attempts had yet been made were Scotland, Wales, the northern region, Yorkshire (apart from Leeds) and London. Even at this advanced stage of the war it was thought worthwhile to proceed with concentration. In the first place, demands for factory space were still urgent and, secondly, concentration was the only means of superseding the outmoded designation procedure. The Board of Trade decided to tackle London first and to defer concentration in outlying areas till later.

The size and structure of the London industry made it the most arduous and ambitious concentration scheme to administer. The Board of Trade wanted to curtail clothing production in North-West and North-East London where labour was extremely scarce and

---

[1] Including St. Albans, Slough, Reading, High Wycombe, Gloucester, Swindon, Bath and Stroud.

[2] Birmingham itself remained scarlet.

concentrate it in Central London where labour was relatively plentiful. This should have been simple since over 60,000 of the 80,000 clothing workers in the London area were employed in the central area.[1] But even for the clothing industry London contained an exceptionally large number of small firms; the average number of workers employed there in each firm was 34, while in Leeds it was 119. Moreover, in the East End there was a strongly rooted tradition of out-working. The administrative complications involved can therefore well be imagined. But in any case a high proportion of London firms preferred to remain outside the concentration scheme. Of 2,775 firms in the area less than half took part in concentration arrangements. Concentration in the London area was not completed until June 1944, and by this stage of the war the advantages of nucleus status may well have seemed insufficient—particularly to high-grade firms who had no wish to promise to make seventy-five per cent. of utility or Service clothing.

In the remaining clothing areas—Scotland, Wales, Yorkshire (excluding Leeds), Southern and Eastern England—proper concentration was impossible, for production was either very scattered or else on a very small scale. A 'debased' form of concentration was therefore introduced. Firms wishing to regard themselves as nuclei had to group themselves in units of fifty or more workers and nominate a principal firm in order to simplify the issue of cloth certificates.

Designation was finally withdrawn from all firms on 1st June 1944 —exactly two years after the first complete designation list had been published. In accordance with the intentions of the Board of Trade it had been superseded by concentration. Table 28 shows the results of concentration up to April 1944—that is, before the concentration schemes had been completed in London or in the 'outlying' districts in Scotland, Wales and so on. Final figures including these districts are not available, but in the London scheme alone nucleus certificates were eventually issued to 502 principal and 609 out-working firms.

Clothing Concentration at 30th April, 1944

TABLE 28

No. of nucleus certificates issued	No. of nucleus sub-certificates (out-workers)	No. of closed firms	Total A.L.F.s of nucleus firms	Total labour force of nucleus firms May 1942	Factory space released (including space released before concentration)
912	201	336	105,059[2]	173,657	2,966,000 square feet

[1] Central London included Stepney, Hackney, Shoreditch, Camden Town, Holloway and the Edgware Road as well as the West End.

[2] Including 468 juveniles and 121 part-timers outside the approved labour force.

According to these figures the releases of labour and factory space were certainly useful. The predominance of small firms in the industry meant that the amount of useful factory space to be released was limited, but the two million square feet released through concentration were important and all but 50,000 square feet was used by Factory Control. The labour force of the nucleus firms had in theory been reduced by about twenty per cent. The figure for the approved labour force does not, of course, show the effective reduction in the clothing labour force. Labour remained with firms which had stood outside concentration; in some areas firms were unable to recruit labour up to their approved labour forces: in others, the Ministry of Labour had not reduced firms down to their approved strengths. It was not only the total labour releases from nucleus firms that were important: concentration had also made a real contribution towards releasing labour where it was most needed. In Birmingham, for example, the total approved labour force was twenty-three per cent. of the employment of the same firms in June 1942, in Derby it was thirty-seven per cent., in Scotland and London it was eighty-five per cent. and in Leeds seventy-five per cent.

Concentration in the clothing industry differed fundamentally from the schemes in most other industries. Partly the difference was one of timing—as we have seen, clothing concentration came after production and consumption policy had been formulated; it was introduced when the war economy had reached a more mature stage. But the principles of the clothing schemes were peculiar to itself. Its central feature was the approved labour force. Non-nucleus firms were simply not given an approved labour force, but they were openly permitted to run as best they could. For the concentrating firms the approved labour force was regarded as a sufficient stake in the industry and all questions of compulsory levies or industry-wide compensation funds or fixing standard period turnover were avoided. Moreover, very few firms in fact closed down. For the most part the 'closed firms' in the industry shared in the activities of the nucleus firms, and operated machines on the premises of their concentration partners. In a way, indeed, concentration was simply designation writ large. It was, like designation, a method of releasing labour while safeguarding the Board of Trade's clothing programme. But it was more orderly and more precise than designation; labour withdrawals could more easily be arranged so that they matched production programmes. Moreover, concentration removed one of the chief objections to designation—its inequity. Any firm could join in the concentration scheme and the advantages to be gained thereby. And from the Board of Trade's point of view the more firms that joined in, the better. For nucleus firms made the same promises as designated firms to obey the Board's direction and to produce a high proportion of utility goods; the more concentrated firms there were, therefore, the greater the Board's control over garment production. Concentration did extend the Board's control. In June 1942, when designation had been completed, the Board were allocating cloth to 1,400 designated firms, but by June 1944 they were allocating cloth to over 2,200 nucleus firms.

As for the approved labour force system, it had several advantages. It enabled the Board of Trade to spread labour releases equitably among manufacturers[1] and was sufficiently flexible to allow the production of some garments to be stimulated and others curtailed. It was to prove as useful in expansion as in contraction. The approved labour forces had, however, been nominal figures only, of more use in interdepartmental negotiation than in measuring the actual labour force of a firm. In 1942 and 1943 the Ministry of Labour had frequently been unable to reduce firms to their approved labour force and in 1944 and 1945 it was often to be unable to recruit labour to bring firms up to their approved figures.

We have been considering methods of tying individual clothing firms to a certain labour force. We must now go back to consider the total level of employment in the making-up industry as a whole. The level to which the Government agreed inevitably fluctuated. The labour requirements for the forty-eight coupon civilian ration remained constant at about 180,000–185,000 workers. The changing factor was the clothing demands of the Services. For example, Ministers had contemplated withdrawals of about 37,000 workers from the making-up industry between July 1942 and December 1943. Then, however, in the spring of 1943 heavy cuts—up to fifty per cent. in some garments—were recommended in the clothing requirements of the Services; these meant that the releases were to be 61,000 or about one-fifth of the total labour force of the industry. Appropriate percentage reductions had therefore to be made in each section of the industry and equivalent cuts in the approved labour forces of nucleus firms. For the next few months therefore the problem was one of labour surpluses in the clothing firms. Former Ministry of Supply contractors now under-employed were applying to the Board of Trade for cloth certificates, but the available cloth supplies could not be stretched to include newcomers, nor to provide work for surplus labour in firms supplying the civilian market. The Board were therefore anxious to see the labour withdrawn. At the end of 1943 Service requirements were once more cut by an amount sufficient to release

---

[1] It must be emphasised, however, that whatever the paper releases, or percentage cuts in approved labour forces, the Ministry of Labour's withdrawals of suitable individuals or age-groups went steadily on, mitigated by the deferment of key workers procedure which helped to maintain production in individual firms. These arrangements, common to industry as a whole, will be described in the manpower volume of this series of histories.

a further 30,000 workers. The percentage cuts in each section of the industry were therefore revised and cuts were made in the approved labour forces according to the labour shortages in various parts of the country, e.g. labour forces in scarlet areas were already at residual level and there was no need to release labour in green areas. The percentage cuts in each section of the industry now varied from $33\frac{1}{3}$ per cent. for tailoring and dressmaking to 25 per cent. for underwear, 10 per cent. for industrial overalls and shirts and nil for infants' wear.

At the request of the Ministry of Supply the cut in the heavy tailoring section was reduced from $33\frac{1}{3}$ per cent. to 20 per cent. But even this reduction proved too great. For almost at once demands on capacity, especially in the heavy tailoring section, began to rise and the problem of labour surpluses disappeared. Production of clothing for demobilisation, for relief and for jungle warfare was beginning; owing to the uncertainties of the war the industry was attempting to meet several different contingencies at once. It was soon clear that the clothing industry as a whole could not afford the planned labour releases. In the six months from February 1944, 13,500 workers had been released. Then in September withdrawals of labour from nucleus firms in the Manchester, Leeds, Birmingham and Nottingham areas had to cease. In London clothing firms lost many workers as a result of flying bomb attacks. By October it was not enough to stop withdrawals of labour. The industry, whose concentration had so recently been completed, had to be re-expanded. Skilled clothing workers on being released from munitions work were to be returned to nucleus firms which had less than their approved labour force even though there might be preference vacancies for labour in the area. In addition, workers not needed for preference vacancies could return to clothing firms which had more than their approved labour force. Skilled tailoring firms received even more preferential treatment. Nucleus firms might nominate individual former workers with more than two years' tailoring experience for extraction from munitions and other industries. Approved labour forces for tailoring firms in all regions except London were increased to ninety-five per cent. of the numbers employed in June 1942. The approved labour forces of infants' wear specialists were increased to 110 per cent. of their June 1942 figure. At the same time the clothing industry was urged to increase its hours of work.

By June 1945—after nine months—the recruiting measures had met with some success, but not nearly enough. It had been hoped to obtain 26,500 workers, but only 14,500 returned. There was once more the familiar story—in this industry as in the textile industries, wages were, comparatively, too low and amenities too poor to retain or attract workers.

workers employed by the nucleus firm after the various cuts were made became its permitted labour force.

The Board of Trade had at first hoped that similar firms would combine and turn out a pool product. Firms preferred, however, to join with non-competing firms in order to retain their own identity. The financial arrangements between nucleus and closed firms were mostly of the agency type—that is, the nucleus firms manufactured goods at cost for the closed firms which kept their own selling and often their own packing organisations. Each firm, nucleus or closed, was allowed its yarn ration. Most closed firms tried to keep yarn buying in their own hands, invoicing it at cost to the nucleus firms. Some, however, sold their yarn rations outright to the nucleus firms and closed down their own marketing and buying organisations. Most nucleus firms paid no compensation to the closed firms, but the closed firms received income from the letting or requisitioning of their premises, and some of their necessary expenses, such as care and maintenance of closed factory and plant, were permitted to be charged as expenses of the nucleus firms—that is, were paid for by the consumer in the retail price. Closed firms also made some profits from the merchanting of their share of the combined output. These financial arrangements seem to have worked well and closed firms did not complain about them.

Concentration changed the structure of the hosiery industry to some extent. Firms with out-working branches in small towns and villages tended to close them down, in spite of Ministry of Labour opposition, if by doing this they could achieve the necessary degree of concentration in their main factories. Moreover, on the whole the larger firms in the industry received nucleus status and the smaller firms tended to be the ones which closed. So far as machinery was concerned, the fine-gauge machinery was put out of action because yarn shortage and Service requirements for heavier underwear favoured output from coarser-gauge machines.

Concentration proceeded rapidly. The arrangements made were almost all voluntary; there was practically no nomination by the Government of firms to close. Concentration was more or less complete by September 1941[1] when 436 units had been closed and 342 granted nucleus status. About 180 firms employing less than twenty workers each remained outside the concentration scheme. About five million square feet of factory space were released and the number of workers in the industry fell from 95,300 in March 1941 to 76,600 in October 1941.

Concentration of the hosiery industry was considered by the Board of Trade to be one of the most thorough and successful of all schemes.

---

[1] Warp knitters' plants, hosiery makers-up and dyers and finishers were concentrated later.

Why were hosiery manufacturers willing to allow themselves to be absorbed, very often by their rivals, at so early a stage in the war? The advantages bestowed on nucleus firms were the usual ones—protection from requisitioning of their factory premises and protection of their directable labour from withdrawal without prior substitution. These advantages were not, however, always as great as they seemed. Most hosiery firms are small, and in these cases the premises were not of great interest to the Factory Control. Moreover, the industry is staffed quite largely with non-directable married women so that even if firms did not join concentration schemes they could count on keeping a good deal of their labour. Indeed, those firms that did not co-operate in concentration reaped some advantages. For nucleus firms could not employ more than a certain number of workers, whereas non-co-operators could recruit any non-directable women they could find and also any juvenile labour. Again, the Ministry of Labour could not withdraw labour from nucleus firms without prior substitution, but it had no responsibility for replacing workers who left of their own accord. Some nucleus firms complained that the only real advantage in labour protection that they received compared with non-co-operators was that while the Schedule of Reserved Occupations was in force the works manager of a nucleus firm was reserved from the Services at the age of twenty-five instead of thirty-five.

The majority of the hosiery industry did, however, join the concentration scheme. Probably firms were willing to close because they feared that the Government had or was likely to acquire powers of compulsory closure or, as serious yarn shortages were developing, they may have been afraid that yarn supplies would be restricted to nucleus firms;[1] they would then be forced into liquidation with none of the financial compensations available under concentration. In fact when the utility scheme was developed the capacity of the concentrated industry was barely sufficient to meet the minimum requirements of the hosiery budget so that there was not a great deal of difference in the treatment of nucleus and the non-co-operating firms.

After concentration had been completed, two problems dominated the industry for the remaining years of the war—shortage of yarn and shortage of labour. The most acute problem was the shortage of yarn. In the first eighteen months of the war yarn shortage had been masked by the substantial stocks—especially of wool—which hosiery manufacturers had accumulated. By early 1941, however, yarn supplies for hosiery for home civilian trade were growing scarce. They had been limited by the quota restrictions and, in the case of cotton, by the Cotton Control's system of preference directions, which gave

---

[1] Government contracts were in any case confined to nucleus firms.

priority to Government and export orders. The Materials Committee began in August 1941 to allocate cotton yarn to the hosiery industry for both Service and civilian purposes.[1] Actual deliveries during the summer and autumn of 1941 were, however, less than half the allocation rate. Consumers, on the other hand, were spending more of their coupons on hosiery products than the Board of Trade had at first expected. Something had to be done and the Cotton Control, partly by earmarking capacity and partly by standardising yarns, managed to increase deliveries to the hosiery industry until by the end of 1941 they were over 100 per cent. of the allocation. This increase, allowing for the time lag in production, was not in time to prevent serious hosiery shortages during that winter. As far as wool was concerned, serious shortages in the worsted yarns used by the hosiery industry did not appear until the end of 1941. For the following fifteen months these shortages were acute. Minimum requirements for civilian hosiery garments were met by substituting cotton underwear for wool in the case of men and rayon for cotton in the case of women. Nevertheless, retail stocks reached danger level in the winter of 1941–42.

From the beginning of 1942 supplies of cotton and wool yarn for civilian use were endangered by the increasing demands of the Services. The Board of Trade felt that these demands were excessive. The Services required, for example, 25·5 million lbs. of wool for the year for about four million bodies compared with the 31 million lbs. allowed for the whole of the civilian population. Indeed, out of a total ration of 50 million lbs. of wool to the hosiery industry in 1942 the Board of Trade were for a time receiving an allocation for the civilian market at a rate of only 21 million lbs. or only two-thirds of their requirements. The outlook was even darker, for the hosiery industry's requirements were for worsted yarn and the capacity of the worsted spinning industry seemed nearer 40 than 50 million lbs.; since spinners were instructed by the Wool Control to give first priority to Government contracts, further deficits seemed bound to fall on the civilian ration. Despite the fact that Service clothes were 10–15 per cent. heavier than civilian clothes and that on the whole they had a shorter life, this discrepancy of treatment seemed excessive. The Board of Trade appealed to the Materials Committee which agreed that the civilian ration must not bear the whole brunt of any shortfall in deliveries; forty-five per cent. of such a shortfall should be borne by Service requirements and fifty-five per cent. by civilians. This decision was to some extent cold comfort as the capacity of the worsted spinning industry shrank and Ministry of Supply demands increased. The Wool Control had to warn the Board in

---

[1] The allocation was administered by the Hosiery Rationing Committee.

April 1942 that the deliveries of worsted yarn available for the civilian hosiery ration were likely to be at an annual rate of $16\frac{1}{2}$ million lbs. instead of 21 million lbs.,[1] the meagre current rate.

The Board of Trade had therefore to reduce greatly their demands for hosiery goods. This was done in part by cutting the civilian clothes ration from sixty-six to forty-eight coupons, in part by introducing austerity regulations—the restriction of men's socks to a length of nine inches, the prohibition of the manufacture of girls' gym stockings and so on[2]—and in part by accepting woollen yarns instead of the worsted yarns that were normal in the hosiery industry. The civilian ration of wool hosiery goods continued to exist on a hand-to-mouth basis until in March 1943 there were big cuts in Service clothing requirements which diverted worsted yarn to civilian purposes. Deliveries of worsted yarn for civilian hosiery rose from an average of 6·5 million lbs. per four months' allocation period before March 1943 to an average of 8·2 million lbs. after that date.[3] These increases were offset by reduced deliveries of cotton yarn so that their effect was not to increase the total production of hosiery but to increase the supply of warmer garments.

The shortage of labour for civilian hosiery production was only subsidiary to the shortage of yarn. In the autumn of 1941 Service demands for hosiery had actually decreased; concentrated though the industry was, there had been short-time working because raw material shortages prevented sufficient increases in civilian production to offset the Service cuts and the Ministry of Labour had been encouraged to withdraw redundant labour. When Service demands increased once more at the beginning of 1942, the hosiery industry had 4,000 workers less than the labour force of 65,000 permitted under concentration. By this time the shortage was difficult to remedy for in Leicester, the main centre of the hosiery industry, the munitions industry was expanding rapidly. All the Ministry of Labour could do was to try and rebuild the labour force to 65,000 and to agree to schedule the industry under the Essential Work Order. Later, in March 1943, the reduction of Service demands made possible a release of 5,500 workers from hosiery production out of an actual labour force of about 58,750 workers. This release was spread over the industry by the calculation of revised permitted labour forces in the individual firms. From this time until the end of the war there was little change in the industry's labour force.

---

[1] The total of both woollen and worsted yarns actually delivered to the hosiery industry during the last half of 1942 appears to have been about 11·2 million lbs. See Appendix 12 at the end of this chapter.

[2] See p. 438.

[3] Compared to an average of 7·4 million lbs. of both woollen and worsted yarns before March 1943 and an average of 9·1 million lbs. after that date. See Appendix 12 at the end of this chapter.

In order to mitigate the effects of the shortages of yarn and labour, it was clearly important to ensure that production in the hosiery industry was concentrated only on essential goods. There was some discussion about the form of control—whether manufacturers should be persuaded, by preferential treatment, to manufacture goods according to the wishes of the Board of Trade as in the case of the making-up industry or whether they should be compelled to do so by the issue of directions, as for example in the cotton industry. Both methods of production control cut across the Board of Trade's obligations under the concentration White Paper to nucleus firms. For the White Paper had promised to help safeguard the supplies of raw materials to nucleus firms. Yet production control would obviously mean that some nucleus firms would be given preferential treatment compared with others. The Board were, for this reason, reluctant to establish the control. They were, however, forced to do so in order to tailor their meagre allocation of material to fit civilian needs. In the end, the control over hosiery followed the same pattern as that for the control over the textile industries. Compulsion was used in order to secure planned production: the legal basis was the Apparel and Textiles Order of 1942.[1]

This system of control and the utility hosiery scheme will be described in the next chapter. Here we shall simply mention the institution that exercised the control over the hosiery industry. At the end of March 1942 a Directorate of Civilian Clothing (Hosiery) was established in Leicester. It took over from the Hosiery Rationing Committee the responsibility for policy in distributing yarn though the Committee continued to handle the mechanism of distribution. The system of distributing yarn on the basis of fair shares to manufacturers had broken down and national need was the new criterion. Two trade committees (the War Emergency Committees), one for England and one for Scotland, were set up as a link between the industry and the Directorate who worked together in amicable partnership during the rest of the war. From the summer of 1942 the Ministry of Supply and the Board of Trade agreed to institute 'joint planning' of Service and civilian hosiery requirements and to inform each other in advance of any large-scale new demands likely to arise. Finally, in August 1944, the hosiery production branch of the Ministry of Supply was merged with the Directorate of Civilian Hosiery.

---

[1] The hosiery industry was governed by the Knitted Goods Directions issued under the Order (S.R. & O. 1942, No. 1003), and by a second Order (S.R. & O. 1942, No. 1258), prohibiting the manufacture of any knitted goods except in accordance with directions issued by the Board of Trade.

APPENDIX 11

Labour Force in the Clothing Industry, Great Britain

Thousands

	Tailoring[1]			Hats and Caps[1]			Shirts, Collars[1] Underwear, Overalls, Blouses, etc.			Dressmaking[2] and Millinery			Dress industries[2] not separately specified, e.g. corsets, gloves, umbrellas, etc.			GRAND TOTALS			
	M	F	Total	M	F	Total	M	F	Total	M	F	Total	M	F	Total	M	F	Total	
Mid 1939	66·6	168·0	234·6	11·1	18·5	29·6	10·1	83·4	93·5	11·4	94·0	105·4	7·6	23·8	31·4	106·8	387·7	494·5	1939
Mid 1940	54·8	188·5	243·3	8·2	15·5	23·7	8·9	82·6	91·5	10·0	72·7	82·7	6·8	23·8	30·6	88·7	383·1	471·8	1940
Mid 1941	49·3	192·7	242·0	7·0	16·2	23·2	6·8	70·9	77·7	6·8	63·8	70·6	5·0	19·3	24·3	74·9	362·9	437·8	1941
Mid 1942	41·4	153·2	194·6	5·6	13·5	19·1	5·1	53·3	58·4	6·6	49·8	56·4	3·5	13·6	17·1	62·2	283·4	345·6	1942
Mid 1943	38·0	140·1	178·1	3·8	8·9	12·7	4·7	50·4	55·1	4·9	45·2	50·1	3·0	11·4	14·4	54·4	256·0	310·4	1943
Mid 1944	34·9	123·6	158·5	3·3	8·1	11·4	4·4	45·2	49·6	5·0	42·4	47·4	2·7	10·9	13·6	50·3	230·2	280·5	1944
Mid 1945	37·4	134·8	172·2	3·7	9·0	12·7	4·2	48·3	52·5	6·7	45·6	52·3	2·8	11·4	14·2	54·8	249·1	303·9	1945

[1] All insured workers, males 14–64, females 14–59, both manual and clerical, but excluding non-manual workers earning over £420 p.a. Part-time female workers included, two being counted as one unit.

[2] These figures are the estimated numbers of insured persons in employment in Great Britain in the dressmaking and miscellaneous clothing industries. They do not include part-time workers,

Source: Statistical Digest of the War and Ministry of Labour

APPENDIX 12

Consumption of Yarn in the Hosiery Industry

(a) Total Deliveries of Yarn to the Hosiery Industry

Million lbs.

	1937[1]	1942[2] July–Oct.	1942–43 Nov.–Feb.	1943 March–June	1943 July–Oct.	1943–44 Nov.–Feb.	1944 March–June	1944 July–Oct.	1944–45 Nov.–Feb.	1945 March–June
Cotton[3]	70·6	12·6	13·2	13·5	14·2	15·1	14·8	12·1	11·6	11·5
Woollen and Worsted	63·8	18·7	18·5	14·7	16·0	16·8	16·6	16·0	15·7	15·5
Rayon	20·7	4·6	5·2	5·3	3·9	4·4	4·4	4·4	4·5	4·9
Shoddy	—	—	—	—	0·5	0·4	0·6	0·6	0·7	0·7
Other Yarns	3·5	0·9	1·3	0·8	0·4	0·4	0·4	0·4	0·3	0·3
TOTAL	158·6	36·8	38·2	35·0	35·1	37·1	36·9	33·5	32·7	32·9
Totals over a 12-month period			110·1			109·1			99·2	

[1] *Hosiery Working Party Report.* Original source is Import Duties Act Inquiry, 1937.
[2] Hosiery Control Statistics 8th January 1946, for all figures from 1942 onwards.
[3] Cotton yarn includes spun rayon staple from 1942 onwards.

(b) Analysis of Wartime Consumption of Yarn by the Hosiery Industry

	1942 July–Oct.	1942–43 Nov.–Feb.	1943 March–June	1943 July–Oct.	1943–44 Nov.–Feb.	1944 March–June	1944 July–Oct.	1944–45 Nov.–Feb.	1945 March–June
Government:									
Cotton (estimated)	0·6	0·6	0·4	1·0	1·9	1·6	1·1	1·2	1·0
Woollen and Worsted	11·2	11·4	6·3	7·7	8·4	7·3	6·7	6·5	6·4
TOTAL	11·7	11·9	6·8	8·7	10·2	8·9	7·7	7·7	7·5
Total over a 12-month period		30·4			27·8			22·8	
Civilian:									
Cotton	12·1	12·6	13·1	12·8	11·5	11·3	9·9	9·3	9·5
Woollen and Worsted	7·5	7·2	8·4	8·7	9·0	10·0	9·4	9·1	8·9
Rayon	4·6	5·2	5·3	3·9	4·1	3·9	4·0	4·2	4·5
Shoddy	—	—	0·5	0·5	0·4	0·6	0·6	0·6	0·7
Other	0·9	1·3	0·9	0·4	0·4	0·3	0·4	0·3	0·3
TOTAL	25·1	26·3	28·2	26·4	25·4	26·2	24·2	23·5	23·9
Total over a 12-month period		79·6			78·0			71·7	
Exports:									
Cotton	—	—	—	—	1·1	1·1	1·0	1·1	0·9
Woollen and Worsted	—	—	—	—	—	0·2	0·1	0·2	0·2
Rayon	—	—	—	—	0·3	0·5	0·4	0·4	0·3
Shoddy	—	—	—	—	—	—	—	—	—
Other Yarns	—	—	—	—	—	—	—	—	—
TOTAL	—	—	—	—	1·5	1·8	1·5	1·7	1·5
GRAND TOTAL	36·8	38·2	35·0	35·1	37·1	36·9	33·5	32·9	32·9

CHAPTER XVII

CLOTHING POLICY

(i)

The General Outline

DURING the early months of the war there had been little thought about the problems of clothing the civilian. A scheme for standard clothing had been mooted[1] but neither the Ministry of Supply nor the Board of Trade had been anxious to foster it and the proposal had been allowed to drop. During the first year of the war there were indeed no general shortages of clothing. But by the beginning of 1941 there were well-grounded fears that shortages would soon appear. The limitation of supplies policy was bound before long to reduce the supplies of clothing in the shops and the clothing component of the cost-of-living index was already rising ominously.[2] The introduction of consumer rationing to restrain demand has already been discussed.[3] The task of this chapter is to describe how textile and clothing production was organised in order to honour the ration.

The Board of Trade were always aware that clothes rationing could not work unless the vast majority of the population helped to make it work. The system would have collapsed if there had been really wide-scale evasion or panic buying. These evils might well have arisen if the public had not felt assured that its coupons would be honoured. The Board therefore felt responsible for seeing that there was, broadly, the right amount of the right clothes in the shops at the right time and at the right price. Plentiful supplies of stockings would be no compensation for lack of shoes; it would be no use offering stock-size clothes to outsize people or to children; cotton frocks were not wanted in December. Moreover, unless the price of the majority of clothes was what the majority could afford, many people would suffer severely and there would be a black market in coupons.

The circumstances of war inevitably twisted the normal pattern of supply and demand. Some articles of clothing could not be supplied in sufficient quantities because of particularly severe raw material shortages (for example corset production was hampered for lack of

---

[1] See pp. 87-9.
[2] In January 1941 it was 160 (September 1939=100). By August it had risen to 183.
[3] See Chapter XIV.

rubber and steel). Then the demand for different garments was liable to be different from peace-time requirements; for example, the increase in the birth-rate put a heavy strain on the comparatively few firms specialising in children's clothing. Or again, with a restricted ration consumers would buy more durable and essential goods than formerly. This did indeed happen. For example, between 1942 and 1945 when supplies of boots and shoes were sixty-nine per cent. of 1935 production there were complaints of shortage; whereas the production of gloves was only thirty-nine per cent. of 1935, but there were no complaints.

There were, then, plenty of riddles and the answers to them could not be left to chance. The needs of the public must be met; the strain on the economy was so heavy that waste could not be tolerated. Amid the distortions of war demand could not make itself felt through the price system or even through the rationing system. If production were to be left to find its own level, either a large margin of raw materials would be necessary or else there would be a medley of gluts and shortages. The Board of Trade had, therefore, to plan the production of garments and of cloth for the civilian market—an interference with the normal channels of trade that was far greater than anything they had ever contemplated.

In their relationship with the clothing industries[1] the Board of Trade were in a more difficult position than the Ministry of Supply with whom they had to share the productive capacity for textiles and clothing. The Ministry of Supply not only planned its programme, but it bought the goods outright from the industries; if it had over-estimated requirements it could hold the goods concerned in its stores until demand caught up with supply again. But as we have already emphasised[2] the Board of Trade were not the customer.[3] They had to guess what the customer wanted and if the customer did not like something—such as short socks or trousers without turn-ups—he very often did not buy it. The retailer or manufacturer then suffered loss, and valuable raw material and labour were wasted. Or if the Board's estimates erred on the low side, an essential article of clothing disappeared from the shops. In either case dissatisfaction was very vocal.

For the task of planning the production of civilian clothing three things were essential. First, the Board had to compile a clothing programme or budget. This meant that the Board needed to obtain reasonably accurate estimates of the way coupons were spent by the public and then relate this picture of demand to production possibilities. Secondly, if reasonably durable goods at reasonable prices

---

[1] By 'clothing industries' are meant the textile industries—cotton, rayon and wool—the hosiery industry and the making-up industry.

[2] See Chapter VI.

[3] The question was raised whether the Board should become a direct purchaser. See p. 435.

were to be produced, the Board had to consider not only the quantities of each item of clothing but also the types of article. Thirdly, of course, the Board needed so to control the cloth and textile industries that these two aims could be fulfilled.

The pivot of clothing policy was the budget which was drawn up for four monthly periods. It was the aim of the budget to present the Cotton and Wool Controls with firm programmes of cloth required for home civilian trade within the allocations of raw materials already granted. To obtain these programmes it was necessary to work backwards from estimates of the pattern of the public's coupon expenditure. These estimates had to be translated into terms of garments and the garment estimates into terms of cloth.

This process involved some complicated calculations in which there were only two relative certainties—the size of the population and the amount of raw materials available for the home market. For the first budget, covering the first year of clothes rationing, the estimates were particularly imperfect. Coupon expenditure was calculated only for the 'lower income group' of the population.[1] The 19 million or so people in this class were divided into age-groups and an estimate was made of the minimum amount of the most essential garments that each group needed. The Board of Trade were only concerned to see that this limited programme was met; coupon demand, as interpreted by producers, was to direct the remainder of clothing production.

After mid-1942, the designation of the making-up industry enabled the Board to obtain regular returns from the selected clothing firms showing their forward programmes in terms of garments and of cloth requirements. Moreover, the Board now endeavoured to calculate the coupon expenditure of the whole population. A panel of consumers was established, consisting of about 2,500 families of varied ages and incomes, which reported regularly on their coupon expenditure. In general the information of the consumer panel showed that the proportion of the ration spent on different garments did not vary much from year to year or from family to family. Where possible the information was checked from other sources—from production statistics, special consumer surveys and statistics of retail shortages collected by area distribution officers.

The consumer panel was divided into groups which corresponded with the broad categories into which the population was divided for the issue of clothes coupons—that is, men with the basic clothes ration, men with the basic ration plus the industrial supplement,[2] women with the basic ration, women with the basic ration plus the

---

[1] i.e. all in the wage group of joint family income up to £4 per week (8 millions) and half in the group of joint income of £4–£6 per week (11 millions).

[2] See p. 321.

industrial supplement, boys, girls and infants. The members of the panel were asked about the number of coupons spent, the rate of spending, the proportion of coupons spent on different items of clothing and footwear and the clothing purchases planned in the months ahead. From the consumer panel returns the Board of Trade could calculate the number of different garments per head bought by each of these groups. These figures could then be multiplied by the total national population in each group.[1] After adding a percentage to cover other supplementary coupon issues, and contingencies such as bomb damage, and a small amount to cover black market activities, the Board possessed a summary of the clothing needs of the population for one year expressed broadly in garment categories.

The groupings of garments were then broken down into cloth by types and materials with the help of trade experts. For example, men's overcoats were divided between melton and other fabrics, women's dresses between cotton, rayon and wool cloth, and hosiery between cotton interlock, wool, and rayon locknit.[2] The information on which this analysis was made came from the production figures which were obtained regularly from the making-up and hosiery industries. In planning the budget it was, of course, necessary to take into account prospective shortages of particular materials. For example, the shortage of worsted yarn meant that men had to take more cotton interlock underwear; then a shortage of cotton interlock meant that women had to take more rayon.

After this point the rest of the budget calculations were simple. The agreed number of each type of garment was converted into cloth by means of a standard average yardage per garment or, in the case of hosiery, into yarn by means of average weights. The final stage was the cloth programme sheet showing the total yardage of each cloth required to meet the budget. This was divided very roughly between utility and non-utility in each broad category and then the amount of cloth required for each utility specification could be calculated. The total requirements of cotton and cleaned wool could then be worked out. For hosiery there was a yarn summary sheet showing the amount of cotton, rayon and wool yarn required. Finally,

---

[1] The figures in each group were:

	millions
Men with the basic ration	4
Men with the basic ration plus supplement	10
Women with the basic ration	15·6
Women with the basic ration plus supplement	4
Boys	3·6
Girls	3·4
Infants	2·7

[2] An allowance was made at this stage for the demands for cloth and knitting wool for home-made garments. Garments for special consumers, e.g. industrial overalls, were not included in the garment budget, but an allowance was made for them in the raw material estimates. Coupons were allowed for footwear in the budget.

the annual figures were divided into quarterly periods according to seasonal demands.

From 1942 onwards, when utility production was in full swing and when the production of utility clothes and utility hosiery was being carefully planned, the budget became even more detailed. For it was used to determine the amount of each type of utility cloth and hosiery to be produced. When the clothing summary sheet was prepared it was subdivided to show, for example, the amount of utility and non-utility tweed cloth required for men's jackets; the utility yardage was further subdivided into the various cloth specification numbers. Once the yardages for each specification of cloth had been obtained, the Board of Trade's cloth and yarn estimates could be compared with the forward programmes obtained by the Cotton and Wool Controls from textile manufacturers.[1] While no attempt was made to match the two estimates precisely, the Board's cloth budget was adjusted to take account of known shortages of particular yarns or cloths.

The main purpose of the clothing budget was to provide this firm programme for cloth production. The Board of Trade always watched carefully to see how closely cloth production and cloth deliveries from merchant converters were matching the budget. The Board did not —they could not—watch equally carefully the relationship between the garment requirements set forth in the budget and garment production.

There could indeed be no exact programme of clothing production because the Board of Trade were not directly responsible for the pro-duction of clothes. The whole clothing scheme was based on the maintenance of normal commercial channels for placing orders and the Board had to try to influence the orders in various ways without a strict and direct control over production. They had a strong control over hosiery but not over the making-up industry. Although they had some control over the output of utility clothes by designated firms, an appreciable margin of production was left in the hands of undesig-nated firms about whom the Board knew very little. Moreover, the budget included a considerable amount of non-utility clothes and here the control over production was very slender indeed.

From mid-1942 onwards the Board did their best to influence garment production. Designated makers-up and nucleus hosiery firms had to supply forward estimates of their production programmes and of their requirements for each utility yarn or cloth. The Board of Trade compared these estimates with the budget figures and where there were very obvious gaps they asked manufacturers to modify their production in order to reduce the output of garments which had been over-subscribed and stimulate the production of neglected

---

[1] The detailed conversion of the budgets into cotton and wool yarns and cloths is discussed below in Section (ii).

lines. They did not however issue directions to makers-up. The only legal sanction behind their persuasion was the statutory requirement that each utility cloth might only be made into certain garments.[1] The Board could, however, sometimes influence production by cloth allocation—for example, by giving more cloth to firms making baby clothes and less to firms who wanted the same cloth for, say, women's blouses.

The possibilities of error in the whole of the budget calculations were large. For their forward planning and their knowledge as to how far the plans were being fulfilled the Board of Trade received plentiful figures of production, stocks and sales of cloth and clothing. These were of varying accuracy and completeness. Cotton, rayon and wool producers made regular returns to the Controls of their stocks and of the cloth they had supplied to makers-up and wholesalers; the figures for wool were however less comprehensive than for cotton and rayon. The Board of Trade paid particular attention to the figures they themselves collected showing merchant converters' sales and stocks of finished cotton and rayon cloth; until the end of 1944, however, these figures did not include one of the most important parts of the picture—the converters' stocks of grey cloth.[2] For the output of finished goods the Board collected figures from the hosiery and making-up industries and also received figures giving the output of the boots and shoes industry. The hosiery figures were a pretty complete record of output achieved and output planned and of yarn consumption. The making-up figures also showed production achieved and production planned and in addition cloth consumption and cloth stocks. These figures for making-up, however, only covered designated makers-up and for a time only a proportion of them; undesignated firms made no returns. In addition to all these returns about cloth and finished garments, the Board of Trade also had figures for wholesale and retail sales and stocks of cloth and clothing.

It was, however, difficult to interpret this mass of figures with any degree of certainty. In the first place, returns for any period of time could obviously only be collected when that period had passed. There might be a gap of two months or even four months before the Board of Trade had the information before them. Then the economic process was immensely complicated. Between the processing of raw materials and their appearance in the shops as finished garments there were many stages of production and distribution. It was most difficult to trace stocks through these stages, particularly as the original stocks of cloth were unknown. Moreover, since the Board of Trade did not themselves handle clothing production and distribution they could not always know which of several possible reasons

---

[1] See p. 432.

[2] Even after 1944 the figures were only for utility grey cloth.

caused a sudden fall of stocks. For example, if wholesale stocks of clothing fell, this might be due to increased sales to retailers or to decreased purchases from manufacturers. To interpret the reasons for increased sales to retailers, officials had to consider seasonal factors and the timing of coupon issues. And decreased purchases from manufacturers might be due either to the desire of wholesalers to carry smaller stocks of some particular garments or to their inability to procure supplies. In the latter event shortages of production might be due either to shortages of cloth or of manufacturing capacity in the making-up trades.

There were other difficulties in budgeting besides the interpretation of figures. The budget had to be planned many months in advance of the coupon issue to which it related. There was a long time lag between the processing of the raw materials and their sale as finished garments. This lag varied from garment to garment and lengthened as the war went on; it remained as low as four to eight months for some garments, but rose to as much as a year for some cotton and woollen goods towards the end of the war. Thus, if a shortage of some essential item was not foreseen it was many months before it could be remedied. When errors were made they were magnified by the immense size of the planning operation—a forty-coupon ration meant a total issue of over 2,500 million coupons a year.

Another difficulty in planning ahead came from a rather unexpected quarter—from price-control measures. It was unfortunately fairly common for manufacturers to reduce their production of garments whose ceiling prices they believed were about to be increased. And sometimes when the Board of Trade investigated shortages of particular kinds of production—often shortages of particular sizes—they found that manufacturers had carefully scrutinised the price schedule and were naturally reluctant to make those things on which the price ceilings pressed most heavily.

Altogether it would not be surprising if plans sometimes went awry. It was difficult for the Board of Trade with their indirect methods of control to keep supply and demand for particular garments in close and continuous balance. To take one example: boys' shorts. There were at first shortages due to inadequate output. Then output was expanded or rather over-expanded and the over-expansion continued too long because the shortage did not disappear overnight. Stocks therefore became excessive, buyers struck, output was reduced, but too far and for too long until stocks were once more extremely low.

As far as total supply and demand for clothing were concerned, the Board of Trade's budgeting activities seem to have been reasonably accurate. Some margin of error was, however, inevitable, particularly as the budget during 1942 and 1943 was a minimum one; that is, it made no allowance for contingencies—for under-production of some clothes and over-production of others, for shortages of particular 'types of cloth' and so forth. It was recognised that this would probably lead to some fall of stocks which were in most cases more than sufficient. In the event, however, as we shall see later, stocks fell too far so that it seems that the budget had in fact been slightly 'underplanned'. The supplies of material and labour that had seemed large enough to maintain the clothes ration had not in fact been adequate and the supply of textiles had been maintained by too great a drain on stocks. This underplanning might not by itself have caused any serious trouble. It must, however, have aggravated the difficulties that were arising in the last half of 1944 when the labour force of the cloth and clothing industries was proving unable to meet all the demands placed upon it. The production of cloth and clothing then fell so far that, allowing for the time lag in production, the clothes ration had to be cut at a time when it was least expected —that is, in the eight months from September 1945.[1]

We have carried the description of clothes budgeting methods on to the end of the war. In this description utility production has inevitably been mentioned and we must now turn back to examine this part of the Board of Trade's policy more closely. For it was the Board's answer to the problem of providing reasonably durable clothes at reasonable prices. The continuing rise of clothing prices during the summer of 1941 caused a good deal of concern. Rationing no doubt helped to curb the rise. But it was clear that in part the rise was due to general trading-up; to counteract this, increased supplies of cheaper clothing were needed. The essential clothing scheme,[2] which freed from quota control children's garments and cheaper kinds of cloth and clothing, was designed to release such supplies from stock. But it was only a temporary expedient and in August 1941 the utility clothing scheme was launched as the long-term plan to ensure that adequate supplies of reasonably priced clothing were produced. The utility policy rested on twin controls —control of prices and control of production—and it is not easy to separate the discussion of them. Nevertheless, for the sake of clarity this must be done; here we shall concern ourselves with control of production.[3]

In the early discussions about utility policy during the summer of 1941 it was proposed that utility clothes should simply cover a limited range of popular fabrics which would be cheap and durable enough to give reasonable service; these should be produced in

---

[1] See p. 472.

[2] See p. 554.

[3] The price aspects of the utility policy are discussed below in Chapter XXI.

sufficient quantities to supply the lower income groups. This intention was however modified. Anxious though the Board of Trade were to avoid stimulating consumption, they did not wish utility to become synonymous with 'cheap and nasty'. Moreover the consumer, who wanted good value per coupon, joined with the manufacturers and distributors, who wanted maximum profit per coupon, in pressing for more expensive utility ranges. In the end, the utility policy covered a very wide range and a high standard of clothing.

It took the Board of Trade some ten months after the introduction of the utility scheme to evolve the necessary forms of control over the clothing industries. The types of control varied widely for each branch of the industry, and they will be discussed in detail later.[1] In each case, however, the utility policy had two requirements—first, the introduction of some form of standardised or clearly specified cloth and clothing and, secondly, machinery for restricting the output of non-utility goods and stimulating the production of utility.

Without clear specifications strict price control was impossible. But it was, of course, a lengthy and difficult business to draw them up. The Board of Trade enlisted the help of the industries concerned and of the British Standards Institution. Even so, it was not until June 1942 that specifications of varying precision were introduced for cotton and rayon and wool cloth, hosiery and boots and shoes. Specifications were not introduced for made-up garments except in the case of overalls and women's underwear; utility clothes were simply garments made from utility cloths.[2]

Utility cloth, however, could only be made into utility garments and as from May 1942 only into stated types of utility garments.[3] When in 1942 a list of closer specifications was published for cotton, rayon and wool cloths, separate lists of garments were published; against each garment were shown the number and names of the cloths which might be used in making it. These cloths could be confined to the types of clothing for which they were suitable and maximum prices and margins could be fixed for the garments at each stage until they reached the consumer.[4]

In order to identify utility clothes for the purposes of price control, it was not enough simply to specify utility cloths. The cloths and the garments made from them had to be clearly marked. In November 1941 an Order was issued[5] making it compulsory to apply to utility cloths

---

[1] See Section (ii) of this chapter.

[2] Simplifications of design that were introduced (see pp. 436–9) applied both to utility and non-utility clothes.

[3] e.g. S.R. & O. 1942, No. 1008, and amending Orders.

[4] Export of utility cloth was forbidden. Utility cloth was exempted from purchase tax in August 1942 and for a time it was subsidised (see Chapter XXI).

[5] S.R. & O. 1941, No. 1614.

and garments the distinguishing mark thus:—
Once applied, the mark might not be defaced or
removed. In August 1943 the system of identification was tightened by an Order which required
not only the utility mark to be shown but also the specification
number of the cloth used to make the garment.[1] Detailed regulations about the size of, and method of applying, the utility mark
were also made.[2] Thus utility cloth could be treated legally and
administratively as a distinct commodity, even if it were identical
with a non-utility cloth.

Specification of cloths was not only a method of enforcing price
control. It also helped to economise in labour and materials and thus
reduce manufacturing costs by eliminating uneconomical short runs
and by cutting out unnecessary processes. Moreover, it ensured that
the public received good value for their coupons by getting rid of
many of the unserviceable shoddy goods which had existed before
the war.

It must be emphasised that utility specifications did not kill variety
in clothing. Economists might complain that 'variety is one of the
elements in the standard of living that can be most easily dispensed
with'[3] and that standardisation should go further. But the trade press
and the public disliked the idea of standardisation and at first suspected the utility policy on those grounds. In practice, the difficulty
of enforcing standardisation on a type of production over which
fashion normally exerted such a strong influence was considerable.
It was to some extent overcome by making specifications for utility
cloths but not for utility garments. But even in the case of the closely-
specified cotton and rayon cloths it was the construction of the
cloths[4] and not their colour or design that was laid down; these
variations in finish were enough to conceal the fact of standardisation
from the ordinary consumer. There were, as we shall see, style
restrictions on all garments, both utility and non-utility;[5] but these
were not sufficiently numerous to limit seriously the scope of design
in making-up.

There was one interesting experiment in the design of utility
clothing. Ten well-known fashion designers (all members of the
Incorporated Society of London Fashion Designers) were asked to
prepare designs for women's coats, dresses, blouses and skirts suitable
for utility production. Templates blue-printed like architects'
drawings were made of the designs and these were made available to

---

[1] S.R. & O. 1943, No. 1208.
[2] S.R. & O. 1942, No. 1012.
[3] See *The Economist*, 7th March 1942, p. 317.
[4] See p. 442.
[5] See pp. 436–9.

those manufacturers of utility clothing who asked for them.[1] This scheme gave favourable publicity to utility clothes for women, showing that elegance and fashion were compatible with austerity restrictions and utility prices.[2] Moreover, it promoted economy in designers' labour.

The Board of Trade's efforts to make utility popular were justified. When utility clothes began to appear in substantial quantities in the shops, public reactions were generally favourable.[3] The general comment was that the clothes were of decent quality and at decent prices. The effect on prices was marked; even before purchase tax was removed from utility clothes retailers reported that women's utility coats of comparable if not better quality were selling at about a guinea cheaper than free ranges in the same shop. Or to take another example: children's utility coats were eighteen shillings and sixpence compared with thirty shillings for non-utility of similar quality.

Ideally, if the Board of Trade aimed at achieving anything like the certainty of control over clothing and textile prices which the Ministry of Food had achieved over food prices,[4] clothing and textile products should have been 100 per cent. utility. In practice, however, it was never possible to reach this figure except for a few items like overalls and sheets. Utility production ranged from about sixty to seventy per cent. of output in wool cloths to ninety to ninety-five per cent. of output in hosiery; on average it was about eighty per cent. of total production. There were serious difficulties in raising this proportion.[5] Chief of these were the variety of raw materials and the variety of machinery in normal use, much of which was not suitable for mass-production methods. Moreover, there were a good many firms in the making-up industry which were not equipped for the 'skilled art of making cheap clothes'. Some of them indeed turned with a will to making utility clothes. But others were less adaptable and there would have been no economy in leaving their resources idle; the Ministry of Labour could be relied on to remove from them any labour which could be more usefully employed.

In planning their clothing policy—both the programming of production and the manufacture of utility clothes—the Board of Trade were faced with the problem of the kind of control they should exercise over the clothing industries. There were two alternatives. Either the Board could assume direct responsibility for the production of

---

[1] After the first trade showing over 100 manufacturers asked for them.

[2] Utility clothes probably improved the general style of women's mass-produced clothes by concentrating on 'line' and cutting out unnecessary trimmings.

[3] Reactions were not always so favourable to the style restrictions. See pp. 438, 439.

[4] This is what the Chancellor of the Exchequer had hoped. In fact, of course, the Ministry of Food operated under very different conditions from the Board of Trade. See p. 75.

[5] See H. of C. Deb., Vol. 382, Col. 213. Speech of the President of the Board of Trade.

clothing by becoming a direct purchaser or they could simply guide production into the right channels. The first alternative would mean that the Board could either buy clothing and distribute it through normal trade channels or they could buy the cloth and sell it to manufacturers on the condition that it was made into prescribed clothing. This would have meant setting up a control analagous to that of the Ministry of Supply over Service clothing. The second alternative would mean that neither cloth nor clothing would come into the possession of the Government at any stage; production could be guided either by the selective allocation of raw materials and cloth, or by issuing directions to manufacturers on what they should produce. These alternatives were extensively discussed; but the vast scale of purchase, administration and ownership involved in the first method finally ruled it out. Production would instead be guided.

The difficulty of this method of indirect control was that of forcing a large number of people to make something they did not want to make. There were doubts whether control by raw materials—which in the end was to be the linchpin of the system—would be effective. Certainly, experience hitherto had shown that control of a long chain of manufacture from the raw material end was too remote to be adequate by itself. But the issue of directions was also difficult if only because of the large numbers of firms involved. Finally, clothing policy was enforced by a combination of directions and raw material controls, the proportions varying from industry to industry.

As far as utility clothing was concerned, production could be stimulated either by offering inducements to manufacturers or by threats of compulsion. When utility clothing was introduced in August 1941 the method of inducement was adopted because time was too short to allow any elaborate schemes of compulsion to be worked out. A Woven Textiles (Cloth and Apparel) Order[1] extended the system of quota control for a further nine months and introduced a quota for utility goods roughly double the non-utility quota.[2] In practice this quota inducement was somewhat deceptive. Neither raw material nor coupon issues would have permitted all firms to produce up to the permitted utility level. Indeed, although the utility cloth quota was double the non-utility quota, the garment budget for the last quarter of 1941 was higher for non-utility than for utility. Nevertheless, the Order did do something to stimulate the supply of cheaper goods.[3]

---

[1] S.R. & O. 1941, No. 1281.

[2]

	Utility quota	*Non-utility quota*	
Woven wool cloth .	30%	15% ⎫	base period—year ending
Woven non-wool cloth	20%	9% ⎭	31st March 1940
Knitted cloths . .	50%	25%	base period—year ending 31st May 1940

[3] Utility specifications were at this time loose (see pp. 440–1).

Meanwhile, machinery was being evolved for controlling output more closely. Under the Apparel and Textiles Order of May 1942[1] the Board of Trade assumed the necessary powers to control the manufacture and supply of woven wool and non-wool cloth, knitted goods, corsets, gloves, fur apparel, footwear, hand knitting yarn, felt hat hoods, lace, lace net and bedding. This was simply an enabling Order under which the Board could apply their policies by directions issued to manufacturers and suppliers.[2] As direct control of production came to be applied, quotas were abolished.[3]

One more control over the production of clothing remains to be described—the so-called 'austerity' regulations. These were introduced in the spring of 1942 to save labour and materials by simplifying styles of made-up garments. They applied to utility and non-utility alike. They were drawn up on the advice of twelve advisory panels covering the main sections of the trade,[4] and were published in a series of Orders, the Making-up of Civilian Clothing (Restrictions) Orders of 1942 and 1943.[5]

---

[1] S.R. & O. 1942, No. 1000.

[2] e.g. S.R. & O. 1942, Nos. 1001, 1002, 1003, 1004.

[3] *Ibid.*

[4] Men's outerwear; boys' outerwear; rainwear; shirts and pyjamas; household overalls; industrial overalls; women's and maids' heavy outerwear; women's underwear; women's and maids' blouses and dresses; infants' and girls' light clothing; infants' and girls' heavy clothing; corsets.

[5] The Making of Civilian Clothing (Restrictions) Orders are as follows:

(a) Men's suits (No. 1 Order), S.R. & O. 1942, No. 541	Revoked by S.R. & O. 1944, No. 101.
(b) Men's overcoats and boys' suits (No. 2 Order), S.R. & O. 1942, No. 606	
(c) Men's and boys' shirts and pyjamas (No. 5 Order), S.R. & O. 1942, No. 702	
(d) Household overalls (No. 10 Order), S.R. & O. 1942, No. 1041	Superseded by S.R. & O. 1944, Nos. 6 and 256.
(e) Industrial overalls (No. 12 Order), S.R. & O. 1942, No. 1521	Superseded by (No. 15 Order), S.R. & O. 1942, Nos. 2107 and 2615. Superseded by S.R. & O. 1944, Nos. 6, 256.
(f) Women's and maids' suits and overcoats (No. 4 Order), S.R. & O. 1942, No. 701	Amended by S.R. & O. 1942, No. 1364.
(g) Women's and maids' dresses and blouses (No. 6 Order), S.R. & O. 1942, No. 784	Superseded by (No. 13), S.R. & O. 1942, No. 1541.
(h) Women's underwear (No. 3 Order), S.R. & O. 1942, No. 658	Superseded by (No. 11), S.R. & O. 1942, No. 1436.
(i) Infants' and girls' outerwear (No. 7 Order), S.R. & O. 1942, No. 785	Superseded by S.R. & O. 1944, Nos. 6, 256.
(j) Corsets (No. 8 Order), S.R. & O. 1942, No. 833	Superseded by (No. 16) Order, S.R. & O. 1942, No. 2224; and revoked, except for limitations on use of rubber, by S.R. & O. 1944, No. 1295.
(k) Rainwear, S.R. & O. 1942, No. 882	Superseded by S.R. & O. 1944, No. 786.
(l) Hosiery and knitwear (No. 14 Order), S.R. & O. 1942, No. 1919	Superseded by S.R. & O. 1943, No. 265.

There were several types of restrictions. The first type forbade trimmings such as embroidery, appliqué work, fur or leather trimmings on outerwear or ornamental stitching on underwear. The saving involved in such prohibitions was probably not large, but the speed of production was increased. The purpose of the second type of restriction was economy in scarce raw materials such as steel and rubber. For example, the use of elastic was forbidden in all garments except women's corsets and knickers, infants' clothes, industrial headwear and so on.

The third type of restriction was on the style and design of garments. In women's outerwear, the number of pleats, seams, buttons and buttonholes in a garment was limited and maximum widths for sleeves, belts, hems and collars were fixed. With men's clothing the most celebrated restriction of this kind was the prohibition of trouser turn-ups; but there were also restrictions on the length of shirts, prohibitions on double shirt cuffs and limitations on the number of buttons and buttonholes used. With rainwear a maximum width of skirt for all garments was fixed.

These restrictions had, as their primary aim, economy in the use of cloth, and in this they achieved some success. Shorter shirts without double cuffs could, when produced in large numbers, save a considerable amount of cloth.[1] One large-scale manufacturer of women's cheap coats considered that his firm saved a quarter of a yard both of woollen and of lining cloth in every 'austerity' coat they made. This represented a total yearly saving of 50,000 yards of each type of cloth. Two other Orders of this kind were made, for two specialised types of clothing: the first, the Making of Uniforms (Restrictions) Order,[2] which enforced 'austerity' styles (chiefly simplified pockets) for Army officers' Service dress, and the second, which was not issued until December 1943, the Civilian Clothing (Nurses' Indoor Uniforms) Order[3] which prohibited the trimmings and uneconomical styles of dress which characterised the uniforms of some hospitals.

The fourth type of restrictions were those designed to encourage long runs of production. In a number of the Orders—those relating to goods in which there was a strong fashion element—a limitation was put on the number of basic designs to be made by any firm in any year. Manufacturers of women's underwear were restricted to six shapes for each article produced, manufacturers of women's dresses to 'fifty sets of basic style templates per annum'. Variation in infants' wear, which was particularly scarce, was even more drastically

---

[1] It was estimated that the 2 inches off the length of men's shirt tails and the abolition of double cuffs saved about 4 million square yards of cotton annually, and about 1,000 operatives in the cloth manufacture alone.

[2] S.R. & O. 1942, No. 763.

[3] S.R. & O. 1943. No. 1702.

reduced; one style of 'buster suits, buster rompers, or rompers', two styles of blouses and fifteen styles of infants' and girls' dresses only were permitted. With industrial and household overalls a similar type of restriction was imposed in a rather different form. The manufacture of all domestic and industrial overalls, utility and non-utility, was prohibited, except for garments conforming to specifications drawn up and issued by the British Standards Institution on behalf of the Board of Trade. In the production of overalls the Board of Trade approached most closely to a real policy of standardisation.

Lastly, there were the controls over the making of garments which consisted of positive requirements rather than restrictions: they were designed to set a minimum standard rather than to check the excesses of fashion. These covered all overalls and women's underwear, blouses and dresses and consisted of provisions relating to the sizing of garments and minimum standards of making-up. With women's dresses and overalls the provisions consisted of minimum measurements for each size of garment.[1] With women's underwear and nightwear there was in addition to these size regulations a schedule of making-up requirements,[2] prescribing the standard of sewing, the width, type and finishing of seams to be used in all garments. Specifications for stockings included the type of rayon used, the type of cotton used for top and foot, the length of leg, etc. The specifications for overalls and underwear were the only ones in which the economies and restrictions were made watertight by stipulating the maximum yardage of material to be used for each size of garment.[3]

There were style restrictions not only on woven garments but also on hosiery. These were introduced in September 1942. They were similar to those on made-up woven goods and included limitations on the number of buttons or of pockets on cardigans, prohibition of pockets on pullovers, elimination of the buttoned openings on men's vests and pants, prohibitions of trimmings and ornamental transfers.[4] The most notorious of these measures was the enforcement of the short sock. Maximum leg lengths were fixed for men's and boys' socks —in no case were they to exceed $9\frac{1}{2}$ inches. This measure, designed to save worsted yarn, encountered considerable opposition from the consumer and there was little sale for the short sock so long as stocks of longer socks lasted. The shorter socks had to be down-pointed. When retail stocks of long socks disappeared the problem solved itself —sales resistance to short socks inevitably vanished.

---

[1] Similar minimum measurements were prescribed in the making-up directions under the Apparel and Textiles Order. These regulations applied, however, to utility goods only.

[2] S.R. & O. 1944, No. 6; related specification No. 2; Part II.

[3] When the question of the removal of restrictions was opened in the autumn of 1944, it is interesting to see that the trade manufacturing and distributing organisations were anxious for these minimum making-up standards to be permanently retained.

[4] S.R. & O. 1942, No. 1919 and 1943, No. 1100.

The restrictions on style were a mixed collection which varied in value and in the possibility of enforcing them. They were most valuable where they introduced minimum standards into the industry and least valuable when they tried to control fashion.[1] The effective control over extravagance in fashion lay in the utility ceiling prices and the labour shortage rather than in the restrictions on style. In men's wear the influence of fashion meant resistance to any changes involving economies. Definite savings of cloth were achieved by restrictions on shirts and suits, but evasion was fairly common— certainly at least in bespoke tailoring.[2] The austerity regulations as a whole proved difficult to enforce. A period of grace was given during which garments already cut could be completed in non-austerity styles, but it was difficult to prove that a garment had been cut after the relevant date. The Orders also brought in their train a host of minor licensing problems mostly connected with people who could not wear austerity garments for one reason or another—the disabled, the very tall or the very large and others.[3]

In February 1944 the austerity restrictions for men's outer clothes were removed. For it was decided that the demobilised soldiers could not be offered civilian clothing in austerity styles. The makers-up then maintained with some justification that the simultaneous manu- facture of two types of clothes would not only slow down production but would make the austerity regulations impossible to enforce. In order to clear stocks, austerity suits had to be down-pointed and some were sold to the Ministry of Supply for relief purposes. Manufacturers urged that the other austerity restrictions should also be repealed. But the restriction on the length of men's socks was not removed until November 1945 and the restrictions on other men's hosiery until January 1946.[4] The bulk of the restrictions on women's clothes were not removed until March and April 1946.[5]

We have discussed the general measures by which the Board of Trade's clothing policy was implemented, and we must now study the controls as they were applied to each industry. The variation in method from industry to industry was made necessary partly because the extent of Government control varied so widely and partly because in the summer of 1942 these industries had reached very different stages of economic mobilisation. The Cotton Control was, for example, very different from the Wool Control. And while concen-

---

[1] The prohibition of trimmings, for example, frequently stimulated new kinds of decoration such as metal studs instead of sequins, stencilled designs instead of embroidery, and so on.

[2] e.g. trouser legs could be made longer than necessary and then turned up at home.

[3] Doctors were allowed more than the austerity number of pockets and surgical corsets were free of restrictions on production of a doctor's certificate.

[4] S.R. & O. 1945, No. 1422, and S.R. & O. 1946, No. 124.

[5] S.R. & O. 1946, Nos. 264, 316, 428, 618.

tration had been carried out in the cotton, boot and shoe and hosiery industries, it had not got far in the wool industry and had not yet been attempted in the making-up industry. The labour losses of these industries also varied considerably. For these reasons, therefore, and also because of their own inexperience, the Board of Trade had to proceed by trial and error and by *ad hoc* decisions.

(ii)

The Controls in Detail

The arrangements made with the Cotton and Wool Controls were fundamental to the utility clothing scheme. For unless supplies of marked cloth were adequate and unless the price and making-up conditions attached to them were enforceable, the entire scheme would collapse. The histories of the production of cotton and wool cloth were, however, very different. Cotton and rayon cloths became far more closely specified than wool cloth and control over the production and distribution of cotton and rayon cloth from the spinner to the maker-up was more rigid than the control of wool cloth. The main reason for this divergence was that in September 1941, when utility production began, the shortage of labour and of raw material in the wool industry was not nearly so acute as it was in the cotton industry.

UTILITY COTTON CLOTHS

From the beginning of the utility cloth scheme it was clear that it would be very difficult to lay down minimum quality and maximum price specifications for a wide range of cloths in an industry as complex as the cotton industry. Nevertheless it was done. Before the war the number of varieties of cloths had run into thousands if not tens of thousands, all of them calling for slightly different yarns, weaves and finishes and sometimes varying by only a few threads to an inch. Even though the utility range was in the end wider than had at first been thought necessary, the pre-war number of cloths was drastically reduced.

For a few months after the introduction of the utility scheme control over cotton cloths was still relatively slack in comparison with what it was to become. Specifications were loose and so was control over production. The first cotton utility cloths numbered sixteen and were very simply described, being identified only by name, price and number.[1] For example, Number 301 was 'flannelette and winceyette

---

[1] S.R. & O. 1941, No. 1281.

pyjama cloth, maximum price one shilling per yard'. These became known as the three-figure cloth specifications as opposed to the close four-figure specifications introduced for cotton and rayon nine months later. There was no stipulation as to quality; indeed, any cloth which approximated to a three-figure specification could be submitted to the Manchester Chamber of Commerce Testing House for test and could be classed as utility if it complied with the broad description. Some of these three-figure cloths gave utility a bad name: it could be said that utility at this stage was no more than a convenient label for the varieties of cotton cloths normally consumed by the lower income groups of the community.

In these early months, there was a threefold control over cloth production. First, the Materials Committee allocations imposed an upper limit on the amount of cloth manufactured for the home market. Secondly, under consumer rationing coupons were passed back at every stage of distribution and production until they reached the registered firm (usually in the case of cotton the merchant converter). Thirdly, to bolster these other controls in the early days of rationing there was the Cloth and Apparel Order with its double quota system.[1] All three controls were indirect ones. The Cloth Planning Department of the Cotton Control was not fully functioning and cloth production was still in general organised on traditional lines. On the basis of the Board of Trade's budget for different types of cloth[2] the Control gave merchant converters a percentage allocation of their standard period trade in that cloth. This allocation certificate was passed back to the spinners and was in fact a guarantee of the issue by the Control of a delivery licence for an equivalent quantity of yarn. Thus the merchant converter still retained his position of initiative in the cotton industry. Utility cloths were woven to his order and he could still place orders for a great variety of cloths.

In the early summer of 1942 specifications and production arrangements were both tightened. In May technical descriptions of the new four-figure closely specified cloths were published by the British Standards Institution,[3] and they were made compulsory by directions under the new Apparel and Textiles Order. The list was later extended and by the end of August it included 102 cotton and 69 rayon specifications. All these specifications were for apparel cloths; neither household textiles nor furnishing fabrics were included as yet. What was a four-figure specification? It was, as described by the Board of Trade, an attempt to produce a series of cloths which would be good coupon value and make the right use of raw material, and which could be produced in reasonable bulk from

---

[1] See Chapter XIV, p. 310 for reasons for retaining quota control.

[2] See p. 427.

[3] BS/BOT/24 for cotton cloths and BS/BOT/23 for rayon cloths. See Appendix 13.

available yarns using available machinery. The specification itself
was a highly technical document which defined the type of cotton
yarn which might be used, the fineness or count of yarn employed,
the closeness of the weave (that is, the number of threads per inch
lengthways and crossways of the cloth), the weight of cotton per yard
and the weight of added matter, the degree of shrinkage and the type
of finish—raising, bleaching, printing and so forth—considered
appropriate for the particular cloth construction. Rayon specifications
prescribed the number of threads in the warp and in the selvedge
and the length of shrinkage to be given in finishing.

Discussion about the technical construction of the cloths and the
price margins had gone on all through early 1942 between the Cotton
Control, the Cotton Board, the Shirley Institute, the Manchester
Chamber of Commerce Testing House and various committees of
weavers and converters having special knowledge of each group of
cloths. As a starting point these committees took representative cloths
from each of the ranges already scheduled, working somewhere near
the prices of the three-figure specifications. More elaborate specifications were then worked out. These took account of the raw
materials and spinning and weaving facilities which existed, and the
Control suggested an alternative cloth when it was necessary to avoid
particularly serious strains on productive capacity. In order to
qualify for inclusion in the schedule a cloth had to have—in order of
importance—a substantial consumer demand and good coupon
value. Then it must not be a speciality product and finally it must be
economical of labour. Goods of the lowest quality, provided they
were not plainly a misuse of labour and material, were included as
well as those of better quality. The specifications were planned to fit
in with Service requirements using, for example, neither high counts
needed for surgical dressings nor low counts needed for canvases.
After they had been selected the cloths were subjected to tests for
shrinkage, fastness to washing, waterproofing, etc., before being
finally approved. Each cloth had a maximum selling price, but the
price was not an integral part of the specification as it had been in
the case of the three-figure cloths; the price was published in
separate directions.

The specifications for cloth controlled the exact construction of the
grey (or loom-state) cloth. Colour and design were not restricted
except in so far as the final maximum price discouraged wasteful
small-scale dyeing and printing. At the Utility Fabric Exhibition
held in Manchester in early 1943, where the four-figure cloths were
shown, there were over 2,000 different samples (ranging in price from
one shilling and fourpence to three shillings a yard for cotton and
two shillings to six shillings for rayon) produced from only 160
specifications of cloth.

The four-figure specifications caused something like a revolution in Lancashire cotton trade practice. Standard lines and the consequent economies of long runs were introduced for about eighty per cent. of total home trade production. The scheme showed indeed, as the war-time Deputy Cotton Controller wrote, that 'a wide variety of garments can be produced from a very limited range of weaves and yarns; that continuous running is at least possible for the home trade and that uniform quality can be maintained'.[1] The four-figure specifications were also believed to have helped to establish a high quality in cotton and rayon cloths, especially in matters like fully shrunk fabrics, crease-resisting finishes, tests for fastness to light and washing, etc. Cloths with these virtues were not new. They had been evolved by the 'decadent, dilatory and virtually insolvent textile industry during the previous twenty years'.[2] The trade committees had selected good cloths for the specifications; they had not invented them. By choosing good cloths they banished much mediocre cloth from the market. In future the bulk of cloth produced for the home market was to have these virtues. This technique of quality control was something quite new.

Side by side with the introduction of close specifications for standard lines of cloths there was a great change in Government control over the cotton industry. Planned production was introduced —a concept no less revolutionary than the standard cloths themselves. Hitherto, the Cotton Control had not been much concerned with production of cloth for civilian purposes. Its main concern had been to see that no department placed orders in excess of buying rights. Within the limitations imposed by the system of approved orders, trade continued to move along traditional channels.

By the early months of 1942 it had become clear that more drastic interference with the normal channels of trade would be necessary. For spinning capacity was a serious limitation; production was falling and was only reaching about ninety per cent. of the weight of yarn allocated. This shortfall was unevenly distributed between departments and the burden of arrears fell with disproportionate severity on the home civilian and export allocations. The plight of the civilian allocation was the worse because converters had held back their orders for utility cloths fearing that when the new four-figure specifications were published, three-figure cloths stocks would be unsaleable.[3] In the last period of 1941 they had only placed orders adding up to 11,350 tons of yarn out of a home trade allocation of

---

[1] Lacey, *op cit.*, p. 41.

[2] See the article by H. E. Wadsworth cited in the footnote on p. 375.

[3] In fact they were allowed for a period to give a three-figure cloth a four-figure specification number if the Manchester Chamber of Commerce Testing House passed a cloth sample as suitable.

13,800 tons.[1] The gap between deliveries and the requirements of the home market had to be met from heavy withdrawals of stocks. According to a Board of Trade estimate stocks fell by about half during the period.

The real problem of course was shortage of spinning labour. But the Cotton Control was convinced that careful planning of production would bring some easement. Approved orders were not spread evenly through the industry. The obvious course therefore was to control the spinners' and weavers' own programmes. Moreover planned production would be helped by the new standardisation of cloth, for the Control hoped to wring the most out of available production by introducing all the economies of long runs. The Control had always encouraged departments to plan programmes ahead as far as possible, but now it would enter the planning field itself. It had always been intended that the Control should plan the production of the new four-figure cloths. Then in April 1942 the Minister of Supply directed that the Control should plan the production of all cotton cloths used by his department and in June it was agreed that non-utility civilian production should also be planned. By the last quarter of 1942 seventy per cent. by weight of cloth production was being planned by the Control.

The system worked in the following way. Production was planned quarterly. The Board of Trade budget showed the amount of cloth which would be needed in each category, for example shirtings, split into square yardage. This programme was modified by the Cotton Control if necessary, and then put into production by reserving blocks of spinning and weaving capacity. The Cloth Planning Office of the Cotton Control issued directions to weavers stating the amount of grey cloth of each specification number which was to be delivered each week from a basic date and telling them the name of the merchant converter to whom delivery was to be made.[2] The Yarn Planning Office similarly arranged the production of the appropriate yarns with the spinners, the yarns being supplied to the weavers on condition that they used them in the production of that particular cloth. Thus arrangements for a cloth's spinning and weaving were made before the converter had ordered it. This was the major revolution. The industry was directed to produce the Board of Trade's exact programme, up to the loom-state cloth, and the merchant converter was no longer the initiator.

There remained the supervision of the finishing of the grey cloth and its distribution to the clothing industry. These functions were also normally performed by the merchant converter and they could

---

[1] Unfortunately this created an impression that the Board of Trade had exaggerated the size of the allocation necessary to meet the civilian ration.

[2] This procedure was slightly modified in 1943, see p. 447.

not be transferred to the Cotton Control whose responsibilities ceased when the cloth had been manufactured. The Board of Trade decided that, rather than set up a Government organisation to take over these functions of the merchant converter, the existing system should continue under adequate supervision. The Utility Cloth Office—a department of the Cotton Board—was therefore set up in May 1942 to supervise the conversion of the grey cloth after it left the weaver and the distribution of the finished cloth between converter and maker-up.[1] The services of converters were retained in order that the cloth should be finished, packed and distributed as the trade required.

The Board of Trade were responsible for the production of the designated (or nucleus)[2] makers-up. These firms made returns of their labour forces, their production (including Government work), their use of cloth and their stocks of cloth. The bulk of the utility cloth likely to be available was then shared out among them from June 1942 by the issue of 'key certificates'. These were authorisations to acquire a specified total yardage of utility cloth. Copies of them were sent to the Utility Cloth Office which became the link between the Cotton Control's planned production and the Board of Trade's control of the clothing industry.

The Utility Cloth Office divided the budget requirements for each particular cloth among the appropriate converters.[3] It issued allocation certificates for the right amount of each cloth to them and put them in touch with suitable weavers.[4] The Office thus knew the amounts and types of each cloth to be handled by each merchant converter. It also knew the designated (or nucleus) makers-up and to them it circulated each quarter a list showing the types of fabrics held by the qualified converters. Thus the clothier could select a suitable supplier for each cloth.[5] When the clothier got his utility cloth a sub-certificate was presented to the Utility Cloth Office and the yardage debited against the clothier's key certificate and the converter's allocation. A designated maker-up was not permitted to acquire utility cloth otherwise than through his key certificate nor from anyone except a qualified converter. The converter on his side could only acquire utility cloth up to the amount of his allocation, and during the first weeks of each allocation period he could only supply it against key certificates. When all the key certificates had been met,

---

[1] The Utility Cloth Office also performed special services for the Board of Trade in the release of cotton upholstery cloths to furniture makers, sheets and cotton blankets to priority users, and utility goods to the Ministry of Health.

[2] See Chapter XVI, Section (i).

[3] The number of converters of a cloth ranged from half a dozen to sixty.

[4] This procedure was modified in 1943. See p. 447.

[5] If a firm could not find a supplier, the Utility Cloth Office could direct the supply of cloth from a converter to a maker-up. But this rarely happened; advice and assistance were usually enough.

the Utility Cloth Office permitted a converter to sell any remaining utility cloth to undesignated makers-up and the counter-trade. This was called 'free' utility cloth.[1]

Once the maker-up had found his converter, the two of them could decide details about finishing the grey cloth and draw up their contracts. In order to get the cloth the converter sent a copy of the clothier's sub-certificate to the Cotton Control. The Control's Cloth Planning Department then put the converter into touch with a weaver.

In ordinary commercial contracts it is possible to reverse the flow of production by the cancellation of the order by the clothier, but under the war-time system the manufacture of the cloth was already planned in advance, and if an order were cancelled for any reason— or indeed if the Board of Trade's budget were seriously at fault—the weaver would have become blocked with grey cloth. As a safety valve, therefore, the Board of Trade guaranteed to buy, through British Overseas Cottons Ltd., any cloth left on the weaver's hands by the merchant converter. In fact this insurance was never used, because merchant converters were always willing to take all the grey cloth that was available throughout the period of planned production.

It is clear that at least half the converters' functions had been taken over by the Cotton Control. As total cloth production had also fallen considerably,[2] some thinning out of the converters' ranks became inevitable. On the advice of the Cotton Board converters continued to receive allocations of utility cloths in which they had always dealt, but in order to avoid unworkably small allocations there was a minimum allocation in any one cloth of 5,000 yards per period. Converters were asked for their standard period sales in each cloth. Of 900 converters who replied, 365 qualified for allocations.

The status of a qualified converter carried a specific obligation to observe the directions of the Utility Cloth Office, on pain of losing an allocation. Unqualified converters were left with two alternatives. Either they could combine with a qualified converter, or they could combine with other non-qualified converters to become eligible for the minimum allocation in future periods. These arrangements covered utility cloth only. All converters were free to compete for any non-utility trade available.

---

[1] Returns were then made to the Board of Trade of any unsold balances of cloth, and these were used by the Board as a guide to the next budget. In addition, converters also sent two-monthly returns to the Board of Trade (and the Cotton Board) of deliveries and stocks of finished goods. Three times a year the returns also included stocks of unfinished cloth and the yardage due from weavers. These figures could, however, be misleading, owing to the varying period between the planning of a cloth and its delivery to the maker-up. Some simple items like towels took only two months. Some like coloured handkerchiefs took fifteen months. The period also varied from firm to firm depending partly on the type of finish, the date on which looms became available, etc.

[2] Cotton and rayon cloth for the home market had fallen in 1942 to less than half the estimated production in 1935.

Planned production and the four-figure specifications together formed a very tight control. Quotas for utility cloth[1] were therefore unnecessary and they were in fact abolished by the directions issued under the Apparel and Textiles Order. For non-utility cloth a very small general quota[2] was retained until February 1943 in order to encourage converters holding any utility-type pre-utility cloths to sell them as three-figure cloths instead of as non-utility. By early 1943 converters' stocks had fallen to a normal working stock of about two months' sales. The non-utility quota was therefore abolished, and at the same time permission to supply three-figure cloths against key certificates to the makers-up[3] was also abolished. From this date all utility cloth was four-figure cloth whose production was planned by the Control.

No important changes took place after this date, although there were alterations from time to time in the schedules of specified utility cloths. Any changes were made in the direction of relaxation of the controls. It was found for instance that 'planned marriages' (whereby the Utility Cloth Office told the weaver the name of the converter to whom his cloth was to be delivered) were distasteful to the trade because they had to deal with firms they had never traded with before and neglect their old-established customers. Accordingly it was arranged that after each cloth allocation to converters two weeks would be allowed during which they could arrange the supply of cloth from weavers of their own choice. The Utility Cloth Office then arranged the supply of any unsold balance. This arrangement worked smoothly—the cloth balance at the end of each two weeks' period of grace did not exceed five per cent.—without taking any real powers from the Utility Cloth Office. This system was introduced for rayon in March 1943 and for cotton cloth in the following June. Rayon converters could also choose which cloths they bought— a relaxation which was not permitted in cotton.

The scale of the Cotton Control's activities in planning production can be seen from Table 29. Table 30 shows the yearly proportions of total production of cotton and rayon fabrics represented by utility.

Planned production of cotton cloth had become necessary because the Cotton Control saw no hope of meeting departmental allocations except by assuming drastic powers of control, because the obligation to honour the coupon required exact control over the amount of each cloth produced and because the utility scheme depended on the production of specified cloths of guaranteed quality. In practice the control was never quite so complete nor so smooth working as in

---

[1] See p. 435.

[2] For the first three months it was nine-tenths of one per cent. of trade in the standard year; in the following six months it was raised to three per cent. (S.R. & O. 1942, Nos. 1002 and 1661). Makers-up, of course, held fairly large stocks of non-utility cloth.

[3] S.R. & O. 1942, No. 2633.

Deliveries of Cotton and Rayon Cloths to the Home Market for Civilian Consumption

TABLE 29   Million square yards

	Standard[1] period: 12 months ending 31st March 1940	1943	1944	1945
Cotton apparel cloths	736			
Utility		245	231	215
Non-utility		64	43	41
Rayon apparel cloths	272			
Utility		115	104	113
Non-utility		31	26	33
		Including linen		
Hand and bath towels and towelling . .	44	18	15	12
Tea towels	9	6	4	4
Tablecloths	n.a.	..	..	..
Cotton sheets (including sheets containing cotton waste)	92	17	22	41
Cotton blankets	61	19	20	22
Pillow and bolster cases and pillow cottons .	38	5	7	10
Tickings	38	5	8	11
Down and wadded quilt cloths:				
Cotton	20 }	n.a.	n.a.	7
Rayon	7 }			
Furnishing fabrics:				
Non-utility	135	4	7	6
Curtain cloths:				
Utility		..	..	8
Upholstery cloths		..	..	1
Handkerchiefs	35 (cotton)			
Utility (cotton)		2	4	4
Non-utility (including linen, estimated) .		..	3	4

[1] The standard period figures are taken chiefly from the returns to the Cotton Board; figures for the later years from Board of Trade summaries of returns by converters.

Proportion of Cotton and Rayon Fabric Production for Home Civilian Market represented by Utility

TABLE 30

			per cent.	
	1942 Aug.–Dec.	*1943*	*1944*	*1945*
Cotton apparel cloth	80	79	84	84
Rayon apparel cloth	83	78	81	77

theory. Too much depended, of necessity, upon forward estimates of production which were often upset by unforeseen circumstances. For demands were liable to sudden fluctuations under the stress of war. Moreover, the planning was a cumbrous procedure which was abandoned as soon as the post-war inflow of labour eased the yarn shortage. Nevertheless the results were impressive. Planned production had enabled the ragged edges of output and demand to be trimmed so that the two fitted each other closely—surprisingly closely when it is remembered that output was steadily falling.

UTILITY RAYON CLOTH

Rayon cloth was controlled by the Cotton Control to a very large extent and the description of planned production and the utility scheme in the cotton industry applies in large measure to rayon. The rayon trade has always produced a high proportion of standard yarns so that standard utility cloths were comparatively easy to select. There were initially forty-eight rayon utility cloths—normal trade was about 1,500 cloths—but the actual specifications were more numerous in order to give greater elasticity of production. For instance, there were separate acetate, viscose and mixture specifications for roughly the same cloth in most groups so that temporary shortages in particular yarns would not affect the utility programme; fewer specifications would have produced fewer economies of production. However, in order to obtain the economies of long runs, the Board of Trade's intention was to concentrate production on a few 'winners'; increased yarn allocations would be given for those specifications at the expense of the rest, unless a sudden raw material shortage made a switch-over necessary. Utility cloths represented eighty-three per cent. of rayon production in the second half of 1942 and remained high throughout the war, only sinking to seventy-seven per cent. in the second half of 1945.

It will be remembered that control over rayon production—as against rayon cloth—was not a statutory control but was exercised voluntarily by the rayon producers and only supervised by the Board of Trade and Ministry of Supply.[1] The Board agreed an estimated figure of output with the producers for any one period and allocated it to the various consumers—the cotton and wool industries for home and for export, the hosiery, warp knitting and narrow fabrics industries, etc.—through the Rayon Allocation Office, which was set up for the purpose in November 1941. A firm registered under the Limitation of Supplies Order that wished to place an order with a rayon producer would get a certificate of approval from the Cotton Control. This was notified to the Rayon Allocation Office which authorised the rayon producer to deliver the amount of rayon involved after checking that users were not exceeding their permitted quantities. The Board were thus able to exercise some control over the amount of material which was to go, not only to each industry,

---

[1] See Chapter XV, p. 374.

but also into each type of clothing or into utility or non-utility cloth. The sanction of the scheme was that after February 1942 rayon was not to be delivered except against approved orders—an arrangement similar to that introduced in the cotton industry five months earlier.[1] The Hosiery Rationing Committee issued certificates of approval to the hosiery manufacturers and the warp knitters up to the total of the hosiery allocation. No yarn could be delivered to either industry without an approved order.

As in the case of cotton, the approved order system by itself was not satisfactory because the controlling authority was not really in charge of production but only had to see that approved orders did not exceed allocations. A variety of problems arose. For instance, producers were found to be reserving for throwsters (doublers) a high proportion of their hosiery yarn, whereas utility hosiery—by now the greater proportion of all hosiery being made—had cut out the need for heavily twisted (doubled) yarns and the hosiers' demand for straight yarns to meet the programme could not be met. Therefore, planned production was introduced for rayon in exactly the same way as for cotton. The Cotton Control, in consultation with the producers, arranged rations for each weaver and issued permits to acquire yarns up to this ration. Weavers had to make returns showing how much of each cloth they could produce. The Rayon Allocation Office continued to distribute yarn but the Utility Cloth Office took over the planning of rayon cloth from 1st July 1942 in order to ensure supplies of cloth to the designated makers-up. Allocations of rayon cloth based on past trade were given to merchant converters. These allocations were matched with the requirements of the designated makers-up through the Utility Cloth Office. In all this the rayon utility programme resembled the cotton utility programme.

This control continued more or less unchanged except that in March 1943 the 'planned marriage' system gave way to an arrangement whereby the converter was given two weeks' grace to find a weaver of his own choice and was also allowed to choose which rayon cloths he bought. Unsold balances at the end of the period of grace were dealt with by the Utility Cloth Office. In December 1944 an experiment in the relaxation of controls was made—converters' allocations were abolished but only in utility spun rayon fabrics. This in fact meant a transfer of power to the weaver who could, at least in theory, withhold supplies from a converter; he was not however very likely to do so at a time when weavers were trying to establish post-war trading connections. Vertically organised firms such as Courtaulds, whose weaving allocation was much bigger than their converting allocation, had to undertake not to supply all their cloth to themselves.

---

[1] See Chapter XV, p. 348.

Further relaxation took place in April 1945 when twenty-five per cent. of both spun and continuous filament rayon was freed, that is, twenty-five per cent. of a weaver's total budget could be sold freely to any qualified converter, although the remaining seventy-five per cent. could still only be sold against buying permits.[1] The 'free cloth' was raised to fifty per cent. in the next period and all cloth was free by the end of 1945. Rayon yarn was derationed in January 1946. Rayon weavers were then allowed to acquire any weight of yarn from any producer, but had to guarantee that the full utility programme would have first priority. The safeguard was that it was arranged with each individual weaver how much utility and planned non-utility[2] cloth he was to produce in each period. Rayon producers had to give an undertaking to meet these yarn requirements plus an agreed proportion of non-utility cloth before making any free sales of yarn.

UTILITY WOOL CLOTH

The forms of control which were introduced over the wool industry were much less drastic than those for cotton and rayon.[3] Wool cloths were never more closely specified than the original three-figure specifications, the Board of Trade had great difficulty in routeing cloth to the designated makers-up and nucleus hosiery firms and the proportion of cloth output which was utility was lower than in any of the other industries.

From the beginning of the utility scheme the Wool Control had strongly maintained that close specification of wool cloth was technically impossible because of the wide variation in types of raw material—there were upwards of 7,000 grades of raw wool[4]—and in the types of machinery used in the industry. Two pieces of wool cloth manufactured in the same way from the same raw material would not result in the same article. The result of this was that the schedules of utility wool cloth merely gave descriptions of the various types of wool cloth with their maximum and minimum weights and stated the maximum and minimum prices which might be charged.[5] Within this sliding scale prices were regulated by an agreement made in 1941 between the Wool Textile Delegation and the Central Price Regulation Committee. Under this agreement a stated profit margin was added to the manufacturers' cost of production and sale. Wool cloth departed from the strict pattern of other utility schemes in that

---

[1] Six silk converters were added to the list of qualified rayon converters so that they could receive some of the free rayon although they were not entitled to any 'unfree' rayon.

[2] See p. 444.

[3] See pp. 387–389 for some of the differences in the Cotton and Wool Controls.

[4] See *Wool Working Party Report*, p. 31, for a description of varieties of wool.

[5] S.R. & O. 1942, No. 1001.

there was no guarantee of quality in the Board's specifications and no fixed cash margins such as were introduced for cotton cloth in April 1942. In the case of wool the price determined the specification and not *vice versa*.

There was therefore little prospect that utility wool cloth would fulfil all the hopes of the Board of Trade. Whether closer specification of wool cloths were technically possible or not, it would in practice certainly have been impossible without the Wool Control's support.

There were, therefore, three problems for the Board of Trade. It was necessary first to obtain a fair share of the available wool cloth production for the civilian, secondly to see that deliveries of utility cloths were of the right kinds and of the right proportions to balance the clothing budget, and lastly to see that the supply of these cloths was steered towards those making-up firms which had been designated by the Board of Trade for the production of utility clothing.[1]

The first of the Board's three problems—that of getting an adequate share of the production available—proved the least difficult one. The size of the annual allocation of wool for the home civilian market was raised by the Materials Committee from 50,000 tons greasy to 80,000 tons,[2] which was some help even though there was doubt whether the rate at which rations of wool were distributed bore much relationship to these figures. The greatest easement in the supply problem came from the happy coincidence that as utility production for the civilian began, Service demands for wool cloth fell. The numbers employed on Government work fell considerably during the summer of 1941 and enabled the production of civilian cloths to be increased.

The Board of Trade's second problem—to see that deliveries of utility cloths were of the right kinds and in the right proportions to balance the clothing budget—was more difficult. When the utility scheme began, the Board hoped that at least fifty per cent. of wool cloth would immediately be supplied marked as utility. This could be achieved in one of two ways. Either the Board of Trade could adjust the mechanism of the quota so as to provide a strong inducement to manufacturers and merchants to supply their cheaper cloths marked as utility; or, alternatively, the Wool Control's rationing system could be developed so as to make the issue of raw wool conditional on the supply of a certain quantity of utility cloth. During August and September 1941 considerable correspondence and discussion took place between the Board of Trade and the Wool Control on this question. The Wool Control strongly favoured the latter alternative. From the Board of Trade's point of view, however, there were considerable arguments for retaining the quota for a further period. The arrangements proposed by the Wool Control for using

---

[1] See Chapter XVI.

[2] See Chapter XV, Section (iv).

issues of raw material to encourage the production of utility cloth would only come into force in the wool rationing period November 1941–February 1942, and the cloth manufactured from it would not be delivered to the clothiers for at least another two months. In the intervening period, therefore, quota control would be required to govern the supply of cloth which had already been manufactured. As we have seen, differential quotas for wool were in fact fixed under the Cloth and Apparel Order[1] in order to stimulate the supply of suitable cloths for the home market.

Apart from this quota arrangement, the production of utility wool cloth was organised by the Wool Control. The Board of Trade stated their budget requirements to the Wool Control—the linear yardage required for each specification number—and left the Control to fulfil them. The Control assumed responsibility for obtaining the delivery of the necessary quantities of cloth by issuing (through the Joint Rationing Committee) a special ration for utility cloth to any manufacturer who applied for it on the condition that it was manufactured into utility cloth of the various specification numbers. The arrangement was enforced by a complete system of monthly returns from merchants and manufacturers showing the quantities of cloth delivered under each specification number; in the case of manufacturers returns had to be supported by certificates from the clothiers showing the quantities of cloth received by them.[2] Offers received from manufacturers were compared with the budget requirements, and if a cloth had been over-subscribed manufacturers received only a proportion of the raw material for which they had asked.

This arrangement was essentially the same as that adopted nine months later for the hosiery industry. Its efficiency depended on how accurately the manufacturers' efforts reflected the Board of Trade budget—that is to say, on the speed in adjusting raw wool rations to produce the required result. In the first period of the scheme deliveries of utility cloth in fact showed marked differences from the Board of Trade's budget. Rations had been issued varying from between 137 per cent. and 175 per cent. of the Board's requirements for the more expensive cloths and there appeared to have been little attempt to stimulate production of the cheaper cloths for which the manufacturers' offers were less than the Board of Trade's budget. The result of this negative system of control, whereby the production of cloth reflected the demand from the clothiers primarily, and the Board of Trade's budget only secondarily, was a clear tendency towards trading up. The Wool Control defended this tendency and held that the clothiers' orders were probably a better reflection of the

---

[1] See p. 435.

[2] These returns incidentally gave the Board of Trade a valuable means of checking the use made of utility cloth by the maker-up.

public's requirements than the Board of Trade's budget. The Board of Trade, on the other hand, feared that the cheaper end of the utility programme might become submerged.

Thus during the first six months of the utility scheme the Board of Trade had obtained the raw material they wanted for the home civil programme and the total volume of supplies had been adequate, but the difficulty had been that the supplies had not been closely related to the budget. On the third problem—that of steering cloth supplies to the designated makers-up—very little progress was made. In November 1941 an understanding had been reached between the Board of Trade and the Wool Control that the latter would co-operate in seeing that the output of clothing firms designated for the production of utility clothing was not wrecked by shortages of cloth. By February 1942, however, the Board of Trade were receiving complaints from individual designated firms engaged, in some cases, on the production of those garments where shortages were most severe, that they could not get adequate quantities of cloth. In fact, as it emerged later, the designated firms were receiving less cloth than the undesignated. Returns of cloth deliveries in February 1942 showed that 2,379 thousand yards had been delivered to the designated and 2,387 thousand yards to the undesignated firms. The fundamental point at issue between the Board of Trade and the Wool Control on this, as on the question of delivery of cloths at the cheaper end of the utility scale, was the reluctance of the Control to intervene more than was absolutely necessary in individual firms' trade. The reason for the difficulty experienced by the makers-up in getting supplies was that manufacturers tended to ration their customers on the basis of their pre-war trade.[1] The utility clothing policy, on the other hand, presupposed a good deal of discrimination between clothing firms. Utility garments could only be efficiently produced by a fairly large firm working to eighty per cent. of capacity, and priority in cloth supplies for these firms was therefore essential. The Wool Control, whose prestige in the industry depended to some extent on the support it gave to the idea of fair shares, was unwilling to be a party to this discrimination.

To meet the difficulty, the Board of Trade were compelled themselves to take action. This took the form of a direction under the Cloth and Apparel Order imposing a quota on cloth supplies to individual clothiers. No one firm might receive more than thirty per cent. of the supplies sent to it in the standard period laid down under the main Order, except under licence. These licences were reserved to designated firms.[2] Thus, while old-established customers were

---

[1] The ration was usually thirty to forty per cent. of the pre-war supplies.

[2] Licences were not supplied to designated firms who had more than ten weeks' stocks of a particular cloth in hand, in order that firms with such large stocks could dispose of them to less fortunate firms who could not get supplies.

allowed a proper proportion of supplies of utility cloth, a residue was obtained which could be diverted to those designated makers-up who could make immediate and full use of the cloth. A further licence and direction required wool cloth manufacturers to supply cloth on the receipt of licences from designated firms. This imposition of a further quota on supplies at a time when the main policy of the Board of Trade was to eliminate quotas at the earliest opportunity was an anomaly. However, it seemed to provide the only means of safe-guarding the production of utility garments[1] and of implementing the promise to designated clothiers that adequate supplies of the cloths they needed for utility clothes would be forthcoming. It was feared that this procedure might impose a temporary check on the distribution of cloth, but it did not appear to do so.

These arrangements were introduced temporarily and lapsed with the issue of the Apparel and Textiles Order and the directions issued under it at the end of May 1942.[2] A more permanent and satisfactory solution to the two problems—that of relating production of cloth to the budget requirements and that of steering a substantial propor-tion of utility cloth to the designated firms—was achieved by the key certificate scheme, which has already been described in connection with cotton cloth production.[3] The system for wool was similar. Designated clothing firms had key certificates entitling them to purchase utility wool cloth of each specification number up to a stated amount; these amounts were based on the Board of Trade's budget figure adjusted to the capacity of the wool industry in agree-ment with the Wool Control. In the aggregate these certificates would cover sixty-five per cent. of the programme of utility cloth production, which in itself was planned to absorb eighty per cent. of the total production of the industry for the home market.

Orders for wool cloths placed by designated firms had to be accompanied by a cloth sub-certificate. The total yardage covered by sub-certificates had not to exceed the yardage specified in the main certificate. The Wool Control endeavoured to ensure that supplies of utility cloth were available against the sub-certificates.

Cloth manufacturers were, of course, required to apply the utility mark and specification number to the cloth before they supplied it, and they had to continue to make monthly returns to the Wool

---

[1] It was not unnatural for manufacturers to show a tendency to distribute cloth to old customers, irrespective of whether they were designated or not. One of the results of cutting out the merchants in the wool trade was that manufacturers were often doubtful about the financial stability or trading methods of the unfamiliar designated firms and were reluc-tant to enter into business relations with them. They did not like the business methods of some of the big multiple makers-up and they did not like the bank balances of the small designated firms. The Board of Trade even considered using the wool cloth merchants again.

[2] S.R. & O. 1942, Nos. 1000 and 1001.

[3] See p. 445.

Control of their deliveries of utility cloth of each specification number and also of non-utility cloth.

These arrangements allowed the Board of Trade to steer supplies of utility cloth to the designated clothing firms without that individual direction to which the Wool Control was so strongly opposed. Raw material rations were, after July 1942, only issued to wool manufacturers to fulfil orders already booked by them against cloth certificates. As with cotton and rayon supplies, seventy-five per cent. of utility wool cloth production was to be reserved for designated firms in this way. The remaining twenty-five per cent.—known as free utility—was produced to supply the undesignated firm and the counter trade. Rations for this 'free' cloth were, however, distributed only after holders of cloth certificates had succeeded in placing their orders.

The main structure of control for utility wool cloth production and distribution was thus complete by July 1942, and consequently the existing controls by quota could be relaxed. The controls over the volume and types of wool cloth produced were, therefore, relatively simple, deriving from the absolute administrative powers wielded by the Wool Control; the Wool Controller had the powerful sanction that he could withhold rations from firms. There was no planning of production of the kind introduced by the Cotton Control. Cloth was woven to the order of the clothier, not in obedience to the directions issued by the Control. In wool, the Board of Trade produced a plan and made it the basis of cloth certificates. In cotton, the plan was executed in advance of orders from clothiers. Moreover, in wool a considerable degree of latitude over the type of cloth produced was preserved for there was no close specification of utility wool cloths.

It may be useful to compare here the effectiveness of the methods of control introduced for cotton and rayon on the one hand and wool on the other. The effectiveness of each method must be judged in relation to three questions. First, did it in fact ensure that the right proportion of utility cloth was delivered to the making-up trade? Secondly, what was the real effect of the absence of specifications on the quality of utility wool cloth? Thirdly, how far did planned production and standardised cloths produce economies in cotton production that were not achieved with wool?

Generally speaking, the total volume of cloth supplies whether of cotton, rayon or wool did not present any serious problem to the Board of Trade until 1944. Despite any shortages of particular categories, the total cloth supplies matched the budget more or less satisfactorily. When, however, we come to the proportions of utility and non-utility cloth delivered, the picture is not so uniformly satisfactory. There was a marked difference between the history of cotton and wool cloths:—

Sales of Cloth by Manufacturers for Home Trade

TABLE 31   Annual rate: million sq. yds.

| | Woven Wool Cloth | | | | Woven Non-Wool Cloth | | | | | | | |
| | | | | | Cotton | | | | Rayon | | | |
	Utility	Non-Utility	Total	Percentage of Utility to Total	Utility	Non-Utility	Total	Percentage of Utility to Total	Utility	Non-Utility	Total	Percentage of Utility to Total
1942												
1st half	119	50	169	70	—	—	—	—	—	—	—	—
2nd half	146	37	183	80	234	58	292	80	124	25	149	83
1943	119	43	162	73	244	65	309	79	113	31	144	78
1944	104	55	159	65	232	43	275	84	104	25	129	81
1945												
1st half	119	37	156	76	217	35	252	86	109	31	140	78
2nd half	146	29	175	83	216	47	263	82	116	35	151	77

From the spring of 1942 onwards the Board of Trade's programmes were based on the requirement that eighty per cent. of clothing production should be utility. Whereas the proportion of utility to the whole approached very close to eighty per cent. in cotton and in 1944–45 rose considerably above it, the proportion of utility wool cloth fell steadily for the first two years—from eighty per cent. of total output in the second half of 1942 to sixty-six per cent. in 1944. This was at a time when it would have been reasonable to expect the necessary controls to be firmly established. The proportion of utility wool cloth did indeed rise again to eighty-three per cent. in 1945 but this was mainly due to the new range of more expensive garments added to the utility range at that date rather than to an increase of utility production.

The fall in the proportion of wool cloth manufactured as utility reached its lowest point in the summer of 1944, and the Board of Trade were seriously concerned. Not only was the proportion of non-utility rising, but the quantity of utility cloth produced was not enough to honour the cloth certificates of the makers-up. Various reasons were put forward for the development: the Wool Control explained that the rising proportion of non-utility was due to the manufacturers using up non-utility rations which had accumulated from earlier periods. In other words, their manufacturing capacity was not equal to manufacturing their non-utility rations and supplying the whole current demand from the designated clothing trade, and they were using this position to discriminate against utility and in favour of non-utility production. This situation could not easily have developed in cotton where the production of non-utility as well as utility cloths had been planned by the Control from July 1942 onwards.

There were two possible remedies; either the Wool Control could further restrict the issue of non-utility rations (which in 1944 were limited to twenty per cent. of the total rations issued), or else the utility range could be extended to more expensive cloths. Both courses were adopted. In the period July–October 1944 no rations for non-utility wool cloths were issued. Then, as the Board believed that the increasing proportion of non-utility production was in part the reflection of an increased demand for better quality cloths, they agreed in January 1945 to add a new range of more expensive cloths to the schedule of utility cloths.[1] As a result of these measures the proportion of utility wool cloth deliveries increased, reaching seventy-six per cent. in the first and eighty-three per cent. in the second half of 1945.

The second test of the effectiveness of the control over wool was the quality of utility wool cloths in the absence of close specifications. It is impossible to give a definite answer, but there were complaints from the makers-up who emphasised the poor coupon value offered by the cheapest wool utility cloths; complaints were also received about the quality of boys' three-quarter hose and pit hose. In order to bring their cloths within the utility price ceilings wool manufacturers often economised by 'spinning to lower counts, using fewer picks per yard'[2] and so on. Nevertheless, the Wool Controller maintained that the cheaper utility cloths had been tested and that though they were undoubtedly not durable they were not worse and were probably rather better than comparable cloths before the war. While the Wool Control had resisted for technical reasons the close specification of cloths, it had enforced certain precautions on the quality of utility shoddy cloths. It had insisted that manufacturers applying for rations for these cloths should declare the ingredients from which they were made, and periodically stock was taken of the consumption of these ingredients as a check on the manufacturers' statements. In addition a series of tests which the Control called 'most exhaustive' had been carried out by the Wool Textile Research Association; the results of these tests supported the Wool Controller's contention that there had been no detectable adulteration of these cloths. Probably serious deterioration was avoided for two reasons. First, raw materials were comparatively plentiful. Secondly, the utility wool cloth specifications allowed a certain latitude for rising

---

[1] S.R. & O. 1945, No. 23.
[2] *Wool Working Party Report.*

prices by quoting minimum and maximum prices;[1] this allowed manufacturers to maintain quality to some extent in the face of rising costs and diminishing activity by selling a higher proportion of their output at ceiling prices.

Because the control over wool had greater difficulty than the control over cotton and rayon both in maintaining a high proportion of utility production and a high quality of utility cloth, it made one problem more serious. This was the problem of trading up or concentrating on the more expensive end of the clothing trade. The only satisfactory solution to it was planned production.

There remains one question unanswered: how far did planned production and standardised cloths produce economies in cotton production which were not possible with wool? This will be discussed later in connection with the general question of the economies produced by the utility programme.

UTILITY HOSIERY

The description of the Board of Trade's methods to secure the production of utility cloth in the various textile industries has of necessity included a description of the control exercised over the utility garment manufacturers—that is, the key certificate procedure which enabled the Board to route utility cloth to the nucleus clothing firms and to see that it was made into the prescribed garments.

The hosiery industry, however, did not fit exactly into this pattern because its raw material is yarn and its finished products are finished garments; there is no stage corresponding to cloth production or garment making-up. There was therefore a separate system of control for utility hosiery.

The production of utility hosiery like that of utility cloth was introduced under the Cloth and Apparel Order in September 1941 by fixing separate quotas for utility and non-utility garments—fifty per cent. and twenty-five per cent. respectively of trade in the base period. As there is no intermediate cloth stage in the production of knitted goods, the only thing that could be specified was the finished garment.[2] Specifications for all types of garments were drawn up with the help of manufacturers' representatives; the first list was published in November 1941, together with the maximum prices and margins for them.[3]

Hosiery specifications could not be as close as those for cotton cloth. For machines in the industry are not readily interchangeable and the specifications had to be wide enough to include as much of

---

[1] See S.R. & O. 1943, No. 1209, and 1945, No. 23.

[2] Yarn supplied to the hosiery industry had already been standardised to some extent by the restriction of the range of quality and sizes by the raw material Controls.

[3] S.R. & O. 1941, No. 1614, and subsequent Orders.

the trade as possible in the utility scheme. The list of specifications eventually introduced was long—nearly 430—because the variety of machines and types of yarns prevented mass-produced standard lines but permitted a 'conglomeration of slightly varying types'. Nevertheless, relatively few specifications were introduced for garments that were extravagant in the use of labour—such as fully-fashioned stockings and fine gauge garments. The specifications covered such details as yarn content, method of production, minimum measurements, minimum weight and maximum price. In some cases the specifications improved on the existing practice of the hosiery industry—for example, unshrinkable finishes for some underwear and uniform size markings for socks and stockings were introduced for the first time. There were complaints from the public about the quality of utility hosiery—particularly about women's stockings. Even in this range, however, at least one utility stocking[1] so far improved on the normal cheap rayon stocking that some manufacturers whose businesses had been built on the quantity production of cheap short-life hose complained that it would put them out of business. It was probably the best seamless stocking that had ever been produced in Britain.

The utility scheme began in October 1941; but, since yarn permits were not issued until November-December, utility garment production did not get under way until January 1942. The controls over the hosiery industry in the autumn of 1941 were not well adapted to ensure that sufficient garments of the various types were produced. Indeed they were ill related to one another. Yarn was allocated on the basis of a firm's total pre-war consumption; the limitation of supplies quota was based on home trade in the twelve months ending May 1940, redundancy cuts under concentration had been fixed according to the importance of each type of garment to the consumer. Fortunate was the manufacturer whose raw material cuts, machine activity cuts under concentration and civilian quota bore any relation to each other or to his approved labour force.[2]

Concentration, in particular, complicated the problems of utility production. For though it had left the industry at a size roughly corresponding to the civilian budget, it had not necessarily left in existence those firms which would have been the most efficient producers of utility in the sense of mass-produced standard lines. Once a firm's labour had been dispersed, however, it could not be called back and the Board of Trade had to do the best they could with the existing structure of the industry. This meant the exercise of drastic powers over what the industry produced.

---

[1] Specification No. 731.
[2] See Chapter XVI, Section (ii).

The Directorate of Civilian Hosiery (often referred to as the Hosiery Control) undertook to plan production in the hosiery industry—to issue yarn to the manufacturers in accordance with that plan[1] and to direct the use they could make of it. The old system of allocating yarn to manufacturers on the basis of past performance was dropped. Manufacturers[2] were invited to submit their production programmes for four months ahead to the Control. The figures were added up and the totals of each type of garment compared with the Board of Trade's budget figures. Where garments were 'over-subscribed' offers were cut proportionately and manufacturers were invited to produce other garments which would otherwise be under-produced. Machine capacity set a limit to the possibilities of thus switching production. Production of the over-subscribed garments was therefore concentrated on the more inflexible specialist firms and the non-specialists were asked to manufacture the under-produced garments.

When the production programme had been settled, production directions were sent out to each firm setting out the maximum amount of each utility specification number and the maximum amount of non-utility it might make during the next period. A producer could have any of the quantities increased if the rest of his programme were not in arrears and provided it was possible to supply additional raw materials. Yarn certificates were issued to match up with the Control's programme. The approved labour force of each firm was also related to the amount of its approved production.

For the purposes of enforcement it was necessary to collect returns showing quantities of goods manufactured against agreed programmes every two months. Any shortages—compared with the estimate—could be added to the next period's target figures. Every second month of each four-monthly production period, therefore, these returns of production were sent in together with the manufacturers' projected programmes for the following period. Approvals were sent out from the Board of Trade within the following week or two and were followed in due course by the actual directions and schedules. In this way manufacturers had their approvals about three months before the actual garments were due to be made, and could plan materials and machine capacity well ahead. In the fourth month of each period they sent in returns of their past production only.

About ninety per cent. by volume of the industry's production was covered by this type of direction. There were also, however, about 250 registered non-nucleus firms whose activities were covered by a

---

[1] Through the reconstituted Hosiery Rationing Committee. See Chapter XVI.

[2] They were grouped into three geographical areas each with a production officer and a technical officer to negotiate and agree programmes with each firm in the area. There were also technical enforcement officers to examine the quality of utility goods, production returns, etc.

general direction permitting them to make a fairly long list of garments[1] in stated proportions of utility and non-utility from specified
materials. Some firms which would have been partially or totally immobilised by these restrictions were granted licences negotiated
individually permitting some variation from these directions. The
idea was to get the most useful production possible out of each firm,
but not to put any firm out of business. For the total capacity left
in the industry after concentration was barely sufficient to meet the
hosiery budget requirements.

The other class of firms were the unregistered non-nucleus firms
which, though numerous, only accounted for about one per cent. of
production. About 250 of them received rations in the ordinary way,
but many others continued to exist on the 'free' hand knitting yarn
they could procure. They were supplied with a list of permitted
garments, with no restrictions about raw materials, but they were
limited to £100 worth of trade in each calendar month.[2]

This system of control over the hosiery industry's products continued until after the end of the war. It was a form of planned production more closely akin to the controls exercised by the Wool and
Cotton Controls than to those over the making-up industry. For the
Board through the Hosiery Control issued individual directions to
each firm controlling the number of garments of each utility specification and also the numbers of non-utility garments to be produced.
In the clothing industry the Board exercised no control at all over
the making-up of non-utility woven cloth.[3] There was nothing corresponding in hosiery to the undertaking required from designated
clothing firms about the proportions of utility production to be
undertaken; planned production made it unnecessary.

In fact the proportion of utility hosiery was higher than for any
other type of clothing as Table 32 shows. Between May and August
1942 the proportion of utility garments rose from sixty-seven per cent.
to ninety per cent. By the second half of 1943 the percentage had
risen to ninety-six per cent. (in the case of women's stockings to
ninety-nine per cent.). This was a remarkable achievement[4] in view
of the variation of hosiery machinery and of production costs.

The results of utility and planned production in the hosiery industry were encouraging. In the winter of 1941–42 the most serious
clothing shortages reported by the Board's area distribution officers

---

[1] Various items whose production was undesirable from the raw material point of view
were omitted from the list, e.g. scarves, women's all-wool vests, wool outerwear fabrics, etc.

[2] Goods produced by these firms could, of course, only be sold against coupons and
therefore did not constitute a free supply of garments in any sense.

[3] Except for the style restrictions.

[4] It may be due to the fact that in peace-time the hosiery industry had supplied a large
proportion of its output to the big chain stores which had imposed considerable standardisation on their suppliers.

Percentage (by number) of Total Output of Hosiery Garments for Home Civilian Use represented by Utility Garments

TABLE 32

	MEN'S AND YOUTHS'			WOMEN'S AND MAIDS'			CHILDREN'S			TOTALS			GRAND TOTAL
	Outer-wear	Under-wear	Hose	Outer-wear	Under-wear	Hose	Outer-wear	Under-wear	Hose	Outer-wear	Under-wear	Hose	
1942:													
January	5	49	35	12	55	44	24	51	32	20	52	41	41
February	14	63	48	35	57	53	30	66	55	30	61	52	52
March–April	39	72	52	55	68	56	45	70	66	47	69	58	62
May–June	36	71	54	62	65	69	52	71	71	54	69	68	67
July–August	73	90	80	82	95	90	89	87	95	84	92	90	90
1943:													
January–February	60	89	89	77	91	92	80	87	95	78	89	92	91
July–August	64	93	94	85	97	95	93	90	98	90	94	97	96
1944:													
January–February	65	92	95	90	98	98	95	94	98	91	95	98	96

NOTES: 1. The percentages are based on the output of hosiery manufacturers registered under the Apparel and Textiles Order, and therefore leave out of account a small quantity of supplies from unregistered manufacturers whose turnover was under £100 monthly. Up to June 1942, records were obtained from nucleus firms only, but the output of registered non-nucleus firms and hosiery firms engaged in making-up only which were included after that date would not affect the percentages to any great extent. The figures relate to manufacturers' sales up to June 1942, and to production after that date, and exclude output for direct orders by a government department and for export; supplies for N.A.A.F.I. and local authorities are included.

2. Garments made up from rayon locknit and those made up from knitted fabric by firms not operating knitting machines are excluded from the Table.

3. In arriving at the percentages for the 'total' columns, no attempt has been made to weight the various garments, each item of outerwear and underwear, and each pair of hose being counted as one.

4. *Outerwear*—relates to 'heavy' outerwear only:—i.e. excludes headwear, gloves, scarves, collars, ties, etc.

5. *Children*—relates to all persons under fourteen—i.e. includes infants.

had been in hosiery garments—particularly in underwear and boys' socks. The first aim of the Hosiery Control was to remedy these shortages and in this it succeeded. By January 1943 the Board of Trade were able to say: 'the preliminary totals of manufacturers' own estimates of their production for the period March–June 1943 show that the manipulation of programmes during the past six months has produced results better than we could reasonably have expected . . . although we cannot hope to meet our full requirements with the raw materials available we can be satisfied that hosiery will be produced in approximately the right proportion in relation to the estimated consumer demand. The industry will no longer over-produce women's goods and under-produce everything else'. The Hosiery Control's statistics of civilian production do indeed show considerable increases in the production of men's and children's underwear and men's and children's socks and decreases of women's outerwear and stockings between the latter half of 1942 and the early half of 1943. This is shown in the following Table:

Production of Hosiery Knitted Goods for the Civilian Market[1]
(*Excluding direct and indirect Government contracts*)

TABLE 33

Thousand Dozens

	1942 July–Dec.	1943 Jan.–June	1943 July–Dec.	1944 Jan.–June	1944 July–Dec.	1945 Jan.–June
Underwear:						
Men's	887·5	1,188·5	974·1	900·9	822·6	871·8
Women's	1,660·0	1,612·9	1,464·7	1,434·6	1,338·0	1,420·4
Children's and Infants'	1,192·0	1,400·5	1,307·9	1,302·2	1,236·5	1,214·8
Outerwear:						
Men's	121·0	100·0	88·2	99·3	106·2	119·6
Women's	353·0	259·0	258·1	289·3	276·3	294·3
Children's and Infants'	744·8	806·6	739·0	820·1	799·4	873·9
Footwear (Hose and Socks):						
Men's	1,550·1	1,898·7	1,181·6	930·0	943·6	994·0
Women's	6,707·8	6,224·6	5,527·9	5,669·0	5,529·5	5,734·5
Children's	2,342·8	2,695·6	2,845·4	2,798·0	2,583·2	2,636·2

This contribution towards 'honouring the ration' was important. The possible contribution of planned production to raising productivity in the hosiery industry will be discussed at the end of this chapter.

---

[1] Hosiery Control Statistics based on returns from registered manufacturers (non-registered manufacturers consumed less than one per cent. of the materials allocated to the industry).

THE PRODUCTION OF SPECIAL GARMENTS

We have so far described the Board of Trade's methods to ensure sufficient production of ordinary clothes for the general population. This was not the end of the Board's task. For it was also necessary to see that certain special garments were produced in sufficient numbers. For example, industrial clothing such as pit pants, overalls or agricultural fustians had to be provided; so had ordinary garments in special sizes—the very small or very large—or special garments such as surgical corsets. In volume such demands were very small, but the effort of seeing that they were produced occupied a good deal of the Board of Trade's time and energy. These garments were neglected by the manufacturers either because—as in the case of outsizes—they used more material than was covered by the coupons surrendered by the consumer or because—as in the case of cotton pit pants—the Board had not sufficient knowledge of industrial habits and tastes and had made no budget to cover them. By some means or other production of these neglected garments had to be stimulated.

The remedies varied with the problems. For example, corduroy for agricultural trousers was scarce. The Board of Trade ensured that available supplies of corduroy were made into such trousers by specifying its use in working trousers alone and by asking that it should be supplied only to those firms who were manufacturers of working clothes and little else.[1] Similar action was taken over pit pants. The problem of outsizes was dealt with by permitting a special 'up lift' on utility ceiling prices for ready-made outsize clothes.[2] The maximum prices for men's and women's underwear were raised by twenty per cent., women's outerwear and corsets by fifteen per cent. and men's outerwear by ten per cent. In addition, extra coupons were given to those firms making a substantial proportion of outsize garments.

Two examples may be taken to typify these special problems of the Board of Trade—overalls and corsets. During the early part of 1943, the area distribution officers began to report serious shortages of both household and industrial overalls. All overalls were closely specified and production of them was 100 per cent. utility. Capacity, however, was not sufficient to meet the greatly increased war-time demand for them: for if overalls were to be fit for their purpose they had to be made from restricted counts of yarn woven on particular looms. Various steps were taken to ease the shortage. Makers-up of overalls did not share in the general reduction of the clothing industry's labour force in March 1943. Cuts in Service demands for overalls helped the civilian by releasing labour and Service overall cloth (which was very similar to the industrial overall cloth). The Board of Trade restricted

---

[1] The general public could not, however, be prevented from buying these trousers in the shops if they so wished.

[2] S.R. & O. 1942, No. 886.

the two lighter cloths specified for domestic overalls to the production of industrial overalls[1] and by permitting them to be dyed only in plain colours they hoped to make them unattractive to housewives. Two suitable cotton dress cloths were specified for domestic overalls. By these means the threatened crisis was overcome: from May 1943 the proportion of retailers without any stocks of overalls declined rapidly. The story demonstrates that the Board could remedy a shortage by administrative action; namely, by redistributing supplies of cloth in favour of the more essential uses through their control of cloth distribution to the makers-up and by their control over the purposes for which a cloth might be used.

The corset problem was more difficult to solve. In the first place, total corset production was inadequate. Production was never more than nine to ten million garments a year, whereas there were probably 18 million corset wearers; one war-time corset was hardly likely to last as long as two years. The corset industry had released a high proportion of its resources to the war effort. It had been drastically concentrated and since it was particularly well equipped for making parachutes a number of firms had turned over to Ministry of Aircraft Production contracts. For these reasons, together with air-raid damage, the factory space employed on corset production had been reduced by a third and the labour force engaged on civilian corset production by more than a half. These losses of labour were the more serious since corset production is very specialised, using special methods of manufacture and specially trained labour. It was not only the production figures that were unsatisfactory; quality was equally depressed by the war. Even in peace-time a large section of the industry had produced low-grade garments. In war-time standards were lowered still further because corset production required the three raw materials that were most scarce—cotton cloth (of a specialised and durable type), steel and rubber. The original corset cloths were among the worst in the utility range: a good-quality cloth was not introduced until the summer of 1944 and the supply only became adequate when the Services released a large quantity of cloth suitable for the civilian market. Hard strip steel for corset bones (for which there was no efficient substitute) was not released for corsets until March 1944. Elastic made from synthetic rubber was unsatisfactory, and this shortage was not eased until after the war.

The Board of Trade had to see that the best use was made of corset production. A very tight control was therefore introduced. In the interests of long runs only a very few corset cloths and garments were specified in the appropriate directions under the Apparel and Textiles

---

[1] S.R. & O. 1943, No. 1411.

Order. Only four per cent. of the standard period trade was permitted in non-utility varieties;[1] for an experimental period, indeed, there was a complete prohibition on non-utility corset manufacture. Although corsets were worn by a large number of people, their shortage or inferior quality only caused real hardship to some—to outsizes, or women standing at jobs for long hours, or those who had to wear surgical corsets. The best of the scarce materials were reserved for these classes. On a doctor's certificate surgical corsets could be manufactured free of quota. The priority certificates, however, soon out-ran the productive capacity of the specialist manufacturers and it became necessary to specify the physical conditions which would entitle consumers to priority. The Board of Trade helped outsize women by arranging with individual firms that an increased proportion of their production should be in those sizes. The Board also made some attempt to raise the standard of workmanship of ordinary corsets to compensate for the poor quality materials. Minimum standards were never introduced to safeguard the quality of the lower priced corsets, but makers-up had to mark their corsets with an identification number so that complaints could be taken up with individual firms. With the better manufacturers the problem was one of prices. It was difficult to fix utility ceiling prices which (while ignoring the top end of the trade) were not either too high for the cheaper goods or too low for the medium- and better-class production. The Board of Trade met this difficulty by introducing 'super utility' corsets; this permitted higher prices for proved quality. Under this arrangement manufacturers were invited to produce models made of utility materials but with a design and finish that justified prices higher than the utility ceilings. These models were considered by a trade panel which fixed individual ceiling prices for each approved model. Until the end of the war the 'super utility' production of each firm was limited to eight models a year and fifty per cent. of total production.

HOUSEHOLD TEXTILES

Household textiles must be discussed along with clothing for they competed for the same raw materials and the Board of Trade were of course responsible for their production. In peace-time the proportion of total textile output devoted to household goods—sheets, pillowcases, towels, furnishing fabrics, blankets, and so forth—was high. In 1937 nearly thirty per cent. of the total cotton supplies for home consumption was for household textiles, compared with just over fifty per cent. for all apparel cloths.[2] To this must be added the

---

[1] S.R. & O. 1942, Nos. 1004, 1677.

[2] *Board of Trade, Working Party Reports: Cotton* (H.M.S.O. 1946), p. 18.

large quantity of wool used in making almost three million pairs of wool blankets.

This high consumption could not be justified in war-time especially when nearly a third of it was for relative unessentials such as furnishing fabrics. The Woven Textiles Order of March 1941 accordingly reduced the quantities of household textiles available to the home market to twenty to thirty per cent. of the relevant base-period trade, and the Limitation of Supplies Orders similarly reduced the quantities of bedding to fifty per cent.[1] As in all the limitation quotas, the restrictions did not discriminate sufficiently between essential and unessential goods. When clothes rationing was introduced the Board of Trade's control over household textiles was strengthened. The articles concerned—except furnishing fabrics—were coupon-free to the purchaser; manufacturers, however, could not acquire rationed cloth to make unrationed goods except against coupons issued to them by the Board of Trade. These coupons were issued quarterly; manufacturers received a proportion of the amount of cloth they had used during the year ending 31st March 1941.

Furnishing fabrics as a whole were not coupon-free but rationing had some mitigations. The Wool and Cotton Controls were releasing no more materials for the manufacture of these fabrics, but it was estimated that there was about eighteen months' stock in the hands of manufacturers and retailers. The heavier furnishing fabrics—those weighing more than 7 oz. per square yard supposedly unsuitable for making into clothes—were therefore freed from coupon restriction.[2] This concession proved too generous since some of these heavier materials could in fact quite well be used for dress materials. In June 1942 the heavier materials that were suitable for clothes, such as linens and cretonnes, were therefore rationed at one-third of the coupon rate. This rate also applied to the fabrics weighing less than 7 oz. a yard which had a repeat design more than 15 inches high. All other light furnishing fabrics required the full coupon rate and all other heavy fabrics remained coupon-free.

The next general step in the control of household textiles came with the Cloth and Apparel Order, which reduced the quota for non-utility cloth to nine per cent. of the base-period trade in cotton and fifteen per cent. in wool. If these percentages had been rigidly applied to household textiles many civilians would have suffered real hardship. By the sternest standards sheets could be dispensed with but blankets and towels were necessities. Licences were therefore issued to registered manufacturers to enable them to use cloth in excess of their Cloth and Apparel Order quota: they could use cloth up to fifty per

---

[1] Woven Textiles (No. 7) Order (S.R. & O. 1941, No. 323), and Limitation of Supplies (Miscellaneous) Order (S.R. & O. 1941, No. 700).

[2] S.R. & O. 1941, No. 939.

cent. of their base-period trade in the case of cotton blankets, thirty per cent. in the case of wool blankets and twenty per cent. for towels.[1]

It was anomalous that essential goods like blankets and towels should be left to fight for the diminishing supplies of non-utility cloth, and since household textiles can be readily identified and closely specified they fitted in to the utility scheme quite easily. Maximum prices and specifications about manufacturing and making-up were therefore laid down in June 1942 for towels,[2] tea-towels, cotton sheets and blankets, mattresses and quilts; provision was also made for a national price-controlled—in effect a utility—blanket,[3] and the manufacture of any other blanket was forbidden. For example, towels were restricted to three sizes, in white and grey only, sheets to two types, one in cotton and one in cotton waste, with two sizes in each and blankets to three sizes. Manufacture of all non-utility household textiles and the supply of non-utility bedding were prohibited.[4] In August 1942, when purchase tax was removed from utility cloth and apparel, it remained chargeable for household textiles.[5]

Under the Miscellaneous Textiles (Manufacture and Supply) Directions of June 1942[6] the manufacture of a large class of non-essential goods, such as bedspreads, table-cloths and the heavier types of un-rationed furnishing fabrics was specifically prohibited. Later series of directions prohibited the manufacture of travelling rugs and non-utility pram rugs.[7] The manufacture of the lighter types of furnishing fabrics was not forbidden, but the high coupon rating put them out of the reach of the majority of consumers and their manufacture virtually ceased about this time.

---

[1] The manufacture of quilts had been stopped (alongside that of tablecloths, table napkins and bedspreads) by the Board of Trade's refusal to issue coupons for acquiring cloth, and their prohibition on the use of stocks of cloth for these purposes. Now, however, quilts which were made of cotton waste, and other substitutes for blankets, could be manufactured again.

[2] Towels were put on the ration from October 1942.

[3] Miscellaneous Textiles (Manufacture and Supply) Directions 1942 (S.R. & O. No.1151). Bedding (Manufacture and Supply) Directions 1942 (S.R. & O. No. 1011). Quilts and Quilt Covers (Maximum Prices) Order 1942 (S.R. & O. No. 887). Blankets (Maximum Prices) Order 1942 (S.R. & O. No. 1291). Household Textiles (Manufacture and Supply) Directions 1942 (S.R. & O. No. 1292). Household Textiles (Manufacture and Supply) (No. 2) Directions 1942 (S.R. & O. No. 2344).

[4] i.e. mattresses, pillows, bolsters and quilts. Sleeping-bags were not so prohibited (S.R. & O. No. 1011). Utility bedding was still subject to a quota—$12\frac{1}{2}$ per cent. of the value supplied in the standard period.

[5] They were readily identifiable by the Customs because utility household textiles bore specification numbers under 200 whereas apparel cloths either had four-figure numbers or numbers over 200.

[6] S.R. & O. 1942, No. 1151.

[7] From 31st December 1942 and 31st January 1943 respectively. Household Textiles (Manufacture and Supply) Directions 1942, (S.R. & O. No. 1292). Household Textiles (Manufacture and Supply) (No. 2) Directions (S.R. & O. No. 2344), and (No. 3) Directions (S.R. & O. 1942, No. 2666).

2G

The control exercised over household textiles was thus exceedingly rigid; they were the only goods apart from overalls where manufacture was 100 per cent. utility, and production of unessentials was eliminated.[1] Nevertheless, supplies of even the most essential articles remained woefully inadequate. The quantities of cotton and wool yarn which could be spared from the clothing ration were very limited. Moreover, production difficulties—especially in the case of blankets and mattresses—were aggravated by the diversion of supply to the Services. Thus the production of mattresses increased from 200,000 in 1935 to 280,000 in 1942, but of these only 77,000 were available for the home market. The shortages can be seen from the following Table:

Supplies of Household Textiles for the Home Civilian Market
(Monthly Average for Calendar Months)

TABLE 34

Thousands

	Blankets[2]		Sheets	Towels	Tea Towels, etc.	Mattresses[2]
	Wool	Cotton				
1935 . .	550					200
1942 .						77
1943 .	188	367	250	1,867	900	87
1944 .	226	397	322	1,555	597	100
1945 .	317	418	589	1,249	610	130

By 1944 stocks of all textiles were becoming exhausted, whether in the shops or in the homes, and supplies of curtain materials and bedding were directed to those in greatest need by including them in the priority docket system[3] which limited supplies to the bombed out and the newly married. They remained unobtainable to the general public until after the end of the war.

(iii)

The Results

The edifice of control over the clothing industries had been constructed fairly swiftly. In the nine months between the issue of the

---

[1] Unfortunately, it is impossible to assess the results of the economies.

[2] Including cot size.

[3] See Chapter XIV.

Cloth and Apparel Order and the Apparel and Textiles Order—that is, between August 1941 and May 1942—the main framework of control over civilian cotton, rayon and wool production had been set up, the designation policy had been applied to the clothing industry and the Directorate of Civilian Hosiery had been set up. The control over clothing production was as complete as the Board could make it. After mid-1942 there were no great modifications of the controls. The only obvious changes were the concentration of the clothing industry and the extension of utility production to such items as gloves, handkerchiefs, braces, and household textiles.

It is clear from the previous section that the control over clothing involved a wide variety of production arrangements—directions under the Apparel and Textiles Order, undertakings by makers-up to produce seventy-five per cent. utility goods, the control over the distribution and use of utility cloth supplies, and so forth. The administration of these controls was a heavy burden. The machinery for allocating cloth at four-monthly intervals under individual specification numbers to more than 2,000 designated or nucleus firms was cumbrous and meant a vast amount of work both at headquarters and in the various controls. Various attempts were made to simplify the system but without success. It continued until, in the later stages of the war or after the war, resources were released for civilian production. From November 1944 the clothing budget was no longer divided into cloth specifications and early in 1946 first cloth certificates and then allocations were abandoned. Planned production of cloth ceased with the end of the war; but 'utility'—in the sense of price- and quality-controlled clothes—not only continued after the war but its range was widened by the inclusion of better class, higher priced goods.

It may be that the detailed description of the administration of the Board of Trade's clothing policy has conjured up in the reader's mind the picture of a vast number of bureaucrats seated at their Whitehall desks and laying down in great detail what each firm all over the country should or should not be allowed to make. This would not be a true picture. For the sake of brevity the phrase 'the Board of Trade' has frequently been used to cover the activities of many other bodies who were issuing directions or collecting statistics on their behalf. The utility scheme was devised and the broad outlines of its administration were, it is true, laid down centrally,[1] but its execution depended on the various Controls in such places as Manchester, Bradford, Leicester and on the trade committees like the Hosiery and Wool

---

[1] Much credit for its invention and execution must in fact be given to the business men who had left their peace-time jobs in the clothing industry to become temporary civil servants in the Board.

Rationing Committees who worked under their direction. Innumerable individuals, committees and institutions provided the essential technical information and advice without which the scheme could not have worked; in particular they gave liberally of their time and experience in drawing up the utility specifications. Finally, the whole system depended on the regular and accurate returns provided at frequent intervals by manufacturers and wholesalers throughout the textile and clothing industries—returns which made great demands on depleted war-time staffs but which were vital to the scheme.

The Board of Trade's clothing policy, of course, had to work within certain limits which the Board of Trade could not easily control. The Board of Trade had to reckon both with a gradual decline in the total volume of clothing production and with the claims of the Ministry of Supply on this falling production. The arbitration between the Ministry of Supply's claims on behalf of the Services and the Board of Trade's claims on behalf of the civilian was not very effective. The Materials Committee confined its operations to the allocation of raw materials and yarn and in practice only dealt thoroughly with cotton yarn. The Board of Trade felt that the basic issue of clothes coupons should not be reduced below forty-eight coupons a year. When this level was threatened in 1942 the President felt bound to appeal to his colleagues. 'I cannot accept the view', he said, 'that the Services have first call on all clothing capacity and that the civilian should be left to make do with what may remain after they are satisfied . . . in many cases there is at present nothing to prevent the Government ordering on a scale that leaves wholly inadequate production for the civilian. . . . I am not in a position to criticise [the high level of Service requirements], but at 9·8 million garments a year [for men's underwear] it seems right out of scale with the civilian ration.'

As a result of this complaint, Service and civilian demands for clothing were reviewed by the chairman of the Materials Committee. The first result of this review was a setback for the Board of Trade; civilian programmes for hosiery and boots and shoes, where competition with the Services was most fierce, had to be reduced. In the spring of 1943, however, Service clothing requirements were again reviewed and drastic cuts were agreed; these averaged almost fifty per cent. of the current rate of production and involved the release of some 42,000 workers. Thereafter, although civilian shortages did appear they could no longer be ascribed to serious competition from the Ministry of Supply.

Nevertheless, the civilian shortages that did appear thereafter were very severe indeed. The clothing ration having been maintained at an annual rate of forty-eight coupons fell to a rate of just over forty-one coupons from February to August 1945 and then—when the war was over—to a rate of thirty-six coupons for the period from September 1945 to April 1946.

The fundamental cause of this fall in the ration was a crisis of production. Chapters XV and XVI have already shown that by 1944 all the textile and clothing industries were in difficulties. Their labour forces had dwindled further than anyone had intended and every effort to build them up again met with little success.[1] Not only were employees in the industries disappearing but those that were left were also ageing and tiring; the industries were not attracting their share of school-leavers. The labour shortages were particularly severe in all the yarn-producing sections of the textile industries. In consequence the output of cotton and rayon cloth for making-up and of all kinds of yarn for the hosiery industry fell; wool cloth for making-up was not so seriously affected. The capacity of the heavy tailoring section of the making-up industry was however inadequate to deal with the supplies of wool cloth that were coming forward. Here, too, the labour shortage was serious and the industry could not meet the normal Service contracts, the new contracts for demobilisation clothing that it received from mid-1944 onwards and civilian needs. In other sections of the clothing industry the ruling shortage was that of cloth. But in these sections, too, difficulties were aggravated by problems of capacity—sometimes through the demobilisation clothing contracts, Service contracts for jungle warfare clothing, relief clothing, etc., and sometimes, particularly in the case of women's outerwear, through the effects of the flying-bomb raids on London.

The reflection of these unpleasant facts was seen in many of the figures that were coming before the Board of Trade. For example, deliveries of cotton yarn against the Board's home trade allocation fell as follows:

Deliveries of Cotton Yarn against the Board of Trade allocation

TABLE 35

Yarn, thousand tons

	1943 Quarterly Average	1944				1945			
		Period I	Period II	Period III	Period IV	Period I	Period II	Period III	Period IV
Allocation	15·4	15·0	15·0	14·5	15·1	15·5	15·0	17·0	19·5
Deliveries	16·8	14·9	14·0	12·6	13·5	13·2	13·6	13·8	20·4

[1] See pp. 370, 377, 395–6, 413, 419.

Figures of cloth production likewise fell:

Deliveries to the Home Market of Woven Cloth for Clothing

TABLE 36

Annual rate: million sq. yds.

	Woven Wool Cloth	Woven Non-Wool Cloth	
		Cotton—all types	Rayon—all types
1942:			
February–July.	171	n.a.	n.a.
August–December	183	296	150
1943:			
January–April.	161	344	169
May–August	155	295	135
September–December	171	296	132
1944:			
January–February	163	292	142
March–April	169	288	139
May–June	165	281	129
July–August	150	251	129
September–October	163	282	117
November–December	154	256	120
1945:			
January–February	157	256	144
March–April	160	253	143
May–June	149	248	133
July–August	152	242	136
September–October	187	279	161
November–December	186	269	155

These falls were cushioned—certainly in the case of cotton and rayon[1]—by the existence of large stocks[2] of cloth in the hands of merchant converters. Total deliveries by converters of cotton and rayon cloth—utility and non-utility together—remained above the budget figure until May 1944, but converters' stocks of finished cloth had been falling since the beginning of the year. Deliveries of non-utility cloth had indeed begun to fall at the beginning of 1944 while deliveries of utility cloth were still buoyant. The Board of Trade had for a long time been surprised to see how well deliveries and stocks of non-utility cloth had been maintained; they referred to 'the widow's cruse', or, more plainly, to the holes in the net of control. Nevertheless, the widow's cruse was now emptying itself at a rather unfortunate moment. Deliveries of non-wool cloth were ninety-four per cent. of the budget rate between May and August 1944, ninety-two per cent. between September and December 1944, eighty-three per cent between January and April 1945, and eighty per cent. be-

---

[1] Figures for stocks of wool cloth at various stages were unknown.
[2] Stocks both of grey and of finished cloth.

tween May and August 1945. They climbed back to 100 per cent. in the first four months of 1946.

The failure of cloth deliveries to keep up to the level of the budget must obviously have affected the making-up industry. Unfortunately the figures for garment production and for stocks of cloth in the hands of makers-up were not comprehensive. The Board of Trade could, however, see that hosiery production—the other source of finished garments[1]—was falling.[2]

The figures that first startled the Board of Trade were not production figures but figures for wholesale clothing stocks. Wholesale clothing stocks as a whole[3] had risen throughout the first half of 1943, but from mid-1943 onwards they began to fall. During the first half of 1944 the fall was steep so that by mid-summer 1944 stocks as a whole were below the level for efficient distribution.[4] They continued to fall sharply until the middle of 1945. It is clear that production of cotton yarn, of all types of cloth (except possibly wool) and of hosiery for civilian needs was falling during most of 1944 and 1945 and that this fall was bound to be reflected sooner or later in the clothing ration. During the spring of 1945 the Prime Minister did indeed authorise a twenty per cent. switch of manpower engaged on military clothing to civilian use even though this might entail delay in fulfilling Service demands. In practice, however, the cut was difficult to enforce and by the middle of 1945 only about 10 per cent. of cotton, $7\frac{1}{2}$ per cent. of wool and 10 per cent. of hosiery Service requirements had been cut. There were certain considerable releases of Army blankets and corset cloth, and considerable cuts in production of some articles such as battledress later in the year. But although they marked the first switch from war production to peace production their effect on the home market was largely offset by the increased rate of demobilisation. Permanent improvement in clothing supplies could not be expected until munitions production in the textile and clothing areas was curtailed and the labour began to go back to civilian industries.

Production of textiles and clothing for the home market thus fell for reasons that were in the main outside the Board of Trade's control. It does seem, however, that the Board may have unwittingly aggravated the crisis. In the first place, we must come back to a point that has been mentioned earlier in this chapter—the underplanning of the clothing budget. Rayon and cotton cloth deliveries did not fall below the budget until about May 1944; wool cloth deliveries were never seriously below the budget. Allowing for the time lag in production wholesale clothing stocks should not have been affected until the late

---

[1] Hosiery was, of course, produced from yarn not from cloth.

[2] See Table 33 on p. 464.

[3] There were, of course, variations between particular garments.

[4] i.e. two months' stock.

summer of 1944. These stocks had, however, begun to fall sharply in January 1944. This seems to support the suggestion that the requirements of cloth set forth in the Board of Trade's clothing budget were somewhat, though not wildly, inadequate to meet the ration. The ration, that is to say, had been maintained by drawing on stocks. If this be true the consequences are obvious. It would mean that the Board of Trade had set its claims for raw material and productive capacity too low. Moreover, stocks were consumed before they were needed most—that is, before the crisis in production rose to its height.

Perhaps the most serious consequence of this understatement of requirements was that it obscured from the Board of Trade the difficulties that were crowding in upon them. In April 1944 the Board were still confident that the forty-eight coupon ration could be easily maintained, in June they felt that they could scrape through without cutting the ration, and in September, while they saw that the production outlook was sombre, they thought they could manage by running down stocks. It was not till December that the Board seriously considered a cut in the ration from February 1945 and even then they hoped to restore the ration by September 1945. The understatement of requirements may have clouded the problems, but nevertheless it would be difficult to blame the Board for any slowness to grasp the dangers confronting them. We have already explained the difficulties of interpreting the mass of statistics coming forward and the time lag in collecting them. Moreover, the Board had been quite glad to see some fall in stocks at various stages, for in 1943 they had in many cases grown rather high. Then, too, the uncertainty about the date of the end of the war must be emphasised. For a time there was a hope that the European war might finish by the end of 1944; if it had done so, there would still have been production difficulties but the ration might have been maintained by drawing still further on stocks until production for the home market increased once more.

The crisis in clothing supplies at the end of the war may seem a reflection on the success of the Board of Trade's clothing policy. But it is fair to conclude that for the most part it was due to forces outside the effective control of the Board. There are other criteria for judging the Board of Trade's clothing policy. Was the ration honoured? Were garments produced in the proportions that consumers wanted? Were clothing prices kept down? Did the consumer receive value for his —or her—money? Did simplification and standardisation of production bring economies in time, labour and materials? Some of the answers to these questions are difficult to prove statistically, but there is little doubt that they are all in the affirmative.

The ration was always honoured. In the period of crisis during late 1944 and 1945 which we have just discussed there was a growing volume of complaint about shortages. But the ration was adjusted to the level of supplies before shop shortages grew acute. The Board did indeed wonder at the end of 1944 whether now that the end of the war was so near the public would take a cut in the ration so hardly that it might be preferable to maintain the coupon issue and suffer severe shop shortages and a storm of complaints. The Board decided to hold fast to the principle that the ration must be honoured. This principle had meant that there had never been serious 'coupon clumping'—coupons in the hands of consumers or retailers which could not be spent.

Were garments produced in the proportions that consumers wanted? On the whole the balance between the supply of individual garments and the demand for them was pretty well kept. There were shortages—sometimes serious ones—of items such as industrial overalls, corsets, infants' and children's wear, woollen hosiery and footwear, and there was over-production of some items such as raincoats and the cheaper utility clothes. These difficulties were, however, the exception and the Board of Trade found it possible to remedy most of them.

Clothing policy undoubtedly fulfilled one of its other chief aims— to keep the price of clothing down. No satisfactory price control was ever evolved for non-utility clothes; but, owing largely to the utility scheme, the index of clothing prices had fallen from 195 early in 1942 to 164 by the end of 1943.[1] At a corresponding period of the 1914–18 war prices of clothes were 260 per cent. above the 1914 level and their quality was poor. The public in the Second World War could be satisfied not only with the prices but also with the quality of utility clothing. As we have seen, there were some complaints about some cloths and some garments. But on the whole the clothes were good. Shoddy pre-war clothes were eliminated and the use of such finishes as waterproofing, non-shrinking, and crease-resisting was considerably extended.

The economies of labour and material are perhaps the most difficult of all the results of clothing policy to assess. Any attempt to do so would be a research project of its own demanding detailed investigation into the experience of individual firms. For it seems almost impossible to isolate, amidst the changes of war-time, the effect on efficiency of one or two factors. Some forces in war-time tended to depress productivity—the black-out, the loss of experienced workers and the ageing of the labour force, increased wear and tear on machinery, the decline in the quality of fuel and raw materials. On the other hand, the austerity regulations, planned production and

---

[1] 1st September 1939=100. Part of the fall was, of course, due to the removal of purchase tax from utility clothing but no such remission of taxation would have been feasible without the utility scheme. See Chapters XXI and XXII generally for price control.

standardisation tended to increase productivity. Many sections of the textile and clothing industries were confident that war-time methods had increased their efficiency. In the doubling and weaving sections of the cotton industry most manufacturers believed that their efficiency had increased by ten to fifteen per cent. A sub-committee of the Cotton Working Party, however, when it went very fully into the effect of long runs on costs, concluded that the available information did not warrant an exact answer. It felt, for example, that the traditional costing methods of weavers were insufficiently precise to enable them to ascertain the true structure of costs.[1] The sub-committee believed nevertheless that the war-time experience of working on a smaller number of cloths had clearly demonstrated the economic value of organising production for long runs.

Information about the efficiency of the wool industry is even more scanty. One firm making blankets and flannels reported increased productivity of from fifteen to thirty per cent., brought about by long runs. In woollen weaving as a whole, long runs increased the average number of 'cuts' per warp by about twenty-eight per cent.,[2] which represented a considerable saving in production costs. Certainly the Wool Control, no less than the Cotton Control, exercised its influence towards the longest possible runs; presumably it was therefore convinced of the economies which could thus be obtained.

The finishing section of the textile industries was agreed on the advantages of receiving bulk orders from a reduced number of merchant converters instead of a myriad of small orders. This was particularly true of the dyeing section where full vats account for an average saving of about ten per cent. on processing costs. The chairman of one dyeing association asserted that before the war the yarn-dyeing industry 'was clogged and stifled by an excess of small dyeing quantities brought about by the endless variety of shades in use, with the result that labour expenditure was exceedingly high and the outlay in coal, dyestuffs and chemicals proportionately high'. He believed that a continuation or extension in the post-war period of production on the lines of the utility scheme would do much to solve a most difficult problem.[3]

In the industries producing finished garments—the clothing and hosiery industries—there was also evidence of increased efficiency; this seems, however, to have been produced by the austerity regulations rather than by long runs. In replies to a questionnaire issued to the making-up industry in 1943, two-thirds of the firms showed increases of between twenty-five and seventy-five per cent. in output per worker. These increases were ascribed to austerity regulations

---

[1] *Cotton Working Party Report*, p. 101.

[2] *Wool Working Party Report*, Appendix III.

[3] *The Economist*, 19th May 1942.

and to the longer hours worked. Efficiency must also have been stimulated by the virtual elimination of fashion changes and seasonal trading.

In the hosiery industry at the end of 1942 a labour force equal to only forty-eight per cent. of pre-war strength was consuming seventy-five per cent. of the pre-war volume of yarn. These figures are to some extent deceptive as a test of productivity because the use of coarser yarn and coarser machinery would account for at least part of the increased weight of yarn consumed. Nevertheless, there must undoubtedly have been some increase of efficiency. This was ascribed by the Director of Civilian Hosiery to three causes—the working of a full 48-hour week, long runs, and the simplification of garments. One study, however, suggests that almost all the increased productivity could be accounted for by the economies introduced by style restrictions.[1] For example, the elimination of the buttoned opening in men's vests saved about ten per cent. in manufacturing time and the time spent on making austerity men's pants was about 25–30 minutes per dozen garments compared with nearly $1\frac{3}{4}$ hours per dozen for the pre-war type. There were similar savings on other garments. Moreover, it must be remembered that increased output was obtained by reducing the supply of fully-fashioned stockings and elaborate garments, by failing to eliminate 'seconds' and by eliminating luxury and speciality goods. Comparatively little increased productivity remains, therefore, to be attributed to the economies of long runs. Nevertheless, forty per cent. of the replies received to a questionnaire issued by the Hosiery Working Party state that war-time production lessons had been useful in demonstrating the advantages of standardisation and long runs.[2]

All this evidence about the effect of clothing policy on productivity is unfortunately vague. The burden of it is, however, favourable. These results added to the other benefits of the Board of Trade's clothing policy make only one conclusion possible. That policy as a whole was a great success. The clothing budget saw that the clothing needs of the population were, broadly, met. And the utility scheme was conceived with imagination and administered with skill—both in improvisation and in the execution of settled plans. 'Utility did an excellent war-time job', writes one specialist upon it, 'and even in retrospect it is difficult to suggest improvements.'[3]

---

[1] The authors are indebted to Miss S. A. Taylor for permission to see her thesis *The Policy of Industrial Concentration during the War*, written for a University of London Ph.D. degree.

[2] *Hosiery Working Party Report*, p. 59.

[3] Wadsworth, *op. cit.*

Some Examples of the Four-Figure Cotton Cloth
Institution, July 1942, under

	Speci-fication No.	Description	Type of Finish	Min. width overall in.	Min. weight per sq. yd. oz.	Max. percentage of foreign matter	Min. threads per in. Warp	Weft
FLANNEL-ETTE PYJAMA CLOTHS	3010	Coloured-woven double warp flannelette	Raised	30 36	5½	5	48 double ends =96	45
SHIRTINGS	3020	Bleached, dyed or printed poplin	Bleached and mercerised; dyed and mercerised; Bleached and calendered;	31 36	3½	Nil	102	59
			Printed	31 36	3½	3	102	59
	3031	Oxford	Calendered	28	6½	5	40 double ends =80	41
DRESS CLOTHS	3044	Poplin	Bleached, dyed or printed	36	3	Nil	152	74
	3050	Zephyr, plain	Calendered	36	3½	7	60	55
	3051	Zephyr, striped	Calendered	36	3½	7	60	55
	3052	Check gingham	Calendered	36	3½	7	60	55
LIGHT OVERALL CLOTHS	3060	Cambric	Bleached, dyed or printed	36	3¾	3	76	58
GABAR-DINES	3080	Gabardine	Dyed and water-proofed	54	5¾ pure	Proofing material only	118	61
FUSTIANS	3100	Light corduroy	Dyed	28	13½	10	49	220
LININGS	3995	Coloured-woven check raincoat lining	Desized and waterproofed	54	4½	5	69	64
	3991	Jean (Silesia lin-ing for sleeves, vests, trouser tops and pocket-ing)	Dyed or printed (beetled or schreinered)	39	4½ black 4¼ other colours & prints	1	100	60

NOTE: There were in all 79 specifications of cotton cloths. There were, for example, 10 shirtings and 12 dress cloths. Besides the groups illustrated above there were also terry towelling, heavy overall cloths, velveteen, lingerie, sateen, calico long cloths, flannelette, corset cloths, etc.

Specifications issued by the British Standards

S.R. & O. 1942, No. 1002

MANUFACTURING PARTICULARS

Dye	Max. washing shrinkage		Other details	Width overall	Threads per inch		YARNS			
	Warp %	Weft %		in.	Warp	Weft	Counts		Schedule	
							Warp	Weft	Warp	Weft
Fast to No. 2 washing test	5	2	Weave: Plain (double and warp) Design: Proportion of coloured yarn in warp not to exceed 50%. Design should comprise not more than three colours in addition to bleached, cream or tinted ground Finish: To be raised, not sueded.	31½ 38	46 double ends =92	46	22	14	RF	C
Fast to No. 3 washing test	4	2	Dyed pale shades	32½ 37½	98	62	32	30	RN	D
Fast to No. 3 washing test	4	2	Not mercerised	32½ 37½	98	62	32	30	RN	D
Colours in stripes fast to No. 3 washing test	4	1	Ground weave: Plain (double-end warp). Design: Number of dyed ends not to exceed 60% of the total. Undyed ends to be bleached, weft to be grey.	28½	39 double ends =78	42	22	8	RD	Condenser
Fast to No. 3 washing test	4	2	Finish: Mercerised	38	144	76	2/100	2/100	Egyptian combed and gassed	
Vat or azoic colours, fast to No. 3 washing test	6	2	Design: Self-coloured warp or weft. Bleached weft or warp	36½	59	56	24	24	RD	D
Vat or azoic colours, fast to No. 3 washing test	6	2	Design: Not exceeding 30% of warp threads may be coloured and the remainder bleached. Bleached weft.	36½	59	56	24	24	RD	D
Vat or azoic colours, fast to No. 3 washing test	6	2	Design: Up to 60% coloured threads, remainder bleached	36½	59	56	24	24	RD	D
Vats: fast No. 3 washing test	5	2	Finish: Mercerised or lustre	38½	72	60	24	24	RD	D
Sulphur: fast to No. 2 washing test	—	—	Weave: 2/1 twill. Waterproofness: Bundesmann test max. absorption 40%. Max. penetration 5 c.c.	56	114	64	22	18	Eg.	G
Fast to No. 2 washing test	3	Nil	Grey weight per linear yd., 10 ozs. Finish to be free from odour	32	43	216	2/20	20	RD	C
Fast to No. 2 washing test	—	—	Weave: 2/2 twill. Design: Number of colours (including white if used) shall not exceed 4 in warp and 4 in weft.	55	68	65	20	22	RD	D
—	—	—	Weave 2/1 twill	40½	96	62	24	24	RD	D

There were full details of washing tests, shrinking tests, waterproofing tests, etc., given in the document and other notes about the type of manufacturing particulars referred to and the finishes required.

APPENDIX 14

Summary of Range of Utility Cloths

(excluding wool)[1]

	No. of Specifications		
	Cotton	Rayon	Mixtures
Pyjama cloths	6	—	—
Shirtings	21	—	—
Dress cloths	13	51	3
Light overall cloths	3	1	1
Nursery squares	1	—	—
Bib and feeder cloth	2	—	—
Gabardines	5	—	—
Bedford cords	2	—	—
Corduroys and moleskins . . .	7	—	—
Heavy overall cloths	13	—	—
Pit drawer cloth	1	—	—
Hospital cloths	6	—	—
Velveteens and light corduroys . .	5	—	—
Lingerie	1	11	3
Suitings	3	—	—
Linings	25	12	2
Cloth for mackintoshes	5	—	—
Cloth for oilskins	2	—	—
Corset cloth	11	—	7
Curtain cloths	13	3	5
Towels { Terry 4 / Tea and Kitchen 5 / Huck 3 } .	12	—	—
Sheets	10	2	4
Pillowcases	4	—	2
Cotton blankets	18	—	—
Tickings	15	—	—
Down and wadding quilt cloths . .	2	3	—
Upholstery cloths	3	—	—
Handkerchiefs	8	—	—
TOTAL NUMBER OF CLOTHS .	218	83	27

[1] Wool specifications are excluded because they were based chiefly on weight and price and broad description so that some specifications may include scores of technically different cloths.

Source: Cotton Control

APPENDIX 15

Cotton Cloth Deliveries, 1944 (By Users)

	Piece-goods (yards)	Made-up Articles (number)[1]
Government Departments . .	406,618,340	23,677,530
Industrial Groups . . .	148,759,009	—
Essential Home Services . .	97,938,328	—
Civilian Home Trade . .	321,014,846	3,016,084
Exports	321,014,846	—
GRAND TOTAL—All Users .	1,215,730,417	26,693,614

[1] Made-up articles = sheets, towels, pillowcases, dusters, etc., which are recorded in numbers, not by yardage.

Source: Cotton Control

CHAPTER XVIII

CIVILIAN FOOTWEAR

(i)

The Control of the Industry

BEFORE September 1939 there had been as little consideration of the war-time problems of the civilian uses of leather, particularly in footwear, as there had been of the general problems of civilian clothing. Arrangements had indeed been made for setting up on the outbreak of war a Leather Control as part of the system of raw material Controls. Its main concern however was to make provision for Service requirements, to deal with the export and import licensing of the principal materials of the industry and to exercise a general responsibility for leather prices. There was no question of a policy or policies for controlling the leather and footwear industries or for limiting or shaping civilian consumption.

Even after war had broken out these industries managed for a considerable time to escape any sort of regulation either of production or supply. To help in the export drive, a Leather Footwear and Allied Industries Export Corporation was created, supported by a levy on raw skins and hides. But there was still no control over footwear for the home civilian market. As has been seen[1] the War Cabinet decided in March 1940 that as an anti-inflationary measure a scheme for the production of standard boots and shoes for men, women and children should be worked out. Nothing came of the plan, however; there was indeed throughout 1940 a good deal of uncertainty as to whether the Ministry of Supply or the Board of Trade were responsible for administering footwear policy. Footwear also escaped control under the Limitation of Supplies Order of June 1940—chiefly because it was felt to be impracticable to distinguish between essential and unessential types of footwear.

Nevertheless, there was in the latter half of 1940 a good deal of concern in the Board of Trade about the need for quantitative and qualitative control over the civilian output of the boot and shoe industry. Unfortunately, the manufacturers' views as to the course of policy to be adopted diverged markedly from the views held by Government departments. The manufacturers in the first place wanted the Government to make a statement about the total amounts

[1] See Chapter IV, p. 88.

of footwear in the various categories which it considered to be required to meet the essential needs of the civilian population; they themselves put the total at $93\frac{1}{2}$ million pairs per annum.[1] This the Government not unreasonably refused to do in view of shipping uncertainties. Next, the manufacturers favoured, as a means of limiting the output of the industry, a system of pairage licensing—that is, a restriction on the physical output as opposed to the value of output of the industry. Thirdly, they showed no readiness to co-operate with the Ministry of Supply in enforcing economy measures such as limitation on the use of certain materials or methods of construction. The Board of Trade, on the other hand, were anxious to ensure that the footwear which was manufactured was of a serviceable type. They were afraid that if pairage alone were limited the trade would switch from the cheaper, more essential types of footwear to the more expensive varieties. For this reason they revived the idea of standard footwear and pointed out that this need not involve standardisation of design or construction. But the manufacturers, remembering the failure of the standard boot at the end of the 1914–18 war, would have nothing to do with it; in this they were supported by the Leather Controller. The whole problem of control was further aggravated by the division of responsibility between the Board of Trade and the Ministry of Supply. The Board and the Ministry were independently pursuing their ideas as to the best way of limiting the output of the industry; meanwhile the manufacturers were not slow to suggest that limitation Orders would merely create further unemployment, as they were alleged to be doing in the hosiery industry.

However, the shipping shortage, with its effect on the industry's raw materials, and the need to release labour, made it evident that some form of control would have to be established. The industry still favoured pairage restrictions, which it claimed to be 'simple, equitable, flexible and adjustable', coupled with a rationing of upper leather. The Board of Trade still had in mind the possibility of controlling footwear by a Limitation of Supplies Order. But negotiations were now largely in the hands of the Ministry of Supply, which was unsympathetic to the proposals alike of the industry and of the Board of Trade. It believed that the best way of handling the matter would be to ration upper leather and at the same time to press ahead with formulating footwear specifications which the manufacturers had undertaken to prepare in conjunction with the Leather Control. The rationing of upper leather was intended simply to bring about a cut in consumption; the initial aim was a twenty-five per cent. reduction in civilian usage compared with the first half of 1940. There

---

[1] Viz: men ($1\frac{1}{2}$ pairs per head) $22\frac{1}{2}$ million, women (2 pairs per head) 43 million, children ($3\frac{1}{4}$ pairs per head) 28 million. In 1935 the total had been 132 million pairs of footwear of all kinds.

would be no allocation of the ration as between different classes of footwear, since it was expected that firms would continue to specialise on different types and grades of boots and shoes.

In the end the acquisition and use of upper leather in the manufacture of footwear was controlled by an Order of February 1941.[1] This limited acquisition to seventy per cent. and usage in manufacture to eighty per cent. of amounts acquired and used respectively in the first nine months of 1940. By itself and without supporting measures of economy and standardisation this control could achieve little. It might even—and this was the view of the industry—do harm by making it advantageous for a manufacturer to make fewer shoes, using more leather per pair. Thus it might accentuate the shortages which were beginning to be felt in certain categories of footwear—children's shoes and miners' heavy boots for example.

In March 1941, the Government's concentration of industry policy was launched. By this time, all that had been achieved in the footwear industry was a control of part of its raw materials. From the spring of 1941 onwards, however, the application of the policy of concentration of industry, the extension of measures of price control and the introduction of the utility programme combined to force the pace in the control of the manufacture and distribution of footwear.

The concentration problem was the first to be dealt with. Here it seemed that the licensing of pairage output, which the manufacturers' federation had all along been demanding, would form a useful starting point in a concentration scheme, for it would indicate the share of each manufacturer in the reduced total output of the industry. Taking 1940 as a base year the industry was informed that pairage was to be reduced by the following amounts: men's eighteen per cent., women's twenty-three per cent., boys and girls nil, infants' twelve per cent., fabric footwear forty per cent., slippers and house shoes thirty per cent. The basic figure for total output in the concentration scheme was put at $96\frac{1}{2}$ million pairs,[2] but it was definitely stated that this was no indication of the Government's views as to the minimum essential needs of the civilian population; furthermore, it was added that there was no guarantee that this figure of total output would be maintained. Actual licensing of pairage production did not come into force until December 1941,[3] but the figures given for pairage restriction enabled each firm to measure the contribution that it could make to a grouping arrangement and its status therein. Firms were to make their own concentration arrangements, with the provision that nucleus firms were expected to run their factories at full capacity as measured by their highest monthly output in 1940,

---

[1] S.R. & O. 1941, No. 208.
[2] Men's 20 million, women's 35 million, boys' 7 million, girls' 12 million, infants' $6\frac{1}{2}$ million, fabric footwear 4 million, slippers, etc., 12 million.
[3] S.R. & O. 1941, No. 1858.

adjusted for the lengthening of the normal working week from forty-five to forty-eight hours; but all schemes, of course, had to obtain the approval of the Board of Trade and to satisfy the requirements of the Ministry of Labour and of the Factory and Storage Control. There was no central compensation fund and firms were left to make their own financial arrangements with one another. In fact, the usual arrangement was for the nucleus firm to make footwear from the absorbed firm's materials and to sell the finished product to the absorbed firm at cost, the latter retaining its buying and selling organisation.

By the time of the closing date for voluntary concentration schemes—30th June 1941—applications had been received from about half the industry. Leicester, one of the main centres of the footwear industry, was then almost entirely covered and the Rossendale Valley manufacturers had submitted a group scheme covering thirty-five firms. Sometimes not merely two but three or four manufacturers entered into a concentration arrangement. But there still remained some fifty per cent. of the trade which had not yet submitted concentration proposals and a good deal of hard work had to be devoted during the remainder of the year by the Board of Trade's newly appointed Director of Civilian Footwear to finishing off the whole business. There was some trouble, too, with the Ministry of Labour, which was inclined to treat concentration schemes on a local basis and to be unwilling to agree to them if they appeared likely to release more labour than could be absorbed locally. There was also the problem of the machinery of the industry, which was mostly leased from the British United Shoe Machinery Company. Finally, the Company agreed to waive the rents on machinery rendered idle through concentration and to permit the movement of machinery from one factory to another.

By the summer of 1942 concentration arrangements had been completed. They covered 700 firms which represented practically the whole of the industry, apart from some very small firms employing elderly labour which would have been of little use for other work. 408 nucleus certificates were issued, while 3·8 million square feet of factory space were released, representing about thirty per cent. of the total space available. The labour force of the industry had been reduced by 15,000 or fourteen per cent. since 1940.[1] At the same time Local Advisory Panels were set up consisting of representatives of both sides of the industry with a Ministry of Labour chairman and attended by the labour adviser of the Directorate of Civilian Footwear. The function of these panels was to scrutinise the labour force of nucleus firms so as to ensure that they were using manpower as

---

[1] In 1935 the total labour force of the industry had been 116·6 thousand: it fell to 82·3 thousand in 1942 (see *Board of Trade, Working Party Reports: Boots and Shoes* (H.M.S.O. 1946), p. 64).

efficiently as possible. It is worth noting that output per operative increased between 1942 and 1943 from 1,026·5 to 1,071·2 (weighted pairage) and that part of the credit for this improvement was claimed by the local panels.

While the concentration of the footwear industry may be regarded as successful in the sense that practically the whole of the firms in the industry entered into some form of grouping arrangement, it would be a mistake to overlook certain disadvantages to which concentration, as it was actually carried out, gave rise. From the point of view of civilian requirements the concentrated industry resulting from voluntary groupings based on a fixed pairage factor was probably not well adapted to meeting the strains and stresses which were to develop in the latter half of the war. In an industry characterised by specialised capacity adjusted to the needs for varied outputs there was clearly a danger that concentration along these lines might lead to a loss of the flexibility required to meet the sudden and unexpected changes of global war. Thus the disappearance of rubber supplies, which was unforeseen at the time when concentration was undertaken, called for adaptations and adjustments in the leather footwear industry which were made much more difficult by the rigid pattern of concentration. All that can perhaps be said is that, in 1941 at any rate, the alternative to concentration, namely some form of direct control of production, was not in the field of practical politics.

After concentration the next big influence on the footwear industry was the utility scheme. Proposals for a range of utility footwear, which began to be discussed in the summer of 1941 at the time of the setting up of the Board of Trade's Directorate of Civilian Clothing, were put forward for much the same reasons as those underlying the schemes for utility cloth and clothing. The Director of Civilian Clothing said that what was wanted was reasonably durable footwear to meet the coupon demand of the working classes, such footwear being price-controlled under the new price legislation which was just then coming into force. Still less than in the case of cloth and clothing was anything in the nature of a standard article to be aimed at. Quite apart from the hostility of the manufacturers to standard boots and shoes, the great variety in substances and qualities of leather, coupled with the fact that the most serviceable varieties were reserved for the armed forces, would have precluded any rigid measure of standardisation. The acute raw material shortages, which subsequently developed and which will be discussed later in this chapter, added emphasis to this point, since one of the best ways of dealing with these shortages was to allow scope to the ingenuity and initiative of the manufacturer in making the most of his material. And in fact there had to be some relaxation of the specifications which were laid down.

The procedure which was actually adopted in framing a utility scheme was, after a determination of certain grades of footwear, to arrange for each district of the industry to submit samples of the main categories of footwear in each grade and then to have these samples scrutinised by central committees representing the manufacturers. In all 115 footwear specifications[1] were drawn up, covering men's, women's, boys', girls' and infants' footwear[2] and divided into four grades: cheap, medium, best and extra-best. These grades were related to pre-war price ranges and when the utility scheme was put into force manufacturers themselves were graded according to the 1939 prices of their output and were restricted in their utility production to their appropriate grades. The specifications fell broadly into two parts, first, a description of the types and minimum prices of leather to be used and secondly, a description of the methods of construction to be employed. It was emphasised throughout the discussions on the utility proposals, first, that the aim would be to crystallise in the specifications good, normal practice and, secondly, that there would be no attempt to introduce anything like a standard boot or standard shoe. These specifications represented a cross-section of the output of the industry and covered everything except the following: slippers, house shoes and shoes with fabric uppers, specialities such as surgical footwear and sports footwear, the dearer lines selling above twenty-nine shillings and ninepence pre-war and also some very cheap lines. As far as price fixing was concerned, this was based on costings submitted by manufacturers in the different districts; ceiling prices were agreed which were regarded as applicable to the greater part of the industry and manufacturers were required to charge either these prices or sums equal to their costs of production and sale plus five per cent., whichever were the less. The scheme was put into force by requiring manufacturers to devote fifty per cent. of their licensed production to utility types,[3] the footwear so produced being marked with the utility mark and with the manufacturers' identification numbers which were assigned to them by the Board of Trade. Subsequently, in certain categories of footwear much higher percentages of utility production were prescribed—100 per cent. for men's heavy boots and 75 per cent. for children's and infants' footwear. Provision was made for licensing variations from the specifications and also for granting exemption to a class of firms, for example the surgical boot makers, who were clearly incapable of conforming to the requirements of the utility scheme.

---

[1] In September 1943, 28 additional specifications were introduced, mainly for children's and industrial footwear.

[2] Also heavy mining and agricultural footwear.

[3] This was as from 1st October 1942. When the scheme began in July 1942, the percentage had been fixed at 37½ per cent. to allow for the difficulty manufacturers might experience at the outset in achieving 50 per cent. utility production.

It may perhaps be questioned whether the utility arrangements served any major war-time purpose other than that of price regulation. They helped no doubt, as did other schemes of this kind, in the identification of price-controlled commodities, which was necessary in any really effective measures for the fixing of maximum prices. They did not ensure and were not intended to ensure that the maximum number of pairs of shoes were manufactured from the raw materials available. It was claimed rather that they set minimum standards for the bulk of the footwear which was required to meet the war-time needs of the civilian population. But it may well be argued that after the introduction of rationing the population was capable of looking after itself and that the civilian tended generally to aim at securing the best possible value for his coupons. For example, during the war the pre-war tendency to buy the lighter and less durable footwear would in any case have been reversed. The manufacturers, it may reasonably be suggested, could have been left to meet this demand as best they could with such resources in materials and labour as they could obtain. In fact the utility scheme, with its grading of manufacturers and its ceiling prices, may be regarded rather as an instrument for securing that all the different grades of leather were employed in the manufacture of the sort of footwear that would be required in war-time. As the Working Party on Boots and Shoes pointed out, one of the conditions of the scheme was that it should be able to use up a complete cross-section of the available qualities and types of leather.[1] Thus the scheme should be viewed in the main as an economy measure and associated with the introduction of such general restrictions on footwear manufacture as those on through or three-quarter soling and on decoration.[2]

In any event footwear was clearly a commodity which presented certain technical difficulties for a utility scheme, apart from special war-time difficulties. There is the enormous variety in its raw material, which has already been mentioned. Then there is the fact that the quality of shoes depends so much on good workmanship, something which it is impossible to define.[3] Considerations such as these went some way to justify the dislike which the manufacturers felt for the utility arrangements. On top of these problems came the war-time shortages of materials which called for technical ingenuity rather than adherence to a rigid system of specifications. 'Even with the elaborate machinery of the utility specifications', says the Working Party report, 'it was quite possible for unsatisfactory footwear to be made which conformed to the specifications in the letter if not in the spirit. When to this is added the increased variability, mainly in

---

[1] *Boots and Shoes Working Party Report*, p. 146.

[2] S.R. & O. 1942, No. 1846: 1943, No. 7.

[3] *Boots and Shoes Working Party Report*, p. 147.

a downward direction, of leather and other materials used for shoe-making in war-time and also the fact that many makeshifts had to be resorted to, the marvel is not that some utility shoes did give cause for legitimate complaint by the public, but that the cases were so few.'[1]

Within the general problem of providing enough footwear of reasonable quality for the civilian population there were some special difficulties. Of these, the one that probably attracted most public attention was the supply of children's footwear. There were numerous complaints both about shortages and about the quality of available supplies. The loss of rubber supplies was largely responsible for the shortage, for before the war the use of plimsolls and wellingtons had lessened the wear and tear on leather footwear. To meet the shortage, the President of the Board of Trade directed that the highest possible priority should be given to children's footwear—for example, by licensing a large pairage in children's footwear and a reduced pairage in adults' footwear. There were, however, obvious limits to what could be achieved by measures of this sort. Licensing a large supply of children's shoes did not necessarily mean that output would be increased: many manufacturers found themselves unable to achieve their permitted rate of supply owing to raw material or labour difficulties. Moreover, increased supplies could come only from those firms which had the specialised plant and equipment needed to make children's shoes. In spite of these difficulties, output did increase. Indeed, *per capita* purchases of children's and infants' shoes with leather uppers rose from three pairs in 1935 to 3·2 in 1943 and 3·4 in 1944.[2] Nevertheless this increase was not sufficient to meet the expanded demand.

For the tasks of the later years of the war the mechanism of control over the footwear industry had been much strengthened. During the first year and a half of war there had been, as we have seen, uncertainty as to whether the Ministry of Supply or the Board of Trade were responsible for the industry. But in July 1941 a Director of Civilian Footwear, responsible to the Board of Trade, was appointed; this seemed to make it clear that footwear problems came within the purview of the Board and not of the Ministry of Supply. Nevertheless throughout almost the whole of the war the handling of these problems suffered to some extent from divided authority. The allocation of leather was for some time undertaken by a division of the Leather Control of the Ministry of Supply. Then there was a separate Directorate of Service Footwear, with its own control of leather, its own rationing arrangements and its own system of labour protection. No factory was entirely engaged in making Service footwear, so all

---

[1] *Boots and Shoes Working Party Report*, p. 147.
[2] *The Impact of the War on Civilian Consumption*, p. 95.

Service contractors were subject to two controls. The dual system only disappeared in August 1944, when the Controller of Civilian Footwear (as he was then termed) resigned and the two controls became merged in one Footwear Control under the hitherto Director of Service Footwear and Leather Equipment at the Ministry of Supply.

Some measure of unification of authority had, however, been achieved in 1943 by the setting up of a Footwear Board responsible to the President of the Board of Trade and to the Minister of Supply and consisting of representatives of both departments under the chairmanship of Sir Cecil Weir, then Director-General of Equipment and Stores at the Ministry of Supply. The functions of the Board were to look after both Service and civilian production, to watch the amount of resources in the shape of raw materials, labour and capacity available to the industry and to the repair trade and to report through its chairman to both Ministers if factors outside its control appeared likely to interfere with the production programme.

Apart, however, from these problems of administrative co-ordination there was always the question whether the powers at the disposal of the Footwear Control were adequate to the responsibilities laid upon it. The main statutory instrument of control, as has been seen, was the system of pairage licensing, that is the authorisation to each manufacturer to supply up to a given pairage in the main categories of footwear. Redistribution of output between firms or between classes of footwear could only be achieved through the use of this instrument. This was a different type of arrangement from the system of 'direction' which operated in some other industries. It was fundamentally negative rather than positive and, taken in conjunction with lack of power to allocate raw materials, it could hardly be expected to achieve the best results. There was nothing here like the planned production in cotton textiles and it was perhaps in the nature of the industry that that sort of planning could not be introduced.

Control was applied not only to the production of new shoes but also to repairs. Clearly, leather would be saved if the public were enabled to have their shoes repaired rather than buy new ones. There were, of course, limits to the practicability of this policy. Children, for example, require new shoes because they grow out of old ones and heavy working boots often suffer as much wear and tear on the uppers as on the soles. Moreover, much of the footwear bought in the past was of light construction and unsuited to continuous repair, while much of the plant in the industry was incapable of being adapted to the manufacture of heavier type of shoes. At the end of 1942 a control of repairs was established with a regional organisation incorporated in the Board of Trade's regional system of Factory and Storage Control and linked with the Army's repair controllers.[1] All repairers, except those concerned with rubber footwear, were compelled to register[2] and regulations came into operation in 1943 enforcing economies, for example, by the prohibition of through or long soling.[3] In September 1944 licensing was required for the opening of new businesses or for the movement or extension of existing businesses.[4] Here again, as in the manufacture of footwear, the critical problem was the raw material shortage and here too steps had to be taken to see that leather was properly allocated, not in relation to past usage but in relation to current requirements.

(ii)

The Shortages

The public's demand for boots and shoes was controlled by the general clothes rationing scheme; the Board of Trade did not consider that it would be practicable to introduce special coupons for footwear. In calculating demand the Board were guided by the evidence of their consumer panel for since the total number of coupons was limited this was some guide to the public's real needs. The Board could, of course, try to influence demand by altering the price of footwear in terms of clothes coupons and in 1943 the points value of adults' footwear was increased.[5] But demand for shoes proved fairly inelastic; the changes in coupon values were not followed by any reduction in *per capita* purchases of footwear.[6] This demand was very difficult to meet and shop shortages of particular sizes or grades of footwear were continually experienced. The supply of raw materials and labour constantly limited output.

The two principal materials used in the making of boots and shoes were leather and rubber and in both these the years 1942–43 witnessed the emergence of dangerous scarcities. Supplies of leather were affected by shipping shortages and by heavy sinkings of hides in 1942–43. The overrunning by the Japanese in 1942 of the rubber-growing areas gave rise to such an acute shortage of rubber that the

---

[1] The question of a repair control was first raised in 1942 by the War Office, who asked the Board of Trade to set up a control to deal with the problem of repairs to American Service footwear.

[2] By 1st January 1944 there were 37,209 registrations: 34,120 full-time, 3,089 part-time repairers.

[3] S.R. & O. 1942, No. 2544.

[4] S.R. & O. 1944, No. 1060.

[5] Men's shoes from seven to nine coupons and women's from five to seven.

[6] *Impact of the War on Civilian Consumption*, p. 95.

manufacture of rubber footwear had soon to be prohibited with the exception of industrial knee boots for which a certificate arrangement with priority for essential users had to be devised. Early in 1942 the manufacture of crepe rubber soles and heels was prohibited[1] and soon after the manufacture of women's and children's wellington boots and goloshes was eliminated. In time synthetic rubber and reclaim rubber were used as substitutes for natural rubber, but the difficulties over rubber continued to have serious repercussions upon the supply of children's footwear.

There was only one other material which might be thought to provide in some degree at any rate a substitute for leather or rubber soles and that was wood. Wooden footwear in the form of clogs had been widely used in the industrial areas of the North of England,[2] and the demand for them increased in these areas during the war when they[3] were obtainable coupon free against the certificate of factory inspectors. Here, however, we are concerned rather with the attempts to encourage the use of wood as a soling material. This was a new idea and all sorts of difficulties were encountered in the war-time attempts to produce and market wooden-soled footwear. There were supply difficulties, such as the inability of the Timber Control to release kiln-dried home-grown beechwood, from which the soles were made, and the shortage of kilning capacity. In fact, permission had to be obtained in the spring of 1943 to import wooden soles from Canada. Then there were the technical problems of manufacture to be solved and the opposition of the industry to be overcome. Lastly there was the unpopularity of wooden-soled footwear with the public —it had a tendency to chip and break and it was difficult to repair— and it was not until late in 1944 that its coupon value was reduced to a reasonable level.[4] The Controller of Civilian Footwear considered wooden-soled shoes as an alternative not to leather-soled shoes but to going unshod; he pointed out that they would make additional demands on supplies of upper leather and on leather for repairs. These shoes were, in fact, the response to an acute shortage of soling material and they were to be regarded simply as marginal supplies, not as an attempt to revolutionise the footwear habits of the public.[5]

---

[1] S.R. & O. 1942, No. 30.

[2] Also in the Navy.

[3] That is clogs proper.

[4] Two coupons for adults, one coupon for children, Purchase tax on wooden-soled footwear was not abolished until April 1944.

[5] Production of wooden-soled footwear for civilian use was as follows:—

	Men's	Women's
1944	12,000 (pairs)	1,352,000 (pairs)
1945	1,000 (pairs)	698,700 (pairs)

Source: Leather Control

Out of this production a substantial part of the United Kingdom's relief commitments for footwear were met.

Some attention was devoted to the problem of devising a utility scheme for wooden-soled shoes, but it was found that the variations in manufacturing costs were too wide to make it possible to prescribe a reasonable level of ceiling prices.

Leather, then, remained the principal material for the manufacture of boots and shoes, though, as has been seen, shortages developed both in upper leather and in leather for soling purposes. Upper leather, it has been noted, was rationed from March 1941. Bottom leather was rationed from January 1942 and there was separate rationing of bend leather, the critical element in soling material, from the summer of 1942. The most acute shortage, that in material for soling, developed early in 1943, but difficulties with regard to upper leather were being experienced towards the end of the year. There were various reasons for these shortages. There were the sinkings of hides in 1942–43. But there were also shortages of raw materials at the sources of supply; these were aggravated by the fixing of ceiling prices in the United Kingdom and the United States at levels which led to supplies being held off the market or being directed to other markets where there was no price control. These shortages affected civilian supplies the more severely because the best leather was reserved for Service uses. The President of the Board of Trade found it necessary to make urgent application for the highest possible shipping priority for hides and leather, for requisitioning of leather for civilian purposes in the United States, for purchase of leather in South America and for securing American agreement to the allocation to the United Kingdom of a large share of available hides.

The problem of the division of the world supply of hides had been receiving attention since 1942, when anxiety had begun to be felt about the possibility of a world shortage. In the United Kingdom there had been instituted from the beginning of 1942 a centralised purchase of all imported raw hides, calf skins and tanning materials. At the same time the total output of civilian footwear had been reduced. The picture was very different in the United States where there was as yet no central purchase of hides and where there had been, as between 1939 and 1941, an increase in total purchases of practically every class of footwear.[1] In 1942, however, the two countries began to plan the division of available supplies. In 1943 the Combined Raw Materials Board and the Combined Production and Resources Board examined the problems of hides, leather and footwear. A joint hides and leather mission, with a Canadian representative, went to South America to consult about future purchases and shipments and to look into the supply position in the South American countries.

---

[1] *The Impact of the War on Civilian Consumption*, p. 99. *Per capita* purchases of leather footwear were higher even in 1943 than in 1939 in both U.S.A. and Canada. *Ibid.* p. 40.

The Combined Raw Materials Board also made recommendations for an apportionment of available foreign hides between the United Kingdom and the United States. However, it was only after the joint mission had reported and after the visit of a United States Footwear, Leather and Hides Mission to the United Kingdom that agreement was reached as to a satisfactory basis for the division of supplies of hides and to the setting up of a joint hide control office in Washington. World supplies, including the domestic supplies of the United Kingdom and the United States, were to be shared in the ratio of actual consumption during each country's first year of war—that is in the proportion of $3\frac{1}{2}$ to the United States to 1 to the United Kingdom.[1] The joint hide control office was set up to implement the agreement about division of supplies and to ensure that the ceiling prices were observed in hide transactions.

The prevailing leather shortage clearly demanded that every effort should be made to use available supplies in the most economical manner. Thus the technical committee of the Directorate of Civilian Footwear suggested various technical improvisations that made possible economy in the use of sole leather and these became incorporated in the manufacture of boots and shoes. But the system of leather allocations was for some time inadequate. It was divorced from the control of footwear, being administered by the Directorate of Civilian Leather Supplies on the basis of past usage. It was not until August 1943 that the actual administration of leather rations, as opposed to the purely formal licensing arrangements, was transferred to what was now termed the Footwear Control at Leicester. Only then was sole leather issued not on past usage but on each manufacturer's licensed production in different types and categories. Another possible way of saving leather has already been mentioned. The public could be encouraged to have their shoes repaired rather than buy new ones.

The shortage of labour in the boot and shoe industry was only a little less pressing than the shortage of raw materials. Wastage of labour was a continuous problem for the industry, the average number of persons employed falling from 82,345 in 1942 to 73,546 in 1943 and 71,737 in 1944, as compared with a pre-war (1935) total of 116,567.[2] The people who left were naturally the younger and more productive workers and nothing was done to stop the drift until the somewhat belated application of the Essential Work Order in February 1943. At the same time the Ministry of Labour was taking people out of the industry and the impression was being created that

---

[1] Kips and calf skins were to be shared in the ratio 5·8 to the United States to 1 to the United Kingdom.

[2] Including operatives, administrative, technical and clerical staff, but excluding out-workers.

the manufacture of boots and shoes was not regarded as work of national importance. The increase in productivity which had been achieved after concentration was not maintained and there seems to have been a decline in discipline and in quality of workmanship.

The question of the retention of labour in the industry was brought to a head as a result of the cuts in Service requirements recommended at the end of 1942. The net figure for the release of boot and shoe operatives through these cuts was estimated at 4,500. The Board of Trade, in view of the difficulty of maintaining stocks and supplies of footwear, asked for 1,000 of these operatives to be retained in the industry to meet the requirements of the civilian programme, but the Minister of Labour at first insisted that all the labour released by the cuts should be withdrawn. Finally, in April 1943 the Minister agreed to the proposal of the President of the Board of Trade that 1,000 operatives should be retained and also that, as the industry had already lost a large number of women workers, those released should be mostly men. The detailed operation of these changes was to be carried out in consultation with the advisory labour panels for the industry, which were instructed to bear in mind the importance of maintaining a balanced labour force so as to achieve maximum efficiency in each firm.

In 1944 arrangements were made to assign an approved labour force to each nucleus firm in the industry, covering direct factory workers and maintenance workers and clerical and managerial staff. The Ministry of Labour undertook that, where firms' employment was below the level of their approved labour force, workers, other than men of military age, would not be withdrawn without prior substitution.

Wastage of labour continued, however, in spite of all these arrangements. A joint approach was made by the Ministry of Supply and the Board of Trade to the Ministry of Labour in 1944 with a view to securing sufficient labour to meet the manufacturers' civilian pairage and the requirements of the Services and it was eventually agreed that 1,500 additional operatives should be allocated to the industry. It was also agreed in 1944 that skilled operatives should be directed back into the industry and that arrangements should be made for the voluntary return of workers from the munitions industries. However, shortage of workers persisted and the labour force became more and more unbalanced through lack of women. By the end of the war the labour situation had improved, but it still remained a major obstacle to the increase of output.

CHAPTER XIX

CONTROLS OVER THE MANUFACTURE AND SUPPLY OF MISCELLANEOUS CONSUMER GOODS

(i)

Policy

As successive chapters of this book have shown, there was throughout the Board of Trade's activities from the autumn of 1941 onwards a double theme. The Board were as anxious as ever to divert from civilian industry to war industry all the raw material, labour and factory space that could be spared. But the Board were also increasingly anxious that civilian production should remain adequate for the minimum essential needs of the population. And as we have remarked before, 'essential' for this purpose meant not so much physically essential as essential to morale.

Concern for the consumer was first apparent in the clothing policy that began to develop in the summer of 1941. For other consumer goods policy marched more slowly. Until the summer of 1942 the Limitation of Supplies Orders remained almost the only method of control for these goods. This method had been adequate in the earlier stages of the war when the need had been for simple, fairly drastic weapons with which to cut civilian production. But certain disadvantages had been inherent in the limitation Orders and these were now increasingly apparent. The classes of goods controlled under the Orders were very wide. Class 9, for example, covered metal furniture, cutlery, lighting fittings and domestic hollow-ware—a group of articles that had nothing in common except that they were all made of metal. At first a flat percentage restriction had applied to all goods within a class irrespective of how essential they were. Refinements to the Orders[1] made it possible to discriminate between essential and unessential goods and within the limitation scheme it would have been possible to carry this discrimination still further until the supplies

---

[1] See p. 109: description of the factor system.

of essential goods were quota-free and until supplies of unessential goods were reduced to a negligible quota.

Something like this did happen in the case of pottery. Under the Limitation of Supplies Order manufacturers were prohibited, after 1st December 1941,[1] from supplying pottery of their manufacture for home use except under licence or for Government orders. This prohibition was imposed in order to facilitate a more selective control of supply. This was done by means of two sets of general licences.[2] The first was intended to stimulate the supply of more necessary types of pottery by removing restrictions from the supply of specified articles of undecorated china and earthenware—such articles as cups and saucers, mugs, plates, teapots, meat and vegetable dishes. The second set of licences enabled manufacturers to supply the restricted kinds of pottery up to fifty per cent. of their quota for the first half of the period and to a very reduced extent in the second half of the period.

But whatever refinements were introduced in the limitation Orders there was the inescapable difficulty that the restrictions applied only to supply. The limitation Orders usually permitted free supply between registered persons, and since registered persons included wholesalers, this meant free supply between manufacturers and wholesalers. If wholesalers were for any reason prepared to 'stock up'—they might think production was likely to decrease or they might look forward to the end of the war—the whole intention of the restriction was defeated. There was some evidence that this had happened in one or two industries.[3] Even more important was the fact that the limitation Orders gave the Board no real control over individual manufacturers —no power to compel a firm to make one article rather than another, much less a certain type of article.

This had serious disadvantages. In the first place, as long as the Board of Trade had no control over the range and type of articles made, price control could not be effective.[4] Secondly, if the Board did not interest themselves directly in production they could not really control the war-time destinies of the various manufacturing industries. Until the middle of 1942 the Board had concerned themselves with production in the consumer goods industries (outside clothing and textiles) only indirectly for the purposes of the concentration of production policy. This had some unfortunate results. For the labour demands of the munitions industries had been rising rapidly throughout 1941 and the Board of Trade, in the absence of a direct control over production and over the activities of individual firms and industries,

---

[1] S.R. & O. 1941, No. 1949.

[2] S.R. & O. 1941, No. 1950 and 1942, No. 330.

[3] The de-registration of wholesalers was a remedy for this, but such an arrangement often meant that wholesalers—and consequently the smaller and more remote retailers— were deprived of some of their trade. The Board were therefore reluctant to take this action.

[4] Price control is fully discussed in Chapters XXI and XXII.

had been in no position to stop an excessive drift of manpower away from essential civilian industries. The acute shortages of essential consumer goods that were so difficult to remedy were the inevitable consequence.

Altogether there was a pressing need for more direct methods of control. The first step in this direction was taken in September 1941 when a new hollow-ware Order was issued. Domestic hollow-ware, as we have seen, was grouped with various miscellaneous metal goods for the purposes of the Limitation of Supplies Orders. In December 1940 the quota for the class as a whole had been reduced to twenty-five per cent.[1] By the spring of 1941 there was such an acute shortage of essential hollow-ware that the quota for buckets, kettles and saucepans was raised to fifty per cent. This increased quota was retained until the summer of 1942 when hollow-ware was removed from the scope of the Limitation of Supplies Orders. Meanwhile, in the autumn of 1941, manufacture of hollow-ware was restricted to those who received a licence specifically for that purpose from the Board of Trade. At the same time the British Standards Institution was asked to prepare a schedule of essential goods capable of standardisation; manufacture was in general restricted to the articles included in the schedule. By this means variations in types and sizes were cut by over sixty per cent. and available capacity could be used for the maximum production of essential articles. The way was also open for stricter price control.

No more changes in the methods of controlling miscellaneous consumer goods were made or discussed for another six months. Then the impetus to discussion came from the Lord President's Committee. In March 1942 the war was going badly and the Lord President himself wrote a memorandum urging that civilian consumption should be restricted further and that activities not essential to the war effort should be curtailed in order to save shipping and release resources for the ever-growing needs of war production. The Lord President's Committee agreed that the possibility of further restrictions on civilian consumption should be examined and that the ministers concerned should submit reports to the Committee.

The proposals of the Board of Trade were soon assembled. The field covered by them was not very wide. For the cloth and clothing industries—including production for Government orders—accounted for sixty per cent. of the employment on what were called the 'consumer goods other than food'. About another thirteen per cent. of the employment was in industries which were dealt with mainly by the Ministry of Supply as part of the control over raw materials—for example, rubber, paper and cork manufactures. The remaining

---

[1] The supply of aluminium hollow-ware had been forbidden from October 1940.

twenty-seven per cent. of employment was in industries controlled by the Board of Trade. Most of these miscellaneous industries had been covered by the Limitation of Supplies Orders. There were, however, one or two important industries—in particular furniture and paint and polishes—which were in theory the responsibility of the Board of Trade but which were still controlled only by raw material releases. All these industries had contracted severely by the end of 1941: it was estimated, for example, that the number of people making goods for the home market of the types controlled under the limitation Orders had fallen from about 154,000 in June 1940 to about 64,000 in December 1941. Moreover, it seemed probable that the remaining labour force was largely non-mobile and unadaptable.

The scope for further restrictions in the spring of 1942 was therefore limited. Indeed it was already clear that in a few special cases, such as hollow-ware, production would have to be increased. Nevertheless, there still remained a margin of unessential production and some further squeezing could still be done. The Board of Trade concluded that for this purpose it was necessary to control production; in some cases to prohibit manufacture altogether and in others to limit production as far as possible to price-controlled utility goods in quantities no more than sufficient for essential civilian needs. Experience had shown the difficulty of restricting manufacture for the home civilian market while labour and materials were made available for the same product for other purposes. It was therefore proposed that with very few exceptions—such as fine china for export and linoleum for warships and royal ordnance factory hostels—prohibition would apply to production for all purposes. Prohibition of manufacture would undoubtedly lead to difficulties. In most cases it should be possible to use the labour released by the prohibitions for war production. But there would be some elderly and non-mobile workers who could not be readily absorbed. Some firms who could not turn over to producing essential articles easily and economically would have to close down altogether. The Board of Trade were satisfied that this price was worth paying—that it must be paid if the remaining labour was to be put to better use.

By the end of April 1942, however, ministers' enthusiasm for belt-tightening measures that might prove over-rapid or over-drastic had waned. There seems also to have been a desire to avoid any public controversy that might impede the progress of the fuel rationing plans that the Government was preparing. The Lord President's Committee generally felt that it was desirable to proceed gently. They would have preferred to see the limitation of supplies procedure used to the fullest possible extent before totally prohibiting production, and they were anxious about the hardships that might arise from prohibition. They agreed in principle, however, that there should be a gradual and progressive contraction of the manufacture of less essential consumer goods. It was also agreed that no Orders should be made without consulting the industries concerned.

It was clear that the new controls would not be ready in time to supersede the limitation Order when the current quota period ended on 31st May. The limitation Order[1] was therefore continued for a further two months. Meanwhile discussions proceeded with industry about the form of control and with the Ministry of Labour about the further employment of old and immobile workers. The decision to consult the industries concerned was undoubtedly wise. It could hardly be said that the industries welcomed the Board's policy. But they accepted it with a good grace and certainly did not offer serious opposition.

In the light of the separate discussions with industries the Board of Trade collected together all their proposals for changes in the control of miscellaneous goods into a coherent scheme. In two cases—pottery and pencils[2]—where there had been previous discussions with manufacturers and where action was urgently needed, control over manufacture was imposed in advance of the announcements about the general scheme. From 23rd May 1942 the manufacture of pencils could be carried on only in accordance with directions or a licence from the Board of Trade; the directions that were issued regulated the size and type of pencils to be produced.[3] Then from 1st June domestic pottery could only be manufactured in accordance with directions or a licence from the Board.[4] It was clear from the enabling Order that the powers of direction conferred on the Board were very wide.[5]

By the end of June 1942 the Board had ready their arrangements for all the other industries formerly controlled under the Limitation of Supplies Orders—arrangements that were to operate from 1st August. Some ten classes of goods were to be the subject of Control of Manufacture and Supply Orders. These goods had been chosen after investigation, either because it was desirable to concentrate production on utility or other closely specified articles, or in order to ensure that output went to priority consumers, or to divert manufacture away from areas where labour was very scarce to those where it was most plentiful or, finally, to use to the best advantage very limited supplies of particular raw materials. These Control of Manufacture and Supply Orders would give the Board of Trade any powers they were likely to need. The Orders could lead on to positive production

---

[1] S.R. & O. 1942, No. 1028. Lace goods and mattresses were now controlled under the Apparel and Textiles Order, S.R. & O. 1942, No. 1000, instead of under a Limitation of Supplies Order.

[2] Neither pottery nor pencils was included in the 'stopgap' limitation Order.

[3] S.R. & O. 1942, Nos. 984, 985.

[4] S.R. & O. 1942, No. 1038.

[5] See p. 526.

programmes and they could by inference embody prohibition on manufacture. But individual licensing of firms was a heavy administrative task. It was, therefore, not desirable—and indeed it was not necessary—to extend these methods to all the miscellaneous consumer goods. Some classes of goods therefore remained subject to the Limitation of Supplies Orders; production was to be confined to the more essential articles within these classes. The manufacture of a large variety of unessential articles was to be prohibited in a special Order. In one or two classes, hitherto covered by limitation Orders, essential articles would be freed from control altogether while the unessential articles would be prohibited.

These different arrangements were to apply as follows: floor coverings, hollow-ware and kitchen hardware,[1] metal furniture, domestic electrical appliances, mechanical lighters, sports goods, musical instruments, fountain pens and umbrellas were to be covered by Control of Manufacture and Supply Orders. Hollow-ware was the outstanding example of a control designed to permit the planned production of adequate supplies of closely specified essential articles, and these articles alone. At the same time the control would make it possible for the Board to redistribute supplies about the country.[2] In the case of musical instruments and sports goods, the chief purpose of the control was to regulate supply—to ensure that the limited supplies of these goods went to such people as the Services and schools who needed them most. The controls over fountain pens and umbrellas aimed largely at persuading firms to move civilian production away from the most difficult labour areas. Domestic electrical appliances may be cited as an example of the prohibitions that were inherent in the control over manufacture. The Board of Trade were ready to announce that they would not normally entertain applications for the manufacture and supply of a list of articles such as chafing dishes, toasters, shavers, drink mixers and cigar lighters. For the goods covered by Control of Manufacture and Supply Orders there was normally to be no control of supplies by wholesalers, since it was desirable that stocks should be freed.

The method that combined prohibitions on unessential goods with limitation of supplies quotas for permitted goods was to be applied chiefly to five groups of goods—cutlery, lighting fittings, leather goods, jewellery and toys. The list of prohibitions was pretty extensive. It included, in the case of jewellery, all goldsmiths' and silversmiths' ware, jewellery, and imitation jewellery except clocks, watches, gem diamonds, identification bracelets, cuff links, studs, watch chains and key chains that did not contain gold finer than nine carats, and plain

---

[1] Hitherto neither the production nor the supply of kitchen hardware had been controlled except through raw material allocation.

[2] See Chapter XIII.

wedding rings made according to Board of Trade specification. In cutlery the prohibitions covered spoons and forks made of non-ferrous metals and such articles as soup spoons, coffee spoons, egg spoons, butter knives, grape scissors, asparagus eaters. Toys comprising any rubber, cork, hemp, kapok, celluloid or plastics derived from cellulose, casein or synthetic resin were prohibited with the single exception of table-tennis balls; billiard tables and coin- or disc-operated machines for games were not permitted. Practically all leather goods were prohibited except brief and document cases, unframed handbags, school satchels, wallets and purses, instrument cases, bank cash bags, conductors' cash bags, railway bags and tobacco pouches. Suit cases, travelling bags, steamer trunks, shopping bags, gas-mask cases, cycle bags and tool bags were allowed if they were not made of leather. Manufacturers were to have a three months' period in which to dispose of their stocks of prohibited goods; manufacturers' supply of permitted articles would remain subject to Limitation of Supplies Orders with small quotas ranging from 5 to $12\frac{1}{2}$ per cent.; wholesalers could use their quotas for supplying prohibited or permitted goods.

In two cases—glassware and fancy goods—there was a long list of prohibitions, but manufacture and supply of the remaining permitted articles was freed from all control. Thus in glassware, production would be concentrated on simple tumblers, jugs, mugs and small mirrors and the only 'fancy goods' allowed would be such things as spectacle frames, hair slides and grips and combs, cups, mugs, flapjacks, babies' baths and chambers.

The fate of the two remaining classes of goods hitherto controlled under the Limitation of Supplies Orders should perhaps be mentioned. Photographic goods remained subject to quota but no prohibitions were applied to them. Toilet preparations also remained subject to quota with no prohibitions. But this industry was given a Limitation of Supplies Order of its own in order to tighten up enforcement. One class of goods—polishes—was brought in July 1942 under the limitation of supplies. It had an Order of its own with no prohibition.

When this comprehensive scheme for revisions in control was ready, there was still some doubt whether it was necessary or desirable. There were still fears of hardship to old non-mobile workers, hardship to firms which might have to close down and hardship to industries which might lose all their skilled labour and have difficulty in restarting after the war. Moreover, it did not seem that the total saving of labour to be achieved by cutting out unessential goods would be large—only about 20,000.[1] And of this figure, 7,000 would come from

---

[1] In addition, it was hoped to release 10,000 additional workers by the introduction of new controls over furniture. See the section on furniture.

the floor-coverings industry which was bound to contract severely in any case owing to lack of raw material. Nevertheless the Board of Trade considered that at this stage of the war the effort to secure these releases of labour was worth while. There would, too, be some saving in raw material and at a time when civilian goods were becoming more and more scarce manufacturers would be compelled to cut out fripperies and concentrate on essentials. Moreover, the Board of Trade and the Ministry of Labour had made arrangements to miti- gate hardship. If the labour released by the prohibitions could not be absorbed, the Board would be prepared to issue special licences for a limited manufacture of prohibited goods by approved firms with an approved labour force, provided that the premises were not required by the Factory Control and that materials could be spared. The Board did, indeed, intend to issue these licences very sparingly. If they took too easy a line the whole policy would be brought into disrepute. Licences were to be given only if the labour concerned really could do nothing else. However, the worst hardship would be avoided and with this assurance the policy was approved by the President of the Board of Trade, and all the Orders that the Board had prepared came into operation on 1st August.[1]

Between 1st August 1942 and the end of the war, there were, of course, various further changes in these controls. It proved impossible, for example, to maintain the prohibition on manufacture for all pur- poses including Government orders. It was, therefore, necessary to except from the provisions of all the various Orders goods required as forming an order or part of an order for a Government depart- ment.[2]

The general tendency was to make the controls over particular classes of goods more detailed. This was certainly true of the controls over the manufacture and supply of more essential articles such as pottery and hollow-ware.[3] It was also true of the limitation on sup- plies. In view of enforcement difficulties toilet preparations were brought under a control of manufacture. Limitation of supplies restrictions on toys also gave a great deal of trouble. Production by established manufacturers had been reduced to a trickle and new- comers were making toys from scraps of material and charging fantastic prices. Each Christmas brought an outcry about the supply of toys, their shoddiness and their price. To deal with these com- plaints, general licences were issued towards the end of 1942 and 1943, permitting extra supplies for Christmas.[4] For the period from February 1944 to the end of July 1944 the quota for toys was raised to

---

[1] S.R. & O. 1942, Nos. 1451–1461, 1510, 1620.
[2] S.R. & O. 1943, Nos. 15 and 149.
[3] The developments in the control of pottery are discussed on p. 526 *et seq.*
[4] S.R. & O. 1942, Nos. 2137, 2543; 1943 Nos. 1115 and 1654.

12½ per cent.,[1] and the use of a 'half-factor' doubled the quota for toys and children's indoor games sold at less than 5s. manufacturers' price or 6s. 8d. wholesale. In the spring of 1943 manufacturers' maximum prices for toys were fixed at 10s. and retailers' at £1 4s. 5d.[2]

For leather goods and cutlery the changes in control were designed to regulate the types of certain articles. The manufacture of permitted leather goods, for example, was confined to those of certain sizes, certain materials and a certain number of locks and fittings.[3] As for cutlery, the manufacture of table knives, spoons and forks was regulated as to length and weight of the finished product, materials used, marking, methods of manufacture and prices.[4] The supply of both leather goods and cutlery still remained subject to the limitation of supplies quotas ruling at the time the new Orders were passed.

So far we have discussed changes in the methods of control of miscellaneous goods only as they affected those industries that had been subject to the Limitation of Supplies Orders. But there were of course other restrictions, in particular raw materials restrictions, that affected consumer goods. Most raw materials were, by 1942, covered by some form of licensing. In the case of materials such as steel and cotton, which were allocated to the departments responsible for finished goods, raw material policy could closely match production policy. In a few cases, such as perambulators and bicycles, the Board of Trade found that their powers of allocating raw material allied with close co-operation with the industries were sufficient to make possible a fairly close control over manufacture. But where materials were licensed by the raw material Controls while the Board of Trade were responsible for manufacturing policy, it was much less easy to achieve consistency. This was inevitable, for the two controlling authorities would be working towards different purposes. The Raw Materials Department might wish to prohibit or restrict the use of one raw material in the manufacture of certain goods while the Board of Trade wished to prohibit, control or direct the production of the same goods irrespective of the material. Or the Raw Materials Department might wish to prohibit or restrict the use of a particular material in a range of goods which there was no other reason to control. Or the Raw Materials Department might wish to prohibit or restrict the use of raw material for processing goods which the Board of Trade wished to see made.

Some industries had been controlled from the outset by the Raw Materials Department of the Ministry of Supply and its Controls, and

---

[1] S.R. & O. 1944, No. 60.

[2] Including purchase tax.

[3] S.R. & O. 1943, Nos. 128, 967.

[4] S.R. & O. 1944, No. 1252. The manufacture of other non-prohibited goods, such as carving knives, scissors, etc., was not regulated as to type.

the problem of consistency had not, therefore, arisen. This arrangement was sometimes only common sense—in the case of paper and rubber, for example, the same firms often manufactured both the material and the finished goods. Sometimes, however, the arrangement had just grown. In theory, for example, the Board of Trade were responsible for furniture; but the timber-using industries had been controlled by raw material allocations—not because this was thought to be adequate, but because satisfactory methods of controlling the finished products had not been devised by the spring of 1942.

Side by side with the Board of Trade's controls over consumer goods, there had therefore grown up the controls of the Raw Materials Department. In addition to control by licensing and allocation the Raw Materials Department issued regulations about war-time economy standards for certain goods and it also issued prohibitions. There were, for example, long lists of articles in the manufacture of which the use of cork, rubber or paper was specifically prohibited. For some time the Raw Materials Department and the Board of Trade do not seem to have kept closely in touch with each other about the general policy towards consumer goods. This led to anomalies. For example, the Board of Trade were incensed to find that while they were planning their own long lists of prohibitions, the Ministry of Supply was allowing new stocks of paper for the manufacture of greeting cards. From time to time there were suggestions that the whole problem of division of responsibility for civilian goods and for the consumer should be thrashed out and some concordat reached. But while draft concordats were passing to and fro, the problem had been solved sensibly enough by much closer day-to-day consultation between the officials of the Board of Trade and the Raw Materials Department over the administration of restrictions. When there was an acute shortage of some essential commodity that was controlled primarily by raw materials authorities—toilet paper or teats for babies' bottles—the Board of Trade inevitably came to the fore as the guardian of the consumers' interests and inevitably took responsibility for ensuring increased production. They also became closely involved in production policy towards important articles such as books. And in 1942 the Board of Trade assumed a much closer responsibility for furniture which, as we have seen, had hitherto been controlled by raw material allocations. This control over the manufacture and supply of furniture and the introduction of utility furniture were to be among the most successful of the Board of Trade's schemes for meeting economically the essential needs of civilians in war-time.

The Board of Trade's controls over the manufacture and supply of consumer goods were popularly connected with the idea of utility production. Indeed, when the Board launched their policy for the control of manufacture and supply in the summer of 1942, they had been at some pains to emphasise utility as the constructive part of their policy. Both at a press conference and in Parliament the President had looked forward to the extension of utility production to cover a variety of consumer goods.

It seemed, however, that utility was, at this stage, a rather loose conception that had different meanings for different people. The President had defined utility products as 'goods sufficiently clearly defined for their prices to be fixed—that is important; planned to meet essential needs in a sensible manner and produced in the most economical way possible in terms of material and labour'.[1] This definition had its uses but did not do very much to distinguish between utility goods proper and mere 'standardised' goods. Both involved limitations on the use of materials, the elimination of unnecessary or over-elaborate types of goods and price control. In general, utility schemes were more rigid; utility articles were usually more narrowly specified and they bore a statutory mark of identification. But even this distinction could be overdone; for example, some of the 'standardised' goods also bore statutory marks of identification. In fact the problem of whether certain goods should be full utility or simply 'standardised' turned on rather more subtle considerations.

Sometimes it was just a question of convenience. For example, war-time white pottery was commonly known as utility, and indeed production was confined to essential articles. There had been a good deal of simplification, prices were controlled and the goods were marked, though not with the recognised utility mark. All that was necessary for a full utility scheme was positive specification. There seemed, however, little advantage in prescribing it, especially as it would have involved technical difficulties and waste of labour. So the pottery scheme never became a full utility one. In other cases, goods that were pretty closely specified were not officially designated utility goods because there were some doubts about the reliability of quality or supplies. For whatever the official definition of utility might be, the public had come to believe that utility goods would be good value for money and that they would be forthcoming in reasonable quantities. The word 'utility', according to the President of the Board of Trade, had become a 'noble title'. It would, therefore, be embarrassing to call goods utility when there was no guarantee that supplies could be maintained, or that the quality of the goods could be safeguarded. For example, the quality of hollow-ware was not controlled and the tinware produced was often particularly poor. Tinware could hardly be left out of a utility hollow-ware scheme, but if it was included it might bring the whole scheme into disrepute.

In practice, therefore, the number of proper utility schemes outside

---

[1] H. of C. Deb., Vol. 382, Col. 215.

clothing was small—there were schemes only for utility furniture, utility pencils and utility lighters, But beyond these there were a fair number of goods that were standardised in varying degrees—pottery and hollow-ware, prams, travel goods, wedding rings, brooms and brushes, cutlery and hearth furniture.

The practical application of the Board of Trade's controls over consumer goods can best be studied by examining individual examples; this will be done in the following pages. But first it will be as well to comment on the results of the policy as a whole. One of the first questions that arises is how far the controls over miscellaneous consumer goods succeeded in releasing resources for the war effort and in curtailing civilian consumption. Unfortunately, it is impossible to segregate the effects of all the various influences of war-time life on these industries. Most of the release of labour from these industries had occurred before the era of controls over manufacture and supply. And even after these controls were imposed manpower withdrawals and the absence of replacements for natural wastage of manpower were probably the most powerful single force in squeezing the industries still further.

All one can really say is that the labour force of the miscellaneous consumer goods industries[1] which had fallen from 293,000 in June 1940 to 251,000 in June 1941 fell further to 192,000 in June 1944. A further indication of the resources released for the war effort is in the figures for personal expenditure. Expenditure on household goods[2] at 1938 prices, for example, was about fifty-seven per cent. of the 1938 figure in 1941 and only thirty-five per cent. in 1944.

In addition to releasing resources for the war, a main purpose of the Board of Trade's policy was, of course, to get as much production as possible out of the available resources. Success in this purpose is again very difficult to measure. One can try to compare labour employed with output at different times. Sometimes it is possible to get, in this way, some rough guide. For example, one can say that the monthly rate of pencil production was 13,424,000 in the period July to September 1942 with a labour force of 505 and 14,382,000 in the corresponding period for 1943, with a labour force of 490. But with pottery and hollow-ware, it is difficult to find a common denominator for such diverse articles as cups and mugs, plates, jugs and sauceboats, or pans and kettles, buckets and dustbins. Production of some articles was increased by deliberately reducing the production of others. All it is possible to say is that the labour force of the pottery industry was 24,000 in June 1942 and 22,300 in March 1943, and that production

---

[1] The industries covered by these figures are pottery, hollow-ware, cutlery, linoleum, toys, brushes, footwear, furniture, pens and pencils. The figures include people employed on Government and export work.

[2] This includes household textiles.

of essential articles rose. 21·0 million pieces of domestic pottery were produced in June 1942, 23·1 million pieces in November 1942, and 27·2 million pieces in March 1943. Similarly, the labour force employed on hollow-ware was about 8,000 in the period October–December 1941 and about 8,500 in the period May–July 1943, and 8,600 in May–July 1944. Production of saucepans and stewpans rose from a monthly average of 620,000 in the first period to 1,030,000 and 1,173,000 respectively in the two later periods. All this really shows is that the Board of Trade's efforts to increase the output of the most essential articles with a diminishing or barely increased labour force succeeded. For furniture there are no reliable figures for output before the controls over manufacture and supply were imposed.

Even if it were possible to measure changes in output against changes in the labour force, it would be a large research project outside the scope of this book to try to analyse the causes of changes in the correlations. How much of the changes were due to utility and standardised production, how much to austerity restrictions—the absence of polish on pencils or decoration on pottery—and how much to long production runs through limitation on types? What part did other influences, such as the changing composition of the labour force or shortages of raw materials, play? These are the questions which it would be very interesting and very difficult to answer.

It is not, then, easy to measure the success of the Board of Trade's policy towards essential consumer goods. But at least one can say that the mistakes of the earlier days of the war were rectified, difficult though this was; production of the most essential articles was increased to meet the minimum essential needs of the population, and an effort was made to produce the goods economically through simplification and a reduction in the number of types.

But what of the controls over some of the smaller consumer goods? Were they worth while? It may seem rather incongruous to see an important department within an important ministry concerning itself, at the height of the war, with a whole range of consumer goods, a good many of which seem 'fiddling'—for example, pins and needles, fountain pens, jewellery, handbags, fireguards and fancy goods down to such minutiæ as artificial flowers. But the economy was stretched so taut that this was inevitable. The production of small essential articles was apt to fall very low unless some Government department was taking an interest in them and it was surprising how very important some of these small goods proved to be. Needles, for example, were not only a necessity at home; other countries, including the United States, had always relied very largely on British supplies. And there was little that caused as much public protest as the shortages of odds and ends of babies' equipment. As for the controls over unessential goods, they too proved inevitable. When supplies of consumer goods were so restricted, it was obviously sensible to concentrate labour and materials on making the civilian articles that were essential. The public, moreover, was irritated when it found fripperies in the shops at a time when saucepans or cups or hair-grips were so difficult to buy. As long as the production of unessential goods was not strictly controlled, they provided a happy hunting-ground for some of the more disreputable sections of the community. The controls over raw materials and manpower were not in themselves sufficiently watertight to prevent the diversion of resources to unnecessary production. While the public had money in their pockets and little to spend it on there was a strong temptation for some enterprising people to pour out trashy goods or luxuries—things that by their nature could not be effectively price-controlled.

The administrative costs of the controls over minor consumer goods were not really very heavy. None of the smaller industries occupied more than the time of one junior administrative officer and part of the time of a principal or his equivalent. It is true that the work of licensing exceptions to the prohibition orders was a burden,[1] but it was mostly of a once-and-for-all nature. The controls that bore the greatest cost in administrative labour were those for the essential goods such as furniture, pottery and hollow-ware.

(ii)

Examples of Individual Industries

The Board of Trade's controls over manufacture and supply will be examined in more detail for four separate industries. They have been chosen as illustrations of different problems. First, there is furniture where there was perhaps the most complete of all the controls over civilian production. Next there is pottery which is an example of an industry where control and a semi-utility scheme were developed to remedy acute shortages of essential articles. Thirdly, there are toilet preparations which illustrate the problems of enforcement at their worst. Fourthly, there are sports goods which provide an example of a control imposed mainly in order to control distribution.

DOMESTIC FURNITURE

In 1938 those firms in the British furniture industry with more than ten workers employed 75,900 people.[2] Since only a little capital was needed to start the manufacture of furniture, the industry was composed of a large number of firms, many of them small. It is estimated

---

[1] Between 1st August 1942 and the middle of December 1942 the Board of Trade submitted 900 cases to the Ministry of Labour. A sample test showed that about sixty-six per cent. of the workers concerned were allowed to continue to make prohibited goods.

[2] See *Board of Trade, Working Party Reports: Furniture* (H.M.S.O. 1946).

that in 1938 there were 3,000 or more firms that employed ten or less workers and there were 1,000 firms employing more. Of this thousand less than forty firms employed more than 300 and of these only two employed more than 750. The production of furniture was scattered throughout the country with heavy concentrations in London and High Wycombe.

The furniture industry was quick to feel the impact of war, for it was a large consumer of imported materials. Its main raw materials were timber, plywood and veneers. Before the war Britain was almost entirely dependent for these supplies on outside sources and the furniture industry normally consumed about half the total hardwood imports together with some softwoods and a considerable proportion of the plywood and veneer imports.[1] The acquisition of timber was controlled from the outbreak of war and—by the standards that were then current—pretty strictly controlled. Supplies of timber to the furniture industry were heavily cut. Then in July 1940 it was decided that no more timber was to be released for the production of domestic, kitchen and garden furniture.

These raw material restrictions were not reinforced by any limitation of supplies.[2] Indeed, the Ministry of Supply had dealt heavily with this important consumer goods industry when the Board of Trade's policy for reducing the output of consumer goods was in its infancy. The output of domestic furniture did not, however, cease. Manufacturers were for some time able to live on their stocks of timber. Many of the firms with larger premises turned over some of their spare capacity to the production of aeroplanes, landing craft and various kinds of precision woodworking. There was, however, still sufficient spare capacity in the furniture industry to make it seem a likely candidate for concentration of production in the spring of 1941. For some time the number of small firms was a deterrent. When concentration was actually attempted towards the end of 1941 progress was very slow. For many woodworking factories were partly engaged on war contracts which the supply departments insisted could not be transferred elsewhere. Then, when the idea of utility furniture was mooted, concentration was halted to see how the new scheme would work out.

Until the middle of 1942, the Board of Trade did not worry much about the furniture needs of ordinary civilians. The only arrangement that existed was one made by the Ministry of Health to help the bombed out. Under this scheme furniture was lent to bombed-out people through their local authorities. At the end of three months

---

[1] *Ibid.* The percentage of total plywood imports used by the furniture industry was over forty.

[2] Only cane, wicker and metal furniture were covered by the Limitation of Supplies Order.

borrowers could either buy the furniture or return it. Some of the furniture was bought second-hand by local authorities, but the chief source of supply was furniture made by the Ministry of Works for the Ministry of Health out of an allocation made for the purpose by the Timber Control. As a sequel to this scheme the Timber Control agreed at the end of 1941 to license timber to furniture manufacturers once more so that they might make specific types of furniture. There was no distribution scheme, but it was hoped that these supplies would help the bombed-out. The design of this furniture was not prescribed but production was limited to twenty articles and the maximum timber content of each was fixed. The timber was allocated to manufacturers on the basis of pre-war usage, the rate of release being about one-sixth of pre-war; by the spring of 1942, however, the timber allocation had been reduced to one-eleventh.

By 1942 it was becoming clear that it was not only the bombed-out who needed new furniture. The greatest demand was from newly-married couples who were setting up house and from growing families There was also a demand from people whose standard of living before the war had been low and who were anxious to re-stock their homes with their increased war-time earnings. All these people, however, found it very difficult to buy furniture of reasonable quality at reasonable prices. Supplies had been heavily reduced and stocks of furniture had been used up. Moreover, the shortage of timber had led to the extensive use of poor substitute materials; this encouraged the production of furniture whose shoddiness was often disguised by decorations. From June 1940 the price of new furniture was subject to the Prices of Goods Act, but the Act was ineffective; prices of second-hand furniture were quite uncontrolled. It was not until May 1942 that an attempt was made to impose some more effective measure of price control. Under the powers granted to the Board by the Goods and Services (Price Control) Act the maximum price to be charged for new furniture was limited to the price then current and for second-hand furniture made after 1899 to the first-hand price. These maximum prices when combined with maximum timber content encouraged still further the production of poor quality articles.

The provisions of these rudimentary controls were very difficult to enforce. By this time, however, the Board of Trade were becoming increasingly aware of their responsibilities for ensuring that the minimum essential needs of the consumer were met. The Board were surveying the consumer goods industries to see how this aim could best be reconciled with the need to release still more labour and materials for the war effort. Furniture was one of the industries where the need for action was greatest. On the one hand, many urgent and legitimate demands were not being met. On the other hand, there was still scope for economies in production. Small though the timber allocation of the furniture industry was, it was the equivalent of 40,000–50,000 tons of shipping space a year. Moreover, there were still 30,000 workers employed in the furniture industry—far too high a percentage of the pre-war figure.[1] Firms had kept going at this level by substituting other materials for timber, by illegitimately diverting timber from other purposes and by using stocks.

The Board of Trade's plan for making economies and meeting essential needs was far-reaching. Specifications and prices for a very limited range of utility furniture were to be settled as soon as possible. When this was done, the manufacture of civilian furniture would be prohibited except under licence and licences would be granted only for the production of utility goods. Sales of utility furniture would be allowed only against priority certificates issued by the Board of Trade with the help of the Assistance Board. Once this control was introduced concentration of the furniture industry was to be speeded up. Meanwhile, in the period before the utility scheme could get going an interim control would be needed. This should take the form of the prohibition of unessential articles of furniture; for this purpose essential articles would be, broadly, those for which timber was still being allocated under the Timber Control's arrangements. Maximum prices would be fixed for these articles. The Board of Trade hoped that the new controls over furniture would release some 10,000 workers, in addition to factory space for war production.

These proposals of the Board of Trade were accepted by ministers in June 1942. The interim measure of control came into force on 1st August when the manufacture of all furniture, other than twenty-two articles with a prescribed timber content, was prohibited.[2] New price-control measures for new and second-hand furniture and for hire-purchase charges soon followed. Meanwhile, the Board of Trade were busy working out the main utility scheme.

The scheme had three main parts—they were the control over distribution, the control over prices and the control over production. To a large extent the three parts were interdependent. The system of buying permits was indispensable as a method of confining demand to essential needs and price control was impossible without effective control over production. The controls over distribution and prices are, however, discussed elsewhere in this volume;[3] here we shall be mainly concerned with the controls over production.

The first step in the control of production was to decide on specifications. Early in July 1942 the President of the Board of Trade ap-

---

[1] Of the 30,000 it was estimated that about 15,000 workers were employed on ordinary domestic furniture. The others were presumably making furniture for institutions, Government orders, etc.

[2] S.R. & O. 1942, No. 1452.

[3] See p. 335 for the distribution scheme and p. 587 for price control.

pointed a committee to advise him on this question—to be precise, to advise 'on specifications for the production of utility furniture of good, sound construction in simple but agreeable designs for sale at reasonable prices, having regard to the necessity for the maximum economy of raw materials and labour'. The chairman of the Committee was Mr. (now Sir Charles) Tennyson, an eminent industrial designer, and the membership was made up of one or two leading furniture manufacturers and furniture trade unionists, designers, housing experts and a housewife.

The task of the Advisory Committee in ensuring 'good, sound construction' was difficult, for materials were very scarce. Only off-grades of timber were available and even these were so scarce that timber could only be used for framing. Plywood was wholly unobtainable[1] and its place had to be taken by hardboard. Fortunately there were good supplies of veneers so that the hardboard could be veneered on both sides; this produced a material suitable for framed panels, provided the ends were protected to prevent splitting. The polishes normally used in the furniture trade had to be cut out altogether and matt wax finishes substituted. No plastic materials were to be had. Metals were very scarce and the best forms of stuffing and webbing were unobtainable. Moreover, since uniformity of price and service had to be maintained, design and specification had to take account of the widely differing equipment of manufacturers. Design had in fact to be adapted to the simplest productive processes.

The Advisory Committee decided upon the items of furniture which should be included in the utility range. It was a fairly, but not excessively, austere list. It did not, for example, include the three-piece sitting-room suite so beloved by British homes. But it included a tallboy as well as a dressing chest for bedrooms, bookshelves and an occasional table. For the preparation of sample designs and specifications, a panel of designers was formed from men nominated by the trade on the one hand and by professional design organisations on the other. In the end the Committee chose the work of two of the twelve designers who submitted designs. All this work was quickly done and before the end of September 1942 samples of furniture were made up ready for inspection by the Board of Trade; by the middle of October they were on view to the public.

The range of utility furniture chosen represented two qualities and about three designs for each article. A major point of principle had arisen in the deliberations of the Advisory Committee over this whole question of design. Should utility furniture be produced to fixed specification and fixed designs or should it follow the pattern of utility clothing and leave the question of design to be settled by the

---

[1] A very little was secured from the Timber Control later for use in children's high chairs.

manufacturer within the limits of the specifications? The idea of standardised designs was naturally disliked by the trade. Manufacturers and retailers affirmed that standardised designs would not be well received by the consumer who would expect to be able to buy furniture to his own taste. 'Over and above all questions of design', it was said 'there are a number of standard idiosyncrasies in the public taste in furniture which defy both rules of design and construction'. Moreover, manufacturers felt that by insisting on adherence to one or another of a limited number of designs the benefits of manufacturers' ingenuity in adaptation would be lost.

There were, however, a good many compelling arguments on the other side. The point about the consumer's choice was not very valid since in order to save transport each area would have to be supplied from the factories found there; variety in construction and design must be limited for that reason alone. Freedom of design for manufacturers would, moreover, involve dangers of rank poor design which might in some cases bring utility furniture into disrepute. There were other factors to be borne in mind. For example, utility furniture would be marked as such for sale against buying permits at definite prices. With statutory designs as well as specifications the appropriateness of the marking could be more easily checked and the inspection of quality would be greatly facilitated. Fixed design was the only way to ensure value for money. Again, firms licensed to produce utility furniture would be put in a specially favourable position for the post-war period compared with the closed firms if they could, during the war, use their position to create a special goodwill in designs of their own. The decisive arguments against freedom of design were, however, the need to ensure the maximum economy of production, the importance of precise specification for price control purposes, and the need to get production going as soon as possible. It would be speediest for manufacturers—and would economise in the labour of designers—to use the standard Board of Trade designs. And indeed the drawing up of the specifications would be a much easier and quicker job if it were done with reference to standard designs and drawings.

With all these points in mind the Board of Trade decided that the approved designs must be used—certainly in the initial period of the scheme—for the sake of ease in administration and a rapid production of good quality furniture. In the end this decision was not altered during the remaining years of the war. The standard designs were modified, but freedom of design with a utility scheme came after the war when conditions of manufacture were very different.

Once the question of specification and design had been settled, the way was clear for imposing the control over manufacture. Under a new Domestic Furniture Order,[1] with effect from 1st November 1942,

---

[1] S.R. & O. 1942, No. 2214.

the Board of Trade were able to issue directions regulating the descriptions of goods that might be made, the materials to be used and the processes and methods to be employed in manufacture. Manufacture of domestic furniture could not be undertaken without a licence from the Board of Trade. The Order also introduced the utility mark for furniture,[1] but did not embody the specifications for the making of utility furniture. The idea was that manufacturers were to receive their instructions with their licences.

The Board of Trade agreed with the Timber Control that after 1st November no timber should be allocated for domestic furniture other than utility. Manufacturers were, however, given until the end of January 1943 to complete any furniture in process on 1st November 1942.

How much utility furniture was to be manufactured and which firms were to receive licences to make it? One of the main principles behind the utility furniture scheme was to secure economics of labour and materials by producing only enough to meet essential needs. But even when the Board of Trade had decided which needs were essential—that is, who should receive buying permits—it was extremely difficult to calculate the demand for utility furniture. The marriage rate and the birth rate were ascertainable facts, but no one could know, for example, how many young married couples were living with their parents, or in furnished rooms, how many parents borrowed nursery equipment from friends, and so on. Then, again, it was impossible to know whether utility furniture would be popular or not. However, by a process of 'guestimating' the target production programme for utility furniture was set at 400,000 units[2] per period of four weeks. This total figure had in turn to be translated into terms of specific articles of furniture—so many dining-room suites, so many kitchen tables, etc. There was in addition a separate production programme for nursery furniture. An additional complication arose from the need to split geographically the total demand. For the carriage of furniture about the country was a heavy burden on transport and each area was therefore to be as self-sufficient as possible.

With these rough calculations of demand before them, the Board of Trade had a basis for planning production. Firms had to be chosen to make the right articles in the right quantities in the right places. It was obvious that only a small proportion of the furniture firms could be used. There were 1,150 firms which had had at any rate a nominal

---

[1] A later Order and directions of December 1942 (S.R. & O. Nos. 2581 and 2650 with subsequent S.R. & O. 1943, No. 1612; 1944, No. 1048; 1945, No. 397), gave very specific instructions about the method of applying the utility mark and its placing. Each manufacturer had to apply his designation number to his furniture so that faulty articles could be traced to their source.

[2] For the purpose of buying permits each item of furniture was reckoned in terms of 'units' just as clothing was reckoned in 'points' see, p. 335.

timber quota under the previous production arrangements. Yet the Board of Trade calculated that the programme for utility furniture would occupy at near-full capacity only 150 firms with about forty employees each. During August and September 1942 officials of the Board spent some time in the regions making a list in consultation with Factory Control and the Ministry of Labour of firms likely to be suitable for designation. But this list could not give information about the willingness and ability of firms to produce the specific articles of furniture at reasonable prices, nor sufficient information about costs. When the furniture designs and specifications were settled in October it was therefore decided to ask a considerably larger number of firms whether they wished to apply to be allowed to make utility furniture; the firms were also asked to supply particulars about costs, labour, machines, etc. All the firms with a previous timber quota were therefore sent application forms, excepting only those who had timber quotas so small that they would barely employ one man, those who had not drawn their quota and those who, according to the Machine Tool Control, certainly did not have the right equipment for making utility furniture.

Application forms were sent to 800 firms and 600 applications were received. In weeding these applications all kinds of points had to be remembered. There was the usual need to release labour and factory space in the right places. There was the need to zone production to avoid unnecessary transport. Each firm's machining capacity had to be considered and the availability of kilning capacity for drying home-grown timber. It was also agreed that, for the sake of economical production, firms who were to make utility furniture must devote nearly all their capacity to it; this ruled out many firms—often the large and efficient ones—who had Government contracts. Finally, it was important to ensure that the firms chosen could produce the right quality at the right price.

The trade associations and the trade unions were consulted about the choice of firms. But trouble was unavoidable. Naturally the furniture firms would have preferred to see the work spread. Moreover, the Board of Trade found that very few firms employing less than ten or twelve people were properly equipped to make utility furniture or to make it at a competitive price. The Board were prepared to consider applications by groups of small firms acting as one unit through a processor-wholesaler. But in practice a good many amongst the multitude of small firms in the industry felt themselves squeezed out. The Board, however, stood firm. They were not prepared to relax the requirement that firms on utility furniture should run at full capacity. Nor would they contemplate the use of timber destined for utility furniture in non-utility furniture.

When the utility furniture scheme was launched, it had been emphasised that concentration of the industry would be speeded up. In effect designation of firms to make utility furniture meant concentration. The chosen firms were considered nucleus firms and were given approved labour forces. There was also a compensation scheme for those firms who were not designated and who, unable or unwilling to do war work or repairs or make domestic woodware from 'off-cuts', had to close down their domestic furniture departments. The concentration of the woodworking industry as a whole was left on one side until a Directorate of Woodworking was established in the Ministry of Supply in the spring of 1943. The new director's policy was then to drop the idea of concentration, to load essential firms to full capacity and leave others to the desires of the Ministry of Labour.

The main list of designated firms was not ready until March 1943, but most of the 132 firms included in it had been designated by the end of January. Production of utility furniture therefore began in January. The issue of buying permits to the public also began in January. It was now that the disappointments began. The trouble was not on the demand side. Indeed, the number of units issued by the Assistance Board in the first few months of the scheme came very near the Board of Trade's estimate of 400,000 for a four-week period. The demands for the different articles of furniture also came remarkably close to the Board's estimates. So the production programmes were not at fault. The disappointment lay in the very slow build-up of production itself. In the first three months of 1943 total production was less than thirty per cent. of licensed production. The programmed production was not reached until the very end of 1943.

There were various causes for the lag in production. Many of the manufacturers, it seemed, showed little initiative and had to be nursed like beginners in business. Some did not believe there would be a demand for utility furniture. Others, contrary to their undertakings, had run on with Government orders. There were also technical difficulties over types of construction to which particular firms were not accustomed. Then of necessity the Board had had to designate firms which had no veneer presses, and it was not always easy to arrange for outside veneering to be done. For some time, too, firms had difficulty in obtaining supplies of metal fittings.

The Board did what they could about these difficulties. They had the services of an Adviser on Furniture Production drawn from the trade and also of production officers whose job it was to visit firms and smooth out troubles and also to ensure that the standard of quality was maintained. The Board also got over the metal fittings difficulty by arranging for centralised ordering and supply of approved types of fittings. Moreover, owing to very close collaboration between the Board and the Timber Control, difficulties over timber supplies at a time of acute shortage were much less than might have been expected.

The Board got from the Materials Committee the allocations they needed for the licensed production. But even so there were all kinds of complexities over types of timber. At first, to avoid troubles in the early stages of the scheme, the Timber Control was able to provide imported seasoned timber for the furniture. When it was necessary to turn over to home-grown timber even for nearly all the exterior parts of the furniture, the Board and the Timber Control between them were helpful in finding kilning capacity.

The difficulties that were much less easy to overcome were those of labour. About 15,000 workers were supposed to be employed on domestic furniture when the utility scheme was introduced. The 130 or so designated firms employed at the time of designation only 3,600 people. It was agreed, however, that they should have approved labour forces totalling 5,850 in order to bring the output of each up to something near full capacity. The intention was that the 2,200 workers required to make up these approved labour forces should be found from the undesignated firms who should still be able to yield over 8,000 people for war work. In fact, of course, the Ministry of Labour had great difficulty in building up the labour force to this figure; even by August 1943 designated firms had only 4,200 workers. Scheduling under the Essential Work Order in the summer of 1943 may have stopped some of the drift away from the firms. Meanwhile attempts to find extra labour for the original designated firms went on. But the main method of finding workers was to designate more firms and to achieve thereby the minimum labour force needed to produce the goods. By January 1944 170 firms with a labour force of 5,872 engaged on domestic furniture were designated.

It took a year—up to the beginning of 1944—before production of utility furniture was up to the original planned rate. The deficiencies over this year had of course produced large arrears of orders.[1] Moreover, utility furniture was popular and the number of applications rose. It was therefore necessary to cut demand drastically. For six weeks from the beginning of July no applications for buying permits were admitted and when applications were resumed the maximum permitted quantity for a couple without children[2] was reduced from sixty to thirty units—a very small allowance that was barely sufficient to furnish one room.

By this means the number of units issued monthly was brought to a figure not very different from the current rate of production. But there were still, at the end of 1943, large arrears of orders—about a million units worth—to be worked off. Moreover, there was general

---

[1] This was in spite of the fact that many of the units issued did not materialise into orders. In April 1944 nearly two million issued units had not been used.

[2] This basic allocation was increased by seven units for each additional member of the household including an expected baby.

agreement that as soon as possible the number of units should be increased to somewhere near the former level and that the priority classes should be extended—to cover, for example, the childless couples married in 1939 and 1940. It was therefore agreed at the end of 1943 that the planned rate of output should be increased by three-quarters. This was to be done largely by getting the Director of Woodworking to release the capacity of additional firms to make utility furniture. Owing to urgent last minute demands of the Services for D-Day supplies, the additional capacity could not in the end be released until later in 1944. By the middle of 1944, therefore, production was a bare quarter above the original planned rate.

Meanwhile, after the success of the D-Day landings the feeling that the war would soon end led to a great increase in the demand for utility furniture. Demand also increased as the result of renewed bombing. By the end of 1944 the orders received by manufacturers were double what they had been in the spring of that year. It was clear that output must be substantially increased. The programme was therefore raised to 1,100,000 units for January 1945, rising to 1,500,000 units by June. Materials, labour and capacity appropriate to this rate were allocated to the Board. Still, however, hopes were disappointed as the following figures show:

Utility Furniture Production

TABLE 37

Month		Number of firms making returns	Production (U.F. Units) '000s	Number of persons employed on U.F. (end month)
1943	January	—	28	—
	March	—	194	—
	June	137	259	4,280
	September	158	345	5,366
1944	January	171	420	5,872
	March	170	468	5,997
	June	214	511	7,142
	September	228	537	6,997
1945	January	298	686	8,949
	March	337	847	10,663
	June	400	1,164	13,509
	September	497	1,490	19,091

As the Board of Trade had foreseen, demand increased more rapidly than production. Minor relaxations in supply were made, but it was not until March 1946 that it was possible to restore the maximum issue to the original sixty units.

In spite of all its teething troubles the utility furniture scheme was one of the notable war-time successes on the home front. It brought together many strands of policy—the production of a minimum of domestic furniture of reasonable quality, production with the minimum of raw material, price control, rationing, and release of labour and factory space. It was an imaginatively conceived scheme. And although the allowance of furniture was so austere, the scheme did help to alleviate the personal problems of thousands of families by providing pleasant furniture at reasonable prices. The Board could take credit for the fact that even in the first seven months of the scheme they had provided furniture for some 30,000 homes at the average level of issue of units. And by June 1944 the number of units produced was sufficient for furniture for 17,000 homes a month at the thirty-unit level. This was accomplished, moreover, without undue strain on the war economy. A good deal of timber was used—the 400,000 units a month programme took 150,000 cubic feet of hardwood—or ten per cent. of the country's total hardwood consumption at that time. But the demands in labour were only low—less than 6,000 for the 400,000-units programme.

DOMESTIC POTTERY

The pottery industry illustrates well the changing impact of the war on a civilian industry. It had in peace-time a valuable export trade and therefore an important part in the export drive of the early months of the war. Then from 1941 onwards there were very heavy demands for munition workers in North Staffordshire, the centre of the industry. Finally, such things as cups and plates are considered to be essential in civilised life and when supplies fell too low the Board of Trade had to make special efforts to increase them.

In 1939 the pottery industry employed 80,000 workers. The outlook of the industry just before the war was not, however, very happy. The equipment of many potteries was out of date, and among the workers there was fairly high unemployment and in addition a good deal of ill health due to working on clay. The unemployment was the more serious because in the Stoke-on-Trent area there was no other important industry.

The first demand that was made on the pottery industry was for an increase of exports. Exports of domestic china and earthenware had been worth £2 millions in 1938, and of this about half had gone to the North and South American markets which were of course particularly valuable in war-time. Pottery exports were the more useful in war-time because they presented no raw material complication; they were produced almost exclusively from native clays. They had, therefore, a high conversion value; no problem of finding the shipping for imports arose, and there was no competing warlike use for the raw materials. The pottery export drive was successful. China exports rose from £425,000 in 1938 to over £1 million in 1941 or an average of about 50,000 cwt. in 1940–41 compared with an average of 27,000 cwt. in 1938–39. The earthenware section of the industry could not make the same spectacular response to the export drive because of essential orders at home, but here too exports in 1940 and 1941 were greater than they had been in the preceding years. The quantity of earthenware exported to the United States rose from 54,600 cwt. in 1939 to 67,300 cwt. in 1941 (£295,700 to £486,000 by value).

The first step in Government control over pottery was not taken until June 1940. Then, under the Limitation of Supplies Order, the supply of pottery passing to the shops was limited to 66⅔ per cent. of supplies in the standard period. Pottery manufacturers, however, succeeded in pressing forward the argument that the two-thirds quota for sales to the home market was harmful to their export trade because it meant that home trade could no longer absorb the export 'seconds'. During November 1940, therefore, the pottery manufacturers were allowed a quota of 85 per cent. instead of the normal 66⅔. In fact, however, it became clear that several manufacturers increased their home supplies at the expense of their exports. For the six months from 1st December 1940 the home sales quota was reduced to fifty per cent. of the value of sales in the standard period. Even this restriction was less drastic than it sounded. For according to returns made by the pottery manufacturers to the Board of Trade export orders accounted for about forty per cent. of the output of the industry, and Government orders which were likewise not controlled by the limitation Orders for a further six or seven per cent. The restriction on home sales therefore affected only about half the output of the industry. And within that half supplies to special consumers, such as local authorities, hospitals, Women's Voluntary Services, N.A.A.F.I., and so forth, could be quota free.

Nevertheless the restrictions were now sufficiently severe to threaten the potteries with short-time working. At the same time the demand for workers to man the big new war factories of North Staffordshire was becoming pressing. The pottery industry in the spring of 1941 was therefore an obvious candidate for a concentration scheme. At first pottery concentration did not go very smoothly. On the industry's side there was little enthusiasm. On the Government's side there was slowness in actually demanding the release of workers for munitions and in deciding upon the total number of workers to be released under concentration. At first the only guidance given to the industry was that the volume of contraction expected was equal to twenty-two per cent. of trade or thirty-four per cent. of home trade. In order that this contraction should be achieved firms desiring to qualify for nucleus status were advised to raise their monthly output to that achieved in the best month of the quota period June to

November 1940, and to arrange to transfer the production of other factories so that the transferred production would fill the gap between the peak and current production rate.

There were further difficulties in the early months of concentration about the methods of compensating pottery firms. The manufacturers' federation was anxious from the outset to have an industry-wide pooling scheme. At first, the Government felt that such industry-wide schemes went against the principle of private arrangements between individual firms that was enshrined in the concentration White Paper. However, this attitude soon changed and the Board of Trade agreed that in the pottery industry, as in the cotton spinning and weaving industries, there should be a central compensation scheme provided that manufacturers retained the right to make individual arrangements of the kind contemplated in the White Paper.[1]

In the early summer of 1941 the Board of Trade made it clear that each nucleus group of pottery manufacturers was expected to release a third of its joint labour force. But still very few acceptable schemes were submitted to the Board. Finally, the Board made one considerable concession—one that was out of line with the concentration White Paper. In view of the different types of pottery production and the need to preserve as many export patterns as possible, the Board agreed to waive the condition that nucleus firms must run at full capacity. They agreed that nucleus status might be granted to establishments operating at not less than seventy-five per cent. capacity after the release of thirty per cent. of the labour employed by the nucleus group on 1st April 1941. Labour was to be withdrawn first from non-nucleus establishments. Younger workers were, however, to be withdrawn at once from nucleus establishments and replaced by older workers from non-nucleus firms.

The Board's concession won the co-operation of the producers and by the end of July 1941 concentration schemes had been completed for nearly the whole of the North Staffordshire industry.[2] The industry's labour force did not fall very quickly by the prescribed thirty per cent. By the beginning of December 1941 the numbers employed were about fifteen per cent. less than in April 1941. By the end of March 1942 the labour force was down to about three-quarters of that a year earlier. The fall did not stop here and at its lowest—in June

---

[1] The compensation scheme as it was finally approved consisted of a central fund based on payments made by nucleus firms to provide for closed firms' care and maintenance of premises and plant, the cost of fire-watching, rates, rent, fire insurance, workmen's compensation, etc., and such compensation to closed firms as was necessary to carry out the policy set out in the White Paper. A tribunal consisting of the chairman and secretary of the Federation, together with an independent arbitrator, was to settle claims and compensation questions.

[2] By the time concentration was finally completed 84 establishments were authorised to run with nucleus status and 105 establishments were scheduled as closing down production with an estimated release of factory space of over 2,400,000 square feet.

1944—the industry's labour force was only sixty-eight per cent. of the figure in April 1941 and only fifty-four per cent. of the pre-war figure.

The two main considerations in the concentration discussions had been the protection of the important pottery exporting firms and the need to release labour for munitions. In the summer of 1941 the industry had indeed been warned that it would probably now be necessary to reduce exports except perhaps to the most desirable hard currency countries. Nevertheless, it was not until the end of 1941 that a new consideration—the plight of the home consumer—came to the fore. In June 1941 the home sales quota was reduced to forty per cent. of the standard period. But in the following months evidence began to pile up of severe shortages of essential crockery.

The Board of Trade hoped to alleviate this shortage by modifying the restrictions. Registered manufacturers and wholesalers were permitted to supply without restriction the more essential types of pottery, including cups and saucers, teapots, plates and dishes,[1] provided that they were made of undecorated earthenware or china or of china decorated merely with a narrow plain band or a plain line and edge. Manufacturers were permitted to supply other types of pottery to the value of 50 per cent. of their quota in the first half of the ensuing limitation period and to the value of $7\frac{1}{2}$ per cent. in the second. This was intended to encourage manufacturers to reduce their stocks of decorated and luxury ware without providing a stimulus to further production.

The Board of Trade's hope that there would be an increase in supplies of plain ware corresponding to the decrease in supplies of more expensive decorated ware was disappointed. In March 1942 the quota for decorated ware was reduced once more. But it was already clear that more drastic methods of control were necessary. For it was not the limitation Orders that were mainly responsible for the reduced supplies. It was rather the shortage of labour in the potteries. And because of the export drive nearly the whole of the decrease in output resulting from the withdrawal of labour for munitions work had been felt by the home consumer. While supplies had been falling demand had been increasing. For war brought a great extension of communal feeding and an increase in the number of people eating in more than one place—not only at home but also in Army messes, N.A.A.F.I. canteens, industrial and pithead canteens, emergency feeding centres, British Restaurants, nurseries, and so forth. It was, of course, very difficult to calculate the deficiency in supplies, but it seemed in the spring of 1942 as if current supplies might be falling short of minimum needs by at least 100 million pieces of crockery a year.

---

[1] The complete list was as follows: teacups and saucers, breakfast cups and saucers, mugs, beakers, plates, coffee-pots, teapots, jugs, sauceboats, meat dishes, vegetable dishes, casseroles, pie dishes, bowls, basins, ewers and chambers.

There were two main lines of approach to the problem of increasing domestic supplies with the available labour. First, it was reluctantly agreed that exports must be cut. This was not an easy decision. For fine china was one of the few remaining 'currency' exports to the United States and South American countries. Moreover, since supplies of pottery from Japan had been cut off many Empire and Allied countries were more than ever dependent on British supplies; several of them, such as South Africa, were already experiencing shortages nearly as acute as those in Britain. Nevertheless, it was arranged that all pottery manufacturers should cut their exports by twenty per cent. from 1st May 1942[1] and by a further twenty per cent. from 1st August 1942. From the autumn of 1942 coloured and decorated ware could be exported only to the United States, Canada and Latin America. An export quota system was worked out to ensure that an adequate balance was struck between the needs and currency value of the various markets.

The second line of approach was direct control over production. Under an Order, operative from 1st June,[2] the manufacture of domestic pottery was forbidden except in accordance with directions and licences issued by the Board of Trade. Directions might be made to regulate the types of pottery to be manufactured, to prohibit the manufacture of certain types of pottery, to regulate or prohibit some processes employed, to regulate the quantity of domestic pottery to be made and also the marking of such pottery, to regulate or prohibit the supply of pottery and, finally, to regulate prices. Manufacture was defined to include decoration and domestic pottery to mean pottery and other shaped and fired clay products other than those specified in the schedule to the Order. The exception covered such goods as laboratory, electrical and other industrial porcelain ware designed primarily for nursing, bricks, tiles and sanitary earthenware.

The first directions were issued on the same day as the enabling Order.[3] They prohibited manufacture of domestic pottery other than of the type specified in the schedule to the directions, unless the pottery was for export. The permitted articles for home use were cups, eggcups, mugs, beakers, plates, saucers, teapots, coffee-pots, jugs, meat dishes and vegetable dishes, sauceboats, cooking ware, including pie dishes, bowls, ewers, basins, chambers, hot-water bottles and stoppers, and rolling-pins. This ware was to be made without decoration and was to be white or light ivory only, except in the case of stoneware or ware made from a natural clay body for which a brown or colourless glaze was permitted. These provisions about decoration

---

[1] From 1st May licences were required for the export of domestic pottery to all destinations.

[2] S.R. & O. 1942, No. 1038.

[3] S.R. & O. 1942, No. 1039.

were more stringent than those in the Order of December 1941 that controlled supply. For example, line decorations, coloured bodies and all but a very few types of embossed ware were no longer allowed. It was hoped that by carrying austerity as far as possible few people would be tempted to buy crockery they did not absolutely need. The directions also made provision for the control of prices.[1] All articles of earthenware for which a maximum price was prescribed were to be marked under the glaze with the group letter they had been given for price-control purposes. No other form of mark was permitted on any ware except the manufacturer's name and registered trade mark and in the case of the railway companies the initials of the name of the company. Apart from this concession, the regulation about marking was strictly enforced in spite of protests from all kinds of associations. For the more marking there was, the more labour would be used even in such subsidiary processes as sorting ware.

There were, of course, no longer any restrictions on the volume of pottery manufactured for the home market. The object of the control over manufacture introduced in June 1942 was to get increased supplies of essential articles from the industry by cutting out unnecessary processes such as decoration and the manufacture of unnecessary articles. But the first directions of June 1942 were to the Board of Trade only a beginning—an interim measure pending the working out of much closer specifications of the sizes and types of articles to be produced. Standardisation, it was felt, would bring considerable economies in output. A committee of the pottery industry was therefore established in order to advise the Board on standardisation. The Board of Trade hoped that the committee would select a specified shape, size, thickness, etc., for each type of article—a choice governed by economy in production and durability in use. Then when the Board had approved it, each pottery was to submit to the committee its own shape nearest to the 'standard' for approval, after which it would be required to turn over to its approved shape as rapidly as it could work off its existing moulds.

These hopes were to some extent disappointed. It became clear that there were very real obstacles in the way of enforcing too much standardisation. First and foremost mould-makers and saggar-makers were scarce and production would fall if maximum use were not made of existing moulds and saggars. Then the older skilled workers who had carried out the same operation on the same size and shape of article for years were opposed to changes since they would not earn as much at new work at which they were less proficient. Again, most manufacturers were also exporters and if they were making a particular size or shape for, say, Argentina, it was cheapest to run off a great many at the same time for the home market.

---

[1] These are discussed in the chapter on price control. See pp. 588–9.

Finally, Government departments and institutions had all kinds of special needs. This made it difficult to eliminate some seemingly un-essential sizes or types of article. For example, cafés and canteens needed two sizes of cups for 1d. and 2d. cups of tea. The Army needed pint mugs so that soldiers need make only one journey to their messes. Vegetable dishes were needed for cafés and institutions. And small families had to have, for example, small pudding basins to avoid wastage of food.

In the end, therefore, the advisory committee's conclusions were that it would be well worth while to reduce the number of sizes that might be made of each permitted article, but that there was no advantage in specifying standard shapes. The Board of Trade felt that it might be possible to reduce the number of sizes the committee recommended for each article and also to cut out some permitted articles, such as coffee-pots or sauceboats. On the whole, however, the Board felt that there was not much to be gained by pressing the industry too far. After all, the limitation to certain types of plain white ware plus maximum prices plus the labour shortage would in any case make the maximum simplification necessary in the interests of each individual firm.

Broadly, then, the advisory committee's recommendations were adopted. Under new directions made in October 1942[1] with effect from 1st January 1943, manufacturers were only permitted to make a limited number of types of each kind of article and these had to be either of the capacity or within the limits of size or capacity set out in the directions. Articles were only considered to be of the same type if they were identical in shape, weight and measurement or capacity; in the case of cups, however, no account was taken of the presence or absence of a handle. To give one or two examples: a manufacturer could only make three types of earthenware cups within the limits of 7 to 12 ounces capacity; at least one type was to be less than, and another more than, 9 ounces. Again, ordinary brown teapots were limited to sizes between 10 and 65 ounces capacity and each manufacturer was permitted to make six sizes only. Manufacturers were required to register with their federation the types and sizes of articles they wished to make and from 1st February 1943 they were not permitted to continue the manufacture of other types except for ex-port. Moreover, a committee of manufacturers was set up to advise on the suitability or otherwise of the shapes and sizes chosen. If the analysis of returns made by the manufacturers showed that the pro-duction of any particular size or type of article was relatively too high or too low in comparison with estimated requirements, changes in production were advised. This committee also adopted a minimum standard of thickness in approving shapes.

[1] S.R. & O. 1942, No. 2210.

All these efforts were directed towards getting as much output as possible out of the war-time pottery industry. But a general increase in output was not enough. For the shortage of some particular items was much more serious than that of others. Thus, in the summer of 1942 it became clear that, while supplies of things such as saucers and plates were more than adequate, there was a real scarcity of cups and teapots. Consumer and retailer surveys left no doubt that a total annual production of 96 million cups, mugs and beakers—the rate for May and June 1942—was inadequate. It was, however, extremely difficult to calculate what production ought to be in order to meet minimum essential needs. It was possible to calculate roughly the requirements for Government orders and various catering establishments. But the civilian demand—the rate of breakage and the need for replacement—was a much more doubtful quantity. Estimates wavered betwen 32 million and 194 million cups a year. The Board of Trade made the best guess they could and decided that the aim should be an increase of fifty per cent. in the output of cups, mugs and beakers—that is about 145 millions instead of 95 millions a year—and a fifteen per cent. increase in the output of teapots—about $7\frac{1}{2}$ millions instead of 6·1 millions.

The detailed work of ensuring that production was increased to this extent was entrusted to a special Cup Committee of the manufacturers. This committee asked manufacturers for their weekly production figures and for a target figure of increased production which they undertook to reach. The committee could watch the position and help manufacturers with their difficulties.

The chief difficulty was of course labour. The industry was by the autumn of 1942 below its permitted labour force under concentration. Instead of having over 26,000 workers it only had 22,000 odd. This was in part due to the withdrawal of mobile decorators for munitions work. All other workers except men reaching the age of military service were protected against withdrawal without prior substitution. There had, however, been some voluntary drift away from the industry. The manufacturers felt that if an extra 200 or 300 workers were drafted into the potteries the desired figure of cup production could be reached. The Board of Trade, however, were not willing to make this request to the Ministry of Labour until all other expedients had been tried.

One of the most obvious of these expedients was to transfer labour within the potteries. Could not the few remaining decorators and the makers of saucers and plates transfer to cup-making? This was not as easy as it sounded. For the pottery industry had a highly complicated system of employment. Certain occupations were performed traditionally by men and others by women. Decorators would be loth to move to clay processes, and indeed all changes between departments might involve unwelcome changes in earnings. Nevertheless, it was possible to exaggerate these difficulties. For example, saucer-makers and teaplate-makers like cup-makers were normally women or juveniles, and they should soon pick up sufficient skill to earn at their old rate.

The Board of Trade considered at one time whether production might be increased by reorganising the industry. This really meant a small-scale reconcentration. The original concentration scheme had been framed with an eye to export rather than to the needs of the home market. One or two firms that had been closed were in fact very suitable for the mass production of cups and other essential articles. The Board suggested that these firms might be reopened and that several firms, which, though still open, were inefficient or particularly unsuitable for mass production, should be closed. The labour would be transferred to the more efficient firms. If reopening of closed firms were not possible it might still be worth while closing the inefficient firms—not only in order to find labour for the good firms but also to save fuel. The industry, however, was unenthusiastic about these proposals. It felt that the original concentration scheme had caused wastage of labour—some of the labour released had drifted away into less essential occupation or retirement—and that any reorganisation would probably do the same. Instead, therefore, the committee of the industry promised to keep the inefficient firms up to the mark.

The general efforts to increase production were amply justified. Production of cups, mugs and beakers for January–March 1943 was almost exactly at the rate of 145 millions a year—the target set to the industry. The increase had been achieved by a variety of individual efforts and by the transfer of labour within firms—a process that was hastened when the Essential Work Order was applied to the industry in December 1942. A large part of the increased production consisted, of necessity, of handleless cups.[1] As part of the standardisation policy the Board of Trade had suggested a compulsory handleless cup, but the suggestion had been received unfavourably. Nevertheless, there were not enough handle-makers to keep pace with the increased output of the cup-makers. When there began to be difficulty in selling the handleless cups in the spring of 1943, it was a sure sign that the cup shortage was over.

During the rest of the war other shortages of pottery became prominent from time to time. Sometimes it was large plates that were scarce or it might be pudding bowls or babies' chambers. After the experience of dealing with cups there was a fairly well defined process for meeting each new shortage. Production targets were fixed

---

[1] One unexpected result of fostering the production of handleless cups was that for the first time it became possible to make cups on Saturday morning, for cups are normally made in the morning and the handles put on in the afternoon before the clay gets too dry.

and the industry and the Board considered which alternative articles might be cut and the industry's committee tackled individual manufacturers.

Altogether the pottery industry was a successful example of the Board of Trade's efforts to protect the essential war-time needs of the civilian and of the special users such as Government departments and catering establishments. Supplies were never lavish and the goods provided were austere. The good manufacturers still produced pleasingly designed shapes but colour and decoration vanished, apart from a few export rejects. Sets of crockery also disappeared and it was often difficult even to get a cup and a saucer designed for each other. The main points, however, were that the population had vessels to drink from and plates to eat off and that the pottery industry contributed large numbers of workers to war industry.

TOILET PREPARATIONS

By the end of 1943 the control over the manufacture and supply of toilet preparations was one of the most complicated of the controls over manufacture and supply that had been evolved within the Board of Trade. The controls over most other consumer goods had been imposed in order to ensure the supply of essential articles at reasonable prices and the use in their production of as little labour and material as was compatible with a serviceable article. But this was not true of toilet preparations. It was obvious that production and supply of these goods should be considerably reduced in war-time. An ordinary limitation of supplies procedure might, however, have been sufficient to serve the needs of war if only it had not been for the problem of enforcement. As it was, the control had to be drawn progressively tighter in order to defeat the plans of unscrupulous people who were ready to make use of every loophole in control in order to supply goods illicitly to a public willing to buy unknown goods when known varieties were not available. This illicit manufacture and supply was not only unfair to the straightforward manufacturer of reputable preparations but was a real danger to the buying public who were being supplied with inferior products which were often produced under unhygienic conditions and were sometimes a danger to their health.

Toilet preparations and perfumery were first controlled under the Limitation of Supplies (Miscellaneous) Order of June 1940 with a $66\frac{2}{3}$ per cent. quota. Registered manufacturers could supply controlled goods outside their quota to the usual recognised authorities and small manufacturers did not have to register. In December 1940 the value of supply permitted to registered manufacturers and wholesalers of toilet preparations and perfumery was reduced to twenty-five per cent. of the value for the standard period while the value of supply by unregistered people was reduced from £167 to £100 a month.

About 600 manufacturers of toilet preparations were registered under the Limitation of Supplies Order and many of them also manufactured goods such as soap and medical preparations which were outside the Board of Trade's control. Of this number only about thirty had a considerable turnover. When the industry was concentrated in 1941 the seventy or so firms in the concentration scheme were estimated to employ over seventy per cent. of the labour of the industry. In addition to manufacturers who made up toilet preparations as the whole or as part of their main business many chemists and hairdressers were also manufacturers on a small scale; chemists mixed preparations themselves for sale over the counter and hairdressers made them for use in the course of their business.

It became apparent very soon in the history of the limitation of supplies of toilet preparations that evasion was rife. In the early days the most serious method of evasion was 'invoicing through'. Manufacturers supplied goods direct to a retailer, but invoiced them to a wholesaler who in turn invoiced to the retailer; in this way the supply counted against the wholesaler's quota. There was nothing legally wrong in this provided that the wholesaler did not exceed his quota. Some wholesalers were, however, tempted by the offer of large commissions to exceed their permitted quotas. A number were prosecuted but the widespread destruction of records in the autumn and winter of 1940–41 often made it impossible to obtain sufficient evidence to support legal proceedings.

In October 1941 the Board of Trade put a stop to 'invoicing through' by cutting out the wholesalers' quota. A special Limitation of Supplies (Toilet Preparations) Order[1] introduced a new toilet preparations register in two parts. Manufacturers' names only were entered on Part I of the register. Part II contained the names of export merchants who were not permitted to supply goods to the home market except under licence. Since supplies to 'other registered persons' were free of control, exports were unchecked. 'Invoicing through' was, however, no longer possible. The quota for registered manufacturers remained at about twenty-five per cent. But additional licences were henceforth granted to established firms provided these firms did not employ workers above the number permitted under concentration schemes and provided they realised that they were not entitled to extra supplies of scarce materials. It was hoped that this extra licensing would help to curb the sale of illegally supplied preparations. There were further provisions to curb evasion. The value of permitted sales by unregistered manufacturers was reduced from £100 a month to £41 13s. 4d. a month and this concession was restricted to manufacturers producing controlled goods on the 1st

---

[1] S.R. & O. 1941, No. 1519.

October 1941. Moreover, no unregistered manufacturers were allowed to supply goods of their own manufacture for resale.

As soon as one form of evasion was stopped, other means of flouting the Order were devised. For example, some unregistered persons supplied goods of their own manufacture to the public through buying agents. Or by packing in bulk and arranging for a packer to repack the preparations in small containers, registered manufacturers could supply within their quota excessive quantities of toilet preparations: since the cost of packing was a high proportion of the cost of production, materials valued at £1 might make £25 to £50 worth of finished packed goods. Again, some manufacturers supplied creams with medicinal properties outside their quotas as they were legally entitled to do. But on analysis many of these new creams were found to differ only slightly from toilet preparations, while advertisements, labels or descriptions on the jars showed quite clearly that they were cosmetics in disguise. Other manufacturers supplied small packets of raw materials, unmixed but in proper proportion so that the purchaser could mix the cosmetic which she was unable to buy.

It was therefore clear by 1942 that there were a good many more loopholes in control to be closed. At the same time the toilet preparations industry came under review as part of the Board of Trade's study of ways to reduce unessential activities. Should there be a control of manufacture and supply which would prohibit the manufacture of the most unessential cosmetics and curb illicit manufacture? In the end it was decided not to proceed with this idea. Toilet preparations were considered to be too important a part of morale to be the subject of prohibition. Instead, to meet the needs of the war effort the industry was reconcentrated in order to move production away from the most difficult labour areas. Nucleus firms in these areas were told that they would lose their nucleus status unless they moved. The main advantage offered to them was a quota of fifty per cent. instead of the standard twenty per cent.; this advantage sounded grander than it was for nucleus firms were already receiving licences to exceed their quota by substantial amounts. However, the value of the second concentration compared with the first is shown by the reduction in the permitted labour force of the concentrating firms; for in 1942 it was under 3,000, while in 1941 it exceeded 6,000.

Having ruled out control of manufacture and supply as a means of releasing resources for the war effort, the Board of Trade decided they could not impose it, as the established firms in the industry wished, purely as a means of enforcement; the administrative burden involved would be too heavy. Instead, there was a new Limitation of Supplies (Toilet Preparations) Order which came into force on 1st August 1942.[1] This Order closed more loopholes. Unregistered per-

---

[1] S.R. & O. 1942, No. 1512.

sons could now only supply goods to the general public on the premises where they were made. It also became illegal for any person to supply controlled goods not of his own manufacture to a person buying for resale except in the same quantity and the same container as they were received. Another effort to remove the 'packeting' abuse was the rule that no person other than a manufacturer might pack controlled goods without a licence. Moreover, containers had to be marked with the name and address of the manufacturer and the licensed packer (if any). Medicated toilet preparations were brought within the control to prevent the evasion of quotas by the addition of antiseptics. The standard quota for registered manufacturers was twenty per cent. or £500, whichever was the greater; licences for nucleus firms in approved areas brought their quota up to fifty per cent. Face powder was temporarily freed from quota as the raw materials for it were plentiful.[1] Unregistered manufacturers were still limited to £41 13s. 4d. a month.

In December 1942,[2] the use of certain scarce materials in toilet preparations was prohibited. Even this Order could be evaded. It led, for example, to the disappearance of nail varnish and nail varnish remover. But instead there appeared very similar preparations in containers like those used for nail varnish which purported to stop ladders in stockings. To counteract this the Ministry of Supply prohibited the packing of preparations containing the prohibited solvent in containers holding less than half a pint of the preparation.[3] Another prohibited use of scarce materials was petroleum for hair preparations. Hairdressers, however, were allowed to use these petroleum preparations in the course of their business provided they were unregistered manufacturers supplying controlled goods under the Order.[4]

In 1943 the possibilities of evading the control were much less than they had been, but they were still too great. It was still necessary to establish illegal supply before prosecuting a suspected offender and this was far more difficult than it would have been to prove that goods had been manufactured in contravention of an Order. It was gradually becoming clear that either control should be abandoned as unenforceable or that control should be extended to manufacture as well as supply. Finally, it was decided to control manufacture in spite of the administrative burden involved.

---

[1] From January 1943 it was subject to a separate quota of sixty-five per cent.

[2] S.R. & O. 1942, No. 2605. At the same time the quota period was divided into three monthly periods to spread supplies.

[3] S.R. & O. 1944, No. 404.

[4] S.R. & O. 1943, No. 575. The prohibition on the manufacture and supply of these preparations was removed from 1st January 1944 (S.R. & O. 1943, No. 1683).

From September 1943, therefore, quota control over supplies was abolished and manufacture was subject to individual licences. These licences specified the address at which the manufacturers might make controlled goods, the total value of controlled goods of their own manufacture that they might supply to the home market and the type of controlled article they might supply. In the case of pre-packed goods the licence specified the sizes of the containers and the minimum value to be counted against the licence in respect of each size and type of article covered by the licence. If supply in bulk was permitted the licence specified in addition the percentage of the licensed value that the manufacturer might supply in bulk, the minimum size of the containers to be used and the minimum value to be counted against the licence for each unit.

Additional measures adopted to make illegal manufacture more difficult included prohibiting suppliers from supplying materials used in making toilet preparations except to registered manufacturers and to unregistered manufacturers who made a written declaration that they were qualified to manufacture. There was also a ban on the use by manufacturers of materials that did not belong to them.

The total value of the licences issued to registered manufacturers was generally calculated on a similar basis to the quotas prescribed under the earlier Orders. The rates of the licences issued for the period ending on 31st December 1943 were the same as those laid down from 1st January 1943. Manufacturers could still supply goods in excess of the value of their licences to recognised voluntary bodies supplying goods to the Services. The former unregistered manufacturers were not brought within the licensing scheme and the restrictions on their activities remained substantially unaltered.

In January 1944 the quotas on which licences were based were increased to $33\frac{1}{3}$ per cent. of the standard period for non-nucleus firms and to 75 per cent. for nucleus firms. This was the outcome of a policy permitting the maximum supply that limited factory space, raw materials and packing materials would allow. This policy indeed was considered the strongest weapon to defeat illicit supply.

The control over toilet preparations was obviously an extremely tiresome one. For example, the Orders had prohibited certain normal trade practices because they were being made to serve illegal ends. But it was necessary to license manufacturers to continue some of these practices for *bona fide* purposes. This alone meant the use of many kinds of special licence forms—indeed more than fifty such forms were in current use in September 1944.

One is led to ask first whether the control in the end was successful and, secondly, whether the results were worth all the trouble. The final controls made it much more difficult for black-market operators to escape detection; but it would have been impossible to stamp out illegal activities completely in an industry that required little or no machinery, that used small quantities of raw materials with large profit and that produced goods which were easy to transport. The question how worth while all the effort was is more difficult to answer. The direct benefit to the war effort of stamping out illegal activities cannot have been large. The·issue was much more one of psychology. Control over the established manufacturers was inevitable—labour had to be forced out of them or they had to be encouraged to turn over to Government contracts. But these men were obviously enraged if they saw their market invaded by racketeers. The public too was angry at the appearance of rackets. The price of toilet preparations could only be controlled by the ineffective methods of the Prices of Goods Act, and people disliked seeing profiteering amidst war-time shortages. The complicated toilet preparations control was in effect a response to public demand. Finally, one remark is worth making. When the anti-social sections of society went into battle against the law in the conditions of war it was desirable that the law and the Government should win.

SPORTS GOODS

The number of workers engaged in the manufacture of sports goods was small before the war—only about 7,000. Of 160 manufacturers who made war-time returns, 100 said that in 1938 they were engaged in the manufacture of sports goods only, but these only accounted for fourteen per cent. of the total product of the industry. Some of the big manufacturers of sports goods, for example the large rubber firms, made these goods only as a sideline.

'Appliances, apparatus, accessories and requisites' for 'sports, games, gymnastics and athletics' were bought under the control of the Limitation of Supplies (Miscellaneous) Order 1940; supplies were permitted up to $66\frac{2}{3}$ per cent. of the quantity supplied in the standard period. This quota was gradually reduced and by November 1941 was only twenty-five per cent. The effect of the Orders was, however, largely offset by the granting of a number of general licences under which the supply of sports goods was permitted without restriction to the Services, Service organisations, local authorities and a number of voluntary organisations.

Nevertheless, production declined for other reasons—raw materials were scarce and skilled labour was transferred, especially in the non-specialist firms, to the manufacture of munitions. In February 1941 it was estimated that not more than 2,000 workers were now engaged on making sports goods. The Board of Trade felt that in view of the amount of plant which was not fully employed the industry should be concentrated. In the scheme that was accepted there were only twelve nucleus firms, and, in fact, a great deal of production continued to be carried on by non-nucleus firms. 2,100 workers were covered by nucleus certificates, but of these only 600 were actually making sports goods.

In 1941 production of sports goods declined heavily—it was estimated to be only fifty per cent. of the 1935 level. In some branches, such as the manufacture of hockey sticks, the fall was as much as eighty per cent. During the following year production declined still further—it was not expected to be more than sixty to seventy-five per cent. of the 1941 level. Many of the raw materials used for sports goods were now acutely scarce; the Ministry of Supply now prohibited the use of cork for sports goods and restricted the use of rubber to within very narrow limits.

While production was falling, demand was increasing. The armed forces and women's Services were expanding, junior training corps were formed, sports equipment was to be provided for the civil defence services and the Board of Education and Ministry of Labour were anxious to develop the health and fitness of schoolchildren, adolescents and munition workers. Orders for ex-quota supplies could not be met. Moreover, the system of ex-quota licences had its disadvantages; for example, there was evidence that officers commanding units in the Army had used their privileges to obtain supplies of golf balls for various golf clubs.

Early in 1942, therefore, the Board of Trade called a conference of departments responsible for the large-scale purchase of sports goods and proposed that a system of yearly allocations be introduced. Instead of the system of buying under general licences and certificates which had dissipated supplies, there would be a central buying system for the Services and a central certifying organisation for each class of civilian user. For example, it was hoped that the Board of Education would undertake the responsibility for issuing certificates to all schools and youth organisations. Available supplies would be carefully shared out. For some items of equipment the requirements of Government departments would easily be met by estimated production. In many items, however, cuts would have to be made. It was agreed interdepartmentally that the cuts should be made *pro rata*, the same percentage reduction for each department. The demands of each department were to be accepted without question. All these proposals were agreed.

Having reorganised methods of distribution, the Board of Trade had to give attention to production. Sports goods came under one of the first Control of Manufacture and Supply Orders on 1st August 1942. Manufacture could only be undertaken with the authority of a licence from the Board of Trade and an era of planned production began. This was to ensure that as far as possible supplies of labour and raw materials were concentrated on the manufacture of those goods which were used in communal sports (athletics and gymnastics, boxing, cricket, rugby and association football, hockey other than ice-hockey, netball and volley-ball and rounders) and that the finished articles should be delivered only to persons who had been issued with certificates by Government departments or 'approved associations'. The production of non-priority goods was not expressly forbidden and the Board of Trade reserved the right to allow the supply of sports goods to people not holding certificates. In practice, however, the growing shortage of raw materials reduced the manufacture of fishing tackle and of equipment for such sports as tennis, lacrosse, badminton, rackets, squash, golf, croquet and bowls to very small proportions. Control of the supply of articles used in 'indoor games' was maintained by the Limitation of Supplies Orders. The quota was $7\frac{1}{2}$ per cent. of the standard period with quota-free supplies to approved authorities.

The first production programme for 'priority' sports goods was based on a survey that was made of sales by manufacturers of different types of sports equipment during 1941. From this it was calculated how many of some fifty to sixty articles were likely to be made in 1942 and 1943. Experts were then consulted about the raw material needed for production and the Board of Trade found out from the appropriate authority whether the amounts needed were likely to be available.

The administration of the system of planned production and allocation to users went as well as war-time conditions would allow, but these conditions were always difficult. The labour force of the industry fell and raw materials were more and more scarce. And demand was further increased by the need to meet the sports goods requirements of American troops. Then later the Services were anxious to build up reserves for the demobilisation period. Some of the difficulties were eased by such expedients as economies in the use of raw materials—for example the rubber used in football bladders was reduced from seventy-five per cent. to twenty-five per cent.—and by permitting the sale of existing stocks. All the same, priority demands could not be met—in 1942–43 actual demands for equipment for priority outdoor games were in most cases fifty per cent. in excess of allocations. Apart from supplies to the Services, prisoners of war and to civilian authorities with buying certificates, the Board of Trade themselves maintained a reserve of sports goods for supply to people such as football and cricket teams. At first this reserve took twenty-five per cent. of production, but as shortages grew worse, and as the Services were insistent that their allocations were inadequate, the reserve's demands were reduced to between five and ten per cent. of production.

In the context of a total war effort the history of the control of sports goods is not important. It is, however, a useful illustration of the minutiæ that cannot be ignored in war-time. In a war where there was a good deal of tedium, where the Army had long periods of standing by and where the lives of many children were disrupted, healthy communal exercise was considered necessary to morale. A detailed control had therefore to be imposed on an industry that was even in pre-war days a small one.

CHAPTER XX

CIVILIAN ENGINEERING

DURING the war an overwhelming proportion of the engineering industries was engaged on Government work. These industries were classified as munitions industries and their activities were primarily the responsibility of the supply departments. But the capital equipment of civilian industry could not be ignored. It was essential to the war effort that the gas works and power stations, the railways and the Post Office communication services should keep running. It was no less important that the coal mines should obtain machinery and that equipment for increasing the output of home-grown food should be found.

Outside these large and obvious needs there was a variety of miscellaneous ones. For all civilian industries that were not so unessential as to be closed down needed to maintain their machinery —albeit at a low standard. They had to repair and maintain their existing equipment and in cases of emergency get new machines. Moreover, there was a wide range of goods such as camera equipment, bicycles, wireless sets or scientific instruments that had to be provided for the 'civilian' sector of the economy, even in war-time. In addition, there was the problem of exports. Someone had to decide upon the needs of the export markets for engineering products.

A good many of the responsibilities for civilian engineering products fell clearly within the scope of specific Government departments. The public utilities had their departmental niches, the Ministry of Food must obviously look after the machinery needs of the food industries and the Raw Materials Department after the needs of the industries processing raw materials. But there remained many kinds of machinery for which the Board of Trade, as the residuary legatee among departments, must take responsibility. And the Board of course were responsible for exports.[1]

The Board's controls over engineering were designed to ensure that sufficient—but only just sufficient—machinery and metal goods were released to meet essential needs. The twin pillars on which this control rested were machinery licensing and the distribution of iron and steel. Machinery licensing, it will be remembered, had been established in June 1940 in order to prevent the unnecessary purchase of capital goods. Originally only sixteen classes of machinery and plant were controlled and these, in the main, were either of a type

---

[1] These are discussed in the export policy chapters of this volume.

which would be used in the production of luxury and unessential goods (for example, toilet preparations and confectionery) or such as would be employed in an industry known to possess surplus productive capacity (for example, some of the textile industries). Machinery and plant required by order of a Government department, for export, or as parts for replacement were exempted from licensing. Replacement parts or, as they were subsequently called, repair parts were defined as parts required for servicing or for running repairs to maintain a machine or plant in its existing use and not such as would provide parts or material capable of modifying the method of operating the machine or effecting the rebuilding, refitting, recruitment or remodelling of the whole or part of the machinery.

Between the summer of 1940 and the end of 1942 the scope of machinery licensing was extended until it covered more than ninety classes of goods—a very substantial proportion of the machine-making field.[1] Among the more important classes covered were textile machinery, bakery machinery, paper-making machinery, printing machinery, refrigerating machinery, heavy electrical plant, steam generating plant, furnaces and foundry machinery and plant. Some metal goods that could not really be classified as machinery such as certain metal safes and motor-driven lawn mowers had also been included. And the type of weighing apparatus brought under control covered not only large machines but also personal weighing machines and baby scales. Besides expanding the lists of controlled goods, subsequent orders made it clear that controlled machinery was defined to include any steam generator, prime mover, electrical generator and electric motor exceeding fifteen horse-power (later reduced to five horse-power) used in conjunction with the controlled machinery. Moreover, manufacturers making machinery for their own use were required to obtain a licence before using it. Another restriction introduced was the inclusion of reconditioning as a process of manufacture.

So much machinery was effectively controlled by other Government departments that as machinery licensing was extended to more and more goods there was increasing risk of duplicating control. The goods controlled by other departments were therefore increasingly freed from control by machinery licensing. Sometimes an exception to licensing was embodied in the statutory Order. For example, machinery and plant supplied to a public utility undertaking were excluded from the Order[2] provided the supply of such machinery could only be made under the licence or authority of a Government

---

[1] S.R. & O. 1940, Nos. 1363 and 2179; 1941, Nos. 1063 and 1610; 1942, Nos. 1175 and 2487.

[2] S.R. & O. 1941, No. 1063.

department. And woodworking machinery and plant that could only be supplied under the authority of the Ministry of Supply were also excluded from the Order.[1] More often, however, a general licence was issued in favour of particular items or particular classes of applicants. For instance, a person requiring electrical machinery controlled under the machinery Order for use in connection with a machine tool was authorised to acquire it under a general licence.[2] Again, a general licence was given to mining undertakings to acquire certain kinds of machinery provided they were authorised to do so by the Mines Department.[3] Similarly, founders and steel producers authorised by the supply departments to acquire furnaces, conveyors, foundry machinery, industrial trucks or lifting equipment could be supplied with them without applying to the Board of Trade for a licence. This method of the general licence was useful in helping other Government departments to control the acquisition of certain plant without themselves making statutory Orders.

Machinery licensing was a most valuable method of restricting civilian claims on the engineering industries to a minimum. By December 1944 over 236,000 licences had been issued for machinery valued at nearly £47½ millions while over 54,000 licences for machinery worth over £13 millions had been refused. And in the early days of machinery licensing a good deal had been done by the machinery licensing division to ensure that the capacity released through curtailing civilian work should turn over to war contracts. The existence of the Order and the knowledge that it was rigorously administered undoubtedly prevented many unessential applications.

Useful though machinery licensing was, it was obvious that the system was practicable only as long as 'essential for the war effort' was the sole criterion in judging applications. As soon as munitions contracts began to tail off the criteria would be more complicated; it would not then be within the competence of an administrative officer to pronounce on the different merits of all the customers for a particular type of machinery. A first step towards relaxation of control was therefore taken in August 1943 when an amending machinery licensing Order was made limiting the definition of 'supply' to exclude 'an agreement to supply'.[4] This meant that manufacturers could accept orders for later delivery and could plan ahead for the time when their munitions contracts fell away.

The main problem however remained. Would it be practical to adopt a modified system of licensing as war work was curtailed or should licensing the acquisition and supply of machinery be aban-

---

[1] S.R. & O. 1941, No. 778.
[2] S.R. & O. 1941, No. 1164.
[3] S.R. & O. 1941, No. 1392.
[4] S.R. & O. 1943, No. 1166.

doned altogether? In the twilight between war and peace there would be advantages in keeping some form of licensing. For then the Board could insist on priority of supply for certain agreed purposes or for export. In the end it was decided to switch the emphasis of the control away from the need of the ultimate user towards the production programmes of the engineering firms. From January 1945 therefore the Board of Trade were empowered[1] to give licences for the supply of controlled goods by manufacturers in place of individual licences to acquire to the users of such goods. The licences to manufacturers took the form of bulk licences for approved production programmes. In the first few months of 1945 this policy was necessarily applied only gradually, and even after the war was over individual licensing was retained for classes of machinery where demand was particularly heavy.

The Board of Trade could not have operated the machinery licensing system in the days of individual licensing without the services of men with considerable knowledge of engineering. A body of such men already existed in the machinery licences division of the Import Licensing Department where they had been considering import licences for machinery. Many of these men had been seconded from the Patent Office, where they were authorities in their own field. Now the knowledge they had acquired in dealing with the import of machinery could be used more widely. For the purposes of administering the Machinery and Plant (Control) Order, the machinery licences division was reckoned not as part of the Import Licensing Department but as a division of the Industrial Supplies Department of the Board.

Machinery licensing was one of the main methods of controlling engineering. The other was control over iron and steel. At first the control was operated mainly in order to save steel, but later when steel was less scarce in relation to other factors of production its main object was to economise in labour and capacity in the engineering industries. The Board's control over iron and steel was part of the wider distribution scheme of the Iron and Steel Control. The essence of this scheme was that total supplies of iron and steel were allocated quarterly by the Materials Committee between all the various Government departments. Each department was then responsible for dividing its allocation of steel among the firms for which it was responsible. The Board of Trade had at first a five-fold allocation. One, known as B.T.1, covered the steel requirements of statutory gas undertakings and was administered first by the Gas Section of the Board and then by the Ministry of Fuel and Power. Another, known as B.T.3, was made for one period only to cover certain miscellaneous

---

[1] S.R. & O. 1945, No. 6.

agricultural requirements. The allocation B.T.4 covered the export of goods made of steel, and B.T.5 covered the export of finished steel; both these allocations are dealt with elsewhere in this book. Here in this chapter we are concerned with B.T.2—the allocation for home civilian requirements.

The iron and steel distribution scheme had been formulated primarily with an eye to the needs of contracting departments. All acquisition of iron and steel, whether for direct Government contracts or for any other purpose, had to be authorised on a special Form M. The authorisation on Form M could only be obtained direct from a Government department or through a firm or person who had received authority from a Government department to issue an authorisation. Thus when a purchasing department such as the Ministry of Supply placed a contract for, say, guns it would usually give the contractor an authorisation for the steel required for the whole job of making the guns. The gun-maker, however, would not make every part of the guns himself and would not himself order from steelworks the whole of the tonnage allocated to him. He might therefore pass on his authorisation to the manufacturers of the component parts of the guns. The latter might also sub-authorise part of the tonnage they received to makers of components which they in turn bought. These sub-authorisations were also made on Form M by the person wishing to pass on his authority to quote the symbol, reference and so on given in the main authorisation.

This scheme was not so easy for the Board of Trade because the Board were not a purchasing department. It was not, for them, simply a matter of issuing an M Form for the amount of steel needed for a series of particular contracts. They had to decide how much steel to issue for the manufacture of a great variety of civilian purposes. Between the spring of 1940, when the distribution scheme was established, and the spring of 1941 the Board of Trade did indeed abrogate a good deal of their responsibility for deciding in detail how the B.T.2 allocation should be used. The Board acted as adviser on broad questions of policy and occasionally authorised steel themselves for projects of special importance or urgency. But it was the Iron and Steel Control which licensed the acquisition of iron and steel by individual firms. This licensing had been different from the authorisation system. For the licences had been granted only to persons who themselves wished to acquire finished steel from a steelworks. Authorisations, on the other hand, could be given to anyone and could be passed on by their recipients to other people.

By the end of 1940 it was clear that this division of responsibility was not very satisfactory and that if the Board decided policy they should also be responsible for executing it. The Board therefore began to take over from the Iron and Steel Control the allocation of steel for home civilian purposes and by the early summer of 1941 they were covering practically the whole field.

One of the early difficulties of allocating B.T.2 steel was the complexity of demarcation lines. The allocation was supposed to cover the supply of steel for production and for the repair and maintenance of plant for all home civilian purposes except those specifically defined as coming within the allocation of another department. This formula was vague, but unavoidably so. For there were so many frontiers that they could only be settled piecemeal by degrees and between the departments concerned. Gradually a volume of case law was established and applications for iron and steel could be routed to the right department fairly quickly. For example, it was agreed that steel for A.R.P. equipment, whether required by public authorities or by private individuals or firms, was in general the responsibility of the Ministry of Home Security. The Board of Trade, however, took responsibility for factories' fire-fighting equipment (excluding sprinklers) which normally existed in peace-time and for the authorisation of steel for goods which were normally sold through shops and merchants and which could be used for general purposes as well as for A.R.P.—for example, buckets, torches, goggles and knives.

Again, producers of iron and steel were in general dealt with by the Iron and Steel Control, but while this definition included producers of iron and steel who carried on a subsidiary business as manufacturers of fabricated goods, it excluded manufacturers of fabricated goods who incidentally produced some of their own iron and steel. In some of these cases, where boundaries were blurred, the division of responsibility between the Board and other Government departments rested on agreed lists of firms.

The iron and steel distribution scheme obviously held fairly high opportunities of 'buck passing' between Government departments. To some extent the onus of preventing too much of this game rested on the Board of Trade. The Board indeed were only too anxious to avoid an excessively departmental outlook. They were quite ready to assume responsibility for the repair and maintenance requirements of firms working for several Government departments, even though only a very small percentage of these firms' work was for 'home civilian' purposes. It had also been the Board's policy to treat flexibly applications for small quantities of steel. In part this was a question of administrative routine. Complaints were heard that papers floated round from Government department to Government department, spending a week or two with each one before being passed on without any action having been taken. And there was at least one case of an application for the small sum of nine pounds of steel that went to five departments, including two visits to the Board of Trade. The Board of Trade issued instructions devised to minimise this nuisance. They made it clear that, even if discussions on principle were involved, the Board should authorise the steel at once (especially if the quantity involved was small) as long as it was reasonably certain that the steel should be provided by someone.

The Board of Trade were also prepared to allocate steel from B.T.2 to what could be called 'general service' firms. Two types of manufacturers were involved. First there was the firm wholly or almost wholly engaged on Government contracts. It would be able to obtain authorisations for almost all the steel required for this work without difficulty, but might well find that hundreds or even thousands of M Forms would have to be collected in order to obtain small tonnages of steel required for small vital parts; an example of this would be steel used by a manufacturer of small pumps. Secondly, there was the firm engaged in making small articles and repair parts most of which were supplied in small numbers to many Government departments and contractors; sometimes, however, the firm would have orders for substantial quantities for which it was reasonable to expect it to obtain M Forms.

In the case of the small manufacturers requiring only a few tons of steel a quarter, the Board were prepared to find all their steel from B.T.2. But firms making the same type of equipment on a much larger scale were to get departmental symbols if the aggregate of steel used in the manufacture of these small articles and sold as one order was more than a certain amount. Firms receiving bulk allocations of steel from the Board for general production purposes were to undertake not to collect authorisations on Form M for the steel so received. They were also to make returns to the Board showing the use they had made of the steel received in this way.

The purpose of these Board of Trade arrangements for small orders was to prevent the iron and steel distribution scheme from destroying itself through the nuisance of the small M Form. There was, of course, some danger of duplicate issues of steel when the Board issued steel for purposes that should strictly be covered by departmental symbols. But in any case the error of estimate in the tonnages authorised by any department for particular jobs probably greatly exceeded the theoretical wastage from the double authorisations of small tonnages. It was, however, clear that the issue of steel by the Board for general production purposes could not be extended beyond small orders without imperilling the whole steel distribution scheme.

At the end of 1941 the whole 'general service' principle was rationalised. The iron and steel distribution scheme was modified so that M Forms were no longer required for the purchase of manufactured goods provided that the tonnage of iron and steel combined that was required for each individual order did not exceed one hundredweight. Manufacturers were instead to apply to the Board of Trade or, where appropriate, to the Ministry of Works for bulk authorisations to cover the steel for these small orders. Manufacturers of industrial goods who received these allocations were to undertake that as far as possible they would ensure that the goods they manufactured were supplied for essential purposes only.

These new arrangements could have been criticised as a leakage in the distribution scheme. It seemed, however, that the elimination of the small M Form for manufactured goods should reduce by half the number of M Forms required in the working of the scheme, while the tonnage involved was only about one per cent. of the total.

We have already emphasised that the steel distribution scheme was primarily suited to the needs of the purchasing departments. For them the M Forms were issued with the contracts. The Board of Trade, on the other hand, had to decide how to issue the steel for a wide variety of goods that they themselves did not buy. In time they developed a variety of distribution methods. They were clear from the outset that they could not contemplate issuing M Forms to purchasers of steel goods because of the vast number of authorisations that would be involved. Thus a manufacturer requiring a machine for use in a factory for whose steel requirements the Board were responsible would not be granted a Form M: it was for the manufacturer of the machine to apply for the steel he required for his home civilian trade. Occasionally when an urgent job was being held up the Board would overcome difficulties by granting an M Form to a purchaser. And for a very few types of machinery requiring individually large tonnages of steel the principle was adopted of authorising the steel for making these machines only to the purchasers of the final goods. The effect of this procedure was to subject a class of machinery to licensing without the necessity of making a new Order. The machinery licensing inspector helped by making inquiries into the need for the machines.

Having decided that in general authorisations should go to the manufacturers of machinery the Board had to make up their minds whether to assimilate their procedure as far as possible to that of the supply departments by adopting the 'main contractor' rule. This meant that the Board authorised to manufacturers of steel goods sufficient steel to cover the tonnages that would have to be bought as components. For example, no allocation for electric motors would in theory be made to the electrical industry since this industry would receive enough M Forms to cover its requirements. In practice a certain number of motors would be sold for which M Forms could not be collected; an allocation of steel for oddments like this would therefore be given to the electrical industry.

When it came to actually distributing the steel to manufacturers the Board used bulk allocations wherever possible; that is, manufacturers were given a quarterly allocation of steel. Sometimes these allocations were given in the form of a quarterly ration; this happened usually in the case of smaller goods made for stock. In these cases there was no undertaking to replace the steel used and returns were not normally asked for. A good many of the B.T.2 steel allocations had a replacement basis. The Board of Trade would then specify the kind of orders that they considered essential. Then, at the end of each quarter, manufacturers would furnish returns showing the orders they had executed with B.T.2 steel. If the Board approved these returns, they would replace the steel used. The Board might fix a limit up to which they undertook to replace, impose and special conditions and vary these conditions from period to perioy. It was not possible, of course, to go into great detail about the essentiality of the orders executed. Sometimes a broad rule of thumb could be applied; for example, steel was issued for the manufacture of clocks on the understanding that only factory clocks and alarm clocks were made. Sometimes, too, there were production programmes for the goods concerned. An allocation of cinema equipment for civilian purposes was, for example, agreed with the supply departments. Programming, where it occurred, made the problems of deciding upon the right allocation of steel easy. It was also simple to issue steel for the manufacture of goods covered by machinery licensing. Orders for which licences had been received could be regarded automatically as essential. When the machinery licensing division considered applications for machines needing five tons or more of steel, they consulted their opposite numbers in the Board to make sure that the steel was available. Sometimes, too, machinery licences were endorsed to the effect that no steel was to be granted for manufacture or replacement. Machinery licensing division helped further by securing the agreement of certain manufacturers to effect specific economies in their use of steel.

Sometimes the Board of Trade delegated the responsibility for making home trade bulk allocations to individual manufacturers to the export groups or trade associations of the industries concerned. There were, of course, dangers in this method. The Board had to know what proportion of the industry the group or association covered, and they had to be assured that the allocation would be fairly administered. There were two difficulties in handing over the 'policing' activities; it was necessary to make sure that B.T.2 steel was not used for purposes that should have been symbolised by other departments, and that it was used only for really essential purposes. In some cases these dangers were minimised by the existence of programmes for civilian production. This happened, for example, in the case of bicycles and radios. But on the whole the dangers were sufficient to prevent the practice of granting home trade allocations to export groups from spreading very far in the engineering industries.

The Board of Trade were anxious that as much B.T.2 steel as possible should be issued through bulk allocations to manufacturers. There remained however a fringe of cases where *ad hoc* authorisations had to be made. Sometimes these authorisations were necessary as an interim measure before bulk allocations could be settled. Then there were a certain number of non-recurrent requirements or special requirements which gave the manufacturers claims to steel additional to their rations. To take one example: there was no case in war-time for making general issues of steel to manufacturers of dodg'em cars in fairgrounds. But as 'holidays at home' grew in importance there was a case for giving small specific amounts of steel for the repair of these vehicles.

In addition to issuing steel for the manufacture of civilian goods, the Board of Trade had to issue steel for the repair and maintenance of the plant of manufacturers in both steel-using and non-steel-using industries. Moreover, as we have seen, the Board issued repair and maintenance steel not only for civilian production but also to firms wholly engaged on work for another Government department. The Board in general adhered to their principle that the steel for manufactured goods for repairs must be issued to the producers of those goods and not to the factories requiring them. With a few exceptions, therefore, repair and maintenance authorisations were only given for finished iron and steel. For current repair and maintenance jobs quarterly allocations were appropriate. Large and special repair and maintenance jobs had to be authorised individually. The process of making quarterly allocations for repairs was largely one of trial and error, for there was no knowledge of past usage and few or no means of checking up on whether materials were being used for essential purposes or not. In practice, therefore, arbitrary reductions were made in the steel requirements that firms stated in the knowledge that there would soon be loud complaints if the allocations made were really inadequate. Similarly, by comparing applications of individual firms a clue could be obtained as to whether one firm's application was a wild overstatement or not.

For the purposes of issuing iron and steel for civilian engineering a metals and engineering division was developed within the Industrial Supplies Department of the Board. This division was of course responsible not only for the home trade but also for dealing with the export of iron and steel goods.[1] Inevitably as time went on the functions of the division grew beyond mere authorisation of raw material. In some of the industries—radios or cables or watches or electrical plant or cinema equipment or scientific instruments—the

---

[1] After lend-lease this involved all kinds of difficult policy questions. See Chapters VII, VIII and IX.

Board were responsible for a small corner of a field dominated by the supply departments. This meant that, in order to ensure that the minimum needs covered by the Board were met, the Board joined in the various attempts at inter-departmental production planning. And the Board, too, frequently took the initiative in stimulating the home production of goods that had hitherto been largely imported. Gradually indeed the Board became a real 'production department' for some of the engineering goods; they found themselves dealing with all the complexities of demand and supply.

One example of the Board's activities as a production department was the office machinery industry. In this case the responsibility of the Board did not develop gradually as a result of machinery licensing and raw material allocation. It was deliberately thrust upon the Board. Before the war British production of typewriters had supplied about half the total home requirements.[1] Home production of other types of office machinery—accounting, adding and calculating machines and duplicating and addressing equipment—had been limited to very few types of machines, so that in this field Britain had been almost wholly dependent on imports. When war came the demand for all this equipment rose by leaps and bounds as administrative work and the collection of statistics expanded in the Services, in industry and in Government departments.

By the spring of 1941 demand for office machinery and appliances exceeded supply so greatly that the Government departments concerned felt that one department should be made responsible for production and supply. The Board of Trade agreed to take over this responsibility and in September 1941 a new Directorate of Office Machinery within the Board was ready to begin work.[2] One of the main tasks of the Directorate was to control the use made of machines. At the beginning of 1942 an Order was made prohibiting the supply, use and breaking up of accounting, adding, calculating machinery (including punch card machines), except in accordance with a licence issued by the Board of Trade.[3] This Order, it will be noted, applied not only to those who supplied machines in the course of their business but also to the users of the machines. Licensing therefore covered second-hand and reconditioned machines as well as new ones —a closer control than any other exercised by the Board over acquisition and supply.

At first the Directorate's control over acquisition and supply did

---

[1] *Net domestic consumption* (i.e. home production plus imports less exports)   *Home production*

Standard	Portable	Standard	Portable
57,660	30,852	28,020	18,840

[2] In the interim a sub-committee of the Industrial Capacity Committee of the ministerial Production Executive considered co-ordination of supply and requirements.

[3] S.R. & O. 1942, No. 29.

not cover duplicating and addressing equipment, for these two types of office machinery were covered by machinery licensing. At the end of 1942, however, control was transferred to the Directorate of Office Machinery.[1] For this made it possible to exercise full control over the sales of second-hand machines which would be essential if it should become necessary to requisition machines. Moreover, under the Directorate's licensing system, machines could be traced so that the Directorate could inform firms and Government departments about machines which could be made available.

In May 1943 a sales control was also imposed on typewriters.[2] The supply and acquisition including the hire of all typewriters except second-hand portables was made subject to licence.

Side by side with the controls over the sale and use of office machinery the Directorate had to try to increase supplies. It was possible to stimulate home production of standard typewriters, largely at the expense of the production of portables. Little could be done in war-time, however, about the production of the other types of office machinery since home output was even in normal times so small. It was therefore necessary to ask for imports of these machines under lend-lease. Imports in the later war years were indeed higher than they had been before the war.[3] In the case of typewriters, imports were almost negligible largely because the shortage in the United States was as acute as that in the United Kingdom.

Although the Board's controls over other engineering industries were not as close as that over office machinery the officials of the metals and engineering division developed a pretty close acquaintance with each industry's problems. The standards of different officers in considering applications either for machinery licences or for steel must have varied in their austerity. Owing to the absence of pre-war statistics and to the changes in the boundaries between the steel allocations to B.T.2 and to other Government departments it is impossible to assess with any pretence at accuracy the economies in the use of steel—or of labour and capacity—for B.T.2 purposes. A very rough guess suggested that over the field for which the Board of Trade were throughout responsible the consumption of steel by the end of 1942 was only a third of what it had been in the third quarter of 1940. And even by 1940 there had been a great reduction compared with pre-war. The Board of Trade controls over engineering could thus be counted as a major contribution to the transfer of the engineering industries to war purposes.

---

[1] S.R. & O. 1942, No. 2489.
[2] S.R. & O. 1943, No. 676.
[3] Imports of office machinery into the United Kingdom.

	Tons	£
1938	540	847,000
1943	351	750,000
1944	726	1,500,000

CHAPTER XXI

PRICE CONTROL:
THE EVOLUTION OF POLICY

(i)

The Stabilisation Policy

THE last few chapters of this book have dealt with the activities of the Board of Trade as a production department. The twin aims of these activities were, first, to release resources for the war effort and, secondly, to make sure that sufficient goods were produced to meet the essential needs of the home market. As we have seen, the Board concerned themselves not only with the quantities but also with the types of goods manufactured. To some extent the two went together; the more economical production was, the greater the quantity of goods that could be made with a given amount of labour and raw materials. But there was another reason why the Board took so much interest in the kind of articles to be made. It was important that supplies to the home market should be reasonably priced. Effective price control, however, was impossible unless the goods concerned were clearly specified. Thus one of the motives for closer production control was stricter price control. Effective price control needed further support. It could not function successfully unless demands were curbed by taxation and by forms of consumer rationing.

In 1941 the time was propitious for a new price control measure. Taxation was increased, and although rationing seemed impracticable for consumer goods as a whole, it was introduced for clothing, the most important item. And in 1941 the Board of Trade were ready to control production.

The problem of tightening control over the prices of non-food consumer goods became urgent when the stabilisation policy was introduced. The Chancellor of the Exchequer, in his budget speech of April 1941, announced that the Government intended to stabilise the cost-of-living index number at the existing level of twenty-five to thirty per cent. above that of 1939.[1] This policy was pursued throughout the rest of the war.[2]

---

[1] H. of C. Deb., Vol. 370, Col. 1323.

[2] In his budget speech of April 1944 the Chancellor of the Exchequer stated that the policy would be relaxed to the extent of permitting a rise in this index number to 30 to 35 per cent. above the pre-war level. (H. of C. Deb., Vol. 399, Col. 663.)

The stabilisation policy was based on the official Ministry of Labour cost-of-living index; as we have emphasised before, this index, begun in 1914, had admittedly become obsolete in what it included, what it failed to include and in the weighting of its component elements. Working-class budget investigations undertaken in 1937–38 showed clearly these defects. For example, some articles in which the Board of Trade were particularly interested—women's made-up outerwear, men's and boys' shirts, rayon goods, furniture and carpets were not included in the index. Nor were the charges for such services as boot and shoe repairing and laundrying included. As the war went on, changes in the flow of purchasing power made the index number still more unreal. Reconstruction of the index and also the introduction of a new, supplementary index—an 'iron ration' index number— were considered. But the close relationship between changes in the index number and changes in the wage rates of many occupations made the problem very delicate. Nothing was done therefore until after the war.

It was clear that the Board of Trade could not confine their price-controlling activities to the items in the cost-of-living index. Indeed a policy of control that related simply to the official index would have tended to divert manufacture and supply to the more profitable uncontrolled items. Thus the Board thought rather in terms of the 'real' cost of living. As we have seen, the Prices of Goods Act was applied to many commodities that were not included in the official index and its range was extended during the war to items that would not be classed as necessities—things such as toys, motor bicycles and handbags. As far as the closer forms of price control were concerned, the dividing line between those commodities that could and those that could not be covered was drawn on the basis of practical decisions about the degree of standardisation that it was feasible to impose. The problem was governed not by the official index but by administrative resources and techniques.

Nevertheless, while this was true of the Board's price control measures over the war as a whole, the announcement of the stabilisation programme meant that for the moment attention had to be focused on the cost-of-living index. A long-term measure for controlling the prices of non-food consumer goods was already being drafted but this would have to be laid before Parliament. Even when it became law, some time would elapse before it had much effect, for it could not operate without a whole programme of production and supply controls. Meanwhile, however, something had to be done to arrest the steep rise in clothing prices. Hitherto the rise in the cost-of-living index had been limited by the food subsidies which had been introduced originally as an *ad hoc* measure rather than as part of a coherent plan for price stability. The Treasury pointed out to the

Board of Trade that at the beginning of 1941 clothing prices in the index had risen by sixty per cent. compared with September 1939, while the index as a whole had risen only by twenty-six per cent. and the food component by less than twenty-five per cent. Food prices could not be expected to bear the whole brunt of the stabilisation policy. Some short-term policy for clothing prices was necessary.

By now the problem of introducing some such policy was aggravated by shortages due to the Limitation of Supplies Orders. The shortages were acute for the cheaper ranges of children's and adults' clothing. For manufacturers and distributors had concentrated their limited trade on the more expensive goods. Only rationing combined with the production of specified, effectively price-controlled articles could really cure these difficulties. But the Board of Trade did something to alleviate the problem in July 1941 with an essential clothing programme which freed from quota control children's garments, the cheaper woollen cloths and the cheaper kinds of adult clothing. The programme was expanded in different ways; for example, cloth for working-class clothing might be supplied without the surrender of coupons by makers-up registered for purchase tax. And the scheme was extended from the end of August until the end of October 1941. It was in operation for too short a time to have much effect on production, but it probably did something to ease supplies by releasing stocks.

Meanwhile, the Treasury had suggested that the Board of Trade should at once issue a 'standstill' Order which would peg to the current level the prices of items of clothing in the cost-of-living index. There were, however, fairly obvious objections to this proposal. An Order of this sort would almost inevitably be inequitable as between different businesses. Widely applied, moreover, without any reinforcing production or supply controls it would probably aggravate such maldistribution as then existed in the field of clothing. The main objection of the Board of Trade, however, was the difficulty of enforcing a standstill on prices. Evasion of such an Order, the Board held, would be widespread; a view for which there was undoubtedly much to be said at a time when their existing arrangements for policing measures of price control were very inadequate. Nevertheless, in view of the urgency of the matter—the index number was only four points below the 'stabilisation level'—the President of the Board of Trade expressed his willingness to introduce a standstill Order on a limited range of materials and articles of clothing, defined by reference to a wholesale price ceiling. He would do this, however, only in return for a lifting of purchase tax from the relevant items. But Treasury and Customs and Excise officials were agreed on the impracticability of removing purchase tax from a selected range of articles, and they were, therefore, not prepared to make the concession. In spite of this conflict of opinion, the drafting of a standstill Order went ahead, until at the end of May 1941 ministers became convinced that the Order would on balance be harmful and that the main objects of price stability could be better achieved in other ways. They were impressed by the danger that evasion of the Order might bring the whole system of price control into disrepute, and they accepted the argument of the President of the Board of Trade that the consumer rationing Order, which would shortly be announced, would restrain demand, and thus prices, sufficiently until long-term measures could be put into operation.

(ii)

The Goods and Services (Price Control) Act, 1941[1]

Long-term measures of price control were already being devised. In a memorandum to ministers of February 1941 the President of the Board of Trade had stated that the great and growing excess of demand over supply would lead to substantial rises in prices which the machinery of the Prices of Goods Act would be unable to check. The Board of Trade should, therefore, be empowered to fix maximum prices and maximum margins. Other measures, it was plain, would also be necessary. Plans for commodity specification would have to be introduced. Agreement had also to be reached on the stabilisation of raw material prices; this was fundamental to the carrying out of a programme for the production of specified, price-controlled articles of clothing and footwear.

The prices measure itself was introduced in the House of Commons on 19th June 1941 by the President of the Board of Trade.[2] The President made it plain that no formal piece of legislation could by itself hold down prices, and that such legislation must be firmly based on measures to mop up excess purchasing power through taxation and savings. The explanation he offered for the rises of prices which had occurred—reduced supplies, increased purchasing power, war-time increases of freight and insurance—enforced this point. A new Act was, however, necessary because the Prices of Goods Act had certain obvious defects and omissions, and was inadequate to meet the current situation.

The most important features of the new Bill were the powers taken to fix maximum prices, maximum margins and maximum charges

---

[1] 4 & 5 Geo. 6, ch. 31.
[2] H. of C. Deb., Vol. 372, Cols. 851 *et seq.*

for services.[1] These powers provided entirely new instruments of price control. The maximum price provisions made it possible (*a*) to fix maximum prices for different classes of business, e.g. manufacturers, wholesalers and retailers, (*b*) to require retailers to bring to the notice of their customers the prices fixed for the goods which they sold, (*c*) to arrange for a mark to be applied indicating that the goods which bore it were subject to maximum price regulation and were being sold at the correct price. More important, however, than any formal provision was the fact that the Bill left completely open the question of the basic principles to be adopted in laying down these maximum prices. The price-fixing authorities were not required to take into consideration costs, profits, or current prices in formulating their policy. The techniques and procedures adopted under the Prices of Goods Act were, however, recognised to the extent that 'permitted prices' became maximum prices under the new Bill.

For some commodities, particularly those which could not be fairly closely specified, maximum prices would be inappropriate, and the Act provided that Orders made under it might 'direct that the price shall be computed in such manner and by reference to such matters as may be provided by the Order'. This made it possible to control manufacturers' prices by reference to their costs together with a pre-scribed margin of profit, and distributors' prices by gross overall margins.

The Bill also dealt with two special problems which it was judged from experience under the earlier Act would be sources of trouble to the price-fixing authorities, namely the problem of middlemen and intermediaries, and the problem of second-hand goods.

The problem of the superfluous middleman and of excessive charges levied by intermediaries is of course one that extends far beyond the scope of formal price legislation. In large part the solution lies in effective control over those inflationary movements of prices which enable profits to be reaped simply by commodity buying and selling. Price legislation, however, if effectively enforced can help towards limiting the profits on such transactions. The problem had been aggravated by the introduction of quota control under the Limitation of Supplies Orders. A class of 'quota brokers' had emerged who were prepared, for a commission, to arrange for the transfer of unused quota from one trader to another. The dubiety of some of these transactions lent additional reason to the argument for bringing this type of intermediary under control. The problem was, however, bound to become much less important as control by coupon took the place of control by quota for a wide range of commodities.

The Act dealt with the matter by empowering the making of an

---

[1] The services, it should be noted, were services performed 'in relation to goods'.

Order prohibiting, except under licence, the resale of goods at higher prices otherwise than through the normal channel, manufacturer-wholesaler-retailer.[1] Furthermore, the Board of Trade might by regulation prohibit the giving or taking of commissions for procuring the transference of unexhausted quotas. Margin control would also reinforce these provisions, since the maximum margins prescribed would cover a stage of the distributive process, thus necessitating the sharing of a margin between two or more wholesalers.

Satisfactory control of the prices of second-hand goods proved difficult to achieve, and it might indeed be argued that the balance of advantage lay in leaving such prices uncontrolled. No production problem was involved, whilst high prices would have the effect of bringing on to the market stocks of these goods which would help to ease shortages. In any case the argument in favour of restricting the rise in second-hand prices really only became effective later in the war, when curtailment or closing down of new production diverted demand to the second-hand market.

In devising measures of control for second-hand goods it was clear that there would be great difficulties in enforcing observance of maximum prices. The Act accordingly provided that, if the Board of Trade were satisfied that excessive prices were being charged for any class of second-hand goods, they might make an Order requiring persons selling such goods to be registered; and the Board might under such an Order refuse to register a trader or cancel his registration if he appeared to have been charging excessive prices for the goods in question or to have been a party to any practice which appeared to raise the prices of such goods unduly, subject to an appeal to a referee to be appointed by the Lord Chancellor.

Control by registration of second-hand dealers would have raised serious administrative problems and was not attempted. As will be seen later, effort was made, though with doubtful success, to control second-hand prices by reference to maximum prices based on first-hand prices of comparable goods. Control in this sphere was also applied through the licensing of auctioneers and auctions.

The Board of Trade had incorporated in the new Bill two amendments to the Price of Goods Act which might have acquired significance but for the new techniques of price control which were put into operation in the latter half of the war. In the first place it was decided that the power taken to fix basic prices should be revised. In the original Act the basic price was the price ruling on 21st August 1939, but there were provisions for varying the date of the basic price and for fixing basic prices for goods which had come into existence since that date. It had, however, been found impracticable to make

---

[1] i.e. sales from wholesaler to wholesaler, retailer to wholesaler, or retailer to retailer were prohibited.

any effective use of these provisions, and the Board of Trade were now empowered to fix by Order basic prices for price-regulated goods and also to determine the date of the basic price which should be taken for the purpose of calculating the increase permitted under section four of the original Act.

This amendment was in fact only used on one occasion, in December 1941 to fix basic prices for imported vacuum flasks.[1] There had been numerous complaints of the prices charged for these flasks, and it appeared that certain importers were taking excessive margins and reaping high profits on the trade. It had been difficult to prove the basic price under the provisions of the Prices of Goods Act, and the Order of December 1941 accordingly fixed basic prices, as of 21st August 1939, for importers, wholesalers and retailers of vacuum flasks of different sizes.

The second amendment to the Prices of Goods Act made provision for varying the application of the first schedule to the Prices of Goods Act by omitting or altering any of the items included in it, as well as by adding to them. Thus an Order might be made omitting or varying any of the items of cost which a manufacturer or trader had hitherto been allowed to take into account in calculating his 'permitted' increase of price above the basic price.

At the time when the new Bill was under consideration it seemed likely that the main purpose of this provision would be to withdraw from businesses the permission to take into account diminished turnover in fixing their prices. It was stated in the House of Commons during the debate on the Bill that traders were alarmed that this step might be taken, notwithstanding the fact that diminished turnover was due to restrictions and supply limitations outside their control. The move which the traders feared was not made, and in any case the spreading of overhead costs over a reduced volume of output or sales raised problems which went far beyond the range of any price legislation. In manufacture the Government had already inaugurated its policy of concentrating restricted output into a number of nucleus firms in each industry. So far as distribution was concerned the Committee on Retail Trade had already been appointed to investigate the matter.[2]

In general these two amendments to the Prices of Goods Act lost most of the importance they might have had through the supersession of that Act as an effective instrument of price control. The Central Price Regulation Committee in dealing with applications for the sanctioning of 'permitted prices'[3] had already been working out, independently of the first schedule to the Prices of Goods Act, a

---

[1] S.R. & O. 1941, No. 1964.
[2] See Chapter XII, p. 258.
[3] See p. 81.

schedule of approved costs for the benefit of applicants. This schedule was divided into four parts: (i) materials, (ii) labour, (iii) factory overheads, (iv) general overheads, and special treatment was accorded to, for example, directors' or proprietors' remuneration and advertising expenses. When the new system of price control came into operation the Central Committee's schedule, with only minor alterations, was incorporated in the prices Orders under the heading of 'matters to be regarded in ascertaining makers-up' or 'manufacturers' cost of production and sale'. The only use which appears to have been made of the second amendment was to exclude from the schedule to the original Prices Act premiums payable under the War Damage Act 1941 which were to be treated as payments of a capital nature.[1]

Of the utmost importance in securing observance of the new regulations were the provisions made by the Goods and Services (Price Control) Bill for enforcement. The Prices of Goods Act had depended for its enforcement mainly, it will be remembered, upon complaints about high prices, an arrangement which was both unsatisfactory and inadequate. The new Act now provided for the appointment of inspectors who would assist the Local Price Regulation Committees in seeing that the prices Orders were understood and observed. It was agreed in the summer of 1941 that there should be two grades of inspectors, the first grade being qualified accountants capable of dealing with the more complicated cases, and the second grade being persons of no professional qualifications who could investigate the more simple cases of infringement of the price regulations.[2] These inspectors, who were attached to the Local Price Committees, helped not only in detecting evasions and contraventions of the price regulations but also in the enforcement of the Location of Retail Businesses Order. Furthermore, they gave advice and assistance to the trader who was in genuine difficulty as to how he should price his goods.

Experience had taught another lesson about enforcement—that it was difficult, if not impracticable, unless proper records were kept of transactions in price-controlled commodities. The new Act accordingly made provision for the furnishing of invoices and the keeping of books of account. It provided that where there were dealings in price-controlled goods an Order might be made requiring invoices to be furnished by sellers to buyers. Such an Order might specify the particulars which the invoices should show and might require the buyer to demand an invoice, and, in the event of not receiving an invoice, to notify the appropriate authority. The Act also provided that 'persons selling price-controlled goods or second-hand goods or offer-

---

[1] S.R. & O. 1941, No. 1535.

[2] The numbers of inspectors were at first: Grade I, 12; Grade II, 20. These numbers were raised in 1942 to Grade I, 27; Grade II, 50.

ing price-controlled services' might be required to keep books and accounts, and that these books and accounts might be in a prescribed form and show particulars required in any Order made or notice issued. Under the former provision an invoices Order was made in September 1941[1] requiring the seller of price-controlled goods to furnish an invoice to the buyer within seven days of delivery, the particulars to be shown on the invoice being specified in the Order. Traders who did not receive invoices or invoices containing the specified particulars were required to register a demand for them with the seller of the goods and also to notify the secretary of the Local Price Committee that an invoice had not been furnished in accordance with the provisions of the Order. In the case of a sale of utility cloth or utility apparel the invoice had also to state that the goods were utility and to contain the appropriate specification numbers.

Finally, note should be made of the power taken in the Act to fix different maximum prices and charges for different classes of business. Broadly, this may be taken as referring to manufacturers, wholesalers and retailers. However, Section 17 of the Act provided that the definition of a class of business might be 'framed by reference to any circumstances whatsoever'. One such set of circumstances that it might be convenient to use for framing a definition was clearly that of geographical location. Thus when maximum laundry charges were fixed arrangements were made for fixing different maxima, in the form of percentage increases over pre-war charges, for the different regions of Great Britain. Later again (in 1943), in controlling the prices of woollen and worsted textiles provision was made for differences in overheads and profit margins for the different regions in which these textiles were manufactured.

Other distinguishing criteria might be employed apart from or in addition to those associated with geographical location. Thus in fixing wholesalers' margins it was found both practicable and desirable to distinguish between those who possessed a regular selling organisation and storage premises, and the so-called 'brass-plate wholesalers' who merely arranged for the disposal of goods from manufacturer to retailer. In the case of manufacturers the provision was probably less frequently used, but it proved useful in certain cases to fix different maximum prices for different types of businesses, for example different groups of pottery manufacturers. The problem of the retailers' margins will be fully discussed later, but it may be said here that no provision was made for different maximum margins in spite of the very wide range of retailing conditions and the enormous differences in types of retail unit. Distinctions would presumably have been difficult to draw and in any case impracticable to ad-

---

[1] S.R. & O. 1941, No. 1388.

minister. The proposal for a 'house charge' for high-grade retailers of the Bond Street type was considered but never put into practice.

The possibility of fixing different maximum prices touches on one of the more difficult problems of price control. In any given industry, as defined for the purpose either of a statistical census or of administrative control, there is usually a wide range of costs, a considerable variety of output and the use of different methods of production, including different types of labour. To fix uniform prices for the products of such an industry would appear at first sight to be a difficult task in itself and, if achieved, to be likely to create a formidable group of economic problems for the administrator. Price-fixing in such cases does indeed raise the fundamental issue whether in war-time the high-cost producer or the producer of the finer qualities of commodities can be permitted by the community to acquire and make use of any part of its economic resources. Clearly there is no simple answer to this question. The requirements of the export trade may have to be taken into account, while the resources employed in high-grade production may be immobile and incapable of being adapted or transferred to meeting war requirements. Again, for one reason or another, the efficient low-cost producers may not be able to absorb the production of high-cost firms which have been closed down, and the marginal output of the latter may be lost at a time when any easing of shortages is to be welcomed.

The techniques mentioned above sometimes provided a partial solution. Manufacturers might for the purposes of price control be arranged in groups based on differences in cost or in quality of products. More generally, with the development of utility schemes, the producer whose type of product or methods of production made it impracticable for him to come within the scope of these schemes carried on with such labour and raw materials as were available subject only to the imperfect price control of a standstill Order or a cost-plus regulation. However, the fundamental problem presented by the range of costs persisted. Ceiling prices had to be fixed at a level which would call forth the required volume of production. But given the war-time assumption that profits as well as prices must be limited, the ceiling price by itself appeared an inadequate instrument of control. Hence the ceiling price provisions of the prices Orders were normally reinforced by a supplementary cost-plus control intended to limit the prices and profits of the low-cost producers. Schemes were also put forward with the same purpose for levies on low-cost producers and the pooling of profits.[1]

These problems were not ventilated when the Goods and Services

---

[1] In the control of tanners' margins a levy and equalisation fund were adopted; in dealing with rayon prices it was decided finally that it would be impracticable to have a profit pooling arrangement for the low- and high-cost producers in the industry.

(Price Control) Bill was before Parliament. The Bill was accepted as a necessary measure and was passed with little, if any, opposition. It may have been felt that adequate safeguards existed to prevent any arbitrary or ill-considered use of the new price-fixing powers. Any Order made under the Act (except an Order amending the first schedule of the Prices of Goods Act, which would require an affirmative resolution in both Houses) would be subject to the negative resolution procedure in Parliament—that is, the Order must be laid as soon as possible before Parliament, and might be annulled by a resolution of either House. In contrast to this, it may be noted that neither Orders made under the Prices of Goods Act nor price-fixing Orders made by the Ministry of Food or the Ministry of Supply needed to be placed before Parliament. Another safeguard was the provision that no Orders might be made by the Board of Trade except after consultation with the Central Price Regulation Committee. The Central Price Regulation Committee was a semi-independent body, and, though not formally representative of special interests, included members drawn from different elements in the community, manufacturers, traders, consumers. By its judicious handling of the problems arising under the Prices of Goods Act it had gained the confidence and co-operation of the business community. It might, therefore, be reasonably expected that due weight would be given to business considerations in the formulation and the application of any new price measures.

(iii)

The Formation of Utility Prices

The new price control legislation was first applied where it was most needed—to clothing. In September 1941 the Board of Trade introduced the utility clothing scheme which rested on the two principles of minimum specifications and maximum prices. Enforcement was secured by the device of a special mark which was to be fixed to utility cloth and knitted apparel.

A major scheme of this sort required, of course, many months of testing and improvement. As we have already seen, all kinds of changes were soon made.[1] For example, at the outset specifications were much too loose (for cloth they were merely a matter of weight and price) and as time went on they had to be tightened as much as possible. Then, directions to manufacturers replaced the earlier system of encouraging production by means of quota inducements.

---

[1] See Chapter XVII.

Administrative arrangements also changed, and, as we shall see later, there was a more precise allocation of function between the Board of Trade and the Central Price Regulation Committee.

For some time the structure of price control was incomplete. In the first months of the utility scheme weavers' margins for cotton textiles had not been fixed[1] and there was no sort of control over merchant converters' margins. Finishing charges depended on agreements between the Cotton Board and the respective trade associations that trade price lists, which showed considerable increases over pre-war, would not be changed without consultation with the Cotton Board and the Board of Trade. There had, of course, been no time to check these prices by detailed costings of the firms in the finishing trades. In rayon very little had been done towards securing control of either yarn or cloth prices.

These gaps did not prevent the Board of Trade from applying the new price control fairly swiftly. By the end of 1941 seven utility price Orders had been made fixing maximum prices and margins for the following items: men's, youths', and boys' outer clothing; men's and boys' shirts and pyjamas; women's underwear; women's and maids' outer clothing; women's seamless hose; overalls; utility cloths; utility hosiery. The basis for fixing these prices lay in the specifications for finished cotton, wool and rayon cloths and for knitted apparel contained in the Cloth and Apparel Order of the autumn of 1941.[2] The specifications themselves included a price element, so that the maximum price Orders which were made at this time referred to the garments made from these cloths or to the prices which distributors might charge for the utility cloth or knitted apparel which they sold.

In fixing manufacturers' prices for utility goods the Central Price Committee adopted the basic principle of a cost-plus limitation together with an overriding maximum price. Thus, the maximum price which the manufacturer of utility clothing might charge was defined as his costs of production and sale together with a prescribed profit margin, subject, however, to the requirement that in no case might his price exceed the ceiling price laid down for the relevant item of clothing. The costs which might be taken into account were enumerated and grouped under four main headings: materials, labour, factory overheads, general overheads. Among general overheads, it may be noted, advertising expenses were included but were limited to 'such expenses only as will ensure adequate distribution of products in the home market'.

---

[1] Cash margins covering most cloths were fixed in April 1942, being estimated to give a gross yield (including depreciation) of £9 10s. per 40-inch loom. The effect of these margins on weavers' profits was subsequently investigated by Cotton Board and Ministry of Supply accountants and in view of the high profits apparently being obtained revisions were made in 1944.

[2] S.R. & O. 1941, Nos. 1281, 1374 and 1614.

The explanation of this dual system of control lay in the fact that the ceiling prices recommended by the Central Price Committee, after consultation with representatives of the trades concerned, were set at a level which, it was thought, would enable the bulk of the trade to participate in a utility scheme. Thus, in effect, only the very high-cost producers would be excluded. At the same time the Committee felt that the consumer should enjoy the advantages of low-cost production and therefore proposed that the maximum price should be supplemented by a cost-plus form of control. They were undoubtedly over-sanguine in expecting that competition would restrain the rise of costs and possibly did not appreciate fully the difficulty of enforcing the observance of a cost-plus control over a large number of manufacturers.

The maximum percentage margins on cost for manufacturers or makers-up varied as follows: 4 per cent. (men's and boys' outer clothing, women's underwear, overalls), 5 per cent. (women's seamless hose), 7 per cent. (women's and maids' outer clothing), $7\frac{1}{2}$ per cent. (hosiery). At this stage it can hardly be said that the Central Price Committee had any simple formula in mind in putting forward its recommendations. Later in the war it was agreed that the net profit margins prescribed should yield to the representative firm 10 to 12 per cent. on capital employed. But in the first utility price arrangements, while some attention was paid to the rate of return on invested capital, other considerations played a part. Thus the Central Price Committee felt bound to have some regard to the principle enshrined in the Prices of Goods Act that firms should earn the same net profit per article as they were earning in August 1939. Even the question of jobbing losses on fashion goods which might be marked down at the end of the season was taken into account in the fixing of the margin on women's and maids' outerwear at 7 per cent., rather than 5 per cent. Some allowance has to be made for the lack of time for full consideration of these matters or for obtaining detailed costings from all the trades concerned. The price Orders had to be published as soon as possible, in order that manufacturers should know what prices they would have to work to in undertaking the production of utility clothing. The Central Price Committee was less concerned with the appropriate rates of net profit margin than with the need for ensuring as soon as possible an adequate flow of reasonably priced utility goods on to the market. Nor perhaps did time permit full consideration of such alternative methods of control as the fixing of *gross* profit margins on prime costs as opposed to net margins.[1]

---

[1] The Central Committee were opposed to gross margins for manufacturers on the grounds (a) that a clear distinction could not be drawn between overheads and prime costs, and (b) that enormous variations in overheads existed as between one manufacturer and another.

In their recommendations about wholesale and retail utility prices the Central Committee considered the combination of maximum prices and maximum gross margins to be the most appropriate arrangement. Inevitably they were influenced by the distributors' practice of employing a conventional 'mark-up' of so much per cent. on the cost of goods in order to arrive at selling price.[1] After discussions with the Wholesale Textile Association in the case of wholesalers and the Retail Distributors' Association and Drapers' Chamber of Trade in the case of retailers, it was agreed that the wholesale margin should be 20 per cent. on manufacturer's or maker-up's selling price, the retail margin $33\frac{1}{3}$ per cent. on wholesaler's selling price including purchase tax. These margins were also employed in calculating the overriding maximum prices for wholesaler and retailer.

These arrangements for wholesale and retail prices raised two points of criticism. First, there was the well recognised objection to allowing the retailer to take a profit on the purchase tax. To this the Central Price Committee replied that if the margin had been calculated on an ex-tax basis it would have had to be fixed at a higher rate in order to correspond with the normal retail margin of $33\frac{1}{3}$ per cent. on costs (25 per cent. on returns), and that it would have worked out at 39·86 per cent., an awkward figure for the smaller shopkeeper to handle. Secondly, uniform margins on all sorts of utility goods and for all types of distributors appeared a somewhat crude method of price-fixing. Little information was, however, available about retailers' operating expenses and net profit margins, either on different commodities or in different types of shop, and the prescribed margins in any case could have represented little more than the conventional margins which had been taken in the past on standard lines. In 1942 utility margins were differentiated broadly according to class of goods, but anything like a scientific fixing of margins could not be achieved until more adequate statistical information had been collected.

A further stage in the control of distributors' prices and margins was reached in a Consolidating Order of January 1942. Wholesalers were now divided into two classes. Those who conducted a regular selling organisation for supplying the retail trade and carried in warehouses or other storage premises stocks of goods substantial in relation to their turnover were allowed the full margin of 20 per cent. on cost ($16\frac{2}{3}$ per cent. on returns). For the rest, the so-called 'brassplate' wholesalers, the maximum margin was 5 per cent. on cost. At the same time it was provided that the margins must be calculated on the price paid to the manufacturer by the first pur-

---

[1] The retailer's 'mark-up' was normally calculated as a percentage on turnover.

chaser. This provision was clearly intended to reinforce the limitation imposed on transactions between intermediaries, since it required two or more wholesalers to share the margin. (The retailers' margin was similarly restricted to 33⅓ per cent. on the price paid to the wholesaler by the first purchaser.)

Provision was also made in the Consolidating Order for certain types of composite business, that is, those in which manufacturing functions were combined with wholesaling and/or retailing functions. The question at issue was that of the 'double margin', namely whether the manufacturer might take, in addition to his own margin, the margin prescribed for wholesaler or retailer.[1] The basic principle adopted in dealing with this matter was that a single margin only might be taken, unless certain fairly stringent conditions were satisfied. Thus the manufacturer who wished to take the wholesale or retail margin as well as the manufacturer's margin must have had in the last accounting year before the war a separate wholesale or retail branch with separate accounts and records. Moreover, if he had a wholesale branch which he wished to treat as separate, that branch must have a selling organisation for supplying the retail trade and a warehouse or other storage premises for carrying stocks substantial in relation to the turnover of the branch. Later, similar provisions were enacted for distributing firms which wished to claim both the wholesale and the retail margins. These regulations clearly did not cover businesses which, though supplying their own retail branches, had in effect no separate wholesaling organisation, and in 1943 the clothing multiples agitated for and secured some revision of the provisions about double margins.

This survey of the structure of control that was beginning to be built up in 1941–42 on the foundations of the Goods and Services (Price Control) Act may be completed by reference to two special problems in the sphere of distribution.

First, in order to ensure equity as between different types of business, price regulations had to take account of pre-war conventions and practices in the distributive trades. For example, manufacturers and wholesalers tended, in a period of scarcity, to reduce or abolish discounts that had customarily been given for prompt payment. This led to the provision of a compulsory minimum discount at the rate of 2½ per cent. for payment within a specified period of time, usually one month.[2] This was by no means a completely satisfactory solution; the minimum could easily become a maximum, and even in spite of the provision there appears to have been a tendency for sellers to take advantage of shortages to the disadvantage of their customers. Simi-

---

[1] There was never any question of the manufacturer being allowed three margins when he was in addition both wholesaler and retailer.

[2] For footwear there were compulsory discounts of 5 and 6¼ per cent.

larly, delivery charges had to be taken into account; price Orders were therefore framed so as to include delivery charges in the prescribed maximum prices. Provision was made for a higher wholesale margin on sales to Northern Ireland in those cases such as pottery and hollow-ware where it was the practice for the wholesaler to meet carriage charges both from the manufacturer and to the retailer.

No comprehensive solution was found for the problems of distributive trade practices. Towards the end of the war, with a view to possible legislative action, associations in the textile and clothing trades were circularised in an attempt to find out what pre-war practices had been with regard to cash and settlement discounts and to carriage and packing charges, and what changes in these practices had taken place since the outbreak of war.

The second special distributive problem was that of sales between intermediaries. It will be remembered that this had received attention in the framing of the Goods and Services (Price Control) Act. While the limitation of supplies quotas were in operation it was undoubtedly true that the intervention of an unnecessary number of middlemen between producer and consumer had tended to raise prices unduly. It was notorious that abuses had arisen in the disposal of quotas and in the emergence of quota brokers, which probably led to unnecessary profits and commissions being charged on to the prices of goods. It is, however, less clear that in the later phases of the war the problem was of such dimensions as to warrant the application of special measures which were admittedly difficult to administer and enforce.

In January 1942 a Restriction of Re-sale Order[1] was made with the intention of dealing with the general problem. Briefly the purpose of the Order was to restrict the number of transactions in price-controlled goods, except under licence from the Board of Trade, to one at the wholesale stage and one at the retail stage. It was provided, however, that proof that a transaction was in accordance with pre-war and still prevailing trade usage should be a good defence against a charge of infringement of the Order.

This apparently simple Order turned out to be none too easy to administer. Difficulties arose principally in determining trade usage, in which clearly there was considerable scope for differences of opinion. Moreover, where trade usage had been established there was nothing to prevent speculators from taking advantage of it nor, in such a case, did the Order limit the number of intermediaries through whose hands goods might pass on their way from manufacturer to final consumer.

A second Order, of May 1942, did something to overcome these

---

[1] S.R. & O. 1942, No. 64.

difficulties. It abandoned the criterion of pre-war trade usage, and instead provided that the prohibition on re-sale should not apply to a trader who could show that he had been engaged continually since six months before the war in trading otherwise than in accordance with the requirements of the Order in the class of goods concerned. At the same time, however, the Order provided that the trader should not only satisfy the requirement of continuous dealing since before the war, but must also show that he had reasonable cause to believe that the person from whom he bought such goods had himself bought those goods from the manufacturer or importer thereof. In other words, there must not be more than *two* intervening wholesalers between manufacturer and retailer.

After this second Order had been brought into operation there was good ground for supposing that adequate provision had been made for the genuine need for secondary wholesaling, as, for example, in the remoter country districts. Goods intended for export, otherwise than as packing materials or containers, were ruled to be outside the scope of the Order. Yet a good deal of licensing was still needed, sometimes owing to war-time policies. For example, licences were needed for transactions in goods manufactured by nucleus firms under concentration schemes and sold by closed firms. Again, dealers re-selling second-hand goods had to be licensed.

In addition to the need to restrain price-boosting speculative activities it might have been held that the Order provided an instrument of major policy for the elimination of traders who were surplus to the minimum number needed to distribute greatly reduced supplies of commodities. It was, however, agreed by the Board of Trade that the Order must be regarded simply as a measure of price control and that it would be improper to use it either in conjunction with other measures to release labour and storage space or to force out of business unnecessary wholesalers. There can be no doubt that the problem of securing an organised release of resources from the distributive trades badly needed tackling, but it is clear that the rational and systematic application for this purpose of the Restriction of Resale Order would have presupposed the working out of an orderly scheme of concentration for these trades. That major policy did not exist.

We may perhaps conclude this chapter by referring to a piece of administrative tidying-up which probably helped to make the price control machine run more smoothly. In the first two years of price control there had been some confusion about the responsibilities respectively of the Board of Trade and the Central Price Regulation Committee. This confusion was largely cleared up by the President of the Board of Trade in March 1942 when he suggested that the Board should be primarily responsible for the specification and price-fixing of utility goods, the Committee having the primary responsibility for the fixing of the prices of non-utility goods and services.[1] At the same time a committee representative of the Board and the Central Price Regulation Committee was set up under the chairmanship of the Parliamentary Secretary to the Board of Trade, which, throughout the remainder of the war, handled continuously and effectively the main problems of price control.

---

[1] Manufacturers' utility prices were henceforward fixed (along with the specifications) under Defence Regulation 55 and not under the provisions of the price control Acts.

CHAPTER XXII

PRICE CONTROL: THE SYSTEM
IN OPERATION 1942–45

(i)

Stabilisation Achieved

IT will be remembered that the stabilisation policy as far as the prices of non-food consumer goods were concerned rested on two fundamental assumptions. First, prices of these goods could only be controlled given reasonable stability in the prices of labour and raw materials. Secondly, practical schemes had to be devised for the production to specification of such things as clothing, footwear and furniture; in other words, utility programmes were essential to the policy of price control.

When these programmes had been introduced there had been an understanding between the departments concerned that the prices of the major materials used in the manufacture of utility goods would be prevented from rising. However, this understanding could be interpreted in such a way as to allow rises in raw material prices which would affect non-utility goods and exports, provided that some measure could be devised which would prevent the higher prices from being passed on to the prices of utility goods. It was implied that the Government would be prepared, if necessary, to introduce an element of subsidy either at the raw material stage or at an early stage in the manufacturing process.

Raw material prices had risen considerably at the outbreak of the war, and there were further rises until the stabilisation policy was in operation. Thereafter, the prices of major clothing materials were on the whole effectively kept in control; this is clear from the following table:

Index Numbers of Raw Material and Rayon Yarn Prices

TABLE 38   Dec. 1938 = 100

	Dec. 1939	Dec. 1940	Dec. 1941	Dec. 1942	Dec. 1943	Dec. 1944	Dec. 1945
Raw Cotton	144·9	162·7	167·8	159·8	143·7	215·8	215·8
Raw Wool	125·3	173·5	173·5	173·5	173·5	173·5	168·4
Artificial Silk Yarns	110·2	134·0	159·9	159·9	159·9	159·9	156·9

Source: Board of Trade

In the latter part of the war it was felt that raw material prices were below what might be expected to be the economic level in the post-war period. In 1943, therefore, the Treasury initiated discussions on prices in this period and indicated their desire to move away from the 'artificial' war-time price level. Even in war there was a clear case against subsidising materials which went into exports, for which the maximum return ought to be obtained, particularly since the conditions were those of a sellers' market. And in the field of cotton textiles, as not only raw cotton prices but also yarn and cloth prices were fixed, the profits of a sellers' market went mainly into the pockets of the merchants; here, clearly, there was no justification for specially low raw material prices. The sole justification for retaining artificially low prices for raw materials for exports seemed to be the danger of accentuating inflationary tendencies overseas in Colonies or dependent territories from which Britain drew supplies of primary products.

On this assumption the issue price of raw cotton needed revision. The price had in fact been lowered on two occasions—March 1942 and February 1943—in order to offset rises in spinners' and weavers' wages.[1] The real problem was how to raise the price without affecting the cost-of-living index, that is without affecting the price of utility goods. There appeared to be two main alternatives. A difference could be introduced between home and export prices, as had been done with wool; a higher price would be charged for the material when used in exports. Or the issue price could be raised and a subsidy could be introduced for utility production. A third proposal, namely to levy export duties on textile exports in order to offset the low price of the raw material, seemed to have little to recommend it: the duties would be difficult to assess and would involve a disproportionate expenditure of administrative labour.

Strong objections were put forward against both the former proposals. There was felt to be a good deal of difficulty in charging different prices for a raw material on the basis of final use, since its ultimate use and destination might only be decided at a late stage in the production process. A subsidy, either at the yarn or at the cloth stage, was also at first declared to be quite impracticable; the policing of such a subsidy, it was asserted, would prove an administrative nightmare. In the end, however, it was agreed that a utility cloth subsidy could be introduced at the merchant converter stage. This made it possible not only for the issue price of raw cotton to be put up in April 1944 by $4\frac{1}{2}$d. a pound, but also for further advances which had occurred in December 1943 in spinners', weavers' and doublers' wages to be met without an increase in the prices of utility

---

[1] The reductions were $\frac{1}{2}$d. a lb. in 1942 and 1d. a lb. in 1943.

cloths. A rebate was introduced, payable through the Utility Cloth Office, and calculated on each cloth in such a way as to enable the converters to sell the finished cloths at the prescribed maximum prices and at the same time to take their approved margins despite the increase in grey cloth prices.

Leather prices were also stabilised by means of a subsidy on hides. Some time indeed elapsed before these prices came under any sort of effective control. Leather had become a price-regulated article under the Prices of Goods Act, and investigations by the Central Price Committee showed that tanners' margins in 1940 were excessive. There was, however, some uncertainty as to whether the Ministry of Supply or the Board of Trade should be regarded as the proper authority for dealing with civilian leather and leather prices. In July 1941 it was agreed that the Ministry of Supply should be the responsible authority, and in May 1942 leather was removed from the list of price-regulated articles. The Ministry of Supply became the sole importer of hides and it was easy to pursue a policy of issuing hides to the tanners at prices which, taking account of changes in costs of production, would enable leather prices to remain constant. In 1942 the prices of civilian leathers were thus stabilised at the levels of the autumn of 1941.[1] The stabilisation scheme involved the adoption of a target rate of profit for the industry as a whole of about 8 per cent. on capital employed, which was expressed in terms of rates of profit on aggregate turnover given 'normal' rates of production—5 per cent. for sole leather and full chrome upper leather, and $4\frac{1}{2}$ per cent. for tanned kips. The range of tanners' costs was pretty wide and it was thought desirable to combine with this arrangement a pooling scheme for the equalisation of profits based on a levy on turnover.[2]

Prices of hides were reviewed at quarterly intervals when changes in costs of tanning and in the levels of production were considered. In the sole leather section all the firms submitted accounts; in other sections a representative selection of firms was examined. Invariably it was found that, despite a steady advance in hide prices, the aggregate profit was much in excess of the target rate in each section of the trade. However, it had been agreed that such excess should be met by a retrospective adjustment of hide prices.

The case, so far as exports were concerned, for moving away from an artificially low price was clearly less strong for leather than for cotton textiles. In 1943 it was stated that less than one per cent. of the leather used was finding its way into export commodities. At the same time there was the familiar problem of how to raise export prices

---

[1] Similarly in 1942 the issue prices of tanning materials were stabilised at the level of October 1941.

[2] The Board of Trade, it may be noted, had wanted in 1942 an all-round reduction of 5 per cent. in leather prices. This, however, it was argued, might drive out of production certain high-cost producers.

while maintaining fairly steady prices for home consumption in the interest of the stabilisation programme. Differential prices, that is higher prices for hides used for manufacture for export, and also a sliding scale of export duties for various types of leather were suggested. The former was regarded as impractical; the latter, while not impractical, would be cumbersome and difficult to administer. In view of the small volume of exports the trouble that a scheme of the latter type would involve was clearly not worth while.

Another material, which, though its price did not enter into the official cost-of-living index, was important in the consumer price structure, was rayon. The fact that the prices of rayon goods were not taken into account in the calculation of the official index was perhaps the main reason why the control of rayon yarn prices was both more informal and less satisfactory than, for example, the control of the prices of cotton yarn. There was also during the first two years of war the unsettled question of departmental responsibility for the rayon industry; ultimately the Board of Trade through the Central Price Committee became responsible for the control and supervision of rayon prices.[1] Meanwhile, in 1940 and 1941, there had been advances in rayon yarn prices. After another increase in September 1941 the rayon producers agreed to inform the Board of Trade of any intention to raise prices further and of the amount of increase proposed. Rayon prices remained stable from then onwards.

There were two facts about the rayon industry which complicated the discussions and negotiations during the latter half of the war concerning prices. First, there was the structure of the industry. By far the greater proportion of the output was controlled by the two big firms, Courtaulds and British Celanese. Since the beginning of the war total production had been considerably reduced, but, although one or two units had been closed down, there had not been any concentration scheme covering the whole industry. While it appeared that the most economical arrangement would have been to close down the smaller high-cost firms and to transfer their output, it was argued that this was both impracticable and undesirable, partly on account of the difficulties of transferring labour, partly because the closing down of plants would, it was alleged, involve the deterioration through the action of acid of the machinery of the smaller firms.

Secondly, there was the problem of the war-time levy of threepence a pound on yarn, which had been established in connection with the export drive in order to provide a fund for subsidising exports. This levy, together with the payment of a penny a pound from the profits of the rayon producers, had yielded a surplus in the fund which amounted at the beginning of 1943 to £1¾ millions. The producers'

---

[1] At the beginning of the war control of prices lay with the Ministry of Supply but this control was soon abandoned.

contribution ceased after July 1942 and with the entry of Japan into the war the need for export subsidies to meet Japanese competition vanished. However the levy, which raised the price of yarn, still continued to be paid. The question of taxing the surplus in the fund had to be settled by the end of March 1943, and while the producers suggested that this balance should be reserved for post-war export development or for research for the benefit of the industry as a whole, the Chancellor of the Exchequer decided that there was no ground for interfering with the claim of the Inland Revenue to the whole amount. The levy was, however, continued on the ground that to remove it would upset the price structure of the industry and the complicated system of utility prices; the producers suggested that the proceeds of the levy should now be used to offset higher costs of production and so avoid further increases of price.

A firm control of rayon prices could only have been secured if fairly drastic action had been taken. There was a strong case for abolishing the levy and at the same time making a substantial reduction in the prices of rayon yarn. However, the major obstacle to an effective control of prices appeared to lie in the disparity of costs in the industry. A flat reduction in prices that would be reasonable for the big producers would create difficulties for the smaller firms. The only two practical alternatives seemed to be a cost-plus control with differential prices or uniform prices with a profits pool for the benefit of the high-cost producers. There were precedents for both cost-plus controls and equalisation funds, but both arrangements were regarded as objectionable by the rayon producers. Moreover, wages and costs of materials were rising in 1944, and the opportunity had then passed to enforce a control which might have been practicable earlier in the war.

The prices of most of the major raw materials used in the production of civilian goods could be stabilised by appropriate Government action. These prices, however, were not the only threat to the stability of industrial costs. Coal prices, for example, rose steadily. During the period 1942–45 there were the following rises in price per ton: three shillings (July 1942), one shilling (January 1943), three shillings (February 1944), four shillings (August 1944), three shillings and sixpence (May 1945).

An even greater threat to prices was presented by rising wage rates. The increased costs they caused would, through the operation of margin controls at successive stages, be reflected in a more than proportionate advance in the retail prices of commodities. Government policy towards wages[1] was to rely on the sense of responsibility of employers and trade unionists working through the normal

---

[1] See Cmd. 6294.

machinery of wage negotiation and on their appreciation of the need to avert inflationary developments in the economy. The Government's appeal undoubtedly had some moderating influence. Nevertheless, within a short time demands for wage increases were confronting the authorities responsible for the control of prices with the problem of whether they should concede a fairly wide range of price advances, or should try to hold the existing price level. In 1941 and 1942 wage increases that were either taking place or impending in textiles, clothing, pottery and furniture were all threatening to undermine the structure of price control.

Given the Government's general attitude towards wages the departments concerned with price fixing could do little more than make what was described as a 'fighting retreat' when price increases were claimed on the basis of wage increases. There ought, it was agreed, to be no recognition of terms in wage negotiations making wage advances dependent on price advances. Employers should be expected to meet part at any rate of the cost of wage advances out of their profits and should in any case be warned that for administrative reasons prices could not be frequently changed. However, it was quite clear that in most cases adjustments would have to be made in ceiling prices.[1]

We have already noted the offsetting of the rises in wages in cotton textiles by successive reductions in the issue price of raw cotton and ultimately by a utility cloth subsidy. In 1944 wage increases in the wool and clothing industries necessitated further Government intervention with textile prices. Wage advances took place in the woollen and worsted industries in March 1944, but it was thought that these advances could probably be absorbed without rises of prices, either by deterioration of the quality of cloth, that is by altering the proportions of wool and shoddy in production, or by the use of a coarser count of yarn, without any serious effect on quality. However, the possibility of using a subsidy to hold prices was investigated and it was agreed by ministers that the introduction of a rebate on cloth would be perfectly practicable.

Impending rises in wages in the clothing trades in the early summer of 1944 provided effective support to the arguments for a cloth subsidy. Already in the spring of 1944 the removal of austerity restrictions on men's garments had necessitated a rise in the ceiling prices for men's suits. In the previous year the prices of utility suits had advanced $12\frac{1}{2}$–15 per cent., and it was felt that further rises in clothing prices would endanger the stabilisation policy. The clothing manufacturers were warned that the Government could not accept

---

[1] The measures of simplification and standardisation introduced during the war tended to reduce costs by way of offset; but, on the other hand, the use of less efficient labour tended to raise costs.

the view that a rise in manufacturing costs, from whatever cause, should automatically involve a rise in maximum prices. At the same time, however, investigations showed that over eighty per cent. of suits were being sold at or within five per cent. of the ceiling prices, so that assuming, as appeared to be justified, that the cost-plus provisions were being observed there was little room for absorption of the wage advance by the manufacturers.

A rebate on utility wool cloth was therefore introduced from February 1945, the scheme being administered on behalf of the Board of Trade by the Wool Control. It applied not only to cloths for men's and boys' garments, but to certain cloths which were made up into women's and children's wear, and also to piece-goods sold over the counter.[1] Because of the differences in labour costs the fixing of the appropriate rate of subsidy was a difficult matter, and it was felt that all that could be done would be to offset on the average the increased cost incurred by clothing manufacturers through the recent advance in wages. There were to be two rates of rebate—6d. and 7½d.— applying respectively to the cheaper and the more expensive cloths. This was on the ground that, in fixing ceiling prices for the garments made from the more expensive cloths, allowances had been made for a higher standard of workmanship and that, therefore, the labour cost of these garments was greater. Cloth on which rebate might be claimed was to be marked with the letter S in addition to the utility specification number.

Thus in the end a subsidy policy was applied to both cotton and wool utility textiles in order to offset wage advances.[2] In all their efforts to restrain the rise of clothing prices, the Board of Trade were fulfilling the requirements of the stabilisation policy. By July 1941 the clothing item in the cost-of-living index had risen eighty per cent. above pre-war; the index as a whole had risen by twenty-eight per cent. and food prices by only twenty-one per cent. The clothing element in the index continued to rise until March 1942 when it was ninety-five per cent. above pre-war. Thereafter, as supplies of utility clothing came on to the market, clothing prices ceased to rise and they remained stable until August 1942 when, with the removal of purchase tax on utility cloth and the arrival in the shops of an increasing proportion of utility, a prolonged downward trend began. This achievement marked the end of a phase in which

---

[1] Importance was attached to the extension of the subsidy to cloth sold in this way because (*a*) piece-goods were deliberately overweighted in the index number, and (*b*) the subsidy would not be 'diluted' by making-up costs.

[2] The sums payable on utility cloth subsidies were as follows:—

	1st April 1944–1st April 1945	*1st April 1945–1st April 1946*
	£	£
Cotton cloth .	554,990	2,381,571
Wool cloth .	4,769	2,652,166

the stabilisation policy had rested almost entirely on the food sub-sidies. In January 1942, indeed, the cost-of-living index had remained at the prescribed level only because the Ministry of Food had agreed—reluctantly—to reduce the price of sugar by a penny a pound.

Paradoxically, as the rise in clothing prices was curbed there was a possibility, in the short run at any rate, that the stabilisation policy would be endangered by a fall rather than by a rise of prices. In the autumn of 1942, to offset the decline in clothing prices there had been increases in the prices of various foodstuffs—bread, flour, bacon and butter—and the food index had risen three points. At the end of 1942 the total index seemed about to fall further. The Treasury and the Ministry of Food did not wish to raise food prices again and the Treasury therefore contemplated withdrawing the subsidy on raw cotton.

The Board of Trade took the strongest possible objection to this proposal. Its adoption would mean, they pointed out, that approxi-mately 2,000 articles for which ceiling prices had been fixed would have to be re-costed, and there was insufficient staff for the task. Enforcement difficulties would be increased, and confidence in the structure of price control might be affected. Moreover, it would be much harder to get cloth and clothing prices down after the war under such an arrangement than to hold prices at their current level, and then, later, reduce the subsidy. The Board aimed at maintaining utility prices substantially unchanged throughout the war, and they claimed not only that the subsidy on cotton should not be reduced but that it should if necessary be increased in order to offset rises in spinners' and weavers' wages. It would be much simpler, it was argued, to let food prices rise, since control of these prices was much easier than control of the prices of textiles and clothing. Food prices, that is, should continue to be the controllable, adjustable element in the cost-of-living index.

The Chancellor of the Exchequer, in December 1942, was con-vinced by the Board of Trade's argument about the difficulty of tampering with the utility price structure and suggested that the price of tea should at once rise in order to prevent the threatened fall in the cost-of-living index. The Minister of Food was clearly disturbed by the idea that in the new price situation his department would be called upon to make unpopular, upward adjustments of prices, but ministers agreed at the end of 1942 to a rise in the price of tea. They pointed out that some degree of fluctuation in the index number might be preferable to these artificial movements of food prices and called for an inquiry into the construction of the index. Early in 1943, however, proposals for increases in the prices of bread, flour and sugar were made by the Chancellor, and agreed.

In July 1943, as clothing prices fell further, the Chancellor again proposed an advance in food prices, either a rise in the price of bread or an increase in the price of sugar. Ministers agreed to the increase in sugar as from 1st October 1943, but decided at the same time on a further review of the index. They also invited the President of the Board of Trade to report as to whether the existing arrangements for price control should be extended to classes of consumer goods as yet uncovered. The President's report of January 1944 showed that almost all commodities of importance within the Board's sphere, except newspapers, tobacco and jewellery, had by now been covered by price control Orders.[1]

(ii)

Manufacturers' Prices

The actual forms which price control may take are numerous and varied, but they can be reduced to two fundamental types—control through a maximum or ceiling price, and control based on manufacturers' costs. These two fundamental principles, either alone or in combination with one another, formed the basis of almost all price control legislation.

The maximum price or prices may be fixed with or without reference to some date or period. In the former case there are such arrangements as the standstill price, or the percentage increase in charge over pre-war. Here, of course, there is normally not one maximum but a multiplicity of maxima, a fact which in itself tends to make the control less easy to enforce. Nevertheless, when maximum prices are fixed independently, cost considerations tend to enter the picture: the price-fixing authorities have regard to the supply position, and to the range of costs in the industry.

The fixing of prices on the basis of manufacturers' costs raises a different set of problems. In the form which it usually took, that of cost plus a profit margin, it was open to the familiar objections that it offered an inducement to the inflation of costs and that it gave no incentive to firms to reduce costs by greater efficiency. This was true both of real and of money costs; for example, there was greater readiness to agree to wage advances which could be passed on in the shape of higher prices. The situation was aggravated in the case of firms who were subject to 100 per cent. Excess Profits Tax.

There were also administrative and accountancy difficulties in enforcing cost-plus arrangements. The procedure adopted was en-

---

[1] The report added that price control would have to be applied after the war to goods not at present being produced.

tirely different from that employed on Government contracts. Ministry of Supply accountants, for example, costed Government contracts themselves, on completion of the work and sometimes while it was in progress. Manufacturers of civilian goods, however, were left to do the costing themselves in the light of such meagre information as the price control Orders provided. Board of Trade accountants could only check a small proportion of the firms involved. Moreover, for goods made to Government order, production costs alone were relevant, whereas price control measures referred to costs of production and sale.[1]

Among the smaller traders standards of costing were imperfect and unsatisfactory. General legislation was of little help, particularly in the case of the unincorporated trader: in the Income Tax Acts and the Finance Acts there were no provisions prescribing in any detail the records which firms should keep. The Central Price Committee found the situation so incompatible with proper enforcement of price measures as to recommend, towards the end of the war, special legislation on the subject. A document was also issued to trade associations providing guidance for manufacturers in costing their products and indicating the minimum requirements of a satisfactory costing system.

All this would have helped, but fundamental accounting difficulties would have remained. How, for example, should joint costs be allocated, when a firm was producing together utility and non-utility, for Government and for export? Overheads, again, presented a major problem. There was, it was agreed, no single recognised formula for their allocation; different firms might quite properly adopt different methods of allocation.

Then again, in connection with overheads, there was the problem of estimating turnover. The manufacturer had to price his goods on an estimate of turnover in a future, unspecified, period. The price Orders provided no answer to the problem, and it was found that manufacturers were often content to base their overhead recovery rates on the results of the previous year's operation. Even when adjustments were made, they were too frequently a matter of guesswork, instead of being linked with estimates of future output. Moreover, having fixed their overhead recovery rates manufacturers were often inclined to go on employing them without checking their accuracy.

As there was some evidence of over-recovery of costs it was suggested that steps should be taken to secure that, where during a given period costs had been overestimated, in the following period prices should be so adjusted so to offset the gain which had resulted.

---

[1] Hence arose difficult questions of the proper amounts to be allowed in connection with advertising and marketing expenses.

As things stood there was no legal obligation on the manufacturer to make any adjustment, nor had any rule been laid down as to the period over which the recovery of overheads should be spread. However, there were formidable legal and practical difficulties in the way of this sort of measure. If manufacturers were to be required to make adjustments for over-recoveries of cost should they not also in fairness be permitted to take under-recoveries into consideration? But to grant this would come near to guaranteeing manufacturers a minimum profit, and by enabling them to make subsequent price adjustments to cover errors of estimation would tend to make them less careful in forming estimates. Further, if the matter were to be dealt with statutorily, the price Orders would have to be altered so as to require the manufacturer to price his goods not in accordance with his costs of production and sale, but in accordance with his *reasonable estimate* of these costs, and that would obviously make prosecutions for price offences much more difficult. In the end it was decided not to make any alterations in the Orders but to issue a statement on the subject. This statement warned manufacturers that where, through errors of estimation, notional costs had exceeded realised costs, *prima facie* offences had been committed. Nevertheless, any steps taken by a manufacturer, before complaint was made, to reduce his prices in order to offset such over-recoveries of costs, would be taken into account in considering the gravity of his offence. Similarly, if a manufacturer were found to be exceeding his own maximum price by making adjustment for previous under-recovery of costs, that factor also would be taken into account, though no allowance would be made for it when the ceiling price itself had been exceeded.

In the application of price control to manufacturers three main types of control may be listed:—

- (*a*) Standstill on prices,
- (*b*) Cost plus profit together, where practicable, with an overriding ceiling price,
- (*c*) Cash ceiling price alone.

(*a*) STANDSTILL ON PRICES

When in the early summer of 1942 the range of utility was being extended and the control over utility clothing prices was being tightened, it was clear that some more effective control over non-utility prices than that afforded by the Prices of Goods Act would have to be introduced. A proposal for a 'general margins Order' controlling the prices of all non-utility goods from the manufacturer down to the consumer was abandoned in favour of a series of Orders dealing with certain broad categories of goods. It appeared urgent at this time to deal with cloth and clothing, household textiles and bedding.

The form of control of manufacturers' prices of non-utility goods which could be most easily and quickly imposed and enforced seemed to be to freeze prices as at a given date. The Central Price Committee had suggested that there might be a double control—costs plus a percentage margin, with the current price as an overriding maximum. But the profit margins would take some time to work out, and the cost-plus arrangement would probably be difficult to enforce. It was therefore decided to impose a standstill on prices, though it was felt at the same time that this should be only a temporary measure and should be replaced ultimately by some more permanent arrangement, possibly on a cost-plus basis.

The General Apparel and Cloth Order[1] of 21st July 1942 fixed the maximum prices for non-utility cloth and items of apparel at the level of the current prices, the current price being defined as the price at which the goods in question or comparable goods were being lawfully offered for sale on 30th June 1942. A similar Order of the same date[2] controlled the prices of non-utility household textiles and bedding on a standstill basis. Again, for non-utility footwear, an Order of 19th April 1943[3] fixed the maximum price at the level of the current price, that is the price at which the goods or comparable goods were being lawfully offered for sale on 30th September 1942.

The fixing of the price ruling at a particular date as the maximum price was an arrangement recognised throughout the war as offering serious disadvantages. It would often be unfair in its incidence as between one firm and another, it could easily be evaded by a slight change in the make-up of commodities, and, finally, it was far too rigid for a situation in which costs were frequently changing. In the latter part of the war it was clearly ineffective in restraining the rise in the price of non-utility clothing, as enforcement was quite impracticable.[4]

In April 1943 the Central Price Committee announced that it was considering the amendment of the standstill Order on cloth and apparel prices and invited trade associations and individual manufacturers to put forward suggestions as to alternative measures of control. It was clear then to the Committee that these arrangements, which had been in operation for nine months, had outlived their usefulness and needed to be replaced by something more scientific. Some changes, which substituted a cost-plus control for the standstill, were soon introduced. This was done, for example, in the case of

---

[1] S.R. & O. 1942, No. 1407.

[2] S.R. & O. 1942, No. 1412.

[3] S.R. & O. 1943, No. 525.

[4] Other goods for which the 'standstill' form of control was adopted, with the relevant dates for prices, were hardware and ironmongery (August 1943), unbranded toilet rolls (31st March 1942), toilet preparations (1st December 1942), travel and fancy goods (1st November 1942).

20

children's outerwear,[1] where even at this time it had to be agreed that production was so completely unstandardised that any form of ceiling price control was out of the question. In a few cases the manufacturers pressed for the abandonment of any attempt to control the prices of their non-utility production on the ground that practically the whole of their output was in utility categories and that to undertake price fixing for, say, two per cent. non-utility was not worth the time and trouble involved.

Towards the end of 1944 it was clear that the standstill arrangement was quite ineffective as a measure of price control. It had never been enforced in the courts against any manufacturer; and with the removal of the austerity restrictions on men's garments it would be in fact impossible to enforce it against a manufacturer of such garments, because his goods would not be comparable with goods produced at the time when the standstill was imposed.

The trouble was that it was difficult to see what effective and practicable alternative could be devised. It was impossible to put forward a group of maximum prices which would both offer reasonable protection to the consumer and at the same time enable high-class businesses to continue in operation.[2] In September 1944 the Central Price Committee suggested that in dealing with outerwear there might be a combination of cost-plus with individual ceiling prices for each manufacturer. The Board of Trade, on the other hand, thought that, though there might be serious difficulties of definition, maximum prices could perhaps be fixed for certain broad categories of clothing, and that the problem of the high-class business could be met by licensing it to sell at higher prices. Both these solutions of the problem, however, seemed to be complicated and to require the expenditure of a great deal of administrative labour.

An excessive rise in the prices of non-utility items presented a danger to the utility scheme. The big gap that was emerging between the highest utility price in a particular line and the lowest non-utility price had to be taken into consideration. To some extent the situation was met by increasing the proportion of utility and by extending it into the higher price ranges, though there were limits to what could be done in this direction. There was also some consideration of the up-pointing of non-utility clothing as a means of restricting the demand for it, but the proposal was rejected.

At the end of the war it was felt that there was serious danger of steep price rises, particularly in such items as women's and girls' outerwear. To deal with the situation it seemed that steps must be taken to fix ceiling prices, in spite of the absence of specifications, and

---

[1] S.R. & O. 1944, No. 140.

[2] The high-class businesses did a valuable export trade, so it would not have been wise to close them down.

in the face of the usual objections that such measures of control would hamper initiative and damage the export trade. Accordingly in December 1945, an Order[1] was made fixing cash ceiling prices for certain broadly defined categories of women's and maids' ready-made non-utility outerwear—overcoats, raincoats, mackintoshes, costumes, dresses, skirts, jackets, blouses, jumpers.[2] For example, there was a maximum price of £20 for an overcoat or woollen costume and £15 15s. for a dress. This Order shows clearly the difficulties of imposing any close and effective scheme of price control in the absence of some measure of commodity standardisation. Moreover, there was always the danger of deterioration in the quality of articles subject to nothing more than a ceiling price.

(b) COST PLUS PROFIT (WITH CEILING PRICES)

The type of control adopted for utility clothing and footwear was, as has been seen, embodied in the requirement that manufacturers' prices should not be in excess of their costs of production and sale together with a percentage profit margin thereon, subject to an over-riding maximum price which must in no case be exceeded. The reasons for this dual system of control have already been mentioned, nor need anything further be said about the importance of satisfactory specifications in any effective scheme of control working through maximum prices. It should, however, be pointed out that while close specifications were laid down in 1942 for cotton cloth, there were no specifications for garments apart from the austerity restrictions;[3] in fact any suggestions that clothing would be standardised were scouted.

There were, of course, obvious objections to the cost-plus form of control, though some of these objections had less force when cost-plus was combined with a ceiling price. The main economic objections have already been mentioned, as well as the administrative difficulties of enforcing this type of control over industries composed of numerous small units. There were answers to these objections— for example, that the efficient producer would gain a higher rate of *profit on capital*, in spite of cost-plus, because of increased turnover— but it is doubtful whether the argument had much validity in wartime when the capacity of the efficient producer to increase his turnover was limited by shortages of raw materials and of labour. Perhaps the only significant argument in favour of the cost-plus control was that it afforded some safeguard against the deterioration of quality which might occur when there were merely maximum prices and

---

[1] S.R. & O. 1945, No. 1530.

[2] There were in fact two sets of maximum prices, according to the prices of the cloth out of which the garments were made.

[3] Except in the case of overalls.

specifications were not very close.[1] In any case a satisfactory form of control of prices based on costs plus profit margin required a far closer scrutiny and control of costs of firms than was ever likely to be achieved in civilian industry.

The percentage profit margin permitted on costs varied usually between 4 per cent. and $7\frac{1}{2}$ per cent. These margins, it was estimated, would normally yield a return of something like 10–12 per cent. on the capital of a representative firm. It would, however, be misleading to suggest that anything like a standard rate of profit, either for industry as a whole, or for particular industries, was used in price-fixing arrangements. Probably the major consideration was the rate of profit earned by the representative firm before the war, and the figure mentioned above was taken as corresponding to the normal pre-war profit rate on capital employed in the trades concerned. To consider pre-war rates was in line with the requirements of the Prices of Goods Act, but to do so left unresolved the question whether excessive rates, rates for example in excess of 12 per cent., should be allowed by war-time price policy. There was certainly no frontal attack on monopolistic price or profit levels dating from the pre-war period and it might perhaps be argued that there was no mandate for this under war legislation. However, this attitude could hardly be said to be consistent with equity in the administration of price control legislation, even though it may have been in harmony with a policy of price stabilisation.

Some of the evils of the cost-plus arrangements, such as the tendency to inflate costs, might have been reduced perhaps by the substitution of fixed cash margins for percentage margins. Probably cash margins could only usefully have been introduced where the goods in question could be made subject to fairly close specification; they would not have been applicable, for example, to non-utility goods with a wide variety of design and make-up. The arrangement was only adopted in one instance, that of glass tumblers, where production control had greatly reduced the number of sizes. Here fixed cash margins, varying according to the type of tumbler—$\frac{1}{4}$d., $\frac{1}{2}$d. and 1d.—were prescribed for the manufacturers.[2]

For almost all utility clothing and footwear the structure of price control, as has been seen, rested on a combination of cost-plus and ceiling prices. However, in the case of infants' and girls' utility garments, cost-plus remained the only form of control for the greater part of the war and ceiling prices were not imposed until April 1944. This policy was adopted with a view to encouraging the production of children's utility clothing as much as possible, even the high-class producers thus coming within the scope of the utility scheme. When

---

[1] Improved specifications would have been a better way of dealing with this problem.
[2] S.R. & O. 1943, No. 1469.

ceiling prices were at length imposed it was recognised that these producers would not be able to come within the scheme unless they could modify their styles and reduce their prices.

In some cases it was recognised that initially the ceiling prices had been fixed too high, probably in order to make sure of an adequate stimulus to secure the required volume of utility production. Thus it was felt in 1943 that the ceiling prices for women's utility outerwear were out of line with other utility prices and higher than the bulk of the trade needed. Relatively there was an overproduction of this category of clothing in comparison with that of other categories which were more urgently required, though this sort of maladjustment could of course be corrected by allocation and production control. There was also some evidence of wasteful use of labour and materials. Ultimately, in view of the manufacturers' opposition, only small reductions were made in some of the ceiling prices, but at the same time the profit percentage margin on cost was lowered from 7 per cent. to 5 per cent.[1]

Dissatisfaction with the cost-plus arrangements led in 1943 to the introduction of suggestions for the adoption of a system of 'standard' prices. Under the proposed system there would be, in addition to the ceiling price for a commodity, a standard price some way below the ceiling and based on the costs of the most efficient manufacturers in the industry, to whom it could be expected to yield a profit of something like ten per cent. on cost. Any manufacturer selling at or below this price would be free from cost-plus control and from cost investigation. Above this price the ceiling price would still be effective. The advantages of this arrangement, it was claimed, would be two-fold; first, the more efficient manufacturer would have an incentive to keep his price down and, secondly, the field of control and enforcement of the cost-plus system would be restricted to those manufacturers who continued to sell between the standard price and the ceiling price.

The proposal for a system of standard prices was put to the manufacturers of women's outerwear and rejected by them. The scheme was however approved by the hosiery manufacturers and it was brought into operation in the hosiery industry in June 1945. The aim was to prescribe a standard price covering at least one-third of the volume of total sales at current costs, subject to the price being not less than five per cent. below the appropriate ceiling price. It was not intended that standard prices should apply to all the specifications, since it was considered necessary to retain cost-plus control without the alternative of a standard price in those cases where the specifications were loose enough to allow the manufacturers a good deal of

---

[1] Another initially high profit margin—that on utility hosiery—was reduced from 7¼ per cent. to 6¼ per cent.

latitude. The scheme was on a voluntary basis and manufacturers had to apply to the Hosiery Control for permission to come under the new arrangements. The Control would then ask manufacturers to submit samples of the goods they intended to supply at standard prices, which, if approved, would be specified more closely than in the existing schedules. Approved manufacturers would be free from cost-plus control, though the standard prices were of course maxima and not minima. Probably the weak point in the new arrangements lay in the fact that they did not apply to distributors; it was appreciated that, as only the utility ceiling prices and not the standard prices would be published, it would be difficult to enforce the standard prices through the various stages of distribution.

On the whole conditions were favourable for maintaining unchanged the utility price structure throughout the war. Long runs, simplification and standardisation, operation of plant and machinery to fuller capacity were all factors making for reduction of costs and these things probably served at least to balance the higher costs of labour, due both to rising wage rates and the use of less efficient labour, and of such things as fuel. Thus in 1944 it was pointed out that it had been possible, even after allowing for higher yarn costs,[1] to reduce the ceiling prices of certain hosiery items, partly because of fuller and more accurate costing, but also because manufacturers had gained experience of the production economies which war conditions had made possible. Reduction of advertising and sales expenditure operated in the same direction as these production economies.

Cost-plus control without ceiling prices was an imperfect arrangement, but where commodities were not included in plans for simplification and standardisation, for example in utility or near-utility schemes, it seemed to be in most cases the only practicable way of dealing with prices. Of all the schemes of cost-plus control the most elaborate probably was that which was applied to the woollen and worsted industry,[2] extending to all the woollen textile regions of Great Britain and covering spinners, weavers and conversion processors. Here, too, the number and variety of the products of the industry made anything other than this sort of control seem unworkable. Apart from worsted spinning, where there was a scale of conversion charges in shillings and pence, maximum prices for yarn and cloth were limited to raw material costs plus conversion costs plus a rate of profit which differed according to the section of the trade in which the spinner or weaver was engaged and the region in which his factory was situated. Furthermore, for the purpose of allocating overheads, percentages of full capacity working were laid down

---

[1] There was nothing corresponding to the utility cloth subsidy to offset in the case of hosiery the effect of higher cotton prices.

[2] S.R. & O. 1943, No. 1187.

which varied again with the different sections and regions of the industry.[1] This formed an interesting point of departure from the normal cost-plus arrangement since a spinner or weaver was to allocate overheads on the basis of an *average* percentage of full capacity operation for his section and region. Businesses where power-operated machinery was not employed, and those consisting of members of a household—in effect small businesses—were exempted from the scope of the Order.

Measures were under consideration towards the end of the war to meet, in the case of footwear, the usual objections to a cost-plus form of control. Here it was proposed to introduce an alternative form of margin, viz., a gross rather than a net margin. Thus the Federated Association of Boot and Shoe Manufacturers towards the end of 1944 proposed that the existing standstill control on non-utility footwear prices should be replaced by a dual margin control, the manufacturer being allowed to price his goods on the basis of either (*a*) a net margin on his costs of production and sale, i.e. the ordinary cost-plus arrangement, or (*b*) a gross margin on the prime costs of labour and materials, prices in both cases being maxima. The Central Price Committee favoured the proposal as it was felt that the gross margin alternative would provide an incentive to efficiency on the part of firms with average or less than average overhead costs. The arrangement did not, however, come into operation until September 1946.[2]

(*c*) CEILING PRICES

Rarely was it considered advisable to impose a control which rested simply upon a ceiling price without the support of the cost-plus requirement. It was in any case clear that such an arrangement would not be practicable unless the commodity in question admitted of fairly close specification. Perhaps the most important case of a control of this sort was that over utility furniture, which satisfied the condition which has just been mentioned. Indeed no better example could be quoted than this of a ceiling price control which through close specification and careful costing could be applied effectively to a whole industry. Other commodities controlled simply by ceiling prices were knives, spoons and forks.[3] Where, however, the manufacturers themselves, as it were, provided the specifications, as in the case of branded goods, a control of this sort was fairly straightforward

---

[1] There was also an overriding maximum in that the charges must not exceed the conversion costs of 30th June 1942 by more than a stated percentage.

[2] See S.R. & O. 1946, No. 1413, which allowed the manufacturer the choice between maxima of either aggregate costs plus net margin of 5 per cent., or 'basic costs' (materials, wages of direct labour, delivery charges, machinery royalties), plus gross margin averaging $33\frac{1}{3}$ per cent.

[3] S.R. & O. 1944, No. 1252.

and ceiling prices were thus in effect secured for branded varieties of fountain pens, toilet paper and knitting yarns. In dealing with perambulators an arrangement was adopted which amounted to much the same thing—each manufacturer's production was restricted to a few models for each of which a maximum price was laid down, but even here this control was reinforced by a control of the cost-plus type, i.e. prices must not exceed costs of production and sale together with a net profit margin of 6 per cent.[1]

War-time wireless sets for civilians introduced in the summer of 1944 afforded another example of relatively standardised commodities for which ceiling prices could be fixed. Specifications worked out by the manufacturers were approved by the Radio Production Board and manufacture of all wireless sets was brought under licence. Price maintenance had been universal in the trade. Manufacturers' ceiling prices fixed for battery sets and main sets were £5 2s. od. and £5 13s. 4d. respectively,[2] while the corresponding retail prices were £10 19s. od. and £12 3s. 4d., purchase tax included.

The scheme for control of pottery prices which operated from June 1942 for three years may be considered here, although it was not based on simple ceiling prices. The maximum prices were to be the lowest of three alternatives, the current prices, costs plus 6 per cent., or ceiling prices agreed with the manufacturers. The ceiling prices, it should be noted, applied only to about half the output of earthenware; for all other forms of pottery the control was on the basis of cost-plus or the standstill price. Furthermore, in applying the ceiling prices to certain scheduled items of pottery, manufacturers were divided into three groups, which were intended to be based on differences in the quality of their products. The threefold control was unsatisfactory in various ways. The standstill was, as in other cases, inequitable as between different manufacturers, some of whom had raised their prices shortly before the introduction of the Order, while others were on the point of doing so: cost-plus was less easy to enforce than in other industries because, mainly on account of technical reasons, such as breakages at various stages of production, it was difficult to cost accurately individual items: and, lastly, the grouping of the manufacturers tended to correspond with differences in cost rather than with differences in quality of products. By an Order of 17th May 1945[3] the standstill and cost-plus provisions were abolished and control was enforced through ceiling prices alone, the new ceilings being generally five per cent. above the old ceiling prices. The division of the manufacturers into three groups was

---

[1] S.R. & O. 1942, Nos. 2558, 2322; 1943, No. 135.   S.R. & O. 1943, No. 579, reduced these prices so that no pram could be sold retail at a price exceeding 10 guineas (twin-pram 14 guineas).

[2] S.R. & O. 1944, No. 720.

[3] S.R. & O. 1945, No. 498.

retained and three new sub-classes were created, with ceiling prices lower than those of the main classes.

The price-fixing arrangements adopted for enamelled hollow-ware were similar to those for perambulators. There was a grouping of the articles which might be produced under the various branded names and for each of these items ceiling prices were laid down. To do this meant costing approximately 900 different articles made by seventeen manufacturers with widely differing costs. For identification purposes manufacturers were required to mark their products either with their own brand names or with code letters assigned to them by the Board of Trade.[1]

Before proceeding to consider distributors' prices, we must review the problems of manufacturers' prices as a whole. Early in 1944 the President of the Board of Trade had informed his colleagues that almost all commodities of importance within the Board's sphere except newspapers, tobacco and jewellery had been covered by price control Orders. But a good many articles were still covered by the weak and imperfect control of the Prices of Goods Act. The Act still applied to such things as umbrellas, drugs and toilet requisites, bicycles, clocks and watches and spectacles. There was another weak link in the chain of price control. As production of some goods had ceased and other goods had become almost unobtainable, the second-hand market had grown increasingly important. This market will be discussed later, but it should be emphasised here that prices in it were extremely difficult to control.

Of the different methods of controlling manufacturers' prices that were practised under the Goods and Services (Price Control) Act there was little doubt that the ceiling price was the most effective provided that the articles concerned could be closely specified. Thus, as had been foreseen, price control depended very largely on the possibility of applying fairly rigid specifications to an industry or trade. Where this was not possible, price control met with all kinds of difficulties. The cost-plus system had serious disadvantages and the standstill was a very weak form of control. A combination of different forms of control was hardly more effective as the examples of pottery (already described) and non-utility furniture (for which there was a combination of cost-plus and standstill) proved.

In developing the elaborate structure of price control probably the

---

[1] S.R. & O. 1943, No. 1339.

major problem which confronted the price-fixing authorities, as opposed to the production departments, who were responsible for drawing up specifications, was the range of efficiency and costs and of methods of production and types of product to be found in almost any industry. Should a ceiling price be set at a level at which almost any producer, however inefficient or however high-grade his product, could make a profit, or should it be so low that only the really efficient or the manufacturers of bulk lines could operate beneath or at it, or somewhere between the two? As early as May 1942, the Central Price Committee wanted an amending bill which would enable them to license individual businesses to charge prices higher than the maxima laid down in Orders made under the Goods and Services (Price Control) Act.

Towards the end of the war the need was felt both for a more flexible system of price control and also for some more effective arrangements for controlling the prices of commodities which could not be closely specified. It was foreseen that, with the relaxation of war-time controls and with the return of goods whose production had been either drastically reduced or entirely discontinued during the war, commodities would be coming on to the market which it would be impracticable and undesirable to fit into commodity schemes. Yet, with the end of the war, the danger of inflation and of the breakdown of the stabilisation policy would be very much greater. More effective ceiling prices could probably be fixed if arrangements could be made with individual manufacturers to provide their own specifications, or, on the other hand, if powers were available to license high-grade producers to charge higher prices than those laid down.

After discussion with the principal trade associations therefore a short bill was drafted giving power to fix maximum prices for goods manufactured by particular businesses and maximum charges for services performed by particular businesses. Power was also taken to prescribe 'price-control marks' to be affixed to goods for which maximum prices had been fixed. The manufacturer could thus be required to mark the maximum retail price on the goods which he sold, and this would greatly simplify the task of enforcement.

This bill was not brought forward during the war, but after the war extended powers of price control were acquired by the Board of Trade. Thus Regulation 55AB made under the Supplies and Services (Transitional Powers) Act 1945 enabled the Board to control prices of goods or charges for services without any restriction. (In war, under Defence Regulation 55 control had to be exercised for maintaining supplies and services essential to the life of the community and, so far as the Board were concerned, must form part of a scheme for controlling production or supply.) Furthermore, by Defence

(Price Control) Regulations[1] of 1945, the Goods and Services (Price Control) Act was itself amended. Power was now taken to fix maximum prices and charges for particular businesses, whether of manufacturer or distributor. This would make it possible, as the President of the Board of Trade pointed out, to fix ceiling prices appropriate to the bulk of the trade in any given line, while authorising higher prices for the high-class businesses which made a valuable contribution to the export trade. The Board of Trade were also empowered to prescribe price control marks to be applied to goods and where these marks actually stated the permitted maximum prices this statement was to be taken as itself fixing the maximum price for the commodity in question.[2]

(iii)

Distributors' Prices

The normal arrangement for controlling the prices charged by distributors was to allow them to add to the price paid by them for a commodity a specified percentage, so fixed as to cover the expenses of most traders, and to provide a reasonable net profit, subject in many cases, for example utility clothing and footwear, to an overriding maximum price.

WHOLESALERS

In the price controls for many commodities, for example, in those for clothing, footwear, household textiles and general furniture, wholesalers were divided into two categories. There were those who did and those who did not 'conduct a regular selling organisation for supplying the retail trade' and 'carrying in warehouse, or other storage premises, stocks substantial in relation to their turnover'. For the wholesaler performing only the minimum distributive functions the normal margin was 5 per cent. on the manufacturers' price (or $4\frac{3}{4}$ per cent. on returns). Further differentiations in margins according to the type of wholesaler were made in the hollow-ware and hardware price Orders.

For those who performed the full wholesaling functions the maximum margins varied according to the type of commodity dealt in

---

[1] S.R. & O. 1945, No. 1613.

[2] A precedent for this arrangement was provided by the Ministry of Food's regulations about soap substitutes. These regulations provided for labels on the soap stating the approved price, and the price on the label was to be treated as the maximum price. (S.R. & O. 1943, No. 638.)

and the conditions of trade. The margins permitted on non-utility goods were generally higher than those on utility goods of the same description, though for footwear the same wholesale margin applied —15 per cent. on returns. The maximum margins on utility cloth were 15 per cent., those on utility clothing $16\frac{2}{3}$ or $17\frac{1}{2}$ per cent. (on returns).

The wholesale margins varied in certain cases according to methods of handling or according to conditions of delivery. Thus for glass tumblers the wholesale margin was either $33\frac{1}{3}$ per cent. or $22\frac{1}{2}$ per cent. on cost, according as repacking was or was not involved. Carriage charges were sometimes taken into account where they were high in relation to the value of the commodity, and where it was the custom for the wholesaler to bear all such charges. Thus on pottery delivered to retailers in Northern Ireland higher wholesale margins were permitted, since it was the custom of the trade for the wholesaler to meet out of his margin both inward and outward carriage charges.[1] For the same reason the wholesale maximum margin generally was high, 30 per cent. on cost, for items of domestic pottery other than teapots. It is, however, noticeable that apart from these examples no provision was made for transport costs incurred by distributors. To some extent the explanation may be found in zoning arrangements of one sort or another.[2]

In the case of utility furniture no provision was made for a specific margin for the wholesaler, since it was considered that there would hardly be any place for him in the scheme. Manufacturers could only supply such furniture against the surrender of certificates which would normally be sent direct to them by retailers. Furthermore, the zoning of supplies under this scheme tended towards the elimination of the wholesaler.

RETAILERS

The control of retail prices presented difficult general problems, quite apart from such special problems as the incidence of purchase tax. How could margins be fixed which would give a reasonable, but no more than a reasonable, return to such different types of retail outlet as the small independent shop, the department store, the co-operative, the multiple shop and the chain store? What allowances should be made for war-time changes affecting retailing, the introduction of utility goods, the limitations on advertising and publicity, the withdrawal of staffs? What account should be taken, in

---

[1] S.R. & O. 1943, No. 906. Similarly a wholesaler of enamelled hollow-ware despatching goods from warehouse premises in Great Britain to a retailer in Northern Ireland was permitted a surcharge of $1\frac{1}{2}$ per cent. on the wholesaler's maximum price.

[2] However, in the case of sales of utility furniture made to a customer situated outside a radius of 15 miles from the seller's premises delivery charges 'necessarily and properly incurred, might be added to the price (S.R. & O. 1942, No. 2589).

price fixing, of the need to secure a reduction in the proportion of the national resources devoted to retailing?

The solution of all these problems was hampered by the quite remarkable lack of statistical information covering the retail field. It was clear that at first little more could be done than to take the customary margins on which retailers had hitherto been pricing their goods and make these the basis of price control Orders, with the hope of achieving more scientific measures of control as fuller information became available. For many commodities the fixing of distributors' charges never got beyond this stage. Only after the war was it decided that more adequate information about retail trade should be obtained by means of a Census of Distribution.

The war did, however, see the beginning of a series of yearly inquiries about the retail trade in cloth and apparel; these provided a more scientific basis for margin control than anything else available in the way of statistical information. At the time of the introduction of the utility clothing scheme in 1941–42 the retail margin on such clothing had been fixed at $33\frac{1}{3}$ per cent. on cost (inclusive of purchase tax), i.e. 25 per cent. on returns. This margin had been regarded as inadequate by the retail trade associations concerned —the Drapers' Chamber of Trade, the Retail Distributors' Association and the National Association of Outfitters—and these three associations had decided that in order to support their case they would undertake an inquiry among retailers into the operating expenses of selling cloth and apparel during the trading year February 1941–January 1942.[1]

Their first report, relating to 916 firms and 1,161 establishments in England and Wales, covered retailers in cloth and apparel other than men's wear specialists and concerns substantially engaged in check or weekly payment credit trade.[2] Since the proportion of small businesses participating in the inquiry was much lower than the proportion of large businesses it was decided, in order to produce a balanced sample of trading, to introduce for the smaller turnover groups a rough system of weighting. It should be noticed, however, that even this did not make adequate provision for the smaller traders, and this was recognised in later inquiries when the returns were reweighted on the basis of results derived from the Board of Trade's coupon banking returns. The weighted figures for shops engaged in drapery and general business were as follows:—

---

[1] Before the war the R.D.A. had undertaken a department store operating costs inquiry.

[2] The trade of most of the firms concerned included in addition to cloth and apparel a proportion of other merchandise as well. It was stated, however, that there would be no appreciable difference in the results between firms specialising in cloth and apparel and firms combining this with other work.

Percentage of Net Sales

	Per cent.
Gross margin	29·53
Expenses: remuneration	13·04
rent charges and rates . . .	3·29
other occupancy	1·35
war risks insurance	1·21
commercial insurances . . .	0·31
miscellaneous expenses . . .	3·41
depreciation of equipment . .	0·56
Total expenses (excluding interest) . . .	23·17
Interest on borrowed money . .	0·85
Total expenses (including interest) . . .	24·02
Net Surplus	5·51

The rate of settlement discount received was approximately 2·95 per cent. of purchases (exclusive of purchase tax). This appears to have represented a slight reduction in comparison with discount terms customarily offered before the war by wholesalers and manufacturers.

Analysis of these figures by size groups, based on differences in annual turnover, showed significant variations in margins, expense percentages and surpluses. The lowest expense ratios were shown by the smaller groups with annual turnover between £2,500 and £25,000. Higher ratios were shown by the larger shops and by the smallest group with turnover below £2,500 per annum. The lower expenses ratios of the smaller groups were associated with the following items: remuneration;[1] rent and rates; other occupancy expenses; miscellaneous expenses; depreciation of equipment. It should be remembered that these returns did not cover the multiple shops or the chain stores, whose expenses ratios were certainly lower. Nor, of course, did they include the co-operatives.

The second report, dealing with men's wear specialists, included 288 returns, covering 569 establishments, excluding retailers substantially engaged in cheque or weekly payment credit trade. The percentages of net sales (unweighted figures) were as follows:[2]

---

[1] In the case of the smaller businesses this item covered the remuneration of the working proprietor and his family, and was probably represented by too low a figure for purposes of comparison.

[2] No distinction was drawn between multiple and non-multiple businesses.

	Per cent.
Gross margin	31·75
Expenses: remuneration . . .	13·66
rent charges and rates . .	5·41
other occupancy . . .	1·17
war risks insurance . .	1·56
commercial insurances . .	0·30
miscellaneous expenses . .	3·93
depreciation of equipment .	0·82
Total expenses (excluding interest) . .	26·85
Interest on borrowed money .	0·62
Total expenses (including interest) . .	27·47
Net Surplus	5·51

Here again, as in the case of the drapery shops, there was a tendency for the smaller shops to have the lowest expense ratios.

Thus the case for a higher margin on utility clothing rested to some extent on the evidence with regard to the expense percentages of the larger shops, shops with expensive premises and correspondingly high overheads. They were presumably the shops which the retail trade associations had in mind when, earlier in 1942, they had argued for a 'mark-up' of 33⅓ per cent. instead of the permitted margin of 25 per cent. on returns.

The retail trade associations, taking the average expense percentage for drapery and general business as 23·17 per cent. of net sales, based their claim for a higher margin on the following grounds: first, an estimated fall of money turnover of ten per cent. for the period August 1942–July 1943, as a result mainly of the removal of the purchase tax from utility clothing, and the planned increase in the proportion of utility production with its lower range of prices, secondly, a provision of four per cent. for stock losses and markdowns, thirdly, the need to allow an adequate net profit to cover return on capital, risks and a margin for contingencies.

The Board of Trade, on the other hand, took the view that, while there might be a fall in turnover, there should also be considerable scope for reductions in expenses. Publicity, display, advertising and provision for bad debts should all be reduced to a minimum. Furthermore, retail trade as a whole would have to undergo a process of contraction and amalgamations might be arranged which would reduce costs. The fundamental principle that ought to be observed was that the retail margins should be no more than was required to secure distribution of consumer goods in the simplest and most efficient way, irrespective of pre-war profits and of the expenses of particular businesses. Moreover, in dealing with utility goods there was no case for making provision for mark-downs. Finally, as regards interest and discounts, interest on borrowed money should not be allowed as an item of expense, while the provision that was being made for a compulsory minimum discount of $2\frac{1}{2}$ per cent. on both utility and non-utility cloth and clothing should be taken into account. Taking the figures submitted for the smaller shops with turnover up to £50,000 per annum, and allowing for a fall of turnover in the coming year, the Board arrived at an overall figure for gross margin, which would cover both utility and non-utility sales, of $26\frac{1}{2}$ per cent. This allowed for a $2\frac{1}{2}$ per cent. net profit on sales, which, assuming a turnover of stock of four times a year, would provide a return of 10 per cent. on working capital.

In discussions with representatives of the retailers it soon appeared that they would prefer different margins on different types of goods rather than a single margin, since some goods, women's outerwear for example, were more expensive to sell than others. The Board of Trade were also prepared to introduce a system of differential margins, since higher margins on goods which did not appear in the cost-of-living index, for example women's outerwear, could compensate for lower margins on other commodities. Finally it was decided that there should be three maximum margins—25, $27\frac{1}{2}$ and 30 per cent. on returns—for the various items of utility cloth and clothing as follows:[1]

25 per cent.	*27½ per cent.*	*30 per cent.*
Hosiery.	Rubber-proofed	Women's and maids'
Men's, women's and	garments.	outer clothing.
children's under-	Women's and maids'	Children's outerwear.
wear and nightwear.	raincoats.	Corsets and
Stockings.	Men's, youths' and	brassières.
Overalls.	boys' outer clothing.	
Shirts and pyjamas.		

The maximum margin applicable to most cloths was 25 per cent.[2] For utility household textiles and bedding the maximum margin was also 25 per cent.[3]

---

[1] See S.R. & O. 1942, No. 1408.
[2] See S.R. & O. 1942, No. 1409.
[3] See S.R. & O. 1942, No. 1411.

On the whole it would seem, and indeed it was actually felt at the time, that these margins were pitched on the generous side. In relation to the figure set for the overall margin—26½ per cent.—they would also appear to be high, since traders were able to earn bigger margins on the sale of non-utility goods. The evidence received from later inquiries shows, moreover, that the estimates of future expense ratios were at fault; realised expense ratios were lower than had been forecast, partly because traders succeeded in making economies and partly because money turnover instead of falling actually rose by over ten per cent. There were, of course, overriding maximum prices as well for these items, but they were simply arrived at by applying the maximum retail margins to the wholesalers' ceiling prices. Hence discussion centred round the margins.

Proposals for the fixing of maximum retail margins on non-utility goods were put forward by the Central Price Committee in April 1942. Among other suggestions put forward by the Committee was one for a double system of control through gross and net margins. This would mean that retail distributors' prices would be fixed by allowing them to add a maximum of 'x' per cent. to the sum of the costs of goods and the actual costs of distribution, provided that the total amount did not exceed 'y' per cent. on the cost price of the goods. The main arguments in favour of the double margin were that manufacturers were granted a net profit margin on their total costs, and, probably more important, that it would be difficult to fix margins which would be fair to traders as a whole without fixing them at levels higher than were necessary for many businesses. On the other hand, it was felt that price-fixing arrangements which had to apply to numerous small retailers should be made as simple as possible, and also that in principle the cost-plus type of control should be avoided. Accordingly it was agreed that it was best to follow the generally accepted arrangement for distributors of maximum gross margins.

At this time, when effective price control was in its early stages, there was no attempt to work out appropriate margins on the basis of estimates of costs, turnover and surplus in the retail trades. The inquiries which have been mentioned came into use later. Little more could be done than to refer to the normal pre-war margins which had customarily been taken, and these no doubt formed the only practicable starting point in dealing with the immense variety of commodities for which some sort of control had fairly rapidly to be devised. However, it was appreciated that there were dangers in prescribing maximum margins for non-utility goods much above the level of those laid down for utility, for this would induce traders to prefer the former and to neglect the latter.

It was at length decided that there should be three different

2P

margins, 30 per cent., 33⅓ per cent., and 37½ per cent. on returns; applying as follows:[1]

30 per cent.	*33⅓ per cent.*	*37½ per cent.*
Underwear and nightwear.	Outerwear.	Furs and millinery.[2]
Piece-goods.	Household overalls.	
Industrial overalls.	Corsets and brassières.	
Stockings and socks.	Handkerchiefs.	
Shirts.		

These margins were based on selling price, inclusive of purchase tax, and corresponded to margins on cost of 42·86 per cent., 50 per cent., and 60 per cent. respectively. At the time when these margins were fixed it was intended that they should not be revised upwards during the war, notwithstanding any tendency for the expense ratio to rise in relation to a diminishing turnover.

The margins may have been over-generous for the smaller retailers in populous areas. But there were protests from the traders who did a high-class business or who had high overhead expenses that the margins were inadequate for them and that they ought to be allowed something like the 'house charge' made in the more expensive restaurants. Protests also came from the high-class bespoke tailors who argued that the survival of their businesses was in the national interest on account of their valuable export connections.

Where the trader concerned was also a manufacturer or maker-up the answer was that he would be governed not by the maximum retail margin but by the standstill price applicable to manufacturers, i.e. the price ruling on 30th June 1942. This answer clearly did not cover much of the criticism, but other proposals appeared to be as impracticable as that for a house charge. It was suggested, for example, that non-utility goods whose wholesale value was fifty per cent. above that of corresponding utility items should be freed altogether from price control. Against this it was pointed out that to many non-utility goods there was no utility counterpart, that serious enforcement difficulties would be encountered, that other classes of businesses would probably, if the claim were met, also ask for special treatment, and, finally, that inflationary tendencies would be encouraged.

Some concession to retailers was subsequently made with regard to the margins on men's and boys' shirts, both utility and non-utility. The figures submitted in connection with the operating expenses inquiry by the National Association of Outfitters had shown for men's wear shops a considerably higher expense ratio than that for drapery and general businesses—26·85 per cent. (excluding interest) against 23·17 per cent. Excluding the larger businesses with their higher proportionate expenses it appeared that the average expense

---

[1] S.R. & O. 1942, No. 1407.
[2] In these cases there were no corresponding utility items.

ratio for businesses with a turnover of up to £50,000 per annum was 24 per cent., for which a gross margin of 27 per cent. might be considered reasonable. The figures were admittedly unsatisfactory, since they represented a small sample of a class of specialist shops, and there was no evidence that the margin was inadequate for drapery shops, department stores, multiple shops and co-operatives which handled part of the trade. Shirts did not, however, figure in the cost-of-living index, and it was decided to meet the outfitters' objections by raising the margins on this item. By Orders of 29th March 1943 the margins on men's, youths' and boys' shirts were increased from 25 per cent. to $27\frac{1}{2}$ per cent. on returns (utility) and from 30 per cent. to $33\frac{1}{3}$ per cent. on returns (non-utility).[1] The ceiling prices for shirts were correspondingly raised.

In April 1943 the Board of Trade suggested and the retail trade associations agreed that the experiment of the operating expenses inquiry should be repeated, the new inquiry covering the trading year 1942–43.[2] Since the period covered by the original inquiry the proportion of utility in the shops had increased. Moreover, more accurate estimates of retail turnover were now available and it was possible to introduce a more reliable system of weighting for the different size groups.

The Board now suggested that a statement should be added reconciling the figures of the returns for the new inquiry with the firms' accounts as audited for income tax purposes, but the trade associations felt that the inclusion of such a statement would make the form too complicated and would discourage retailers from filling it up. The Board felt, however, the need for an independent check on the inquiry, partly because it seemed probable that traders who had been doing well had not contributed to the former inquiry and partly because in that inquiry the sample had been overweighted with the results of the larger businesses. The Board of Trade accordingly proposed, and it was agreed, that the accountant inspectors attached to the Local Price Regulation Committees should conduct an independent investigation along the same lines. This supplementary investigation was intended to include thirty retailers in each region who had not made returns to the trade associations' inquiry. It was to cover large, medium and small shops, large towns, small towns and villages and to represent in these categories both those who were and those who were not doing a profitable business.

The 1942–43 operating expenses inquiry was more comprehensive and more detailed than the earlier inquiry. It included 2,485 usable returns (covering 3,572 establishments) as against 1,367 usable re-

---

[1] S.R. & O. 1943, Nos. 335 and 470.

[2] From now on the operating expenses inquiries became the basis of an annual review of retail margins.

turns (covering 2,062 establishments) in the 1941–42 inquiry.[1] Men's outfitters were divided into multiple and non-multiple businesses. The inquiry was extended to cover the Scottish Retail Drapers' Association. Furthermore, as a result of information supplied by the Board of Trade based on the coupon banking returns it was possible to introduce a more accurate system of weighting than had been practicable at the time of the earlier inquiry. This was important in view of the fact that in these returns the small trader was still under-represented. However, it should be noted that the four trade associations which undertook this investigation did not include in their membership the co-operatives, the chain stores, footwear specialists or bespoke tailors.

The analysis of turnover for the trading year 1st February 1942 to 31st January 1943 showed how strikingly the estimates made in the earlier year had been falsified. Turnover had not fallen, as had been expected, but had actually risen. This was true of all turnover groups and applied both to drapery and department stores (+11·3 per cent.) and men's and boys' outfitters (+14·4 per cent.).[2] This increase reflected to some extent the general trading-up tendency of war-time associated with rationing. During the five months succeeding the end of the trading year there had indeed been a decline in turnover in practically all the groups, but this, it was pointed out, was mainly to be explained as a result of the incidence of coupon releases. The net surplus of traders had increased and the fears expressed by their representatives that the permitted margins would not be adequate had, so far at any rate, not been realised.

The weighted aggregates for percentages of gross margin, expenses and surplus to net sales for the trading year 1942–43 were as follows (cash traders):

Retail Margins and Expenses

TABLE 39

	Gross margin (including discounts)	Expenses	Trading Surplus	Interest	Net Surplus
A. NON-MULTIPLES					
Cash Drapers and Dept. Stores					
1. England and Wales	29·56	21·59	7·97	0·63	7·34
2. Scotland	28·60	19·79	8·81	0·39	8·41
Men's Outfitters	30·14	23·10	7·04	0·45	6·59
B. MULTIPLES					
1. Drapers (E.& W.)	30·94	24·41	6·53	0·85	5·68
2. Men's outfitters.	32·91	26·57	6·34	0·47	5·87

[1] The figures here differ from those on pp. 594–595 in that they include firms engaged on check or weekly credit business.

[2] This compared with Bank of England figures of +9·3 per cent. for department stores and +0·1 per cent. for all reporting organisations. The latter included, in addition to the department stores, the co-operatives and multiples whose trading experience had been less favourable.

Perhaps the chief point brought out by a comparison of these returns with those for the earlier year was the reduction which had taken place in the expense percentage, a fact probably attributable to economies in retailing combined with a larger money turnover.[1] A significant feature, however, of this as of the earlier inquiry was the variation in expense percentages shown by a detailed analysis of the different size groups. This variation added, of course, to the difficulties experienced in fixing reasonable retail margins.

The data collected by the accountant inspectors in their inquiry were based on a much smaller sample—325 returns as against 2,485. They showed, however, considerably lower expense ratios than those yielded by the trade associations' operating expenses inquiry: for cash drapers in England and Wales a ratio of 19·69 per cent. and for non-multiple and multiple outfitters 19·55 and 24·06 per cent. respectively.

In deciding on future policy there were two main questions which had to be considered. There was, first, the question of the level of money turnover which was to be expected in the coming year. This was a matter on which even in war-time there could be a divergence of opinion and the margin of error attaching to any estimates of turnover is an indication of the difficulty of achieving anything like scientific precision in the fixing of margins. Secondly, there was the problem of deciding how far to take account, when fixing margins, of the high expense ratios of the very small traders.

On the question of the future level of money turnover there was a sharp difference of view between the Board of Trade and the retail trade associations. The trade associations, arguing from the experience of the first five months of the trading year 1943–44, maintained that there would be a fall of turnover.[2] The Board, on the other hand, pointed out that the incidence of clothing coupon releases made these figures an unreliable guide to the future, and held that there would not be a fall but a rise in turnover for the year 1944–45 in which any newly fixed margins would begin to be effective. This rise, first put at 10 per cent. and then at 6 per cent. over the level of turnover in 1942–43, would, it was estimated, take place because a decline in the number of coupons received by retailers would be more than offset by a rise in the average money expenditure per coupon, due to trading-up. Moreover, in considering the heavy fall in retail turn-

---

[1] This was still true after the earlier returns had been re-weighted on the basis of the coupon information.

[2] The following turnover figures may be noted:—

Percentage change in turnover as compared with previous year

	1943	1944
Retail trade inquiry	−6·44	+13·20 (non-multiple
Bank of England—retail trade returns:—		cash businesses)
1. Apparel (incl. footwear)	−9·9	+16·0
2. All non-food	−5·7	+ 9·1

over for the months February–June 1943 in comparison with the previous year,[1] allowance should be made for the fact that these figures were heavily weighted with the turnover of the cheap multiples whose trading experience had been less fortunate than that of the ordinary draper or outfitter.

With regard to the level of margins, it appeared that the average gross margin, under existing provisions as to margin control, would amount to 29½ per cent. over the whole field of cloth and apparel. Over this field the expense ratio, as revealed by the 1942 figures, amounted to 22 per cent., showing a net surplus of 7·5 per cent. But these averages concealed appreciable variations both as between turnover groups and as between individual businesses. Thus the largest businesses with annual turnover of £250,000 and upwards had obtained a gross margin about one per cent. above the general average, with expenses at about the average level. On the other hand, the smallest businesses with turnover up to £2,500 per annum obtained about the average gross margin, with expenses more than three per cent. above the average. For businesses of intermediate size both gross margins and expenses were below the general average.[2]

The small trader was really the focus of the problem. For a quarter of those in the smallest group the 1942–43 expense ratio had exceeded the average permitted margin, and half of this quarter had expenses of over 35 per cent. However, this group had the highest average remuneration expense of any (15·4 per cent. against an average 13·0 per cent.) and much the highest rent charges (5·3 per cent. against an average of 3·4 per cent.). The reliability of these figures for small traders might be questioned; the remuneration figure was doubtful and the rent figure probably included in many cases charges for living accommodation. Furthermore, it was felt that small traders were more likely to participate in these inquiries if they were doing badly. Therefore in building up the maximum margins it might be considered reasonable to ignore this group and to allow for an expense percentage which would cover the bulk of traders with turnover of £5,000–£25,000 per annum.

The whole question of retail trade policy, in both its political and its economic aspects, was involved. The small trader had shown that he could exert considerable political influence, while there was not enough evidence available to indicate whether the small shop could be eliminated without inconvenience to the consumer. Again, was it always clear that the small trader was less 'efficient'? Finally, any margin arrangements which would adversely affect the small shop would conflict with the 'fair shares' policy which was designed to

---

[1] As shown by the Bank of England retail trade statistics.

[2] These were group averages and the ratios for individual businesses would vary a good deal more widely.

protect the traders with a turnover up to £5,000 a year.[1] Perhaps part of the small trader's problem was due to the fact that he was less able than the larger trader to cut down expenses in war-time.

The Board of Trade felt that there was a clear case for a reduction in the retail margins on cloth and apparel. The 1942–43 figures revealed a net profit on turnover of 6 per cent.—a higher profit than that which the retail associations themselves claimed. Turnover, it was argued, would rise while the absolute amount of retailers' trading expenses would not be significantly different from what it was in 1942. The retailers' net surplus, the Board thought, might be cut to as low a figure as 3 per cent.[2]

The Board also held that in future the margins for non-utility should be the same as those fixed for corresponding categories of utility items. There was no evidence to show that in general the expenses of selling non-utility were higher than the expenses of retailing utility, except in the case of furs and millinery for which there were no utility equivalents. There was, on the other hand, the danger in higher margins on non-utility that they gave traders a strong incentive to deal in non-utility rather than utility.[3] Finally, in a general revision of margins opportunity might be taken to reduce the margins on women's and children's outerwear to the level of that prescribed for men's and boys' outerwear.

Strong opposition to these proposed changes was manifested in the spring and early summer of 1944 by the retail trade associations, and in face of this opposition the Board of Trade modified their original proposals and in July 1944 put forward the following scheme of margin reduction:[4]

	UTILITY Percentage on returns	NON-UTILITY Percentage on returns (ex-tax)
1. Women's outerwear . . .	30 (30)	$33\frac{1}{3}$ ($33\frac{1}{3}$ cum tax)
2. Children's and infants' outerwear	$27\frac{1}{2}$ (30)	30 ($33\frac{1}{3}$ cum tax)
3. Men's and boys' outerwear .	$27\frac{1}{2}$ ($27\frac{1}{2}$)	30 ($33\frac{1}{3}$ cum tax)
4. Underwear and overalls . .	25 (25)	$27\frac{1}{2}$ (30 cum tax)
5. Cotton piece-goods . . .	25 (25)	$27\frac{1}{2}$ (30 cum tax)
6. Other piece-goods . . .	25 (25)	$27\frac{1}{2}$ (30 cum tax)

(NOTE: Existing margins in brackets.)

[1] See p. 274.

[2] The retail traders had in 1942, in the fixing of the utility margins, agreed to this figure, but they argued subsequently that they had accepted it only for utility, not for their trade as a whole. They also rejected the argument that the figure accorded with the provisions of the Prices of Goods Act—viz. that real turnover had been halved, so that the profit margin should be half the pre-war rate.

[3] The traders scouted this argument, pointing out that the authorities should be able by their production and supply controls to determine the proportion of utility coming on to the market.

[4] The Board's original proposals were that all utility margins should be reduced by $2\frac{1}{2}$ per cent. and that non-utility margins should be converted to an ex-tax basis at the corresponding utility percentages.

While the co-operatives and the multiple shops expressed themselves as satisfied with the proposed changes, the representatives of the retail trade associations still maintained a vigorous opposition. They claimed a figure of 4 per cent. for mark-downs and stock losses, as against the Board's 3 per cent., and a minimum of 6 per cent. net surplus as providing a reasonable return on capital.[1] Then there was the problem of the estimate of future turnover, which became complicated so far as the London area was concerned by the effects of the flying-bomb attacks. Part also of the retailers' case was based on the argument that margins fixed with reference to average expenses and expense ratios would bear hardly on particular sections of the trade and particular retailers with higher than average ratios. They told the President of the Board of Trade, 'your advisers have little conception of the trades which they are undertaking to control'.

To this the President replied that the control of retail prices through the fixing of maximum gross margins of general application had worked satisfactorily and was indeed the only practicable method of control in existing circumstances. In deciding on the appropriate margins he could no more be guided by the expenses of the particular businesses with the highest costs than by those of the businesses with the lowest costs.

Further discussion failed to bring about agreement as to a reduction in the margins. Eventually, however, in November 1944, the traders' representatives accepted the proposal that there should be no reduction in the utility margins, nor in the non-utility margins, but that these latter should be expressed in future on an ex-tax as opposed to a cum-tax basis. The Parliamentary Secretary to the Board stated that if the traders agreed to this there would be no further investigation of costs and margins until the end of the trading year 1945–46. Failure to agree, he pointed out, would involve a fresh investigation to be undertaken immediately with a view to providing as soon as possible information on which a decision could be based. Thus the retailers had won their case; the fixing of margins on an ex-tax as opposed to a cum-tax basis was not in fact brought about until May 1946,[2] and retail margins were not reduced until well after the end of the war.

Before concluding the discussion of retailers' margins the special arrangements for footwear may be mentioned. In controlling the retail prices of footwear it was decided to have two margins, depending upon the grade of shoe. Thus for utility footwear the maximum margin for the better grades was $33\frac{1}{3}$ per cent. on returns, for the

---

[1] The ratio of capital to turnover varied, of course, according as retailers did or did not own their premises.

[2] S.R. & O. 1946, No. 750.

inferior grades 30 per cent. Similarly, in the case of non-utility foot-wear two maximum margins were laid down. For footwear selling at or above certain prices (men's 27s. 6d., women's 20s.) the margin was 35 per cent. on returns excluding purchase tax, for footwear selling below these prices the margin was 33⅓ per cent. The reasons for this differentiation were twofold: first, the better footwear cost more, in time and trouble, to sell; secondly, a single margin adequate for the overall expenses of retailing either utility or non-utility footwear would have raised unduly the prices of the cheaper goods which formed by far the larger proportion of total supplies.

DISTRIBUTORS' PRICES: SPECIAL PROBLEMS

(a) *Cash Margins*

The price-fixing authorities were well aware of the objections that could be made to a system of control which laid down maximum charges for distributors on the basis of the addition of gross percentage margins to buying prices. In the first place, any changes in manu-facturers' costs and prices were accumulated through these margins on to the final price charged to the consumer. Secondly, there was a fair amount of evidence that the system tended to encourage the trading-up characteristic of war-time, that is, the substitution of more expensive for cheaper articles. Manufacturers declared that they were continually being pressed by their wholesale and retail customers to charge more for their commodities, either by evasion of the price Orders or by the equally undesirable method of using more labour and materials per unit of commodity.

Some attention was, therefore, paid to the practice adopted by the Ministry of Food of fixing cash margins. Percentage margins corre-sponded to the retailer's conventional mark-up, and it was clear that in certain fields there was no alternative to them. But where goods had been specified, as in utility or near-utility schemes, it seemed that it might be practicable to prescribe a fixed sum in cash instead of the usual percentage figure. In one case, that of utility handkerchiefs, cash margins for wholesalers and retailers were prescribed;[1] in general, however, the matter never got beyond the stage of tentative discussion. The procedure for food prices was not a very reliable guide, since the commodities with which the Ministry of Food dealt were more highly standardised than most of those for which utility schemes had been devised. Probably, too, the range and variety of retail outlets would have made it very difficult to fix reasonable cash margins, and in any event the task would have been a heavy one. When the matter was considered in 1944 the end of the war was in sight, and margins fixed then would have had to be revised to suit

[1] S.R. & O. 1943, No. 1693.

post-war conditions, so that it was hardly worth while pursuing the problem any further.[1]

(b) Purchase Tax

Purchase tax was related to price control policy in two ways. First, the tax entered into prices, and so its removal from items entering into the working-class cost-of-living index should assist the stabilisation programme. With the introduction of utility schemes a practicable policy of this sort could be applied, and purchase tax was taken off the following items: utility cloth and clothing (3rd August 1942), utility footwear (1st June 1942), utility furniture (1st January 1943), and utility household textiles (3rd May 1943). The second problem was that of the relation of the tax to the retail margin. Should the margin be calculated on an ex-tax or a cum-tax basis?

When the tax was being debated in Parliament in 1940 the Financial Secretary to the Treasury had stated that retailers would not be justified in taking a profit on the tax.[2] Then, in the autumn of 1941, when utility margins were being laid down, the Central Price Committee had recommended that, purely as a matter of convenience, they should be calculated on a cum-tax basis, i.e. on cost price plus tax, rather than on an ex-tax basis. The general fixing of retail margins in the summer of 1942 raised the matter again; it was now mainly a question of the non-utility margins, since, as has been seen, the tax was being removed from utility cloth, clothing and footwear.

When the margins were fixed in 1942 the cum-tax basis was adopted, i.e. the maximum percentage margin was to be calculated on the cost of the goods to the retailer inclusive of purchase tax. This was partly because the margins looked smaller when expressed in that way and partly, perhaps, because the calculation was said to be easier. Traders generally seemed to reckon prices and margins on a cum-tax basis, though some calculated the tax separately.

However, by 1943 the Central Price Committee had come round to the view that the margins ought to be fixed on the basis of cost exclusive of tax. There was, it was felt, always the suspicion that under the existing arrangements the trader might be taking a profit on the tax, or that attempts would be made to get the Customs authorities to over-assess goods for purchase tax. Moreover, the cum-tax arrangement logically required the recalculation of the margins whenever the rate of purchase tax was altered. In two price Orders of 1942 the retail margins had been fixed on a tax-exclusive basis because the goods covered by the Orders (quilts and pottery) paid tax at varying rates. Then from 1943 onwards the new procedure

---

[1] As was recognised at the time it would probably have been more practicable to fix cash margins for wholesalers than for retailers, since the former were fewer in number and could price their goods more accurately.

[2] See Chapter IV, p. 85.

began to be adopted: the margins for non-utility footwear, for toys, for enamelled hollow-ware and for hardware were all fixed on the basis of cost exclusive of tax.[1] However, as has already been seen, it took some time before the ex-tax arrangement was generally adopted and the maximum margins for non-utility clothing were not fixed on this basis until after the end of the war.[2]

A further problem of some awkwardness was that of the correct pricing of utility goods after the tax on them had been removed, or rather of the stocks of such goods which had already paid tax. It was not considered advisable to give traders complete freedom to dispose of such stocks on a tax-paid basis and it was accordingly decided to allow them to price these stocks on a tax-inclusive basis for a month or two, after which the goods would have to be sold at tax-free prices.[3]

(c) Composite Businesses

The problem of the composite businesses, of the firm, for example, which performed both wholesaling and retailing functions, has already been mentioned.[4] As has been seen the policy adopted was not to allow these firms to take more than one margin unless it could be shown that they possessed distinct wholesale and retail branches with separate records and effective wholesaling organisations. However, the clothing multiples who supplied their own retail branches claimed that the single margin was not adequate for them and an investigation of their average margins and selling expenses supported their case. It was accordingly decided that the clothing multiples which supplied not less than ten retail branches from a central warehouse should be allowed an additional margin of 5 per cent. for their wholesale branches on both utility and non-utility items.[5]

(iv)

Control of Service Charges, Hire-purchase Charges, Auctions, Second-hand Prices

SERVICE CHARGES

The Goods and Services (Price Control) Act made it possible, as has been seen, to control the charges made for services.[6] Orders were

---

[1] S.R. & O. 1943, Nos. 525, 615, 1338, 1480.

[2] S.R. & O. 1946, No. 750.

[3] For utility clothing concessions, subject to certain conditions, extended the period until the end of January 1943.

[4] See p. 566.

[5] S.R. & O. 1943, Nos. 335 and 470. The concession was extended to firms which but for air-raid damage would have been supplying not less than ten retail branches from a warehouse (S.R. & O. 1943, No. 851).

[6] Strictly, services performed in relation to goods (Goods and Services Act, S.2).

subsequently made controlling the charges for laundering, boot and shoe repairs and furniture storage.

Civilian laundry charges were controlled by fixing the maximum percentage increase in charges that might be made over 'basic charges', i.e. the charges made for laundering during the week beginning 21st August 1939. Different percentage increases were fixed, after costing investigations, for different areas and for this purpose the United Kingdom was divided into fifty-three areas. At the beginning of 1944 these maximum percentage increases varied from 41·7 (Birkenhead and Wallasey area) to 12½ (Cumberland and Westmorland area).[1] As a result of wage increases these percentages were raised generally in April 1944.[2] Further increases were authorised in July 1945, the labour situation having deteriorated and laundries being unable at current charges to cover their overheads on a reduced turnover.[3]

Boot and shoe repair charges were controlled on the same principle. After an interim measure of June 1942,[4] an Order of November 1942[5] provided for a system of maximum percentage increases in charges, distinction being made between different types of repairer. For the repair factories, defined as establishments in which twenty-five or more persons were engaged on repairs, the maximum percentage increase over pre-war charges was 29·2 per cent. For other repairers the maximum percentage increase permitted was 33⅓ per cent. over pre-war. Special provision was made for the 'cut price' repairers of pre-war days, for whom the latter percentage increase would be uneconomic, in order to prevent them from being driven out of business or doing their work with inferior or shoddy material. To meet their case a scale of maximum charges, in shillings and pence, for specified repairs was laid down in a schedule to the Order and the repairer could, if he chose, agree to be bound by this scale rather than by the prescribed maximum percentage increase. In effect, therefore, the scale represented a series of minimum rather than maximum charges, which would safeguard the position of this class of repairer. These permitted maximum percentage increases and maximum charges persisted until wage increases necessitated their revision in 1944.[6]

The control of charges for furniture storage, introduced in 1942,[7] operated along different lines. The maximum charges permitted were the lower of two alternatives—current charges or a scale of cash

---

[1] S.R. & O. 1944, No. 20.
[2] S.R. & O. 1944, No. 258.
[3] S.R. & O. 1945, No. 937.
[4] S.R. & O. 1942, No. 989.
[5] S.R. & O. 1942, No. 2249.
[6] S.R. & O. 1944, No. 1192.
[7] S.R. & O. 1942, Nos. 837 and 1202.

charges which varied according as the goods were stored in London or elsewhere and according to the total amount of storage space occupied.[1] A further Order of December 1943 extended the range of goods covered to include hotel and canteen furniture and prescribed maximum charges for handling and overhauling, fixing them at the level of the charges current during April–June 1942.[2] At the end of the war, with the disappearance of the costs of firewatching, a general reduction was made in the maximum cash rates prescribed for furniture storage.

The possibility of bringing the charges for dyeing and cleaning under control was also considered. The major difficulty in imposing a control of this sort was the familiar one of devising a schedule of maximum rates which, while appropriate to the bulk of the trade, would not prove quite uneconomic for the high-class firms. It seemed fairly clear that in any Order controlling these charges special provision would have to be made for this type of firm. However, it was decided in 1944 to drop the proposal for control and to rely instead on the growing forces of competition.

HIRE-PURCHASE CHARGES

The need in war-time to limit and control civilian consumption to the fullest possible extent made it doubtful whether any form of hire-purchase or instalment purchase should be permitted, or whether, if permitted, any restriction should be imposed on the charges made. However, it was agreed that there was a case for allowing, under proper control, the hire-purchase of certain commodities which were important elements in consumption and for which the hire-purchase arrangement could be regarded as the normal method by which the poorer consumer would spread the payment for these items over a period of time. Thus it was held that the goods for which special provision could be made should be essential, that their cost should be large in relation to the average weekly income, and that the normal distribution and price control arrangements affecting them should not be disturbed if such special provision were made. To a large extent the commodities in question were those for which it had been decided that new production must be drastically curtailed or even prohibited and the control came therefore to be linked mainly with the control of second-hand goods.[3] The general conditions of hire-purchase arrangements were rigidly prescribed and a maximum charge of 20 per cent. was laid down. For other commodities than those for which provision was made hire-purchase charges were prohibited.

---

[1] i.e., lower rates for bulk storage.
[2] S.R. & O. 1943, No. 1651.
[3] For example, furniture, cycles, motor cycles, sewing machines, carpets and rugs, wireless sets, domestic cooking, heating and cleaning appliances, deaf aids, perambulators.

AUCTIONS

Control of auctions was first introduced by Orders of May 1942.[1] At first a general licence for conducting auctions was given to members of any of three auctioneers' associations—the Auctioneers and Estate Agents Institute, the Chartered Surveyors Institute and the Incorporated Society of Auctioneers. A statutory declaration was required of the owner of the goods to be sold at auction. Subsequently, it was decided that the privilege accorded to members of these three bodies was too widely drawn and liable to abuse. The general licence was therefore withdrawn and it was provided that every auction sale must be individually licensed.[2] At the same time the statutory declaration required was replaced by an ordinary declaration. It may be noted that the ceiling prices laid down in 1944 for scheduled items of furniture were applicable also to auction sales.[3]

SECOND-HAND PRICES

The control of the prices of second-hand goods proved administratively to be one of the most difficult problems of price control. It might indeed have been doubted whether the results achieved were commensurate with the administrative labour expended. For a strong case could be made out for allowing the stimulus of free prices to elicit the largest possible supply of second-hand goods in order to relieve war-time scarcities due to the curtailment of new production. It was, however, this very fact—the curtailment of new production—which made the problem a significant one; people had to resort increasingly to the supply of second-hand goods in order to meet their needs for durable articles, carpets, rugs and furniture, for example. There was a 'ramp' in second-hand furniture; and it would hardly have been politically practicable to leave second-hand prices free from control.

The difficulties of control were pretty obvious. The ultimate source of supply lay with private individuals who were much less easy to control than business firms. The goods were sold through various channels[4] many of which bore little resemblance to the normal outlets of the retail market. The most serious problem of all, however, was the type of price control to be imposed—whether through maximum price or maximum margin—on this heterogeneous assortment of goods.

The first Order attempting a control of the prices of second-hand goods was made in May 1942[5] and stated that the maximum price

---

[1] S.R. & O. 1942, Nos. 816 and 897.

[2] S.R. & O. 1943, No. 58.

[3] S.R. & O. 1944, No. 767.

[4] For example through advertisements in papers only identifiable by box numbers, or through auctions.

[5] S.R. & O. 1942, No. 815.

to be charged for second-hand price-controlled goods in the course of business of a second-hand dealer should be the first-hand price; and also required dealers to keep a stock record of certain second-hand goods and to put on such goods tickets displaying their maximum prices.

The weaknesses in this control soon became evident. The enforcement of the first-hand price as a ceiling proved difficult if not impracticable, even after this price had been redefined with six different meanings.[1] Furthermore, an increasing proportion of the business in second-hand goods tended to pass through other hands than those of the recognised dealers and to be conducted at uncontrolled prices. In yet other cases dealers masqueraded as private persons in order to escape control.

The abuses associated with dealings in second-hand furniture were so glaring that special steps were taken to control second-hand furniture prices.[2] The margin of the second-hand dealer was fixed at 50 per cent. of the price paid, whether to a private person or at an auction.[3] Furthermore, it was seen to be necessary to control repair charges, since the margin control could be nullified by dealers who carried out, or alleged that they had carried out, repairs and added the charges for these repairs to the buying price before calculating their margin. Maximum charges were accordingly prescribed for repairs to second-hand furniture—actual cost of labour and materials plus overheads plus 6 per cent. net profit margin on the aggregate of these items; further, the second-hand dealer was allowed his 50 per cent. margin on the original buying price only, not on the buying price plus the repair charge.[4]

These controls can hardly have been very effective. Not only did the prices of second-hand furniture continue to rise but the price situation became chaotic. There was often a wide range of selling prices for the same category of furniture, not only as between different shops in the same town, but even within a shop. It was common to find good furniture selling for less than bad, or, if at a higher price, for much less than was proportionate to its superior quality. Antique furniture had probably risen in price least of all. Mass-produced furniture, which was in greatest demand, had risen to three, four, five or even six times its pre-war prices. One could not speak of a market but only of 'an unorganised welter of selling prices'.

It was now agreed that if there was to be a control of second-hand

---

[1] S.R. & O. 1943, Nos. 393 and 395.

[2] Antique furniture, defined originally as furniture proved to have been made before 1831, was excluded from control. This definition was later amended so as to refer to furniture more than 100 years old.

[3] S.R. & O. 1942, No. 1530. If there was more than one dealer the margin had to be shared. S.R. & O. 1942, No. 2402.

[4] S.R. & O. 1942, No. 2402.

furniture there must be effective ceiling prices other than the first-hand prices which it had proved impracticable to enforce. Accordingly furniture in common use was divided into a number of categories and, with the help of a committee of experts from the furniture trades, a schedule of maximum prices was drawn up. In building up these prices three classes were distinguished embracing all the known varieties of wood of which furniture was made, while sub-divisions of these classes were based on the size of the article, the number of drawers and other fitments and characteristics which are the main factors determining the value of items. Furniture covered by these arrangements was described as 'scheduled furniture'.[1]

This firmer price control[2] applied to new furniture, other than utility, to second-hand furniture and to furniture reconstructed under licence from the Board of Trade. It controlled sales whether made through the normal retail market, through second-hand dealers, by auction or on commission. It did not supersede but reinforced the existing controls, which were, for new furniture, costs plus 6 per cent. net profit margin and, for the second-hand dealer, 50 per cent. margin on the price paid to the original private owner. For un-unscheduled furniture, on the other hand, there was no change in the form of control, although opportunity was taken to simplify the definition of the first-hand price.[3]

Here we have perhaps the biggest attempt made, outside the field of the utility schemes, to tackle the problem of fixing effective maximum prices for a heterogeneous group of commodities. In one respect, namely in applying both to new and to second-hand goods, it was unique. It also stands apart from other price-control arrangements in that it was not supported by any production control aiming at standardisation and simplification. It is an example of what can be achieved in the way of price control at the cost of considerable expenditure of time and effort.

---

[1] The following is a list of items of scheduled furniture: wardrobe and cupboard; dressing chest, dressing table, writing table; chest with cupboard or drawers, millinery chest, miniature wardrobe; washstand; small pedestal cupboard; bedstead; bed springs; divan; chair; fireside chair; easy chair and settee; sideboard; dresser; table.

[2] S.R. & O. 1944, Nos. 765, 767, 768.

[3] Other changes introduced by the new Orders were (a) the fixing of maximum repair charges at actual cost of materials and direct labour plus 125 per cent. of direct labour costs for overheads and profit and (b) the provisions that second-hand dealers should see and note the particulars of identity cards of buyers and sellers and that auctioneers should see and record the details of identity cards of buyers.

(v)
Review

In considering the application of administrative manpower to devising and enforcing measures of price control, it may well be asked whether the results achieved were commensurate with the time and labour expended. Clearly nothing in the way of a precise answer can be given to a question of this sort. It would, for example, be quite inadequate to refer to the relative stability of the cost-of-living index number or of the non-food elements in the index numbers. Moreover, account would have to be taken of other measures—financial measures in the field of taxation and savings and direct controls such as rationing and licensing—before any balanced judgment could be arrived at. It would be impossible to decide how far the price stability that was maintained to a large extent during the latter half of the war was due to any single one of these measures.

It can of course be said quite generally that the economy was exposed to the usual inflationary tendencies that express themselves in time of war. On the one hand there was the shortage of supplies of consumer goods, as resources to make them were diverted to war purposes; on the other there was an expanding aggregate money income. Therefore without measures to curb and restrain demand, since supply *ex hypothesi* could not be increased, control of price movements would have been well nigh impossible.

But even given the existence of measures of rationing, taxation and compulsory saving, it is difficult to estimate the effectiveness of price control. There were so many different forms of price control and though they all, in one way or another, aimed at limiting the entrepreneur's profit margin, they varied in their success in realising this aim. And, indeed, in trying to limit profits they may have ignored the effect upon other elements in price. For example, there certainly was some tendency for entrepreneurs under cost-plus control to inflate costs.

It is impossible to generalise about the effect of price control on profit margins; the field of manufacture covered by price measures was too varied and too extensive. Under the prevailing conditions, however, of commodity shortage, inflationary pressure and a decrease of competition, profit margins almost certainly tended to widen. It is, therefore, reasonable to suppose that price control measures did curb this tendency. In distribution there was a still greater range and variation of supply conditions, so that here in any case price control could probably have achieved very little. In fact lack of information about the distributive trades and, of more importance, the political significance of the retailer combined to prevent any very effective control of the prices charged to the final consumer.

It would, however, be misleading to look at price measures by themselves and to ignore the production controls that normally accompanied them in the latter part of the war. This raises another difficulty for anyone who tries to estimate the effect of price control on commodity prices. Though we have seen how difficult it is to calculate the effects of utility schemes on productivity it is reasonable to assume that these schemes, through standardisation and through making possible long runs in production, did exert an influence over costs. It may thus plausibly be argued that utility measures rather than formal instruments of price control were responsible for securing a high and continuing degree of price stability. And in taking account of utility schemes a good deal of emphasis would also have to be placed on the enormously increased opportunities for enforcement of price legislation which they provided. Certainly there was a marked contrast between the stability of the prices of commodities for which production—not necessarily utility—schemes could be arranged in some detail and the movements of the prices of articles whose production it proved either impracticable or undesirable to control in any rigid manner. Schemes for standardisation of production made it possible to stabilise the official cost-of-living index number and it was this achievement that was politically and economically important. Nevertheless, this was a very different matter from stabilisation of the level of prices of consumption goods as a whole.

It would be wrong to focus too much attention on the economic aspects of price control. For the social and psychological implications were equally important. Even had doubts about the effectiveness of price control in realising its proclaimed objectives been greater than they actually were, it would have been impossible for the Government to have ignored the effects on public opinion of an official attitude of indifference towards concrete price problems. Profit control and profit taxation would not have been sufficient by themselves to allay public suspicion and distrust. In the last resort, therefore, price control may be regarded partly as a social measure and partly as a means of influencing trade union attitudes towards greater restraint in pressing wage claims.

APPENDIX 16

Utility Prices

The following two tables are given as examples of the level of utility prices. These and other prices can be studied in the relevant statutory rules and Orders. The Orders for apparel are S.R. & O. 1941, Nos. 1386, 1467, 1613, 1675, 1691, 1943; S.R. & O. 1942, Nos. 886, 1408, 1967; S.R. & O. 1943, Nos. 335, 949, 1667, 1693; S.R. & O. 1944, Nos. 11, 219, 430; S.R. & O. 1945, Nos. 184, 303, 435.

Orders for bedding are S.R. & O. 1942, Nos. 2425; S.R. & O. 1943, No. 881; S.R. & O. 1944, No. 12; S.R. & O. 1945, No. 571.

Orders for household textiles are S.R. & O. 1942, No. 2425; S.R. & O. 1943, No. 880; S.R. & O. 1945, No. 894.

TABLE (a)

Retailers' permitted overriding maximum prices for selected items of men's utility apparel, as in force on 31st December 1941, 1942, 1943, 1944, and on 30th August 1945

Note: P.T. = Purchase Tax. No P.T. appears for cotton interlock.

Description of item	Specification No.	1941	1942		1943	1944	30th Aug. 1945
		s. d.	s. d. *With P.T.*	s. d. *No P.T.*	s. d.	s. d.	s. d.
Trousers, unlined, grey union flannel, ready made	201	15 7	15 7	14 4	15 1	15 1*	15 1
Trousers, unlined, worsted flannel, ready made	214	29 7	31 2	28 9	27 10	27 10*	27 10
Jacket, ready made, woollen tweed	204	31 1	31 2	28 9	31 11	31 11*	31 11
Suit, ready made, woollen tweed	206	67 5	67 6	62 2	66 7	66 7*	66 7
Suit, ready made, Scottish or Yorkshire tweed	209	96 5	96 8	89 1	94 2	94 2*	94 2
Suit, made to measure, Scottish or Yorkshire tweed	209	108 11	112 3	103 5	108 6	108 6*	108 6
Raincoat, cotton gaberdine (chest 34 to 42 inches)	308	38 11	38 11	35 10	35 10	35 10	37 3
Overcoat, ready made, woollen tweed	212	89 5	96 8	89 1	89 5	89 5	89 5
Overcoat, ready made, navy melton	211	54 5	54 6	50 3	52 2	52 2	52 2
Fustian trousers, unlined ($10\frac{1}{2}$ oz.)	310	19 5	19 6	17 11	23 8	23 8	23 8
Overall (bib and brace, jean)	311	10 11	—	9 8	9 8	9 8	9 8
Shirt, unlined, no collar, drill	303	7 9	7 9	6 11	7 6	7 6	—
Shirt, unlined, collar attached, drill	303	8 4	8 4	7 5	8 0	8 0	—
Pyjamas, flannelette or winceyette striped pyjama cloth	301	12 0	12 0	10 8	10 10	10 10	—
Shirt, cotton interlock	501	4 6	4 0		4 0	4 0	4 0
Trousers, cotton interlock	502	4 6	4 0		4 0	4 0	4 0
Athletic vest, cotton interlock	503	2 6	2 3		2 3	2 3	2 3
Athletic trunks, cotton interlock	504	2 6	2 3		2 3	2 3	2 3
Shirt, all wool, unshrinkable finish	513	12 5	11 1		11 1	11 1	11 1
Trousers, all wool, unshrinkable finish	514	12 5	11 1		11 1	11 1	11 1
Half hose, all wool, unshrinkable finish	521	2 11	2 7		2 7	2 7	2 7
Half hose, wool and cotton	523	2 8	2 $4\frac{1}{2}$		2 $4\frac{1}{2}$	2 $4\frac{1}{2}$	2 $4\frac{1}{2}$
Cap, grey flannel	201	—	3 11	3 2	3 2	3 2	3 2
Gloves, leather	111	—	12 3		12 3	12 3	13 3
Gloves, knitted, woollen	705	—	3 $2\frac{1}{2}$		3 $2\frac{1}{2}$	3 $2\frac{1}{2}$	3 $2\frac{1}{2}$
Handkerchiefs, plain white, hemstitched	61	—	$9\frac{1}{2}$		$7\frac{3}{4}$	$7\frac{3}{4}$	$7\frac{3}{4}$
Handkerchiefs, coloured bordered	63	—	$10\frac{3}{4}$		$8\frac{3}{4}$	$8\frac{3}{4}$	$8\frac{3}{4}$
Braces, dyed web	Type I	—	—		2 $10\frac{1}{2}$	2 $10\frac{1}{2}$	2 $10\frac{1}{2}$

* An additional allowance could be charged if the garments were not of *austerity* patterns, provided that they were of such a size that Purchase Tax would be chargeable if they were not utility goods.

TABLE (b)

*Retailers' maximum selling prices for certain items of new utility furniture as in force on 31st December 1942, 1943, 1944, and on 27th August 1945**

Type of article	Model No.	Exterior timber and exterior varnish	1942 £ s. d.	1943 £ s. d.	1944 £ s. d.	27th Aug. 1945 £ s. d.
Wardrobe, 4 ft.	1	Oak†	15 16 6			
Wardrobe, 4 ft.	1	Mahogany	17 4 9			
Dressing chest with mirror, 3 ft.	3	Oak	8 15 0			
Dressing chest without mirror, 3 ft.	3	Oak	8 11 0			
Dressing chest with mirror, 3 ft.	3	Mahogany	10 10 0		As for 1942	
Dressing chest, without mirror, 3 ft.	3	Mahogany	9 6 9			
Tallboy, 2 ft. 9 in.	5	Oak	9 5 3			
Tallboy, 2 ft. 9 in.	5	Mahogany	10 2 6			
Divan, 2 ft. 6 in.	5		5 13 6			
Kitchen cabinet	3		11 10 6			
Kitchen chair	4		14 3			
Sideboard	1	Oak	10 7 0			
Dining chair	3	Oak	1 10 0			
Bedchair	3		3 19 6			
Curb, 4 ft.	8		17 0			
Playpen	2		1 19 6			
Cot (with mesh)	1		2 9 9			
Convertible high chair	4		2 5 6			
Child's low chair	5		1 1 9			
Bedstead, 3 ft.	6	Oak	2 16 6	2 16 6	2 16 6	3 6 0
Bedstead, 3 ft.	6	Mahogany	2 19 6	2 19 6	2 19 6	3 7 0
Bedstead, 4 ft. 6 in.	6	Oak	4 7 3	4 7 3	4 7 3	R 4 13 0‡ / F 4 15 0‡
Bedstead, 4 ft. 6 in.	6	Mahogany	4 11 0	4 11 0	4 11 0	R 4 14 6‡ / F 4 16 6‡
Bed settee	4		13 4 0	13 4 0	13 9 0	13 9 0
Kitchen table, 4 ft. by 3 ft.	1		3 8 6	3 8 6	3 8 6	4 0 0‡
Dining table	2	Oak	5 15 3	5 15 3	5 15 3	6 8 0‡
Open arm easy chair	2		3 12 0	3 12 0	3 16 0	3 16 0
Set shelves	6	Oak	1 12 0	1 12 0	1 12 0	2 4 0‡

* Sources for figures: 1942, S.R. & O. No. 2589; 1943, S.R. & O. No. 363; 1944, S.R. & O. No. 766 and No. 1049; 1945, S.R. & O. No. 881 and No. 909.

† The term 'oak' in Column 3 was superseded in 1944 by a symbol indicating exterior timber or exterior varnish 'not of mahogany'.

‡ The 1944 prices remained in force for articles ordered before 25th January 1945.

R = Article with a rigid mattress.   F = Article with a folding mattress.

617

CHAPTER XXIII

CONCLUSION

(i)

Post-War Questions

LONG before the war came to an end much thought and attention had been devoted to the numerous and difficult problems which would arise, both in Stage II—the period between the end of hostilities in Europe and the termination of the war with Japan—and also in the long term. Already in February 1941 a Cabinet Committee on Reconstruction under the chairmanship of the Minister without Portfolio had been set up, and later in the same year the problems of the post-war reconstruction of industry began to be considered in the Board of Trade.

At first very little time and very little staff could be spared for reconstruction, but from 1943 onwards a steadily increasing amount of thought was devoted to it. There was still only a handful of staff engaged solely on reconstruction affairs, but the officers engaged in current work became increasingly involved in peace-time problems. The production departments of the Board considered the problems of the industries with which they were closely concerned and the future of the controls they operated. The 'general services' departments of the Board—such as the Industrial Supplies Department and the Statistics Department—took part in many discussions with other ministries about post-war raw material requirements and the distribution of manpower. After D-Day this planning ahead absorbed more energy than current day-to-day work. The few pages that follow do not attempt a thorough account of all this activity; they are only a cursory survey of some of the more general problems that were studied.

In large part the problems that were investigated were those of the transition period between the end of the war with Germany and the end of the war with Japan. The duration of this period was put first at two years, but this estimate was subsequently reduced to eighteen months. The difficulties were primarily those of reconversion, the turning over of industry from war production to production of other sorts. There were also what might be regarded as long-term problems, such as the possibility of establishing in Great Britain new manufactures which would replace goods previously imported, or again the problems of management or of industrial design. Long-term policy was, however, often linked to short-term policy. The balanced distribution of industry, for example, touched all sorts of policies in relation to the transition period, the policies to be adopted, for example, with regard to the termination of war contracts or the release of surplus Government factories.[1]

The main objectives of policy could be set down clearly. They were, first, the rapid expansion of the export trade in view of the gravely adverse balance of payments. Secondly, there was the continuance of the policy of price stabilisation, which would be the more necessary and the more difficult as the demand for civilian goods expanded in a period of shortages. Probably this would mean an extension of the range of utility schemes and of price-fixing. Thirdly, there was the need for provision for capital investment in work of high social priority, such as housing. There was also, of course, the need to make a start on the urgent problem of re-equipping industry, whose capital equipment had in many cases been sadly neglected during the war. Fourthly, full employment must be maintained; this problem was perhaps over-stressed at the time, but was likely to arise if 'patches of unemployment . . . develop where the industrial system fails to adapt itself quickly enough to peace-time production'.[2]

These objectives were to be pursued while maintaining at the same time a full war effort against Japan. There would also of course be new calls on the economy represented by the contribution which the United Kingdom would be called upon to make to relief and rehabilitation in Europe.

In its approach to these problems the Government showed that it had learnt the lessons of the period succeeding the armistice of 1918. Then there had been an intense boom with rising prices, accompanied by a good deal of social unrest, followed by an economic collapse. To a large extent this instability had been due to an over-hasty removal of controls. But even if this experience had not been available it would have been quite clear that there could be no wholesale scrapping of controls after the end of the war with Germany. Shortages of labour and materials would preclude that in any case.[3] Therefore control of most materials and of end-products would have to continue. There would very probably be a public demand for decontrol and this would have to be resisted; it would, however, be made plain that the Government were taking steps to remove as soon as possible all unnecessary controls. Probably the most awkward prob-

---

[1] It is not suggested that location of industry problems were the only problems involved in these policies.

[2] Cmd. 6527, p. 7.

[3] Furthermore, the danger, while the war with Japan was in progress, of unfavourable reactions in the United States would have to be taken into account.

lem likely to arise in the maintenance of economic controls would be that of retaining in positions of control business men who had come into Government service in war-time. As normal production revived not only would these men be wanting to get back to their firms but also the question would arise, in a much more intense form than that in which it had shown itself during the war, of their relation to other firms, particularly rival firms, in the industries to which they belonged. Nevertheless controls must be retained; not just isolated controls but the whole interlocking system, at any rate until shortages had been alleviated. Nor was anything like a scramble for surplus war stocks, such as had occurred after 1918, with high prices and speculation, to be permitted.

The need to expand exports reinforced the other arguments for the retention of controls which would be able in the transition period to limit home demand. There was a very obvious danger to be expected from the competing pull of the home market which would drive up prices and divert supplies to the domestic consumer. Indeed it was not clear that there was any other direct method of forcing an expansion of exports,[1] though export controls would of course be relaxed and export facilities extended. Meanwhile manufacturers, realising the amount of leeway that would have to be made up if they were to face post-war competition from well-equipped American industries, were asking that they should be permitted to undertake the manufacture of prototypes, to prepare estimates and specifications and to renew contacts with overseas customers. There were also certain items of new equipment which would considerably improve the competitive position of certain industries and on which therefore a start should be made as soon as possible. Unfortunately it was not practicable, until near the end of the war, to release the resources, particularly the skilled workmen—the draughtsmen and the designers—who would be needed to put these plans into operation.

As a means of countering another very obvious danger, that of post-war inflation, price-control measures and rationing schemes would, the Government realised, have to be retained. Indeed, since the production of some goods which had stopped during the war would begin again, the range of price control would have to be extended. Moreover, steps would have to be taken to deal with the threat to price control which would come from the expansion of non-utility production.

Plainly, therefore, the general structure of internal controls of supply, manufacture and consumption would be needed in the transitional period. The bulk of production of clothing and textiles would have to continue to be of utility price-controlled types. Rationing of

---

[1] Compare the Limitation of Supplies Order of 1940.

clothes would be maintained until supplies were sufficient to permit a ration of something over 100 coupons per head. Controls of in-essentials would also, it was thought, have to be kept on, because even though there were strong arguments for removing them—to meet public criticism and to save administrative labour—to abolish control would probably lead to the diversion of labour from more important things, namely exports and essential home requirements. At the same time, however, every effort would be made to simplify all these con-trols and to make them more flexible. There would be progressive relaxation during the transition period.

The immediate problem to be dealt with was that of the recon-version of industry. From early in 1943 discussions had been opened up with industries inviting them to indicate what they would need, in order to start up normal production, in the way of release of premises and of particular types of skilled labour, and to state what obstacles they foresaw to the resumption of full normal activity. The earlier discussions were perhaps somewhat premature. They may have given the impression that facilities for experimental work would be made available more rapidly than proved to be the case, and they were undertaken at a time when the real nature of the reconversion problem had barely emerged. Moreover, the problem was one for individual firms, not for industries.

In May 1944 the Government issued a White Paper on Employ-ment Policy.[1] Chapter II of this White Paper dealt with 'the transi-tion from war to peace' and outlined the main problems which would arise. It referred, as has already been mentioned, to the danger that 'patches of unemployment may develop' and stated that the Govern-ment was making preparations to reduce this unemployment to a minimum,

(a) by assisting firms to prepare to switch over their capacity to peace-time production as quickly as possible;

(b) by finding out in advance where the skilled labour which would gradually become available for civilian work would be most urgently required;

(c) by arranging, so far as war conditions permitted, that labour and raw materials would be forthcoming for urgent civilian work and ensuring that the machinery of allocation devised in war-time would be adaptable to the special conditions likely to obtain after the end of the war in Europe;

(d) by arranging, so far as possible, that curtailment of munitions production should take place in areas where the capacity and labour could be used for civilian products of high priority;

(e) by arranging that the disposal of surplus Government stocks should not prejudice the re-establishment and development of

---

[1] Cmd. 6527.

the normal trade channels for producing and distributing
similar goods;

(*f*) by regulating the disposal of Government factories in such a
way as to help towards the early restoration of employment.

Investigation of these problems was related to the experience of the
period following the armistice of 1918. What was clearly to be
avoided was encouragement of the sort of speculative movements
which had played a part in the boom and collapse of 1919–21. The
change-over must be an orderly one. But there was also the experience of the inter-war years, in which one of the major industrial problems had been that of the depressed areas. 'It will be an object of
Government policy', the White Paper stated, 'to a secure a balanced
industrial development in areas which have in the past been unduly
dependent on industries specially vulnerable to unemployment'.[1]
Reconversion policy would have to take this objective into account.

One aspect of this policy was concerned with the release of firms
from war contracts. There was the awkward problem in the first
instance of deciding whether, in order to avoid the wastage of
valuable materials, these contracts should be abruptly terminated or
whether, in the interests of stability of employment, a less drastic
policy should be pursued. Some firms, for example textile firms,
would of course find little difficulty in switching over from production
for Government to production for civilian use; for others, such as aircraft firms, the problem would be more serious, and in such cases it
seemed that the tapering off of contracts would be the best arrangement. Meanwhile it was agreed that, though the Service and supply
departments would have some difficulty in indicating the firms whose
output they would require during the war with Japan, the Board of
Trade should draw up a priority list of industries and firms for
release from war contracts. This would show the regions where contracts should be terminated quickly, either because they were
development areas[2] or because labour was needed for production of
high priority which was localised there.

There were also problems about factory space which required
urgent consideration. On the one hand there was the need to clear
factories as soon as possible of the stocks which had been stored in
them. This reinforced the argument for the early termination of war
production which would merely lead to the piling up of unwanted
stores. Factories requisitioned for war production also had to be
cleared. There was also the problem of the disposal of surplus Government factories. It was decided that the general rule should be that
factories should not be sold to the highest bidder, but should be leased
for a period of ten years, the firm that secured the lease being also

---

[1] Cmd. 6527, p. 11.

[2] The new name for the old depressed or special areas.

granted the option to acquire the reversion of the factory at a value to be agreed.[1] Considerations to be taken into account in allocating factories would be

    (i) the need for a balanced distribution of industry,

    (ii) the need to expand the export trade,

    (iii) the need to maintain a suitable war potential,

    (iv) considerations of town and country planning,

    (v) the ability of applicants to make use of a factory with the minimum of alterations.

Another problem, which had already appeared some time before the end of the war, was that of the disposal of surplus stocks. It was a problem with which manufacturers were much concerned, because they were afraid that a policy of over-hasty disposal would ruin the market for their output. After the 1914–18 war a Disposals Board had been set up which had offered surplus stocks for sale in the open market, and there had been no control over dealers' prices and margins. Government departments were agreed that this sort of thing should not happen again, despite any financial advantage which might accrue from sales at highest possible prices. There would have to be orderly disposal through the trades concerned, with proper control of prices. At the same time, in view of the acute shortages of consumer goods, there could be no justification for a policy of destroying surplus stocks or of unduly withholding them from the market. In any case the problem should not be exaggerated. There were world-wide shortages and there were in particular the relief needs of liberated areas. And it proved indeed that there was little need to fear the dumping of surplus stocks on the home market.[2]

In 1942 arrangements had been made by the Ministry of Supply and the Board of Trade for the disposal of reconditioned Service clothing. The Board of Trade opened a register for dealers in second-hand reconditioned clothing and instigated the formation of a reconditioned and salvaged clothing merchants' association. This association was responsible, subject to direction from the Board of Trade, for allocating the clothing, the Board, in consultation with the Central Price Committee, fixing dealers' margins and final prices. The Ministry of Supply had also in 1941 reached agreement with the Society of Motor Manufacturers and Traders over the disposal of surplus motor vehicles.

Furthermore, the Board of Trade provided for the setting up in 1944 of a Surplus Textiles Corporation, under the ægis of the Whole-

---

[1] The main reasons for leasing were the time which would be taken for prices to settle at a normal level and the desire of firms, particularly small firms, not to lock up their assets in buildings.

[2] What has been said above refers to *consumer* goods. For certain capital goods, e.g. machine tools, of which Government at the end of the war held 200,000 items worth £150 millions, there *was* a serious problem. *cf. British War Economy, op. cit.*, pp. 537–38.

sale Textile Association. Membership was to be confined to traders who had had a turnover of not less than £25,000 in the standard year (1939) and who had been continuously in business since that time. This was, in original intention, a war-time measure, and it was clear that other interests, for example those of the textile industries, would have to be taken into consideration in post-armistice disposals.

The principle that was to be adopted was that of an orderly disposal of surplus stocks through the appropriate trade channels, and Government policy was set out in a White Paper which appeared in July 1944.[1] The relevant supply department, usually the Ministry of Supply, would be designated as a disposal department, and would arrange for the 'sorting, assembling, cataloguing and reconditioning (where appropriate)' of surplus goods and would 'make the contracts for sale'. One department—in the case of almost all consumer goods it would be the Board of Trade—would be 'primarily responsible for deciding the method of disposal, for fixing margins and prices, for settling the rate at which goods will be released, and for conducting the necessary discussions with trade and industry'. The President of the Board of Trade summarised this policy in a debate in the House of Commons of July 1944,[2] and pointed to the contrast with the measures which had been taken after 1918.

In these various ways steps were being taken to implement the pledges which had been given in the White Paper on Employment Policy about the transition period. It must, however, be remembered that what was being drawn was mostly the outline of the picture and the details had yet to be filled in. There were the uncertainties about the requirements of the war with Japan and about the need for relief of liberated areas. There would remain serious labour shortages and a scarcity of many raw materials would still be experienced. Thus there could be no rapid and wholesale reopening of factories which had been closed under the policy of concentration of industry. Even after the war with Japan had ended shortages of labour enforced selective deconcentration of cotton mills. Moreover, in addition to these uncertainties there was the vast question of what the future pattern of trade and exchange would be.

The problems which have been discussed have been mainly those of the transition period. But attention was, of course, being devoted at the same time to long-term problems, problems which would be encountered, not necessarily for the first time, after the end of the war with Japan. Of these, perhaps the most significant in our field was that of the location of industry. It was a problem which had received much attention in the nineteen-thirties, culminating in the Barlow

---

[1] Cmd. 6539.
[2] H. of C. Deb., Vol. 402, Cols. 614–615.

Report published shortly after the outbreak of war.[1] It clearly affected policy towards the transition period as well as long-term policy. In the third chapter of the White Paper on Employment Policy the recommendations of the Barlow Committee about the balance and diversification of industry in what were now termed 'development areas' were fully supported. Steps would be taken to deal with the problem of local unemployment, it was stated, by influencing the location of new enterprises, by removing obstacles to the transference of workers from one area to another and by the provision of training facilities. The Board of Trade would be the department through which the Government policy in this field would be carried out.

Lord Beveridge had said of food control in the 1914–18 war that from it 'little can be learned of permanent application'; and, again, 'The most intricate experiments of the Ministry [of Food] . . . are those farthest removed from any possible task of peace; little if anything learned in them can be of use again, save in a civilisation bent again on self-destruction'.[2] What he has said applies in large part to the experiments described in this volume. Even where it might appear at first sight that the war had yielded experience of permanent value, for example with regard to the efficient organisation of production, further investigation shows that the data are too unreliable and the conditions too abnormal to provide much useful information about the way in which peace-time production could be organised. Similarly, a study of the reconversion programme reveals little more than the problems arising in the dismantling of an elaborate structure built up purely for destructive purposes. The emphasis on a comprehensive and adequate policy for location of industry represented on the other hand the determination that pre-war evils should not again become rooted in the economy. Study of the ingredients of this policy was perhaps the only contribution of these years to economic and social progress.

(ii)

Summing-up

We have just outlined the plans that were being made towards the end of the war for reconversion of industry to peace-time purposes and for dealing with the inescapable problems of the transition period. But this volume has predominantly been concerned with a very different group of problems, the problems of the civilian sector

---

[1] Cmd. 6153.

[2] *British Food Control*, p. 344.

of a war economy. It has not, it must be admitted, covered the whole
of that sector. The stories of the feeding of the civilian population, of
the provision of transport and fuel for that population during the war
period, are told in other volumes in this series. But the policies which
we have analysed and the apparatus of controls which we have
described have centred round a closely linked group of problems
which have a significance of their own in the general economic
strategy of the war. Primarily the question that has been raised has
been: How far were Government measures successful in releasing
resources from civilian uses, so as to make them available for war
purposes of one kind or another with the minimum of friction and of
waste and of disturbance to general economic stability? This question
has dominated either directly or indirectly most of the discussion of
this volume. As a secondary issue there has been the problem of
securing and maintaining balance and equity within the contracted
sphere of the civilian economy itself.

The inadequacy in a major war of financial and fiscal measures
and the need for supplementing such measures by physical controls
have been stated clearly by Professor Robbins in *The Economic
Problem in Peace and War*. The fiscal doctrine, or, as he puts it, the
theory that 'if Government is willing to tax sufficiently drastically
and to arrange its borrowing on a non-inflationary basis, there need
arise no occasion for more direct controls'[1] is inapplicable to a war
waged on the scale of that of 1939–45. 'When we come', Professor
Robbins says, 'to the wars of our own age, with their vast demands
on men and materials, their acute scarcities, and their utter domina-
tion of the field of business confidence, then, as I see it, the fiscal theory
loses its cogency'.[2] In the first place, then, the magnitude of the
shift of resources required has to be taken into account; and, in the
second place, there is the question of speed, for resources have to be
transferred at a rate more rapid than anything experienced under
normal peace-time circumstances. Thus, even if we disregard the
political possibility of applying the fiscal theory of a war economy, it
is clear that to rely on the mechanism of the market, to depend upon
movements of factor prices and commodity prices to effect, without
serious inflationary consequences, the shift of resources from peace-
time to war-time uses would be hopelessly impracticable. Allocations,
rationing, production controls, limitation of supplies are inevitable.

However, in laying emphasis on the need for direct controls over
production, supply and demand, two points should not be overlooked. The first point is that direct controls are helped a good deal
by the adoption of the appropriate financial and fiscal measures.
A moderate dose of inflation, it has been generally recognised, assists,

[1] *Op. cit.*, p. 31.
[2] *Op. cit.*, p. 33.

particularly in the early stages, the transference of resources. On the other hand taxation helps to curb demand and thus limits expenditure on commodities which it is impracticable to ration. Secondly, direct controls can be operated successfully in war-time because they have the backing of public opinion behind them. Professor Robbins has well pointed out, with regard to the price-fixing regulations, that anyone who knows the machinery which was supposed to work these regulations must admit that it would have been completely inadequate for its purpose if there had not existed a strong disposition to co-operate on the part of traders and merchants.[1] Quite clearly a picture of the civilian economy which referred only to the controls enforced by Statutory Rule and Order would be a gross misrepresentation. Equally it is true that controls which are not described in this volume, the controls on labour and materials, were of vital importance in moving resources from civilian to war uses, and that often the chief credit for what was achieved must be given to them. The justification for using end-product control as a supplement to labour and material controls is that the former is more direct and immediate in its effect and can be employed more selectively. Finally, it must be emphasised that what was built up was not an apparatus into which every element of the civilian economy fitted neatly and tidily. There were productive activities which were allowed to continue with very little, if any, control simply because the factors of production responsible for them had no alternative use. And there were other activities which escaped control because they were so divided up among a multiplicity of small independent units that the administrative problems of handling them were too formidable. Similarly with demand; there are some demands that are so variable and intermittent that the normal rationing methods are inapplicable.

The overseas trade policies which have been discussed are similarly to be interpreted in terms of physical as opposed to financial measures. Exports, directly or indirectly, were a contribution to the war effort, and the early attempts to expand them and the later plans to contract them represent the estimates made at different times of the value of that contribution. The significant fact is that the carrying out of policy was envisaged in terms of physical control—limitation of home demand to make exports available or market direction or planning of exports—rather than in terms of financial expedients, such as exchange depreciation or discrimination or export subsidies.

When the central problem—the release of resources from civilian uses—had been solved, there was still the problem of maintaining stability and of securing fairness in distribution in the civilian sector. Hence came the application and intensification of price control

---

[1] *Op. cit.*, p. 45.

measures, the framing of the utility schemes and the introduction of consumer rationing. Price control played its part in conjunction with other measures in restraining inflationary tendencies which, if they had been allowed to get out of control, would have caused much economic and social disturbance. Utility schemes and near-utility schemes helped the enforcement of price control and made available a supply of reasonably priced consumer goods. Though there was criticism of utility, it did provide some guarantee of quality, allowance being made for war-time shortages; for the poorest sections of the population it actually represented an improvement in living standards. Rationing embodied the principle of 'fair shares', a principle unknown to the peace-time economy; and rationing and utility taken together ensured a measure of equity in the distribution of a restricted supply of consumer goods without which unity and co-operation on the home front might have been seriously prejudiced. In these and other ways the principles of a war economy were fairly effectively enforced. Thus, though the war inevitably meant loss of conveniences and deprivation of conventional necessities, it was nowhere attended with serious economic distress. Government policy helped, not only through rationing, but also through investigations such as had never been undertaken before, of the needs of consumers, both geographical and social needs, and through action taken to correct serious maldistribution of supplies. But consumer policy was also made easier by the war-time co-operation of the civilian population, which showed itself in a general readiness to accept a much cruder and more imperfect satisfaction of varied wants than would be tolerated under normal economic circumstances.

The studies in this volume then have emphasised the significance of physical controls, first in releasing resources to serve directly or indirectly the purposes of the war effort, and, secondly, in applying to the civilian sector, thus confined and restricted, the principles of a war economy. The techniques of these controls have been described and analysed, and it is only necessary here to survey the general principles underlying them. On the one hand they can be distinguished broadly as applying to production, supply and use or consumption. On the other hand they can be classified according to the stage at which they operated—to initial factors of production, such as raw materials, to intermediate products or to end-products. Most of the controls which have been discussed have been controls of end products, whether capital or consumer goods. But there was also the policy of concentration of industry, which was enforced by control in the sense that controls of labour and materials were the sanctions behind it.

The historical development of these controls was from the distribution stage of the economic process backwards towards production and forwards towards consumption. They were operated within the framework of private enterprise, and control of supply meant on the whole less interference with the activities of the private entrepreneur than control of the processes of production. But as scarcities became more acute controls moved towards production and restricted the entrepreneur's freedom to manufacture what he liked in the way he liked. What was thus achieved was greater simplification of process and greater standardisation of product. Again, however, it must be emphasised that though this meant far more interference with the private enterprise system than had been contemplated even in the early months of the war, it did assume, and was indeed inconceivable without, the co-operation of the business community.

Again, control of supply was a good deal simpler from the point of view of administrative technique than control of consumption, though it was inevitable that with the pressure of scarcities increasing some form of rationing would have to be imposed. It is not easy to frame a rationing system which will, however imperfectly, allow for unequal, irregular and variable wants, and even if paper schemes can be devised they may make a disproportionate claim on administrative labour in their execution. The difficulties of controlling clothing consumption, which were thus a good deal more awkward than those of food control, were met by a system of points rationing. For some other commodities it was possible, with some degree of arbitrariness, to mark off those categories of people with the more urgent wants and to restrict supplies to them. For other commodities, again, such as teapots or saucepans, it would have been impracticable to formulate any workable rationing scheme.

It would clearly be impossible to measure statistically the success of this apparatus of controls in achieving the major objective, the release of resources from civilian uses. Independently of these controls factors of production moved into war uses, partly through normal economic motives, partly for patriotic reasons, and partly through the application of other measures such as direction of labour. Nor has it proved possible to estimate what might be termed the indirect release of factors of production through the more efficient organisation of the restricted level of civilian output. Concentration was a policy of this sort, aiming at the production of a given (reduced) level of output with the minimum total usage of overhead factors, by working a limited number of plants to capacity. But when we try to measure changes in efficiency which might be ascribed to concentration of production arrangements we are confronted with changes in the quality both of factors of production and of products which make comparisons difficult if not impossible.[1] Quite apart from concentration there were utility schemes and austerity measures which

---

[1] *Cf.* L. Rostas, *Comparative Productivity in British and American Industry*, pp. 44–5.

2R

in a certain sense made labour more productive. And again obviously it is impossible to say how much labour and materials which would otherwise have had to be devoted to new building were saved through the co-ordination of requirements for factory and storage space.

On the other hand, measurement has been made of the contributions from various sources towards the real cost of the war and this measurement enables us to estimate the pressure exerted by the war effort upon the different parts of the civilian economy.[1] It has been estimated that 40 per cent. of this cost was derived from increased output, 20 per cent. from reduced consumption, 20 per cent. from reduced domestic capital outlay, $18\frac{1}{2}$ per cent. from larger drafts on overseas capital, the remaining $1\frac{1}{2}$ per cent. coming from smaller Government non-war expenditure. The first item reflects partly the slack in the economic system, the failure to use fully before the war the nation's available resources, partly the use in war of reserves of labour which had not previously been in the market for employment. And in so far as these reserves were made up of housewives hitherto engaged on work in the home the figures quoted fail to make allowance for the reduction in household services which the absorption of these women into war work involved. The second item provides an indication of the war-time fall in consumption, though it understates the fall in real value to the extent that no account is taken of changes in the quality of what was consumed, for example, the reduced size of newspapers or the substitution of undecorated for decorated pottery. Most of this decrease had taken place by 1941.[2] The same proportion of the cost of the war as that provided by reduced consumption was contributed by the running down of domestic capital, through failure to maintain and replace fixed capital and through declines in stocks.[3] Nearly the same proportion was met by a deterioration in the international economic position of the United Kingdom through realisation of overseas assets, often at serious loss, and through the incurring of new obligations to overseas countries. These proportions provide some guidance, if the necessary qualifications be made, to those who seek an answer to the old question as to the distribution over time of the burden and costs of a war. In any case they serve to emphasise the contribution of capital depletion at home and abroad to Britain's post-war economic difficulties.

There was a significant disparity in the economic experiences of the civilian economies of the United Kingdom, the United States and Canada.[4] Thus while the level of consumption in the United King-

---

[1] Cmd. 6784, and *The Economist*, 13th April 1946, pp. 589 *et seq.*

[2] *The Impact of the War on Civilian Consumption*, p. 24.

[3] No account has, however, been taken of the post-war values of war assets.

[4] *Cf. The Impact of the War on Civilian Consumption.*

dom had fallen by 1943 by twenty per cent. from the pre-war level, and by the end of the war was still appreciably below that level, consumption in the United States and Canada actually increased during the war.[1] There were differences in the general patterns of consumption which will be considered later, but it is clear that the choice expressed in the phrase 'guns or butter' existed for the United Kingdom, whereas, broadly speaking, it did not exist for the United States and Canada. The explanation of this striking divergence can be given in fairly simple terms: there was a good deal more slack to be taken up in the economies of the transatlantic countries, and they were not affected to the same degree by shipping difficulties; while the United States, coming as they did later into the war, could live on the 'hump' of stocks which had already been exhausted in the United Kingdom.[2] The influence of this disparity on the issues discussed in this volume has been seen in the difficulties of planning the supply of civilian goods to third countries from the United Kingdom and the United States. It was in fact an expression of the economic preponderance of the United States, a preponderance which was an obstacle at times to joint planning in the field of exports.

The effects of the controls can be traced a good deal more clearly in the altered pattern of consumption. This altered pattern was almost wholly due to planned limitation of supplies and to rationing. 'It can be said with confidence that the very great changes in the pattern of consumer purchases which took place in all these countries [United Kingdom, United States, Canada] did not reflect consumers' own free choice. American consumers did not wish to spend their money on "other personal effects" instead of motor vehicles, nor did the British want to switch from clothing to entertainment. Changes such as these were mainly due to legal limitations on the purchase of various goods or to sheer lack of supplies.'[3]

In the United Kingdom personal expenditure on consumers' goods and services, revalued at 1938 prices, varied as follows (1938 = 100):[4]

1939	1940	1941	1942	1943	1944	1945
100	90	87	85	84	86	91

and personal expenditure fell, as a proportion of gross national expenditure, from eighty-four per cent. in 1938 to sixty per cent. in 1943. But these war-time changes in the level of consumption as a whole—a steep fall down to 1943 followed by a slight rise to 1945— concealed marked divergences in the movement of different groups of items. These divergences can be traced in Table X of the Statistical Appendix.

---

[1] *Ibid*, p. 21.
[2] *Ibid*, p. 22.
[3] *Ibid*. p. 29.
[4] The indices are based on the figures of *The Statistical Digest of the War* (H.M.S.O. 1951).

It should be noted that the consumption of some groups of items actually increased from 1941 onwards, namely reading matter, travel, communication services and entertainments. This was true not only of aggregate, but also of *per capita* consumption.[1] It was true also of two other groups—beer and tobacco. In the main these increases can be explained either by special war-time factors, as in the case of travel and communication services, or by the fact that the resources which could have been transferred to war purposes were small in relation to the amount of consumer expenditure involved, as in the case of entertainments.[2] Secondly, where falls in consumption did occur, they were in very different proportions. The biggest fall was in motor vehicles, since the purchase of new vehicles by the private individual was practically discontinued. Purchases of furniture and furnishings in 1944 were only one-fifth of what they had been in 1938. On the other hand, purchases of clothing in 1944 were rather more than half purchases in 1938. These differences are, of course, to be explained, as has already been pointed out, in terms not of consumer choice but of policy. On the one hand the more durable goods required in their production materials and labour which were in strong demand for war purposes. On the other hand curtailment of production of these goods involved less sacrifice for consumers as a whole, since in most cases the life of existing articles could be prolonged. It is worth noting that even in the United States and in Canada *per capita* purchases of cars and also of household metal products and of electrical equipment were sharply reduced.[3] But percentage cuts in broad groups of consumer goods do not tell the whole story. Within these groups there were many individual items production of which ceased completely. Thus the whole pattern of consumer expenditure was much distorted, and it was some time after the war before a normal distribution of this expenditure was attained. Two war-time effects of these changes which deserve consideration were the heightened importance of second-hand goods, which provided some tricky problems in price control, and the much increased emphasis on repairs to the durable goods whose production had been curtailed.

The problems and policies which we have just been discussing have been those of a self-contained economy. The economy of the United Kingdom was very far from being self-contained, partly because it drew supplies not only of food and raw materials but also of finished goods from overseas, partly because it was itself a source of supply to other, dependent, economies. The problem of the allocation of resources was therefore not merely one of allocation

---

[1] *Cf. The Impact of the War on Civilian Consumption*, p. 26.

[2] *Ibid.*, p. 25.

[3] *Ibid.*, pp. 26–7.

between civilian and war uses but between home civilian, war and export uses. Fundamentally, in war as in peace, exports are an indirect means of satisfying home requirements. But in war this straightforward economic proposition is soon found to offer only imperfect guidance as to the right export policy to be pursued. For one thing, 'political' exports acquire an importance unknown in the peace-time economy. Goods have to be sent abroad in order to prevent neutral countries falling into the arms of the enemy, to maintain good relations with friends and Allies, and to further the purposes of economic warfare. Then again, considerations of the prices that overseas buyers will pay and of earnings in foreign currency have to be overruled by special war-time considerations, such as the need for sustaining dependent economies which are important sources of food and raw materials. Furthermore, the currency factor itself acquires a new significance owing to the far greater range and intensity of currency restrictions. Finally, the whole question of the cost of exports has to be reconsidered, partly because of the demands which they make on scarce shipping, partly because of their effects upon the domestic economy. For under the full employment conditions of a war economy an increase of exports would divert resources from more urgent uses.

Thus a policy of minimum exports, that is to say, exports at the lowest level compatible with securing necessary supplies from overseas and maintaining abroad certain indispensable political and economic conditions rather than a policy of export stimulation seems to satisfy the requirements of total war. In 1940, before it was seen that massive assistance from the United States would be available and when there were unemployed resources at home, there was some ground for launching an export drive; but even then its undiscriminating character could only be justified in terms of its effect upon the psychology of the home manufacturer and of the overseas suppliers who wanted to be assured that they would ultimately receive payment for their goods. After the introduction of lend-lease the picture changed completely, and with the intensification of the war effort the policy of minimum exports was forced upon the United Kingdom. The results were seen in a reduction of the volume of exports to thirty per cent. of the pre-war level. All exports suffered in this reduction, but principally of course those which competed with war production for scarce materials and labour. In the case of coal, the very steep reduction in exports—from 35·9 million tons in 1938 to 2·6 million tons in 1944—reflected a fundamental change in the industry's output which was to have most serious effects on Britain's post-war trade.

This export policy would have been inevitable, quite apart from the economic preponderance of the United States. But taken in conjunction with this preponderance it threatened seriously to weaken the post-war international economic position of the United Kingdom. It soon became plain that with the loss of invisible sources of income and with the accumulation of indebtedness to overseas countries the United Kingdom would, in order to achieve international equilibrium, require not merely to restore but considerably to surpass its pre-war export volume. Hence every effort was made towards the end of the war to regain the export freedom which had been temporarily sacrificed and to prepare the way for a great expansion of export trade.

Finally, the question may be asked, what was the effect of the building of this apparatus of control and this machinery of planning upon the administrative system and administrative techniques? With what success was the Government machine adapted and enlarged so as to absorb and digest a whole new set of economic and social problems? What were the special features of these problems and what effect had the handling of them on the Government's relations with manufacturers, traders and the general public?

In the ten years between the onset of the great depression and the outbreak of war the scope of Government intervention in the economic life of the community had indeed increased. A complete tariff system had been introduced and quotas had been imposed to restrict and divert the flow of imports into the country. Internally the Government had sponsored schemes which aimed at alleviating the economic difficulties of such basic industries as coal, cotton and agriculture. It had given encouragement to the reorganisation of the iron and steel industry. These schemes did, however, no more than provide a framework within which, it was hoped, the profitability of private enterprise would be restored. They were administered by private enterprise itself and they operated mainly through the limitation of competition in prices and output. They were not really schemes for Government control of industry; rather did they embody the then popular idea of self-government in industry.

Thus, although there had been a considerable growth of interventionism the Government had not in these years been involved directly in the control of industry. And even for some time after the outbreak of war the approach to those controls over industries which have been discussed in this volume was tentative and, to some extent, along pre-war lines. Thus supply was controlled rather than production, while in concentration voluntary schemes were preferred to the imposition on industry of a co-ordinated plan. It was only from 1942 onwards that the policy of telling firms what they were to produce and how they were to produce it was substituted for the policy of arranging things in such a way that the private entrepreneur of his own initiative would do what the Government wanted him to do.

These developments imported quantitative and qualitative changes into the administrative structure. In the first place they called for an increase of staff, though, as has been mentioned in Chapter VI, this increase was not as great as might have been expected.[1] As the new work to be done frequently demanded specialised knowledge, professional men and business men with the necessary qualifications had to be recruited; yet, as has been pointed out, the greater part of the Board of Trade's war-time activities was conducted by permanent civil servants or temporary civil servants not taken from industry.

Secondly, control and more especially planning could not have succeeded, could perhaps barely have been attempted, without much fuller quantitative information than was available about industry and trade before the beginning of the war. Regular statistics of production, supplies and stocks were needed and they were developed. Nor was it only a matter of industrial and trade statistics. Investigation was made into the pattern of consumer spending and the geographical distribution of consumer goods.

Thirdly, the war-time policies for civilian industries required close and continuous co-operation between administrators and business men. The formulation of the general principles of policy was the responsibility of the administrator, but in the elaboration of these principles and in their application to the complex details of industrial and market organisation he necessarily sought the help of the industrialists and traders concerned. In the Industrial and Export Council, moreover, there was an even closer and more direct association of administrators and business men than would be suggested by what has just been said. The business members of that Council became in effect part of the administrative structure and were responsible for expounding and applying policies to their fellow industrialists. But at the same time they were interpreting and expressing the views of the business community to the administrator, and they were therefore not just business men transformed into temporary civil servants. On the other hand, the application and enforcement of industrial policies strengthened business association though the war-time invention of export groups had little opportunity to prove its worth, and the use of the trade association as an instrument of Government policy was less marked than might have been expected.

Fourthly, the administrator found himself compelled to take an interest in the consumer and his needs to an extent unparalleled in peace-time. In peace the market mechanism had been trusted to do the job of supplying the varied wants of consumers. But when war-

[1] See p. 135.

time controls had interfered with the market mechanism and when the principle of 'fair shares', unknown in peace, had been introduced, the Government had in effect to assume a broad measure of responsibility for seeing that the basic requirements of all sections of the population were covered. This meant not only a study of these requirements but also adaptation of production and supply in order to meet them.

Fifthly, there was the development of the field of public relations, a development common to all Government departments during the war. Public relations in its widest sense meant more than just keeping the public of manufacturers, traders and consumers informed of Government measures through press notices and pamphlets on subjects such as price control and rationing. It meant as well the provision on the spot of help towards the understanding and working of these measures. It included a certain amount of publicity in connection with the utility schemes. Furthermore, it was persuasive in its efforts, for example through a 'make do and mend' campaign, to induce the public to make the most economical and effective use of the stocks of goods which it possessed.

Lastly, there was the expenditure of effort on the policing and enforcing of a vast number of Statutory Rules and Orders. This involved everything from detective problems of tracking down coupon offenders to the checking by accountants of manufacturers' costs to see that they were conforming to the requirements of the price regulations. Here again there were new problems created by war, problems which might have been serious and disturbing but for the co-operation of traders and the public. The black market existed but it went nowhere near undermining the clothes rationing scheme.

All these problems, toward the solution of which the administrator's pre-war experience gave little assistance, were not only handled but handled with a fair measure of success. Generally the central economic issues were foreseen, and plans were evolved to meet them and were effectively carried through. Probably the only major example that can be given of failure to see a problem in perspective and to deal with it consistently is that of the Board of Trade's treatment of retail trade. By and large the difficulties that cropped up were not those of a faulty economic policy but were due to the rapidity with which war developments overtook policy.

But this is not to say that the results obtained were commensurate with the administrative labour expended in achieving them. Chapter X has shown reason to doubt the value of the time and effort devoted to working out and applying concentration schemes in the less important industries. Similarly one may question the worthwhileness of some of the effort put into the promotion of exports, particularly when the balance of payments problem had been transformed by lend-lease. All that can be said, however, is that such waste of resources as occurred was inevitable for the experiments that occupied the Board of Trade in war-time were quite new in the history of British government.

All this war-time experience had an important bearing on post-war arrangements. As a general principle war-time controls were not scrapped after the end of hostilities as they had been after World War I, but were retained to deal with an economic situation of shortage and inflation.[1] Thus the Board of Trade continued to administer the controls which they had operated during the years 1939–45, though in an atmosphere increasingly hostile to regulations and restrictions. They even expanded their own sphere of activity through the transference to them of the Ministry of Supply Controls, except those over iron and steel, non-ferrous metals and engineering. They also acquired new responsibilities in the application of a policy with regard to location of industry. But the background to this apparatus of control had completely changed. Whereas in the war there had been a single objective—the winning of the war—there now emerged a multiplicity of aims. Perhaps the only aims on which there was general agreement were, first, that of expanding much above the pre-war level the volume of exports and, secondly, that of restraining and moderating the tendency to inflation inherent in the post-war situation. As well as, and partly as an outcome of, this dis-agreement about objectives there was the controversy over the respec-tive merits and demerits of physical and financial controls. With increasing supplies and with the collapse of war-time unity of purpose this controversy grew sharper. Some of the war-time problems still existed and some of the war-time solutions were still applicable, but behind the façade of control new problems, demanding new solutions, had emerged.

---

[1] The only control which was abandoned shortly after the end of the war was the control over entry into retail trade.

Statistical Appendix

TABLE I

Numbers employed in certain industries in Great Britain[1]

Thousands

	1939	1940		1941		1942		1943		1944		1945
	June	June	Dec.	June	Dec.	June	Dec.	June	Dec.	June	Dec.	June
Cotton spinning and weaving .	339·9	363·8	339·2	276·1	237·3	233·8	231·0	227·3	223·5	220·1	214·9	212·9
Woollen and worsted . .	207·6	222·3	212·1	195·3	176·1	162·1	152·3	143·5	136·0	129·1	127·5	129·8
Silk and rayon .	72·2	75·7	65·7	58·6	52·7	50·0	47·5	45·9	45·4	44·1	44·7	45·9
Hosiery and lace .	139·3	136·9	123·4	110·9	92·6	81·4	77·6	74·3	69·1	67·9	68·2	69·6
Tailoring . .	234·6	243·3	238·7	242·0	208·0	194·6	190·7	178·1	165·0	158·5	158·2	172·2
Shirts, collars, etc.	93·5	91·5	83·1	77·7	66·4	58·4	56·8	55·1	52·1	49·6	47·7	52·5
Boots and shoes .	135·0	132·9	129·8	127·8	118·9	107·0	99·9	96·3	93·7	92·2	91·9	95·3
Furniture, uphol-stery, etc. .	138·4	107·7	93·7	78·2	72·9	70·4	68·5	61·5	59·6	57·8	58·3	62·4
Glass manufacture (excluding bottles and scientific glassware) .	30·6	28·3	27·8	25·9	25·2	26·1	24·9	24·4	24·4	24·3	25·1	25·7
Pottery, earthen-ware, etc. .	67·0	59·3	55·2	52·1	44·5	39·7	37·5	36·7	36·6	36·2	37·1	39·0

Source: Ministry of Labour and National Service

TABLE II

Percentage of total manpower engaged on orders for the Forces and for the home and export markets[1]
June 1944

Percentages

	Manufacture of equipment and supplies for the Forces	Orders for export	Orders for the home market
Cotton spinning and weaving . . .	37	21	42
Woollen and worsted	43	13	44
Silk and rayon	50	20	30
Hosiery and lace	26	8	66
Tailoring	38	2	60
Shirts, collars, etc.	26	2	72
Boots and shoes	18	1	81
Furniture, upholstery, etc. . .	52	0	48
Glass manufacture (excluding bottles and scientific glassware) . . .	40	11	49
Pottery, earthenware, etc. . . .	12	28	60

Source: Ministry of Labour and National Service
[1] Males under 65 and females under 60, but excluding non-manual workers earning over £420 per annum. Part-time female workers are included, two being counted as one unit. Owing to differences in definitions, etc., these figures do not necessarily agree with manpower figures in the text.

TABLE III

Value and volume of the external trade of the United Kingdom[1]

	1938	1939	1940	1941	1942	1943	1944	1945
VALUE (£ millions)								
Imports:								
Total imports . . .	920	886	1,152	1,145	997	1,234	1,309	1,104
Retained imports . . .	858	840	1,126	1,132	992	1,228	1,294	1,053
Exports:								
Exports of United Kingdom produce and manufactures .	471	440	411	365	271	234	266	399
Re-exports	62	46	26	13	5	6	15	51
VOLUME INDEX:[2] (1938=100)								
Retained imports:								
Total	100	97	94	82	70	77	80	62
Food, drink and tobacco .	100	94	78	72	73	78	74	60
Raw materials and articles mainly unmanufactured .	100	98	105	62	63	59	61	60
Articles wholly or mainly manufactured . . .	100	100	112	121	72	94	102	62
Exports:								
Total	100	94	72	56	36	29	31	46
Articles wholly or mainly manufactured:								
Total	100	94	76	62	40	31	35	45
Textiles . . .	100	101	80	69	55	36	36	41
Metals	100	87	65	47	29	23	29	42
Other	100	100	91	83	46	41	42	55

[1] The figures for 1942 to 1945 exclude imports, exports and re-exports of munitions.
[2] Quantities revalued at 1938 prices and expressed as a percentage of the value of imports or exports in 1938.

Source: Board of Trade

TABLE IV

Retained imports
Analysis by classes and selected groups[1]

£ millions

	1938	1939	1940	1941	1942	1943	1944	1945
I. Food, drink and tobacco:								
Total . . .	417·8	387·5	412·3	419·4	433·7	511·0	510·4	464·1
A. Grain and flour .	72·9	54·5	93·3	89·6	53·5	66·0	64·3	76·7
D. Meat . . .	90·1	92·8	96·8	118·7	148·8	166·8	161·7	107·8
E. Dairy produce .	79·3	75·3	62·2	66·3	84·4	85·3	91·1	75·7
F. Fresh fruit and vegetables . .	36·3	33·8	26·9	4·4	5·4	2·3	8·2	15·9
G. Beverages and cocoa preparations . .	40·4	34·9	40·3	41·1	36·3	49·9	49·3	48·7
I. Tobacco . . .	22·5	12·7	8·7	17·9	20·5	41·6	32·6	51·8
Other food . .	76·3	83·5	84·1	81·4	84·8	99·1	103·2	87·5
II. Raw materials and articles mainly unmanufactured:								
Total . . .	218·0	216·5	326·3	224·7	236·1	262·7	278·3	279·9
E. Wood and timber .	42·6	36·9	37·7	24·8	20·4	32·6	35·9	45·7
F. Raw cotton and cotton waste . . .	28·3	33·0	49·8	35·8	52·6	53·7	42·0	46·5
G. Wool, raw and waste, and woollen rags .	30·1	31·8	62·5	21·9	27·4	19·0	35·7	29·2
J. Seeds and nuts for oil, oils, fats, resins and gums . . .	30·0	30·4	44·4	39·5	39·8	55·3	53·4	46·1
Other Class II .	87·0	84·4	131·9	102·7	95·9	102·1	111·3	112·4
III. Articles wholly or mainly manufactured:								
Total . . .	215·2	228·9	381·5	480·4	308·9	438·8	474·7	289·7
C. Iron and steel and manufactures thereof	14·6	18·5	48·1	69·0	47·0	58·9	32·9	6·2
D. Non-ferrous metals and manufactures thereof .	31·8	36·0	58·8	56·6	60·3	83·7	65·7	16·6
F. Electrical goods and apparatus . .	3·0	2·7	4·1	2·6	2·7	8·2	23·9	18·7
G. Machinery . .	20·3	22·4	38·5	49·6	32·3	40·6	39·4	18·3
O. Chemicals, drugs, dyes and colours .	13·1	15·4	16·9	15·4	18·8	22·0	23·7	18·6
P. Oils, fats and resins, manufactured .	43·0	44·7	70·7	93·0	100·3	152·5	220·4	142·8
R. Paper, cardboard, etc.	14·8	15·6	16·3	5·0	4·6	4·6	6·4	11·5
Other Class III .	74·6	73·6	128·1	189·2	42·9	68·3	62·3	57·0
Total retained imports .	858·0	839·5	1,126·1	1,132·4	992·2	1,227·9	1,293·7	1,052·7

[1] As defined in the Accounts relating to Trade and Navigation of the United Kingdom.
Source: Board of Trade

TABLE V

Exports of the produce and manufactures of the United Kingdom Analysis by classes and selected groups[1]

£ millions

	1938	1939	1940	1941	1942	1943	1944	1945
I. Food, drink and tobacco:								
Total	35·9	35·7	33·4	27·8	18·4	19·0	22·9	55·7
G. Beverages and cocoa preparations	13·8	15·9	19·6	17·0	11·5	11·0	10·7	15·2
I. Tobacco .	4·9	5·0	4·8	5·6	4·3	5·2	5·1	12·1
Other food	17·2	14·8	9·0	5·2	2·6	2·8	7·1	28·4
II. Raw materials and articles mainly unmanufactured:								
Total	57·0	54·5	36·2	15·7	10·2	9·4	8·1	15·1
A. Coal	37·4	38·3	25·3	8·0	6·0	6·4	5·0	6·6
Other Class II	19·6	16·2	10·9	7·7	4·2	3·0	3·1	8·5
III. Articles wholly or mainly manufactured:								
Total	365·2	338·1	334·1	316·1	236·6	201·4	229·9	306·8
C. Iron and steel and manufactures thereof	41·7	32·9	31·2	19·0	9·9	6·1	8·6	20·9
D. Non-ferrous metals and manufactures thereof	12·3	12·7	12·4	7·6	7·0	6·7	4·7	12·1
F. Electrical goods and apparatus .	13·6	11·3	13·2	11·4	11·2	11·1	12·6	13·8
G. Machinery	57·2	47·0	36·2	30·9	29·9	27·9	40·9	46·2
I. Cotton yarns and manufactures .	49·7	49·1	49·3	44·7	40·1	34·2	37·1	42·7
J. Woollen and worsted yarns and manufactures	26·8	26·7	28·7	29·8	25·1	18·5	15·3	21·6
K. Silk and artificial silk yarns and manufactures	5·5	5·9	8·7	11·8	16·4	12·7	16·4	17·3
O. Chemicals, drugs, dyes and colours .	22·2	22·7	27·6	25·0	24·0	27·9	29·4	38·2
S. Vehicles (including locomotives, ships and aircraft)	45·1	40·0	31·5	35·7	9·2	8·8	13·4	20·2
Other Class III	91·1	89·8	95·3	100·2	63·8	47·5	51·5	73·8
Total exports of the produce and manufacture of the United Kingdom .	470·8	439·5	411·2	365·4	271·3	233·5	266·3	399·3

[1] As defined in the Accounts relating to Trade and Navigation of the United Kingdom.
Source: Board of Trade

TABLE VI

Imports
Analysis by source

£ millions

	1938	1939	1940	1941	1942	1943	1944	1945
TOTAL . . .	919·5	885·5	1,152·1	1,145·1	996·7	1,233·9	1,309·3	1,103·7
British countries[1] .	371·5	358·1	548·5	515·0	456·3	479·8	517·2	522·6
Foreign countries .	548·0	527·4	603·6	630·1	540·4	754·1	792·1	581·1
Europe . . .	308·2	283·3	149·8	64·4	66·8	60·0	82·0	129·8
Africa . . .	63·4	68·7	95·7	86·6	102·4	106·4	122·5	101·4
Asia . . .	123·6	115·3	165·0	125·5	87·7	88·4	92·2	93·6
Oceania . . .	120·7	105·6	154·0	103·6	100·4	82·4	98·0	111·4
North America . .	199·3	199·4	428·3	602·8	505·0	739·4	745·7	526·8
Central and South America and West Indies . . .	104·3	113·2	159·3	162·2	134·4	157·3	168·9	140·7

[1] Including protectorates, mandated territories and trust territories of members of the Commonwealth and territories under condominium.

Source: Board of Trade

TABLE VII

United Kingdom exports
Analysis by destination

£ millions

	1938	1939	1940	1941	1942	1943	1944	1945
TOTAL . . .	470·8	439·5	411·2	365·4	271·3	233·5	266·3	399·3
British countries[1] .	234·8	216·6	247·4	232·2	175·0	149·2	169·8	213·9
Foreign countries .	236·0	222·9	163·8	133·2	96·3	84·3	96·5	185·4
Europe . . .	172·2	158·6	95·3	66·5	46·0	37·6	58·7	142·8
Africa . . .	73·6	68·5	69·0	70·4	60·9	56·7	65·9	83·4
Asia . . .	78·1	68·1	72·9	67·6	35·9	26·5	37·1	56·2
Oceania . . .	58·2	48·8	63·3	53·1	45·1	40·1	46·6	49·6
North America . .	44·0	51·9	66·3	70·9	49·9	43·1	41·2	42·7
Central and South America and West Indies . . .	44·7	43·6	44·4	36·9	33·5	29·5	16·8	24·6

[1] Including protectorates, mandated territories and trust territories of members of the Commonwealth and territories under condominium.

Source: Board of Trade

TABLE VIII

Woven cloth, household textiles, hosiery and footwear. Supplies for home civilian use

	Unit	1935	1942	1943	1944	1945
Woven cloth for clothing						
Woven wool cloth:						
Total . . .	Million sq. yds.	—	173	162	159	166
Utility . . .	Million sq. yds.	—	128	119	104	133
Non-utility . . .	Million sq. yds.	—	45[1]	43	55	33
Woven non-wool cloth:						
Total . . .	Million sq. yds.	—	371	454	404	403
Utility . . .	Million sq. yds.	—	299	358	336	330
Non-utility . .	Million sq. yds.	—	72[2]	96	68	73
Wool hand-knitting yarn .	Million lb.	—	—	8·7	9·4	11·1
Household textiles:						
Blankets:[3]						
Wool	Millions	6·49	—	2·26	2·70	3·80
Cotton	Millions	—	—	4·40	4·76	5·02
Sheets	Millions	—	—	3·00	3·87	7·06
Pillowcases . . .	Millions	—	—	5·82	7·56	10·78
Towels:						
Hand and bath . .	Millions	—	—	18·5	15·1	12·5
Other	Millions	—	—	14·7	10·7	9·8
Hosiery						
Men's and youths':						
Socks and stockings .	Million pairs	90[4]	35·4	33·4	20·1	23·9
Pullovers and cardigans .	Millions	—	1·8	1·9	2·3	2·8
Vests	Millions	—	8·4	10·9	8·4	8·8
Pants and trunks .	Millions	—	10·1	13·9	9·1	9·6
Women's and maids':						
Stockings and socks .	Million pairs	280[4][5]	160·4	140·6	131·3	134·2
Jumpers and cardigans .	Millions	—	6·6	5·3	6·0	6·2
Vests	Millions	—	19·6	17·8	15·8	17·1
Children's:						
Socks and stockings .	Million pairs	90[4][6]	51·0	66·0	61·8	61·7
Underwear . . .	Million pieces	—	23·2	31·4	26·9	26·8
Footwear[7]						
Total production for all uses	Million pairs	132·5	108·2	102·7	99·7	99·8
Production for home civilian use:						
Total	Million pairs	129·0	90·3	89·4	87·4	87·7
Leather uppers:						
Total . . .	Million pairs	105·0	74·7	75·5	74·1	73·7
Men's . . .	Million pairs	29·3	16·7	14·7	12·6	12·9
Women's . . .	Million pairs	46·4	31·2	29·6	28·1	28·2
Children's . .	Million pairs	29·3	26·9	31·2	33·3	32·6
Fabric uppers . .	Million pairs	5·5	5·9	5·0	4·1	4·4
Slippers . . .	Million pairs	18·4	9·7	9·0	9·2	9·6

[1] Total for eleven months converted to yearly rate.
[2] Total for five months converted to yearly rate.
[3] Including cot size.
[4] Approximate figure for 1937.
[5] Stockings only.
[6] Including women's and maids' socks.
[7] Excluding rubber footwear.

Source: Board of Trade

TABLE IX

Pottery, hollow-ware and brushes. Production and supplies for home civilian use

Millions

	1943		1944		1945	
	Produc-tion	For home civilian use	Produc-tion	For home civilian use	Produc-tion	For home civilian use
Pottery:						
Cups, mugs and beakers .	138·7	108·9	125·9	94·9	108·8	80·2
Saucers and small plates	83·8	52·8	80·1	49·4	78·9	47·1
Large plates . . .	53·7	25·1	51·2	26·8	46·7	23·9
Teapots and coffee pots .	8·7[1]	7·3[1]	8·8	7·4	8·1	6·4
Cooking ware (all types) .	4·1[2]	3·6[2]	4·3	3·7	4·7	4·2
Hollow-ware:						
Kettles . . .	5·8	5·2	5·7	5·1	7·6	7·2
Saucepans and stewpans	11·7	10·9	13·3	12·6	18·0	16·9
Dustbins . . .	1·18	0·71	1·11	0·97	1·47	1·37
Brushes and brooms:						
Household type . .	45·9	34·7[3]	43·3	32·4	43·6	35·6
Paint and paste . .	17·9	10·5[3]	17·2	10·8	20·1	14·2
Toilet	38·0	22·9[3]	38·1	23·9	43·2	28·0

[1] Coffee pots included from March 1943 only.
[2] Until February 1943 including pie and baking dishes only.
[3] First three months of 1943 include exports.

Source: Board of Trade

TABLE X

Personal expenditure on consumers' goods and services revalued at 1938 prices

£ millions

	1938	1939	1940	1941	1942	1943	1944	1945
Food	1,305	1,310	1,145	1,082	1,114	1,076	1,137	1,154
Alcoholic beverages . . .	285	296	276	288	267	269	274	297
Tobacco	177	182	178	196	206	204	205	225
Rent, rates and water charges .	491	504	508	502	497	498	503	506
Fuel and light	197	199	203	205	199	187	193	197
Durable household goods . .	234	219	164	115	81	67	60	82
Other household goods . .	54	55	52	48	42	40	40	40
Clothing	446	444	372	275	273	247	275	279
Books, newspapers and magazines	64	63	59	61	63	67	73	77
Private motoring . . .	127	113	38	30	17	8	8	25
Travel	163	156	137	155	181	193	196	224
Communication services . .	29	29	27	27	31	37	42	40
Entertainments . . .	64	61	53	75	87	89	90	94
Other services	483	467	432	411	373	350	343	369
Other goods	177	177	162	131	109	110	113	120
Income in kind of the armed forces	17	28	66	97	105	135	151	147
Less Foreign tourists' expenditure in the United Kingdom . .	−43	−34	−8	−11	−21	−48	−84	−39
Personal expenditure in the United Kingdom	4,270	4,269	3,864	3,687	3,624	3,529	3,619	3,837
Personal expenditure abroad .	34	38	24	28	45	73	92	85
TOTAL . . .	4,304	4,307	3,888	3,715	3,669	3,602	3,711	3,922

Source: Central Statistical Office

TABLE XI

Working-class cost-of-living index

(Prices at 1st September 1939 = 100)

	Food	Rent (including rates)	Clothing	Fuel and light	Other items included	All items
1st September 1939 .	100	100	100	100	100	100
1st December 1939 .	114	100	118	107	106	112
1st June 1940 . .	115	101	137	116	117	117
30th November 1940	125	101	155	120	123	126
31st May 1941 .	123	101	177	124	127	129
1st December 1941 .	120	101	191	126	130	130
1st June 1942 . .	115	101	195	127	147	128
1st December 1942 .	119	101	181	132	150	129
1st June 1943 . .	120	101	168	134	160	128
1st December 1943 .	122	101	164	134	163	128
1st June 1944 . .	122	101	165	139	163	129
1st December 1944 .	122	101	167	145	163	130
1st June 1945 . .	123	102	167	151	163	132
1st December 1945 .	122	102	166	151	163	131

649

TABLE XII

Wholesale price index numbers (prices at September 1939 = 100)

	1939 Dec.	1940 June	1940 Dec.	1941 June	1941 Dec.	1942 June	1942 Dec.	1943 June	1943 Dec.	1944 June	1944 Dec.	1945 June	1945 Dec.
All articles . . .	114·5	127·3	140·3	144·3	147·6	151·3	152·9	154·5	154·7	157·3	158·3	161·3	160·5
Industrial materials and manufactures . .	112·4	126·6	139·6	144·9	147·1	147·8	150·8	152·0	153·9	158·1	160·3	162·9	162·8
Industrial materials and manufactures (excluding fuel):													
Basic materials	120·0	149·1	155·5	164·4	167·8	165·3	167·2	171·2	174·8	183·2	184·3	184·4	185·4
Intermediate products	110·3	121·3	141·8	146·2	148·0	148·5	151·1	151·3	152·3	155·6	155·5	160·5	161·8
Manufactured articles	109·6	117·8	129·6	133·4	135·0	136·8	138·9	138·6	140·6	142·0	143·9	144·9	145·2

Source: Board of Trade

650

TABLE XIII

Index numbers of wholesale stocks of clothing
(Average quantity held in stock in 1943 = 100)

	1943	1944	1945
January	86	105	61
February	90	100	51
March	90	92	47
April	91	86	45
May	97	83	47
June	106	85	52
July	118	84	57
August	114	69	52
September	105	62	46
October	101	58	46
November	102	58	51
December	103	63	60

Source: Board of Trade

TABLE XIV

Index numbers of stocks of footwear

(Average quantity held in stock in 1943 = 100)

| Month | Men's boots and shoes (including industrial) | | | | | | Women's boots and shoes | | | | | | Children's boots, shoes and sandals | | | | | |
| | A FIRMS | | | B FIRMS | | | A FIRMS | | | B FIRMS | | | A FIRMS | | | B FIRMS | | |
	1943	1944	1945	1943	1944	1945	1943	1944	1945	1943	1944	1945	1943	1944	1945	1943	1944	1945
January	111	98	67	107	119	100	111	97	78	111	115	74	108	119	121	89	137	106
February	115	93	65	106	119	92	116	92	76	110	109	71	117	126	127	89	134	106
March	116	89	62	96	114	94	118	95	68	103	104	66	115	136	118	93	134	105
April	108	85	61	98	118	96	109	91	63	103	100	64	101	125	112	95	133	98
May	104	83	59	96	120	99	103	88	58	94	97	61	96	119	101	89	123	91
June	97	83	59	96	123	98	98	86	59	95	98	64	91	119	100	92	137	102
July	95	84	60	104	132	105	97	91	59	99	103	62	93	130	102	103	139	99
August	94	71	55	96	125	99	94	73	56	96	92	59	90	106	88	97	119	96
September	88	65	50	93	112	90	86	69	50	90	79	62	92	103	81	104	104	93
October	88	65	48	99	107	92	86	70	49	95	79	74	91	103	80	111	100	98
November	90	65	50	101	106	91	89	74	54	101	77	76	98	110	88	115	104	110
December	94	64	49	109	104	93	93	74	58	107	73	82	108	114	94	126	110	114

A FIRMS are those showing stocks held both at the wholesale and at the retail stage.

B FIRMS are those showing stocks held at the wholesale stage only.

Source: Board of Trade

TABLE XV

Index numbers of retail stocks of clothing and footwear

(Average value of stocks in 1942 = 100)

Month	Dress materials					Women's, girls' and infants' wear					Men's and boys' wear					Boots and shoes				
	1941	1942	1943	1944	1945	1941	1942	1943	1944	1945	1941	1942	1943	1944	1945	1941	1942	1943	1944	1945
January	78	94	101	89	58	72	83	100	84	73	83	96	99	102	74	101	117	84	81	69
February	93	103	105	87	47	79	87	109	85	75	91	100	104	94	67	108	118	97	88	71
March	103	105	107	88	41	88	92	115	90	79	97	99	108	94	68	112	115	85	78	58
April	114	108	104	84	36	93	97	114	90	84	99	99	106	96	71	109	110	82	80	60
May	115	110	102	81	36	93	102	113	91	85	98	103	111	101	74	109	106	78	78	57
June	116	106	101	80	36	100	102	115	97	94	105	100	113	101	76	105	97	75	79	58
July	118	97	102	79	34	97	102	112	94	98	105	100	117	100	77	107	96	76	84	57
August	114	99	101	73	32	96	107	113	88	97	104	101	117	92	73	110	91	74	72	57
September	115	98	94	67	26	102	113	105	85	96	108	104	113	88	69	113	93	72	68	49
October	112	93	92	62	26	102	110	100	80	93	111	101	113	87	70	119	86	71	66	53
November	107	92	91	58	27	102	110	98	81	91	113	100	116	89	71	122	87	75	66	56
December	105	95	86	55	31	90	95	85	69	75	105	95	101	71	51	122	83	77	64	54

Source: Board of Trade

Index

INDEX

(The suffix letter 'n' denotes a footnote)

Accountants, 111, 135, 328, 559, 579, 599
Accountancy standards, 76, 559, 560, 579
Admiralty, 371
Agricultural hand tools
    exports, 160, 169, 171
Agricultural machinery
    exports, 177, 180–182
Agriculture, 9, 10, 286, 634
Aircraft industry, 8
Allen, G. C., *British Industries*, 5n; *Introduction to The Economic Organisation of England*, 8n;
    Lessons of the British War Economy, 231n
Aluminium, 25, 65, 108, 152
Anderson, Sir John (now Lord Waverley)
    Lord President of the Council, 240, 501—*See also Lord President's Committee*
    Chancellor of the Exchequer, 552n
Anglo-American Trade Agreement, 22, 32, 59
Argentine, 60, 64, 67, 139n, 140, 143, 144, 145, 146, 193, 195, 200
    —*See also South America*
Ashley, W. J., *The Economic Organisation of England*, 8n
Assistance Board, 312, 327, 335, 336, 514, 519
Auctions
    control of, 557, 610
Australia
    exports to, 54, 72, 140, 141, 189, 190, 195, 200
    import control in, 72
    United Kingdom wool purchases, 381
    —*See also British Empire Commonwealth Supply Council, Dominions*

Babies' clothing, 307
    —*See also Children: clothing*
Babies' equipment, 290, 298, 507, 511, 530
Baillieu, Sir Clive, 51
Balance of payments
    between the wars, 6 7
    war-time, 15, 16, 20, 25, 26, 44, 61
    post-Second World War, 158–159, 161, 619
    —*See also Exports, Foreign Exchange, Lend-Lease*
Bank of England
    exchange control and, 93
    import control and, 22
    retail trade statistics, 13, 14, 263
Bankruptcy, 230, 256, 258, 405
Banks, joint stock
    coupon banking and, 326
Beale, Sir Samuel, 162
Beaverbrook, Lord
    Minister of Aircraft Production, 235, 240
    Minister of Supply, 322
Bedding, 469
    distribution of, 293, 300, 301, 337
    price control, 580, 581, 596
    —*See also Blankets, Household Textiles, Sheets*
Bedding industry, 225
Belgium, 35, 49
Beveridge, Sir William (now Lord), 205, 625
Bevin, Mr. Ernest, Minister of Labour, 221, 223, 226, 495
Bicycles
    control of, 506
    exports, 35, 160, 170–171, 185, 198
    prices, 83, 589
Bicycle industry, 8

Birth-rate, 425
Black market, 327, 328, 536
——*See also Limitation of Supplies Orders: enforcement*
Black-out material, 16, 77, 93n, 106, 307
Blankets, 3, 287, 288, 300, 333, 392, 468, 469, 470
    distribution, 337
    price control, 469
Blockade, 30, 33n, 39, 633
    export control and, 11, 14, 39, 40, 42, 43, 143
Board of Trade[1]
    as a production department, 124–126, 425, 435, 544, 550
    Industrial and Export Council, 136, 162, 211
    Industrial Supplies Department, 45, 133, 134, 543, 549, 618
    organisation of, 134
    Parliamentary Secretary of, 569, 604
    President of
        Mr. Oliver Stanley, 46, 47, 78
        Sir Andrew Duncan, 35, 51, 58, 68, 322
        Mr. Oliver Lyttelton, 108, 137, 138, 208, 219, 236, 237, 240, 258, 259, 312,
            313, 554, 555
        Mr. Hugh Dalton, 160, 161, 162, 222, 223, 224, 272, 472, 491, 492, 495, 497,
            508, 514, 568, 578, 589, 604
        Sir Stafford Cripps, 279, 591
    staffing, 135–136, 634–635
    transference of functions from Ministry of Supply to, 637
Bolivia, 60
——*See also South America*
Bombing, 105, 110n, 112, 204, 235, 237, 240, 257, 260, 261, 265, 273, 276, 277, 284,
    358, 398, 413, 466, 473
    clothes coupons for bombed-out, 312
    furniture for bombed-out, 512, 513
    supplies of consumer goods to bombed areas, 105, 112, 283, 293–295, 296, 299
    war damage compensation, 267
Books, 23n, 25, 107, 264, 507
Boots and Shoes——*See Footwear*
Borrowing policy, 12, 626
——*See also Saving*
Bournemouth, 288
Bowley, A. L., *Some Economic Consequences of the Great War*, 5n
Brand, R. H., *War and National Finance*, 3n
Branded goods
    price control of, 81, 87
Brazil, 60, 140n, 144, 146n, 178, 179, 180, 201
——*See also South America*
British Celanese Ltd., 573
British Empire
    exports to, 30, 40, 66, 72, 120, 122, 139, 140, 141, 143, 146, 149, 153, 158, 174,
        175, 176, 184, 185, 191, 196, 198, 199
    ——*See also Australia, Canada, Colonies, Commonwealth Supply Council, Dominions, India,*
        New Zealand, South Africa, Southern Rhodesia, West Africa, West Indies
British Market Research Bureau, 297n
British Philatelic Association, 25n, 66
British Standards Institution, 432, 438, 441, 500
Brooms and brushes, 300, 509
Budgets, 75, 122
——*See also Chancellor of the Exchequer, Stabilisation, Taxation*
Building industry, 8, 235, 248, 249
Burma, 64, 140n

Canada
    consumption in, 630–632
    export programming and, 178, 180, 181
    exports to, 45, 64, 67, 141, 143, 144, 189, 191, 192, 193, 194, 199, 200, 522, 526

---

[1] The Board is mentioned throughout the book. For the Board's attitude to any subject readers should look up that subject. The entries under Board of Trade in the index refer only to organisation.

imports from, 22, 24, 31, 126, 492
Carpets, 109
Carpet industry
    concentration of production, 214, 221, 227
Cartels, 16
Censorship, 43, 74
Census of Production, 13, 113, 307, 308, 400n
Chambers of Commerce, 52, 96, 327, 347
    Association of British Chambers of Commerce, 44
Chamberlain, Mr. Neville, Prime Minister, 51, 61
Chancellor of the Exchequer
    Sir John (now Lord) Simon, 32, 42, 43, 54
    Sir John Anderson (now Lord Waverley), 552n
    Sir Kingsley Wood, 18, 56, 122, 209, 552, 574, 577, 578
Cheap money, 10
Chemicals
    exports, 12
    imports, 30
Chemicals industry, 16
Children, 3, 290
    clothing for, 402, 404, 425, 431, 477, 584
    footwear for, 491, 494
Chile, 60, 64, 140n, 146n, 159
    —*See also South America*
China, 178, 179
Churchill, Mr. Winston, Prime Minister, 156, 163, 240, 312, 395, 475
Civil servants, 22, 110, 135, 136
Clapham, J., *An Economic History of Modern Britain*, 5n
Clocks
    imports, 23, 24, 25, 27, 120
    prices, 44, 589
Cloth
    budget—*See Clothing: budget*
    deliveries to home market
        cotton, 443, 448, 474
        rayon, 474
        wool, 474
    price control
        non-utility, 580 *et seq*
        utility, 560, 563, 596
            cotton, 442, 563, 571, 572
            rayon, 563
            wool, 450, 451, 459, 563, 576
            removal of purchase tax from, 606
    stocks of, 474
        cotton, 444, 447
    utility, 432
        control over use of, 432
        production controls generally, 435–436
            cotton, 440–449
            rayon, 443–451
            wool, 452–459
            cotton, rayon and wool compared, 456–459
        proportion of total production represented by,
            cotton, 448, 457
            rayon, 448, 449, 457
            wool, 452, 456, 457, 458
        specifications generally, 432, 433, 562
            cotton, 440, 441, 442, 443, 563, 583
                economies through, 443, 444
                quality control through, 441, 442, 443
            rayon, 440, 441, 442, 443, 449, 563
                economies through, 449
            wool, 440, 451, 458, 459, 563
        subsidies on, 571, 575, 576, 577
        supplies of, 456
    —*See also Cotton and cotton goods, Cotton industry, Rayon and rayon goods, Rayon industry, Wool and wool goods, Wool industry*

Clothing
  austerity regulations, 317, 419, 432n, 436–439, 575, 582, 583
    economies through, 437, 439, 477–479
  budget, 297, 408, 425, 426–431, 441, 453, 454, 471, 475–476
    statistics for, 429, 476
  —*See also Clothing rationing: consumers' panel*
  children's, 402, 404, 425, 431, 477, 584
  demobilisation clothing, 396, 413, 473
  Directorate of Civilian Clothing, 486
  distribution of, 273, 274, 293, 295, 298, 299, 300, 333–334
  —*See also Clothing rationing*
  effects of policy on productivity, 477–479
  essential clothing scheme, 431, 554
  Government contracts, 402, 405, 406, 407, 408, 412, 413
  imports, 23, 25n, 35
  industrial, 285, 291–292, 307, 319, 465
    distribution schemes, 333–334
  level of supplies, 424, 431, 554, 632
  —*See also Clothing rationing: size of ration*
  minimum standards for, 438, 439
  outsize garments, 298, 311, 327, 465
  prices generally, 18, 75, 82, 87, 88, 89, 123, 347, 404n, 424, 430, 431, 477, 553, 554, 575, 576, 577, 578, 598, 599
    children's clothing, 582, 584
    non-utility clothing, 580 *et seq.*
    utility, 434, 560, 563, 564, 575, 576, 584, 585, 593, 596, 603
      removal of purchase tax from, 606
  production planning, Chapter XVII *passim*
  reconditioned Service clothing, 623
  retail sales, 254
  standard clothing
    First World War, 4–5
    Second World War, 16–17, 87–89, 106, 424
  stocks of, 315, 431
    retail, 313, 429
    wholesale, 313, 314, 429, 430, 475, 476
  trading up, 295, 329, 431, 453, 459, 554, 600, 601, 605
  utility, 75, 123, 345, 405, 412, 428, 431–481 *passim*
    overalls, 432, 438, 465
    post-war, 471, 620
    production controls, 405, 406, 412, 432, 435–436, 562
    proportion of production represented by, 434
    public reactions to, 433, 434
    quality generally, 477
    specifications for, 432, 562, 583
    standardisation generally, 433
    templates for, 433–434
  —*See also Cloth, Footwear, Hosiery, Limitation of Supplies Orders*
Clothing industry—*See generally Chapter XVI*
  cloth supplies to, 406, 408, 412, 428, 429, 445, 446, 454–456
    'key certificates', 445, 455
  clothes rationing and, 310–311
  concentration of production, 210, 221, 401, 406–412
    results, 410–412
  control of, 401, 428–429, 434–435, 471
  designation policy, 403–406, 426
  Limitation of Supplies Orders and, 98, 100, 401
  manpower for, 131, 134, 400, 401, 402, 403, 404, 405, 411, 412, 413, 421, 473
  statistics, 400, 401, 406, 407, 426, 427, 429, 445
  structure, 400–401, 410
  wages in, 413
Clothing rationing, Chapter XIV *passim*, 13, 18, 75, 88, 122, 213, 283, 288, 296, 401, 441, 629
  babies' clothes, 307, 318
  children's clothes, 317–318, 329
  civilian uniforms, 322–323
  consumers' panel, 297, 298, 329, 426–427, 491
    wardrobe check, 298, 329–331

coupon banking, 254, 325–327, 600
coupon floats, 327
demobilisation and, 324
effects of, 329–331
    on prices, 555
enforcement, 312, 325, 327–329
    lost coupons, 325, 326, 328–329
expectant mothers, 318
honouring the ration, Chapter XVII *passim*
industrial workers, 318–322, 329
issue of coupons, 311, 315, 327, 341–342
Merchant Navy and, 324–325
passing back of coupons, 307, 308, 310, 311, 325, 326
pointings, 307, 308, 309, 316, 317, 319, 339–340, 491, 582
post-war, 620, 621
prisoners of war and, 324
proposals for schemes, 303–312
provisions of first Order, 313
Services' uniforms, 323
size of ration, 307–309, 314–315, 472, 473, 476
special schemes, 317 *et seq.*
statistics for, 297, 307, 308
towels and tea-towels, 319
Coal—*See Fuel*
Coal exports, 65, 71, 633
Coal industry, 10
Colombia, 60, 140n
   —*See also South America*
Colonies, 72, 93, 94, 153, 168, 173, 181, 191, 195, 571
   —*See also West Africa, West Indies*
Combinations in British industry, 10
Combined Food Board, 181
Combined Munitions Assignment Board, 159
Combined Production and Resources Board, 170, 174, 175, 177, 178, 179, 181, 182, 493
Combined Raw Materials Board, 156, 493, 494
Commercial policy
   post-war, 61
Committee of Imperial Defence
   Manpower Sub-Committee, 12
Committee on Restraint of Trade, 81
Commonwealth Supply Council, 174, 175, 176, 181
Competition
   decline in, 6, 9
Concentration of production, Chapter X *passim*, 18, 113, 114, 115, 121, 122, 124, 129, 242, 253, 256, 258, 287, 296, 499, 558, 628, 629
   compensation, 208–209, 216–217, 231, 256, 271, 357
   results of, 224–233
   White Paper on, 207, 209, 215, 352, 353, 357, 358, 389, 405, 420, 524
   For concentration of individual industries—*See the headings for those industries, viz.:*
     Clothing industry, Cotton industry, Cutlery industry, Footwear industry, Furniture industry, Hosiery industry, Jute industry, Lace industry, Paint industry, Paper industry, Photographic goods industry, Pottery industry, Rayon industry, Retail trade, Silk industry, Sports goods industry, Toilet preparations industry, Toy industry, Woodworking industry, Wool industry
Consumer needs, Chapter XIII *passim*, 122, 123, 124, 261, 273, 277, 278, 281, 628
   Adviser on Consumer Needs, 282n, 296
   Consumer Needs Department, 294, 298, 299, 300, 301, 302, 338
     area distribution officers, 277, 294, 295, 296, 298, 299, 300, 302, 426, 463
   statistics, 296–297, 302
Consumption generally
   war-time fall in, 630–632
     international comparisons, 630–632
Contractors' plant, 159
Controls generally, 3, 18, 93, 96, 102, 108, 247, 511, 626–629, 634, 637
   —*See also Cloth: Utility, Clothing: rationing, Exports: licensing of, Imports, control over, Limitation of Supplies Orders, Manpower: controls over, Manufacture and supply controls, price control, Raw materials: control over*
Co-operative societies
   —*See under Retail trade and Retail trade: organisations*

Corsets, 109, 298, 424, 465–467, 475
    concentration of production, 225, 466
    prices, 467
Cost of living, 16, 18, 75, 77, 82, 122, 553
    index number, 18, 75, 82, 89, 122, 123, 424, 477, 552, 553, 554, 571, 573, 576, 577, 578, 596, 599, 606, 613, 614
Costs—*See generally Price control and Retail trade*
Cotton and cotton goods
    cloth production, 343, 369, 474, 475
    cloth stocks, 429, 474
    cloth, utility
        production controls, 440–449, 456–459
        proportion of total production represented by, 448, 457
        specifications, 432, 440, 441, 442, 443, 563, 583
        subsidy on, 571–572
    exports, 7, 12, 43, 45–49, 52, 60, 63–64, 87, 93, 94, 95, 96, 98, 105, 139–142, 143, 148, 177–180, 187–192, 343, 345, 347, 350, 351, 571
        British Overseas Cottons Ltd., 63–64, 190, 345–346, 351, 446
        export control, 43, 141, 345, 350
        export levies, 46, 47, 63
        export planning, 177–180, 350, 371
        export subsidy, 63
        standardisation of export cloths, 10, 63, 142, 188–190, 351
    Government contracts, 93, 95, 97, 98, 346, 349, 350, 355, 361, 362
    Indian exports, 141, 167, 177, 178, 179, 180, 188
    limitation of supplies of, 35, 48, 55, 93–99, 104–107
    prices and price control, 16, 46, 47, 63, 76, 77, 87, 94, 343, 345, 347, 359, 442, 563, 570, 571, 572
    raw cotton imports, 28, 29n, 33, 93, 95, 97, 126, 139, 351, 352, 354, 364, 398
    raw cotton levy, 63, 345
    raw cotton rationing, 95, 96, 347, 353
    raw cotton stocks, 96, 351, 352, 398
    United States exports, 191, 192
    yarn allocations, 127n, 140, 141, 187, 188, 189, 191, 347, 348–349, 351, 397, 443, 473, 506
    yarn deliveries, 140, 187, 188, 191, 348, 349, 351, 354, 355, 356, 365, 368, 370, 443, 473, 475
    yarn output, pre-war, 343
Cotton Board, 43, 46, 47, 48, 52, 63, 64, 95, 139, 140, 185, 188, 189, 190, 337, 344, 350, 352, 356, 358, 360
    composition of, 46–47, 345
    functions of, 46–47, 345, 361, 362, 363, 370, 372, 388, 442, 446, 563
    Utility Cloth Office, 350, 445, 446, 447, 450, 572
Cotton Control and Controller, 46, 48, 49, 51, 63, 188, 190, 344, 345, 347, 348, 349, 350, 351, 353, 354, 355, 356, 360, 361, 366, 369, 370, 371, 372, 377, 418, 439, 442, 449, 450, 468
    approved order system, 347, 348, 443
    differences between Wool Control and, 387–389, 439
    licensing of looms, 356, 357
    licensing of spinners and doublers, 220, 232, 354, 356
    licensing of yarn deliveries, 349
    preference directions, 48–49, 96, 99, 105, 347, 354, 417
    production planning, 188, 190, 348, 349–351, 364, 388, 441, 443–449
        effects of, 478
Cotton Industry Reorganisation Act, 47, 48, 87, 344
Cotton industry
    amenities in, 360, 371
    between the wars, 7–8, 343
    concentration of production, 197, 211, 219, 220, 225, 230, 231, 233n, 345, 347, 351–367
        compensation, 357–363, 365
        results of, 354–355, 357, 361, 362, 363, 364–367
        spinning section, 353–355
        waste spinning section, 355
        doubling section, 355–356
        weaving section, 356–357
        finishing section, 360–363
    deconcentration, 366

export merchants, 95, 141, 189, 190, 191
in First World War, 352
machinery in, 197, 198, 343, 357–358, 360, 372
manpower in, 8, 127n, 129n, 132, 133, 140, 343, 346, 355, 356, 365, 366, 367–372, 379, 389, 392, 444, 473
    productivity of, 367, 368, 371–372
merchant converters, 141, 344, 349, 350, 441, 444, 445, 446, 450, 474, 563, 571
productivity generally, 478
rationalisation in, 10
raw material supplies to, 46, 64, 346, 351, 352, 355, 364, 374, 389, 398
Shirley Institute, 442
structure of, 343–344, 389
wages in, 571, 577
Cotton Textile Mission to U.S.A.: Report (Platt Report), 371–372
Cotton Working Party Report, 8n, 344n, 356n, 357n, 467n, 478n
Court, W. H., *Coal*, 128n
Courtaulds Ltd., 450, 573
Cripps, Sir Stafford, President of the Board of Trade, 279, 591
Cuba, 67, 195
Customs and Excise, 43, 74, 152, 312, 327, 554, 606
Cutlery, 102, 185, 198, 503, 504, 506, 509
    prices, 587
Cutlery industry
    concentration of production, 225, 226

Dalton, Mr. Hugh, President of the Board of Trade, 160, 161, 162, 222, 223, 224, 272, 472, 491, 492, 495, 497, 508, 514, 568, 578, 589, 604
D'Arcy Cooper, Sir F., 51, 56, 61
Demobilisation
    clothes rationing and, 324
    —See also Clothing: demobilisation
Department of Overseas Trade, 11, 39, 51, 66
Depressed areas (pre-war)
    wartime prosperity of, 287, 301–302
Distribution
    generally, 1, 122–123
    of consumer goods, 273–275
        geographical, 283–289, 292, 293, 300–302
    schemes, 332–338
        buying permits, 333–337
        priority dockets, 334–335, 337
        furniture, 335–336
        furnishing, 337
        bedding, 337–338
Distributive trades, 8, 13
    —See also Retail trade, Wholesalers
Dollars
    for tobacco, 26
    reserves, 138
    shortage of, 15, 20, 22, 24, 26, 31–33, 60, 93, 137
    —See also Balance of payments, Exports, Lend-Lease
Dominions, 35, 61, 139, 175, 176
    exports to, 62, 66, 72, 73, 140, 141, 153, 175, 176, 188, 191, 199
    import restrictions in, 72, 73, 153, 188
    industrialisation in, 72, 73
    —See also Australia, British Empire, Canada, Commonwealth Supply Council, New Zealand, South Africa, Southern Rhodesia
Drapers' Chamber of Trade
    —See under Retail trade: organisations
Drapers' Record, 257
Duncan, Sir Andrew, President of the Board of Trade, 35, 51, 58, 68, 322
Dutch East Indies, 63, 140, 185

Economic Policy Committee, 101
Economist, The, 137n, 273, 304, 365n, 370n, 478n
Eden, Mr. Anthony, 148n, 160

Egypt, 33
    exports to, 140, 153
Eire, 30, 42, 140n, 142, 143
Electrical goods, 8, 41, 503
Electricity supply industry, 8
Engineering industries, 44, 66, 68, 69, 92, 103, 104, 122, Chapter XX *passim*
    —*See also Machinery: Licensing of*
Evacuation, 257, 284, 285
Exchange control, 11, 16, 21, 26, 27, 61, 65, 66
    Exchange Requirements Committee, 93, 97
Exchange discrimination, 50, 51, 627
Exports
    between the wars, 7, 8, 9
    credits for, 11, 56–59
    'currency earning' exports—*See under Export drive: also* 120, 137, 138, 139, 140, 143,
        144, 146, 184, 193, 194, 195, 196, 198, 199, 200
    currency gradings, 138
    effect of lend-lease on, 20, 119–120, Chapters VII and VIII *passim*, 633
    export companies, 62–64
    Export Council, 51, 52, 53, 54, 56, 59, 70, 211
    Export Credits Guarantee Department, 56–59
    Export Credits Insurance, 56–59
    Export Guarantees Act, 57
    export drive, 1, 11–12, 16, 17, 20, 50–73, 119–120, 137, 138, 232, 385, 386, 392,
        482, 620, 627, 633
    export groups, 52, 53, 54, 55, 59, 67, 70, 548, 549
    'frustrated' exports, 143, 185, 186, 193, 334
    Government marketing, 11
    in First World War, 2
    Indian, 141, 167 177, 178, 179, 180, 188
    Japanese, 141
    levies for, 46, 47, 62–64, 194, 195, 573, 574
    licensing of, 1, 4, 11, 14, 39–43, 65, 66, 70, 72, 141, 142, 147, 150, 151, 152, 185,
        186, 194, 195, 197, 198, 199
    manpower for, 50, 54, 65, 66, 68, 69, 100
    merchants, 52, 95, 110, 141, 144, 145, 188, 189, 190, 191, 194
    planning of, 20, 120, Chapter VII, VIII, IX *passim*
    post-war export drive, 159, 161, 163, 165, 169, 387, 633–634
    pre-war plans for, 11–12, 39–41
    prices of, 6, 47, 50, 51, 54, 62, 63, 571, 572–573
    programming
        Combined Export Markets Committee, 84, 85, 86, 160, 167, 169, 170, 171, 172
        statistics, 158, 167, 168, 178
    publicity, 48, 50, 53, 54, 62, 64
    raw materials for, 11–12, 39, 43, 44, 45, 49, 50, 53, 54, 64, 65, 67, 68, 69, 70, 71,
        95, 96, 100, 102, 142, 150, 151, 152, 153, 154, 161, 162, 164, 165, 193
    reduction of, 20, 64–72, Chapter VII *passim*, 184, 633
    re-export trade, 27, 29, 30
    selective export policy, 20, 44–45, 53–54, 71, 120, Chapters VII, VIII, IX *passim*, 633
    shipping for, 64, 65, 185, 186, 633
    subsidies for, 11, 46, 47, 48, 50, 62–64, 195, 571, 573, 574, 627
    tax relief for, 56
    Commodities
        agricultural equipment, 160, 169, 171, 177, 180–182
        bicycles, 35, 160, 170–171, 185, 198
        cotton goods, 7, 12, 43, 45–49, 60, 63, 64, 87, 93, 94, 95, 96, 98, 105, 139–142,
            143, 148, 177–180, 187–192, 343, 345, 347, 350, 351, 571
        engineering goods, 12, 44, 65, 67, 68, 69, 70, 71, 103, 145, 146, 147, 149, 151,
            152, 154, 155, 172, 177, 197, 198
        glassware, 50n, 60, 65n, 71
        hemp goods, 152, 196–197
        jute goods, 144, 196–197
        leather and leather goods, 35, 41, 53, 60, 64, 174
        linen goods, 35, 49, 65, 67, 144, 196, 197
        paper and paper goods, 41, 65n, 168
        pottery, 60, 65n, 198, 199, 200, 215, 232, 522, 523, 525, 526
        rayon goods, 62–63, 178, 187, 194–196, 573, 574
        whisky, 200

wool goods, 7, 12, 45, 46, 60, 93, 95, 142–143, 178, 193–194, 384, 385, 386, 387, 392, 394
Countries and areas to which United Kingdom exports went:—
    Australia, 54, 72, 140, 141, 189, 190, 195, 200
    British Empire, 30, 40, 66, 72, 120, 122, 139, 140, 141, 143, 146, 149, 153, 158, 174, 175, 176, 184, 185, 191, 196, 198, 199
    Canada, 45, 64, 67, 71, 141, 143, 144, 189, 191, 192, 193, 194, 199, 200, 522, 526
    Egypt, 140, 153
    France, 34, 35, 36, 40, 65
    India, 64, 140, 175, 197–198
    Iran, 140, 153
    New Zealand, 72, 140, 141, 142, 195, 199
    Portugal, 140n, 144, 153
    South Africa, 67, 140n, 141, 143, 144, 185, 186
    South America, 45, 59–62, 64, 67, 140, 143, 144, 145, 146, 147, 158, 159, 160, 161, 185, 189, 193, 195, 196, 199, 522, 526
    sterling area, 15, 36, 138, 140n
    Turkey, 64, 65, 140n, 144, 153
    U.S.A., 45, 59–62, 64, 67, 71, 140, 143, 144, 193, 194, 195, 199, 200, 522, 523, 526
    —*See also Lend-Lease, Limitation of Supplies Orders*

Factory Acts, 241, 319
Factory space
    Control of Factory and Storage Space, 121, 134, 204, 217, 227, Chapter XI *passim*, 405, 406, 485, 491, 518
        regional organisation, 241, 244, 245, 250, 251
        registers, 239, 241–243
        Location of Industry Order, 245, 246, 247
    release of, 18, 101, 104, 112, 113, 114, 121, 204, 205, 206, 207, 217, 220, 222, 223, 224, 225, 227, 229, 230, 231, 352, 363, 364, 367, 390, 405, 406, 409, 411, 416, 417, 485, 505, 518, 630
    post-war reconstruction, 621
Fancy goods, 504
Feaveryear, A. E., article on retail trade in the *Economic Journal*, 14n
Federation of British Industries, 44, 77, 304
Films
    foreign exchange for, 26, 31
First World War
    controls over civil industry and trade, 3–5
    effects of, 5–6
Flax, 25, 35, 49, 65, 67, 92, 126, 196
Food
    export licensing, 41
    imports, 21, 23, 24n, 26, 27, 28, 30, 32, 36, 121
    lend-lease, 149
    prices, 16, 18, 75, 77, 82, 84, 123, 149, 554, 577, 578, 605
    subsidies, 18, 28, 123, 553, 577
    Ministry of, 26, 27, 28, 30, 36, 37, 38, 74, 120, 259, 271, 350, 540, 562
        buying programmes of, 21
        export licensing and, 42
        lend-lease and, 121, 149
        prices and, 75, 84, 149, 577, 605
        rationing and, 304, 311, 312, 318, 327
        storage and, 234, 237, 238
Footwear—*See generally Chapter XVIII*
    children's, 491, 494
    exports, 177, 484
    Government contracts, 472, 491, 492, 497
    imports, 23
    level of supplies, 477, 493
    prices and price control, 82, 486, 488, 489, 490, 495, 581, 584, 587, 604, 605, 606, 607
    rationing of, 308, 309, 316, 490, 493
        —*See also Clothing: rationing*
    repairs, 492–493
        control over, 492–493

Footwear, *contd.*
    repairs, charges, 553, 608
    rubber, 333–334, 491, 494
    sales of, 264, 265
    standard
        in First World War, 4, 485
        in Second World War, 16–17, 88, 106, 484, 485, 486, 488, 489
    utility, 486, 488, 489, 490, 495
    wooden, 494, 495
Footwear industry—*See generally Chapter XVIII*
    concentration of production, 210, 212, 214, 220, 225, 231, 232, 486, 487
        compensation, 487
    control organisation, 491–492
        Director (later Controller) of Civilian Footwear, 487, 491, 494
        Footwear Board, 492
        Footwear Control, 492
    machinery, 120, 487
    manpower, 129n, 132, 133, 485, 487, 493, 496, 497
        productivity, 488, 497
    pairage licensing, 485, 486, 491, 492
    raw materials for, 485, 486, 488, 490, 491, 493, 494, 495, 496
    Boots and Shoes Working Party Report, 487, 490
    —*See also Clothing, Leather*
Ford, P., article on retail trade in the *Economic Journal,* 13n
Foreign exchange
    in First World War, 3–4
    pre-war plans, 11
    war-time shortage, 14, 15, 16, 17, 20, 21, 22, 23, 27, 28, 43, 44, 68, 71, 93, 97, 113,
        137, 138, 144, 184
        —*See also Dollars, Exchange Control, Exports, Lend-Lease*
Foreign investments, 4, 6, 16, 138
Foreign Office, 22, 45
Foreign Secretary (Mr. Eden), 148n, 160
France
    exports to, 34, 35, 36, 40, 65
    fall of, 15, 17, 20, 29, 36, 65, 92, 127
    imports from, 22, 23n, 24, 25n, 27, 28, 29, 33, 34–36
Freight rates, 16, 28, 58, 61, 72, 76
Fruit
    imports, 28, 31, 32, 61
Fuel
    allocation of, 126, 128
    economies, 207–208, 229–230, 364, 367
    prices, 76, 82, 574, 586
    rationing, 501
    shortage, 121, 247
    —*See also Coal, Ministry of Fuel and Power*
Full employment, 619
    White Paper on Employment Policy, 621–622, 624, 625
Furnishing fabrics
    distribution schemes, 336–337, 520, 521
    rationing of, 316, 468, 469
    utility, 441
Furniture: *See generally Chapter XIX Section (ii)*
    early control over, 501, 507, 512, 513, 514
    expenditure on, 632
    imports, 23n
    metal, 109, 503, 512n
    sales of, 264, 265
    secondhand prices, 298, 513, 514, 611–612
    storage, 608–609
    utility
        designation of firms, 518–519
        distribution scheme, 301, 335–337, 514, 522
            pointings, 335
        introduction of scheme, 335, 507
        output, 336, 517, 519, 520, 521
        price control, 335, 514, 522, 587, 592

removal of purchase tax, 606
production control, 514, 516–517
    Adviser on Furniture Production, 519
    Production Officers, 125, 519
specifications, 514, 515–516, 522
'zoning' of, 336, 516, 517, 518, 592
Furniture industry
    concentration of production, 225, 512, 519
        compensation, 519
    Government contracts in, 512, 518, 519
    manpower for, 129n, 132, 133, 511, 514, 518, 520, 521, 522
    raw materials for, 127, 512, 513, 515, 517, 519, 522
    structure of, 511–512
Furniture Working Party Report, 511
Furs, 27, 109, 307

General Post Office
    clothes coupons and, 311, 312, 318, 325, 326, 327
Germany
    exchange control in, 27
    import control in, 27
    industry in, 5, 9
Glassware
    exports, 50n, 60, 65n, 71
    imports, 23, 24n, 25
    prices of, 82, 584, 592
    prohibitions on manufacture, 504
Gold reserves, 138
Gramophone record industry, 55
Great depression, 9, 389
Greece, tobacco from, 33
Greenwood, Mr. Arthur, Minister without Portfolio, 67, 115, 203, 237, 618

Hammond, R. J., *Food*, 221n
Hancock, W. K., and Gowing, M. M., *British War Economy*, 20n, 21n, 43n, 101n, 108n, 205n, 389n, 623n
Harriman, Mr. Averell, 166
Harrison and Mitchell, *The Home Market*, 14n
Hats, 307
Hat industry, 210, 222
Hemp and hemp goods, 28, 30, 196, 197
    Lend-Lease restrictions 153
Henderson, Mr. Craig, 259
Henderson, H. D., *The Cotton Control Board*, 352n
Hire purchase, 514, 609
Hollow-ware, 102, 108, 122, 124, 168, 210, 500, 501, 503, 505, 508
    distribution of, 273, 274, 288, 289, 291, 293, 295, 299, 300, 301
    output, 509, 510
    price control, 589, 591, 607
    rationing proposals, 304, 306, 332–333
Hosiery
    Directorate of Civilian Hosiery, 320, 461, 479
    Government contracts for, 418, 419, 420, 472
    in First World War, 4
    level of supplies of, 394, 463–464, 475
    limitation of supplies of, 414, 415, 460
    pure silk stockings, 107
    rationing of, 308, 309, 316, 418, 419
    —See also Clothing: rationing
    utility
        price control of, 563, 564, 585–586
        production controls for, 428, 459–464
        proportion of production represented by, 434, 462, 463
        specifications, 459–460, 563
        —See also Clothing generally

Hosiery industry—*See generally Chapter XVI, section (ii)*
    allocations of yarn to, 414–415, 416, 417, 420, 450, 460, 461
    austerity restrictions and, 419, 438
    between the wars, 8, 414
    concentration of production, 210, 213, 214, 217, 218, 220, 225, 231, 232, 415–417, 460
        compensation, 416, 417
    manpower for, 129n, 414, 416, 417, 419
    planned production in, 420, 461–462
    productivity in, 478–479
    statistics, 415n, 427, 429, 461
    structure of, 414, 416
    yarn supplies to, 394, 414, 415, 417–419, 422, 423
Hosiery Working Party Report, 414n, 479
Household textiles
    distribution of, 300, 301
    prices and price control of, 82, 467–470, 580, 581, 596, 606
    utility, 441
    —*See also Blankets, Furnishing fabrics, Towels*
Housing conditions, 291
Hull, Mr. Cordell, 32, 61, 162
Hyndley, Lord, 51

Imperial preference, 9, 61
Import Duties Act Inquiry, 13, 113
Imports
    between the wars, 6–7
    control over, 3, 4, 9, 11, 14, 16, 18, Chapter II *passim*
        administration of, 22, 23, 24, 25, 38, 543
        consumer goods, 21, 22
        extent of, 27, 28
        machinery, 23, 24
        political difficulties of, 22, 23, 31–36
        post-war, 61
        from British Empire, 22, 23n, 24, 28, 33
        from Canada, 22, 24, 31, 126, 492
        from France, 22, 23n, 24, 25n, 27, 28, 29, 33, 34–36
        from United States, 22, 23, 26, 31–33, 61, 73
        in Colonies and Dominions, 30, 72, 185, 186
    prices of, 6, 76
    programmes, 29, 30
    quotas for, 9
    specific commodities:—
        cotton, 28, 29n, 33, 93, 95, 97, 126, 139, 351, 352, 354, 364, 398
        food, 21, 23, 24n, 26, 27, 28, 30, 32, 36, 121
        fruit, 28, 31, 32, 61
        raw materials, 21, 25, 26, 27, 28, 29, 126–127
        tobacco, 26, 27, 31, 32, 33
        torch batteries, 84
        wool, 29, 139, 142, 380, 381, 384
        —*See also Lend-Lease*
India
    combined planning and, 167, 175, 177–180
    exports from, 141, 167, 177, 178, 179, 180, 188, 197, 201
    exports to, 64, 140, 175, 197–198
Industrial and Export Council, 136, 162, 211, 635
Inflation
    in First World War, 4
    post-war, 590
    pre-war plans against, 12–13
    war-time, 12–13, 14, 16, 18, 75, 77, 119, 121, 122–123, 136, 286, 303, 598, 626
    —*See also Clothing: rationing, Price control, Rationing, Saving, Stabilisation, Taxation*
Inland Revenue, 271
Insurance
    income from, 7
International trade, 6–7, 8, 9, 10
Inter-war period, 6–10

Iran
    exports to, 140, 153
Iron and steel
    allocation of, 49–50, 53, 67–70, 127, 506, 543–549
    Control, 543, 544, 545
    exports, 7, 41, 49–50, 67–70, 144, 145, 146, 147, 148, 152, 164, 197–198, 544, 549
    home production, 126–127
    imports, 25
    —*See also Machinery*
Iron and steel industry, 7, 634
    concentration in, 221, 225, 226
    raw materials for, 126
    statistics, 13

Japan, 5, 64, 141, 187, 365, 574, 618, 619
Jewellery
    imports, 23n, 24n
    limitation of supplies, 102, 503
Jewellery industry
    concentration of, 219
Jute and jute goods, 35, 43, 144, 145n, 196, 197, 214, 221, 227
    lend-lease restrictions, 153
Jute industry
    concentration of, 221, 225

Kahn, A. E., *Great Britain in the World Economy*, 6n
Keynes, Lord, 148, 163

Lace exports, 7
Lace industry, 101
    concentration, 219, 221, 225, 226, 231
Lacey, R., article on 'Cotton's War Effort' in *Manchester School of Economic and Social Studies*, 346n, 348n, 353n
Laundries, 129n, 132
    charges, 553, 560, 608
Leak, H., article in *Journal of the Royal Statistical Society*, 10n
Leather
    Control and Controller, 484, 485, 491
    exports, 35, 41, 53, 64, 174
        levy, 64
    international allocation, 495, 496
    prices, 82, 84, 484, 495, 572, 573
    subsidy, 572
    rationing of, 212, 485, 486, 491, 496
    supplies of, 491, 493, 495, 496
    —*See also Footwear*
Leather goods
    exports of, 60
    imports of, 23n
    limitation of supplies of, 503, 504, 506
Leather goods industry
    concentration of, 218, 219, 222, 225
Lend-Lease
    Act, 18, 33, 59, 119, 364
    Administration, 150, 153, 154, 155, 157, 164, 165, 166, 167, 168, 175n, 180n
    consumer goods under, 120–121
    distribution of goods received under, 149
    effects on British exports, 20, 119–120, 145–157, 158–165, 166, 167, 184, 187, 195, 197, 198, 633
    for stage II, 160, 161, 162, 163, 164, 165
    military supplies under, 163
    prices of lend-lease supplies, 147
    raw material supplies received under, 126

Lend-Lease, *contd.*
    reciprocal aid, 162
    —*See also Exports, United States*
Levies
    cotton, 10, 47, 48, 63, 345, 571
    concentration of production, 209, 217, 357
    concentration of retail trade, 267, 268, 271
    rayon, 62, 573, 574
Limitation of Supplies Orders, Chapter V *passim, also* 17, 18, 30, 35, 48, 54–56, 185,
    202, 204, 205, 207, 208, 210, 212, 213, 218, 219, 221, 253, 256, 257, 262, 282, 283,
    285, 286, 293, 306, 307, 313, 347, 373, 401, 414, 415, 482, 499, 500, 501, 502, 503,
    504, 554
    administration of, 96, 98, 110, 111, 112, 113, 114
    clothes rationing and, 310
    disadvantages of, 112, 498–499
    enforcement, 98, 111–112
    ex-quota supplies, 104, 105, 106, 107, 109, 113, 286
    transfer of quotas, 107, 115
Linen goods
    exports, 35, 49, 65, 67, 144, 196, 197
    imports, 28, 34
    limitation of supplies, 35, 54–56, 97, 98, 105, 106, 110
Linoleum, 109, 337
Linoleum industry
    concentration of, 218, 221, 225, 227
Location of industry, 112, 113, 114, 135, 215, 217, 221, 222, 228, 234, 247, 248, 250,
    252, 404, 407, 408, 619, 622, 624–625
    Barlow Report, 625
Location of Industry Order, 245–247, 250n
London Chamber of Commerce, 25
Lord President of the Council (Sir John Anderson), 240, 501
Lord President's Committee, 136, 222, 223, 238, 241, 252, 312, 500
Lyttelton, Mr. Oliver
    Minister of Production, 173, 175
    President of the Board of Trade, 108, 137, 138, 208, 219, 236, 237, 240, 258, 259,
        312, 313, 554, 555

Machinery
    concentrated firms', 209, 216, 228, 231
    exports, 12, 44, 65, 67, 68, 69, 70, 71, 103, 145, 146, 147, 149, 151, 152, 154, 155,
        172, 177, 197, 198
    for civilian industry, Chapter XX *passim*, 92
    imports and import control, 22, 23, 24, 25, 35, 37
    lend-lease imports, 120
    licensing of, 18, 68, 103–104, 540–543, 548
    repair and maintenance of, 545, 549
    —*See also Engineering industries, Iron and Steel*
Machine tools, 5, 40, 114, 120, 175
Maizels, A., article in *Journal of the Royal Statistical Society*, 10n
Make-do and mend campaign, 289, 636
Manchester Chamber of Commerce, 441, 442
Manchester Guardian, 304
Manpower
    budgeting, 130–133
    controls over, 101, 130, 133, 205, 228, 366, 370, 495, 511, 619, 627, 628, 629
    Essential Work Order, 129, 130, 132, 369, 393, 419, 494, 520
    for civilian industry, 3, 18, 92, 99, 100, 101, 108, 112, 113, 114, 121, 122, 126,
        128–133, 203, 204, 205, 221, 222, 223, 224, 225, 226, 227, 228, 229, 283, 505,
        509, 621, 622
    for exports, 11, 50, 54, 66–67, 68, 69, 70, 100, 101, 121, 197, 198, 205
    for Services and War production, 18, 92, 99, 108, 112, 114, 116, 121, 128–133, 198,
        204, 205, 214, 221, 222, 223, 227, 228, 229, 247, 352, 353, 357, 358, 366, 367,
        369, 370, 402, 405, 406, 409, 411, 499
    full employment, 286
    releases under concentration, 205, 207, 208, Chapter X *passim*, 354, 355, 357, 363,
        365, 366, 367, 390–392, 524
    Schedule of Reserved Occupations, 66, 128, 129, 130, 205, 208, 230, 233, 280, 417
    statistics, 13

unemployment, 17, 50, 67, 97, 99, 100, 101, 112, 113, 121, 203, 204, 287, 343, 392, 522, 619, 621, 625
For manpower in individual industries see under the headings for those industries, viz., *Clothing industry, Cotton industry, Footwear industry, Furniture industry, Hosiery industry, Paper industry, Printing industry, Pottery industry, Rayon industry, Retail trade, Wool industry*
—*See also Ministry of Labour*
Manufacture and supply, controls over, Chapters XIV, XV, XVI, XVII, XVIII *passim*
for clothing and footwear, Chapter XIX *passim* for miscellaneous consumer goods, also 3, 16, 18, 93, 115, 121, 123, 207, 220, 222, 226, 233, 247, 283, 286, 297, 299, 620, 621
effects on distribution, 334
prohibitions, 501, 503, 504, 505, 507, 514, 526
results of, 509–511
Materials Committee, 127, 128, 179, 347, 348, 382, 385, 418, 441, 452, 472, 520, 543
Mattresses, 101, 109, 337, 470
Medical supplies, 152, 165, 174, 177
Mercantile Marine Department, 11
Merchant Navy
and clothes rationing, 324
Meynell, Sir Francis, 282n
Middle East, 64, 185
Middle East Supply Centre, 172, 175n
Miners
and clothes rationing, 320, 321
Mines Department, 11n, 41n, 74, 320
Minister of Aircraft Production (Lord Beaverbrook), 235, 240
Ministry of Aircraft Production, 125, 235, 240, 371, 378, 466
Ministry of Economic Warfare, 22, 33, 42, 43n, 45, 51, 74
—*See also Blockade*
Ministry of Food—*See under Food*
Ministry of Fuel and Power, 11n, 76, 120, 128, 543
Ministry of Health, 512, 513
Ministry of Home Security, 292n, 545
Minister of Labour (Mr. Bevin), 221, 223, 226, 495
Ministry of Labour, 54, 66, 76, 99, 100, 112, 113, 121, 129, 130, 131, 132, 133, 204, 205, 206, 208, 214, 215, 217, 221, 222, 223, 224, 226, 228, 229, 253, 256, 259, 262, 278, 280, 321, 327, 353, 370, 371, 376, 377, 390, 391, 392, 393, 394, 402, 403, 404, 405, 406, 407, 408, 409, 416, 417, 419, 485, 494, 495, 505, 518, 519, 520, 537
—*See also Manpower*
Minister without Portfolio (Mr. Arthur Greenwood), 67, 115, 203, 237, 618
Minister of Production (Mr. Oliver Lyttelton), 173, 175
Ministry of Production, 221, 222, 223, 249, 250, 252, 407
Ministry of Shipping, 22, 30
Minister of Supply (Lord Beaverbrook), 322
Ministry of Supply, 11, 25, 29, 38, 51, 74, 94, 99, 106, 113, 120, 121, 204, 371, 380, 383, 444, 449, 482, 483, 489, 490, 495, 500, 506, 507, 512, 519, 540, 623, 624
buying programmes of, 21, 27, 28
clothing industry and, 403, 404, 408, 412, 413, 420, 472
concentration of production and, 210
contracts procedure of, 579
cotton industry and, 46, 345, 347, 357
export licensing and, 42
prices, 76, 80, 83, 87, 562, 572
rayon industry and, 374, 376
restrictions on civilian goods, 506, 507
standard clothing and, 88
storage and, 237, 238
Ministry of Works, 199, 206, 234, 236, 239, 243, 249, 250, 513, 547
Central Register, 234, 236
Morale, 3, 122, 124, 125, 289, 498, 533
Morgenthau, Mr., 60
Most-favoured-nation clause, 22
Motor-cars, 5, 8, 92, 107, 632
exports, 35, 68, 197
imports, 23, 24n, 27
Motor-car industry, 8, 55
Multiple Shops' Federation—*See under Retail trade: organisations*
Musical instruments, 503

Mutual Aid Agreement, 62

National Association of Outfitters
    —See under Retail trade: organisations
National Chamber of Trade
    —See under Retail trade: organisations
National Union of Manufacturers, 44, 78
Needles, 510
New Zealand
    exports to, 72, 140, 141, 142, 195, 199
    import restrictions in, 72
    United Kingdom wool purchases in, 381
Non-ferrous metals, 126, 128, 164
Northern Ireland, 30, 49, 67, 74, 98, 196, 301, 374, 375, 592
Nylon, 375n, 378

Office machinery, 177, 550–551

Paint industry, 501
    concentration of production, 210, 225, 226
Paper and paper manufactures
    allocation of, 127
    exports, 41, 65n, 168
    imports, 25, 126
    supplies to home market, 92, 507
Paper industry
    concentration of production, 210, 218, 221, 226
    manpower for, 131, 132, 133
Pares, R., article in *Lessons of the British War Economy*, 124n
Patent Office, 23, 543
Pencils, 129n, 502, 509
Perambulators, 122, 298, 506, 509
    prices, 83
Peru, 60, 140n
    —See also South America
Photographic goods, 28, 35, 504
    concentration of production, 226
Poland, 57
Population
    war-time movements, 283–285, 292–293
Ports
    diversion of shipping, 286
    storage in, 237, 249
Portugal, 64, 65, 140n, 144, 153
Postage stamps, 25n, 66
Post-war problems, 228, 230, 231, 618–625, 637
    after First World War, 619, 622
    disposal of surplus stocks, 621–622, 623–624
    industrial design, 619
    location of industry, 619, 622, 624–625
    price control, 619, 620
    reconversion of industry, 621
    release of Government factories, 619, 622, 623
    termination of contracts, 619, 622
Pottery
    distribution of, 273, 274, 289, 293, 298, 299, 300
    exports, 60, 65n, 198, 199, 200, 215, 232, 522, 523, 525, 526
    Government contracts for, 199, 206, 523, 528
    imports, 23, 24n
    limitation of supplies of, 56, 102, 109, 499, 523
    manufacture and supply controls, 499, 502, 505, 526
    output, 509, 510, 527, 529, 530
    prices and price control, 82, 527, 588–589, 592
    rationing proposal, 304, 306, 332, 333
    shortage, 122, 124, 525, 530

standardisation of, 509, 527, 528
undecorated, 333, 525, 526, 527
utility, 508
Pottery industry
    concentration of, 206–207, 210, 214–215, 220, 225, 227, 232, 523–524, 530
        compensation, 524
    manpower for, 66–67, 101, 132, 199, 214, 215, 333n, 510, 522, 523, 524–525, 529, 531
Pre-war planning, 11–14
Prices
    exports, 6, 47, 50, 51, 54, 62, 63, 571, 572–573
    imports, 6, 76
    resale price maintenance, 81, 87
    rises generally, 12, 14, 16, 76, 89, 267, 424
Price control generally, Chapters IV, XXI, XXII *passim*, 3, 14, 16, 17, 18, 94, 96, 123, 262, 627, 628
    auctions, 557, 610
    branded goods, 81, 87, 556, 558, 587, 588
    cash margins, 605
    ceiling prices, 561, 563, 564, 578, 582, 583–589, 590, 591, 597, 612
    Central Price Regulation Committee, 78, 79, 80, 81, 82, 83, 84, 85, 86, 87, 90, 451, 558, 559, 562, 563, 564, 565, 568, 569, 572, 573, 579, 581, 582, 587, 590, 597, 606, 623
        Local Price Regulation Committees, 78, 84, 90, 260, 261, 559, 560, 599
    clothing, planning and, 430
    coal, 76, 574
    composite businesses, 566, 607
    concentration and, 271
    'cost-plus', 561, 563, 564, 574, 578, 581, 582, 583–587, 588, 589, 597, 613
    departmental responsibility, 76, 83, 84, 86, 87, 572, 573
    distributors' prices, 78, 79, 80, 81, 83, 85, 86, 87, 556, 558, 560, 563, 565, 566–567, 591–607
    enforcement, 76, 79, 89, 91, 554, 559, 562, 577, 579, 581, 582, 585, 598, 611, 627, 628
    extent of, 578, 589
    First World War, 4–5
    food, 16, 18, 75, 77, 82, 84, 123, 149, 554, 577, 578, 605
    Goods and Services (Price Control) Act, 79, 123, 338, 513, 555 569
    Government surplus stocks, 623, 624
    hire purchase, 609
    manufacturers' prices, 78, 79, 81, 83, 84, 86, 87, 556, 558, 559, 560, 561, 563, 564, 578–591
        high-cost producers, 561, 573, 574, 582, 590
    maximum prices, 555 556, 560, 561, 563, 565, 578, 581, 590–591
    middlemen, 556–557, 565–566, 567, 568
    political importance of, 614
    post-war, 590–591, 619, 620
    Prices of Goods Act, 16, 77–86, 89, 96, 97, 123, 305, 513, 536, 553, 555, 556, 557, 558, 562, 564, 580, 584, 589, 603n
    production control and, 89, 499, 500, 501, 508, 552, 553, 554, 555, 614
    —*See also specifications and,*
    purchase tax and, 76, 85, 86, 565, 604, 606–607
    raw materials, 16, 76, 77, 80, 83, 84, 86, 87, 147, 570, 571
    retailers' prices, 560–561, 565, 592–605
        expenses inquiries, 593–595, 598, 599–602
        high-cost firms, 598, 604
        —*See also distributors' prices*
    second-hand prices, 556, 557, 610–612
    services
        dyeing and cleaning, 609
        footwear repairs, 608
        furniture storage, 608–609
        laundries, 608
    specifications and, 89, 123, 432, 440, 552, 553, 562, 583, 584, 587, 589, 614
    —*See also production control and,*
    standard prices, 585–586
    standstill Orders, 554–555, 561, 578, 580–583, 587, 588, 598
    stocks, 80, 85, 86
    treatment of costs, 79–80, 559, 561, 563, 578, 579, 580, 592
    utility generally, 89, 561, 596
    wage increases and, 575, 578

Price control generally, *contd.*
    wholesalers' prices, 557, 560, 565, 567, 568, 591–592
    —*See also distributors' prices*
    For prices and price control of individual commodities see under the headings for
       these commodities, viz.: *Bedding, Bicycles, Blankets, Clocks, Cloth, Clothing, Corsets,*
       Cotton and cotton goods, Cutlery, Footwear, Fuel, Furniture, Glassware, Hollow-ware,
       Hosiery, Household textiles, Leather, Perambulators, Pottery, Radios, Rayon and rayon
       goods, Torches, Toys, Umbrellas, Vacuum flasks, Watches, Wool and wool goods
       — *See also Clothing rationing, Stabilisation policy, Taxation*
Prime Minister (Mr. Neville Chamberlain), 51, 61
    (Mr. Winston Churchill), 156, 163, 240, 312, 395, 475
Printing industry
    Concentration of production, 210
    manpower for, 131, 132
Priority of production direction, 69
Prisoners-of-war
    clothes rationing and, 324
Productivity
    between the wars, 8
    effects of war-time controls on, 477–479, 486, 495, 509–512, 529, 614
Profits, 12, 78, 103
    —*See generally Price control*
Profiteering, 4–5, 16, 77, 78, 614
    Act, 1919, 4–5
Public opinion, 302
Public relations, 636
Publishers' Association, 25

Quebec Conference, 163

Radio sets, 28, 120, 125, 270
    price control, 588
Rationalisation
    between the wars, 9–10, 202, 206
    —*See also Concentration of production*
Rationing
    consumer goods generally, 12–13, 16, 75, 89, 115, 123, 283, 303, 304–306, 332–333,
       552, 554, 613, 626, 627, 628, 629
    food, 304
    —*See Clothing: rationing*
Raw materials
    control over, 3, 18, 26, 92, 93, 95, 96, 102, 108, 127, 128, 142, 151, 152, 208, 210,
       247, 306, 310, 435, 500, 506, 507, 511, 618, 627, 628
    export licensing and, 40, 41, 151, 152
    for exports, 11, 43, 44, 45, 46, 49, 50, 53, 54, 55, 65, 67, 68, 69, 70, 71, 95, 96, 102,
       119, 138, 139, 142, 151, 152, 153, 155, 161, 162, 193, 195, 196
    imports of, 21, 25, 26, 27, 28, 29, 126, 127
    international allocation of, 156, 175
    lend-lease restrictions and, Chapters VII, VIII *passim*, 195, 197, 198
    lend-lease supplies of, 126
    pre-war planning of, 11
    prices of, 16, 76, 77, 80, 83, 84, 86, 87, 147, 570, 571
    stocks of, 119, 127
    supplies for home market, 92, 93, 95, 96, 100, 102, 106, 107, 108, 113, 126, 127,
       128, 212, 214, 282, 283, 538
Raw materials industries
    concentration of production, 210, 221, 226
    —*See also Cotton industry: concentration, Iron and steel industry: concentration, Jute industry:*
       concentration, Paint industry: concentration, Rayon industry: concentration, Silk industry:
       concentration, Wool industry: concentration
Rayon and rayon manufacturers
    exports, 62–63, 178, 187, 194–196, 573, 574
       Central Rayon Office, 62, 194, 196
       Export Group, 62
       levy for, 62, 194, 573–574
       standardisation of clothes, 194, 196

Government contracts, 373, 375, 376
—*See also under rayon strong yarn*
limitation of supplies of, 48, 55, 97, 98, 100, 104, 105, 106, 373
cloth output, 474, 475
cloth stocks, 474
cloth: utility, 373, 377
    production controls, 443–451, 456–459
    proportion of total production represented by, 448, 449, 457
    specifications, 440, 441, 442, 443, 449, 563
prices, 62, 375, 563, 573–574
rayon strong yarn, 375–376
Silk and Rayon Control, 374, 376, 378
yarn allocations, 373, 374, 449, 450, 451
    Rayon Allocation Office, 374, 376, 449, 450
Rayon industry
    between the wars, 8, 62
    concentration of production, 210, 225, 376, 573
    manpower for, 129n, 373, 376, 377
    pre-war production, 373
    structure of, 372–373, 376, 573
    war-time output of, 373
Razor blades, 289, 290
Reciprocal aid
    —*See under Lend-lease*
Reddaway, W. B., article in *Lessons of the British War Economy*, 303n
Regional organisation, 66, 134–135
    Factory Control, 134, 239, 241, 244, 245, 250
Relief for liberated territories, 179, 180, 439, 492n, 619
Rent, 43
    retailers', 269, 270
Restrictive practices, 10
Retail Distributors' Association
    —*See under Retail trade: organisations*
Retail trade
    bankruptcies in, 256, 258
    bombing and, 112, 257, 260, 261, 265, 273, 276, 277, 293–295
    chain stores, 261, 262, 263n, 273, 599
    concentration schemes, 253, 256, 257, 258, 259, 262, 267, 268, 269, 270, 271, 272, 280
        compensation, 258, 259, 261, 267, 268, 269, 270, 271
    Co-operative societies, 88, 255, 257, 262, 263n, 265, 270, 271, 272, 275, 599, 600, 604
    department stores, 255, 257, 262, 263n, 265, 600
    expenses in, 263, 264, 266, 593–595, 598, 599–602
    food shops, 254, 259, 266, 270, 271, 276, 280
    manpower for, 131, 132, 253, 256, 259, 262, 263, 264, 265, 266, 267, 271, 272, 280, 281
    multiple shops, 255, 257, 262, 263n, 265, 271, 272, 273, 275, 599, 604
    organisation of, 254, 255, 256, 259
    political aspects of, 255, 256, 257, 259, 279, 602, 614
    premises in, 243, 265, 267, 271, 272, 278, 281
    price control and, 77–89, 260, 262, 263, 267, 271, 305, 560–561, 565, 592–605
    restriction on entry into, 260, 261
        Location of Retail Businesses Order, 261, 269, 272, 275, 276–279, 300, 559
        post-war, 273
        registration of withdrawing traders, 275, 276, 278
    retailers' panel, 300
    Retail Trade Committee, 253, 258–272, 273, 558
    'small' trader, 255, 257, 260, 261, 262, 265, 266, 267, 270, 271, 273, 281, 594, 601, 602, 603
    statistics, 13, 14, 253–255
    wages, 266
    organisations
        Co-operative Union, 259
        Co-operative Congress, 265, 270
        Drapers' Chamber of Trade, 259, 269, 565, 593
        Multiple Shops Federation, 259, 265, 267
        National Association of Outfitters, 593, 598
        National Chamber of Trade, 78, 259, 270
        Retail Distributors' Association, 80, 259, 265, 565, 593

Retail trade, *contd.*
    organisations
        Scottish Chamber of Trade, 259
        Trade Unions, 266, 270, 272
Reynaud-Simon Agreement, 34
Robbins, L., *The Economic Problem in Peace and War*, 625, 626
Roosevelt, Mr. Franklin D., 60, 156, 163
Rostas, L., *Comparative Productivity in British and American Industry*, 629n
Royal Navy
    clothes rationing and, 324
Rubber, 126, 127, 333–334, 488, 491, 493
Rubber goods, 333–334, 507
Russia, 178, 179, 187

Sandbags, 16, 77, 78
Sanitary towels, 290, 298
Saving, 16, 75, 101, 102, 122, 305, 555, 613
Scientific instruments, 41, 549
Scientific instruments industry, 8
Scottish Chamber of Trade
    —*See Retail trade: organisations*
Seaham Harbour, 288
Services
    clothes rationing and, 323–324
    clothing demands of, 472, 473, 475
    demands for consumer goods, 285, 537, 538
    surplus goods from, 334
Sheets, 333, 337
    —*See Household textiles*
Shipbuilding industry, 10
Shipping
    diversion from West to East Coast ports, 237, 286
    for exports, 64, 65, 185, 186
    income from, 7
    in First World War, 4
    pre-war plans for, 11, 15, 21
    war-time, 18, 29, 30, 95, 107, 113, 126, 127, 167, 169, 171, 181, 185, 186, 192, 194, 198, 221, 232, 483, 491, 493
Shopping habits, 286–287
Silk and silk goods
    civilian production, 378
    exports, 65n, 378
    imports, 378
    lend-lease restrictions on, 153
    limitation of supplies of, 101, 106
Silk industry
    between the wars, 8
    concentration of production, 210, 378
Simon, Sir John (now Lord), Chancellor of the Exchequer, 32, 42, 43, 54
Smith, H., *Retail Distribution*, 253n
Society of Motor Manufacturers and Traders, 623
South Africa, 67, 140n, 141, 143, 144, 185, 186
South America
    exports to, 45, 59–62, 64, 67, 140, 143, 144, 145, 146, 147, 158, 159, 160, 161, 185, 189, 193, 195, 196, 199, 522, 526
    leather supplies from, 493
    surpluses in, 59–61
    trade mission to, 59–61
Southern Rhodesia, 143, 175, 185
Spain, 64, 65, 144
'Special' areas (pre-war)
    —*See Depressed areas*
Specifications
    —*See Utility policy generally*
Sports goods, 125
    control over, 503, 536–539
Sports goods industry
    concentration of production, 219, 222, 225, 536, 537

Stabilisation policy, 18, 77, 122–123, 552–555, 570–578, 590, 606, 614, 619
Stage Two (period between defeat of Germany and defeat of Japan), 160, 161, 162, 163, 164, 165, 618 *et seq.*
Stamp, Lord, 43, 44, 50, 56, 70, 71
Standard clothing and footwear
    in First World War, 4–5
    in Second World War, 16–17, 87–89, 106, 424
Standardisation generally, 75, 89, 123, 262, 507–509, 575n, 586, 629
    —*See also Cloth: utility, Clothing: utility, Cotton and cotton goods: exports: standardisation of cloths, Footwear: utility, Furniture: utility, Hosiery: utility, Pencils, Pottery: utility, Rayon: exports: standardisation of cloths, Wool: exports: standardisation of cloths*
Stanley, Mr. Oliver, President of the Board of Trade, 46, 47, 78
Staple industries
    between the wars, 7–10
    rationalisation in, 10
Statistics generally, 13, 17, 113, 124, 125, 302, 364, 635
    clothes rationing, 297, 307, 308
    clothing policy, 472, 476
    consumer needs, 296–297
    exports, 158, 187
    export programming, 158, 167, 168, 178
    retail trade, 13, 14, 253–255
Sterling depreciation, 16, 44, 59, 76
Sterling area, 15, 22, 28, 29, 30, 66
    exports to, 30, 138, 140n
Sterling balances, 15, 28, 138, 144, 159
Stettinius, Mr., 154, 155, 157, 158
Stocks generally, 122, 237, 282, 287, 299, 309, 503, 631
    conservation of, 96, 100, 107
    consumers', 298
    prices of, 80, 85, 86
    raw materials, 119, 127
    retail, 113, 282, 294, 295, 297, 303
    —*See also Clothing stocks, Cotton: raw cotton stocks*
Storage space, Chapter XI *passim*
Strabolgi, Lord, 56n
Streat, Sir Raymond, 51, 63
Subsidies generally, 77
    agricultural, 9
    cotton, 46, 47, 48, 63
      exports, 11, 46, 47, 48, 50, 62 64
    food, 18, 28, 553, 577
    to industry, 10
    utility cloth, 571–572, 576, 577
Switzerland
    imports from, 23, 27n

Tariffs, 9, 61, 634
Taxation, 12, 16, 75, 101, 102, 122, 209, 271, 305, 552, 555, 613, 626, 627
    Excess Profits Tax, 56, 578
    purchase tax, 56, 61, 76, 85, 86, 108, 264n, 303, 432n, 469, 554, 565, 604
      removal from utility goods, 606
    relief for exports, 56
Taylor, Miss S. A., 479n
Tennyson, Sir Charles, 515
Textiles
    exports, 60, 61, 93, 94, 97, 139, 177–180
    Government orders, 93, 94, 95, 97
    home sales, 48, 49, 55, Chapter V *passim*, 283
    imports, 23, 25n
    limitation of supplies of, Chapter V *passim*, 17, 18, 35
    prices, 82
    —*See Cotton, Rayon, Silk, Wool*
Timber
    allocation of, 70, 71, 92, 93, 127, 512, 513, 514, 517, 519, 520
    Control, 513, 514, 517, 519, 520
    exports, 41

Timber, *contd.*
    imports, 25, 126
    supplies generally, 127, 512
Times, The, 304
Titmuss, R. M., *Problems of Social Policy,* 283, 285
Tobacco
    duties on, 61
    imports, 26, 27, 31, 32, 33
    storage, 249
Toilet preparations
    control over, 125, 504, 505, 531–536
    prices, 589
Toilet preparations industry, 101
    concentration of production, 210, 222, 225, 532, 533
Torches, 16
    lend-lease imports of bulbs, 120
    prices, 76, 83
Torch batteries, 25, 84, 122, 290–291
Towels, 334, 469, 470
Toys
    imports of, 23n, 24n
    limitation of supplies of, 102, 503, 504, 505, 506
    prices, 506, 607
Toy industry
    concentration of production, 210, 219, 226
Trade associations, 22, 35, 45, 347, 350, 518, 579, 581, 590
    concentration of production, 206, 207, 211, 231
    export licensing and, 42
    export groups and, 52, 53
    import licensing and, 22, 25
    iron and steel allocations and, 548
    prices and, 77, 81, 87
    retail trade and, 259, 260, 593 *et seq.*
Trade missions, 59–62
Trade Union Congress, 319, 320
Trade unions, 518
Trading up, 295, 329, 431, 453, 459, 554, 600, 601, 605
Transport, 247, 286, 296, 336, 353, 364, 516, 592
Treasury, 21, 26, 33, 45, 51, 76, 93, 138, 140, 148, 209, 303, 553, 554, 571, 606
    —See also Chancellor of the Exchequer
Turkey
    exports to, 64, 65, 140n, 144, 153
    tobacco from, 32, 33
Typewriters, 171, 551

Umbrellas, 503
    prices, 589
United Kingdom Commercial Corporation, 64
United States of America
    administration in, 170, 172, 179, 192
    aid to United Kingdom, 4, 17, 18, 71, 119
    Ambassador to United Kingdom, 26, 32, 148
    Anglo-American Trade Agreement, 22, 32, 59
    Commodity Credits Corporation, 33
    concentration of industry in, 166, 173, 180
    Congress, 31, 33, 61n
    consumption in, 630–632
    cotton industry in, 372
    export programming with other countries, 120, 165–183
    export trade of, Chapters VII and VIII *passim,* 191, 192
    growth of economic power of, 5, 6
    imports from, 22, 23, 26, 31–33, 61, 73
    in First World War, 3
    leather supplies, 493, 494
    munitions production in, 15
    munitions requirements from, 31
    Neutrality Act, 15

President of, 60, 156, 163
raw materials from, 126
steel from, 69, 70, 147
tariffs in, 60, 61
tobacco exports, 26, 32, 33
trade mission to, 61–62
trade with South America, 59–62
United Kingdom Ambassador to, 156, 160, 161
United Kingdom exports to, 45, 59–62, 64, 67, 71, 140, 143, 144, 193, 194, 195, 199, 200, 522, 523, 526
United Kingdom import restrictions and, 22, 31–33
United States troops in United Kingdom, 124, 493, 538
War Production Board, 166, 179, 180
—*See also Anglo-American Trade Agreement, Combined Food Board, Combined Munitions Assignment Board, Combined Production and Resources Board, Combined Raw Materials Board, Lend-Lease*
Uruguay, 140, 143
—*See South America*
Utility policy generally, 89, 501, 502, 507–509, 510, 586, 628
influence on productivity, 433, 443, 614, 630
post-war, 619
utility mark, 433
—*See Cloth: utility, Clothing: utility, Footwear: utility, Furniture: utility, Hosiery: utility, Pencils, Pottery: utility*

Vacuum cleaners, 23n, 24n
Vacuum flasks
price control, 558
Venezuela, 60
—*See also South America*

Wadsworth, H. E., article on utility clothing in *Review of Economic Studies*, 375n, 443n, 479n
Wages, 12, 16, 76, 122, 125, 128, 133, 266, 286, 407n, 413, 570, 571, 574–575, 578, 586, 614
War Cabinet
and balance of payments, 17
and clothes rationing, 312
and Factory Control, 238, 240
and exports, 43
and import control, 31
and manpower, 129, 130, 205
and standard clothing, 16, 88, 482
War Cabinet Offices
Economic Section of, 138
War insurance, 16, 76
War-time Social Survey, 298
Watches
exports, 66
imports, 23n, 24n, 25, 27
prices, 83, 589
Watch industry, 549
Weir, Sir Cecil, 51, 490
West Africa, 140n, 185, 190, 191, 195
West Indies, 64, 140n, 171, 195
Whisky exports, 96, 97
Whitehaven, 289
Wholesalers, 96, 97, 98, 99, 103, 110, 111, 243, 557, 568
price control and, 557, 560, 565, 567, 568, 591–592
stocks, 96
—*See also Limitation of Supplies Orders*
Wholesale Textile Association, 14, 292, 565, 624
Willingdon, Lord, 59
Winant, Mr., United States Ambassador to United Kingdom, 148n
Wines and spirits
imports, 28, 30
Women's Voluntary Services, 104, 112, 293, 313, 327, 523

Wood, Sir Kingsley, Chancellor of the Exchequer, 18, 56, 122, 209, 552, 574, 577, 578
Woodworking industry
    concentration of production, 519
Wool and wool goods
    cloth output, 474, 475
    cloth: utility, 381, 384, 386, 389, 393
        production controls, 452–459
        proportion of production represented by, 434, 452, 456, 457, 458
        specifications, 440, 451, 458, 459, 563
        subsidy on, 575, 576
    exports, 7, 12, 45, 46, 60, 93, 142–143, 178, 186, 193–194, 384, 385, 386, 387, 392, 394 also 95
        company for, 64
        levies for, 64, 386
        licensing of, 43, 142, 386
        National Wool Textile Export Corporation, 64, 386
        National Wool Textile Export Group, 386, 387
        standardisation of cloths, 143, 194
    Government contracts, 380, 381, 382, 383, 385, 386, 388, 392, 393, 394, 395
    home trade in, 93, 95, 106, 142, 380, 381, 384, 385
    prices and price control
        raw wool, 570
        wool goods, 82, 84, 451, 586–587
            utility cloth, 450–451, 459, 563, 576
    raw wool allocations, 127, 142–143, 193, 382–387, 388, 452
    raw wool imports, 29, 139, 142, 380, 381, 384
    raw wool rationing, 45, 95, 452, 453
    raw wool stocks, 142, 193, 382, 384
    yarn allocation to hosiery industry, 414, 415, 417, 418, 419
Wool Control and Controller, 51, 380, 381, 383, 384, 385, 386, 387, 388, 389, 390, 391, 393, 394, 395, 418, 451, 468
    control over cloth production, 387–388
    differences between Cotton Control and, 387–389, 439
    exports and, 45, 142–143
    organisation and functions of, 380–382
    pre-war plans, 380, 387
    prices and, 576
    rayon long staple yarn and, 374, 375, 389
    utility cloth and, 451, 452, 453, 454, 455, 456, 457, 458
Wool industry
    concentration of production, 210, 221, 225, 389–392
        financial arrangements, 390
        results, 390
    deliveries of cotton to, 349n
    export merchants, 143, 193–194
    manpower in, 131, 142, 193, 379, 381, 382, 383, 384, 389, 390, 391, 392–396, 473
    merchants, 382n
    output in, 381–382, 394, 399
    productivity generally, 478
    raw wool supplies, 382, 384, 387, 389, 395
    statistics, 429
    structure of, 378–380, 389
    wages in, 575
Wool Textile Delegation, 25, 82, 84, 380, 390, 451
Wool Working Party Report, 379n, 389n, 451n, 458n, 478n
Woolton, Lord, 87